CTIA

Consolidated Treaties & International Agreements

Current Document Service: United States

2008

Volume 1

Containing

Department of State Documents 08-01 through 08-15
and 08-18 through 08-36

Senate Treaty Documents 110-15 through 110-20

Oceana®
NEW YORK

OXFORD
UNIVERSITY PRESS

Oxford University Press, Inc., publishes works that further Oxford University's objective of excellence in research, scholarship, and education.

Published by Oxford University Press, Inc.
198 Madison Avenue, New York, New York 10016

This volume should be cited as **2008-1 CTIA.**

ISSN 1053-9905
ISBN: 978-0-19-973222-7

Note to Readers:

This publication is designed to provide accurate and authoritative information in regard to the subject matter covered. It is based upon sources believed to be accurate and reliable and is intended to be current as of the time it was written. It is sold with the understanding that the publisher is not engaged in rendering legal, accounting, or other professional services. If legal advice or other expert assistance is required, the services of a competent professional person should be sought. Also, to confirm that the information has not been affected or changed by recent developments, traditional legal research techniques should be used, including checking primary sources where appropriate.

(Based on the Declaration of Principles jointly adopted by a Committee of the American Bar Association and a Committee of Publishers and Associations.)

How to Use Consolidated Treaties & International Agreements

The **Consolidated Treaties & International Agreements** set contains all treaties and agreements in a given year to which the United States is a party. The agreements and treaties are made available by the Department of State and the Senate, as explained below.

The Department of State, under 1 U.S.C. §§ 112a and 112b, is obligated to report to Congress all international agreements and treaties to which the United States is a party within 60 days after the agreement or treaty has entered into force. The Department of State is also required to make available on their website within 180 days after the treaty or agreement has entered into force all reported agreements and treaties meeting the requirements for publication status in the U.S. government publication, *United States Treaties and Other International Agreements.* The Department of State numbers each agreement or treaty with a prefix based on the year reported and a suffix based on the order the agreement or treaty arrived to the Legal Affairs Office. For example, for the year 2010, the agreements would be numbered 10-01, 10-02, etc., and for 2011, the agreements would be numbered 11-01, 11-02, and so on.

The Senate, on the other hand, has a different procedure for formalizing and numbering treaties. All treaties requiring the Senate's consent to ratification are first submitted to the Senate Foreign Relations Committee for its review and recommendation. Thereafter, the treaty is introduced to the full Senate for its consent to ratification by a two-thirds vote of all members present. Once the Senate consents to its ratification, the treaty is presented to the President for formal ratification. However, the treaty is made available to the public upon the completed review and recommendation of the Foreign Relations Committee, although parts of the treaty text may remain concealed for security reasons. Senate treaty documents may remain in committee for many congressional sessions; thus, a treaty may be negotiated and signed in one year but not ratified until many years later. However, the treaty document is numbered based on the session the treaty was introduced to the Senate. For example, the Treaty between the United States of America and Japan on Mutual Legal Assistance in Criminal Matters was assigned as Senate Document No. 108-12, meaning it was introduced to the Senate during the 108th session of Congress and it was the 12th treaty submitted to the Foreign Relations Committee.

The editorial staff of the Law Division of Oxford University Press, Inc. (*fka* Oceana Publications) monitors the Department of State and the Senate throughout the year and gathers the agreements and treaties as they become available. Each agreement and treaty document is assigned an internal CTIA number and a subject. The CTIA number is used to track the agreement or treaty and its associated amendments, extensions and protocols. Each agreement or treaty document is assigned a CTIA prefix number with a suffix of ".000"; amendments, protocols and/or extensions of the agreement or treaty are assigned the same CTIA prefix, but a sequential CTIA suffix (*i.e.*, 2525.000 (main agreement), 2525.001 (amendment)).

The **Consolidated Treaties & International Agreements** set is organized by document number, beginning with the Department of State agreements and treaties, followed by the Senate treaty documents, and may also include any agreements for the year between the American Institute of Taiwan and the Taipei Economic and Cultural Representative Office. The Table of Contents for each volume provides all the key elements of the treaties published in the volume—agreement or treaty short title, date and place of signature and country.

The **Consolidated Treaties & International Agreements** set also contains three indices to help the reader locate documents.

The first index, Appendix I, organizes the treaties published in the volume by country and then by subject. Each treaty title includes the Department of State or Senate document number and the Oceana print citation.

The second index, Appendix II, is a complete listing of all multilateral agreements published in the volume. Each treaty title includes the Department of State or Senate document number and the Oceana print citation.

The third index, Appendix III, is the topical index, organizing each treaty published in the volume under its assigned subject in alphabetical order by country name and with the appropriate Department of State or Senate document number and Oceana print citation.

Table of Contents

* The Department of State did not make these agreements available to the public.

State Department Document Number: 08-01

Agreement Between the United States of America and the Republic of Kazakhstan Regarding Cooperation and Mutual Assistance Between Their Customs Services

Signed at Washington D.C.,
November 18, 1997
Entered into force August 21, 2000

CTIA DOCUMENT NUMBER: 13378.000

The Government of the United States of America and the Government of the Republic of Kazakhstan,

CONSIDERING that offenses against Customs laws are prejudicial to the economic, fiscal and commercial interests of their respective countries,

CONSIDERING the importance of assuring the accurate assessment of Customs duties and other taxes,

CONVINCED that action against Customs offenses can be made more effective by cooperation between their Customs Services,

HAVE AGREED as follows:

ARTICLE 1
DEFINITIONS

For the purposes of the present Agreement,

1. "Customs laws and regulations" shall mean such laws and regulations enforced by the Customs Services concerning the importation, exportation, and transit of goods, as related to Customs duties and other taxes, or to prohibitions, restrictions and other similar controls respecting the movement of goods across national boundaries.

2. "Customs Services" shall mean, in the United States of America, the United States Customs Service, Department of the Treasury, and, in the Republic of Kazakhstan, the General Customs Administration.

3. "Offense" shall mean any violation of the Customs laws and regulations as well as any attempted violation of such laws and regulations.

ARTICLE 2
SCOPE OF ASSISTANCE

1. The Parties agree to assist each other in preventing, investigating, and repressing any offense within the competence of their respective Customs Services, in accordance with the provisions of the present Agreement.

2. Assistance as provided in this Agreement shall, upon request, also include all information apt to ensure the accurate assessment of Customs duties and other taxes by their respective Customs Services.

3. Assistance as provided in paragraphs 1 and 2 shall be provided for use in all proceedings within the competence of their respective Customs Services, whether judicial, administrative, or investigative. Such assistance shall include, but not be limited to, proceedings on classification, value, fines, penalties, forfeitures and other characteristics relevant to the enforcement of the Customs laws and regulations.

4. The Parties agree to provide each other the widest range of assistance possible in the area of technical cooperation in Customs matters. Such assistance may include, but not be limited to:

a) training and assistance in developing specialized skills for Customs personnel;

b) exchange of information and experience in the use of technical interdiction and detection equipment;

c) exchange of experts knowledgeable in the field of Customs problems, interdiction and detection practices;

d) exchange of professional, scientific, and technical data dealing with Customs laws, regulations, and procedures; and

e) any other technical cooperation that the Parties may deem appropriate.

5. This Agreement is intended to enhance and supplement mutual assistance practices presently in effect between the Parties. All assistance under the present Agreement by either Party will be performed in accordance with its domestic laws and regulations.

ARTICLE 3
OBLIGATION TO OBSERVE CONFIDENTIALITY

1. Information, documents, and other communications received in the course of mutual assistance may only be used for the purposes specified in the present Agreement, including the use in judicial or administrative proceedings. Such information, documents, and other communications may be used for other purposes only when the supplying Party has given its express consent.

2. Inquiries, information, documents, and other communications received by either Party shall, upon request of the supplying Party, be treated as confidential. The reasons for such a request shall be stated.

3. Any intelligence, documents, or other information communicated or obtained under this Agreement shall be afforded in the receiving country the same protection in respect of confidentiality and official secrecy as applies in that country to the same kind of intelligence, documents, and other information obtained in its own territory.

ARTICLE 4
EXEMPTIONS FROM ASSISTANCE

In cases where the requested Party is of the opinion that compliance with a request would infringe upon its sovereignty, security, public policy, or other substantive national interest, assistance can be refused or compliance may be made subject to the satisfaction of certain conditions or requirements.

ARTICLE 5
FORM AND SUBSTANCE OF REQUESTS FOR ASSISTANCE

1. Requests pursuant to the present Agreement shall be made in writing. Documents necessary for the execution of such requests shall accompany the request. When required because of the exigency of the situation, oral requests may also be accepted but shall be confirmed in writing as soon as possible.

2. Requests pursuant to paragraph 1 of this article shall include the following information:

a) the authority making the request;

b) the nature of the proceedings;

c) the object of and the reason for the request;

d) the names and addresses of the parties concerned in the proceedings, if known; and

e) a brief description of the matter under consideration and the legal elements involved.

ARTICLE 6
CHANNEL

1. Assistance shall be carried out by direct communication between officials designated by the heads of the respective Customs Services.

2. In case the Customs Service of the requested Party is not the appropriate agency to comply with a request, it shall transmit the request to the appropriate agency.

ARTICLE 7
EXECUTION OF REQUESTS

1. The requested Customs Service shall endeavor to seek any official measures necessary to carry out the request.

2. The Customs Service of either Party may, upon request, conduct on behalf of the requesting Party any necessary investigation or gather information within its competence, including the questioning of experts, witnesses and persons suspected of having committed an offense against the Customs laws and regulations.

3. The Customs Service of either Party may, upon the request of the other Party, undertake verification, inspection and fact-finding inquiries in connection with matters within the competence of their Customs Service and referred to in the present Agreement.

4. Upon request, the requested Party may permit officials of the requesting Party to be present in its territory to serve as a liaison and, if appropriate, provide any information or assistance with regard to the request for assistance.

5. A request by a Party that a certain procedure be followed shall be complied with, subject to the laws of the requested Party.

6. The requesting Party shall, upon request, be advised of the time and place of the action to be taken in response to the request, so that such action may be coordinated.

7. In the event that the request cannot be complied with, the requesting Party shall be promptly notified of that fact, with a statement of the reasons for the refusal.

8. The execution of any request for assistance pursuant to this article, shall be subject to laws and regulations of the requested Party.

ARTICLE 8
FILES, DOCUMENTS AND WITNESSES

1. Originals of files, documents and other materials shall be requested only in cases where copies would be insufficient. Upon specific request, copies of such original files, documents and other materials shall be appropriately authenticated.

2. Originals of files, documents, and other materials which have been transmitted shall be returned at the earliest opportunity; rights of the requested Party or of third parties relating thereto shall remain unaffected.

3. The Customs Service of one Party shall authorize its employees, upon the request of the Customs Service of the other Party, to appear as witnesses in judicial or administrative proceedings in the territory of the other Party and to produce such files, documents or other materials or authenticated copies thereof, as may be considered essential for the proceedings.

4. With the agreement of the requested Party, authorization may be given for officials specially designated by the requesting Party to consult, in the offices of the requested Party, the relevant books, registers and other documents or data media held in those offices, take copies thereof, or extract any information or particulars relating to the offense.

ARTICLE 9
COSTS

1. The Parties shall waive all claims for reimbursement of costs incurred in the execution of the present Agreement, with the exception of expenses for witnesses, fees of experts, and costs of interpreters other than government employees.

2. Transportation costs and expenses for witnesses, experts, and interpreters shall be borne by the requesting Party.

3. If expenses of a substantial and extraordinary nature are or will be required to execute the request, the Parties shall consult to determine the terms and conditions under which the request will be executed, as well as the manner in which the costs shall be borne.

ARTICLE 10
SPECIAL INSTANCES OF ASSISTANCE

1. Upon request, the Customs Services shall inform each other whether goods exported from the territory of one Party have been lawfully imported into the territory of the other Party. The information shall, upon request, contain the Customs procedure used for clearing the goods.

2. The Customs Service of one Party, upon request of the Customs Service of the other Party, shall, to the extent of its ability, exercise special surveillance of:

a) means of transport suspected of being used in offenses within the territory of the requesting Party;

b) goods designated by the requesting Party as the object of a clandestine trade of which it is the country of destination; and

c) particular persons known or suspected by the requesting Party of being engaged in an offense.

3. The Customs Services of the Parties shall, upon request, furnish each other all available information regarding activities which may result in offenses within the territory of the other Party.

4. In cases which could involve substantial damage to the economy, public health public security, or any other vital interest of the other Party, such information shall be supplied without being requested.

5. The Customs Services of the Parties shall, upon request, provide documentation relating to transportation and shipment of goods showing value, disposition, and destination of those goods.

ARTICLE 11
IMPLEMENTATION OF THE AGREEMENT

The Customs Service, Department of the Treasury of the United States of America and the General Customs Administration of the Republic of Kazakhstan, may communicate directly for the purpose of dealing with matters arising out of the present Agreement, and, after consultation, shall issue administrative directives for the implementation of the present Agreement, and shall endeavor by mutual accord to resolve problems or doubts arising from the interpretation or application of the Agreement.

ARTICLE 12
ENTRY INTO FORCE AND TERMINATION

1. This Agreement shall enter into force on the ninetieth day following the date on which the Parties notify one another by an exchange of diplomatic notes that they have accepted its terms, and that all necessary national legal requirements for entry into force have been fulfilled.

2. The Parties agree to meet in order to review this Agreement at the end of five years counted from the date of its entry into force, unless they notify one another in writing that no review is necessary.

3. This Agreement may be terminated by written notice through diplomatic channels and shall cease to be in force six months after such notice has been given.

IN WITNESS WHEREOF, the undersigned, being duly authorized by their respective Governments, have signed this Agreement.

DONE at Washington, this eighteenth day of November, 1997, in duplicate, in the English and Kazak languages, each text being equally authentic. In the event of divergence, the English-language text shall prevail.

FOR THE GOVERNMENT OF THE UNITED STATES OF AMERICA:

[Signature]

FOR THE GOVERNMENT OF THE REPUBLIC OF KAZAKHSTAN:

[Signature]

State Department Document Number: 08-02

Agreement Between the United States of America and the Republic of Azerbaijan Concerning the Provision of Training Relating to Defense Articles Under the United States International Military Education and Training (IMET) Program

Effected by Exchange of Notes at Baku,
May 8 and June 14, 2002
Entered into force June 14, 2002

CTIA Document Number: 13379.000

Diplomatic Note

No. 208/2002

The Embassy of the United States of America presents its compliments to the Ministry of Foreign Affairs of the Republic of Azerbaijan and has the honor to refer to earlier discussions between representatives of our two governments regarding the furnishing of defense articles, related training, to include training related to defense articles under the U.S. International Military and Education Training Program, and other defense services from the United States of America to the Republic of Azerbaijan.

In accordance with previous discussions, it is proposed that the Republic of Azerbaijan agree to the following points.

A. Unless the consent of the Government of the United States of America has been first obtained, the Republic of Azerbaijan shall not:

(I) Permit any use of such defense articles or related training including training materials or other defense service by anyone not an officer, employee, or agent of the Republic of Azerbaijan;

(II) Transfer or permit any officer, employee, or agent of the Republic of Azerbaijan to transfer such articles or related training including training materials or other defense services by gift, sale, or otherwise; or

(III) Use or permit the use of such articles or related training including training materials or other defense services for purposes other than those for which provided.

B. Articles or related training including training materials or defense services shall be returned to the Government of the United States of America when they are no longer needed for the purposes for which they were furnished, unless the Government of the United States of America consents to another disposition.

C. Net proceeds of sale received by the Republic of Azerbaijan in disposing of, with prior written consent of the Government of the United States of America, any defense article furnished by the Government of the United States of America on a grant basis, including scrap from any such defense article, shall be paid to the Government of the United States of America.

D. The Republic of Azerbaijan shall maintain the security of such articles, related training including training materials, and other defense services; it shall provide substantially the same degree of security protection afforded to such articles or related training including training materials or other defense services by the Government of the United States of America; it shall, as the United States may require, permit continuous observation and review by, and furnish necessary information to, representatives of the Government of the United States of America with regards to the use thereof by the Republic of Azerbaijan.

E. The Government of the United States of America may also from time to time make the provision of articles, services, and related training furnished under other authority (except the United States Arms Export Control Act) subject to the terms and conditions of this agreement.

A Diplomatic Note from the Ministry of Foreign Affairs stating that the foregoing points are acceptable to the Government of the Republic of Azerbaijan shall, together with this note, constitute an agreement between the two governments, which shall enter into force on the date of the Ministry's reply.

The Embassy of the United States of America avails itself of this opportunity to renew to the Ministry of Foreign Affairs assurances of its highest consideration.

Embassy of the United States of America,
Baku, 8 May 2002

The Ministry of Foreign Affairs of the Republic of Azerbaijan has the honor to confirm that the proposals set forth in U.S. Embassy Note #208/2002 are acceptable to the government of the Republic of Azerbaijan and that the U.S. Embassy's note and this note in reply shall constitute an agreement between the two governments which shall enter into force on this date.

(UNREVIEWED TRANSLATION FOR INFORMATION ONLY)

U.S. Department of State Office of
Language Services Translating Division

LS No. 12-2008-0167
Azerbaijani/English MG/PH

TRANSLATION

[emblem]

REPUBLIC OF AZERBAIJAN

MINISTRY OF FOREIGN AFFAIRS

Embassy of the United States of America
Baku

No.: *844-10* [handwritten]

Urgent

The Ministry of Foreign Affairs of the Republic of Azerbaijan expresses its respect to the Embassy of the United States of America in Baku and has the honor to communicate the following:

Taking into account the replacement of the phrase “Republic of Azerbaijan” with the phrase “the Government of the Republic of Azerbaijan” in Articles “A” and “D”, the Government of the Republic of Azerbaijan confirms the acceptance of the proposals reflected in the Embassy’s note numbered 208/2002 and dated May 8, 2002, and, expressing the agreement between the governments of the two countries, confirms that the Embassy’s note, along with this response note, enter into force effective today.

Taking advantage of this opportunity, the Ministry of Foreign Affairs of the Republic of Azerbaijan once again expresses its respect to the Embassy of the United States of America in Baku.

Baku, June [?] *14*, 2002

[round stamp: Azerbaijani Republic/Ministry of Foreign Affairs/

Secretariat/emblem]

[initials]

[stamp in English] 17 June 2002

State Department Document Number: 08-03

Fifth Amendment to the Strategic Objective Grant Agreement (Assistance Agreement) for Basic Education of September 30, 2002, as Amended, Between the United States of America and the Arab Republic of Egypt, with Attachment

Signed at Cairo, September 30, 2007
Entered into force September 30, 2007

CTIA DOCUMENT NUMBER: 11007.002

"Certified to be a true copy of the original document signed by John Groarke, Acting USAID Director, and Fayza Aboulnaga, Minister of International Cooperation." "This Amendment to the Assistance Agreement grants $45,316,608.58 to the Government of Egypt for Basic Education."

Signature
John Cardenas
Legal Advisor

USAID Assistance Agreement No. 263-0286

Fifth Amendment ("Amendment"), dated 30 SEP 2007 to the Strategic Objective Grant Agreement (now known as "Assistance Agreement"), dated September 30, 2002, between the Arab Republic of Egypt ("A.R.E." or "Grantee") and the United States of America, acting through the United States Agency for International Development ("USAID") (collectively, the "Parties") for Basic Education.

SECTION 1. The Agreement is hereby amended as follows:

A. The Title of the Agreement is amended by deleting "Strategic Objective Grant Agreement between the Arab Republic of Egypt and the United States of America for Basic Education" and substituting "Assistance Agreement between the Arab Republic of Egypt and the United States of America for Basic Education" therefor.

B. Article 1 is amended in its entirety to read as follows:

Article 1: Purpose

The purpose of this Assistance Agreement (the "Agreement") is to set out the understanding of the parties named above (the "Parties") in connection with the Objective described below.

C. Article 2 is amended in its entirety to read as follows:

Article 2: Objective, Program Areas and Program Elements.

Section 2.1. Objective, Program Areas. In order to further the foreign assistance objective of Investing in People (the "Objective"), the Parties hereto agree to work together by focusing on activities in the area of Education.

Section 2.2. Program Elements. In order to achieve the Objective, the Parties agree to work together to achieve results in: Basic Education and Higher Education. Within the limits of the definition of the Objective in Section 2.1, this Section 2.2 may be changed by written agreement of the authorized representatives of USAID and the Ministry of International Cooperation without formal amendment of this Agreement.

Section 2.3. Annex 1, Amplified Description. Annex 1, will be amended through an implementation letter to amplify the above Objective and describe the Program Elements, Program Sub-Elements and Indicators that will be used to measure the progress and achievement in each of the Program Areas. Within the limits of the definition of the Objective set forth in Section 2.1, Annex I may be changed by written agreement of the authorized representatives of the Parties without formal amendment to the Agreement.

D. Articles 3, 4 and 7 are amended to substitute the term "Objective" for "Strategic Objective and Result."

E. Article 3, Section 3.1(a) is amended by deleting "Two Hundred Fifty Two Million Nine Hundred Eighteen Thousand Two Hundred Nine United States ("U.S.") Dollars ($252,918,209)" and substituting "Two Hundred Ninety Eight Million Two Hundred Thirty Four Thousand Eight Hundred Seventeen United States ("U.S.") Dollars ($298,234,817)" therefor.

F. Article 4, Completion Date, is amended by deleting "September 30, 2010" and substituting "December 31, 2011" therefor.

G. Attachment 1.1 of Annex 1 of the Agreement is deleted in its entirety and replaced by the Attachment 1. 1 attached hereto.

SECTION 2. *Language of Amendment.* This Fifth Amendment is prepared in both English and Arabic. In the event of ambiguity or conflict between the two versions, the English language version will prevail.

SECTION 3. Except as specifically amended or modified herein, the Agreement shall remain in full force and effect in accordance with all of its terms.

SECTION 4. *Ratification.* The A.R.E. will take all necessary action to complete all legal procedures necessary for ratification of this Fifth Amendment and will notify USAID of such ratification.

SECTION 5. *Effectiveness.* This Fifth Amendment shall enter into force when signed by both Parties hereto.

IN WITNESS WHEREOF, the Arab Republic of Egypt and the United States of America, each acting through its respective duly authorized representatives, have caused this Fifth Amendment to be signed in their names and delivered in Cairo on September 30, 2007.

ARAB REPUBLIC OF EGYPT	UNITED STATES OF AMERICA
BY: [Signature]	BY: [Signature]
NAME: Fayza Aboulnaga	NAME: John Groarke
TITLE: Minister of International Cooperation	TITLE: Acting Director, USAID/Egypt

Implementing Organizations

In acknowledgement of the foregoing Agreement, the following representative of the implementing organization has subscribed his name:

BY: [Signature]

NAME: Dr. Yousry Saber Hussein El-Gamal

TITLE: Minister of Education

Implementing Organizations

In acknowledgement of the foregoing Agreement, the following representative of the implementing organization has subscribed his name:

BY: [Signature]

NAME: Dr. Hany Mahfouz Helal

TITLE: Minister of Higher Education & Minister of State for Scientific Research

ILLUSTRATIVE FINANCIAL PLAN USAID Contribution ($) NO. 263-0286.00

Budget Input	Previous USAID Obligation $	FY 2007 This Obligation $	Total Obligations to Date $	Anticipated Future USAID/ Cairo Obligations $	Total Planned USAID Contribution $
Education Reform and Piolts	180,664,209	0	180,664,209	0	180,664,209
Training	36,455,000	0	36,455,000	0	36,455,000
NGOs Services and Scholarsh	26,400,000	0	26,400,000	0	26,400,000
Project Management (per.Audit, ass. Evalu.)	9,399,000	0	9,399,000	0	9,399,000
Subtotal	**252,918,209**	**0**	**252,918,209**	**0**	**252,918,209**
3.2 Education	0	45,316,608	45,316,608	71,479,392	116,796,000
3.2.1 Basic Education	0	35,003,268	35,003,268	60,479,392	95,482,660
3.2.2 Higher Education	0	10,313,340	10,313,340	11,000,000	21,313,340
Total	**252,918,209**	**45,316,608**	**298,234,817**	**71,479,392**	**369,714,209**

* The A.R.E. Contribution from the FT-800 Account represents payment for the employer share of social insurance and airfare.

STATE DEPARTMENT DOCUMENT NUMBER: 08-04

AGREEMENT BETWEEN THE UNITED STATES OF AMERICA AND BELIZE REGARDING THE STATUS OF MEMBERS OF THE ARMED FORCES OF THE UNITED STATES AND CIVILIAN PERSONNEL OF THE UNITED STATES DEPARTMENT OF DEFENSE TEMPORARILY PRESENT IN BELIZE IN CONNECTION WITH MILITARY TRAINING, EXERCISES, HUMANITARIAN ACTIVITIES AND OTHER AGREED PURPOSES

EFFECTED BY EXCHANGE OF NOTES AT BELMOPAN,
JULY 2 AND OCTOBER 29, 2007
ENTERED INTO FORCE OCTOBER 29, 2007, WITH EFFECT
FROM APRIL 24, 2007

CTIA DOCUMENT NUMBER: 13380.000

No. 07/038

Diplomatic Note

The Embassy of the United States of America presents its compliments to the Ministry of Foreign Affairs, and has the honor to refer to recent discussions between representatives of our two governments regarding issues related to United States military and Department of Defense civilian personnel (defined as members of the United States Armed Forces and civilian employees of the United States Department of Defense, respectively, hereafter referred to collectively as United States personnel) and United States contractors (defined as non-Belizean companies and firms, and their employees who are not nationals of Belize, under contract to the United States Department of Defense) who may be temporarily present in Belize in connection with military training, exercises, humanitarian activities, and other activities as mutually agreed.

As a result of these discussions, the Embassy proposes that United States personnel be accorded the privileges, exemptions, and immunities equivalent to those accorded to the administrative and technical staff of a diplomatic mission under the Vienna Convention on diplomatic relations of April 18, 1961; that United States personnel may enter and exit Belize with United States identification and with collective movement or individual travel orders; that Belize authorities shall accept as valid all professional licenses issued by the United States its political subdivisions or states thereof to United States personnel for the provision of services to authorized personnel; and that Belize authorities shall accept as valid, without a driving test or fee, driving licenses or permits issued by the appropriate United States Authorities to United States personnel for the operation of vehicles. The Embassy further proposes that United States personnel be authorized to wear uniforms while performing official duties and to carry arms while on duty if authorized to do so by their orders.

The Government of Belize recognizes the particular importance of disciplinary control by United States armed forces authorities over United States personnel and, therefore, authorizes the Government of the United States to exercise criminal jurisdiction over United States personnel while in Belize. The Government of the United States recognizes that United States personnel should respect the laws of Belize.

The Embassy further proposes that the United States Department of Defense and United States personnel shall not be liable to pay any tax or similar charge assessed within Belize and that the United States Department of Defense and United States personnel may import into, export out of, and use in Belize any personal property, equipment, supplies, materiel, technology, training, or services in connection with activities under this Agreement. Such importation, exportation, and use shall be exempt from any inspection, license, other restrictions, customs duties, taxes, or any other charges assessed within Belize. The Governments of the United States of America and Belize shall cooperate to take such measures as may be necessary to ensure the security and protection of United States personnel, property, equipment, records, and official information in Belize.

The Embassy proposes that vessels and vehicles operated by or, at the time, exclusively for the United States Department of Defense be permitted to enter, exit, and move freely within the territory of Belize, and that such vehicles (whether self-propelled or towed) shall not be subject to the payment of overland transit tolls. Vessels and aircraft owned or operated by or, at the time, exclusively for the United States Department of Defense shall not be subject to the payment of landing, parking, or port fees, pilotabe charges, lighterage, and harbor dues at facilities owned and operated by the Government of Belize. Aircraft owned and operated by or, at the time, exclusively for the United States Department of Defense shall not be subject to payment of navigation, overflight, terminal or similar charges when in the territory of Belize. The United States Department of Defense shall pay reasonable charges for services requested and received at rates no less favorable than those paid by the Armed Forces of Belize. Aircraft and vessels of the United States Government shall be free from boarding and inspection.

The Embassy also proposes that the United States Department of Defense may contract for any materiel, supplies, equipment, and services (including construction) to be furnished or undertaken in Belize without restriction as to choice of contractor, supplier, or person who provides such materiel, supplies, equipment or services. Such contracts shall be solicited, awarded and administered in accordance with the laws and regulations of the Government of the United States of America. Acquisition of articles and services in Belize by or on behalf of the United States Department of Defense in connection with activities under this Agreement shall not be subject to any taxes or similar charges in Belize.

The Embassy further proposes that United States contractors shall not be liable to pay any tax or similar charge assessed within Belize in connection with activities under this Agreement and that such contractors may import into, export out of, and use in Belize any personal property, equipment, supplies, materiel, technology, training, or services in fulfillment of contracts with the United States Department of Defense in connection with activities under this Agreement. Such importation, exportation, and use shall be exempt from any license, other restrictions, customs duties, taxes, or any other charges assessed within Belize.

The Embassy proposes that United States contractors shall be granted the same treatment as United States personnel with respect to professional and driver's licenses.

The Embassy proposes that United States personnel shall have freedom of movement and access to and use of mutually agreed transportation, storage, training, and other facilities required in connection with activities under this Agreement.

The Government of Belize recognizes that it may be necessary for the United States Armed Forces to use the radio spectrum. The United States Department of Defense shall be allowed to operate its own telecommunication systems (as telecommunication is defined in the 1992 Constitution and Convention of the International Telecommunication Union). This shall include the right to utilize such means and services as required to ensure full ability to operate telecommunication systems, and the right to use all necessary radio spectrum for this purpose. Use of the radio spectrum shall be free of cost to the United States Government.

Further, the Embassy proposes that the Parties waive any and all claims (other than contractual claims) against each other for damage to, loss, or destruction of the other's property or injury or death to personnel of either Party's Armed Forces or their civilian personnel arising out of the performance of their official duties in connection with activities under this Agreement. Claims by third parties for damages or loss caused by United States personnel shall be resolved by the United States Government in accordance with United States laws and regulations.

Finally, the Embassy proposes further that our two Governments, or their designated representatives, may enter into implementing arrangements to carry out the provisions of this Agreement.

If the proposals set forth herein are acceptable to the Government of Belize, the Embassy proposes that this note, together with the Ministry's reply to that effect, shall constitute an Agreement between the two Governments, which shall enter into force on the date of the Ministry's reply, with effect from April 24, 2007, and which may be terminated by either Party upon twelve months written notification to the other Party through diplomatic channels of its intent to terminate.

The Embassy of the United States of America avails itself of this opportunity to renew to the Ministry of Foreign Affairs of the Government of Belize the assurances of its highest consideration.

Embassy of the United States of America,
Belmopan, July 2, 2007.

MINISTRY OF FOREIGN AFFAIRS AND FOREIGN TRADE

P.O. Box 174
NEMO Building
Belmopan, BELIZE C.A.
Tel: (501) 822-2322 / 2167
Fax: (501) 822-2854
E-mail: belizemfa@btl.net

Our Reference: FA/BR/17/07 (2)

NOTE NO. 695

Embassy of the United States of America
Belmopan

Monday, October 9, 2007

The Ministry of Foreign Affairs and Foreign Trade of Belize presents its compliments to the Embassy of the United States of America and has the honour to refer to the latter's note 07/038 of July 2, 2007 which reads as follows:

> "The Embassy of the United States of America presents its compliments to the Ministry of Foreign Affairs, and has the honor to refer to recent discussions between representatives of our two governments regarding issues related to United States military and Department of Defense civilian personnel (defined as members of the United States Armed Forces and civilian employees of the United States Department of Defense, respectively, hereafter referred to collectively as United States personnel) and United States contractors (defined as non-Belizean companies and firms, and their employees who are not nationals of Belize, under contract to the United States Department of Defense) who may be temporarily present in Belize in connection with military training, exercises, humanitarian activities, and other activities as mutually agreed.
>
> As a result of these discussions, the Embassy proposes that United States personnel be accorded the privileges, exemptions, and immunities equivalent to those accorded to the administrative and technical staff of a diplomatic mission under the Vienna Convention on diplomatic relations of April 18, 1961; that United States personnel may enter and exit Belize with United States identification and with collective movement or individual travel orders; that Belize shall accept as valid all professional licenses issued by the United States, its political subdivisions or states thereof to United States personnel for the provision of services to authorized personnel; and that Belize authorities shall accept as valid, without a driving test or fee, driving licenses or permits issued by the appropriate United States authorities to United States personnel for the operation of vehicles. The Embassy further proposes that United States personnel be authorized to wear uniforms while performing official duties and to carry arms while on duty if authorized to do so by their orders.
>
> The Government of Belize recognizes the particular importance of disciplinary control by United States armed forces authorities over United States personnel and, therefore, authorizes the Government of the United States to exercise criminal jurisdiction over United States personnel while in Belize. The Government of the United States recognizes that United States personnel should respect the laws of Belize.
>
> The Embassy further proposes that the United States Department of Defense and United States personnel shall not be liable to pay any tax or similar charge assessed within Belize and that the United States Department of Defense and United States personnel may import into, export out of, and use in Belize any personal property, equipment, supplies, materiel, technology, training or services in connection with activities under this Agreement. Such importation, exportation, and use shall be exempt from any inspection, license, other restrictions, customs duties, taxes, or any other charges assessed within Belize. The Governments of the United States of America and Belize shall cooperate to take such

measures as may be necessary to ensure the security and protection of United States personnel, property, equipment, records, and official information of Belize.

The Embassy proposes that vessels and vehicles operated by or, at the time, exclusively for the United States Department of Defense may be permitted to enter, exit, and move freely within the territory or Belize, and that such vehicles (whether self-propelled or towed) shall not be subject to the payment of overland transit tolls. Vessels and aircraft owned or operated by or, at the time, exclusively for the United States Department of Defense shall not be subject to the payment of landing, parking, or port fees, pilotage charges, lighterage, and habor dues at facilities owned and operated by the Government of Belize. Aircraft owned and operated by or, at the time, exclusively for the United States Department of Defense shall not be subject to payment of navigation, overflight, terminal or similar charges when in the territory of Belize. The United States Department of Defense shall pay reasonable charges for services requested and received at rates no less favorable than those paid by the Armed Forces of Belize. Aircraft and vessels of the United States Government shall be free from boarding and inspection.

The Embassy also proposes that the United States Department of Defense may contract for any materiel, supplies, equipment, and services (including construction) to be furnished or undertaken in Belize without restriction as to choice of contractor, supplier, or person who provides such materiel, supplies, equipment or services. Such contracts shall be solicited, awarded and administered in accordance with the laws and regulations of the Government of the United States of America. Acquisition of articles and services in Belize by or on behalf of the United States Department of Defense in connection with activities under this Agreement shall not be subject to any taxes or similar charges in Belize.

The Embassy further proposes that United States contractors shall not be liable to pay any tax or similar charge assessed within Belize in connection with activities under this Agreement and that such contractors may import into, export out of, and use in Belize any personal property, equipment, supplies, materiel, technology, training, or services in fulfillment of contracts with the United States Department of Defense in connection with activities under this Agreement. Such importation, exportation, and use shall be exempt from any license, other restrictions, customs duties, taxes, or any other charges assessed with Belize.

The Embassy proposes that United States contractors shall be granted the same treatment as United States personnel with respect to professional and drivers' licenses.

The Embassy proposes that United States personnel shall have freedom of movement and access to and use of mutually agreed transportation, storage, training, and other facilities required in connection with activities under this Agreement.

The Government of Belize recognizes that it may be necessary for the United States Armed Forces to use the radio spectrum. The United States Department of Defense shall be allowed to operate its own telecommunication systems (as telecommunication is defined in the 1992 Constitution and Convention of the International Telecommunication Union). This shall include the right to utilize such means and services as required to ensure full ability to operate telecommunication systems, and the right to use all necessary radio spectrum for this purpose. Use of the radio spectrum shall be free of cost to the United States Government.

Further, the Embassy proposes that the Parties waive any and all claims (other than contractual claims) against each other for damage to, loss, or destruction of the other's property or injury or death to personnel of either Party's Armed Forces or their civilian personnel arising out of the performance of their official duties in connection with activities under this Agreement. Claims by third parties for damages or loss caused by United States personnel shall be resolved by the United States Government in accordance with United States laws and regulations.

Finally, the Embassy proposes further that our two Governments, or their designated representatives, may enter into implementing arrangements to carry out the provisions of this Agreement.

If the proposals set forth herein are acceptable to the Government of Belize, the Embassy proposes that this note, together with the Ministry's reply to that effect, shall constitute an Agreement between the two Governments, which shall enter into force on the date of the Ministry's reply, with effect from

April 24, 2007, and which may be terminated by either Party upon twelve months written notification to the other Party through diplomatic channels of its intent to terminate.

The Embassy of the United States of America avails itself of this opportunity to renew to the Ministry of Foreign Affairs of the Government of Belize the assurances of its highest consideration.

Embassy of the United States of America,

Belize City, July 2, 2007."

The Ministry of Foreign Affairs and Foreign Trade of Belize has the further honor to inform the Embassy of the United States of America that the proposals set forth above in the Embassy's note number 07/038 of July 2, 2007, are acceptable to the Government of Belize and to confirm that the Embassy's note and this note shall constitute an Agreement between the two Governments, which shall enter into force on the date of this note, with effect from April 24, 2007.

The Ministry of Foreign Affairs and Foreign Trade of Belize avails itself of this opportunity to renew to the Embassy of the United States of America the assurances of its highest consideration.

STATE DEPARTMENT DOCUMENT NUMBER: 08-05

MEMORANDUM OF UNDERSTANDING BETWEEN THE UNITED STATES OF AMERICA AND THE PEOPLE'S REPUBLIC OF CHINA REGARDING CERTAIN MEASURES GRANTING REFUNDS, REDUCTIONS OR EXEMPTIONS FROM TAXES OR OTHER PAYMENTS

SIGNED AT GENEVA, NOVEMBER 29, 2007
ENTERED INTO FORCE NOVEMBER 29, 2007

CTIA DOCUMENT NUMBER: 13381.000

Whereas the United States of America ("United States") filed requests for consultations with the People's Republic of China ("China") on 2 February 2007 and 27 April 2007 pursuant to Articles 1 and 4 of the World Trade Organization (WTO) Understanding on Rules and Procedures Governing the Settlement of Disputes, Article XXII:1 of the WTO General Agreement on Tariffs and Trade 1994, Articles 4 and 30 of the WTO Agreement on Subsidies and Countervailing Measures, and Article 8 of the WTO Agreement on Trade-Related Investment Measures, regarding certain measures granting refunds, reductions or exemption from taxes or other payments (DS358);

Whereas China and the United States held constructive consultations in Geneva on 20 March and 22 June 2007;

China and the United States have agreed as follows:

1. During the consultations, the United States described its concerns about the WTO-consistency of tax preferences provided under:

(a) the *Circular of the Ministry of Finance and the State Administration of Taxation Concerning the Issues of Tax Credit To Enterprise Income Tax for Purchase of Domestically Produced Equipment by Enterprises with Foreign Investment and Foreign Enterprises*, CaiShuiZi [2000] No. 49, issued on 14 January 2000, and the *Circular of the State Administration of Taxation on Printing and Issuing the Measures On Tax Credit To Enterprise Income Tax for Purchase of Domestically Produced Equipment by Enterprises with Foreign Investment and Foreign Enterprises*, GuoShuiFa [2000] No. 90, issued on 18 May 2000; and

(b) the *Circular on Printing and Issuing the Interim Measures on Credit and Exemption of Enterprise Income Tax for Investment in Domestically Made Equipment for Technological Renovation*, CaiShuiZi [1999] No. 290, issued by the Ministry of Finance and the State Administration of Taxation on 8 December 1999.

In this regard, China has explained that legal instruments of at least equal legal stature to the circulars identified in sub-paragraphs (a) and (b) above, will contain provisions stating that these circulars are repealed, and will be issued by the competent authorities, by 31 December 2007, effective no later than 1 January 2008. China confirms that the tax preferences under the circulars identified in sub-paragraphs (a) and (b) above will not be reinstated.

2. During the consultations, the United States described its concerns about the WTO-consistency of tax preferences provided under:

(a) Article 9 of the Provisions of the State Council on the Encouragement of Foreign Investment, GuoFa [1986] No. 95, issued on 11 October 1986 (hereinafter "State Council Provisions"); Article 6 of the Income Tax Law of the People's Republic of China on Enterprises with Foreign Investment and Foreign Enterprises, Order No. 45, promulgated on 9 April 1991 (hereinafter "FIE Income Tax Law"); and Article 75, paragraph 1, section 8 of the Rules for the Implementation of the Income Tax Law of the People's Republic of China on Enterprises with Foreign Investment and Foreign Enterprises, Decree No. 85, issued by the State Council on 30 June 1991 (hereinafter "FIE Income Tax Implementing Rules");

(b) Article 8 of the *State Council Provisions*; Article 6 of the *FIE Income Tax Law*; and Article 75, paragraph 1, section 7 of the *FIE Income Tax Implementing Rules*; and

(c) Article 10 of the *State Council Provisions*; Articles 6 and 10 of the *FIE Income Tax Law*; and Article 81 of the *FIE Income Tax Implementing Rules*.

China confirms that, effective 1 January 2008, the *Enterprise Income Tax Law of the People's Republic of China*, Order No. 63, promulgated on 16 March 2007 (hereinafter "*Enterprise Income Tax Law*"), repeals the *FIE Income Tax Law*. In addition, China has explained that legal instruments to be issued by, and made effective no later than, 1 January 2008, will contain provisions stating that the *FIE Income Tax Implementing Rules* are repealed. With the abolition of the *FIE Income Tax Law* and the *FIE Income Tax Implementing Rules*, Articles 8, 9 and 10 of the *State Council Provisions* will no longer be valid. China has further explained that, in accordance with its schedule of administrative regulations revision, Articles 8, 9 and 10 of the *State Council Provisions* will be eliminated by a legal instrument no later than 1 January 2009. The legal instruments repealing the *FIE Income Tax Implementing Rules* and Articles 8, 9 and 10 of the *State Council Provisions* will be issued by the competent authorities and be of at least equal legal stature to the legal instruments being repealed. China confirms that the tax preferences under the legal provisions identified in sub-paragraphs (a), (b) and (c) above will not be reinstated.

3. During the consultations, the United States described its concerns about the WTO-consistency of tax and other preferences provided under:

(a) Article 7 of the FIE Income Tax Law; Article 73, paragraph 1, section 6 of the FIE Income Tax Implementing Rules; and Section XIII of the Catalogue of Encouraged Foreign Investment Industries (hereinafter "Encouraged Catalogue") within the Catalogue for the Guidance of Foreign Investment Industries, Order [2004] No. 24, issued by the National Development and Reform Commission and the Ministry of Commerce on 30 November 2004 (hereinafter "Catalogue"); and

(b) the *Circular of the State Council Concerning the Adjustment in the Taxation Policy of Imported Equipment*, GuoFa [1997] No. 37, issued on 29 December 1997; and Section XIII of the *Encouraged Catalogue*.

In this regard, China has explained that, in accordance with its economic and social development, it revised the *Catalogue* on 31 October 2007, which revision will take effect as of 1 December 2007. China confirms that Section XIII of the *Encouraged Catalogue* dated 30 November 2004 will not be reinstated.

4. During the consultations, the United States described its concerns about the WTO-consistency of the *Enterprise Income Tax Law*, including Articles 25, 28, 31 and 57 thereof. China has explained that these provisions do not provide for the offering of any income tax preference contingent upon the use of domestic over imported goods or upon export performance. China has further explained that, notwithstanding the fact that Article 57 of the *Enterprise Income Tax Law* authorizes the continuation of certain income tax preferences beyond 1 January 2008, it will not be implemented or applied so as to introduce or permit the continuation of the income tax preferences being repealed by virtue of the actions described in paragraphs 1 through 3 of this Memorandum of Understanding. These limitations will be made explicit under fully authoritative legal measures, and will be effective, no later than 1 January 2008.

5. During the consultations, the United States described its concerns about the WTO-consistency of an exemption for certain foreign-invested enterprises from payments to the State for worker allowances, provided under Article 3 of *State Council Provisions*.

China has explained that, at the time the State Council promulgated the *State Council Provisions*, Article 11 of the *State Council Regulations on Labor Management in Sino-Foreign Joint Ventures*, GuoFa [1980] No. 199 (26 July 1980), required foreign-invested enterprises to make such payments to the State. China has confirmed, however, that because this requirement was eliminated by the *State Council Decision on Abolition of Certain Administrative Regulations Promulgated Prior to the End of 2000*, Order No. 319 (6 October 2001), the exemption provided under Article 3 of the *State Council Provisions* is no longer operative. China confirms that Article 3 of the *State Council Provisions* may no longer serve as a legal basis to exempt foreign-invested enterprises from making payments required by Chinese law, regulation, or other official measure.

6. During the consultations, the United States described its concerns about the WTO-consistency of value-added tax (VAT) refunds provided under the *Circular of the State Administration of Taxation on Printing and Issuing the Interim Measures for the Administration of Tax Refund to Enterprises with Foreign Investment for the Purchase of Domestically Produced Equipment*, GuoShuiFa [1999] No. 171, issued on 20 September 1999, and the *Circular of the State Administration of Taxation and National Development and Reform Commission on Printing and Issuing the Interim Measures for the Administration of Tax Refund for the Purchase of Domestically-Produced Equipment in Foreign Investment Projects*, GuoShuiFa [2006] No. 111, issued on 24 July 2006.

In this regard, China has stated that these circulars do not create a preference, either in law or on a *de facto* basis, for the use of domestic over imported goods in connection with purchases of domestically-produced equipment when viewed in relation to the *Circular of the State Council Concerning the Adjustment in the Taxation Policy of Imported Equipment*, GuoFa [1997] No. 37, issued on 29 December 1997, in connection with purchases of imported equipment. China has confirmed that, in implementing the above-mentioned legal instruments as well as any new legal instruments that affect the operation of the above-mentioned legal instruments, it will ensure that imported equipment receives VAT treatment under terms and conditions no less favorable than those applicable to domestically-produced equipment.

7. China and the United States agree to communicate in a timely manner with respect to the implementation of the actions described above, including provision of related new legal instruments.

8. This Memorandum of Understanding is without prejudice to the rights and obligations of China and the United States under the WTO Agreement.

Done in Geneva, on 29 November 2007, in two copies in Chinese and English respectively, each text being equally authentic.

[Signature]	[Signature]
For the Government of the People's Republic of China	For the Government of the United States of America

State Department Document Number: 08-06

Air Transport Agreement Between the United States of America and Georgia, with Annexes

Signed at Washington D.C., June 21, 2007
Entered into force December 6, 2007

CTIA DOCUMENT NUMBER: 13382.000

The Government of the United States of America and the Government of Georgia (hereinafter, "the Parties");

Desiring to promote an international aviation system based on competition among airlines in the marketplace with minimum government interference and regulation;

Desiring to facilitate the expansion of international air transport opportunities;

Desiring to make it possible for airlines to offer the traveling and shipping public a variety of service options at the lowest prices that are not discriminatory and do not represent abuse of a dominant position, and wishing to encourage individual airlines to develop and implement innovative and competitive prices;

Desiring to ensure the highest degree of safety and security in international air transport and reaffirming their grave concern about acts or threats against the security of aircraft, which jeopardize the safety of persons or property, adversely affect the operation of air transportation, and undermine public confidence in the safety of civil aviation; and

Being Parties to the Convention on International Civil Aviation, opened for signature at Chicago on December 7, 1944;

Have agreed as follows:

Article 1
Definitions

For the purposes of this Agreement, unless otherwise stated, the term:

1. "Aeronautical authorities" means, in the case of the United States, the Department of Transportation, or its successor, and in the case of Georgia, the Ministry of Economic Development, and any person or agency authorized to perform functions exercised by the Ministry of Economic Development.

2. "Agreement" means this Agreement, its Annexes, and any amendments thereto;

3. "Air transportation" means the public carriage by aircraft of passengers, baggage, cargo, and mail, separately or in combination, for remuneration or hire;

4. "Convention" means the Convention on International Civil Aviation, opened for signature at Chicago on December 7, 1944, and includes:

a. any amendment that has entered into force under Article 94(a) of the Convention and has been ratified by both Parties, and

b. any Annex or any amendment thereto adopted under Article 90 of the Convention, insofar as such Annex or amendment is at any given time effective for both Parties;

5. "Designated airline" means an airline designated and authorized in accordance with Article 3 of this Agreement;

6. "Full cost" means the cost of providing service plus a reasonable charge for administrative overhead;

7. "International air transportation" means air transportation that passes through the airspace of the territory of more than one State;

8. "Price" means any fare, rate or charge for the carriage of passengers (and their baggage) and/or cargo (excluding mail) in air transportation charged by airlines, including their agents, and the conditions governing the availability of such fare, rate or charge;

9. "Stop for non-traffic purposes" means a landing for any purpose other than taking on or discharging passengers, baggage, cargo and/or mail in air transportation;

10. "Territory" means the land areas under the sovereignty, jurisdiction, protection, or trusteeship of a Party, including all land areas within its internationally recognized borders, the territorial waters adjacent thereto and the airspace above them;

11. "User charge" means a charge imposed on airlines for the provision of airport, air navigation, or aviation security facilities or services including related services and facilities.

Article 2
Grant of Rights

1. Each Party grants to the other Party the following rights for the conduct of international air transportation by the airlines of the other Party:

a. the right to fly across its territory without landing;

b. the right to make stops in its territory for non-traffic purposes; and

c. the rights otherwise specified in this Agreement.

2. Nothing in this Article shall be deemed to confer on the airline or airlines of one Party the rights to take on board, in the territory of the other Party, passengers, their baggage, cargo, or mail carried for compensation and destined for another point in the territory of that other Party.

Article 3
Designation and Authorization

1. Each Party shall have the right to designate as many airlines as it wishes to conduct international air transportation in accordance with this Agreement and to withdraw or alter such designations. Such designations shall be transmitted to the other Party in writing through diplomatic channels, and

shall identify whether the airline is authorized to conduct the type of air transportation specified in Annex I or in Annex II or both.

2. On receipt of such a designation, and of applications from the designated airline, in the form and manner prescribed for operating authorizations and technical permissions, the other Party shall grant appropriate authorizations and permissions with minimum procedural delay, provided:

a. substantial ownership and effective control of that airline are vested in the Party designating the airline, nationals of that Party, or both;

b. the designated airline is qualified to meet the conditions prescribed under the laws and regulations normally applied to the operation of international air transportation by the Party considering the application or applications; and

c. the Party designating the airline is maintaining and administering the standards set forth in Article 6 (Safety) and Article 7 (Aviation Security) of this Agreement.

Article 4
Revocation of Authorization

1. Either Party may revoke, suspend or limit the operating authorizations or technical permissions of an airline designated by the other Party where:

a. substantial ownership and effective control of that airline are not vested in the other Party, the Party's nationals, or both;

b. that airline has failed to comply with the laws and regulations referred to in Article 5 (Application of Laws) of this Agreement; or

c. the other Party is not maintaining and administering the standards as set forth in Article 6 (Safety).

2. Unless immediate action is essential to prevent further noncompliance with subparagraphs 1b or 1c of this Article, the rights established by this Article shall be exercised only after consultation with the other Party.

3. This Article does not limit the rights of either Party to withhold, revoke, limit or impose conditions on the operating authorization or technical permission of an airline or airlines of the other Party in accordance with the provisions of Article 7 (Aviation Security).

Article 5
Application of Laws

1. While entering, within, or leaving the territory of one Party, its laws and regulations relating to the operation and navigation of aircraft shall be complied with by the other Party's airlines.

2. While entering, within, or leaving the territory of one Party, its laws and regulations relating to the admission to or departure from its territory of passengers, crew or cargo on aircraft (including regulations relating to entry, clearance, aviation security, immigration, passports, customs and quarantine or, in the case of mail, postal regulations) shall be complied with by, or on behalf of, such passengers, crew or cargo of the other Party's airlines.

Article 6
Safety

1. Each Party shall recognize as valid, for the purpose of operating the air transportation provided for in this Agreement, certificates of airworthiness, certificates of competency, and licenses issued

or validated by the other Party and still in force, provided that the requirements for such certificates or licenses at least equal the minimum standards that may be established pursuant to the Convention. Each Party may, however, refuse to recognize as valid for the purpose of flight through its own territory, certificates of competency and licenses granted to or validated for its own nationals by the other Party.

2. Either Party may request consultations concerning the safety standards maintained by the other Party relating to aeronautical facilities, aircrews, aircraft, and operation of the designated airlines. If, following such consultations, one Party finds that the other Party does not effectively maintain and administer safety standards and requirements in these areas that at least equal the minimum standards that may be established pursuant to the Convention, the other Party shall be notified of such findings and the steps considered necessary to conform with these minimum standards, and the other Party shall take appropriate corrective action. Each Party reserves the right to withhold, revoke, or limit the operating authorization or technical permission of an airline or airlines designated by the other Party in the event the other Party does not take such appropriate corrective action within a reasonable time.

Article 7
Aviation Security

1. In accordance with their rights and obligations under international law, the Parties reaffirm that their obligation to each other to protect the security of civil aviation against acts of unlawful interference forms an integral part of this Agreement. Without limiting the generality of their rights and obligations under international law, the Parties shall in particular act in conformity with the provisions of the Convention on Offenses and Certain Other Acts Committed on Board Aircraft, done at Tokyo September 14, 1963, the Convention for the Suppression of Unlawful Seizure of Aircraft, done at The Hague December 16, 1970, the Convention for the Suppression of Unlawful Acts against the Safety of Civil Aviation, done at Montreal September 23, 1971, and the Protocol for the Suppression of Unlawful Acts of Violence at Airports Serving International Civil Aviation, done at Montreal February 24, 1988.

2. The Parties shall provide upon request all necessary assistance to each other to prevent acts of unlawful seizure of civil aircraft and other unlawful acts against the safety of such aircraft, of their passengers and crew, and of airports and air navigation facilities, and to address any other threat to the security of civil air navigation.

3. The Parties shall, in their mutual relations, act in conformity with the aviation security standards and appropriate recommended practices established by the International Civil Aviation Organization and designated as Annexes to the Convention; they shall require that operators of aircraft of their registry, operators of aircraft who have their principal place of business or permanent residence in their territory, and the operators of airports in their territory act in conformity with such aviation security provisions.

4. Each Party agrees to observe the security provisions required by the other Party for entry into, for departure from, and while within the territory of that other Party and to take adequate measures to protect aircraft and to inspect passengers, crew, and their baggage and carry-on items, as well as cargo and aircraft stores, prior to and during boarding or loading. Each Party shall also give positive consideration to any request from the other Party for special security measures to meet a particular threat.

5. When an incident or threat of an incident of unlawful seizure of aircraft or other unlawful acts against the safety of passengers, crew, aircraft, airports or air navigation facilities occurs, the Parties shall assist each other by facilitating communications and other appropriate measures intended to terminate rapidly and safely such incident or threat.

6. When a Party has reasonable grounds to believe that the other Party has departed from the aviation security provisions of this Article, the aeronautical authorities of that Party may request immediate consultations with the aeronautical authorities of the other Party. Failure to reach a satisfactory agreement within 15 days from the date of such request shall constitute grounds to withhold, revoke, limit, or impose conditions on the operating authorization and technical permissions of an airline or airlines of that Party. When required by an emergency, a Party may take interim action prior to the expiry of 15 days.

Article 8
Commercial Opportunities

1. The airlines of each Party shall have the right to establish offices in the territory of the other Party for the promotion and sale of air transportation.

2. The designated airlines of each Party shall be entitled, in accordance with the laws and regulations of the other Party relating to entry, residence, and employment, to bring in and maintain in the territory of the other Party managerial, sales, technical, operational, and other specialist staff required for the provision of air transportation.

3. Each designated airline shall have the right to perform its own ground-handling in the territory of the other Party ("self-handling") or, at its option, select among competing agents for such services in whole or in part. The rights shall be subject only to physical constraints resulting from considerations of airport safety. Where such considerations preclude self-handling, ground services shall be available on an equal basis to all airlines; charges shall be based on the costs of services provided; and such services shall be comparable to the kind and quality of services as if self-handling were possible.

4. Any airline of each Party may engage in the sale of air transportation in the territory of the other Party directly and, at the airline's discretion, through its agents, except as may be specifically provided by the charter regulations of the country in which the charter originates that relate to the protection of passenger funds, and passenger cancellation and refund rights. Each airline shall have the right to sell such transportation, and any person shall be free to purchase such transportation, in the currency of that territory or in freely convertible currencies.

5. Each airline shall have the right to convert and remit to its country, on demand, local revenues in excess of sums locally disbursed. Conversion and remittance shall be permitted promptly without restrictions or taxation in respect thereof at the rate of exchange applicable to current transactions and remittance on the date the carrier makes the initial application for remittance.

6. The airlines of each Party shall be permitted to pay for local expenses, including purchases of fuel, in the territory of the other Party in local currency. At their discretion, the airlines of each Party may pay for such expenses in the territory of the other Party in freely convertible currencies according to local currency regulation.

7. In operating or holding out the authorized services on the agreed routes, any designated airline of one Party may enter into cooperative marketing arrangements such as blocked-space, code-sharing or leasing arrangements, with

a) an airline or airlines of either Party;

b) an airline or airlines of a third country; and

c) a surface transportation provider of any country;

provided that all participants in such arrangements (i) hold the appropriate authority and (ii) meet the requirements normally applied to such arrangements.

8. Notwithstanding any other provision of this Agreement, airlines and indirect providers of cargo transportation of both Parties shall be permitted, without restriction, to employ in connection with international air transportation any surface transportation for cargo to or from any points in the territories of the Parties or in third countries, including transport to and from all airports with customs facilities, and including, where applicable, the right to transport cargo in bond under applicable laws and regulations. Such cargo, whether moving by surface or by air, shall have access to airport customs processing and facilities. Airlines may elect to perform their own surface transportation or to provide it through arrangements with other surface carriers, including surface transportation operated by other airlines and indirect providers of cargo air transportation. Such intermodal cargo services may be offered at a single, through price for the air and surface transportation combined, provided that shippers are not misled as to the facts concerning such transportation.

Article 9
Customs Duties and Charges

1. On arriving in the territory of one Party, aircraft operated in international air transportation by the designated airlines of the other Party, their regular equipment, ground equipment, fuel, lubricants, consumable technical supplies, spare parts (including engines), aircraft stores (including but not limited to such items of food, beverages and liquor, tobacco and other products destined for sale to or use by passengers in limited quantities during flight), and other items intended for or used solely in connection with the operation or servicing of aircraft engaged in international air transportation shall be exempt, on the basis of reciprocity, from all import restrictions, property taxes and capital levies, customs duties, excise taxes, and similar fees and charges that are (a) imposed by the national authorities, and (b) not based on the cost of services provided, provided that such equipment and supplies remain on board the aircraft.

2. There shall also be exempt, on the basis of reciprocity, from the taxes, levies, duties, fees and charges referred to in paragraph 1 of this Article, with the exception of charges based on the cost of the service provided:

a. aircraft stores introduced into or supplied in the territory of a Party and taken on board, within reasonable limits, for use on outbound aircraft of an airline of the other Party engaged in international air transportation, even when these stores are to be used on a part of the journey performed in the territory of the Party in which they are taken on board;

b. ground equipment and spare parts (including engines) introduced into the territory of a Party for the servicing, maintenance, or repair of aircraft of an airline of the other Party used in international air transportation;

c. fuel, lubricants and consumable technical supplies introduced into or supplied in the territory of a Party for use in an aircraft of an airline of the other Party engaged in international air transportation, even when these supplies are to be used on a part of the journey performed in the territory of the Party in which they are taken on board; and

d. promotional and advertising materials introduced into or supplied in the territory of one Party and taken on board, within reasonable limits, for use on outbound aircraft of an airline of the other Party engaged in international air transportation, even when these stores are to be used on a part of the journey performed in the territory of the Party in which they are taken on board.

3. Equipment and supplies referred to in paragraphs 1 and 2 of this Article may be required to be kept under the supervision or control of the appropriate authorities.

4. The exemptions provided by this Article shall also be available where the designated airlines of one Party have contracted with another airline, which similarly enjoys such exemptions from the

other Party, for the loan or transfer in the territory of the other Party of the items specified in paragraphs 1 and 2 of this Article.

Article 10
User Charges

1. User charges that may be imposed by the competent charging authorities or bodies of each Party on the airlines of the other Party shall be just, reasonable, not unjustly discriminatory, and equitably apportioned among categories of users. In any event, any such user charges shall be assessed on the airlines of the other Party on terms not less favorable than the most favorable terms available to any other airline at the time the charges are assessed.

2. User charges imposed on the airlines of the other Party may reflect, but shall not exceed, the full cost to the competent charging authorities or bodies of providing the appropriate airport, airport environmental, air navigation, and aviation security facilities and services at the airport or within the airport system. Such charges may include a reasonable return on assets, after depreciation. Facilities and services for which charges are made shall be provided on an efficient and economic basis.

3. Each Party shall encourage consultations between the competent charging authorities or bodies in its territory and the airlines using the services and facilities, and shall encourage the competent charging authorities or bodies and the airlines to exchange such information as may be necessary to permit an accurate review of the reasonableness of the charges in accordance with the principles of paragraphs 1 and 2 of this Article. Each Party shall encourage the competent charging authorities to provide users with reasonable notice of any proposal for changes in user charges to enable users to express their views before changes are made.

4. Neither Party shall be held, in dispute resolution procedures pursuant to Article 14, to be in breach of a provision of this Article, unless (a) it fails to undertake a review of the charge or practice that is the subject of complaint by the other Party within a reasonable amount of time; or (b) following such a review it fails to take all steps within its power to remedy any charge or practice that is inconsistent with this Article.

Article 11
Fair Competition

1. Each Party shall allow a fair and equal opportunity for the designated airlines of both Parties to compete in providing the international air transportation governed by this Agreement.

2. Each Party shall allow each designated airline to determine the frequency and capacity of the international air transportation it offers based upon commercial considerations in the marketplace. Consistent with this right, neither Party shall unilaterally limit the volume of traffic, frequency or regularity of service, or the aircraft type or types operated by the designated airlines of the other Party, except as may be required for customs, technical, operational, or environmental reasons under uniform conditions consistent with Article 15 of the Convention.

3. Neither Party shall impose on the other Party's designated airlines a first-refusal requirement, uplift ratio, no-objection fee, or any other requirement with respect to capacity, frequency or traffic that would be inconsistent with the purposes of this Agreement.

4. Neither Party shall require the filing of schedules, programs for charter flights, or operational plans by airlines of the other Party for approval, except as may be required on a non-discriminatory basis to enforce the uniform conditions foreseen by paragraph 2 of this Article or as may be specifically authorized in an Annex to this Agreement. If a Party requires filings for information purposes,

it shall minimize the administrative burdens of filing requirements and procedures on air transportation intermediaries and on designated airlines of the other Party.

Article 12
Pricing

1. Each Party shall allow prices for air transportation to be established by each designated airline based upon commercial considerations in the marketplace. Intervention by the Parties shall be limited to:

a. prevention of unreasonably discriminatory prices or practices;

b. protection of consumers from prices that are unreasonably high or restrictive due to the abuse of a dominant position; and

c. protection of airlines from prices that are artificially low due to direct or indirect governmental subsidy or support.

2. Prices for international air transportation between the territories of the Parties shall not be required to be filed. Notwithstanding the foregoing, the designated airlines of the Parties shall continue to provide immediate access, on request, to information on historical, existing, and proposed prices to the aeronautical authorities of the Parties in a manner and format acceptable to those aeronautical authorities.

3. Neither Party shall take unilateral action to prevent the inauguration or continuation of a price proposed to be charged or charged by (i) an airline of either Party for international air transportation between the territories of the Parties, or (ii) an airline of one Party for international air transportation between the territory of the other Party and any other country, including in both cases transportation on an interline or intraline basis. If either Party believes that any such price is inconsistent with the considerations set forth in paragraph 1 of this Article, it shall request consultations and notify the other Party of the reasons for its dissatisfaction as soon as possible. These consultations shall be held not later than 30 days after receipt of the request, and the Parties shall cooperate in securing information necessary for reasoned resolution of the issue. If the Parties reach agreement with respect to a price for which a notice of dissatisfaction has been given, each Party shall use its best efforts to put that agreement into effect. Without such mutual agreement, the price shall go into effect or continue in effect.

Article 13
Consultations

Either Party may, at any time, request consultations relating to this Agreement. Such consultations shall begin at the earliest possible date, but not later than 60 days from the date the other Party receives the request unless otherwise agreed.

Article 14
Settlement of Disputes

1. Any dispute arising under this Agreement, except those that may arise under paragraph 3 of Article 12 (Pricing), that is not resolved by a first round of formal consultations may be referred by agreement of the Parties for decision to some person or body. If the Parties do not so agree, the dispute shall, at the request of either Party, be submitted to arbitration in accordance with the procedures set forth below.

2. Arbitration shall be by a tribunal of three arbitrators to be constituted as follows:

a. Within 30 days after the receipt of a request for arbitration, each Party shall name one arbitrator. Within 60 days after these two arbitrators have been named, they shall by agreement appoint a third arbitrator, who shall act as President of the arbitral tribunal;

b. If either Party fails to name an arbitrator, or if the third arbitrator is not appointed in accordance with subparagraph a of this paragraph, either Party may request the President of the Council of the International Civil Aviation Organization to appoint the necessary arbitrator or arbitrators within 30 days. If the President of the Council is of the same nationality as one of the Parties, the most senior Vice President who is not disqualified on that ground shall make the appointment.

3. Except as otherwise agreed, the arbitral tribunal shall determine the limits of its jurisdiction in accordance with this Agreement and shall establish its own procedural rules. The tribunal, once formed, may recommend interim relief measures pending its final determination. At the direction of the tribunal or at the request of either of the Parties, a conference to determine the precise issues to be arbitrated and the specific procedures to be followed shall be held not later than 15 days after the tribunal is fully constituted.

4. Except as otherwise agreed or as directed by the tribunal, each Party shall submit a memorandum within 45 days of the time the tribunal is fully constituted. Replies shall be due 60 days later. The tribunal shall hold a hearing at the request of either Party or on its own initiative within 15 days after replies are due.

5. The tribunal shall attempt to render a written decision within 30 days after completion of the hearing or, if no hearing is held, after the date both replies are submitted. The decision of the majority of the tribunal shall prevail.

6. The Parties may submit requests for clarification of the decision within 15 days after it is rendered and any clarification given shall be issued within 15 days of such request.

7. Each Party shall, to the degree consistent with its national law, give full effect to any decision or award of the arbitral tribunal.

8. The expenses of the arbitral tribunal, including the fees and expenses of the arbitrators, shall be shared equally by the Parties. Any expenses incurred by the President of the Council of the International Civil Aviation Organization in connection with the procedures of paragraph 2b of this Article shall be considered to be part of the expenses of the arbitral tribunal.

Article 15
Registration with ICAO

This Agreement and all amendments thereto shall be registered with the International Civil Aviation Organization.

Article 16
Termination

Either Party may, at any time, give notice in writing to the other Party of its decision to terminate this Agreement. Such notice shall be sent simultaneously to the International Civil Aviation Organization. This Agreement shall terminate at midnight (at the place of receipt of the notice to the other Party) immediately before the first anniversary of the date of receipt of the notice by the other Party, unless the notice is withdrawn by agreement of the Parties before the end of this period.

Article 17
Amendments

The Parties shall agree to any amendments of this Agreement in a separate Protocol which, upon its entry into force, shall form an integral part of this Agreement. Any such Protocol shall enter into force on the date of the later note in an exchange of diplomatic notes between the Parties confirming that each Party has completed the necessary internal procedures for entry into force of the Protocol.

Article 18
Entry into Force

This Agreement and its Annexes shall enter into force on the date of the later note in an exchange of diplomatic notes between the Parties confirming that each Party has completed the necessary internal procedures for entry into force of this Agreement.

IN WITNESS WHEREOF the undersigned, being duly authorized by their respective Governments, have signed this Agreement.

DONE at Washington, this twenty-first day of June, 2007, in duplicate, in the English and Georgian languages, each text being an authentic text. In case of any divergence of interpretation between the two language texts, the English text shall prevail.

FOR THE GOVERNMENT OF THE UNITED STATES OF AMERICA:

[Signature]

FOR THE GOVERNMENT OF GEORGIA:

[Signature]

ANNEX I
Scheduled Air Transportation

Section 1
Routes

Airlines of each Party designated under this Annex shall, in accordance with the terms of their designation, be entitled to perform scheduled international air transportation between points on the following routes:

A. Routes for the airline or airlines designated by the Government of the United States:

1. From points behind the United States via the United States and intermediate points to a point or points in Georgia and beyond.
2. For all-cargo service or services, between Georgia and any point or points.

B. Routes for the airline or airlines designated by the Government of Georgia:

1. From points behind Georgia via Georgia and intermediate points to a point or points in the United States and beyond.
2. For all-cargo service or services, between the United States and any point or points.

Section 2
Operational Flexibility

Each designated airline may, on any or all flights and at its option:

1. operate flights in either or both directions;
2. combine different flight numbers within one aircraft operation;
3. serve behind, intermediate, and beyond points and points in the territories of the Parties on the routes in any combination and in any order;
4. omit stops at any point or points;
5. transfer traffic from any of its aircraft to any of its other aircraft at any point on the routes; and
6. serve points behind any point in its territory with or without change of aircraft or flight number and may hold out and advertise such services to the public as through services;

without directional or geographic limitation and without loss of any right to carry traffic otherwise permissible under this Agreement; provided that, with the exception of all-cargo services, the service serves a point in the territory of the Party designating the airline.

Section 3
Change of Gauge

On any segment or segments of the routes above, any designated airline may perform international air transportation without any limitation as to change, at any point on the route, in type or number of aircraft operated; provided that, with the exception of all-cargo services, in the outbound direction, the transportation beyond such point is a continuation of the transportation from the territory of the Party that has designated the airline and, in the inbound direction, the transportation to the territory of the Party that has designated the airline is a continuation of the transportation from beyond such point.

ANNEX II
Charter Air Transportation

Section 1

A. Airlines of each Party designated under this Annex shall, in accordance with the terms of their designation, have the right to carry international charter traffic of passengers (and their accompanying baggage) and/or cargo (including, but not limited to, freight forwarder, split, and combination (passenger/cargo) charters):

1. Between any point or points in the territory of the Party that has designated the airline and any point or points in the territory of the other Party; and

2. Between any point or points in the territory of the other Party and any point or points in a third country or countries, provided that, except with respect to cargo charters, such service constitutes part of a continuous operation, with or without a change of aircraft, that includes service to the homeland for the purpose of carrying local traffic between the homeland and the territory of the other Party.

B. In the performance of services covered by this Annex, airlines of each Party designated under this Annex shall also have the right: (1) to make stopovers at any points whether within or outside of the territory of either Party; (2) to carry transit traffic through the other Party's territory; (3) to combine on the same aircraft traffic originating in one Party's territory, traffic originating in the other Party's territory, and traffic originating in third countries; and (4) to perform international air transportation without any limitation as to change, at any point on the route, in type or number of aircraft operated; provided that, except with respect to cargo charters, in the outbound direction, the transportation beyond such point is a continuation of the transportation from the territory of the Party that has designated the airline and in the inbound direction, the transportation to the territory of the Party that has designated the airline is a continuation of the transportation from beyond such point.

C. Each Party shall extend favorable consideration to applications by airlines of the other Party to carry traffic not covered by this Annex on the basis of comity and reciprocity.

Section 2

A. Any airline designated by either Party performing international charter air transportation originating in the territory of either Party, whether on a one-way or round-trip basis, shall have the option of complying with the charter laws, regulations, and rules either of its homeland or of the other Party. If a Party applies different rules, regulations, terms, conditions, or limitations to one or more of its airlines, or to airlines of different countries, each designated airline shall be subject to the least restrictive of such criteria.

B. However, nothing contained in the above paragraph shall limit the rights of either Party to require airlines designated under this Annex by either Party to adhere to requirements relating to the protection of passenger funds and passenger cancellation and refund rights.

Section 3

Except with respect to the consumer protection rules referred to in the preceding paragraph, neither Party shall require an airline designated under this Annex by the other Party, in respect of the carriage of traffic from the territory of that other Party or of a third country on a one-way or round-trip basis, to submit more than a declaration of conformity with the applicable laws, regulations and rules referred to under section 2 of this Annex or of a waiver of these laws, regulations, or rules granted by the applicable aeronautical authorities.

STATE DEPARTMENT DOCUMENT NUMBER: 08-07

AMENDMENT NUMBER SIX TO THE STRATEGIC OBJECTIVE GRANT AGREEMENT OF SEPTEMBER 11, 2003, AS AMENDED, BETWEEN THE UNITED STATES OF AMERICA AND THE REPUBLIC OF MOZAMBIQUE, FOR THE HIV/AIDS PROGRAM, WITH ATTACHMENTS

SIGNED ON JULY 31, 2006
ENTERED INTO FORCE JULY 31, 2006

CTIA DOCUMENT NUMBER: 13383.001

Strategic Objective Grant Agreement 656-009
Amendment 6

This Strategic Objective Grant agreement Amendment Number Six is entered into between the Republic of Mozambique (the "Grantee") and the United States of America, acting through the U.S. agency for International Development ("USAID").

WHEREAS the Grantee and USAID (the "Parties") executed this Strategic Objective Grant Agreement for the HIV/AIDS Program (the "Agreement") on September 11, 2003;

WHEREAS the Parties previously amended the Agreement on January 20, 2004, on September 20, 2004, on May 13, 2005, on September 30, 2005, and on April 27 2006; and

WHEREAS the Parties now desire to execute this Amendment Number Six to the Agreement to:

1) Reflect an increase in the USAID Contribution to the Grant in the amount of Thirty Million Six Hundred Fifty Seven Thousand Six Hundred United States (U.S.) Dollars ($30,657,600), to support the on-going implementation of activities under the Agreement under the USAID Country Strategic Plan (CSP) for Mozambique 2004–2010); and

2) Include the amount of Eleven Million Seven Hundred Seventy Eight Thousand Two Hundred Forty Two U.S. Dollars ($11,778,242) in the "USAID/Washington Instruments" line item contained in the Illustrative Financial Plan.

NOW THEREFORE, the Parties hereby agree that the Agreement is hereby amended as follows:

1. Article 3. Section 3.1.(a). "*The Grant*," is amended by deleting "Forty Five Million One Hundred Fifty Five Thousand Five Hundred Eight U.S. Dollars ($45,155,508)" and by substituting "Seventy Five Million Eight Hundred Thirteen Thousand One Hundred Eight U.S. Dollars ($75,813,108)."

2. Annex 1 of the Agreement, Amplified Program Description, is modified to incorporate Attachment 2 to this Amendment 6, "Fourth Supplement to the Amplified Program Description".

3. Attachment No. 1 (Illustrative Financial Plan) to Annex 1 of the Agreement is deleted in its entirety and is replaced with Attachment No. 1 (Illustrative Financial Plan) attached hereto.

SECTION 2. Except as specifically amended or modified herein, the Agreement shall remain in full force and effect in accordance with all of its terms.

SECTION 3. *Effective Date*. This Amendment to the Agreement shall enter into force when signed by both Parties hereto.

IN WITNESS WHEREOF, the Government of the Republic of Mozambique and the Government of the United States of America, each acting through its respective duly authorized representatives, have caused this Amendment to be signed in their names and delivered as of the day and year written above.

For the Government of the United States of America

[Signature]
KEVIN ARMSTRONG
Acting Director
U.S. Agency for International Development
Date: 27. 07. 2006

Pelo Governo da Republica de Moçambique

[Signature]
ALCINDA ANTóNIO DE ABREU
Ministra
Ministério dos Negócios Estrangeiros e Cooperação

Strategic Objective Grant Agreement 656-009
Amendment 4
Attachment 2

FOURTH SUPPLEMENT TO THE AMPLIFIED PROGRAM DESCRIPTION

This Supplement is an integral part of the Amplified Program Description to the HIV/AIDS Program, Strategic Objective Grant Agreement ("Agreement") 656-009.

The purpose of this Supplement is to describe new activities related to the treatment of tuberculosis that are being introduced into the HIV/AIDS Program.

Tuberculosis is the major opportunistic infection that affects people living with HIV and AIDS, yet there is limited collaboration between the HIV/AIDS and TB programs in Mozambique. Since morbidity and mortality rates among TB/HIV co-infected patients are high, the development and implementation of new models of collaboration and integration between TB and HIV programs must be a high priority.

New Activities

New TB activities implemented under the program will contribute to the achievement of Result 3, Provide Care to People Infected and Affected by HIV/AIDS, Including Orphans and Vulnerable Children.

The objective of new activities is to expand care and strengthen the integration of TB and HIV care and treatment services.

Illustrative activities to be carried out include:

- Establish HIV testing services at TB clinics in Manica and Sofala provinces;
- Strengthen the referral system for co-infected TB-HIV clients identified at TB clinics to improve their access to other clinical and support services, including anti-retroviral therapy, as appropriate;
- Train physicians, nurses and counselors at existing TB clinics to apply a new treatment model; and
- Train health care workers to improve screening of HIV clients for TB.

Strategic Objective Grant Agreement 656-009
Annex 1

Monitoring and Evaluation

The indicators that will be used to measure the impact of new activities have yet to be finalized, but are likely to include:

- Number of TB clinic patients at selected sites who receive voluntary HIV counseling and testing services; and
- Number of health care workers trained to apply new TB-HIV treatment model.

Strategic Objective Grant Agreement 656-009
Annex 1
Amendment 6

Attachment 1 to Annex 1

	Strategic Objective Grant Agreement No. 656-009 Illustrative Financial Plan USAID Contribution (USD)			
Elements	**Previous USAID Obligations**	**This Obligation**	**Obligations to Date**	**Total Planned USAID Contribution**
Result 1 - Provide Treatment to HIV-infected People	2,684,243	4,642,500	7,326,743	6,415,300
Result 2 - Prevent New HIV Infections	19,520,377	9,440,620	28,960,997	27,607,100
Result 3 - Provide Care to People Infected and Affected by HIV/AIDS, Including Orphans and Vulnerable Children	19,212,459	12,347,782	31,560,241	28,766,200
Result 4 - Strengthen Policy and Systems for HIV/AIDS Response	957,307	1,150,000	2,107,307	2,035,400
Management Support	2,781,122	3,076,698	5,857,820	5,990,800
Sub-Total (USAID/ Mozambique)	**45,155,508**	**30,657,600**	**75,813,108**	**70,814,800**
Sub-Total (USAID/ Washington Instruments)	13,139,138	11,778,242	24,917,380	21,585,200
Total Expected USAID Assistance Obligated and Planned	**58,294,646**	**42,435,842**	**100,730,488**	**92,400,000**
Additional Expected USAID Assistance				**194,330,500**
Expected USAID Assistance to be planned				**286,730,500**

State Department Document Number: 08-08

Amendment Number Eight to the Strategic Objective Grant Agreement of September 11, 2003, as Amended, Between the United States of America and the Republic of Mozambique, for the HIV/AIDS Program, with Attachments

Signed on August 9 and 13, 2007
Entered into force August 13, 2007

CTIA Document Number: 13383.002

Strategic Objective Grant Agreement 656-009

Amendment 8

This Strategic Objective Grant agreement Amendment Number Eight is entered into between the Republic of Mozambique (the "Grantee") and the United States of America, acting through the U.S. Agency for international Development ("USAID").

Whereas the Grantee and USAID (the "Parties") executed this Strategic Objective Grant Agreement for the HIV/AIDS Program (the "Agreement") on September 11, 2003;

Whereas the Parties previously amended the Agreement on January 20, 2004, on September 20, 2004, on May 13, 2005, on September 30, 2005, on April 27, 2006, on July 31, 2006, and on May 4, 2007; and

Whereas the Parties now desire to execute this Amendment Number Eight to the Agreement to:

1) Reflect an increase in the USAID Contribution to the Grant in the amount of Forty Five Million Three Hundred Thirty Four Thousand Seven Hundred and Seven United States (U.S.) Dollars ($45,334,707), to support the on-going implementation of activities under the Agreement under the USAID Country Strategic Plan (CSP) for Mozambique 2004-2010); and

2) Include the amount of Eighteen Million Nine Hundred Sixteen Thousand Six Hundred Sixty Eight U.S. Dollars ($18,916,668) in the "USAID/Washington Instruments" line item contained in the Illustrative Financial Plan; and

3) To realign the indicative planned level of assistance for each Result over the life of the Agreement.

NOW THEREFORE, the Parties hereby agree that the Agreement is hereby amended as follows:

1. Article 3. Section 3.1.(a). "*The Grant*," is amended by deleting "Ninety One Million Three Hundred Seventy Thousand Four Hundred Eight U.S. Dollars ($91,370,408)"and by substituting "One Hundred Thirty Six Million Seven Hundred Five Thousand One Hundred Fifteen U.S. Dollars ($136,705,115)."

2. Annex 1 of the Agreement, Amplified Program Description, is modified to incorporate Attachment 2 to this Amendment 8, "Fifth Supplement to 'the Amplified Program Description".

3. Attachment No. 1 (Illustrative Financial Plan) to Annex 1 of the Agreement is deleted in its entirety and is replaced with Attachment No.1 (Illustrative Financial Plan) attached hereto.

SECTION 2. Except as specifically amended or modified herein, the Agreement shall remain in full force and effect in accordance with all of its terms.

SECTION 3. *Effective Date*. This Amendment to the Agreement shall enter into force when signed by both Parties hereto.

IN WITNESS WHEREOF, the Government of the Republic of Mozambique and the Government of the United States of America, each acting through its respective duly authorized representatives, have caused this Amendment to be signed in their names and delivered as of the day and year written above.

For the Government of the United States of America

____

[Signature]
TODD HANSON AMANI
Director
U.S. Agency for International Development
Date: August 13, 2007

Pelo Governo da Republica de Moçambique

____

[Signature]
ALCINDA ANTÓNIO DE ABREU
Ministra
Ministério dos Negócios Estrangeiros e Cooperação

Strategic Objective Grant Agreement 656-009
Amendment 8
Attachment 2

Fifth Supplement to the amplified Program description

This Supplement is an integral part of the Amplified Program Description for the HIV/AIDS Program approved and implemented under Strategic Objective Grant Agreement 656-009.

The purpose of this Supplement is to describe the expanded array of activities related to HIV/AIDS prevention, treatment, care, and mitigation that will be implemented as part of the U.S. President's Emergency Plan for AIDS Relief (PEPFAR), also known as the Emergency Plan.

A number of activities to be implemented with PEPFAR funding under this Agreement were described in the previous Supplements to the Amplified Program Description. Activities previously described are expected to continue. This Supplement describes activities to further expand HIV/AIDS-related services in Mozambique, focusing on the following areas:

1. Improving the lives of orphans and other vulnerable children affected by HIV/AIDS; and extending and optimizing quality of life for HIV-infected individuals and their families, through the provision of clinical, psychological, spiritual, social and prevention services.

2. Expanding prevention activities, including condom social marketing, focusing on high-prevalence areas and high-risk groups, to avert new infections and to increase acceptance of and demand for voluntary counseling and testing, prevention of mother-to-child transmission, and care and treatment services.

3. Helping prevent new infections, promote uptake of new HIV/AIDS care and treatment services, reduce stigma and discrimination, and strengthen Mozambican systems and institutional and social capacity to meet the challenges of a true national response to HIV/AIDS.

Within these areas and those described in the Amplified Program Description as previously amended, the following new activities are planned:

- One activity will improve the health and nutritional status of the most vulnerable children and of PLWHA receiving anti-retroviral treatment, in order to increase treatment adherence and reduce potential negative effects of the drugs. In coordination with the Ministry of Health (MOH) and the Ministry of Women and Social Assistance (MMAS), this activity will focus on the implementation of food-based interventions in the context of ART both at the clinical setting and within the household.

- A second activity will support the MOH to assess the current state of male circumcision in Mozambique. Results of this assessment will provide information for the MOH in considering potential next steps such as training of health workers and public health messages.

- A third activity will support capacity building for Mozambican networks, associations, and national and local organizations, to enhance their abilities in the areas of program planning, implementation, monitoring and evaluation, aimed at fostering self-sufficiency and sustainability. All organizations will be part of the integrated health network system. This support is expected to increase their capacity to solicit, receive and account for funds, sub-grant to member organizations and report results to donors.

As the design of the activities described above proceeds, further consultations between USAID, the GRM, and other partners will continue, to ensure that assistance provided under this Agreement is used efficiently and effectively to achieve the Results as stated in the Agreement.

Strategic Objective Grant Agreement 656-009
Annex 1
Amendment 8

Attachment 1

Strategic Objective Grant Agreement No. 656-009
Illustrative Financial Plan
USAID Contribution (USD)

Elements	Previous Obligations	Budget Realigment	This Obligation	Obligations to Date	Total Planned USAID Contribution
Result 1 - Provide Treatment to HTV infected People	**12,146,743**	**−129,270**	**9,550,520**	**28,193,704**	**21,956,493**
Result 2 - Prevent New HIV Infections	**31,058,297**	**−297,278**	**16,046,961**	**45,859,873**	**51,544,658**
Result 3 - Provide Care to People Infected and Affected by HIV/AIDS, including Orphans and Vulnerable Children	**38,700,241**	**150,000**	**14,801,576**	**53,501,817**	**54,709,832**
Result 4 - Strengthen Policy and Systems (or HIV/AIDS Response	**2,307,307**	**276,548**	**1,650,000**	**3,957,307**	**6,975,903**
Management Support	**7,157,820**	**0**	**3,285,650**	**10,443,470**	**10,443,470**
Sub-Total (USAID/ Mozambique)	**91,370,408**	**0**	**45,334,707**	**136,705,115**	**145,630,356**
Sub-Total (USAID/ Washington Instruments)	24,917,380	0	18,916,668	43,834,048	40,277,807
Total Expected USAID Assistance Obligated and Planned	**116,287,788**	**0**	**64,251,375**	**180,539,163**	**185,908,163**
Additional Expected USAID Assistance					100,822,337
Expected USAID Assistance to be Planned					**286,730,500**

Strategic Objective Grant Agreement 656-009 *Amendment 8*			
HIV/AIDS Program SOAG 656-009 Amendment 8 Financial Plan			
PO Drafter:	**H Silva**	**Signature**	**Date: 06/01/07**
HIV Program Officer	**N Lentini**	**Signature**	**Date: 06/14/07**
HIV Acting Team Leader:	**N McCharen**	**Signature**	**Date:** 6/14/07
PO:	**G Mendes**	**Signature**	**Date:** June 19, 2007
RLA:	**D Keene**	**e-mail**	**Date:** 06/22/07
A/Controller:	**W Butler**	**Signature**	**Date:** 7/3/07
Portuguese:	**L Capelao**	**Signature**	**Date:** 5/7/07
A/Program Officer:	**G Mendes**	**Signature**	**Date:**7/5/07

SO9 SOAG AMDT No. 08

Accounting Classification

CO No.:	**656-SOAG-656-0090-08**	**FUNDS AVAILABLE** **8/3/07**
Program Area:	A11	
Program Element-	A047	
Fund:	2007 GAI-X7	
USD:	45,334,707.00	

State Department Document Number: 08-09

Memorandum of Understanding Between the United States National Aeronautics and Space Administration and the Italian Space Agency Concerning the Gamma-Ray Large Area Space Telescope Mission

Signed on February 22 and March 7, 2007
Entered into force December 4, 2007

CTIA DOCUMENT NUMBER: 13384.000

Preamble

The United States National Aeronautics and Space Administration (hereinafter referred to as "NASA"), and

The Italian Space Agency (hereinafter referred to as "ASI"),

Collectively hereinafter referred to as "the Parties":

CONSIDERING that NASA is developing the Gamma-ray Large Area Space Telescope (GLAST) mission;

CONSIDERING that NASA is engaged in a vigorous, long-term exploration program that is designed to improve our understanding of the universe;

CONSIDERING mat ASI has a well-defined strategy in the field of gamma-ray astronomy starting from the national BeppoSAX mission, followed by the Italian participation on the NASA Swift mission, and in developing the national small mission AGILE;

RECOGNIZING that ASI is interested in joining with NASA as a key participant on the GLAST mission;

RECALLING the interim agreement of November 11, 2004, between NASA and ASI, addressing an interest to pursue activities together on GLAST;

HAVE AGREED as follows:

Article 1 - Scope

1.1. This Memorandum of Understanding (MOU) defines the responsibilities, ways, and means, as well as the terms and conditions, by which the cooperation between the Parties shall be conducted within the framework of NASA's GLAST mission.

1.2. The primary activities addressed in this MOU concern the participation in the development of the Large Area Telescope (LAT) tracker subsystem and in the LAT scientific investigations by ASI and its related entity, the National Institute of Nuclear Physics (INFN).

Article 2 - The GLAST Mission

2.1. NASA's GLAST mission is designed to identify and study nature's highest energy particle accelerators, measuring, with two instruments, the spectra and temporal histories of gamma rays in the energy range from 10 keV to 300 GeV. The LAT, the primary GLAST instrument, covers the energy range 20 MeV to 300 GeV. The GLAST Burst Monitor (GBM) instrument complements the LAT, monitoring the sky for transients in the energy range 10 keV to 25 MeV.

2.2. GLAST is expected to observe at least ten times as many active galactic nuclei and stellar-mass black holes as previously detected in the gamma-ray band. It is intended to study pulsars and supernova remnants, gamma-ray bursts, the diffuse galactic and extragalactic high-energy gamma-ray backgrounds, and solar flares. GLAST is also designed to search for annihilation-line radiation from weakly interacting massive particles that may account for much of the dark matter in the universe.

Critical mission milestones (estimated)	
Launch:	No Earlier Than November 2007
Primary Science Phase:	60 Days After Launch for 5 Years
Critical mission parameters	
Nominal Orbit:	550 km
Inclination:	28.5 degrees
Nominal Lifetime:	5 years (10-year goal)

Article 3 - Programmatic Responsibilities of NASA

NASA shall use reasonable efforts to fulfill the responsibilities below:

3.1. Provide overall program management for the GLAST mission, including design, development, integration, launch, and operations.

3.2. Establish and support the GLAST Science Working Group (SWG), appoint a Project Scientist to serve as the SWG lead, and support, jointly with the United States Department of Energy (DOE), the LAT instrument team.

3.3. Arrange for the design of the GLAST mission, including requirements definition, design and development of subsystem specifications, verification plans, and overall mission requirements.

3.4. Provide overall management of the development of the LAT flight instrument including the silicon tracker subsystem.

3.5. Support the design and development of the LAT prototype and flight silicon tracker readout electronics and collaborate with ASI and its related entities on the design and development of the LAT tracker support structure subassemblies.

3.6. Integrate, with assistance from ASI and ASI's related entities, the tracker modules into the LAT instrument assembly and perform associated testing and calibration in the United States with assistance from ASI and its related entities.

3.7. Conduct, in the United States, a high-altitude balloon flight of GLAST instrument engineering models.

3.8. Provide the interfaces and data necessary for the ASI Science Data Center (ASDC) to serve as a mirror data site for the LAT science database at the LAT Instrument Operations Center (LIOC).

3.9. Establish and maintain a NASA GLAST Science Support Center (GSSC) consistent with GLAST mission data use policy as described in the GLAST Project Data Management Plan (PDMP).

3.10. Provide opportunities for participation of the general scientific community in the GLAST Guest Observer Program and Key Project opportunities defined in the GLAST PDMP.

3.11. Seek suggestions from ASI on candidate names of Italian scientists to participate as reviewers when the GLAST Guest Observer peer review teams are being formed.

Article 4 - Programmatic Responsibilities of ASI

ASI shall use reasonable efforts to fulfill the responsibilities below:

4.1. Participate, with its related entities, in the development of the LAT tracker subsystem, build eighteen tracker towers, and provide them directly to the Stanford Linear Accelerator Center (SLAC).

4.2. Ensure that INFN fulfills its GLAST-related responsibilities, including the provision of the LAT tracker hardware and operations expertise, LAT science planning, and data analysis, as needed.

4.3. Support LAT instrument team meetings and reviews, as appropriate.

4.4. Establish and maintain a mirror data site of the LAT science database, participate in the development of the GLAST/LAT data analysis software, and lead the development of and make available for the use of the GLAST LAT collaboration, the software for the publication of LAT catalogs and the distribution of high level data products via the World Wide Web.

4.5. Provide for the necessary interfaces to allow the ASDC to serve as a mirror site for the LAT data at the LIOC.

4.6. Participate as members of the LAT science team and in the LAT science investigation in accordance with the data use policy as described in the PDMP.

4.7. Provide suggestions to NASA on candidate names of Italian scientists to participate as reviewers when the GLAST Guest Observer peer review teams are being formed.

Article 5 - Rights in and Distribution of Scientific Data

5.1. Data generated under this MOU shall be treated in accordance with the GLAST data use policy as described in the PDMP.

5.2. The Parties shall have the right to use the data (processed and unprocessed) at any time for support of their respective responsibilities but shall not prejudice the mission investigators' first publication rights, which are established in accordance with paragraph 5.1 above.

5.3. The Parties and their investigators shall have immediate access to scientific data obtained by their respective investigations. The Parties shall work to ensure that all investigators have access to other telemetered science and engineering data relevant to the calibration/validation of the respective investigations.

Article 6 - Program and Project Management

This Article describes general management and organizational responsibilities. Each Party is responsible for the management of its activities as identified in Articles 3 and 4 above.

NASA Headquarters

6.1. The NASA Astrophysics Division Director, within the Science Mission Directorate, is responsible for the overall NASA Astrophysics Observation Program, is supported by mission-specific program executives, and is responsible for oversight of all NASA Astrophysics flight program activities, as well as formal programmatic liaison with ASI and liaison and coordination with other United States Government agencies.

6.2. The GLAST Program Executive is responsible for the definition, integration, and assessment of all activities related to the GLAST mission.

6.3. The GLAST Program Scientist is the primary point of contact for international discussions of science policy.

6.4. The GLAST Program Executive is the principal point of contact for NASA in the performance of this MOU.

NASA Goddard Space Flight Center (GSFC)

6.5. NASA has designated GSFC to lead the formulation and implementation of the GLAST mission. A GLAST Project Office has been established for this purpose, and a GLAST Project Manager has been assigned. This Project Office is part of the GSFC.

ASI Headquarters

6.6. The ASI Headquarters, Observation of the Universe, is responsible for overall programmatic and science management of the ASI-sponsored universe observation activities. Within this directorate, the Astrophysics Office is responsible for all activities regarding NASA GLAST cooperation. ASI has designated a GLAST Program/Project Manager and GLAST Program/Project Scientist to manage ASI contributions to GLAST. ASI also has designated a contract manager to manage the primary GLAST implementation contract.

6.7. The GLAST Program/Project Scientist is the principal point of contact for ASI in the performance of this MOU.

Article 7 - Transfer of Goods and Technical Data

The Parties are obligated to transfer only those technical data (including software) and goods necessary to fulfill their respective responsibilities under this MOU, in accordance with the following provisions, notwithstanding any other provision of this MOU:

7.1. All activities of the Parties will be carried out in accordance with their national laws and regulations, including those pertaining to export control and the control of classified information.

7.2. The transfer of technical data for the purpose of discharging the Parties' responsibilities with regard to interface, integration, and safety shall normally be made without restriction, except as provided in 7.1 above.

7.3. All transfers of goods and proprietary or export-controlled technical data are subject to the following provisions. In the event a Party or its related entity (e.g.; contractor, subcontractor, grantee, cooperating entity) finds it necessary to transfer goods or to transfer proprietary or export-controlled technical data, for which protection is to be maintained, such goods shall be specifically identified and such proprietary or export-controlled technical data shall be marked. The identification for goods and the marking on proprietary or export-controlled technical data will indicate that the goods and proprietary or export-controlled technical data shall be used by the receiving Party or related entities only for the purposes of fulfilling the receiving Party's or related entity's responsibilities under this MOU, and that the identified goods and marked proprietary technical data or marked export-controlled technical data shall not be disclosed or retransferred to any other entity without the prior written permission of the furnishing Party or its related entity. The receiving Party or related entity shall abide by the terms of the notice and protect any such identified goods and marked proprietary technical data or marked export-controlled technical data from unauthorized use and disclosure. The Parties to this MOU will cause their related entities to be bound by the provisions of this Article related to use, disclosure, and retransfer of goods and marked technical data through contractual mechanisms or equivalent measures.

7.4. All goods exchanged in the performance of this MOU shall be used by the receiving Party or related entity exclusively for the purposes of this MOU. Upon completion of the activities under this MOU, the receiving Party or related entity shall return or, at the request of the furnishing Party or its related entity, otherwise dispose of all goods and marked proprietary technical data or marked export-controlled technical data provided under this MOU, as directed by the furnishing Party or related entity.

Article 8 - Intellectual Property

8.1. For the purposes of this Article, "Related Entity" includes but is not limited to contractors, subcontractors, grantees, or cooperating entities (or any lower tier contractor, subcontractor, grantee, or cooperating entities) of a Party.

8.2. Patents

a. Nothing in this MOU shall be construed as granting, either expressly or by implication, to the other Party any rights to, or interest in, any inventions of a Party or its Related Entities made prior to the entry into force of, or outside the scope of, this MOU, including any patents or other forms of protection (in any country) corresponding to such inventions.

b. Any rights to, or interest in, any invention made in the performance of this MOU solely by one Party or any of its Related Entities, including any patents or other forms of protection (in any country) corresponding to such invention, shall be owned by such Party or, subject to paragraph 2.d of this Article, such Related Entity.

c. It is not anticipated that there will be any joint inventions made in the performance of this MOU. Nevertheless, in the event that an invention is jointly made by the Parties in the performance of this MOU, the Parties shall, in good faith, consult and agree as to: a) the allocation of rights to, or interest in, such joint invention, including any patents or other forms of protection (in any country) corresponding to such joint invention; b) the responsibilities, costs, and actions to be taken to establish and maintain patents or other forms of protection (in any country) for each such joint invention; and c) the terms and conditions of any license or other rights to be exchanged between the Parties or granted by one Party to the other Party.

d. With respect to any invention created in the performance of this MOU and involving a Related Entity, allocation of rights between a Party and its Related Entity to such invention, including any patents or other forms of protection (in any country) corresponding to such invention, shall be determined by such Party's laws, regulations, and applicable contractual obligations.

8.3. Copyrights

a. Nothing in this MOU shall be construed as granting, either expressly or by implication, to the other Party any rights to, or interest in, any copyrights of a Party or its Related Entities created prior to the entry into force of, or outside the scope of, this MOU.

b. Any copyrights in works created solely by one Party or any of its Related Entities, as a result of activities undertaken in performance of this MOU, shall be owned by such Party or Related Entity. Allocation of rights between such Party and its Related Entities to such copyrights shall be determined by such Party's laws, regulations, and applicable contractual obligations.

c. For any jointly authored work, should the Parties decide to register the copyright in such work, they shall, in good faith, consult and agree as to the responsibilities, costs, and actions to be taken to register copyrights and maintain copyright protection (in any country).

d. Subject to the provisions of Articles 7 and 9, each Party shall have an irrevocable, royalty-free right to reproduce, prepare derivative works, distribute copies to the public, and perform publicly and display publicly, and authorize others to do so on its behalf, any copyrighted work resulting from activities undertaken in the performance of this MOU for its own purposes, regardless of whether the work was created solely by, or on behalf of, that Party or jointly with the other Party, and without consulting with or accounting to the other Party.

Article 9 - Publication of Public Information and Results

9.1. The Parties retain the right to release public information regarding their own activities under this MOU. The Parties shall coordinate with each other in advance concerning releasing to the pu. blic information that relates to the other Party's responsibilities or performance under this MOU. As appropriate, full acknowledgement shall be made by both Parties of the role of the other Party in the GLAST mission.

9.2

a. The Parties shall make the final results obtained from the GLAST mission available to the general scientific community through publication in appropriate journals or by presentations at scientific conferences as soon as possible and in a manner consistent with good scientific practices.

b. Each Party shall have an irrevocable, royalty-free right to reproduce, prepare derivative works from, distribute to the public copies of, present publicly, and authorize others to do so on its behalf, the scientific information included in each such publication or presentation for its own purposes. The royalty-free right shall exist irrespective of any copyright protection applicable to each such publication or presentation.

9.3. The Parties acknowledge that the following data or information does not constitute public information and that such data or information shall not be included in any publication or presentation by a Party under this article without the other Party's prior written permission: 1) data furnished by the other Party in accordance with Article 7 of this MOU which is export-controlled, classified or proprietary; or 2) information about an invention of the other Party before a patent application has been filed covering the same, or a decision not to file has been made.

Article 10 - Financial Arrangements

10.1. Each Party will bear the costs of discharging its respective responsibilities, including travel and subsistence of personnel and transportation of all equipment and other items for which it is responsible.

10.2. The ability of the Parties to carry out their obligations is subject to the availability of appropriated funds. Further, it is understood that NASA's ability to carry out its overall responsibilities under this MOU is also subject to DOE funding necessary to complete its contributions to development of the LAT, and DOE contributions are also subject to the availability of appropriated funds.

10.3. The Parties understand that ASI's ability is also subject to INFN funding necessary to complete its contributions, and the INFN contribution is also subject to the availability of appropriated funds.

10.4. Should either NASA or ASI encounter budgetary problems that may affect the activities to be carried out under this MOU, the Party encountering the problems will notify and consult with the other Party as soon as possible. NASA and ASI also agree to monitor the funding status of their respective related entities and notify and consult with the other Party as soon as possible should their related entities encounter budgetary problems.

Article 11 - Customs Clearance, Taxes, Immigration and Ownership

11.1. In accordance with the laws and regulations in force in each Party's respective country, each Party shall facilitate free customs clearance and waiver of all applicable customs duties and taxes for equipment and related goods necessary for the implementation of this MOU. In the event that any customs duties or taxes of any kind are nonetheless levied on such equipment and related goods, such customs duties or taxes shall be borne by the Party of the country levying such customs duties or taxes. The Parties' obligation to facilitate duty free entry and exit of equipment and related goods is fully reciprocal.

11.2. Subject to applicable laws and regulations, each Party shall facilitate provision of the appropriate entry and residence documentation for the other Party's personnel who enter, exit, or reside within its territory in order to carry out the activities under this MOU.

11.3. Equipment provided by ASI pursuant to this MOU will remain the property of ASI. Equipment provided by NASA pursuant to this MOU will remain the property of NASA.

Article 12 - Exchange of Technical Personnel

12.1. Each Party may temporarily locate a mutually agreed-upon number of its personnel at the other Parry's respective facilities in the United States and Italy to participate in technical activities described in this MOU. Each Party shall provide workspace and necessary office equipment to accommodate the other Party's personnel that shall be temporarily located in the United States and Italy. Salary and all other personnel expenses, such as living and travel expenses, shall be borne by the employing Party of the technical representative(s) throughout the duration of their assignment. Arrangements for, and all conditions relating to, the personnel relationships, shall be agreed to and jointly documented in writing between NASA and ASI. These personnel shall comply with the safety and security rules and regulations of the hosting Party.

Article 13 - Registration of Space Objects

13.1. NASA shall request that the U.S. Government register GLAST in accordance with the 1975 Convention on Registration of Objects Launched into Outer Space (the Registration Convention). NASA shall retain jurisdiction and control over the space objects it registers.

13.2. Registration pursuant to this paragraph shall not affect the rights or obligations of either Party or its Government under the 1972 Convention on International Liability for Damage Caused by Space Objects.

Article 14 - Liability

14.1. The Parties agree that a comprehensive cross-waiver of liability among the Parties and their related entities will further participation in space exploration, use, and investment. The cross-waiver of liability shall be broadly construed to achieve this objective. The terms of the waiver are set out below.

14.2. The following terms, as used in this Article are defined below:

a. The term "Party" has the meaning specified in the Preamble;

b. The term "related entity" means:

(i) a contractor, subcontractor, or sponsored entity of a Party at any tier;

(ii) a user or customer of a Party at any tier;

(iii) a contractor or subcontractor of a user or customer or sponsored entity of a Party at any tier; or

(iv) scientific investigators.

The term "related entity" may also include another State or an agency or institution of another State, where such State, agency, or institution is an entity as described in (i) through (iv) above or is otherwise involved in the activities undertaken pursuant to this MOU.

The terms "contractors" and "subcontractors" include suppliers of any kind.

c. The term "damage" means:

(i) bodily injury to, or other impairment of health of, or death of, any person;

(ii) damage to, loss of, or loss of use of any property;

(iii) loss of revenue or profits; or

(iv) other direct, indirect, or consequential damage.

d. The term "launch vehicle" means an object or any part thereof intended for launch, launched from Earth, or returning to Earth that carries payloads or persons, or both;

e. The term "payload" means all property to be flown or used on or in a launch vehicle; and

f. The term "Protected Space Operations" means all activities pursuant to this MOU, including launch vehicle activities and payload activities on Earth, in outer space, or in transit between Earth and outer space. "Protected Space Operations" begin at die signature of this MOU and ends when all activities done in implementation of this MOU are completed. "Protected Space Operations" include, but are not limited to:

(i) research, design, development, test, manufacture, assembly, integration, operation, or use of launch or transfer vehicles, payloads, or instruments, as well as related support equipment and facilities and services; and

(ii) all activities related to ground support, test, training, simulation, or guidance and control equipment and related facilities or services.

The term "Protected Space Operations" excludes activities on Earth that are conducted on return from space to develop further a payload's product or process for use other than for the joint activity in question.

14.3. a. Each Party agrees to a cross-waiver of liability pursuant to which each Party waives all claims against any of the entities or persons listed in subparagraphs (i) through (iii) below based on damage arising out of Protected Space Operations. This cross-waiver shall apply only if the person, entity, or property causing the damage is involved in Protected Space Operations and the person, entity, or property damaged is damaged by virtue of its involvement in Protected Space Operations. The cross-waiver shall apply to any claims for damage, whatever the legal basis for such claims, against:

(i) the other Party;

(ii) a related entity of the other Party; or

(iii) the employees of any of die entities identified in subparagraphs (i) and (ii) immediately above.

b. In addition, each Party shall extend the cross-waiver of liability, as set forth in subparagraph 14.3.a above, to its own related entities by requiring them, by contract or otherwise, to agree to waive all claims against the entities or persons identified in subparagraphs 14.3.a (i) through 14.3.a (iii) above.

c. Notwithstanding the other provisions of this section, this cross-waiver of liability shall not be applicable to:

(i) claims between a Party and its own related entity or between its own related entities;

(ii) claims made by a natural person, his/her estate, survivors, or subrogees for bodily injury, other impairment of health, or death of such natural person, except where the subrogee is a Party to this MOU or has otherwise agreed to be bound by the terms of this cross-waiver;

(iii) claims for damage caused by willful misconduct;

(iv) intellectual property claims;

(v) claims for damage resulting from a failure of a Party to extend the cross-waiver of liability, as set forth in subparagraph 14.3.b, or from a failure of a Party to ensure that their related entities extend the cross-waiver of liability as set forth in subparagraph 14.3.b; or

(vi) contract claims between the Parties based on the express contractual provisions.

d. Nothing in this Article shall be construed to create the basis for a claim or suit where none would otherwise exist.

e. For avoidance of doubt, this cross-waiver of liability includes a cross-waiver of liability arising from the 1972 Convention on International Liability for Damage Caused by Space Objects where the person, entity, or property causing the damage is involved in Protected Space Operations and the person, entity, or property damaged is damaged by virtue of its involvement in Protected Space Operations.

f. In the event of third-party claims for which the Parties may be liable, the Parties will consult promptly to determine an appropriate and equitable apportionment of any potential liability and on the defense of any such claims.

Article 15 - Mishap Investigation

15.1 In the case of a mishap or mission failure, the Parties agree to provide assistance to each other in the conduct of any investigation, bearing in mind, in particular, the provisions of Article 7. In the case of activities that might result in the death of or serious injury to persons, or substantial loss of or damage to property as a result of activities under this MOU, the Parties agree to establish a process for investigating any such mishap as part of their program/project implementation plans.

Article 16 - Amendment

16.1. This MOU may be amended or extended by written agreement of the Parties.

Article 17 - Consultation and Settlement of Disputes

17.1. The Parties' respective points of contact, identified in Article 6.4 and 6.7, shall consult promptly with each other on all issues involving interpretation or implementation of this MOU. These points of contact will attempt to resolve all issues arising from the implementation of this MOU.

17.2. In the case of a question of interpretation or implementation of the terms of this MOU, such questions that cannot be resolved by the Parties' respective points of contact shall be referred for joint resolution to the NASA Associate Administrator for Science Mission Directorate and the ASI Director of the Observation of the Universe, or their designees; and if unresolved at this level, to the NASA Administrator and the ASI President, or their designees, for joint resolution.

Article 18 - Entry into Force and Termination

18.1. This MOU shall enter into force upon signature by the Parties and the conclusion of an agreement to be effected by an exchange of diplomatic notes incorporating its terms and conditions. This MOU shall remain in force until February 28, 2013, to permit completion of the GLAST mission and data-analysis period. This MOU may be extended by mutual written agreement of the Parties, provided that the agreement effected by the exchange of notes remains in force. The interim agreement of November 11, 2004, shall terminate upon entry into force of this MOU.

18.2. Either Party may terminate this MOU at any time by giving the, other Party at least six months written notice of its intent to terminate. Termination of this MOU shall not affect a Party's continuing rights and obligations under Articles 5, Rights in and Distribution of Scientific Data; 7, Transfer of Goods and Technical Data; 8, Intellectual Property; 11, Customs Clearance, Taxes, Immigration and Ownership; and 13, Liability, that shall continue to apply after the expiration or termination of this MOU. In the event of termination, the Parties shall endeavor to minimize the negative impacts of any such termination on the other Party.

Done in duplicate in the English language.

[Signature]

For the United States National Aeronautics and Space Administration

Date: February 22, 2007

[Signature]

For the Italian Space Agency

Date: 07 MAR. 2007

STATE DEPARTMENT DOCUMENT NUMBER: 08-10

AGREEMENT BETWEEN THE UNITED STATES OF AMERICA AND THE EUROPEAN COMMUNITY ON THE COORDINATION OF ENERGY-EFFICIENCY LABELLING PROGRAMS FOR OFFICE EQUIPMENT

SIGNED AT WASHINGTON D.C., DECEMBER 20, 2006
ENTERED INTO FORCE DECEMBER 28, 2006

CTIA DOCUMENT NUMBER: 13385.000

The Government of the United States of America and the European Community, hereinafter "the Parties";

DESIRING to maximise energy savings and environmental benefits by stimulating the supply of and demand for energy-efficient products;

TAKING INTO ACCOUNT the Agreement between the Government of the United States of America and the European Community on the Coordination of Energy-Efficient Labelling Programs for Office Equipment, done on 19 December 2000, and its annexes, as amended (hereinafter "the 2000 Agreement");

SATISFIED by the progress made under the 2000 Agreement;

CONVINCED that additional benefits will be achieved by continuing mutual efforts on ENERGY STAR;

HAVE AGREED AS FOLLOWS:

ARTICLE I
General Principles

1. A common set of energy-efficiency specifications and a common logo shall be used by the Parties for the purpose of establishing consistent targets for manufacturers, thereby maximising the effect of their individual efforts on the supply of and demand for such product types.

2. The Parties shall use the Common Logo for the purpose of identifying qualified energy-efficient product types listed in Annex C.

3. The Parties shall ensure that common specifications encourage continuing improvement in efficiency, taking into account the most advanced technical practices on the market.

4. The Common Specifications strive to represent not more than 25 percent of models for which data is available at the time the specifications are set while also taking other factors into consideration.

5. The Parties shall endeavour to ensure that consumers have the opportunity to identify efficient products by finding the label in the market.

ARTICLE II
Relation to the 2000 Agreement

This Agreement supersedes in its entirety the 2000 Agreement.

ARTICLE III
Definitions

For the purposes of this Agreement:

(a) "ENERGY STAR" means the service mark designated in Annex A and owned by the United States Environmental Protection Agency ("U.S. EPA");

(b) "Common Logo" means the certification mark designated in Annex A and owned by U.S. EPA;

(c) "ENERGY STAR Marks" means the "ENERGY STAR" name and the Common Logo, as well as any versions of these marks that may be developed or modified by the Management Entities or Program Participants, as herein defined, including the sign or marking contained in Annex A of this Agreement;

(d) "ENERGY STAR Labelling Program" means a program administered by a Management Entity using common energy-efficiency specifications, marks, and guidelines to be applied to designated product types;

(e) "Program Participants" means manufacturers, vendors, or resale agents that sell designated, energy-efficient products that meet the specifications of and who have chosen to participate in, the ENERGY STAR Labelling Program by registering or entering an agreement with the Management Entity of either Party;

(f) "Common Specifications" are the energy-efficiency and performance requirements, including testing methods listed in Annex C, used by Management Entities and Program Participants to determine qualification of energy-efficient products for the Common Logo.

ARTICLE IV
Management entities

Each Party hereby designates a management entity responsible for implementation of this Agreement (the "Management Entities"). The European Community designates the Commission of the European Communities ("Commission") as its Management Entity. The United States of America designates the U.S. EPA as its Management Entity.

ARTICLE V
Administration of the ENERGY STAR Labelling Program

1. Each Management Entity shall administer the ENERGY STAR Labelling Program for the energy-efficient product types listed in Annex C, subject to the terms and conditions set forth in this Agreement. Program administration includes registering Program Participants on a voluntary basis, maintaining Program Participant and compliant product lists, and enforcing the terms of the Guidelines for Proper Use of the ENERGY STAR Name and Common Logo set forth in Annex B.

2. The ENERGY STAR Labelling Program shall use the Common Specifications listed in Annex C.

3. To the extent that each Management Entity takes effective measures to educate consumers about the ENERGY STAR Marks, it shall do so in accordance with the Guidelines for Proper Use of the ENERGY STAR Name and Common Logo set forth in Annex B.

4. Each Management Entity shall bear the expenses for all of its activities under this Agreement.

ARTICLE VI
Participation in the ENERGY STAR Labelling Program

1. Any manufacturer, vendor or resale agent may enter the ENERGY STAR Labelling Program by registering as a Program Participant with the Management Entity of either Party.

2. Program Participants may use the Common Logo to identify qualified products that have been tested in their own facilities or by an independent test laboratory and that meet the Common Specifications set forth in Annex C, and may self-certify product qualification.

3. The registration of a Program Participant in the ENERGY STAR Labelling Program by the Management Entity of one Party shall be recognised by the Management Entity of the other Party.

4. To facilitate the recognition of Program Participants in the ENERGY STAR Labelling Program in accordance with Paragraph 3 above, the Management Entities shall cooperate in order to maintain common lists of all Program Participants and products that qualify for the Common Logo.

5. Notwithstanding the self-certification procedures specified in Paragraph 2 above, each Management Entity reserves the right to test or otherwise review products that are or have been sold within its territories (in the territories of the European Community Member States in the case of the Commission) to determine whether the products are certified in accordance with the Common Specifications set forth in Annex C. The Management Entities shall communicate and cooperate fully with one another to ensure all products bearing the Common Logo meet the Common Specifications set forth in Annex C.

ARTICLE VII
Program coordination between the Parties

1. The Parties shall establish a Technical Commission to review implementation of this Agreement, composed of representatives of their respective Management Entities.

2. In principle, the Technical Commission shall meet annually and shall consult at the request of one of the Management Entities to review the operation and administration of the ENERGY STAR Labelling Program, the Common Specifications set forth in Annex C, product coverage, and the progress in achieving the objectives of this Agreement.

3. Nonparties (including other governments and industry representatives) may attend meetings of the Technical Commission as observers, unless otherwise agreed by both Management Entities.

ARTICLE VIII
Registration of the ENERGY STAR Marks

1. The U.S. EPA, as owner of the ENERGY STAR marks, has registered the marks in the European Community as Community Trade Marks. The Commission shall not seek or obtain any registration of the ENERGY STAR marks or any variation of the marks in any country.

2. The U.S. EPA undertakes not to consider as an infringement of these marks the use, by the Commission or by any Program Participant registered by the Commission, of the sign or marking contained in Annex A in accordance with the terms of this Agreement.

ARTICLE IX
Enforcement and non-compliance

1. In order to protect the ENERGY STAR marks, each Management Entity shall ensure the proper use of the ENERGY STAR marks within its territory (within the territories of the European Community Member States in the case of the Commission). Each Management Entity shall ensure that the ENERGY STAR marks are used only in the form that appears in Annex A. Each Management Entity shall ensure that the ENERGY STAR marks are used solely in the manner specified in the Guidelines for Proper Use of the ENERGY STAR Name and Common Logo set forth in Annex B.

2. Each Management Entity shall ensure that prompt and appropriate action is taken against Program Participants, whenever it has knowledge that a Program Participant has used an infringing mark or has affixed the ENERGY STAR marks to a product that does not comply with the Specifications set forth in Annex C. Such actions shall include, but not be limited to:

(a) informing the Program Participant in writing of its non-compliance with the terms of the ENERGY STAR Labelling Program;

(b) through consultations, developing a plan to reach compliance; and

(c) if compliance cannot be reached, terminating the registration of the Program Participant, as appropriate.

3. Each Management Entity shall ensure that all reasonable actions are taken to end the unauthorised use of the ENERGY STAR marks or use of an infringing mark by an entity that is not a Program Participant. Such actions shall include, but shall not be limited to:

(a) informing the entity using the ENERGY STAR marks of ENERGY STAR Labelling Program requirements and the Guidelines for Proper Use of the ENERGY STAR Name and Common Logo; and

(b) encouraging the entity to become a Program Participant and register qualified products.

4. Each Management Entity shall immediately notify the Management Entity of the other Party of any infringement of the ENERGY STAR marks of which it has knowledge as well as the action taken to end such infringement.

ARTICLE X
Procedures for amending the Agreement and for adding new Annexes

1. Either Management Entity may propose an amendment to this Agreement and may propose new annexes to the Agreement.

2. A proposed amendment shall be made in writing and shall be discussed at the next meeting of the Technical Commission, provided that it has been communicated to the other Management Entity at least sixty days in advance of such meeting.

3. Amendments to this Agreement and decisions to add new annexes shall be made by mutual agreement of the Parties. Amendments to Annexes A, B, and C shall be made according to the provisions of Articles XI and XII.

ARTICLE XI
Procedures for amending Annexes A and B

1. A Management Entity seeking to amend Annex A or Annex B shall follow the procedures set forth in paragraphs 1 and 2 of Article X.

2. Amendments to Annexes A and B shall be made by mutual agreement of the Management Entities.

ARTICLE XII
Procedures for amending Annex C

1. A Management Entity seeking to amend Annex C to revise existing Specifications, or to add a new product type ("Proposing Management Entity") shall follow the procedures set forth in paragraphs 1 and 2 of Article X, and shall include in its proposal:

(a) a demonstration that significant energy savings would result from revising the Specifications or adding the new product type;

(b) as appropriate, energy consumption requirements for various power consumption modes;

(c) information on the standardised testing protocols to be used in evaluating the product;

(d) evidence of existing non-proprietary technology that would make possible cost-effective energy savings without negatively affecting product performance;

(e) information on the estimated number of product models that would meet the proposed specification and approximate market share represented;

(f) information on the views of industry groups potentially affected by the proposed amendment; and

(g) a proposed effective date for the new Specifications, taking into consideration product life cycles and production schedules.

2. Proposed amendments that are accepted by both Management Entities shall enter into force on a date mutually agreed by the Management Entities.

3. If, after receipt of a proposal made in accordance with paragraphs 1 and 2 of Article X, the other Management Entity ("Objecting Management Entity") is of the view that the proposal does not meet the requirements specified in Paragraph 1 above or otherwise objects to the proposal it shall promptly (normally by the next Technical Commission Meeting) notify the Proposing Management Entity in writing of its objection and shall include any available information supporting its objection; for example, information demonstrating that the proposal, if adopted, would likely:

(a) disproportionately and unfairly confer market power on one company or industry group;

(b) undermine overall industry participation in the ENERGY STAR labelling program;

(c) conflict with its laws and regulations; or

(d) impose burdensome technical requirements.

4. The Management Entities shall make best efforts to reach agreement on the proposed amendment at the first meeting of the Technical Commission following the proposal. If the Management Entities are unable to reach agreement on the proposed amendment at this Technical Commission meeting, they shall seek to reach agreement in writing prior to the subsequent Technical Commission meeting.

5. If, by the end of the subsequent Technical Commission meeting, the Parties are unable to reach agreement, the Proposing Management Entity shall withdraw its proposal; and with respect to proposals to revise existing Specifications, the corresponding product type shall be removed from Annex C by the date agreed upon in writing by the Management Entities. All Program Participants shall be informed of this change and of the procedures to be followed to implement this change.

6. When preparing new Common Specifications or revising existing Common Specifications, the Management Entities shall ensure effective coordination and consultation among themselves and with their respective stakeholders, particularly with regard to the content of the working documents and timelines.

ARTICLE XIII
General provisions

1. Other environmental labelling programs are not covered by this Agreement and may be developed and adopted by either of the Parties.

2. All activities undertaken under this Agreement shall be subject to the applicable laws and regulations of each Party and to the availability of appropriated funds and resources.

3. Nothing in this Agreement shall affect the rights and obligations of any Party deriving from a bilateral, regional or multilateral agreement into which it has entered prior to the entry into force of this Agreement.

4. Without prejudice to any other provisions of this Agreement, either Management Entity may run labelling programs with respect to product types not included in Annex C. Notwithstanding any other provisions of this Agreement, neither Party shall hinder the import, export, sale or distribution of any product because it bears the energy-efficiency marks of the Management Entity of the other Party.

ARTICLE XIV
Entry into force and duration

1. This Agreement shall enter into force on the date upon which each Party has notified the other in writing that its respective internal procedures necessary for its entry into force have been completed.

2. This Agreement shall remain in force for a period of five years. At least one year prior to the end of this period, the Parties shall meet to discuss renewal of this Agreement.

ARTICLE XV
Termination

1. Either Party may terminate this Agreement at any time by providing three months written notice to the other Party.

2. In the event of termination or non-renewal of this Agreement, the Management Entities shall inform all Program Participants which they have registered of the termination of the joint program. Moreover, Management Entities shall inform the Program Participants which they have registered that each Management Entity may continue the labelling activities under two separate individual programs. In this case, the European Community labelling program will not use the ENERGY STAR marks. The Commission shall ensure that itself, the Member States of the European Community and any Program Participants which it has registered cease using the ENERGY STAR

marks by the date agreed upon in writing by the Management Entities. The obligations contained in this Article XV (2) shall survive the termination of this Agreement.

ARTICLE XVI
Authentic languages

Done in duplicate at Washington D.C. on the twentieth day of December in the year two thousand and six in the Czech, Danish, Dutch, English, Estonian, Finnish, French, German, Greek, Hungarian, Italian, Latvian, Lithuanian, Maltese, Polish, Portuguese, Slovakian, Slovenian, Spanish and Swedish, languages, each of these versions being equally authentic. In case of difficulties concerning interpretation, English shall prevail.

For the Government of the United States of America	For the European Community
[Signature]	[Signature]

State Department Document Number: 08-11

Agreement Between the United States of America and the Republic of Uganda Concerning the Program of the Peace Corps in the Republic of Uganda

Signed at Kampala, December 10, 2007
Entered into force December 10, 2007

CTIA DOCUMENT NUMBER: 13386.000

The Government of the United States of America (hereinafter "the United States"); and the Government of the Republic of Uganda (hereinafter "Uganda"), recognizing the importance of developing mutually advantageous relationships and cooperation between their countries, have agreed as follows:

Article I

1. The Government of the United States shall furnish such Peace Corps Volunteers as maybe requested by the Government of Uganda and approved by the Government of the United States to perform mutually agreed tasks in Uganda.

2. The Volunteers shall work under the immediate supervision of governmental and private organizations in Uganda designated by the two governments.

3. The Government of the United States shall provide training to enable die Volunteers to perform their tasks in the most effective manner.

Article II

1. The Government of Uganda shall accord equitable treatment to the Volunteers and personnel performing functions under contract with the Peace Corps and their dependents and property; accord them and their property full aid and protection, including treatment no less favorable than that accorded generally to nationals of the United States residing in Uganda; and fully inform, consult, and cooperate with representatives of the United States with respect to all matters concerning them.

2. The Government of Uganda shall exempt the Volunteers and persons performing functions under contract with the Peace Corps who are not citizens or permanent residents of Uganda from all taxes on payments that they receive to defray their living costs, on income derived from their Peace Corps work, and on income from other sources outside Uganda; from all customs duties or other charges

on their personal property introduced into Uganda for their own use; and from all other taxes or other charges (including immigration/visa fees), except license fees. The Government of Uganda shall issue residence permits and visas (including multiple-entry visas), without fee or other charge, to Volunteers and persons performing functions under contract with the Peace Corps.

Article III

1. The Government of the United States shall provide the Volunteers, the Peace Corps Representative, and staff of the Representative with such limited quantities of equipment and supplies as the two governments may consider necessary to enable the Volunteers to perform their tasks effectively.

2. The Government of Uganda shall exempt from all taxes (including value-added taxes), customs duties, and, other charges any equipment, supplies, and other goods and services introduced into or acquired in Uganda by the Government of the United States, or any contractor financed by it, for use hereunder.

Article IV

1. To enable the Government of the United States to discharge its responsibilities under this agreement, the Government of Uganda shall receive a Peace Corps Representative and such staff of The Representative (including employees and contractor personnel as designated by the Peace Corps Representative), and members of their families forming part of their households, as are acceptable to the Government of Uganda, Notwithstanding the provisions of any other agreement, the Government of Uganda shall exempt such person, and members of their families forming part of their households, who are not citizens or permanent residents of Uganda from all taxes on income derived from their Peace Corps work or other sources outside Uganda, from all customs duties and other charges on their personal property introduced into Uganda for their own use, and from all other taxes or other charges (including. immigration/visa fees), except license fees. In addition, such persons and members of their families forming part of their households, shall be accorded status equivalent to that accorded administrative and technical staff personnel of the diplomatic mission of the United States, except they shall not be accorded immunities.

2. The Government of Uganda shall issue residence permits and visas (including multiple-entry visas), without fee or other, charge, to the Peace Corps Representative, staff, and individuals performing functions under this agreement, and members of their families forming part of their households.

Article V

The Government of Uganda shall; exempt from investment and deposit requirements and currency, controls all funds introduced into Uganda for use in accordance with this agreement by the Government Of the United States or contractors financed by it Such funds shall be convertible into die currency of Uganda at the highest rate that is not unlawful in Uganda.

Article VI

1. Appropriate representatives of the two governments may from time to time make such arrangements with respect to Peace Corps Volunteers and Peace Corps programs in Uganda as appear necessary or desirable for the purpose of implementing this agreement.

2. Any disputes arising under this agreement shall be resolved amicably by the two governments.

Article VII

The undertakings of each government herein are subject to the availability of funds.

Article VIII

This agreement may be amended from time to time by mutual consent of the two governments. Any such amendment shall be in writing. In the event of a conflict between this agreement and a future agreement regarding cooperation to facilitate assistance between the United States and Uganda, this agreement shall prevail concerning, the Peace Corps program.

Article IX

This agreement shall enter into force on the date of signature and shall remain in force until ninety days after the date of any written notification from either government to the other of its; intention to terminate the agreement. This agreement supersedes the Agreement between Uganda and the United States Relating to the Establishment of a Peace Corps Program in Uganda of November 16, 1964, which shall terminate upon entry into force of this agreement.

Done at Kampala, Uganda on this 10th day of December 2007, in the English language.

FOR THE GOVERNMENT OF THE UNITED STATES OF AMERICA:

[Signature]

MR. RONALD. A. TSCHETTER
DIRECTOR, PEACE CORPS

FOR THE GOVERNMENT OF REPUBLIC OF UGANDA:

[Signature]

HON. ISAAC ISANGA MUSUMBA, MP,
MINISTER OF STATE FOR REGIONAL COOPERATION ALSO HOLDING PORTFOLIO OF MINISTER OF FOREIGN AFFAIRS

STATE DEPARTMENT DOCUMENT NUMBER: 08-12

AGREEMENT BETWEEN THE DEPARTMENT OF HEALTH AND HUMAN SERVICES OF THE UNITED STATES OF AMERICA AND THE GENERAL ADMINISTRATION OF QUALITY SUPERVISION, INSPECTION AND QUARANTINE OF THE PEOPLE'S REPUBLIC OF CHINA ON THE SAFETY OF FOOD AND FEED

SIGNED AT BEIJING, DECEMBER 11, 2007
ENTERED INTO FORCE DECEMBER 11, 2007

CTIA DOCUMENT NUMBER: 13243.000

The Department of Health and Human Services ("HHS") of the United States of America ("United States") and the General Administration of Quality Supervision, Inspection and Quarantine ("AQSIQ") of the People's Republic of China ("China") (hereinafter referred to together as "the Parties"):

Understanding the mutual benefits of protecting the public health through bilateral cooperation and exchange between the Parties with regard to the safety of food and feed;

Appreciating the long-standing collaboration between the United States Food and Drug Administration of HHS ("HHS/FDA") and AQSIQ and the history of the AQSIQ registration and certification program;

Desiring to continue to work together to protect the safety and health of consumers and animals in the United States and the customs territory of China to prevent, intervene, and respond to any safety issues related to food and feed exported from one country to another;

Recognizing that such cooperation can improve and promote the health of people in the United States and in China, and enhance confidence in safety of food and feed exported from one country to another;

Have agreed as follows:

Article I
Purpose

The purpose of this Agreement is to establish a bilateral cooperative mechanism regarding food and feed safety. Such a mechanism may include current and future registration and certification systems. The mechanism aims to provide the Parties with information to use in judging whether an imported product meets the requirements of the importing country.

Article II
Definitions

For purposes of this Agreement, the following definitions shall apply.

1. "Covered Products" means food and feed under the jurisdiction of both Parties.

2. "Designated Covered Product" means a Covered Product that has been designated for inclusion in any phase of the cooperative mechanism regarding food and feed safety. Designated Covered Products are listed in the Annex.

3. "Feed" means articles under the jurisdiction of both Parties that are used for food or drink for animals other than humans, including articles used for components of such article and including vitamins or herbs meant to supplement the diet not regulated as drugs. Feed includes feed ingredients, feed additives, and feed that contains veterinary drugs, whether processed, semi-processed, or raw.

4. "Firm" means any business in either the customs territory of China or the United States that is engaged in the manufacture, production, growing, processing, packing, testing, holding, transporting, distribution, or export of food or feed.

5. "Food" means articles under the jurisdiction of both Parties that are used for food or drink for humans, including articles used for components of any such article.

6. "HHS/FDA Requirement" means any U.S. law, regulation or other requirement, including any amendment adopted after the date of entry into force of this Agreement, concerning food or feed that is administered or enforced by HHS/FDA.

7. "AQSIQ/CNCA Requirement" means any Chinese law, regulation or other requirement, including any amendment adopted after the date of entry into force of this Agreement, concerning food or feed that is administered or enforced by AQSIQ or the Certification and Accreditation Administration ("AQSIQ/CNCA").

8. "AQSIQ/CNCA Registered Establishment" means an Establishment that AQSIQ/CNCA has registered meets Chinese relevant registration Laws/regulations and HHS/FDA Requirements pursuant to the Annex.

9. "HHS/FDA Registered Establishment" means an Establishment that has registered with HHS/FDA pursuant to the U.S. Federal Food, Drug, and Cosmetic Act under 21 U.S.C. 350d.

10. "Establishment" means any Finn's site or facility within the customs territory of China or in the United States that is engaged in the manufacture, producing, growing, processing, packing, testing, holding, transporting, distribution, or export of food or feed.

Article III
General Principles

1. The Parties shall engage in regulatory cooperation regarding the export of Covered Products from the customs territory of China to the United States and Covered Products produced in the United States and exported to the customs territory of China as set out in Article V and as further defined in Work Plans to be agreed upon by the Parties.

2. Each Party shall engage in information-sharing as set out in Article IV to improve its understanding of, and to gain greater confidence in, the other Party's regulatory system and as further defined in Work Plans to be agreed upon by the Parties. As specified in Article IV, each Party shall share

relevant information with the other Party, including on laws, regulations, areas of jurisdiction, and public health and safety.

3. The Parties shall engage in regulatory cooperation regarding improving the safety of food and feed as set out in Articles IV and V and as further defined in Work Plans to be agreed upon by the Parties.

4. The Parties shall hold annual meetings between HHS/FDA and AQSIQ leaders to discuss and evaluate progress under this Agreement, among other things.

Article IV
Information Sharing

The Parties shall exchange information on their regulatory systems and other public-health matters concerning Covered Products as follows:

1. A Party may provide information to the other Party in the English or the Chinese language.

2. The Parties shall exchange copies of, and other relevant information concerning, their respective laws and regulations relating to food and feed safety.

3. Each Party shall immediately notify the other Party of significant risks to public health related to product safety, manufacturing conditions, recalls, and other instances that involve imminent or significant danger to health, or the gross deception of consumers with regard to Covered Products. Such notification shall occur within two (2) calendar days of the discovery of the significant risk to public health or gross deception of consumers. Each Party shall promptly respond to requests from the other Party for information concerning any such notification, including contact information for the Establishments or other entities concerned. Such response shall normally occur within five (5) calendar days of the request from the other Party unless otherwise specified in the Work Plan. The Work Plan shall include specific commitments to ensure the timeliness of any such notification or response.

Article V
Regulatory Cooperation

The Parties shall:

1. Develop and set out in the Work Plan strategies to control the transshipment of potentially unsafe Covered Products.

2. Develop appropriate regulatory cooperative activities, including training programs and scientific discussions or cooperation, intended to support the long-term stability and effectiveness of the registration and certification programs for Covered Products. For each training program or other cooperative activity that requires travel or other organizational costs, each Party shall bear its own costs of participation. Appropriate regulatory cooperative activities may include the following:

   a. development of laboratory and risk-assessment methodologies, including performing analyses on request by the other Party;

   b. work on identifying and discussing significant differences in maximum residue levels (MRLs) of veterinary drugs used in food-producing animals;

   c. exchange of scientific, technical, and regulatory information about compliance and enforcement programs of each Party;

d. identification of, and work on the mitigation and elimination of, significant human-health and animal-health concerns associated with the incidental or intentional chemical, radiologic, or microbiological contamination of human and animal foods (for example contamination with copper sulfate, dioxin or polychlorinated biphenyls);

e. identification of any substitution or addition of a substance to an ingredient in food or feed or to a food or feed product that reduces the quality of the ingredient or the product, or makes it appear of greater value than it is, when the substitution or addition has not been clearly revealed to the recipient; and

f. exchange of information regarding mandatory, pre-market review/approval processes for food ingredients.

3. Report any science and technology cooperation to the Joint Commission on Scientific and Technological Cooperation established under the Agreement Between the Government of the United States of America and the Government of the People's Republic of China on Cooperation in Science and Technology, signed at Washington January 31, 1979.

4. Develop a streamlined process for facilitating (e.g., issuing a letter of invitation), no later than five (5) calendar days after receipt of a request from a Party, inspections of Establishments by the requesting Party. Such inspection may be conducted with or without providing advance notice (as specified in the request) to the Establishment concerned.

5. Exchange their respective web links that identify requirements for import into their respective customs territories for Covered Products. Each Party shall post the web link of the other Party on its website within thirty (30) calendar days of receipt of the web link.

Article VI
Rights

1. For the purpose of using AQSIQ/CNCA registration and/or certification to inform decision-making regarding the admissibility of Covered Products for entry into the United States, both Parties shall endeavor to agree on all criteria and procedures that AQSIQ/CNCA uses to implement the registration and certification provisions of this Agreement. For greater certainty, all Covered Products offered for import into the United States shall be subject to HHS/FDA Requirements and all other relevant U.S. laws and regulations.

2. Both Parties shall endeavor to agree on all criteria and procedures that HHS/FDA uses to implement the registration obligations under this Agreement. For greater certainty, all Covered Products exported to the customs territory of China shall be subject to AQSIQ Requirements and all other relevant Chinese laws and regulations.

3. For greater certainty, nothing in this Agreement shall be construed to require a Party or any other relevant Government official to base any decisions on admission of any Covered Product on any list or other information the other Party may provide.

Article VII
Administration

1. Within fifteen (15) calendar days of the date of entry into force of this Agreement, each Party shall notify the other Party in writing of its primary points of contact for coordinating all bilateral activities under this Agreement, including coordinating meetings, exchanging information, and sending and receiving notifications.

2. The Parties hereby establish a Working Group. Within thirty (30) calendar days of the date of entry into force of this Agreement, each Party shall identify relevant policy and technical experts of each Party to serve on the Working Group.

3. Within sixty (60) calendar days of the date of entry into force of this Agreement, the Working Group shall hold its first meeting to develop a Work Plan that:

a. further details the specific activities each Party shall perform pursuant to this Agreement within the first 12-month period following the date of entry into force of this Agreement and time lines for completion of each such activity; and

b. includes, as appropriate, performance measures to evaluate the success of each activity.

4. Within 120 calendar days of the date of entry into force of this Agreement, the Working Group shall finalize the Work Plan for the first 12-month period following the date of entry into force of this Agreement. The Parties shall assess the Work Plan at the conclusion of the 12-month period.

5. For each subsequent 12-month period, the Working Group shall meet to develop a Work Plan that further details specific activities that each Party shall perform pursuant to this Agreement within that period and, as appropriate, includes performance measures to evaluate the success of each such activity. The Parties shall assess each such Work Plan at the conclusion of the relevant period.

6. The Work Plan for each 12-month period, when adopted by the Parties, shall include binding commitments for the effective and timely implementation of this Agreement. Each Party shall make the Work Plan for the first twelve (12) months, and each subsequent year, publicly available on its respective website.

7. Within 180 calendar days of the date of entry into force of this Agreement, high level representatives of the Parties shall meet to discuss the implementation of and review progress under this Agreement and related matters.

8. Thereafter, the high level representatives of the Parties shall meet on an annual basis to discuss and review the implementation of and progress under this Agreement and related matters. Unless the Parties otherwise agree, the location of these annual meetings shall alternate between the United States and China. The Parties may convene additional technical or program-level meetings on an as-needed basis in any mutually agreeable location.

Article VIII
Performance Measures

1. The Parties shall collaboratively evaluate and discuss progress under this Agreement on an annual basis, including the effectiveness of the program, pursuant to the Annex.

2. HHS may base its evaluation of such progress on, among other things, the following:

a. the rate of refusal by HHS/FDA of Designated Covered Products exported from the customs territory of China and offered for import into the United States, as compared to the overall rate of refusal in calendar year 2007 or other relevant period by HHS/FDA of Designated Covered Products exported from the customs territory of China and offered for import into the United States;

b. the overall percentage of Designated Covered Products exported from the customs territory of China and offered for import into the United States that do not come from AQSIQ/CNCA Registered Establishments or are not certified; and

c. the volume, frequency and significance in terms of public health hazard of recalls of Designated Covered Products in the United States, including counterfeit Covered Products, exported from the customs territory of China and offered for import into the United States as compared to the volume, frequency and significance of such recalls in 2007 or other relevant period.

3. AQSIQ may base its evaluation of such progress on, among other things, the following:

a. the rate of refusal by AQSIQ of Designated Covered Products exported from the United States and offered for import into the customs territory of China, as compared to the overall rate of refusal in calendar year 2007 or other relevant period by AQSIQ of Designated Covered Products exported from the United States and offered for import into the customs territory of China;

b. the overall percentage of Designated Covered Products exported from the United States and offered for import into the customs territory of China that do not come from HHS/FDA Registered Establishments; and

c. the volume, frequency and significance in terms of public health hazard of recalls of Designated Covered Products in the customs territory of China, including counterfeit Covered Products, exported from the United States and offered for import into the customs territory of China as compared to the volume, frequency and significance of such recalls in 2007 or other relevant period.

Article IX
Final Provisions

1. Nothing in this Agreement precludes the Government of the United States or the Government of China from taking any measure to protect the public health of the citizens of its respective country. Each Party affirms that it shall work with its country's national, state/provincial, or municipal bodies, as appropriate, to implement this Agreement fully.

2. Nothing in this Agreement shall be construed to affect the rights or obligations of the United States or China under any other agreement in force between the United States and China.

3. The Parties shall endeavor to resolve any dispute regarding the implementation or interpretation of this Agreement through timely consultations.

4. This Agreement shall enter into force upon signature by both Parties and shall remain in force for a period of five (5) years, unless terminated by either Party. On the last day of the five-year period, and of each subsequent five-year period, the Agreement shall automatically be renewed for another five-year period, unless either Party notifies the other Party that it wishes to terminate the Agreement at least sixty (60) calendar days prior to the last day of the relevant five year period. In addition, either Party may terminate the Agreement upon sixty (60) calendar days' written notice to the other Party. The Parties may amend the Agreement at any time, by mutual written agreement of the Parties.

5. All Annex provisions are incorporated in, and integral to, this Agreement. Each Party shall undertake all activities under this Agreement in accordance with its country's laws and regulations.

Done at Beijing, this 11th day of December, 2007, in duplicate in the English and Chinese languages, each text being equally authentic.

[Signature]

For THE DEPARTMENT OF HEALTH AND HUMAN SERVICES OF THE UNITED STATES

[Signature]

For THE GENERAL ADMINISTRATION OF QUALITY SUPERVISION, INSPECTION AND QUARANTINE OF THE PEOPLE'S REPUBLIC OF CHINA

ANNEX
Section I. Determination of Designated Covered Products

Work under this Agreement will be implemented in a phased approach, beginning with an initial defined list of Designated Covered Products. The Parties shall conduct a formal evaluation of the outcomes of these programs for the initial Designated Covered Products. Based on the determination of the success of this first phase, the defined list of Designated Covered Products will be expanded to include additional Covered Products.

A. Factors

After consulting with each other, the Parties shall designate which Covered Products to include on the list of Designated Covered Products in each phase as appropriate based on the following factors:

a. potential or actual, direct or indirect risk to the public health associated with the product, based on testing, inspection results or other information both Parties deem relevant;

b. the rate of refusal by one Party of admission of the Covered Products into its territory or of problems associated with the Covered Products before, during or after entering the domestic commerce of the importing country, including product recalls, safety alerts, and enforcement actions;

c. fraudulent or deceptive labeling or indications of any substitution or additions of a substance to a Covered Product or an ingredient of a Covered Product that reduces the quality of the ingredient or product or makes it appear of greater value than it is, without clearly revealing such substitution or addition to the recipient in the importing country; and

d. the feasibility of implementing an effective and timely Work Plan with respect to the product.

B. First Phase - Designated Covered Products

1. The Parties agree that the following Covered Products, for which there are high import refusal rates and associated risk, shall be included in the first phase:

a. Low-acid canned products or acidified food;

b. Pet food/pet treats of plant origin or animal origin;

c. Ingredients of food and feed, i.e., wheat gluten and rice protein; and

d. All aquaculture farming products other than molluscan shellfish.

Details about these product categories will be further defined through the Work Plan agreed by the Parties.

2. Upon agreement, the Parties may designate additional Designated Covered Products for inclusion in any subsequent phase of the registration and certification programs. This process shall be detailed in the Work Plan.

Section II. Controls for Exports

1. The Parties acknowledge the successes of the AQSIQ/CNCA registration and certification programs in China, (e.g., in restoring confidence and improving the safety of ceramic ware imported from the customs territory of China). The Parties desire to build upon these successes of these long established programs to help ensure the safety of other food and feed imported from China.

2. Based on the success of the registration and certification programs, detailed below, HHS/FDA will use registration and certification information provided to it by AQSIQ to inform HHS/FDA

import entry decisions, which may include a reduction in the rate of examination of Designated Covered Products that are part of the registration and/or certification program.

A. General

1. With respect to Covered Products that have been designated in accordance with Section I. A. of this Annex, AQSIQ/CNCA has already established and shall continue:

a. a registration program that requires all Establishments of Designated Covered Products for export from the customs territory of China to the United States to register with AQSIQ/CNCA; and

b. a certification program that is expanded to cover Designated Covered Products for export from the customs territory of China to the United States that provides for such products to be certified by AQSIQ as meeting HHS/FDA Requirements.

2. The Parties shall consult regarding the development of the registration and certification programs. These programs shall be implemented in phases and for the first phase shall cover the Designated Covered Products set forth in Section I.B.I of this Annex and for subsequent phases shall cover the Covered Products as designated in accordance with Section LA. of this Annex. The program shall expand to other products for subsequent phases contingent on the success of the preceding phase. In addition, based on the success of the preceding phase, the Parties may agree that with respect to a later phase that this Agreement shall be modified to include limitations on the export of any shipment of Designated Covered Products from the customs territory of China to the United States that AQSIQ has not certified as meeting HHS/FDA Requirements. The Parties may discuss in the future amending the Agreement to reflect the role of recognized third party testing and certification in promoting product safety.

3. HHS/FDA shall provide AQSIQ with copies of all relevant HHS/FDA Requirements, updated as appropriate, with respect to Designated Covered Products.

4. HHS/FDA shall promptly notify ASQIQ/CNCA about Designated Covered Products refused entry into the United States. Details for this notification system, including the timing and the mechanism, will be further defined in the Work Plan.

5. HHS/FDA commits to explore finding a mechanism to notify AQSIQ/CNCA about Designated Covered Products not accompanied by an AQSIQ/CIQ certificate.

6. Details for this notification system, including the timing and the mechanism, will be further defined in the Work Plan.

7. In the event that an Establishment shipping Designated Covered Products to the United States does not have an AQSIQ/CIQ certificate or in the event that a shipment of Designated Covered Product offered for import into the United States is not accompanied by an AQSIQ/CIQ certificate, and HHS/FDA deems that Establishment or shipment meets HHS/FDA Requirements, HHS/FDA shall notify AQSIQ and the Parties shall discuss the situation, as warranted.

B. Registration

1. With regard to Designated Covered Products for shipment to the United States, AQSIQ/CNCA shall:

a. ensure it registers only Establishments that meet HHS/FDA Requirements;

b. monitor each AQSIQ/CNCA Registered Establishment to ensure that it continues to meet HHS/FDA Requirements; and

c. ensure each AQSIQ/CNCA Registered Establishment is informed of all applicable HHS/FDA Requirements.

2. Pursuant to the program maintained in accordance with Section I.A.1 of this Annex, AQSIQ shall require that all Establishments of Designated Covered Products for export to the United States register with AQSIQ/CNCA. Each registration shall include the following:

a. the name and address of the Establishment;

b. a list of all Designated Covered Products associated with the Establishment; and

c. the name and contact information (including phone number) of the owner, manager, or other senior official responsible at the Establishment.

3. AQSIQ/CNCA shall require AQSIQ/CNCA Registered Establishments to inform ASQIQ/CNCA upon any changes in the information provided in its registration and to provide updated information.

4. AQSIQ/CNCA shall conduct annual inspections of all AQSIQ/CNCA Registered Establishments to ensure each AQSIQ/CNCA Registered Establishment meets HHS/FDA Requirements. AQSIQ/CNCA shall inspect each AQSIQ/CNCA Registered Establishment within 180 calendar days of the date of registration as a baseline for annual inspections thereafter. AQSIQ/CNCA shall revoke or suspend the registration of any Establishment that it determines, as a result of an inspection or otherwise, does not meet HHS/FDA Requirements.

5. AQSIQ/CNCA shall provide HHS/FDA a list of all AQSIQ/CNCA Registered Establishments, and the Designated Covered Products of each such Establishment ("List of AQSIQ/CNCA Registered Establishments"), via a secure electronic system. AQSIQ/CNCA shall provide HHS/FDA the first List of AQSIQ/CNCA Registered Establishments within thirty (30) calendar days of the date of entry into force of this Agreement, and shall update the list every ninety (90) calendar days from the date it provides the first List of AQSIQ/CNCA Registered Establishments.

6. Within fifteen (15) calendar days of receiving the List of AQSIQ/CNCA Registered Establishments or any updates, HHS/FDA shall publish it on its website.

7. HHS/FDA shall provide AQSIQ/CNCA a list of all Establishments registered with HHS/FDA. HHS/FDA shall provide this list to AQISQ/CNCA, via a secure electronic system, within thirty (30) calendar days of the date of entry into force of this Agreement, and shall update the list every ninety (90) calendar days from the date it provides the first list of AQSIQ/CNCA Registered Establishments.

8. AQSIQ/CNCA shall notify HHS/FDA in writing of all AQSIQ/CNCA Registered Establishments that have failed inspection or whose registration AQSIQ/CNCA has suspended, revoked or denied and the reasons therefor. AQSIQ/CNCA shall provide HHS/FDA this information, including a description of the problems identified, within two (2) calendar days of the failure, denial, revocation, or suspension, via secure electronic transmission.

9. AQSIQ/CNCA shall require AQSIQ/CNCA Registered Establishments to notify AQSIQ/CNCA within three (3) calendar days of detection of any failure to meet HHS/FDA Requirements or of any contamination, major defect, or any other safety concern with regard to a Covered Product for export to the United States. AQSIQ/CNCA shall transmit any such notification to HHS/FDA within three (3) calendar days of the time AQSIQ/CNCA receives it. HHS/FDA shall transmit such notification to the U.S. Department of Homeland Security's Customs and Border Protection as appropriate.

10. AQSIQ shall ensure it has and uses a system to enable the tracing of Designated Covered Products from the source of production or manufacture to exportation to assist in containing and resolving safety problems. AQSIQ shall cooperate with HHS/FDA to ensure that AQSIQ's system is effective. The Work Plan shall further specify the forms or specific types of cooperation to be undertaken.

11. AQSIQ/CNCA shall maintain documents on file related to reviews, inspections, testing, recalls, compliance, and any other assessment of a AQSIQ/CNCA Registered Establishment.

AQSIQ/CNCA shall make such records available to HHS/FDA within five (5) calendar days of an HHS/FDA request.

12. Upon agreement by both Parties, AQSIQ shall facilitate periodic audits or reviews of the AQSIQ/CNCA registration program by HHS/FDA.

C. Certification

1. If the China Entry-Exit Inspection and Quarantine Bureau ("AQSIQ/CIQ") determines a shipment meets HHS/FDA Requirements, it shall issue a certificate that contains a unique identifying number and attests that the shipment meets HHS/FDA Requirements. AQSIQ/CIQ shall issue a certificate for a shipment of Designated Covered Products for export to the United States only if such shipment meets HHS/FDA Requirements.

2. To avoid counterfeiting of certificates or the falsification of information, within sixty (60) calendar days of the date of entry into force of this Agreement, AQSIQ and HHS/FDA shall designate technical experts to work together to develop the technological capabilities to implement a secure electronic system or other secure means to transmit certificate and to receive information.

3. Once the secure electronic system is established, AQSIQ/CIQ shall provide HHS/FDA a copy of each certificate issued pursuant to the certification program maintained pursuant to Section II.A.1.b. of this Annex via a secure electronic transmission within three (3) calendar days of the issuance of the certificate. AQSIQ should notify the exporter of the shipment for which AQSIQ issued the certificate that it should provide the certificate's unique identifying number to the importer of record in the United States, or to any intermediate party responsible for transmitting entry filing information to the importer of record in the United States. AQSIQ should notify the exporter or intermediate party that it should provide the unique identifying number electronically to the United States customs authorities along with the entry filing for each shipment.

4. AQSIQ shall immediately revoke a certificate of any shipment of Designated Covered Products for export to the United States if it determines that a shipment does not meet HHS/FDA Requirements. AQSIQ may base a revocation of a certificate on inspection or testing results or any other information that comes to the attention of Chinese or United States authorities to indicate that the product does not meet HHS/FDA Requirements. AQSIQ shall notify HHS/FDA of any revocation with three (3) calendar days of the revocation.

5. Upon agreement by both Parties, AQSIQ shall facilitate periodic audits or reviews of the AQSIQ certification program by HHS/FDA.

6. AQSIQ shall monitor the safety of Designated Covered Products by conducting a testing program that provides, as determined by HHS/FDA, a high level of statistical confidence in the quality of such products offered for import into the United States.

D. Additional Provisions

1. HHS/FDA may request AQSIQ to conduct an investigation regarding any Covered Products exported from the customs territory of China that HHS/FDA has reason to believe may pose a health or safety risk to public health or safety of U.S. citizens. AQSIQ shall respond to HHS/FDA within three (3) calendar days of receipt of the request and shall promptly conduct a thorough investigation. With regard to AQSIQ/CNCA Registered Establishments, AQSIQ shall notify HHS/FDA within fifteen (15) calendar days of an inspection request of:

a. information relating to the source of the health or safety risk;

b. the steps taken to remedy the risk; and

c. the outcome of any remediation.

With regard to non-AQSIQ/CNCA Registered Establishments, AQSIQ shall notify HHS/FDA of the above information as soon as it becomes available.

2. AQSIQ shall inform HHS/FDA of the results of its investigation within three (3) calendar days of completing its investigation. The Work Plan shall further detail requirements and performance measures related to requested investigations.

3. Upon the agreement of AQSIQ/CNCA, HHS/FDA may participate fully in any annual or other AQSIQ inspection of any AQSIQ/CNCA Registered Establishment.

4. HHS/FDA will consult with AQSIQ/CNCA, and shall be permitted to conduct an inspection of any AQSIQ/CNCA Registered Establishment within five (5) calendar days of notifying AQSIQ. AQSIQ shall facilitate HHS/FDA's inspection, including by ensuring, at HHS/FDA's request, that such inspections are conducted without providing advance notice to the AQSIQ/CNCA Registered Establishment.

5. Upon the agreement of HHS/FDA, AQSIQ/CNCA may conduct an audit of any refusal of a Covered Product within five (5) calendar days of notifying HHS/FDA. HHS/FDA shall facilitate AQSIQ/CNCA's audit including by providing relevant information at AQSIQ/CNCA's request (e.g., the test methods and procedures as well as test results.)

6. To the extent possible, HHS/FDA shall notify AQSIQ/CNCA of significant potential negative impact, based on scientific investigation, on human or animal health relating to food and feed imported from the customs territory of China as soon as HHS/FDA becomes aware that there may be a link with a product imported from the customs territory of China. The Parties shall discuss the data in an effort to better understand the situation.

7. For any shipment of Covered Products for export to the United States that AQSIQ determines does not meet, or appears not to meet, HHS/FDA Requirements, or if AQSIQ obtains information or has other reason to believe that a shipment poses a risk to public health, AQSIQ shall notify HHS/FDA in writing, including the reasons therefor and other information that may assist in HHS/FDA in identifying the shipment and the supplier, within three (3) calendar days of its determination.

8. In addition to other provisions of this Agreement, AQSIQ shall not permit the export to the United States of any Covered Product that it has evidence is unsafe.

9. Except in extraordinary circumstances, each Party shall observe the following procedures: Each Party shall publish on its website and in the relevant government publication (i.e., HHS/FDA, the Federal Register; AQSIQ, the Ministry of Commerce of People's Republic of China (MOFCOM) Gazette), all proposed regulations and other measures related to Designated Covered Products and allow a reasonable period of time for all interested parties to submit comments. Each Party shall consider such comments and, at the time it adopts final regulations, address in writing significant, substantive comments received from interested persons during the comment period and explain any substantive revision made to the proposed regulations. Each Party shall also publish on its website, and in the relevant government publication, all final regulations, and measures related to Designated Covered Products and allow a reasonable amount of time before implementation and enforcement.

STATE DEPARTMENT DOCUMENT NUMBER: 08-13

AGREEMENT BETWEEN THE DEPARTMENT OF HEALTH AND HUMAN SERVICES OF THE UNITED STATES OF AMERICA AND THE STATE FOOD AND DRUG ADMINISTRATION OF THE PEOPLE'S REPUBLIC OF CHINA ON THE SAFETY OF DRUGS AND MEDICAL DEVICES

SIGNED AT BEIJING, DECEMBER 11, 2007
ENTERED INTO FORCE DECEMBER 11, 2007

CTIA DOCUMENT NUMBER: 13242.000

The Department of Health and Human Services ("HHS") of the United States of America ("United States") and the State Food and Drug Administration ("SFDA") of the People's Republic of China ("China") (hereinafter referred to together as "the Parties"):

Understanding the mutual benefits of protecting the public health through improved cooperation between the Parties with regard to monitoring and regulating the safety of drugs and medical devices;

Desiring to work together to better ensure the safety and quality of Drugs, Excipients, and Medical Devices; and

Recognizing that such cooperation can improve the health of the citizens of both the United States and China and enhance confidence in the regulation of Drugs, Excipients, and Medical Devices in both countries;

Have agreed as follows:

Article I
Purpose

The purpose of this Agreement is to establish methods of cooperation between the Parties that will provide the Food and Drug Administration within HHS ("HHS/FDA") with additional information about products exported from the customs territory of China to the United States, provide SFDA with increased sharing of information about products exported from the United States to China, and encourage further regulatory cooperation between the Parties regarding Drug and Medical Device regulation.

Article II
General Principles

A. The Parties shall engage in regulatory cooperation regarding the export of Drugs, Excipients, and Medical Devices from the customs territory of China to the United States and Drugs, Exipients, and

Medical Devices produced in the United States and exported to the customs territory of China as set out in Article VI and as further defined in Work Plans to be agreed upon by the Parties.

B. The Parties shall engage in information-sharing to improve their mutual understanding of, and to gain greater confidence in, each Party's regulatory system as set out in Article V and as further defined in Work Plans to be agreed upon by the Parties. As specified in Article V, each Party shall share relevant information with the other Party, including on relevant laws, regulations, areas of jurisdiction, and public health and safety.

C. The Parties shall engage in regulatory cooperation regarding improving the authenticity, quality, safety, and effectiveness of Drugs, Excipients, and Medical Devices as set out in Articles IV and VI and as further defined in Work Plans to be agreed upon by the Parties.

D. The Parties shall commit to annual meetings between senior Agency leaders to discuss and evaluate progress under this Agreement, among other things.

Article III
Definitions

For purposes of this Agreement the following definitions shall apply:

A. "API" or "Active Pharmaceutical Ingredient" means any substance or mixture of substances intended to be used in the manufacture of a drug (medicinal) product and that, when used in the production of a drug, becomes an active ingredient of the drug product. Such substances are intended to furnish pharmacological activity or other direct effect in the diagnosis, cure, mitigation, treatment, or prevention of disease or to affect the structure and function of the body.

B. "Counterfeit Drugs and Medical Devices" means a product that is deliberately and fraudulently mislabeled with respect to identity and/or source. Counterfeiting can apply to branded and generic products and may include products with correct ingredients, with wrong ingredients, without active ingredients, with incorrect quantity of active ingredient, or with fake packaging.

C. "Designated Drugs and Designated Medical Devices" means a Drug (including APIs) and Excipients or Medical Device, respectively, designated for inclusion in each phase of implementation, based on criteria established in Article IV. A.

D. "Drug" means any material commonly used for human pharmaceutical use. The term includes the following materials:

1. Finished-dosage forms (including both over-the-counter ("OTC") and prescription drugs);
2. Drug substance, or active pharmaceutical ingredients ("APIs");
3. Biologic drugs (e.g., vaccines and monoclonal antibodies); and
4. Products taken by mouth intended to supplement the diet that:

(i) bear or contain one or more of the following dietary ingredients: a vitamin; a mineral; an herb or other botanical; an amino acid; a dietary substance for use in humans to supplement the diet by increasing the total dietary intake; or a concentrate, metabolite, constituent, extract or combination of any of the above; and

(ii) meet any one of the following characteristics:

— are not clearly labeled as dietary supplements; or

— contain claims to diagnose, cure, mitigate, treat, or prevent disease; or

— contain substances that are regulated by HHS/FDA as APIs.

E. "Excipient" means any components other than APIs that are commonly used in a pharmaceutical product. These components may include vehicles and additives, such as dyes, flavors, binders, emollients, fillers, lubricants, and preservatives.

F. "Firm" means any business within the customs territory of China or within the United States that is engaged in the manufacture (including processing) and distribution (including export) of Drugs, Excipients, and Medical Devices.

G. "HHS/FDA Requirements" means any U.S. laws, regulations or other requirements, including any amendment adopted after the date of entry into force of this Agreement, concerning Drugs, Excipients, and Medical Devices that are administered or enforced by HHS/FDA.

"SFDA Requirements" means any Chinese laws, regulations or other requirements, including any amendment adopted after the date of entry into force of this Agreement, concerning Drugs, Excipients, and Medical Devices that are administered or enforced by SFDA.

H. "Medical Device" means any instrument, apparatus, machine, implant, in vitro reagent, or similar or related article, intended for use in the diagnosis of disease or other conditions, or in the cure, mitigation, treatment, or prevention of disease in humans, or intended to affect the structure or any function of the human body, and which is not a drug.

I. "SFDA-Registered Firm" means a Firm that SFDA has determined meets SFDA Requirements and that is registered with SFDA.

"HHS/FDA-Registered Firm" means a firm that complies with U.S. registration and listing requirements and that is registered with HHS/FDA.

J. "Facility" means any Firm's site within the customs territory of China or in the United States that is engaged in manufacturing, producing, processing, packing, testing, holding, transporting, distributing, or exporting Drugs, Excipients, and Medical Devices.

Article IV
Import/Export Tools

A. Determination of Designated Drug and Designated Medical Devices

This Article will be implemented in a phased approach, beginning with a defined list of Designated Drugs and Designated Medical Devices. The Parties shall conduct a formal evaluation of the implementation of this Article for the products designated in paragraph 2 at the conclusion of the 12-month period described in Article VII.D and annually thereafter. Based on the Parties' determination of the success of this program, the Parties may agree to add or delete specific Drugs, Excipients, and Medical Devices. Timing for the evaluation will be established through the Work Plan.

1. *Factors*. The Parties shall consult on the designation of which products to include in each phase, as appropriate, based on the following factors:

a. potential or actual, direct or indirect risk to the public health associated with the product, based on testing, inspection results or other relevant information;

b. the rate of refusal of admission in either Party's country or of problems associated with the product before, during or after entering the domestic commerce of the other Party's country, including product recalls, safety alerts and enforcement actions;

c. fraudulent or deceptive labeling or indications of any substitution or additions of a substance to a product or an ingredient of a product that reduces the quality of the ingredient or product or makes it appear of greater value than it is, without clearly revealing such substitution or addition to the recipient in the importing country;

d. promotion or advertising of products intended for consumers of the importing country, beyond the products' approved indications for use; and

e. the feasibility of implementing an effective and timely Work Plan with respect to the product.

2. *First Phase - Designated Drugs and Designated Medical Devices.*

The Parties agree that the first phase shall include products designated by each Party. Designated Drugs shall include any substance or chemical that may be used as an API for any Designated Drug under this Agreement, even if the entity manufacturing or distributing the substance or chemical does not identify the product as an API. Details on these designations shall be determined through the Work Plan. Designated Drugs and Designated Medical Devices shall include:

a. SFDA-Designated Drugs:

i. Recombinant Human Insulin

ii. Lysine Fat and Lysine Salt

iii. Cefoperazone and its salts

iv. Paclitaxel injection

v. Penicillin and its finished dosage form

vi. Diagnostic kit for blood screening, specifically, for HIV/AIDS and Hepatitis B & C

b. SFDA-Designated Medical Devices:

i. Intraocular Lenses

ii. Cardiac pacemakers

c. HHS/FDA-Designated Drugs:

i. Gentamicin sulfate

ii. Atorvastatin

iii. Sildenafil

iv. Dietary supplements intended for erectile dysfunction or sexual enhancement

v. Human Growth Hormone

vi. Oseltamivir

vii. Cephalosporins manufactured in facilities that also manufacture non-cephalosporin drugs

viii. Glycerin

d. HHS/FDA-Designated Medical Devices:

i. Glucose test strips

ii. Condoms

B. Registration and Collaboration on Designated Drugs and Designated Medical Devices

1. With respect to Designated Drugs and Designated Medical Devices:

a. For those designated by HHS/FDA, SFDA shall require that all Firms that manufacture Designated Drugs and Designated Medical Devices intended for export to the United States are registered by SFDA.

b. For those designated by SFDA, HHS/FDA shall provide SFDA with the following available information as agreed to in the Work Plan:

i. the facilities that manufacture the products;

ii. information from the product approval or clearance package;

iii. recalls, warning letters, and enforcement actions; and

iv. reported post-marketing adverse events

2. HHS/FDA shall consult with SFDA to assist SFDA in understanding HHS/FDA Requirements for Designated Drugs and Designated Medical Devices.

3. HHS/FDA and SFDA shall review the HHS/FDA Requirements for the Designated Drugs and Designated Medical Devices and the SFDA Requirements for the Designated Drugs and Designated Medical Devices to understand the differences and identify the means to ensure the quality, safety, and authenticity of Designated Drugs and Designated Medical Devices, given different regulatory systems.

4. SFDA shall maintain documents on file related to reviews, inspections, testing, recalls, compliance, and any other assessment of a Firm of Designated Drugs and Designated Medical Devices. SFDA shall make such records available to HHS/FDA within 7 work days of an HHS/FDA request.

C. Future Collaboration on Registration and Certification

The Parties agree to pursue activities to better understand the differences and the gaps between HHS/FDA and SFDA requirements and establish mechanisms to address those gaps. Specifically, SFDA shall actively create conditions to enable SFDA to certify that HHS/FDA Requirements are met for firms producing Designated Drugs and Designated Medical Devices intended for export to the United States. Once these new conditions mature for SFDA, the Parties may agree to modify this Agreement to include provisions that provide for the certification of products, exported from the customs territory of China to the United States, to HHS/FDA requirements, and for appropriate export control mechanisms.

D. Product Integrity and Security

1. The Parties shall cooperate on the establishment of the pedigree (chain-of-custody) systems, as follows, for those Drugs designated under Article IV A. that are identified in the Work Plan as being at risk for counterfeiting;

a. The Parties shall establish and implement measures, including pedigree requirements, to further ensure the integrity and security of Designated Drugs. The Parties shall collaborate with each other on the establishment of such pedigree requirements for both domestic and exported Designated Drugs.

b. The Parties shall establish and implement pedigree systems. The pedigree shall include information on Designated Drugs and their manufacturers as follows:

i. product information (drug name, manufacturer, product registration or identification number);

ii. item information (unique product serial number, dosage form, strength, container size, lot number, expiration date);

iii. information about each party to the transaction (including company name, street address, license number, contact person, and telephone number); and

iv. transaction information (date product was shipped from seller, date received by purchaser),

c. Each Party shall establish and implement standards for a comprehensive electronic tracking system for each unique package.

2. The Parties shall also work on the following product integrity and security measures for all Drugs:

a. Each Party shall enhance enforcement against entities that fail to provide a pedigree, provide a false pedigree, or fail to comply with any other provisions related to the integrity or security of Drugs.

b. Each Party shall develop a program to inform and educate supply-chain stakeholders and the public on how to avoid and minimize their risk of receiving a misbranded, adulterated or Counterfeit Drug or Medical Device, and how to report suspect drugs, excipients, medical devices and suspicious parties.

c. SFDA and HHS/FDA shall respond rapidly to, and investigate reports of, Drugs, Excipients, and Medical Devices suspected of being misbranded, adulterated, or counterfeited. SFDA and HHS/FDA shall also notify each other of any such reports and the steps they have taken or plan to take to investigate the report. SFDA and HHS/FDA shall also report Counterfeit Drugs to the World Health Organization (WHO).

d. Each Party shall take steps to adopt and implement regulations and practices (e.g., good distribution practices) and guidelines (e.g., pharmacovigilance, rapid response for counterfeits) consistent with those established by the World Health Organization (WHO) including with respect to Counterfeit Drug identification and prevention, including the enforcement of laws and regulations that encompass APIs, Excipients, and finished-dosage forms misidentified as to source and composition. Details of the collaboration on standards shall be determined through the Work Plan.

e. Each Party shall endeavor to enhance cooperative activities with its appropriate law-enforcement and regulatory authorities to actively investigate and prosecute individuals or entities that manufacture, sell, distribute, handle, test, trade, or export misbranded, adulterated, or Counterfeit Drugs, Excipients, and Medical Devices. Each Party shall actively participate in the WHO's International Medical Products Anti-Counterfeiting Taskforce (IMPACT), and the Permanent Forum on International Pharmaceutical Crime (PFIPC).

Article V
Information Sharing

The Parties shall exchange information related to Drugs, Excipients, and Medical Devices and their respective regulatory systems concerning Drugs, Excipients, and Medical Devices, on a timeframe and with updates as agreed to in the Work Plan, as follows:

A. A Party may provide information to the other Party in the English or Chinese language.

B. The Parties shall exchange copies of and other relevant information concerning their respective laws and regulations.

C. HHS/FDA and SFDA shall provide each other with copies of all relevant HBS/FDA and SFDA Requirements, updated as appropriate, with respect to Designated Products.

D. Each Party shall provide to the other Party a list of all registered API manufacturers, and the products they manufacture, in its respective country.

E. Each Party shall notify the other Party of serious adverse health consequences or death relating to product safety, manufacturing conditions, recalls, serious adverse event reports, and other instances or the gross deception of consumers. Each Party shall promptly respond to requests from the other Party for information concerning any such risk, including contact information for the Firms or other entities concerned. The Work Plan shall include specific commitments to ensure the timeliness of any such notification or response.

F. HHS/FDA shall work with SFDA to better understand the Global Harmonization Task Force (GHTF) National Competent Authority Reporting (NCAR) program, to support both Parties' actively reporting any serious adverse events that involve medical devices into the NCAR program.

G. Each Party shall notify the other Party of its determination that a shipment of Drugs, Excipents, or Medical Devices has been shipped to the other Party's country, for which there is a reasonable probability that the use of, or exposure to, the product will cause serious adverse health consequences or death. The notification shall:

1. Be in writing;
2. Be made within 24 hours of the determination;
3. Include the reasons for the determination; and
4. Include, as it becomes available, other information that may assist the other Party to identify the shipment and the supplier.

H. Within 30 calendar days of entry into force of this Agreement, each Party shall provide the other with a list of Firms that manufacture Drugs and Medical Devices in its country and are registered in its country, and the products each Firm manufactures. SFDA shall provide to HHS/FDA the list of Drug, Excipients, and Medical Device manufacturers in the customs territory of China that SFDA has determined to be out of compliance with SFDA Requirements, when such a list becomes available.

I. Within 30 calendar days of a request from HHS/FDA, SFDA shall provide HHS/FDA inspection reports requested by HHS/FDA for SFDA-Registered Firms that manufacture or distribute Drugs, Excipients, or Medical Devices that have been or will be exported to the United States. SFDA shall notify HHS/FDA within 10 calendar days of becoming aware of inspection results that indicate significant deficiencies or fraud associated with firms that manufacture or distribute Drugs, Excipients, or Medical Devices that SFDA determines have been or will be exported to the United States. Once HHS/FDA has addressed any remaining remote access issues, HHS/FDA will grant SFDA access to an electronic database of HHS/FDA inspection results.

J. Each Party shall notify the other Party of any Counterfeit Drug, Excipient, or Medical Device found in its country, including information about the source and distribution.

Article VI
Regulatory Cooperation

The Parties shall accomplish the following tasks, as it relates to Drugs, Excipients, and Medical Devices:

A. Develop and set out in the Work Plan specific steps and measures to prevent and control Counterfeit Drugs, Excipients and Medical Devices.

B. Develop appropriate regulatory cooperative activities, including training programs and scientific discussions or cooperation, intended to support the long-term stability and effectiveness of the registration and certification programs. For each training or other cooperative activity that requires travel or other organizational costs, each Party shall bear the cost for its respective participants. Appropriate regulatory cooperative activities may include:

1. development and coordination of the training programs for Chinese inspectors;

2. technical exchanges and training relating to the use of Good Clinical Practice (GCP)s to ensure the safety of human subjects and the collection of valid clinical data; and

3. training and exchange on the development of evaluation review methods, inspection techniques, establishment of computer databases, evaluation report standard formats, and the development of technical guidance documents, and laws and regulations.

C. The Parties shall cooperate on the implementation of standards.

1. The Parties shall develop through the Work Plan details of collaboration on the establishment of internationally-recognized standards. These standards may include:

a. the International Pharmaceutical Excipients Council's standards for excipients;

b. International Conference on Harmonization of Technical Requirements for Registration of Pharmaceuticals for Human Use (ICH) Guidelines, including ICH Q7A Current Good Manufacturing Practice Guideline for APIs;

c. Pharmaceutical Inspection Cooperation Scheme (PIC/S) GMP Standards for Finished-Dosage Form Pharmaceuticals; and

d. Global Harmonization Task Force Standards, including ISO 13485 medical device requirements.

2. Upon request, HHS/FDA shall provide assistance to SFDA regarding internationally-recognized standards.

D. Each Party shall develop a streamlined process for facilitating (e.g., issuing a letter of invitation) an inspection by a Party in the other Party's country no later than 5 calendar days after receipt of such a request from a Party. Such inspection may be conducted with or without providing advance notice (as specified in the request) to the establishment concerned. The performance measure for this activity shall be the number of days that elapse between the Party's request and the other Party's response in facilitating the inspection.

E. Each Party may request the other Party to conduct an investigation regarding any Drug, Excipient, or Medical Device, exported from the other Party's country to the Party's country, that the Party has reason to believe may pose a risk to public health or safety. The Party shall respond to the requesting Party within 3 calendar days of the receipt of the request, informing the requesting Party of its decision on whether or not to conduct an investigation. If the decision is to conduct an investigation, the Party shall notify the requesting Party within 15 calendar days from the decision to conduct the investigation of:

1. information relating to the source of the health or safety risk;

2. steps taken to remedy the risk; and

3. the outcome of any remediation.

The Work Plan shall set out requirements and performance measures related to investigations under this paragraph.

F. HHS/FDA may fully participate in any annual or other SFDA inspection of any SFDA— or HHS/FDA—Registered Firm in the customs territory in China exporting to the United States.

G. Except in extraordinary circumstances, each Party will observe the following procedures: each Party shall publish on its website(s) all proposed regulations and other measures related to Designated Drugs and Designated Medical Devices and allow a reasonable period of time for all interested parties to submit comments. Each Party shall consider such comments and, at the time final regulations are adopted, address in writing significant, substantive comments received from interested persons during the comment period and explain any substantive revision made to the proposed regulations. Both Parties shall also publish on its website all final regulations and measures related to Designated Drugs and Designated Medical Devices and allow a reasonable amount of time before implementation and enforcement. Both Parties shall also publish all of the information listed above in the relevant government publication (i.e., HHS/FDA, the Federal Register). Pending the designation of a single relevant government publication for this purpose in China, SFDA shall ensure its website is kept current, so as to assure transparency in rulemaking.

H. HHS/FDA shall report any science and technology cooperation to the Joint Commission on Scientific and Technological cooperation established under the Agreement between the Government of the United States of America and the Government of the People's Republic of China on Cooperation in Science and Technology, signed at Washington January 31, 1979.

Article VII
Administration

A. Within 15 calendar days of the date of entry into force of this Agreement, each Party shall notify the other Party in writing of its primary points of contact for coordinating all bilateral activities under this Agreement, including coordinating meetings, exchanging information, and sending and receiving notifications.

B. The Parties hereby establish a Working Group. Within 30 calendar days of the date of entry into force of this Agreement, each Party shall identify relevant policy and technical experts of each Party to serve on the Working Group.

C. Within 60 calendar days of the date of entry into force of this Agreement, the Working Group shall hold its first meeting to develop a Work Plan that:

1. further details specific activities each Party shall perform pursuant to this Agreement within the first 12-month period following the date of entry into force of this Agreement and time lines for the completion of each such activity; and

2. includes, as appropriate, performance measures to evaluate the success of each such activity.

D. Within 120 calendar days of the date of entry into force of this Agreement, the Working Group shall finalize the Work Plan for the first 12-month period following the date of entry into force of this Agreement. The Parties shall assess the Work Plan at the conclusion of the 12-month period.

E. For each subsequent 12-month period, the Working Group shall meet to develop a Work Plan that further details specific activities that each Party shall perform pursuant to this Agreement within that period and, as appropriate, that includes performance measures to evaluate the success of each such activity. The Parties shall assess each such Work Plan at the conclusion of the relevant period.

F. The Work Plan for each 12-month period, when adopted by the Parties, shall include binding commitments for the effective and timely implementation of this Agreement. Each Party shall make the Work Plan for the first 12 months, and each subsequent year, publicly available on its respective website.

G. Within 180 calendar days of the date of entry into force of this Agreement, high-level representatives of the Parties shall meet to discuss and review the implementation of and progress under this Agreement and related matters.

H. Thereafter, the high-level representatives of the Parties shall meet on an annual basis to discuss and review the implementation of and progress under this Agreement and related matters. Unless the Parties otherwise agree, the location of these annual meetings shall alternate between the United States and China. The Parties may convene additional technical or program-level meetings on an as-needed basis in any mutually agreeable location.

I. For each provision in this Article, each Party shall notify the other Party within 24 hours of determining it will be unable to meet an agreed-upon deadline, for such reasons as U.S. or Chinese holidays, or for any other reason, and will provide the reason for the delay. The Parties may then agree to modify the timelines and establish a new delivery date. Such notification shall occur through the designated points of contact established as per Article VII. 1.

Article VIII
Performance Measures

A. The Parties shall evaluate and discuss progress under this Agreement on an annual basis, including the effectiveness of SFDA's registration program established pursuant to the Work Plan. HHS/FDA may base its evaluation of such progress on, among other things, the following:

1. the rate of refusal by HHS/FDA of Drugs, Excipients, and Medical Devices exported from the customs territory of China and offered for import into the United States, as compared to the overall rate of refusal in calendar year 2007 or other relevant period by HHS/FDA of Drugs, Excipients, and Medical Devices exported from the customs territory of China and offered for import into the United States; and

2. the volume, frequency and significance in terms of public health hazard of recalls of Drugs, Excipients, and Medical Devices in the United States, including Counterfeit Drugs and Medical Devices, exported from the customs territory of China and offered for import into the United States as compared to the volume, frequency and significance of such recalls in 2007 or other relevant period.

B. SFDA may base its evaluation of such progress on, among other things, the following:

1. a rate of refusal of Designated Drugs and Designated Medical Devices approved by HHS/FDA offered for import into the customs territory of China, as compared to the overall rate of refusal in the previous calendar year;

2. the overall percentage of Designated Drugs and Designated Medical Devices exported from the customs territory of the United States and offered for import into the customs territory of China that are determined as unqualified based on the supervised sample testing; and

3. the volume frequency, and significance in terms of public health hazard of recall of drugs and medical devices in China, including Counterfeit Drugs and Medical Devices, exported from the United States and offered for import into the customs territory of China as compared to the volume, frequency and significance of such recalls in the previous calendar year.

Article IX
Final Provisions

A. Nothing in this Agreement precludes the Government of United States or the Government of China from taking any measure to protect the public health or the citizens of its respective country.

HHS/FDA and SFDA affirm that it shall work with its country's national, state, provincial, or municipal bodies, as appropriate, to implement this Agreement fully.

B. Nothing in this Agreement shall be construed to affect the rights or obligations of the United States or China under any other agreement in force between the United States and China.

C. HHS/FDA actions with regard to Drugs, Excipients, and Medical Devices shall be governed by HHS/FDA Requirements and all other existing U.S. laws and regulations.

D. SFDA actions with regard to Drugs, Excipients, and Medical Devices shall be governed by SFDA Requirements and all other existing Chinese laws and regulations.

E. The Parties shall endeavor to resolve any dispute regarding the implementation or interpretation of this Agreement through timely consultations.

F. This Agreement shall enter into force upon signature by both Parties and shall remain in force for a period of two years, unless terminated by either Party. On the last day of the two-year period, and of each subsequent two-year period, the Agreement shall automatically be renewed for another two-year period, unless either Party notifies the other Party that it wishes to terminate the Agreement at least 60 calendar days prior to the last day of the two-year period. In addition, either Party may terminate the Agreement upon 60 calendar days' written notice to the other Party. The Parties may amend this Agreement at any time by mutual written agreement.

DONE at Beijing, this 11th day of December, 2007, in duplicate in the English and Chinese languages, each text being equally authentic.

[Signature]

FOR THE DEPARTMENT OF HEALTH AND HUMAN SERVICES OF THE UNITED STATES OF AMERICA

[Signature]

FOR THE STATE FOOD AND DRUG ADMINISTRATION OF THE PEOPLE'S REPUBLIC OF CHINA

STATE DEPARTMENT DOCUMENT NUMBER: 08-14

AGREEMENT BETWEEN THE UNITED STATES OF AMERICA AND MALTA CONCERNING COOPERATION TO SUPPRESS THE PROLIFERATION OF WEAPONS OF MASS DESTRUCTION, THEIR DELIVERY SYSTEMS, AND RELATED MATERIALS BY SEA, WITH APPENDIX

SIGNED AT WASHINGTON D.C., MARCH 15, 2007
ENTERED INTO FORCE DECEMBER 19, 2007

CTIA DOCUMENT NUMBER: 13387.000

The Government of the United States of America and the Government of Malta, (hereinafter, "the Parties");

Deeply concerned about the proliferation of weapons of mass destruction (WMD), their delivery systems, and related materials, particularly by sea, as well as the risk that these may fall into the hands of terrorists;

Recalling the 31 January 1992 United Nations Security Council Presidential statement that proliferation of all WMD constitutes a threat to international peace and security, and underlines the need for Member States of the UN to prevent proliferation;

Also recalling United Nations Security Council Resolution 1540 (2004), which calls on all States, in accordance with their national legal authorities and legislation and consistent with international law, to take cooperative action to prevent illicit trafficking in nuclear, chemical or biological weapons, their means of delivery, and related materials;

Recalling further the Convention on the Prohibition of the Development, Production, Stockpiling and Use of Chemical Weapons and on their Destruction, done at Paris 13 January 1993; the Treaty on Nonproliferation of Nuclear Weapons, done at Washington, London and Moscow 1 July 1968; and the Convention on the Prohibition of the Development, Production and Stockpiling of Bacteriological (Biological) and Toxin Weapons and on their Destruction, done at Washington, London and Moscow 10 April 1972;

Further recalling the International Ship and Port Facility Security Code, adopted by the International Maritime Organization (IMO) on 12 December 2002;

Acknowledging the widespread consensus that proliferation and terrorism seriously threaten international peace and security;

Convinced that trafficking in these items by States and non-state actors of proliferation concern must be stopped;

Guided by the Statement of Interdiction Principles for the Proliferation Security Initiative;

Inspired by the efforts of the IMO to improve the effectiveness of the Convention for the Suppression of Unlawful Acts against the Safety of Maritime Navigation, done at Rome 10 March 1988;

Reaffirming the importance of customary international law of the sea as reflected in the 1982 United Nations Convention on the Law of the Sea;

Committed to cooperation to stop the flow by sea of WMD, their delivery systems, and related materials to or from States or non-state actors of proliferation concern;

Have agreed as follows:

Article 1
Object, Purpose and Scope

1. The object and purpose of this Agreement is to promote cooperation between the Parties to enable them to prevent the transportation by sea of items of proliferation concern.

2. The Parties shall carry out their obligations and responsibilities under this Agreement in a manner consistent with the principles of international law pertaining to the sovereign equality and territorial integrity of States and freedom of navigation, on the basis of the principle of reciprocity.

3. The Parties shall cooperate to the fullest extent possible, subject to the availability of resources and in compliance with their respective laws.

Article 2
Definitions

For the purposes of this Agreement, unless the context otherwise requires:

1. "Proliferation by sea" means the transportation by ship of weapons of mass destruction, their delivery systems, and related materials to or from States or non-state actors of proliferation concern.

2. "Weapons of mass destruction" (WMD) means nuclear, chemical, biological and radiological weapons.

3. "Related materials" means materials, equipment and technology, of whatever nature or type, that are related to and destined for use in the development, production, utilization or delivery of WMD.

4. "Items of proliferation concern" means WMD, their delivery systems, and related materials.

5. "States or non-state actors of proliferation concern" means those countries or entities whose activities should be impeded or stopped because they are or are believed to be engaged in: (1) efforts to develop or acquire WMD or their delivery systems; or (2) trafficking (either selling, receiving, or facilitating) of WMD, their delivery systems, or related materials.

6. "Security Force Officials" means for:

   a. the United States, uniformed or otherwise clearly identifiable members of the United States Coast Guard and the United States Navy, who may be accompanied by clearly identifiable law enforcement officials of the Departments of Homeland Security and Justice, and other clearly identifiable officials duly authorized by the Government of the United States of America and notified to the Competent Authority of the Government of Malta; and

   b. Malta, uniformed or otherwise clearly identifiable members of the Armed Forces of Malta, the Malta Police Force and the Department of Customs, and other clearly identifiable officials duly authorized by the Government of Malta and notified to the Competent Authority of the United States.

7. "Security Force vessels" means warships and other vessels of the Parties, or of third States as may be authorized in accordance with Articles 5 and 9 of this Agreement, on which Security Force Officials of either or both Parties may be embarked, clearly marked and identifiable as being on government non-commercial service and authorized to that effect, including any vessel and aircraft embarked on or supporting such vessels.

8. "Suspect vessel" means a vessel used for commercial or private purposes in respect of which there are reasonable grounds to suspect it is engaged in proliferation by sea, as determined pursuant to Article 5 of this Agreement.

9. "International waters" means all parts of the sea not included in the territorial sea, internal waters and archipelagic waters of a State, consistent with international law.

10. "Competent Authority" means for the United States, the Commandant of the United States Coast Guard (including any officer designated by the Commandant to perform such functions), and for Malta, the Commander of the Armed Forces of Malta (including any officer designated by the Commander to perform such functions).

Article 3
Cases of Suspect Vessels

1. Subject to paragraph 2 of this Article, operations to suppress proliferation by sea pursuant to this Agreement shall be carried out only against suspect vessels:

a. having the nationality of one of the Parties and entitled to fly its flag, or

b. registered under the law of one of the Parties under a bareboat charter, notwithstanding an underlying registration in another State not Party to this Agreement, or

c. without nationality or assimilated to vessels without nationality.

2. Such operations shall not be carried out under this Agreement against vessels registered under the law of one of the Parties while bareboat chartered in another State not party to this Agreement.

Article 4
Operations in and over National Waters

This Agreement does not authorize the conduct of operations to suppress proliferation by sea by one Party in and over the waters of the other Party.

Article 5
Operations in International Waters

1. Authority to Board Suspect Vessels. Whenever the Security Force Officials of one Party ("the requesting Party") encounter a suspect vessel claiming nationality in the other Party ("the requested Party") located in international waters, the requesting Party may request through the Competent Authority of the requested Party, that it:

a. confirm the claim of nationality of the suspect vessel; and

b. if nationality is confirmed:

i. authorize the boarding and search of the suspect vessel, cargo, and persons found on board by Security Force Officials of the requesting Party; and

ii. if evidence of proliferation is found, authorize the Security Force Officials of the requesting Party to detain the vessel, as well as items and persons on board, pending instructions conveyed through the Competent Authority of the requested Party as to the actions the requesting Party is permitted to take concerning such items, persons and vessels.

Each authorization to act shall be in writing between the Competent Authorities. Nevertheless, in urgent circumstances, an authorization to act may be granted orally by the Competent Authority of the requested Party. An oral authorization to act shall be confirmed in writing forthwith by the Competent Authority.

2. Contents of Requests. Each request should be in writing and contain the name of the suspect vessel, sufficiently reliable information forming the basis for the suspicion, the geographic position of the vessel, the IMO number if available, the homeport, the port of origin and destination, and any other identifying information. Nevertheless, in urgent circumstances, a request may be made orally, but shall be confirmed in writing forthwith.

The requested Party shall acknowledge to the Competent Authority of the requesting Party in writing, by e-mail or by facsimile, its receipt of any written or urgent oral request immediately upon receiving it.

3. Responding to Requests

a. If the nationality is verified and the requested Party is satisfied with the basis for suspicion that the vessel is a suspect vessel, and that the information provided by the requesting Party is sufficiently reliable, the requested Party may:

i. decide to conduct the boarding and search with its own Security Force Officials;

ii. authorize the boarding and search by the Security Force Officials of the requesting Party, subject to conditions if deemed appropriate;

iii. decide to conduct the boarding and search together with the requesting Party; or

iv. nevertheless, deny permission to board and search.

b. The requested Party shall answer through its Competent Authority requests made for the verification of nationality and authorization to board within four hours of its acknowledgment of the receipt of such requests unless the requested Party requests additional time to answer.

c. If the nationality is not verified or verifiable within the four hours, the requested Party shall, through its Competent Authority:

i. nevertheless stipulate that it does not object to the boarding and search by the Security Force Officials of the requesting Party; or

ii. refute the claim of the suspect vessel to its nationality.

d. Either Party, consistent with the other provisions of this Agreement, may subject its authorization under this paragraph to conditions, including obtaining additional information from the requesting Party, and conditions relating to responsibility for and the extent of measures to be taken. Information to be provided in response to such a request shall be exchanged in a timely manner by the Competent Authorities; however, the requesting Party may notify the requested Party if it is providing additional information through established information sharing channels.

e. Notification to the Master. Prior to the boarding being conducted, the flag State may, in coordination with the requesting Party, transmit to the Master of the suspect vessel notice that it has authorized the requesting Party to board the vessel.

4. Right of Visit. Notwithstanding the foregoing paragraphs of this Article, the Security Force Officials of one Party ("the first Party") are authorized to board suspect vessels claiming nationality in the other Party that are not flying the flag of the other Party, not displaying any marks of its registration or nationality, and claiming to have no documentation on board the vessel, for the purpose of locating and examining the vessel's documentation. If documentation or other physical evidence of nationality is located, the foregoing paragraphs of this Article apply. If no documentation or other physical evidence of nationality is available, the other Party will not object to the first Party assimilating the vessel to a ship without nationality consistent with international law.

5. Use of Force. The authorization to board, search and detain includes the authority to use force in full compliance with the provisions of Article 11 of this Agreement.

6. Shipboarding Otherwise in Accordance with International Law. This Agreement does not limit the right of either Party to conduct boardings of vessels or other activities consistent with international law whether based, *inter alia*, on the right of visit, the rendering of assistance to persons, vessels, and property in distress or peril, or an authorization from the Flag or Coastal State, or other appropriate bases in international law.

Article 6
Jurisdiction over Detained Vessels

1. Limitations. Neither Party shall undertake the exercise of jurisdiction and performance of functions in the territory of the other Party.

2. Jurisdiction of the Parties. In all cases covered by Article 5 concerning the vessels of a Party ("the flag State") located in international waters, jurisdiction rests with the flag State over a detained vessel, cargo or other items and persons on board (including seizure, forfeiture, arrest, and prosecution). However, the flag State may, subject to its Constitution and laws, consent to the exercise of jurisdiction by the other Party in accordance with the provisions of this Agreement.

3. Jurisdiction in the contiguous zone of a Party. In a zone contiguous to its territorial sea, described as the contiguous zone, a Party may exercise the control necessary, *inter alia*, to prevent the infringement of its customs, fiscal, immigration or sanitary laws and regulations within its territory or territorial sea. In all cases not covered by Article 5 involving the vessel of one Party that arise in the contiguous zone of the other Party and in which both Parties have authority to board in accordance with their respective jurisdictions.

a. except as provided in subparagraph (b), the Party which conducts the boarding shall have the right to exercise its authorized jurisdiction;

b. in cases involving suspect vessels fleeing from the territorial sea of a Party in which that Party has the authority to board and to exercise jurisdiction, that Party shall have the right to exercise its authorized jurisdiction.

4. Disposition Instructions. Consultations as to the exercise of jurisdiction pursuant to paragraphs 2 and 3 of this Article shall be undertaken between the Competent Authorities without delay.

5. Form of waiver. Where permitted by its Constitution and laws, waiver of jurisdiction may be granted verbally, but as soon as possible it shall be recorded in a written note from the Competent Authority and be processed through the appropriate diplomatic channel, without prejudice to the immediate exercise of jurisdiction over the suspect vessel by the other Party.

Article 7
Points of Contact

Each Party shall identify to the other Party, and keep current, through its Competent Authority the points of contact for communicating with its national authorities competent to receive and act at any time to requests under Article 5 for verification of nationality and authority to board, search and detain suspect vessels, and for instructions as to the exercise of jurisdiction under Article 6, and to receive and act on notifications under Article 8, and to respond to requests for technical assistance under Article 18 in addition to any other communication necessary for the implementation of this Agreement.

Article 8
Exchange of Information, Notification of Results of Shipboardings and Actions Taken

1. Model Forms. The Parties shall use the model forms appended to this Agreement for communications pursuant to this Agreement, except as otherwise provided in this Agreement. The Competent Authorities of the Parties may, by mutual agreement, amend or replace in accordance with their laws the model forms annexed to this Agreement.

2. Exchange of Operational Information. The-Competent Authorities of both Parties shall endeavor to exchange operational information on the detection and location of suspect vessels and shall maintain communication with each other as necessary to carry out the purpose of this Agreement.

3. Protection of classified information and material. Each Party shall protect classified information and material from unauthorized disclosure at all times in accordance with such requirements as the requesting Party may specify or as otherwise agreed by the Parties.

4. Notification of Results. A Party conducting a boarding and search pursuant to this Agreement shall promptly, and in any case not later than 48 hours, notify the other Party of the results thereof through their Competent Authorities, following the conclusion of the boarding and search. Such notification shall be effected through the Competent Authorities of the Parties.

5. Status Reports. Each Party, in compliance with its laws, shall timely report at least every month to the other Party, through their Competent Authorities, on the status of all investigations, prosecutions and judicial proceedings and other actions and processes, arising out of the application of this Agreement.

Article 9
Conduct of Security Force Officials

1. Compliance with Law and Practices. Each Party shall ensure that its Security Force Officials, when conducting boardings and searches pursuant to this Agreement, act in accordance with its applicable national laws and policies and consistent with international law and accepted international practices.

2. Boarding and Search Teams

   a. Boardings and searches pursuant to this Agreement shall be carried out by Security Force Officials from Security Force vessels as may be authorized on a case-by-case basis.

   b. Neither Party shall be required to authorize a boarding from a vessel or aircraft of a third State that it would consider adverse to its interests.

   c. The boarding and search teams may carry personal weapons.

Article 10
Safeguards

1. Where a Party takes measures against a vessel in accordance with this Agreement, it shall:

   a. take due account of the need not to endanger the safety of life at sea;

   b. take due account of the safety and security of the vessel and its cargo;

   c. not prejudice the commercial or legal interests of the Flag State;

   d. ensure, within available means, that any measure taken with regard to the vessel is environmentally sound under the circumstances;

   e. ensure that persons on board are afforded the protections, rights and guarantees provided by international law and the boarding State's law and regulations;

   f. ensure that the master of the vessel is, or has been, afforded at any time the opportunity to contact the vessel's Flag State, and, subject to preserving the safety and security of operations, is, or has been, afforded the opportunity to contact the vessel's owner or manager.

2. All reasonable efforts shall be taken to avoid a vessel being unduly detained or delayed.

Article 11
Use of Force

1. All uses of force pursuant to this Agreement shall be in strict accordance with the applicable laws and policies of the Party conducting the boarding and with applicable international law.

2. Each Party shall avoid the use of force except when and to the degree necessary to ensure the safety of Security Force vessels and officials, and where Security Force Officials are obstructed in the execution of their duties.

3. Any use of force pursuant to this Article shall not exceed the minimum degree of force that is necessary, proportional and reasonable in the circumstances.

4. Boarding and search teams and Security Force vessels have the inherent right to use all available means to apply that force reasonably necessary to defend themselves or others from physical harm.

5. Any use of force by the Party conducting a boarding and search pursuant to this Agreement shall be immediately reported with all necessary details to the Competent Authority of the other Party.

Article 12
Exchange and Knowledge of Laws and Policies of Other Party

1. Exchange of Information. To facilitate implementation of this Agreement, each Party, shall endeavor to ensure the other Party is appropriately informed of its respective applicable laws and policies, particularly those pertaining to the use of force.

2. Knowledge. Each Party shall endeavor to ensure that its Security Force Officials are knowledgeable concerning the applicable laws and policies in accordance with this Agreement.

Article 13
Points of Contact

1. Information. Each Party shall inform the other Party through their Competent Authorities, and keep current, the points of contact for communication, decision and instructions under Articles 4 and 5, and notifications under Articles 6 and 8, of this Agreement.

2. Availability. The Parties shall ensure that the points of contact have the capability to receive, process and respond to requests and reports at any time.

Article 14
Disposal of Seized Property

1. Disposal of Property. Assets seized in consequence of any operation undertaken pursuant to this Agreement shall be disposed of in accordance with the laws of that Party exercising jurisdiction in accordance with Article 6 of this Agreement.

2. The seizing Party may transfer in accordance with its laws forfeited assets or proceeds of their sale to the flag State Party after deducting therefrom all expenses directly and reasonably connected with the seizure and disposal and any share thereof which any Party may in accordance with its legislation be entitled to.

Article 15
Disputes and Consultations

1. Disputes. Disputes arising from the interpretation or implementation of this Agreement shall be settled by mutual agreement of the Parties. Where mutual agreement cannot be reached after a reasonable time, the Parties may, by mutual agreement, seek settlement of the dispute by another peaceful means of their own choice, including, but not limited to, arbitration.

2. Evaluation of Implementation. The Parties agree to consult as necessary to evaluate the implementation of this Agreement and to consider enhancing its effectiveness. The evaluation shall be carried out at least once a year.

3. Resolving Difficulties. In case a difficulty arises concerning operations under this Agreement, either Party may request consultations with the other Party to resolve the matter.

Article 16
Claims

1. Injury or Loss of Life. Any claim for injury to or loss of life of a Security Force Official of a Party while carrying out operations arising from this Agreement shall normally be resolved in accordance with the laws of that Party.

2. Other Claims. Any other claim submitted for damage, harm, injury, death or loss resulting from an operation carried out by a Party under this Agreement shall be resolved in accordance with the domestic law of the Party to which the claim is brought and international law.

3. Consultation. If any damage, harm, injury, death or loss is suffered as a result of any action asserted to have been taken by the Security Force Officials of one Party in contravention of this Agreement, including action taken on unfounded suspicions, or if any improper, disproportionate or unreasonable action is asserted to have been taken by a Party, the Parties shall, without prejudice to any other legal recourse which may be available, consult at the request of either Party with a view to resolving the matter and deciding any questions relating to compensation or payment.

4. No Waiver of Other Rights. Neither Party thereby waives any rights it may have under international law to raise a claim with the other Party through diplomatic channels.

Article 17
Technical Assistance

The Competent Authority of one Party ("the Requesting Party") may request, and the Competent Authority of the other Party may authorize, Security Force Officials to provide technical assistance, such as specialized assistance in the boarding and search of suspect vessels, including vessels of the Requesting Party wherever located (provided that any activity in a marine area under the sovereignty of a third State has been authorized by that State), and for the boarding and search of suspect vessels located in the territory or waters of the requesting Party.

Article 18
Miscellaneous Provisions

Nothing in this Agreement:

(a) precludes the Parties from otherwise agreeing on operations or other forms of cooperation to suppress proliferation;

(b) alters the rights and privileges due any person in any administrative or judicial proceeding conducted under the jurisdiction of either Party;

(c) shall be construed as creating any private right of action for any individual or entity;

(d) prejudices in any manner the positions of either Party regarding the international law of the sea.

Article 19
Entry into Force

This Agreement shall enter into force upon an exchange of notes indicating that the necessary internal procedures of each Party have been completed.

Article 20
Termination

1. Notification. This Agreement may be terminated at any time by either Party upon written notification to the other Party through the diplomatic channel.

2. Effective Date. Such termination shall take effect 90 days from the date of notification.

Article 21
Continuation of Actions Taken

This Agreement shall continue to apply after termination with respect to any administrative or judicial proceedings arising out of actions taken pursuant to this Agreement

IN WITNESS WHEREOF, the undersigned, being duly authorized by their respective Governments, have signed this Agreement.

DONE AT Washington, this 15th day of March, 2007.

[Signature]	[Signature]
FOR THE GOVERNMENT OF THE UNITED STATES OF AMERICA	FOR THE GOVERNMENT OF MALTA

APPENDIX: MODEL FORMS

Model Form: STEP 1
Request for Confirmation of Nationality and Request for Authorization to Board and Search Suspect Vessel Pursuant to Article 5 of the Agreement

Date/Time (GMT (Z)): _______________

Reference (Vessel Name): _______________

To: _______________________________
(insert identification of the Competent Authority of Requested Party)

Telephone: _______________

Fax: _______________

e-mail: _______________

From _______________________________
(insert identification of the Competent Authority of Requesting Party)

Telephone: _______________

Fax: _______________

e-mail: _______________

□ If this box is checked, then this request confirms an urgent oral request made previously by [*the United States of America directed to the Operations Center of the Armed Forces of Malta*] [*Malta directed to the United States Coast Guard National Command Center*].

Pursuant to Article 5 of the Agreement between the Government of the United States of America and the Government of Malta Concerning Cooperation to Suppress the Proliferation of Weapons of Mass Destruction, their Delivery Systems, and Related Materials by Sea (hereinafter, the "Agreement"), the Security Force Officials of [*name of Requesting Party*] have encountered a suspect vessel claiming nationality in [*name of the Requested Party*] located in international waters. Accordingly, [*name of Requesting Party*] invites [*name of the Requested Party*]'s attention to following information and requests.

1. Name/hull number/flag of Security Force Vessel on scene: __________
2. Available Description of Suspect Vessel:
   a. Vessel's name: _______________
   b. Claimed flag: _______________
   c. Call Sign: _______________
   d. IMO number: _______________
   e. Port & year of registry: _______________
   f. Type of vessel: **(Check one)**

      □ Container

      □ Tanker

      □ Bulk carrier

□ Pleasure craft

□ Fishing vessel

□ Cruise ship

□ Other: _______________

g. Length of vessel: _______________

h. Last port of call (LPOC): _______________

i. Date of LPOC: _______________

j. Next port of call (NPOC): _______________

k. Date of NPOC: _______________

l. Claimed cargo: _______________

m. Purpose of voyage: _______________

3. Suspect vessel's position:

a. Latitude: _______________

b. Longitude: _______________

c. Geographic reference: _______________

d. Course/Speed: __________/__________

4. Persons on board, if known:

a. Number: _______________

b. Name of Master: _______________

c. Nationality of Master: _______________

d. Master's date of birth: _______________

5. Reasonable grounds to suspect that vessel is engaged in proliferation by sea: (include, if possible, a brief description of the suspect cargo, including any relationship to relevant multilateral or national export control lists, such as the Nuclear Suppliers Group Trigger List)

____

____

____

____

____

____

____

____

____

____

____

□ If this box is checked, relevant information is being provided through established information sharing channels.

6. Estimated duration indicated for the boarding based on current information (this is only an estimate and subject to substantial change depending on circumstances encountered; if this request is approved, the [*name of Requesting Party*] shall keep [*name of Requested Party*] apprised of developments and changed circumstances that may decrease or increase the duration of the boarding):

____

7. Action Request: The [*name of Requesting Party*] requests [*name of the Requested Party*]:

a. Confirm the claim of nationality of the suspect vessel; and

b. If nationality is confirmed:

(1) Authorize the boarding and search of the suspect vessel, cargo and the persons found on board by [*name of the Requesting Party*] Security Force Officials; and

(2) If evidence of proliferation is found, authorize the Security Force Officials of the [*name the of Requesting Party*] to detain the vessel, as well as items and persons on board, pending instructions conveyed through [*name of the Competent Authority of the Requested Party*] as to the actions the [*name of the Requesting Party*] is permitted to take concerning such items, persons and vessels.

Signature/Date/Time (GMT (Z)): ______________________________

Model Form: STEPS 2-4
Response to Requests for Confirmation of Nationality and Authorization to Board and Search Suspect Vessel Pursuant to Article 5 of the Agreement

Date/Time (GMT (Z)): ______________

Reference (Vessel Name): ______________

To: ____________________________
(insert identification of the Competent Authority of Requested Party)

Telephone: ______________

Fax: ______________

e-mail: ______________

From: ____________________________
(insert identification of the Competent Authority of Requesting Party)

Telephone: ______________

Fax: ______________

e-mail: ______________

□ If this box is checked, then this authorization confirms an urgent oral authorization given previously by [*the United States of America directed to the Operations Center of the Armed Forces of Malta*] [*Malta directed to the United States Coast Guard National Command Center*].

THIS SPACE INTERNATIONALLY LEFT BLANK

STEP 2: CONFIRMATION OF NATIONALITY

In response to your request of [*date/time GMT (Z) from request form*] for confirmation of nationality of [*name of suspect vessel*] pursuant to article 5 of the Agreement between the Government of the United States America and the Government of Malta Concerning Cooperation to Suppress the Proliferation of Weapons of Mass Destruction, their Delivery Systems, and Related Materials by Sea (hereinafter, the "Agreement"), the [*name of Requested Party*] hereby:

CHECK ONLY ONE OF THE BOXES:

□ Confirms that the [*name of suspect vessel*] is presently lawfully registered [*in the American Register of Ships*] [*under the Merchant Shipping Act (CAP. 234) of the Laws of Malta*] and is entitled to fly the flag of the [*name of Requested Party*] (see paragraph 2 of request).

□ Can neither confirm nor deny that [*name of suspect vessel*] is registered [*in the American Register of Ships*] [*under the Merchant Shipping Act (CAP. 234*) of the Laws of Malta], but nevertheless stipulates that it does not object to the boarding and search by the Security Force Officials of the Requesting Party (see paragraph 2 of request).

□ Denies that the [*name of suspect vessel*] is presently lawfully registered [*in the American Register of Ships*] [*under the Merchant Shipping Act (CAP. 234) of the Laws of Malta*] and therefore is NOT entitled to fly the flag of the [*name of Requested Party*].

STEP 3: IF NATIONALITY IS CONFIRMED or STIPULATED, THEN COMPLETE STEP 3—

Further to your request, the Government of the [*name of the Requested Party*] hereby:

CHECK ONLY ONE OF THE BOXES:

□ Authorizes, **subject to completion of the procedures in Step 4 below**, the boarding and search of [*name of suspect vessel*] by Security Force Officials of [*name of boarding Party*] from [*name and nationality of boarding platform*] in international waters; and if evidence is found on board that the [*name of suspect vessel*] is engaged in proliferation by sea, detain the vessel as well as items and persons on board, pending instructions from [*name of the Requested Party*] regarding the actions the [*name of Requesting Party*] is permitted to take concerning the [*name of suspect vessel*], as well as items and persons on board.

□ Authorizes the boarding and search of [*name of suspect vessel*] by Security Force Officials of [*name of boarding Party*] from [*name and nationality of boarding platform*] in international waters; and if evidence is found on board that the [*name of suspect vessel*] is engaged in proliferation by sea, detain the vessel as well as items and persons on board, pending instructions from [*name of the Requested Party*] regarding the actions the [*name of Requesting Party*] is permitted to take concerning the [*name of suspect vessel*], as well as items and persons on board. The Requested Party does not intend to transmit notice of authorization for the boarding to the Master. Accordingly, the Requesting Party may execute this authorization forthwith.

□ Is prepared to authorize the boarding and search of [*name of suspect vessel*] by Security Force Officials of [*name of boarding Party*] in international waters, but not from [*name and nationality of boarding platform*]. Please identify to [*name of Requested Party*] an alternative platform, if available, and [*name of Requested Party*] will consider the request and respond accordingly.

□ Decides to conduct the boarding and search with its own Security Force Officials and proposes the following additional instructions:

____

____

____

____

□ Decides to conduct the boarding and search together with the Security Force Officials of the Requesting Party and proposes the following rendezvous instructions:

____

____

____

____

____________________ __________

□ Denies authorization to stop, board, and search the [*name of suspect vessel*] on the following grounds:

CHECK THE APPROPRIATE BOX OR BOXES:

□ According to the information officially submitted by to the Government of the [*name of the Requested Party*] there are not reasonable grounds to suspect that the said vessel is engaged in proliferation by sea.

□ It was not possible for the Parties to mutually agree on certain additional conditions relating to the Authorization required by the Government of the [*name of the Requested Party*] in its capacity as the Requested Party.

□ The Government of the [*name of the Requested Party*], in its capacity as the Requested Party, decided that under the present circumstances it is more appropriate and efficient to conduct the boarding and search of [*name of suspect vesse*l] with its own Security Force Officials at a later date.

□ Other: ______________________________

____

□ The present authorization is given to the [*name of the Requesting Party*] subject, in addition to the terms and safeguards of the Agreement, .to the following additional conditions mutually agreed between the Parties:

□ None

□ ______________________________

□ ______________________________

□ ______________________________

□ ______________________________

STEP 4: INSTRUCTIONS REGARDING TRANSMITTAL OF NOTIFCATION TO THE MASTER

- The [*name of the Requesting Party*] shall notify the [*name of the Requested Party*] by [*identify mode(s) of communication*] of the time that it wishes to conduct the boarding and when notification to the Master should be given.
- Thereafter, [*the name of the Requested Party*] shall notify the [*name of the Requesting Party*] by [*identify mode(s) of communication*] when it has transmitted to the Master of the suspect vessel notice that it has authorized the boarding.
- [*Name of the Requesting Party*] may thereafter execute this authorization.

Signature/Date/Time (GMT (Z)): ______________________________

Model Form: STEP 5
Arrangements for Transmittal of Notice to the Master of a Suspect Vessel that the Flag State has Authorized a Boarding Pursuant to the Agreement

Date/Time (GMT (Z)): ______________

Reference (Vessel Name): ______________

To: ____
(insert identification of the Competent Authority of Requested Party)

Telephone: ______________

Fax: ______________

e-mail: ______________

From: ____
(insert identification of the Competent Authority of Requesting Party)

Telephone: ______________

Fax: ______________

e-mail: ______________

STEP 5: INSTRUCTIONS REGARDING TRANSMITTAL OF NOTIFCATION TO THE MASTER:

- The [*name of the Requesting Party*] wishes to conduct the boarding at [*date & time GMT (Z)*]
- The [*name of the Requesting Party*] recommends notification of the boarding be transmitted to the Master be given [*instructions on date & time GMT (Z)*]

Absent urgent circumstances, where a request for Confirmation of Nationality and Authorization to Board and Search and relevant authorization may be respectively submitted or granted orally pursuant to Article 5 of the Agreement, the [*name of the Requesting Party*] shall await notification from [*name of the Requested Party*] by [*identify mode(s) of communication described by the Requested Party in Step 4 above*] that it has transmitted to the Master of the suspect vessel notice that it has authorized the boarding.

Signature/Date/Time (GMT (Z)): ____________________________

Model Form: STEP 6
Confirmation of Transmittal of Notice to the Master of a Suspect Vessel that the Flag State has Authorized a Boarding Pursuant to the Agreement

Date/Time (GMT (Z)): _______________

Reference (Vessel Name): _______________

To: ____

(insert identification of the Competent Authority of Requested Party)

Telephone: _______________

Fax: _______________

e-mail: _______________

From: ____

(insert identification of the Competent Authority of Requesting Party)

Telephone: _______________

Fax: _______________

e-mail: _______________

STEP 6: CONFIRMATION OF TRANSMITTAL OF NOTIFCATION TO THE MASTER:

The [*name of the Requested Party*] confirms that it has transmitted to the Master of the suspect vessel notice that it has authorized the boarding. Consequently, the [*name of the Requesting Party*] may exercise the previous authorization granted to board the suspect vessel.

Signature/Date/Time (GMT (Z)): ______________________________

Model Form: STEP 7
Report of Results of Boarding and Search of Suspect Vessel Pursuant to Article 5 of the Agreement

Date/Time (GMT (Z)): ______________

Reference (Vessel Name): ______________

To: ____
(insert identification of the Competent Authority of Requested Party)

Telephone: ______________

Fax: ______________

e-mail: ______________

From: ____
(insert identification of the Competent Authority of Requesting Party)

Telephone: ______________

Fax: ______________

e-mail: ______________

In accordance with authorization previously granted pursuant to article 5 of the Agreement between the Government of the United States America and the Government of Malta Concerning Cooperation to Suppress the Proliferation of Weapons of Mass Destruction, their Delivery Systems, and Related Materials by Sea (hereinafter, the "Agreement"), the Security Force Officials of [*name of Requesting Party*] boarded the suspect vessel [*name of suspect vessel*]. Accordingly, [*name of Requesting Party*] invites [*name of the Requested Party*]'s attention to following information and requests:

1. Boarding logistics:
    1. Time boarding commenced (GMT (Z)): ______________
    2. Position at time of boarding: ______________
    3. Resistance or opposition to boarding: ______________
    4. Number of persons in boarding team: ______________
2. Evidence of proliferation by sea:

    CHECK ONLY ONE OF THE BOXES:

    □ The boarding yielded no evidence of proliferation by sea.

    □ The boarding yielded the following evidence that the vessel is engaged in proliferation by sea:

    ____

    ____

    ____

    ____

    ____

3. Persons on board:

Name & Position	Nationality	Date of Birth	Document Number

4. Other evidence or issues:

____

____

____

____

5. Intentions/request for disposition instructions:

CHECK ONLY ONE OF THE BOXES:

□ Due to the absence of evidence of proliferation by sea, the [*name of Requesting Party*] intends to conclude the boarding and release the vessel.

□ Based on the evidence described above, the [*name of Requesting Party*] requests from [*name of Requested Party*] authorization to divert and direct the suspect vessel to [*name of place or port*] to continue the boarding and space/cargo accountability dockside. Pursuant to authority previously granted, the [*Requesting Party*] will detain the vessel as well as items and persons on board, pending instructions from the [*name of the Requested Party*] regarding the actions the [*name of Requesting Party*] is permitted to take concerning the [*name of suspect vessel*], as well as items and persons on board.

□ Based on the evidence that the vessel is engaged in proliferation by sea set forth above, the [*name of Requesting Party*] requests from [*name of Requested Party*] disposition instructions with respect to the vessel, cargo, and persons on board. Pursuant to authority previously granted, the [*Requesting Party*] will detain the vessel as well as items and persons on board, pending instructions from the [*name of the Requested Party*] regarding the actions the [*name of Requesting Party*] is permitted to take concerning the [*name of suspect vessel*], as well as items and persons on board.

Signature/Date/Time (GMT (Z)): ______________________________

Model Form
Miscellaneous Communications Regarding Suspect Vessel Pursuant to the Agreement

Date/Time (GMT (Z)): _______________

Reference (Vessel Name): _______________

To: ____

(insert identification of the Competent Authority of Requested Party)

Telephone: _______________

Fax: _______________

e-mail: _______________

From: ____

(insert identification of the Competent Authority of Requesting Party)

Telephone: _______________

Fax: _______________

e-mail: _______________

____

____

____

____

____

____

____

____

____

____

____

____

Signature/Date/Time (GMT (Z)): ___________________

STATE DEPARTMENT DOCUMENT NUMBER: 08-15

AGREEMENT BETWEEN THE UNITED STATES OF AMERICA AND THE REPUBLIC OF COLOMBIA CONCERNING THE PROGRAM FOR THE SUPPRESSION OF ILLICIT AERIAL TRAFFIC IN NARCOTIC DRUGS AND PSYCHOTROPIC SUBSTANCES (AIR BRIDGE DENIAL), WITH ANNEXES

SIGNED AT BOGOTA, DECEMBER 20, 2007
ENTERED INTO FORCE JANUARY 1, 2008

CTIA DOCUMENT NUMBER: 13388.000

The Government of the United States of America ("USG") and the Government of the Republic of Colombia ("GOC") (collectively, the "Parties"), concerned about the continuing illicit trafficking in narcotic drugs and psychotropic substances into, within, and through Colombia;

Recalling that under the 1962 General Agreement for Economic, Technical and Related Assistance between the Government of the United States of America and the Government of Colombia ("1962 Agreement"), the USG has agreed to furnish certain economic, technical, and related assistance;

Recalling that the 1988 United Nations Convention Against Illicit Traffic in Narcotic Drugs and Psychotropic Substances ("1988 Convention") requires the Parties to consider entering into bilateral agreements to carry out, or to enhance the effectiveness of, its provisions;

Recognizing that the illicit trafficking in narcotic drugs and psychotropic substances has had a major negative impact on Colombian efforts to achieve economic and social progress, under the democratic rule of law;

Desiring to reinforce the bilateral program for the control of narcotic drugs and psychotropic substances as set forth in the 2004 Annex to the 1962 General Agreement for Economic, Technical and Related Assistance between the Government of the United States of America and the Government of Colombia ("2004 Annex");

Have agreed as follows:

ARTICLE I
GENERAL

A. This Agreement, commonly referred to as the "Air Bridge Denial Agreement" or "ABD Agreement" ("the Agreement"), shall be the bilateral instrument that governs the Air Bridge Denial Program and the use of Air Bridge Denial Program assets in support of suppression of illicit maritime trafficking in narcotic drugs and psychotropic substances ("SSIMT"), as set out below and in the Annexes and Appendix to this Agreement.

B. The program described herein is designated as the Program for the Suppression of Illicit Aerial Traffic in Narcotic Drugs and Psychotropic Substances ("Air Bridge Denial Program" or "ABD Program"). The Parties agree to support the ABD Program in order to strengthen the capability of the GOC to eliminate illicit aerial trafficking in narcotic drugs and psychotropic substances in the airspace of the Republic of Colombia. Subject to the availability of appropriated funds, the USG may provide aerial tracking equipment, training, spare parts, communications equipment, support equipment, maintenance technician services, advisory assistance by USG ABD Program representatives, and other support to the ABD program.

C. The Colombian Air Force ("FAC") shall be responsible for the ABD Program. The FAC shall oversee operations undertaken within the ABD Program and shall coordinate with the other Colombian institutions involved in the ABD Program and the United States Joint Interagency Task Force South ("JIATF-S"). The FAC shall perform the day-to-day administration of the provisions of this Agreement with the assistance of the Narcotics Affairs Section ("NAS") of the U.S. Embassy in Colombia. The U.S. Department of Defense, through JIATF-S, may provide aerial assets to the ABD program and shall exercise tactical control of those U.S. aircraft that participate in the ABD Program.

D. An "ABD mission" is a mission undertaken in furtherance of the ABD Program. An "SSIMT mission" ("Annex C mission") is a mission that uses funding and assets provided to the ABD Program to support the ongoing efforts of the United States, Colombia, and other partner nations to counter illicit maritime trafficking in narcotic drugs and psychotropic substances in the Caribbean Sea and Pacific Ocean. ABD missions shall take priority over SSIMT missions, unless otherwise agreed by JIATF-S and the FAC.

ARTICLE II
ABD PROGRAM DESCRIPTION

A. Under the ABD Program, non-commercial aircraft flying in Special Zones of Air Control (as defined in Article III(B)(2)) could be subject to special surveillance by ground and aerial detection assets to determine whether the aircraft is reasonably suspected to be primarily engaged in illicit drug trafficking (as defined in paragraph F). The Appendix to Annex A contains factors to be considered in determining whether the aircraft is reasonably suspected of being primarily engaged in illicit drug trafficking. Safety procedures to be used in the ABD Program are contained in Annex A and shall be used by the personnel and representatives of both parties in implementing the ABD Program.

B. Air Safety Monitors, Ground Safety Monitors, and JIATF-S (collectively, the "safety oversight triad") verify compliance with the procedures contained in Annexes A and C.

C. An "ABD event" is the application of the operational and safety procedures described in this Agreement to a particular civil aircraft.

D. As used in this Agreement, "interception" means the act by a tracker or interceptor aircraft of approaching and remaining near an aircraft, with the goal of identifying that aircraft and, if necessary, directing it back to its planned route, escorting it out of restricted or prohibited airspace or the Special Zones of Air Control, or instructing it to land.

E. In accordance with Article 2 of the Convention for the Suppression of Unlawful Acts Against the Safety of Civil Aviation, done at Montreal, September 23, 1971, to which both the United States and Colombia are parties:

(1) an aircraft is considered to be in flight at any time from the moment when all its external doors are closed following embarkation until the moment when any such door is opened for

disembarkation; in the case of a forced landing, the flight shall be deemed to continue until the competent authorities take over responsibility for the aircraft and for persons and property on board;

(2) an aircraft is considered to be in service from the beginning of preflight preparation of the aircraft by ground personnel or by the crew for a specific flight until twenty-four hours after any landing; the period of service shall, in any event, extend for the entire period during which the aircraft is in flight as defined in subparagraph (1) above.

F. An aircraft is "reasonably suspected of being primarily engaged in illicit drug trafficking" when a sufficient basis exists to reasonably suspect that the primary purpose of the operation of an aircraft in service is:

(1) the illicit transport of narcotic drugs or psychotropic substances (as defined in the 1988 Convention), or the travel of the aircraft to the place where it illicitly receives narcotic drugs or psychotropic substances or the return of the aircraft after illicitly moving narcotic drugs or psychotropic substances, or

(2) the transport of proceeds that directly result from an illicit transaction in such narcotic drugs or psychotropic substances (or the travel of the aircraft to the place where it delivers or receives the proceeds).

G. If any GOC or USG participant in the ABD Program has reason to believe that persons not willfully engaged in illicit drug trafficking are on board an aircraft, that aircraft shall not be considered to have a primary purpose of illicit drug trafficking.

H. The pilot, crew, and passengers of all aircraft subject to action under the ABD program are presumed not to be engaged in illicit drug trafficking. The highest priority for the ABD Program is to have the intercepted aircraft land safely at the nearest GOC-controlled landing strip, where law enforcement personnel may take control of the aircraft. As detailed in Annex A, the use of deadly force shall be undertaken only as a last resort.

I. Continued USG support for the ABD Program is conditioned upon consistent, strict adherence to the safety procedures in Annex A to this Agreement, including the International Civil Aviation Organization ("ICAO") radio and visual communication procedures for interception contained in Annex 2 to the Convention on International Civil Aviation, done at Chicago on December 7, 1944; U.S. Congressional authorization and appropriations of funds; and completion of all requirements under relevant U.S. laws and procedures.

J. The operation of tracker or detection and monitoring aircraft used in the ABD Program shall be subject to the rules, regulations, and procedures in force in Colombia, unless other procedures have been agreed upon by the Parties regarding these matters.

ARTICLE III
RESPONSIBILITIES OF THE GOVERNMENT OF COLOMBIA

A. The GOC agrees to assign specialized personnel sufficient to meet operational requirements. The GOC is responsible for all related costs for such personnel, including but not limited to salaries, benefits, and travel within Colombia, except as otherwise provided for in this Agreement or agreed to by the Parties. Subject to the availability of appropriated funds, the GOC shall ensure effective day-to-day operation of the ABD Program by providing adequate funding for normal administrative and related expenses, such as rents and utilities. GOC personnel may be trained through financing provided by the USG, by personnel of the USG or by GOC personnel certified by the USG as instructors.

B. The GOC shall:

(1) ensure compliance with the procedures in Annexes A and C to this Agreement;

(2) designate Special Zones of Air Control ("ZECAs"). ZECAs are sections of Colombian national airspace delineated by the FAC, in coordination with the Special Administrative Unit of the Civil Aviation Agency of the GOC. The ZECAs shall be clearly defined and their existence clearly and widely disseminated prior to the commencement of activities under the ABD Program. The ZECAs shall only cover areas where there is sufficient basis to reasonably suspect that there are routes used for illicit trafficking in narcotic drugs or psychotropic substances and may not be designated over areas that are heavily populated. The geographical coordinates of the ZECAs are attached hereto as Annex B to this Agreement;

(3) on an annual basis, or as changes occur, widely promulgate, throughout the civil aviation community via NOTAM and other appropriate means, notice of the existence and location of the ZECAs and the procedures that the FAC shall use to order intercepted aircraft to land, including the consequences of non-compliance;

(4) establish a safety oversight program and provide Air Safety Monitors (ASM) and Ground Safety Monitors (GSM). In conjunction with JIATF-S, these safety monitors comprise the "safety oversight triad" and verify compliance with the procedures contained in Annexes A and C;

(5) ensure that the GOC pilots, the Mission Commander Officers, and the Air and Ground Safety Monitors are proficient in English, including functional comprehension of common-use and specialized aviation terminology, and are familiar with agreed-upon communication protocols for the operational implementation of the ABD Program;

(6) carry out through the Ministry of Defense the follow-up and supervision for the adequate daily implementation and management of the ABD Program;

(7) permit, at the USG's request, a USG representative to be present on board any aircraft provided under this agreement to observe aircraft operations;

(8) publish the pertinent documents and information so that the owners and pilots of civil aircraft know the following requirements when operating civil aircraft in Colombia. Each civil aircraft is required to:

(a) file a flight plan before taking off (or if filing before takeoff is not possible, as soon as possible after taking off);

(b) contact the nearest air traffic service as soon as possible after takeoff;

(c) continuously monitor the proper air traffic service radio frequency and, where necessary, establish two-way communications with the air traffic service. In cases where it is impossible to make contact with the proper air traffic service, maintain an open channel on ICAO emergency frequencies;

(d) be familiar with aerial intercept and radio and visual communication procedures promulgated by ICAO in Annex 2 to the Chicago Convention;

(e) keep activated the transponder equipment with the code assigned by the Special Administrative Unit of the Civil Aeronautics;

(f) obtain permission before flying over FAC restricted areas; and

(g) refrain from staying over night at non-controlled air fields in which the FAC has prohibited over night stays.

(9) furnish all necessary documents and information to the USG to enable the USG to make semi-annual reviews and yearly certifications relating to the operation and safety of the ABD Program;

(10) provide, insofar as possible and according to availability, appropriate aircraft to carry out the ABD Program; and

(11) be responsible for all maintenance and operations of the aircraft and associated equipment.

C. The GOC shall not use USG assistance, whether provided for purposes of the ABD program or otherwise, to fire warning shots at or damage, render inoperative, or destroy any aircraft in service unless the agreed-upon ABD Program procedures are followed. Nothing in the Agreement is intended to preclude or limit the GOC's ability to use force in defense of self or others at any time. "USG assistance," includes but is not limited to: funding; intelligence; information; radar data; logistical support; command, control and communications support; equipment; maintenance; and training provided by the USG.

D. All GOC agencies involved in implementing the ABD Program agree to minimize operational costs directly borne by the USG. In particular, any aircraft to which the USG provides maintenance support under this Agreement shall remain within the mutually established hourly flight limits, unless a case-by-case exception is requested and approved in advance through consultations between the Parties. The Parties shall review the number of hours on a monthly basis to determine if yearly expenditure targets are being met.

E. Unless provided for otherwise in a separate transfer agreement, the GOC shall not use or permit the use of any assistance provided at any time under this Agreement for purposes other than counternarcotics without the consent of the USG. The USG's ability to consent to exceptional uses of ABD assistance may be subject to limitations imposed by U.S. law.

F. The GOC shall not use or permit the use of any assistance mentioned in Section E, if the ABD program is suspended or terminated, unless the GOC has first obtained consent of the USG.

ARTICLE IV
RESPONSIBILITIES OF THE GOVERNMENT OF THE UNITED STATES

A. The USG intends to transfer to the GOC the title to five (5) SR-560 aircraft and one (1) Cessna 182 aircraft.

B. The USG intends to transfer to the GOC special aviation tools and test equipment, spare parts and support equipment associated with the aircraft described in the previous section.

C. The USG intends to transfer to the GOC the facilities built in support of the ABD Program.

D. The USG intends to effect the transfers decribed in Sections A, B and C by separate transfer agreements reached by both Parties.

E. Unless otherwise agreed by both Parties, the USG shall provide logistical support required for the operation of the SR-560 aircraft in the FAC units made available by the GOC, subject to the availability of appropriated funds.

F. Subject to the availability of appropriated funds, the USG intends to provide training, operations, and equipment maintenance support to the FAC to support the ABD Program. All USG-funded training shall be in accordance with current U.S. Department of State Bureau of International Narcotics and Law Enforcement ("INL") Air Bridge Denial operations and aircrew training syllabi, by INL-approved instructors. Training may be formal, informal, on-the-job training, or a mixture of all types. All training shall be focused on developing an aviation infrastructure capable of safely and effectively continuing Colombian operations after the termination of USG support.

G. The USG shall ensure that semi-annual reviews and a yearly certification of the ABD Program are conducted, in accordance with the relevant U.S. law, including 22 U.S.C. section 2291-4 (as amended).

H. The USG shall assist the GOC in providing safety oversight through the use of the JIATF-S Operations Center. This portion of the "safety oversight triad" shall also verify compliance with the established procedures that are contained in Annexes A and C. The USG shall assist the GOC in ensuring that the FAC Ground and Air Safety Monitors are proficient in English, and are familiar with agreed-upon communication protocols for the operational implementation of this ABD Program.

I. The USG acknowledges that, in the event that the USG suspends or terminates USG-provided support, the GOC may suspend or terminate future USG access to Colombian information and support provided under this Agreement.

ARTICLE V
FUNDING

A. Disbursement of USG funds for procurement of goods and services referred to in this Agreement shall be subject to the availability of appropriated funds for that purpose and shall be made as charges against sub-obligating documents prepared and issued by the USG.

B. Funds obligated by the USG that have not been sub-obligated within twelve months following the close of the fiscal year in which this Agreement has entered into force may be de-obligated by the USG. The United States Department of State may extend the sub-obligation period upon a request from the GOC.

ARTICLE VI
PROPERTY AND PERSONNEL

The treatment of property and personnel under this Agreement shall be in accordance with Article V of the 2004 Annex, with the exception that funds resulting from any insurance payment or settlement for damaged USG-furnished equipment must be used to implement drug trafficking control projects in support of this Agreement.

ARTICLE VII
PROCUREMENT

Procurements under this Agreement shall be made in accordance with Article IX(2) of the 2004 Annex.

ARTICLE VIII
TRAINING OF PERSONNEL

Training of personnel under this Agreement shall be done in accordance with Article VI of the 2004 Annex.

ARTICLE IX
EVALUATION

Evaluation of the ABD Program and its assets under this Agreement shall be in accordance with Article VII of the 2004 Annex, with the addition that:

(1) The Parties shall jointly monitor and evaluate the implementation of the ABD Program to include, but not be limited to:

(a) an examination of the adequacy and appropriateness of existing ZECAs;

(b) an assessment of whether the relevant ABD Program personnel are or remain proficient in English and Spanish in order to implement the terms of this Agreement; and

(c) an assessment to verify that GOC and USG information was used in a manner consistent with the goals and procedures of the ABD Program in those instances where warning shots were fired or force was used against an aircraft in service, whether pursuant to or outside of the ABD Program.

(2) On an annual basis, the USG and GOC shall issue a joint status and evaluation report on the ABD program. The status and evaluation report shall include a summary of USG and GOC ABD Program contributions, a record of activities performed, objectives achieved, and related basic data.

ARTICLE X
AIRCRAFT ACCIDENTS

The purpose of an Accident Investigation Board is to determine the cause of an accident and recommend corrective actions in the areas of training, operational procedures, maintenance, and equipment with the objective of preventing future accidents. In the event of an accident involving any aircraft engaged in operations under the ABD Program or SSIMT, the Parties shall consult and decide on the need for a Combined Accident Investigation Board and the procedures for that Board within 30 days of the accident. All members of a Combined Accident Investigation Board shall have access to all relevant damaged material/equipment, information, files, and reports.

ARTICLE XI
CURRENCY EXCHANGE

Currency exchange under this Agreement shall be in accordance with Article V of the 1962 Agreement.

ARTICLE XII
TAXES AND DUTIES

Treatment of taxes and duties shall be in accordance with Article IV of the 1962 Agreement.

ARTICLE XIII
STATUS OF USG PERSONNEL IN COLOMBIA

USG personnel present in Colombia in connection with implementation of this Agreement shall be accorded the same privileges and immunities enjoyed by Special Missions in accordance with Article III of the 1962 Agreement.

ARTICLE XIV
HUMAN RIGHTS

Human rights issues under this Agreement shall be addressed in accordance with the Preamble of the 2004 Annex, and the Parties shall act consistent with that text.

ARTICLE XV
ANNEXES

The Annexes to this Agreement shall be deemed an integral part of this Agreement.

ARTICLE XVI
FINAL PROVISIONS

A. This Agreement shall enter into force from January 1, 2008 and supersede the "Agreement between the Government of the United States of America and the Government of the Republic of Colombia Concerning the Program for the Suppression of Illicit Aerial Traffic in Narcotic Drugs and Psychotropic Substances" signed at Bogota on March 14, 2007"

B. Amendments to this Agreement may be made as agreed by the Parties. All amendments to this Agreement shall be in writing. The amendments shall enter into force immediately upon signature by both Parties unless otherwise specified in the amendments.

C. Either Party may temporarily suspend ABD Program operations pending a joint review in accordance with Article IX herein. Such suspension shall take effect upon notification of one Party in writing to the other of such suspension. Either Party may suspend its assistance to the ABD Program, in part or in full, if it believes that the other Party has failed to comply with its responsibilities under this Agreement.

D. The USG reserves the right to terminate any or all assistance provided under this Agreement or to take other appropriate measures if an agency of the GOC to or through which assistance is being provided under this Agreement or a key individual of such agency or any recipient of scholarships, fellowships, or training financed under this Agreement is found to have been convicted of a narcotic drugs or psychotropic substances offense or to be or have been engaged in illicit trafficking in narcotic drugs or psychotropic substances.

E. Nothing in this Agreement modifies or alters the obligations between the Parties provided for in other international agreements to which either is a party; nor is anything in this Agreement intended to prejudice the position of either Party with regard to the international law of the sea.

F. The Parties agree to review the terms of this Agreement at the time when USG maintenance and operation support for the aircraft described in Article IV.A terminates. This agreement will remain in force until it is terminated or replaced.

G. Either Party may terminate this Agreement by giving the other Party 90 days' written notice prior to such termination. In addition, the USG may terminate this Agreement if a Presidential Determination required by U.S. law is no longer in effect for this Program effective on the date the USG notifies Colombia of such a change. Termination of this Agreement shall cancel any obligations of the Parties to make contributions pursuant to this Agreement, except for payments of commitments entered into with third parties prior to the notice of cancellation of the Agreement. Additionally, notwithstanding such termination, it is expressly understood that the obligations under Article VI of this Agreement, relating to the use of property, shall remain in force after termination of the Agreement.

Done this 20 day of December, 2007, at Bogotá, in duplicate in the English and Spanish languages, each text being equally authentic.

FOR THE GOVERNMENT OF THE UNITED STATES	POR EL GOBIERNO DE LA REPÚBLICA DE COLOMBIA
[Signature]	[Signature]
William R. Brownfield Ambassador	Juan Manuel Santos C. Ministro de Defensa Nacional

ANNEX A: AIR INTERDICTION PROCEDURES

The Parties agree to comply with the following procedures in connection with the ABD Program. These procedures are designed to protect against loss of life in the air and on the ground in connection with the ABD Program and to meet the domestic legal requirements of each Party.

I. General

A. Under the ABD Program, aircraft may be damaged, rendered inoperative, or destroyed only if (1) if they are reasonably suspected of being primarily engaged in illicit drug trafficking as determined using the factors set forth in the Appendix, as well as other relevant information gathered before and during the detection, sorting, identification, monitoring, and interception phases of each ABD event, and (2) they fail to comply with instructions from the Colombian Air Force ("FAC").

B. At a minimum, the USG shall provide the following participants for the ABD Program:

(1) a JIATF-S Tactical Commander, who exercises command and control of USG ABD assets through the JIATF-S Joint Operations Center ("JOC");

(2) a JIATF-S Command Duty Officer, who is the Tactical Commander's senior watch officer at the JIATF-S JOC;

(3) a Host Nation Rider Assistant, who is a USG representative who assists the Host Nation Rider. The Host Nation Rider Assistant shall be proficient in Spanish;

(4) the Air Force South Air Operations Coordination Cell ("AAOCC"), located in the Colombian Air Force Command and Control Center ("CCOFA", its initials in Spanish), which shall assist in coordination, information exchange, and analysis between JIATF-S and the CCOFA.

C. At a minimum, the GOC shall provide the following participants for the ABD Program:

(1) the Commander of the Colombian Air Force ("COFAC"), who oversees the ABD Program, approves the progression through the ABD phases discussed herein, and exercises command and control of GOC ABD assets;

(2) the Battle Commander Officer ("OCB"), who transmit the COFAC's orders to the ODM;

(3) the Mission Director Officer ("ODM"), who transmits orders from the OCB to the tracker and interceptor aircraft and supervises compliance by GOC tracker and interceptor aircraft with the procedures and orders detailed herein;

(4) a FAC Liaison Officer, who is assigned to JIATF-S and coordinates the planning, information exchange and analysis between JIATF-S and the CCOFA;

(5) a Host Nation Rider, who makes identification of tracks of interest, if possible, and helps coordinate GOC actions in furtherance of the ABD Program. The Host Nation Rider shall have access to equipment necessary for the purposes of coordinating operations with the CCOFA and, in certain instances, directing such operations;

(6) a Ground Safety Monitor, who is the safety oversight triad's representative in the CCOFA during ABD operations;

(7) an Air Safety Monitor, who is the FAC's representative on GOC tracking aircraft. The Air Safety Monitor observes decisions made by GOC personnel, communicates with the Ground Safety Monitor(s) and the JIATF-S Command Duty Officer, and reports to them whether the agreed-upon procedures are being followed.

D. Subject to the specific exceptions contained in this Agreement, the GOC is solely responsible for all operational actions relating to each ABD event and the program. The OCB shall inform the

Ground Safety Monitor of the COFAC's intentions to proceed to the next phase of an ABD event prior to proceeding to the next phase.

E. Any of the USG ABD participants (including those listed in paragraph B of this section) may notify the GOC of any USG objection to an operational decision made by the GOC, but shall have no authority to take, recommend, or order any particular GOC action under the ABD Program, except as specified in this Agreement. In addition, if at any point during an ABD event any of the USG ABD participants (including those listed in paragraph B of this section) objects, the USG immediately shall cease to provide assistance to that ABD event, except to the extent that the cessation of USG assistance would create safety-of-flight issues. USG assistance to the ABD event may resume if objections are resolved.

F. Operational areas for the detection, identification and monitoring of civil aircraft over the Pacific Ocean and the Caribbean Sea shall be jointly determined by JIATF-S and the FAC. These activities shall be conducted in a manner consistent with international aviation law and the international law of the sea. The FAC shall not initiate Phases I, II, or III with any aircraft so monitored (nor shall it give directions to follow an interceptor's instructions or to land) unless and until that aircraft enters into a ZECA.

G. Phase I of the ABD Program, as described herein, may be implemented everywhere in Colombian airspace. Phase II may only be initiated within a ZECA. The GOC shall make all reasonable efforts to ensure that Phase III, if reached, also only be initiated within a ZECA. However, although not desirable, it is possible that Phase III might occur outside a ZECA, prompted by an identification of an aircraft reasonably suspected of being primarily engaged in illicit drug trafficking within a ZECA, because of the time involved in completing the procedures.

H. Under the ABD Program the GOC shall not enter into Phase II or Phase III (as described herein) when:

(1) an aircraft is reasonably identifiable as a state or commercial aircraft;

(2) it knows or should know that an aircraft is operating in accordance with a flight plan filed with air traffic authorities of Colombia, or of the country in which the flight originated, that does not contain false information and has not, without justification, significantly departed from the flight plan;

(3) the pilot of an aircraft is reasonably believed to be incapacitated. This provision does not apply if there exists sufficient reason to conclude that the report of unlawful interference is being used as a trick in order to avoid the use of force by the FAC; or

(4) an aircraft is reasonably believed to have been subject to unlawful interference or its pilot appears to be under duress (except if the aircraft poses an imminent threat to persons outside of the aircraft). This provision does not apply if there exists sufficient reason to conclude that the report of unlawful interference is being used as a trick in order to avoid the use of force by the FAC.

If any USG or GOC participant in an ABD event has reason to believe that one or more of these conditions is met, that interception shall be terminated immediately. However, these procedures are not intended to preclude the GOC from conducting efforts to identify and monitor these categories of aircraft through radio contact, visual identification, or by other means.

I. If there is a loss of communications among any of the members of the safety oversight triad, USG or GOC agencies or personnel during Phases I, II, or III of an ABD event, as described herein, the GOC or USG ABD participants (including those in paragraph B of this section) may require that the ongoing ABD event terminate. The departure of a tracking aircraft from the scene after the FAC has initiated an ABD ground event shall not be deemed to constitute a loss of communications if there is a second GSM in the CCOFA who is following the event, as described in section VII.F. herein, and is in active communication with the interceptor.

J. The Parties shall take the necessary steps to ensure that each of their nationals or representatives, when participating in the ABD Program, is fully familiar with the contents of this Annex, including its Appendix, and Annex B.

II. Detection, Sorting, and Identification

When the GOC detects or is informed of an aircraft operating in a ZECA that is a candidate for possible ABD action (a "track of interest"), information on that aircraft shall be gathered (sorted) by the GOC from all reasonably available sources, including radar systems, radio and visual contact with the aircraft, electronic systems (which help verify whether the plane is traveling on a filed flight plan and what type of plane it is), and relevant air traffic control centers, to begin to determine whether the aircraft is reasonably suspected to be primarily engaged in illicit drug trafficking. That determination shall be made by the OCB in the CCOFA, using the factors set forth in the Appendix, as well as other information provided to GOC and USG participants in the ongoing action.

III. Monitoring

If the GOC reasonably suspects that an aircraft is primarily engaged in illicit drug trafficking, that aircraft shall be tracked and monitored. If tracking is intermittent, positive re-identification shall be made with reasonable certainty before the ABD event may continue. If the GOC has been unable to identify the track of interest as a legitimate track, the aircraft shall be considered suspect by the FAC under FAC procedures and may be intercepted.

IV. Interception (Phase I)

A. The interception phase (Phase I) includes attempts to contact the intercepted aircraft by radio and, if necessary, by visual signals in order to determine the identity of the pilot or intercepted aircraft.

In Phase I the GOC shall attempt to:

(1) determine with greater certainty the identity of the intercepted aircraft. The tracker or interceptor aircraft shall take all reasonable measures, including the use of night vision devices, to identify the intercepted aircraft by visual or electronic observation of the nationality markings, registration number, and any other license number or identifying features or markings on the intercepted aircraft;

(2) gather any further information regarding the intercepted aircraft that may help determine whether the intercepted aircraft is reasonably suspected to be primarily engaged in illicit drug trafficking (see the Appendix to this Annex);

(3) establish communications with the intercepted aircraft through the use of radio communications or visual signals; and

(4) order the intercepted aircraft to land at the nearest suitable airfield, if factors continue to support a determination that the aircraft is primarily engaged in illicit drug trafficking.

B. The interceptor aircraft shall maneuver relative to the intercepted aircraft in conformance with the interception maneuver procedures promulgated by ICAO in Annex 2 to the Chicago Convention in order to:

(1) avoid endangering the lives of persons on board the intercepted aircraft;

(2) permit the unimpeded and continuous visual observation of the intercepted aircraft; and

(3) allow communications to be established with the intercepted aircraft through the use of radio communications or visual signals.

C. The interceptor aircraft first shall attempt to establish contact with the intercepted aircraft in flight using radio communications procedures promulgated by ICAO in Annex 2 to the Chicago Convention ("ICAO radio communication procedures"), making sure to attempt contact using both emergency frequencies 121.5 MHZ and 243 MHZ and normal UHF and VHF civil aviation frequencies for the area of operation (hereinafter, "the appropriate frequencies"). Radio communications shall use the English and Spanish languages and, where possible, the language of the country of registry, if known. Whenever radio contact can be established with the intercepted aircraft, the interceptor aircraft shall interrogate the pilot of the intercepted aircraft to determine its status.

D. If radio contact cannot be established with the intercepted aircraft, the interceptor aircraft shall use the visual signals for interception promulgated by ICAO in Annex 2 to the Chicago Convention ("ICAO visual signals") to attempt to establish communication.

E. If there continues to be a reasonable suspicion that the aircraft in flight is primarily engaged in illicit drug trafficking, the interceptor aircraft shall contact the intercepted aircraft using ICAO radio communications procedures and using the appropriate frequencies or, if radio contact cannot be established, through the use of ICAO visual signals, and order the intercepted aircraft to land at a designated place suitable for a safe landing.

F. An aircraft for which there is sufficient basis to reasonably suspect that it is primarily engaged in illicit drug trafficking shall be classified as "hostile" by the FAC under FAC procedures if, after being identified and intercepted, it does not comply with the procedures and instructions given by the FAC interceptor during Phase I.

V. Use of Warning Shots (Phase II)

Phase II consists of the firing of warning shots, using ammunition containing tracer rounds, in order to demonstrate to the pilot of the intercepted aircraft that he must comply with the interceptor's order. If all of the procedures required under this Agreement have been followed, if the information gathered continues to indicate that an aircraft is reasonably suspected of being primarily engaged in illicit drug trafficking, and if the aircraft fails to respond to the interceptor's order to land, the GOC may, in accordance with the following, move to Phase II.

A. In Phase II, the Colombian interceptor aircraft shall not fire warning shots until he requests and receives authorization. All such requests must be reviewed by the COFAC. The COFAC may approve such request after verifying that all procedures required under this Agreement have been followed. The OCB shall inform the Ground Safety Monitor of the recommendation he intends to make to the COFAC.

B. In advance of firing warning shots, the interceptor aircraft shall attempt to warn the intercepted aircraft, using ICAO radio communications procedures and using the appropriate frequencies, that warning shots shall be used if the intercepted aircraft refuses to comply. Unless the safety of flight prevents it, warning shots shall be fired from a position slightly ahead of the wing line and parallel to the course of the intercepted aircraft to ensure that the intercepted aircraft is not in the line of fire. In the event that the safety of flight or technical limitations prevent warning shots from being fired from the position described above, the pilot of the interceptor aircraft shall make every reasonable effort to make the warning shots visible to the pilot of the intercepted aircraft. The aircraft firing the warning shots shall make every reasonable effort to avoid shooting the intercepted aircraft, any other aircraft in the vicinity, or persons or property on the ground.

VI. Firing of Weapons at Intercepted Aircraft (Phase III)

A. The GOC shall not fire weapons at an intercepted aircraft if:

(1) the aircraft has met one or more of the conditions contained in section I.H above;

(2) the tracking of the intercepted aircraft has been intermittent and positive re-identification has not been made with reasonable certainty; or

(3) the aircraft is operating in proximity to a populated area or the action being taken could reasonably be expected to result in loss of innocent life in the air or on the ground.

B. If, after warning shots are fired under Phase II, the intercepted aircraft does not acknowledge or follow the interceptor's directions, the Colombian interceptor aircraft may only fire weapons at the intercepted aircraft if it requests and receives permission to do so (Phase III). All such requests must be reviewed by the COFAC. The COFAC may approve such request after verifying that all procedures required under this Agreement have been followed. The OCB shall inform the Ground Safety Monitor of the recommendation he intends to make to the COFAC.

C. Upon receipt of the COFAC's authorization, the interceptor aircraft shall warn the intercepted aircraft, using ICAO radio communications procedures and using the appropriate frequencies, that it shall be fired upon if it refuses to comply. The force used against the intercepted aircraft shall not be in excess of the minimum necessary to disable it, starting with a minimum level of fire in an attempt to persuade the intercepted aircraft to land as directed. The intercepted aircraft shall be given a reasonable opportunity to obey the previously issued orders to land before the interceptor uses additional force. Levels of force may be increased if the intercepted aircraft continues to refuse to follow the interceptor's directions. It is acknowledged that even the minimum level of force could result in loss of life. If the intercepted aircraft has landed or been shot down, the interceptor aircraft or tracker aircraft shall give immediate notice to the CCOFA of the location of the intercepted aircraft. Additionally, the GOC shall initiate the actions required in section VII.K.

VII. Procedures on the Ground

A. When an ABD event has entered Phase I, the FAC shall alert the command and control center of the Colombian National Police ("CNP"), the JOC of the Joint Military Forces Command, and appropriate aviation authorities of those locations at which an intercepted aircraft might be forced to land.

B. Any ABD event against an aircraft on the ground shall only commence if the full safety oversight triad is in place. If, after the FAC initiates an ABD ground event, the ASM cannot continue with the mission, the GOC must have (in addition to JIATF-S) a minimum of one additional GSM in the CCOFA to assist the primary GSM in ensuring that communications with the interceptor are being monitored and that procedures are being followed.

C. Any use of airborne weapons against the aircraft on the ground must be expressly authorized by the COFAC.

D. If an aircraft reasonably suspected to be primarily engaged in illicit drug trafficking lands at or is located at an airfield at which units of the CNP or military forces are present; those units shall attempt to take control of the aircraft for law enforcement purposes.

E. If an aircraft reasonably suspected to be primarily engaged in illicit drug trafficking lands, or, is located at an airfield at which units of the CNP or military forces are not present, units of the CNP or military forces shall make all reasonable attempts to reach the aircraft in a timely manner and take control of it for law enforcement purposes.

F. If an aircraft reasonably suspected to be primarily engaged in illicit drug trafficking lands, or, is located at an airfield where units of the CNP or military forces are not present, and CNP or military forces are unable to arrive at the location of the aircraft within a reasonable period of time (calculated by the on-station loiter time of the tracker aircraft) or in sufficient numbers to control the situation, they shall notify the FAC immediately. Once the FAC is notified, the COFAC may consider whether to proceed with the ABD ground event. The following rules shall govern the event:

(1) the CNP or military forces shall notify the FAC immediately of their inability to arrive within a reasonable time or in sufficient numbers to control the situation;

(2) if the aircraft was located on the ground, or if the aircraft was tracked in flight but Phase I was not completed, or if the aircraft was tracked in flight and Phase I was completed but the aircraft was not continuously monitored, the GOC shall perform the following procedures:

(a) the interceptor aircraft first shall make two passes over the aircraft, rocking its wings and flashing its navigational lights. The passes shall be made at an altitude adequately low to be heard by individuals on the ground. Simultaneously, the interceptor shall attempt to establish contact with the located aircraft using ICAO radio communications procedures, making sure to attempt contact using the appropriate frequencies, including the frequency of uncontrolled aerodromes (122.9 MHZ). Radio communications shall use the English and Spanish languages and, where possible, the language of the country of registry, if known. The pilot shall attempt to obtain information from the pilot of the located aircraft, and shall inform the CCOFA of the physical characteristics of the aircraft and its proximity to buildings or populated areas. (Ground Phase I)

(b) if there continues to be a reasonable suspicion that the located aircraft is primarily engaged in illicit drug and the located aircraft does not respond to the attempts to contact it, the interceptor aircraft shall attempt to warn the located aircraft, using ICAO radio communications procedures and using the appropriate frequencies, that warning shots will be used if the located aircraft refuses to respond. If the located aircraft continues to fail to respond to the warning, the interceptor may, after obtaining permission from the COFAC, fire warning shots, i.e., shots not aimed directly at the located aircraft, while at the same time informing the aircraft on the appropriate frequencies that it is currently firing warning shots and that if its instructions are not followed the located aircraft will be rendered inoperative. (Ground Phase II);

(c) if, after warning shots are fired, the located aircraft does not acknowledge or follow the interceptor's directions, the Colombian interceptor aircraft may only fire weapons at the located aircraft if it requests and receives permission to do so. All such requests must be reviewed by the COFAC. The COFAC may approve such request after verifying that all procedures required under this Agreement have been followed. The OCB shall inform the GSM of the recommendation he intends to make to the COFAC. (Ground Phase III)

(3) if the aircraft was tracked in flight, lands, and has been under continuous monitoring, and Phase I, II, or III have been completed in flight with respect to that aircraft, the FAC may proceed from sub-paragraph (2)(b), without undertaking sub-paragraph (2)(a).

G. The use of airborne weapons against an aircraft on the ground is only permitted in accordance with the procedures described in paragraph F.

H. The procedures in paragraph F shall apply during any attempt by an aircraft reasonably suspected of being primarily engaged in illicit drug trafficking to takeoff without permission. If an aircraft described in paragraph D succeeds in taking off and had been the subject of prior aerial tracking, the aerial event shall be reinitiated from the furthest aerial phase completed. If an aircraft succeeds in taking off but had not been the subject of prior aerial tracking, the aerial event shall be initiated from Phase I.

I. All events in which Phase II and III actions are taken against an aircraft on the ground without a tracker must still be reviewed in accordance with section VIII herein.

J. With regard to each paragraph above, the force used against an aircraft on the ground, following the procedures set forth in this section VII, shall not be in excess of the minimum necessary to prevent it from taking off.

K. Search and Rescue: To the extent possible, the GOC, with the support of participating USG agencies, shall conduct search and rescue operations involving intercepted or located aircraft. Airborne assets, if available, shall remain on the scene as long as possible, report the location of downed aircraft, render assistance as able, and, if so equipped, record through audio and visual means post-event efforts and actions.

L. If, with regard to an aircraft intercepted or located on the ground that is reasonably suspected to be primarily engaged in illicit drug trafficking, the GOC observes cargo being offloaded from that aircraft onto ground-based or water-based conveyances, the GOC may follow those conveyances by air to gather information on such conveyances, including their identity and destination.

VIII. Review of ABD Events

A. The USG, represented by JIATF-S, and the GOC, represented by the Chief of Air Operations of the FAC, shall jointly review ABD events that proceed to Phase II or Phase III. All other ABD events shall be jointly reviewed by the NAS and the FAC. The onboard tapes of all aircraft engaged in ABD events shall be the primary basis for these reviews and each Party shall provide access to all onboard tapes involving a particular ABD event for purposes of conducting a review of that event. In addition, each Party shall receive copies of all onboard tapes of tracker aircraft involving ABD events that proceed to Phase II or Phase III. The USG and GOC shall keep all onboard tapes of ABD events that they possess, in accordance with their laws and regulations, and in any event in accordance with the following schedule:

(1) For ABD events that proceed to Phase II or Phase III, for at least one year; and

(2) For ABD events that proceed only to Phase I, the NAS and the FAC shall keep SR-560 or C-26 recordings, and ASM, GSM, and FAC records for at least 30 days.

B. For ABD events that proceed to Phase II or Phase III, the USG and GOC each shall produce a memorandum summarizing each event, evaluating whether procedures were followed, reviewing any errors or anomalies, and proposing corrective actions, if any, to be taken. Any differences in views shall be addressed in consultations between the Parties.

Appendix 1 to Annex A: Criteria for Determining Whether an Aircraft is Reasonably Suspected of Being Primarily Engaged in Illicit Drug Trafficking

The following factors should be considered before and during Phase I in determining whether an aircraft is reasonably suspected of being primarily engaged in illicit drug trafficking:

(1) Did the aircraft fail to file a required flight plan?

(2) Is it inexplicably flying outside the route designated in its approved flight plan?

(3) Is it not using the assigned transponder code?

(4) Is it flying at an inexplicably low altitude?

(5) Is it flying at night with its lights out?

(6) Does the aircraft have false (or no) tail numbers?

(7) Are the windows blacked out?

(8) Does the physical description of the aircraft match the description of an aircraft previously used in illicit drug trafficking?

(9) Is there signal or human intelligence indicating that the aircraft is primarily engaged in illicit drug trafficking?

(10) Is the aircraft flying without permission over a FAC restricted area in a ZECA?

(11) Is the aircraft parked at night at a non-monitored air field (in which over night stays are prohibited) without permission by FAC?

(12) Have all attempts to identify the aircraft failed?

(13) Has the aircraft failed to respond to all attempts to communicate?

(14) Has the aircraft ignored the FAC's orders?

(15) Have any objects been jettisoned from the aircraft?

(16) Is there any other information suggesting that the aircraft is primarily engaged in illicit drug trafficking?

(17) Is there any inf ormation suggesting that the aircraft is not primarily engaged in illicit drug trafficking?

ANNEX B: ZECA COORDINATES

1	07° 13' 08" N	15	05° 27' 50" N
	77° 52' 59" W		74° 11'48" W
2	08° 40' 36.3" N	16	05° 08' 28" N
	77° 22'13.8" W		75° 11' 15" W
3	08° 51' 30" N	17	07° 01' 15" N
	77° 18' 00" W		74° 42' 34" W
4	12° 38' 09" N	18	07° 01' 15" N
	71° 28' 07" W		75° 33' 52" W
5	12° 17' 38" N	19	06° 32' 00" N
	71° 00' 00" W		76° 13' 31" W
6	12° 28' 58.56" N	20	05° 40' 48" N
	71° 07' 21.71" W		72° 54' 24" W
7	12° 06' 04" N	21	03° 18' 47" N
	70° 55' 02" W		72° 58' 38" W
8	11° 53' 15.14" N	22	03° 18' 47" N
	70° 57' 13.27" W		73° 56' 53" W
9	11° 46' 07.2" N	23	04° 36' 05" N
	71° 07' 21.5" W		73° 56' 53" W
10	11° 49' 14.64" N	24	02° 34' 51" N
	71° 12' 31.35" W		74° 56' 40" W
11	11° 50' 54.5" N	25	01° 28' 28" N
	71° 19' 29.6" W		75° 29' 17" W
12	07° 00' 00" N	26	00° 25' 16" N
	72° 00'12" W		76° 14' 50" W
13	06° 09' 22" N	27	01° 27' 24" N
	72° 11' 48" W		79° 22' 56" W
14	06° 10' 48" N	28	07° 04' 17.18" N
	74° 03' 54" W		77° 56' 08.91" W

NOTES:

- The joining of coordinates 1 and 2 follows the Colombia – Venezuela border.
- The joining of the coordinates 11 and 25 follows the border between Colombia and Venezuela, Brazil, Peru and Ecuador.
- The joining of the coordinates 3 and 4, and 26 and 27, and the width of the operational area by the sea to which the ZECAs extend, is defined by the FAC, in coordination with the NAS.

ANNEX C: USE OF ABD ASSETS IN SUPPORT OF SUPPRESSION OF ILLICIT MARITIME TRAFFICKING IN NARCOTIC DRUGS AND PSYCHOTROPIC SUBSTANCES

The Parties agree to comply with the following procedures in connection with the use of ABD assets in support of suppression of illicit maritime trafficking in narcotic drugs and psychotropic substances ("SSIMT"). The procedures outlined below are designed to ensure standardization among the Joint Interagency Task Force South ("JIATF-S"), Colombian Air Force ("FAC"), and Colombian Navy ("ARC") operations, in a manner consistent with the roles and missions of the Colombian armed forces, and meet the domestic legal requirements of each Party. Additional implementing arrangements may be coordinated among JIATF-S, FAC, and ARC.

I. General

A. The purpose of using the Cessna Citation SR-560 for SSIMT is to support the ongoing efforts of the United States, Colombia, and other nations to counter illicit maritime trafficking in narcotic drugs and psychotropic substances in the Pacific Ocean and Caribbean Sea. ABD missions shall take priority over SSIMT missions, unless otherwise agreed to by JIATF-S and the FAC.

B. Operational areas of SSIMT shall be jointly determined by JIATF-S and the FAC. SSIMT missions shall be conducted in a manner consistent with international aviation law and the international law of the sea.

C. The maximum number of monthly hours that the SR-560 aircraft shall be allowed to fly in support of SSIMT shall be 120 hours per month. The U.S. Embassy, in coordination with the FAC and JIATF-S may jointly change the designated number of SSIMT hours.

D. For purposes of SSIMT, the SR-560 shall be under the operational control of the FAC and tactical control of JIATF-S. JIATF-S shall notify CCOFA of any tactical decisions concerning the SR-560.

E. At a minimum, the GOC shall provide the following participants for SSIMT: the COFAC; the FAC Chief of Air Operations ("JOA"), the COLNAV Chief of Naval Operations ("JONA"), the director of the COLNAV Center of Operations ("DICOA"), the OCB; a GSM; an ASM; the ODM; the FAC and COLNAV Liaison Officers assigned to JIATF-S. The OCB transmits the COFAC's orders to the ODM. The ODM transmits orders from the OCB to the SR-560 aircraft and supervises compliance by SR-560 aircraft with the procedures and orders detailed herein. The FAC and COLNAV Liaison Officers assigned to JIATF-S coordinate SSIMT missions among JIATF-S, the JOA, and the JONA. The ASM and GSM shall be qualified in English. The GSM(s) is the FAC's representative at the Colombian Air Force Command and Control Center ("CCOFA") during SSIMT missions. The GSM shall relay all JIATF-S tactical decisions to CCOFA and, when necessary, assist with the transition from SSIMT to ABD or from ABD to SSIMT. The ASM is the FAC's representative on SR-560 aircraft responsible for communicating with the GSM(s) and JIATF-S, and shall report/pass all collected information to JIATF-S and the CCOFA.

F. At a minimum, the USG shall provide the following participants: a JIATF-S Tactical Commander; a JIATF-S Command Duty Officer (CDO); and a Host Nation Rider (HNR) Assistant, when required. The Host Nation Rider Assistant shall be fluent in Spanish. The JIATF-S Tactical Commander exercises tactical control of the aircraft through the JOC. The JIATF-S Command Duty Officer is the Tactical Commander's senior watch officer at the COC. The AAOCC, which is located in the CCOFA, shall assist in coordination, information exchange, and analysis among JIATF-S, CCOFA, and COA.

II. SSIMT Procedures

A. SSIMT missions are executed under three categories:

1. Scheduled/Pre-planned SSIMT. Mission dates, times and search areas shall be determined by JIATF-S based upon actionable intelligence and/or historical trafficking trends. Missions shall be coordinated among JIATF-S, and CCOFA.

2. Alert-launched SSIMT. Ad hoc (immediate, time sensitive and unscheduled) missions in support of actionable intelligence from USG or GOC. These missions shall be coordinated among JIATF-S, CCOFA, and the COA.

3. Transition missions. JIATF-S shall transfer tactical control of the SR-560 to the FAC when a mission that was originally designated for SSIMT is re-tasked for an ABD event. The FAC shall transfer tactical control of the SR-560 to JIATF-S when a mission originally designated for ABD is re-tasked for SSIMT.

B. The SR-560 shall conduct SSIMT missions in accordance with procedures previously established for them by JIATF-S, the COLAF, and COLNAV. Information concerning the surface tracks shall be collected via radar systems, electro-optical and infrared sensors, radio transmissions, and visual sightings.

(1) For each surface track, the ASM shall report as much of the following information as possible:

(a) Vessel Name;

(b) Vessel Length;

(c) Vessel Flag;

(d) Vessel Type;

(e) Vessel Position;

(f) Vessel Course;

(g) Vessel Speed; and

(h) Suspect activities in which vessel or crew members are engaged, if any.

(2) Suspicious activity may include, but is not limited to, the following:

(a) An unusual number of antennae

(b) No radar reflectors (especially on sailboats)

(c) Equipment missing or in disrepair (especially on fishing vessels)

(d) Covered or blackened windows

(e) An unusual amount of fuel drums or containers on deck

(f) Water containers or bladders on deck

(g) Vessel name painted over or on a plaque

(h) Missing or conflicting registration numbers

(i) No flag or too many flags displayed

(j) An unusual attitude displayed by crew (ignoring presence)

(k) An excessive number of people on board for type of vessel

(l) New paint or patch work visible

(m) Crew jettisons material

(n) A false waterline

(o) Failure of vessel to respond when called / signaled via normal methods

(p) Unusual maneuvering or positioning; e.g. fishing vessel not on fishing grounds, change in speed / course upon detection

(q) Hull scratches or damage (indicating alongside / transfer ops w/ other vessel)

(r) Low profile vessel (LPV) characteristics.

C. Upon detection of a surface track of interest in coordination with the COLNAV and JIATF-S, the SR-560 should maneuver and attempt radio communications with the STOI. Once radio contact with the surface track of interest is established, Right of Approach (ROA) questions should be used to determine the following:

(1) Name of the vessel

(2) Nationality of the vessel

(3) Home port

(4) Official registration number

(5) Last port of call

(6) Next port of call

(7) Purpose of voyage.

State Department Document Number: 08-18

Arrangement Between the Nuclear Regulatory Commission of the United States of America and the Autoridad Regulatoria Nuclear de Argentina for the Exchange of Technical Information and Cooperation in Regulatory and Safety Research Matters, with Addendums

Signed at Rockville and Buenos Aires,
December 4 and 28, 2007
Entered into force December 28, 2007

CTIA Document Number: 13389.000

The Nuclear Regulatory Commission of the United States (hereinafter the NRC) and the Autoridad Regulatoria Nuclear de Argentina (hereinafter the ARN) (hereinafter the "Parties");

Having a mutual interest in a continuing exchange of information pertaining to regulatory matters and of the standards required or recommended by their organizations for the regulation of safety and environmental impact of nuclear facilities;

Having similarly cooperated under the terms of the Arrangement between the NRC and the Ente Nacional Regulador Nuclear for the exchange of technical information and cooperation in regulatory and safety research matters, signed on September 17, 1996;

Noting that the Autoridad Regulatoria Nuclear de Argentina in April 1997 succeeded the Ente Nacional Regulador Nuclear as the nuclear regulatory body in Argentina;

Having most recently cooperated under the Arrangement between the NRC and the Autoridad Regulatoria Nuclear de Argentina for the exchange of technical information and cooperation in regulatory and safety research matters, signed on January 8 and 18, 2002;

Having indicated their mutual desire to continue their established cooperation for another five years;

Have agreed as follows:

I. SCOPE OF THE ARRANGEMENT

1. Technical Information Exchange

To the extent that they are permitted to do so under the laws, regulations, and policy directives of their respective countries, the NRC and the ARN agree to exchange the following types of technical information relating to the regulation of designated nuclear energy facilities and their environmental impact and to nuclear safety research programs:

a. Topical reports concerning safety, safeguards, physical protection, decommissioning, waste management, and environmental effects written by or for one of the Parties as a basis for, or in support of, regulatory decisions and policies.

b. Documents relating to significant licensing actions and safety and environmental decisions affecting nuclear facilities.

c. Documents describing the NRC process for licensing and regulating U.S. nuclear facilities and equivalent documents on Argentine nuclear facilities.

d. Information in the field of reactor safety research, either in the possession of one of the parties or available to it. Exchanges in the field of reactor safety research may require a separate agreement if determined to be necessary by one or both of the parties. Each party will transmit immediately to the other information concerning research results that requires early attention in the interest of public safety, along with an indication of significant implications.

e. Reports on operating experience, such as reports on nuclear incidents, accidents and shutdowns, and compilations of historical reliability data on components and systems, and information on emergency planning and response for power reactor programs.

f. Regulatory procedures for the safety, safeguards (materials accountancy and control and physical protection), waste management, and environmental impact evaluation of nuclear facilities.

g. Early advice of important events, such as serious operating incidents and government-directed reactor shutdowns, that are of immediate interest to the parties.

h. Copies of regulatory standards required to be used, or proposed for use, by the parties.

2. Cooperation in Safety Research

The terms of cooperation for joint programs and projects of nuclear safety research and development, or those programs and projects under which activities are divided between the two Parties, including the use of test facilities and/or computer programs owned by either Party, will be considered on a case-by-case basis and may be the subject of a separate agreement if determined to be necessary by one or both of the Parties. When not the subject of a separate agreement, the terms of cooperation may be established by an exchange of letters between the Parties, subject at least to the terms and conditions of the present agreement. Temporary assignments of personnel by one Party in the other Party's agency will also be considered on a case-by-case basis and will, in general, require a separate exchange of letters.

3. Training and Assignments

Within the limits of available resources and subject to the availability of appropriated funds and to the provisions of this Arrangement, each Party will assist the other Party in providing opportunities for training and assignments in the areas covered by this Arrangement to the other Party. Unless otherwise agreed in a particular case, all salaries, allowances and travel expenses incurred will be paid by the Party that incurs them.

II. ADMINISTRATION

1. The exchange of information under this Arrangement will be accomplished through letters, reports, and other documents, and by visits and meetings arranged in advance. A meeting will be held annually, or at such times as mutually agreed, to review the exchange of information, to recommend revisions to the provisions of the Arrangement, and, to discuss topics within the scope of the

exchange. The time, place, and agenda for such meetings will be agreed upon in advance. Visits which take place under this Arrangement, including their schedules, will have the prior approval of the administrators referred to in Section II.2 below.

2. An administrator will be designated by each party to coordinate its participation in the overall Exchange under this arrangement. The administrators will be the recipients of all documents transmitted under the exchange, including copies of all letters, unless otherwise agreed. Within the terms of the exchange, the administrators will be responsible for developing the scope of the exchange, including agreement on the designation of the nuclear energy facilities subject to the exchange, and on specific documents and standards to be exchanged. One or more technical coordinators may be appointed as direct contacts for specific disciplinary areas. These technical coordinators will assure that both administrators receive copies of all transmittals. These detailed arrangements are intended to assure, among other things, that a reasonably balanced exchange providing access to equivalent available information from both sides is achieved and maintained.

3. The administrators will determine the number of copies to be provided of the documents exchanged. Each document will be accompanied by an abstract in English, 250 words or less, describing its scope and content.

4. The application or use of any information exchanged or transferred between the Parties under this Arrangement will be the responsibility of the receiving Party, and the transmitting Party does not warrant the suitability of such information for any particular use or application.

5. Recognizing that some information of the type covered in this Arrangement is not available within the agencies which are Parties to this Arrangement, but it is available from other agencies of the governments of the Parties, each Party will assist the other to the maximum extent possible by organizing visits and directing inquiries concerning such information to appropriate agencies of the government concerned. The foregoing will not constitute a commitment of other agencies to furnish such information or to receive such visitors.

6. Nothing contained in this Arrangement will require either Party to take any action which would be inconsistent with the laws, regulations, and policy directives of its country. Should any conflict arise between the terms of this Arrangement and those laws, regulations, or policy directives, the Parties will consult before any action is taken. No nuclear information related to sensitive nuclear technology will be exchanged under this Arrangement.

7. Unless otherwise agreed, all costs resulting from cooperation pursuant to this Arrangement will be the responsibility of the Party that incurs them. The ability of the Parties to carry out these obligations is subject to the appropriation of funds by the appropriate governmental authority and to the laws and regulations applicable to the Parties.

III. EXCHANGE AND USE OF INFORMATION

1. General

The Parties support the widest possible dissemination of information provided, created or exchanged under this Arrangement, subject to the requirements of each Party's national laws, regulations and policies and the need to protect proprietary and other sensitive or privileged information, and subject to the provisions of the Intellectual Property Annex, which is an integral part of this Arrangement.

2. Definitions

a. The term "information" means unclassified nuclear energy-related regulatory, safety, Safeguards, waste management, scientific, or technical data, including information on results or methods of assessment, research, and any other knowledge provided, created or exchanged under this Arrangement.

b. The term "proprietary information" means information created or exchanged under this Arrangement which contains trade secrets or other privileged or sensitive commercial information (such that the person having the information may derive a commercial benefit from it or may have a commercial advantage over those who do not have it), and may only include information which:

(1) has been held in confidence by its owner;

(2) is of a type which is customarily held in confidence by its owner;

(3) has not been transmitted by the owner to other entities (including the receiving Party) except on the basis that it be held in confidence;

(4) is not otherwise available to the receiving Party from another source without restriction on its further dissemination; and

(5) is not already in the possession of the receiving Party.

c. The term "other confidential or privileged information" means non-classified information, other than "proprietary information," which has been transmitted and received in confidence under this Arrangement and is protected from public disclosure under the laws, regulations, or policies of the country of the Party providing the information, or is otherwise restricted by the provider.

3. Marking Procedures for Documentary Proprietary Information

A party receiving documentary proprietary information pursuant to this Arrangement will respect the privileged nature of such information, provided that such proprietary information is clearly marked with the following (or substantially similar) restrictive legend:

> "This document contains proprietary information furnished in confidence under an Arrangement dated *28 DEC 2007* between the United States Nuclear Regulatory Commission and the Autoridad Regulatoria Nuclear de Argentina and will not be disseminated outside these organizations, their consultants, contractors, and licensees, or concerned departments and agencies of the Government of the United States and the Government of Argentina, without the prior written approval of *(name of transmitting Party)*. This notice will be marked on each page of any reproduction hereof, in whole or in part. These limitations will automatically terminate when the proprietary information is disclosed by the owner without restriction."

This restrictive legend shall be respected by the Parties to this Arrangement. Proprietary information bearing this restrictive legend shall not be made public or otherwise disseminated in any manner unspecified or contrary to the terms of this Arrangement without the prior written consent of the transmitting Party. Proprietary information bearing this restrictive legend shall not be used by the receiving Party or its contractors and consultants for any commercial purposes without the prior written consent of the transmitting Party.

4. Dissemination of Documentary Proprietary Information

A. In general, proprietary information received under this Arrangement may be disseminated by the receiving Party without prior consent to persons within or employed by the receiving Party, and to concerned Government departments and Government agencies in the country of the receiving Party, provided:

(1) such dissemination is made on a case-by-case basis to persons or departments and agencies having a legitimate need for the proprietary information; and

(2) such proprietary information shall bear the restrictive legend appearing in Section III.3 of this Arrangement.

B. Proprietary information received under this Arrangement may be disseminated by the receiving Party without prior consent to contractors and consultants of the receiving Party located within the geographical limits of that Party's territory, provided:

(1) that the proprietary information is used by such contractors and consultants only for work within the scope of their contracts with the receiving Party relating to the subject matter of the proprietary information, and shall not be used by such contractors and consultants for any other private commercial purposes; and

(2) that such dissemination is made on a case-by-case basis to contractors and consultants having a legitimate need for the proprietary information and who have executed a non-disclosure agreement; and

(3) that such proprietary information shall bear the restrictive legend appearing in Section III.3 of this Arrangement.

C. With the prior written consent of the Party furnishing proprietary information under this Arrangement, the receiving Party may disseminate such proprietary information more widely than otherwise permitted under the terms set forth in this Arrangement. The Parties shall endeavor to grant such approval to the extent permitted by their respective national laws, regulations and policies, provided:

(1) that the entities receiving proprietary information under Section III.C of this Arrangement, including domestic organizations permitted or licensed by the Receiving Party to construct or operate nuclear production or utilization facilities, or to use nuclear materials and radiation sources, have a legitimate need for the proprietary information and have executed a non-disclosure agreement; and

(2) that the entities receiving proprietary information under Section III.C of this Arrangement, including domestic organizations permitted or licensed by the receiving Party to construct or operate nuclear production or utilization facilities, shall not use such proprietary information for any private commercial purposes; and

(3) that those entities receiving proprietary information under Section III.C of this Arrangement that are domestic organizations permitted or licensed by the receiving Party, agree to use the proprietary information only for activities carried out under or within the terms of their specific permit or license.

5. Marking Procedures for Other Confidential or Privileged Information of a Documentary Nature

A Party receiving under this Arrangement other confidential or privileged information will respect its confidential nature, provided such information is clearly marked so as to indicate its confidential or privileged nature and is accompanied by a statement indicating

a. that the information is protected from public disclosure by the government of the transmitting Party; and

b. that the information is transmitted under the condition that it be maintained in confidence.

6. Dissemination of Other Confidential or Privileged Information of a Documentary Nature

Other confidential or privileged information may be disseminated in the same manner as that set forth in Section III.4, Dissemination of Documentary Proprietary Information.

7. Non-Documentary Proprietary or Other Confidential or Privileged Information

Non-documentary proprietary or other confidential or privileged information provided in seminars and other meetings organized under this Arrangement, or information arising from the attachments of staff, use of facilities, or joint projects, will be treated by the Parties according to the principles specified for documentary information in this Arrangement; provided, however, that the Party communicating such proprietary or other confidential or privileged information has placed the recipient on notice as to the character of the information communicated.

8. Consultation

If, for any reason, one of the Parties becomes aware that it will be, or may reasonably be expected to become, unable to meet the non-dissemination provisions of this Arrangement, it will immediately inform the other Party. The Parties will thereafter consult to define an appropriate course of action.

9. Other

Nothing contained in this Arrangement will preclude a Party from using or disseminating information received without restriction by a Party from sources outside of this Arrangement.

IV. FINAL PROVISIONS

1. This Arrangement will enter into force upon signature and, subject to paragraph 2 of this Article, will remain in force for a period of five (5) years. It may be extended for a further period of time by agreement of the Parties.

2. Cooperation under this Arrangement will be governed by the laws and regulations of the Parties' respective countries. Any dispute or question between the Parties concerning the interpretation or application of this Arrangement arising during its term will be settled by mutual agreement of the Parties.

3. Either Party may withdraw from the Arrangement upon written notice to the other Party of its intent to withdraw. Such withdrawal shall be effective 180 days following the date of such notification.

4. All information protected by provisions of this Arrangement as proprietary or other confidential or privileged information will remain so protected for the duration of this Arrangement and after this Arrangement has expired or been terminated, unless otherwise agreed by the Parties in writing.

DONE at Rockville on the 4th day of December 2007 and at Buenos Aires on the 28th day of December 2007, in English.

FOR THE NUCLEAR REGULATORY COMMISSION OF THE UNITED STATES:

[Signature]

Dale E. Klein, Chairman

FOR THE AUTORIDAD REGULATORIA NUCLEAR DE ARGENTINA:

[Signature]

Raul Racana, Chairman

ADDENDUM "A"
ARN-USNRC Safety Research Exchange
Areas In Which the USNRC Is Performing or Sponsoring Safety Research

1. Reactor Vessel and Piping Integrity
2. Aging of Reactor Components
3. Reactor Equipment Qualification
4. Thermal Hydraulic Code Applications and Maintenance
5. Plant Performance
6. Human Performance
7. Core Melt and Reactor Coolant System Failure
8. Reactor Containment Safety
9. Containment Structural Integrity
10. Seismic Safety
11. Probabilistic Risk Assessment
12. Severe Accident Analysis
13. Radiation Protection and Health Effects
14. Radionuclide Transport and Waste Management
15. Nuclear Fuel Analysis
16. Dry Cask Storage and Transport
17. Decommissioning
18. Advanced Reactor Designs
19. Fire Protection

ADDENDUM "B"
USNRC-ARN Nuclear Safety Research Exchange Areas in which the ARN is Performing or Sponsoring Safety Research

- Regulatory Procedures for Environmental Impact Evaluation of Nuclear Facilities
- Thermal Hydraulic Code Applications and Maintenance
- Radiation Protection and Health Effects
- Reactor Pressure Vessel Integrity – *Surveillance Program*
- Neutronic Code Applications
- Severe Accidents – *Deterministic Calculations for PHWR Reactors*
- Piping Integrity – *Break Preclusion Concept*
- PHWR Reactors – *Operating Experience.*

INTELLECTUAL PROPERTY ADDENDUM

Pursuant to Section III of this Arrangement:

The Parties shall ensure adequate and effective protection of intellectual property created or furnished under this Arrangement and relevant implementing arrangements. The Parties agree to notify one another in a timely fashion of any inventions or copyrighted works arising under this Arrangement and to seek protection for such intellectual property in a timely fashion. Rights to such intellectual property shall be allocated as provided in this Addendum.

I. SCOPE

1. This Addendum is applicable to all cooperative activities undertaken pursuant to this Arrangement, except as otherwise specifically agreed by the Parties or their designees.

2. For purposes of this Arrangement, "intellectual property" shall mean the subject matter listed in Article 2 of the Convention Establishing the World Intellectual Property Organization, done at Stockholm, July 14, 1967, and may include other subject matter as agreed by the Parties.

3. This Addendum addresses the allocation of rights, interests, and royalties between the Parties. Each Party shall ensure that the other Party can obtain rights to intellectual property allocated in accordance with this Addendum by obtaining those rights from its own participants through contracts or other legal means, if necessary. This Addendum does not otherwise alter or prejudice the allocation between a Party and its nationals, which shall be determined by that Party's laws and practices.

4. Disputes concerning intellectual property arising under this Arrangement should be resolved through discussions between the concerned participating institutions or, if necessary, the Parties or their designees. Upon mutual agreement of the Parties, a dispute shall be submitted to an arbitral tribunal for binding arbitration in accordance with the applicable rules of international law. Unless the Parties or their designees agree otherwise in writing, the arbitration rules of the United Nations Commission on International Trade Law (UNCITRAL) shall govern.

5. Termination or expiration of this Arrangement shall not affect rights or obligations under this Addendum.

II. ALLOCATION OF RIGHTS

1. Each Party shall be entitled to a non-exclusive, irrevocable, royalty-free license in all countries to translate, reproduce, and publicly distribute scientific and technical journal articles, reports, and books directly arising from cooperation under this Arrangement. All publicly distributed copies of copyrighted work prepared under this provision shall indicate the names of the authors of the work unless an author explicitly declines to be named.

2. Rights to all forms of intellectual property, other than those rights described in Section II.1., above, shall be allocated as follows:

a. Visiting researchers, for example, scientists visiting primarily in furtherance of their education, shall receive intellectual property rights under the policies of the host institution. In addition, each visiting researcher named as an inventor shall be entitled to share in a portion of any royalties earned by the host institution from the licensing of such intellectual property.

b. (1) For intellectual property created during joint research, for example, when the Parties, participating institutions, or participating personnel have agreed in advance on the scope of work, each Party shall be entitled to obtain all rights and interests in its own country. Rights and interests in third countries will be determined in implementing arrangements. If research is not designated as "joint research," rights to intellectual property arising from the research will be allocated in accordance with paragraph II.2.a, above. In addition, each person named as an inventor shall be entitled to share in a portion of any royalties earned by either institution from the licensing of the property.

(2) Notwithstanding paragraph II.2.b. (1), above, if a type of intellectual property is available under the laws of one Party but not of the other Party, the Party whose laws provide for this type of protection shall be entitled to all rights and interests worldwide. Persons named as inventors of the property shall nonetheless be entitled to royalties as provided in paragraph II.2.b. (1), above.

III. BUSINESS CONFIDENTIAL

In the event that information identified in a timely fashion as business-confidential is furnished or created under this Arrangement, each Party and its participants shall protect such information in accordance with applicable laws, regulations, and administrative practices. Information may be identified as "business-confidential" if a person having the information may derive an economic benefit from it or may obtain a competitive advantage over those who do not have it, the information is not generally known or publicly available from other sources, and the owner has not previously made the information available without imposing in a timely manner an obligation to keep it confidential.

STATE DEPARTMENT DOCUMENT NUMBER: 08-19

AGREEMENT ON MUTUAL RECOGNITION OF RESULTS OF CONFORMITY ASSESSMENT PROCEDURES BETWEEN THE UNITED STATES OF AMERICA AND JAPAN, WITH ANNEX

SIGNED AT WASHINGTON D.C., FEBRUARY 16, 2007
ENTERED INTO FORCE JANUARY 1, 2008

CTIA DOCUMENT NUMBER: 13105.000

EMBASSY OF THE UNITED STATES OF AMERICA

Tokyo, November 21, 2007

His Excellency,
Nobutaka MACHIMURA,
Minister of State,
Minister of Foreign Affairs
ad interim of Japan.

Excellency:

I have the honor to acknowledge the receipt of Your Excellency's Note of today's date, which reads as follows:

> "I have the honor to refer to Article 15 of the Agreement on Mutual Recognition of Results of Conformity Assessment Procedures between Japan and the United States of America done at Washington on February 16, 2007, which provides that the Agreement shall enter into force on the first day of the second month following the date on which the Parties exchange diplomatic notes informing each other that they have completed their respective internal procedures necessary for the entry into force of this Agreement.
>
> I have further the honor to inform Your Excellency that the internal procedures necessary for the entry into force of this Agreement in respect of Japan have been fulfilled. The Agreement will accordingly enter into force on the first day of the second month following the date of Your Excellency's Note informing me that the internal procedures necessary for the entry into force of this Agreement in respect of the United States of America have been fulfilled."

I also have the honor to inform Your Excellency that the internal procedures necessary for the entry into force of this Agreement in respect of the United States of America have been fulfilled.

The Agreement on Mutual Recognition of Results of Conformity Assessment Procedures between the United States of America and Japan done at Washington on February 16, 2007, will, therefore, enter into force on January 1, 2008 in accordance with Article 15 of the Agreement.

I avail myself of this opportunity to renew to Your Excellency the assurance of my highest consideration.

[Signature]
J. Thomas Schieffer
Ambassador

Translation

Tokyo, November 21, 2007
His Excellency
Mr. John Thomas Schieffer
Ambassador of the United States of America in Japan

Excellency,

I have the honor to refer to Article 15 of the Agreement on Mutual Recognition of Results of Conformity Assessment Procedures between Japan and the United States of America done at Washington on February 16, 2007, which provides that the Agreement shall enter into force on the first day of the second month following the date on which the Parties exchange diplomatic notes informing each other that they have completed their respective internal procedures necessary for the entry into force of this Agreement.

I have further the honor to inform Your Excellency that the internal procedures necessary for the entry into force of this Agreement in respect of Japan have been fulfilled. The Agreement will accordingly enter into force on the first day of the second month following the date of Your Excellency's Note informing me that the internal procedures necessary for the entry into force of this Agreement in respect of the United States of America have been fulfilled.

I avail myself of this opportunity to renew to Your Excellency the assurance of my highest consideration.

Nobutaka MACHIMURA
Minister of State
Minister of Foreign Affairs
ad interim of Japan

AGREEMENT ON MUTUAL RECOGNITION OF RESULTS OF CONFORMITY ASSESSMENT PROCEDURES BETWEEN THE UNITED STATES OF AMERICA AND JAPAN

The UNITED STATES OF AMERICA and JAPAN (hereinafter referred to as "the Parties");

CONSIDERING the traditional friendly relations that exist between the Parties;

RECOGNIZING that mutual recognition of the results of conformity assessment procedures is an important means of enhancing market access between and economic activity in the respective territories of the Parties;

RECOGNIZING that such mutual recognition requires each Party to have confidence in reliability of conformity assessment procedures of the other Party;

BEARING IN MIND the obligations of the Parties as Members of the World Trade Organization (hereinafter referred to as the "WTO"), and being conscious, *inter alia*, of their obligations under the Agreement on Technical Barriers to Trade included in Annex 1A (hereinafter referred to as the "Agreement on Technical Barriers to Trade"), and the Agreement on Trade-Related Aspects of Intellectual Property Rights included in Annex 1C (hereinafter referred to as the "Agreement on Trade-Related Aspects of Intellectual Property Rights"), of the Marrakesh Agreement Establishing the World Trade Organization (hereinafter referred to as the "WTO Agreement"); and

RECOGNIZING that an agreement providing for mutual recognition of the results of conformity assessment procedures is of particular interest to suppliers of equipment;

HAVE AGREED AS FOLLOWS:

ARTICLE 1
PURPOSE OF THE AGREEMENT

This Agreement establishes procedures for the acceptance by a Party of the results of conformity assessment procedures conducted by conformity assessment bodies located in the territory of the other Party for equipment within the scope of this Agreement, with the objective of facilitating economic activity related to such equipment in and between the territories of the Parties.

ARTICLE 2
DEFINITIONS

1. For the purposes of this Agreement:

(a) the term "conformity assessment procedure" means a procedure to determine whether equipment or a process complies with the Technical Regulations of a Party;

(b) the term "conformity assessment body" means a body that conducts conformity assessment procedures;

(c) the term "Technical Regulations" means relevant laws, regulations, and administrative provisions of a Party set out in Section I of the Annex pertaining to technical requirements for equipment, conformity assessment procedures, and the criteria for designation;

(d) the term "Designating Authority" means an authority of a Party identified in Section II of the Annex with the power to designate, monitor, withdraw the designation of, suspend the designation of, and remove the suspension of the designation of conformity assessment bodies located in the territory of that Party;

(e) the term "designation" means the designation of a conformity assessment body in accordance with Article 5 and the procedures set out in Section III of the Annex;

(f) the term "criteria for designation" means the criteria with which conformity assessment bodies located in the territory of a Party must comply in order to obtain and maintain designation by the Designating Authority of that Party, and that are set out in the Technical Regulations of the other Party and the relevant ISO/IEC Guide and Standard set out in Section III of the Annex;

(g) the term "designated conformity assessment body" means a conformity assessment body located in the territory of a Party designated by the Designating Authority of that Party in accordance with Article 5 and the procedures set out in Section III of the Annex;

(h) the term "Regulatory Authority" means an authority of a Party identified in Section IV of the Annex with the power to regulate the equipment within the scope of this Agreement with respect to compliance with the Technical Regulations of that Party;

(i) the term "registration" means the registration of a conformity assessment body in accordance with the procedures set out in Article 6;

(j) the term "registered conformity assessment body" means a conformity assessment body registered in accordance with the procedures set out in Article 6;

(k) the term "results of conformity assessment procedures" means a determination, reached through conducting conformity assessment procedures, of whether equipment or a process complies with the Technical Regulations of a Party and includes certificates and marks of conformity reflecting an affirmative determination; and

(l) the term "days" means calendar days.

2. All terms used in this Agreement that are not defined in paragraph 1 have the meaning assigned to them in the ISO/IEC Standard set out in Section V of the Annex.

ARTICLE 3
GENERAL PROVISIONS

1. This Agreement applies to conformity assessment procedures for the telecommunications terminal equipment and radio equipment covered by Section VI of the Annex and for processes associated with that equipment. This Agreement applies regardless of the location of the supplier or the country of origin of the equipment, including where the country of origin of the equipment is other than the United States or Japan.

2. Each Party shall accept, in accordance with this Agreement, the results of conformity assessment procedures that a registered conformity assessment body located in the territory of the other Party conducts for equipment within the scope of this Agreement that determine that the equipment or a process associated with that equipment complies with the Technical Regulations of the Party.

3. The results of conformity assessment procedures referred to in paragraph 1 may be based on tests conducted by a laboratory regardless of its location, including where the laboratory is located in a country other than the United States or Japan.

4. The Annex is an integral part of this Agreement and sets out the following:

(a) Technical Regulations of each Party;

(b) The Designating Authority of each Party;

(c) Procedures of each Party for designating conformity assessment bodies;

(d) The Regulatory Authority of each Party;

(e) The ISO/IEC Standard for terms not defined in this Agreement;

(f) The equipment within the scope of this Agreement for each Party;

(g) Information for registration of conformity assessment bodies; and

(h) Co-chairs of the Joint Committee.

5. Each Party shall:

(a) make publicly available its Technical Regulations and any amendments it makes thereto;

(b) make publicly available a list of registered conformity assessment bodies;

(c) notify the other Party and provide corrected information on registered conformity assessment bodies, if the information the Party has provided in a proposal to register the conformity assessment body becomes inaccurate and the inaccuracy could affect the operation of this Agreement; and

(d) notify the other Party if it names a Designating Authority or Regulatory Authority other than the authority identified in Section II and IV of the Annex, respectively.

6. Each Party shall respond to inquiries from the other Party regarding:

(a) conformity assessment procedures within the scope of this Agreement and Technical Regulations of the Party, including inquiries concerning the specific article, annex, section, or part, of the Technical Regulations of the Party that is applicable to such conformity assessment procedures;

(b) implementation of this Agreement; and

(c) any proposed change in its Technical Regulations before it takes effect.

7. Each Party recognizes that cooperation with conformity assessment bodies is essential to ensuring that conformity assessment bodies located in a territory of a Party understand and comply with the criteria for designation, including the Technical Regulations of the other Party, and to that end, should encourage training sessions and other exchanges of information with conformity assessment bodies as a means to enhance their ability to benefit from this Agreement.

8. Each Party should also encourage conformity assessment bodies located in its territory to include conformity assessment bodies located in the territory of the other Party in activities organized to promote understanding of the Technical Regulations of the Party.

ARTICLE 4
DESIGNATING AUTHORITY

1. Each Party shall ensure that its Designating Authority identified in Section II of the Annex has the necessary power to designate, monitor, conduct verification of, withdraw the designation of, suspend the designation of, and remove the suspension of the designation of, the conformity assessment bodies in its territory.

2. If a Party appoints one or more bodies to evaluate conformity assessment bodies, such appointment shall not affect the obligations of the Designating Authority set out in this Agreement.

ARTICLE 5
DESIGNATION

1. The Designating Authority of each Party shall apply the procedures set out in Section III of the Annex in determining whether to designate conformity assessment bodies in its territory for purposes of this Agreement.

2. Each Party shall ensure, through appropriate means such as audits, inspections, or monitoring, that registered conformity assessment bodies in its territory comply with the criteria for designation.

3. Each Party shall, on the request of the other Party, provide information to the other Party on methods the Party uses to designate conformity assessment bodies.

ARTICLE 6
REGISTRATION

1. The following procedures shall apply to the registration of a conformity assessment body:

(a) If a Party seeks to register a designated conformity assessment body under this Agreement, the Party shall submit a proposal to the other Party and the Joint Committee. The proposal shall be in writing and include (i) a proposed text of a Joint Committee decision to register the conformity assessment body signed by the proposing Party's co-chair of the Joint Committee and (ii) the information for registration of the conformity assessment body identified in Section VII of the Annex.

(b) The Party receiving the proposal shall evaluate whether the conformity assessment body complies with the criteria for designation. If the Regulatory Authority of the receiving Party requires additional information to evaluate the conformity assessment body's compliance with the criteria for designation, it may request the information from the proposing Party through the Designating Authority of the proposing Party. A request for additional information under this subparagraph shall suspend the 30-day period referred to in subparagraph (c) until the date on which the receiving Party receives the information.

(c) Within 30 days after the date on which it receives a proposal referred to in subparagraph (a), the receiving Party shall notify the proposing Party and the co-chairs of the Joint Committee in writing whether it accepts or rejects the proposal, in accordance with subparagraph (d) or (e), based on its evaluation of whether the conformity assessment body complies with the criteria for designation.

(d) If the receiving Party accepts the proposal, that Party's co-chair of the Joint Committee shall sign the proposed text of the Joint Committee decision, which shall then constitute a decision of the Joint Committee registering the conformity assessment body. The receiving Party shall include a copy of the decision in its notification under subparagraph (c). The registration of the conformity assessment body shall take effect on the date on which the receiving Party's co-chair of the Joint Committee signs the decision.

(e) If the receiving Party does not accept the proposal,

(i) the receiving Party shall include in its notification under subparagraph (c) the reasons therefor, and

(ii) at the request of either Party, the Joint Committee shall discuss the matter within 60 days after it receives notification under subparagraph (c). The Joint Committee may request the proposing Party to verify whether the conformity assessment body complies with the criteria for designation. Paragraphs 2 and 3 of Article 9 shall apply *mutatis mutandis* to a verification requested pursuant to this paragraph.

2. The receiving Party shall accept the results of conformity assessment procedures conducted by a registered conformity assessment body located in the territory of the other Party from the date of a decision of the Joint Committee registering the conformity assessment body under paragraph 1(d).

ARTICLE 7
WITHDRAWAL AND SUSPENSION OF DESIGNATION AND TERMINATION AND SUSPENSION OF REGISTRATION

1. Each Party shall ensure that its Designating Authority withdraws its designation of a registered conformity assessment body when the Designating Authority determines that the conformity assessment body no longer complies with the criteria for designation.

2. If a Designating Authority of a Party withdraws its designation of a registered conformity assessment body, the Party shall immediately notify the other Party and the co-chairs of the Joint Committee. A notification under this paragraph shall be considered to be a decision of the Joint Committee to terminate the registration of the conformity assessment body, unless the Joint Committee decides otherwise. The termination shall take effect on the date on which the other Party's co-chair of the Joint Committee receives the notification. The other Party shall accept the results of conformity assessment procedures conducted by the conformity assessment body before the date on which the Designating Authority of the Party withdrew the designation of the conformity assessment body.

3. If a Designating Authority of a Party suspends its designation of a registered conformity assessment body, the Party shall immediately notify the other Party and the co-chairs of the Joint Committee. A notification under this paragraph shall be considered to be a decision of the Joint Committee to suspend the registration of the conformity assessment body. The suspension of registration shall take effect on the date on which the other Party's co-chair of the Joint Committee receives the notification under this paragraph. The other Party shall accept the results of conformity assessment procedures conducted by the conformity assessment body before the date on which the Designating Authority of the Party suspended the designation of the conformity assessment body.

4. If a Designating Authority of a Party removes its suspension of the designation of a registered conformity assessment body, the Party shall immediately notify the other Party and the co-chairs of the Joint Committee. A notification under this paragraph shall be considered to be a decision of the Joint Committee to remove the suspension of registration of the conformity assessment body. The removal of the suspension of registration shall take effect on the date on which the other Party's co-chair of the Joint Committee receives notification under this paragraph. The other Party shall accept the results of conformity assessment procedures conducted by the conformity assessment body from the date of the removal of the suspension of registration.

ARTICLE 8
CONTESTATION

1. If a Party considers that a registered conformity assessment body located in the territory of the other Party does not comply with the criteria for designation, the Party may notify the other Party and the co-chairs of the Joint Committee that it contests the conformity assessment body's compliance with the criteria for designation. The notification shall be in writing and include the reasons for the contestation. The Joint Committee shall discuss the matter within 60 days after the date on which the Party makes the notification.

2. Thirty days after the date on which the Joint Committee receives a notification under paragraph 1, the notification shall be considered to be a decision of the Joint Committee to suspend the registration of the conformity assessment body, unless the Joint Committee decides otherwise within the 30 days. The contesting Party shall accept the results of conformity assessment procedures conducted by the conformity assessment body before the date of the suspension.

3. The registration of the conformity assessment body shall remain suspended until the contesting Party withdraws the contest or the Joint Committee decides to remove the suspension of the registration of the conformity assessment body, whichever occurs first. The contesting Party may withdraw the contest by notifying the other Party and the co-chairs of the Joint Committee. A notification under this paragraph shall be considered to be a decision of the Joint Committee to remove the suspension. The contesting Party shall accept the results of conformity assessment procedures conducted by the conformity assessment body from the date of the removal of the suspension.

ARTICLE 9
VERIFICATION

1. The Joint Committee may request a Party to verify whether a registered conformity assessment body located in the territory of that Party complies with the criteria for designation. The request shall be in writing and include the reasons for the request.

2. The requested Party shall conduct the verification in a timely manner. One or more representatives of the Regulatory Authority of the other Party may, as appropriate, participate as an observer in the verification, provided that, prior to the start of the verification, the conformity assessment body agrees to such participation.

3. The requested Party shall promptly notify the other Party and the co-chairs of the Joint Committee of the results of the verification.

ARTICLE 10
JOINT COMMITTEE

1. The Parties hereby establish a Joint Committee composed of one or more representatives of each Party. The Joint Committee shall be co-chaired by a representative of each Party as set out in Section VIII of the Annex.

2. The Joint Committee shall have the authority to take decisions concerning:

(a) registration, suspension of registration, removal of suspension of registration, and termination of registration of conformity assessment bodies as provided in Articles 6, 7, and 8; and

(b) requests for verification as provided in Articles 6 and 9.

3. The Joint Committee shall adopt rules of procedure.

4. The Joint Committee shall convene at the request of either Party.

5. The Joint Committee shall take decisions by agreement of the co-chairs of the Joint Committee or as provided in this Agreement. All decisions of the Joint Committee shall be in writing.

6. The Joint Committee may consider any matter related to the operation of this Agreement.

7. The Joint Committee shall confirm that each Party makes publicly available a list of conformity assessment bodies that are registered under this Agreement.

8. The Joint Committee shall establish appropriate means, including relevant contact points, for the Parties to exchange the information and respond to inquiries referred to in paragraphs 5 and 6 of Article 3 and paragraph 3 of Article 5.

9. A Party may bring any question or concern it may have regarding the interpretation or application of this Agreement to the Joint Committee, which shall seek to answer the question or resolve the concern in a manner that is acceptable to the Parties.

ARTICLE 11
REGULATORY AUTHORITY

The Regulatory Authority of a Party may request a registered conformity assessment body located in the territory of the other Party to answer questions or provide information concerning the results of conformity assessment procedures the conformity assessment body has conducted. Responses by registered conformity assessment bodies to such requests shall be voluntary. The Parties recognize that responses to such requests shall not affect the power of the Designating Authority of the other Party. The Regulatory Authority of a Party shall notify the Designating Authority of the other Party regarding requests made to the conformity assessment body under this Article.

ARTICLE 12
CONFIDENTIALITY

Each Party shall maintain, in accordance with its laws and regulations, the confidentiality of any information provided to it as confidential in connection with the operation of this Agreement and the disclosure of which would prejudice the legitimate commercial interests of particular enterprises, public or private.

ARTICLE 13
HEADINGS

The headings of the Articles of this Agreement are included for convenience of reference only and shall not affect the interpretation of this Agreement.

ARTICLE 14
MISCELLANEOUS PROVISIONS

1. Nothing in this Agreement shall require either Party to accept standards or technical regulations of the other Party.

2. Nothing in this Agreement shall be construed to limit the authority of a Party to:

(a) determine the level of protection it considers appropriate with regard to health or safety, including the safety and effectiveness of medical devices and radiological health, the environment, or misleading or deceptive practices;

(b) take such measures as it considers necessary to protect health or safety, including with regard to the safety and effectiveness of medical devices and radiological health, or the environment or to prevent misleading or deceptive practices; or

(c) take all other appropriate measures whenever it ascertains that particular equipment does not meet its Technical Regulations or other laws, regulations, or administrative provisions or policies governing such equipment.

3. Nothing in this Agreement shall be construed to affect the rights or obligations of either Party under the WTO Agreement, including the Agreement on Technical Barriers to Trade or the Agreement on Trade-Related Aspects of Intellectual Property Rights.

ARTICLE 15
ENTRY INTO FORCE

This Agreement shall enter into force on the first day of the second month following the date on which the Parties exchange diplomatic notes informing each other that they have completed their respective internal procedures necessary for the entry into force of this Agreement.

ARTICLE 16
AMENDMENTS

1. This Agreement may be amended by agreement between the Parties. The Parties may amend Section I, II, IV, V, or VIII of the Annex by agreement between the Government of the United States and the Government of Japan through an exchange of diplomatic notes.

2. If there is any change in the laws or regulations of a Party that renders any of the information set out in Section I, II, IV, or VIII of the Annex no longer accurate or complete, the Party shall initiate, in a timely manner, an exchange of diplomatic notes between the Government of the United States and the Government of Japan in accordance with paragraph 1 to revise the relevant Section.

ARTICLE 17
TERMINATION

Either Party may notify the other Party in writing of its intention to terminate this Agreement. If a Party gives such notice, this Agreement shall terminate 180 days after the date on which the other Party receives the notice.

IN WITNESS WHEREOF, the undersigned, being duly authorized, have signed this Agreement.

Done in duplicate at Washington, this sixteenth day of February, 2007 in the English and Japanese languages, both texts being equally authentic.

For the United States of America: For Japan:

[Signature] [Signature]

ANNEX

Section I
Technical Regulations

UNITED STATES	JAPAN
1. Communications Act of 1934, as amended by the Telecommunication Act of 1996 (Title 47 of the United States Code) and amendments thereto; 2. Title 47 of the Code of Federal Regulations (hereinafter referred to as "47 CFR") as follows and amendments thereto: Part 2 Frequency Allocations and Radio Treaty Matters; General Rules and Regulations Part 11 Emergency Alert System (EAS) Part 15 Radio Frequency Devices Part 18 Industrial, Scientific, and Medical Equipment Part 20 Commercial Mobile Radio Services Part 22 Public Mobile Services Part 24 Personal Communications Services Part 25 Satellite Communications Part 27 Miscellaneous Wireless Communications Services Part 68 Connection of Terminal Equipment to the Telephone Network Part 73 Radio Broadcast Services Part 74 Experimental Radio, Auxiliary, Special Broadcast and Other Program Distributional Services Part 78 Cable Television Relay Service Part 80 Stations in the Maritime Services Part 87 Aviation Services Part 90 Private Land Mobile Radio Services Part 95 Personal Radio Services Part 97 Amateur Radio Service Part 101 Fixed Microwave Services; and 3. Administrative provisions related to the laws and regulations set out in paragraphs 1 and 2.	1. Telecommunications Business Law (Law No. 86, 1984) and amendments thereto; 2. Ordinance concerning Terminal Facilities etc. (Ordinance of the Ministry of Posts and Telecommunications No. 31, 1985) and amendments thereto; 3. Ordinance concerning Technical Conditions Compliance Approval etc. for Terminal Equipment (Ordinance of the Ministry of Internal Affairs and Communications No. 15, 2004) and amendments thereto; 4. Radio Law (Law No. 131, 1950) and amendments thereto; 5. Ordinance Regulating Radio Equipment (Radio Regulatory Commission Regulations No. 18, 1950) and amendments thereto; and 6. Ordinance concerning Technical Regulations Conformity Certification etc. of Specified Radio Equipment (Ordinance of the Ministry of Posts and Telecommunications No.37, 1981) and amendments thereto.

Section II
Designating Authority

UNITED STATES	JAPAN
National Institute of Standards and Technology (NIST) or an authority succeeding this institute	Ministry of Internal Affairs and Communications or an authority succeeding this ministry

Section III
Procedures for Designating Conformity Assessment Bodies

UNITED STATES	JAPAN
1. The Designating Authority of the United States may appoint a body or bodies to evaluate conformity assessment bodies. The Designating Authority of the United States shall ensure appointed bodies comply with the requirements of ISO/IEC Standard 17011 and are competent to evaluate conformity assessment bodies' competence to conduct conformity assessment procedures with respect to the Technical Regulations of Japan.	1. The Designating Authority of Japan may appoint a body or bodies to evaluate conformity assessment bodies. The Designating Authority of Japan shall ensure appointed bodies comply with the requirements of ISO/IEC Standard 17011 and are competent to evaluate conformity assessment bodies' competence to conduct conformity assessment procedures with respect to the Technical Regulations of the United States.
2. The Designating Authority of the United States or the appointed body or bodies shall evaluate whether a conformity assessment body complies with the criteria for designation set out in the Technical Regulations of Japan and ISO/IEC Guide 65 and ISO/IEC Standard 17025.	2. The Designating Authority of Japan or the appointed body or bodies shall evaluate whether a conformity assessment body complies with the criteria for designation set out in the Technical Regulations of the United States and ISO/IEC Guide 65 and ISO/IEC Standard 17025.
3. The Designating Authority of the United States shall determine, based on the results of the evaluation made pursuant to paragraph 2, whether the conformity assessment body complies with the criteria for designation. If the Designating Authority of the United States determines that the conformity assessment body complies with the criteria for designation, the Designating Authority may designate the conformity assessment body.	3. The Designating Authority of Japan shall determine, based on the results of the evaluation made pursuant to paragraph 2, whether the conformity assessment body complies with the criteria for designation. If the Designating Authority of Japan determines that the conformity assessment body complies with the criteria for designation, the Designating Authority may designate the conformity assessment body.
4. When evaluating whether a conformity assessment body complies with the criteria for designation, the Designating Authority or the appointed body or bodies of the United States shall consider whether the conformity assessment body understands the Technical Regulations of Japan.	4. When evaluating whether a conformity assessment body complies with the criteria for designation, the Designating Authority or the appointed body or bodies of Japan shall consider whether the conformity assessment body understands the Technical Regulations of the United States.

Section IV
Regulatory Authority

UNITED STATES	JAPAN
Federal Communications Commission (FCC) or an authority succeeding this commission	Ministry of Internal Affairs and Communications or an authority succeeding this ministry

Section V
The ISO/IEC Standard for Terms Not Defined in this Agreement

ISO/IEC Standard 17000: 2004, Conformity Assessment—Vocabulary and General Principles

Section VI
Equipment within the Scope of this Agreement

UNITED STATES	JAPAN
Any equipment subject to certification, as defined in 47 CFR 2.907, that falls within the scope of the 47 CFR parts listed in paragraph 2 of Section I of the Annex, except Unintentional Radiators and Industrial, Scientific, and Medical Equipment as defined in 47 CFR 15.3(z) and 47 CFR 18.107(c), respectively.	1. Any equipment defined as Specified Radio Equipment in Radio Law (Law No.131, 1950) and amendments thereto; and 2. Any equipment defined as Terminal Equipment in Telecommunications Business Law (Law No. 86, 1984) and amendments thereto.

Section VII
Information for Registration of Conformity Assessment Bodies

UNITED STATES	JAPAN
1. Information identifying the conformity assessment body, including the name, contact person, mailing address, telephone number, and electronic mail address, for the conformity assessment body;	1. Information identifying the conformity assessment body, including the name, contact person, mailing address, telephone number, and electronic mail address, for the conformity assessment body;
2. The equipment for which the conformity assessment body is authorized to conduct conformity assessment procedures (scope of designation);	2. The equipment for which the conformity assessment body is authorized to conduct conformity assessment procedures (scope of designation);
3. The intervals at which the Designating Authority or the appointed body or bodies shall re-evaluate whether the conformity assessment body continues to comply with the criteria for designation; and	3. The intervals at which the Designating Authority or the appointed body or bodies shall re-evaluate whether the conformity assessment body continues to comply with the criteria for designation; and
4. Documentation on the evaluation of the conformity assessment body's compliance with the criteria for designation.	4. Documentation on the evaluation of the conformity assessment body's compliance with the criteria for designation.

Section VIII
Co-chairs of the Joint Committee

UNITED STATES	JAPAN
For the United States, the co-chair of the Joint Committee shall be as follows: 1. For functions referred to in Articles 6 and 7 relating to registration, termination of registration, suspension of registration, and removal of suspension of registration of, conformity assessment bodies located in the territory of Japan: FCC 2. For functions referred to in Articles 6 and 7 relating to registration, termination of registration, suspension of registration, and removal of suspension of registration of, conformity assessment bodies located in the territory of the United States: NIST 3. For functions referred to in Article 8 relating to contestation concerning a conformity assessment body located in the territory of the United States: NIST 4. For functions referred to in Article 8 relating to contestation concerning a conformity assessment body located in the territory of Japan: FCC 5. For functions referred to in Article 9 relating to verification of conformity assessment bodies located in the territory of the United States: NIST 6. For functions referred to in Article 9 relating to verification of conformity assessment bodies located in the territory of Japan: FCC 7. For all other functions: Office of the U.S. Trade Representative (USTR).	For Japan, the co-chair of the Joint Committee shall be the Ministry of Foreign Affairs for all functions.

STATE DEPARTMENT DOCUMENT NUMBER: 08-20

AGREEMENT BETWEEN THE UNITED STATES OF AMERICA AND THE REPUBLIC OF SIERRA LEONE REGARDING THE REDUCTION OF CERTAIN DEBTS OWED TO, GUARANTEED BY, OR INSURED BY THE UNITED STATES GOVERNMENT AND ITS AGENCY

SIGNED AT FREETOWN, JUNE 7, 2007
ENTERED INTO FORCE JANUARY 29, 2008

CTIA DOCUMENT NUMBER: 13390.000

The United States of America (the "United States") and the Republic of Sierra Leone ("Sierra Leone") agree as follows:

ARTICLE I
Application of the Agreement

1. Pursuant to the recommendations contained in the Agreed Minutes on the Reduction of the Debt of the Republic of Sierra Leone, signed on January 24, 2007, the applicable domestic laws of the United States and Sierra Leone, and the September 1999 commitment of the President of the United States to provide 100 percent debt forgiveness of eligible debt to certain Heavily Indebted Poor Countries that have reached Completion Point, the United States and Sierra Leone hereby agree to the reduction of certain Sierra Leonean payments due as a result of debts owed to, guaranteed, or insured by the United States Government and its Agency.

2. This Agreement will be further implemented by a separate agreement (the "Implementing Agreement") between Sierra Leone and the United States Department of Agriculture ("USDA") with respect to PL-480 Agreements.

ARTICLE II
Definitions

1. "*Contracts*" mean

(a) credits extended under PL-480 agreements ("PL-480 credits") having original maturities of more than one year, which were extended to the Government of Sierra Leone or its public sector, or covered by a guarantee of the Government of Sierra Leone or its public sector, pursuant to an agreement concluded with the United States before June 20, 1999 and

(b) the bilateral debt rescheduling agreements concluded between the United States and Sierra Leone on August 21, 1987, April 19, 1993, January 11, 1995, August 7, 1996, April 29, 2002, and April 25, 2003, as amended.

Debt service due as a result of debts described above and affected through special payments mechanisms or other external accounts is covered by this Agreement.

A table listing the relevant contracts to be included under the debt reduction is attached hereto as Annex A.

2. "Relevant Principal" means the total amount of principal outstanding as of December 1, 2006, including Accrued Interest and any principal and interest in arrears (including Late Interest, if any), on Contracts, as defined in Article II, paragraph 1 of this Agreement.

3. "Accrued Interest" means interest accrued under the relevant Contracts from the last interest maturity date through November 30, 2006, inclusive, computed at the rate specified in the Contracts.

4. "Late Interest" means interest charges accruing from the contractual payment date of principal and interest due and not paid through November 30, 2006, inclusive.

5. "Minute" means the Agreed Minutes on the Reduction of the Debt of the Republic of Sierra Leone, signed on January 24, 2007.

6. "Participating Creditor Countries" means creditor countries that are signatories to the Agreed Minutes on the Reduction of the Debt of the Republic of Sierra Leone, signed on January 24, 2007.

7. "Completion Point" means' December 14 and December 15, 2006, the dates on which the Boards of the International Development Association of the World Bank and the International Monetary Fund ("IMF"), respectively, decided that Sierra Leone had reached its Completion Point, as defined under the Enhanced Debt Initiative for Heavily Indebted Poor Countries.

8. "Agency" means USDA.

ARTICLE III
Terms and Conditions of Cancellation

1. One hundred percent of the Relevant Principal, as defined in Article II, paragraph 2, is hereby cancelled.

A table summarizing the amount of Relevant Principal owed to the United States and its agencies and cancelled hereby is attached hereto as Annex B.

2. Adjustments in the amounts of Relevant Principal may be made in writing, as necessary and by mutual consent.

ARTICLE IV
General Provisions

1. Sierra Leone shall seek to secure from its external public or private creditors not participating in the Minute reduction arrangements on terms comparable to those set forth in the Minute for credits of comparable maturity, committing to avoid treatment more favorable than that accorded to the Participating Creditor Countries, as more specifically defined in the Minute.

2. Except as may be modified by this Agreement, all terms of the Contracts remain in full force and effect.

3. Upon entry into force, this Agreement will supersede the Agreement between the United States of America and the Republic of Sierra Leone Regarding the Consolidation and Reduction of Certain Debts Owed To, Guaranteed By, or Insured by the United States Government, dated April 25, 2003, as amended.

ARTICLE V
Suspension or Termination

1. The United States may suspend or terminate this Agreement by giving sixty (60) days written notice to Sierra Leone. In particular, the United States may suspend or terminate all or part of this Agreement, if the Participating Creditor Countries determine that Sierra Leone has not met its obligations under the Minute, including those of comparable treatment. If the United States terminates all or part of this Agreement, all payments consolidated and cancelled under this Agreement shall be due and payable immediately following notification to Sierra Leone of the exercise by the United States of this right of termination.

2. This Agreement may be amended or modified by mutual consent of the United States and Sierra Leone.

ARTICLE VI
Entry into Force

This Agreement shall enter into force following signature of the Agreement and written notice to Sierra Leone by the United States that all necessary U.S. domestic legal requirements for entry into force of the Agreement have been fulfilled.

Done at Freetown, Sierra Leone, in duplicate, in the English language, this seventh day of June, 2007.

[Signature]

FOR THE UNITED STATES
OF AMERICA:

Ambassador Thomas N. Hull, III
Ambassador to the Republic of Sierra Leone

[Signature]

FOR THE REPUBLIC OF
SIERRA LEONE:

The Honorable John O. Benjamin
Minister of Finance

ANNEX A
Contracts Subject to Reduction

USDA

77SL1 – 8/18/1977
78SL1 – 8/31/1978
79SL1 – 8/23/1979
80SL1 – 8/8/1980
81SL1 – 3/25/1981
82SL1 – 7/28/1982
83SL1 – 4/29/1983
84SL1 – 4/23/1984
85SL1 – 5/9/1985
86SL1 – 5/5/1986
87SL1 – 6/10/1987
88SL1 – 6/16/1988
89SL1 – 9/27/1988
90SL1 – 6/8/1990
92SL1 – 3/4/1992
93SLA – 4/19/1993
95SLA – 1/1 1/1995
96SLA – 8/7/1996

ANNEX B
SUMMARY OF RELEVANT PRINCIPAL
(thousands of U.S. dollars)

USDA	$ 58,254
TOTAL	$ 58,254

STATE DEPARTMENT DOCUMENT NUMBER: 08-21

AGREEMENT BETWEEN THE UNITED STATES OF AMERICA NAVY AND THE PERUVIAN NAVY REGARDING THE ASSIGNMENT OF FOREIGN LIAISON OFFICERS, WITH ANNEX

SIGNED AT WASHINGTON D.C. AND LIMA,
OCTOBER 31 AND NOVEMBER 23, 2007
ENTERED INTO FORCE NOVEMBER 23, 2007

CTIA DOCUMENT NUMBER: 13391.000

Preamble

The United States Navy and the Peruvian Navy, each referred to herein individually as a "Party" and together as the "Parties", desiring to establish formal liaisons between the Parties, hereby agree to the following terms and conditions regarding the assignment of naval officers to serve as Liaison Officers between the Parties, within their government facilities.

Article I
Definitions

In addition to any terms defined in other provisions of this Agreement, the following terms shall have the following meanings when used herein:

1.1 "Classified Information" shall mean official information that is generated by or for the Government of the United States of America or the Peruvian Government or that is under the jurisdiction or control of one of them, and which requires protection in the interests of national security of that government and is so designated by the assignment of a national security classification by that government. The information may be oral, visual, electronic, or in documentary form, or in the form of material, including equipment or technology.

1.2 "Contact Officer" shall mean a U.S. Navy official designated in writing to oversee and control all contacts, requests for information, consultations, access, and other activities of foreign Liaison Officers who are assigned to, or are visiting, the United States Navy, its components or subordinate organizations. Likewise, it could be a functionary of the Peruvian Navy to administer and to coordinate the requirements of the Liaison Officers of the United States Navy.

1.3 "Controlled Unclassified Information" shall mean unclassified information of a Party to which access or distribution limitations have been applied in accordance with national laws, policies, and regulations of such Party. It includes United States Navy and Peruvian Navy information that is exempt from public disclosure or subject to export controls.

1.4 "Host Government" shall mean the national government of the Host Party.

1.5 "Host Party" shall mean the Party to which the Liaison Officer acts as a liaison pursuant to an assignment by a Parent Party under Article III.

1.6 "International Visits Program (IVP)" shall mean the program established to process visits by, and assignments of, foreign representatives to United States Navy its components and contractor facilities. It is designed to ensure that Classified and Controlled Unclassified Information to be disclosed to foreign nationals has been properly authorized for disclosure to their governments; that the requesting foreign government provides a security assurance on such foreign nationals and their sponsoring organization or firm, when Classified Information is involved in the visit or assignment, and that administrative arrangements (e.g., date, time and place) for the visit or assignment are provided.

1.7 "Liaison Officer" shall mean a naval officer from the Parent Party who, upon approval or certification of the Host Party or Government, is authorized by the Parent Party to act as its official representative in connection with programs, projects, or agreements of interest to the Parties' Governments.

1.8 "Parent Government" shall mean the national government of the Parent Party.

1.9 "Parent Party" shall mean the Party that assigns a Liaison Officer pursuant to Article III.

Article II
Scope

2.1 During the term of this Agreement, subject to the agreement of the Parties, each Party may assign personnel from its armed forces to serve in the capacity of Liaison Officer to the other Party in accordance with the terms of this Agreement.

2.2 The establishment of each Liaison Officer position under this Agreement shall be based upon the demonstrated necessity of and the mutual benefit of this position to the Parties. Once established, each Liaison Officer position shall be subject to periodic review by either Party to ensure that the position continues to be required by, and is of mutual benefit to, the Parties. The Parties agree that a Liaison Officer position shall be subject to elimination when it is no longer required by, or of mutual benefit to, either Party. In case that one of the parties cannot designate, at some time a Liaison Officer for unforeseen reasons to the Institutions, unless the applicable Party states otherwise, this does not mean this position is not necessary, but will be covered when the conditions change that prevented this designation.

2.3 The commencement of the tour of duty of a Liaison Officer shall be subject to all requirements imposed by the Host Party or its Government regarding formal certification or approval of Liaison Officers. Liaison Officers assigned by their Parent Party to locations within the United States of America shall be requested pursuant to the International Visits Program (IVP), as defined in Paragraph 1.6 of this Agreement.

2.4 Unless otherwise agreed, the normal tour of duty for a Liaison Officer shall be two years.

2.5 As a general rule an individual may serve as a Liaison Officer to only one major military command of the Host Party, at any point in time.

Article III
Duties and Activities

3.1 The Liaison Officer shall represent the Parent Party to the Host Party. The Liaison Officer shall not perform duties that the Host Government, by law or regulation, reserves to its own officials or employees, nor shall the Liaison Officer provide any labor or services to the Host Government or its agencies, including the Host Party.

3.2 The Liaison Officer is required to comply with all applicable Host Government policies, procedures, laws and regulations. The Host Party shall assign a Contact Officer to provide guidance to the Liaison Officer concerning policies, procedures, laws and regulations of the Host Party, and to take the necessary measures to ensure that activities are consistent with the requirements and the purposes of this Agreement.

3.3 The Liaison Officer may request access to Host Party facilities by submitting a request to the Contact Officer. Said access to Host Party facilities may be granted if such access promotes the purposes of this Agreement, is consistent with the terms of any applicable certification or approval properly issued by the Host Government, and is permitted under the applicable policies, procedures, laws and regulations of the Host Government. Approval of such requests shall be at the discretion of the Host Party. Any requests for access that exceed the terms of any applicable certification or approval shall be submitted through the International Visits Program (IVP).

3.4 The Liaison Officer shall not be granted access to technical data or other information of the Host Party, whether classified or not classified, except as authorized by the Host Party, and only to the extent necessary to fulfill the Liaison Officer's functions under this Agreement.

3.5 All information to which the Liaison Officer is granted access while serving as a liaison to the Host Party shall be treated as information provided to the Parent Government in confidence and shall not be further released or disclosed by the Liaison Officer to any other person, firm, organization, or government without the prior written authorization to do so from the Host Government. Disclosure of information to the Liaison Officer shall not be deemed to be a license or authorization to use such information for any purpose other than the purposes described in Article II.

3.6 The Liaison Officer shall not be permitted to participate in exercises, deployments, or civil-military actions, unless expressly authorized to do so by both the Host and Parent Parties.

3.7 The Parent Party shall not place or keep a Liaison Officer in duty assignments in which direct hostilities with forces of third countries are likely to occur or have commenced, unless approved in writing by the Parent Party and Host Party.

3.8 The Liaison Officer shall be required to comply with the dress regulations of the Parent Party but, if requested by the Host Party, shall also wear such identification necessary to identify the Liaison Officer's nationality, rank and status as a Foreign Liaison Officer. The order of dress for any occasion shall be that which most closely conforms to the order of dress for the particular unit of the Host Party where the Liaison Officer is located. The Liaison Officer shall be required to comply with the customs of the Host Party with respect to the wearing of civilian clothing.

3.9 Prior to the commencement of a Liaison Officer's tour, the Parent Party shall notify the Host Party of the specific Parent Party organization that shall exercise operational control over the Liaison Officer and, if different, the Parent Party organization that shall provide administrative support, to the Liaison Officer and dependent(s).

3.10 At the end of a Liaison Officer's tour, or as otherwise agreed by the Parties, the Parent Party may, subject to the provisions of Article 2.2, replace the Liaison Officer with another naval officer who meets the requirements of this current Agreement.

Article IV
Financial Arrangements

4.1 The Parent Party shall bear all costs and expenses of the Liaison Officer, including, but not limited to:

4.1.1 All pay and allowances of the Liaison Officer;

4.1.2 All travel by the Liaison Officer and dependents, including, but not limited to, travel to and from the country of the Host Party;

4.1.3 The expenses of luggage, baggage and installation, so much for from and to, clerical support, medical and orthodontist services, unless otherwise specified in a pertinent an international agreement.

4.1.4 Subject to the Parent Party's domestic law and policies, compensation for loss of, or damage to, the Liaison Officer's personal property or the property of the Liaison Officer's dependents;

4.1.5 The expenses for preparation and transfer of the mortal remains and burial, in case the death of the Liaison officer or any of the individual responsible for.

4.1.6 The qualification, structured or not, of the Liaison officer, independently of the orientation sessions on the requirements of the Host Party who provides the Contact Officer.

4.2 Host Party shall provide the Liaison Officer with office facilities, equipment, supplies and services that the Liaison Officer may need to comply with this current Agreement.

Article V
Security

5.1 The Host Party shall establish the maximum substantive scope and classification levels within which the disclosure of any Classified Information or Controlled Unclassified Information to the Liaison Officer shall be permitted. The Host Party shall inform the Parent Party of the level of security clearance required to permit the Liaison Officer access to such information. The Liaison Officer's access to such information and facilities shall be consistent with, and limited by the terms of the Liaison Officer's assignment, the provisions of this Article and any other agreement between the Parties or their Governments concerning access to such information and facilities. In addition, access shall at all times be limited to the minimum required to accomplish the purposes of this current Agreement, and, at its discretion, the Host Party can prohibit the Liaison Officer's right of access to any of the Host Party facilities or computer systems or require that such access be supervised by Host Party personnel.

5.2 Each Party shall cause security assurances to be filed, through the Peruvian Embassy in Washington, DC, in the case of Peruvian personnel, and through the U.S. Embassy in Peru in the case of United States of America personnel, stating the security clearances for the Liaison Officer being assigned by such Party. The security assurances shall be prepared in accordance with the procedures established by the Host Party and shall be forwarded through prescribed channels in compliance with stipulated Host Party procedures. For the United States of America, the prescribed channel is the International Visits Program (IVP), as defined in paragraph 1.6 of this current Agreement.

5.3 The Parent Party shall ensure that each Liaison officer assigned is fully cognizant of, and complies with, applicable laws and regulations concerning the protection of proprietary information (such as patents, copyrights, practical knowledge, and trade secrets), Classified Information and Controlled Unclassified Information disclosed to the Liaison Officer. This obligation shall apply both during and after termination of an assignment as a Liaison Officer. Prior to undertaking the assigned duties, the Liaison Officer shall be required to sign the certification included in Annex A. Only the naval officers that execute this certification shall be permitted to serve as Liaison Officers with the United States Navy.

5.4 The Parent Party shall ensure that the Liaison Officer, at all times, complies with the security laws, regulations and procedures of the Host Government. Any violation of security procedures by a Liaison Officer during their assignment shall be reported to the Parent Party for appropriate action. Upon request by the Host Party, the Parent Party shall remove the Liaison Officer who violates security laws, regulations, or procedures during their assignment.

5.5 All Classified or Controlled Unclassified Information, if disclosed, to the Liaison Officer shall be considered to be Information furnished to the Parent Party, and shall be subject to all provisions and safeguards provided for under the General Security of Military Information Agreement (GSOMIA) in force between the United States and Peru dated January 12, 1999.

5.6 The Liaison Officer shall not take custody of Classified Information or Controlled Unclassified Information in tangible form (for example, documents or electronic files), except for the following situation:

5.6.1 Courier. The Liaison Officer may assume custody of releasable documentary information to act as couriers only when they are authorized in writing by their government to assume responsibility as an agent of their government. Documents shall be packaged and receipted for in compliance with the Host Party requirements.

Article VI
Technical and Administrative Matters

6.1 The Host Party's certification or approval of an individual as a Liaison Officer shall not bestow diplomatic or other special privileges on the naval officer, except for specifically-requested by the Parent Party.

6.2 To the extent authorized by laws and regulations of the Host Government, and in accordance with Article IV of this Agreement, the Host Party may provide such administrative support as is necessary for the Liaison Officer to fulfill the purposes of this Agreement.

6.3 Tax exemptions, customs or import duties, or similar charges for the Liaison Officer or the Liaison Officer's dependents shall be governed by applicable laws and regulations or by international agreement between the Host Government and the Parent Government.

6.4 If the Host Party provides the Liaison Officer with office space, the Host Party shall determine the normal working hours for the Liaison Officer. Access outside of normal working hours will be coordinated through the Host Party Contact Officer to the Command Security Officer.

6.5 The Parent Party shall ensure that the Host Party is informed of any absences of the Liaison Officer as far in advance as possible.

6.6 The Liaison Officer and the authorized dependents shall be provided care in military medical and dental facilities to the extent permitted by applicable national law, policy, and international agreement. Where a reciprocal agreement for health care exists between the Parties, the access entitlement of the Liaison Officer and dependents is specified. For personnel covered by such an agreement, care is generally provided free of charge. All Liaison Officers and dependents not covered by a reciprocal agreement may be offered health care in military facilities, on a reimbursable basis. Where military facilities are not available, the Liaison Officer shall be responsible for all medical and dental costs incurred by self and dependents. The Parent Party shall ensure that the Liaison Officer and dependents are physically fit prior to the Liaison Officer's tour of duty. The Parent Party must inform the Host Party of any special medical needs the Liaison Officer or dependents may require prior to the Liaison's Officer's tour of duty. The Parent Party shall have the responsibility of familiarizing itself with the medical and dental services the Liaison Officer and dependents shall have available, and the costs of, and the procedures for use of such services.

6.7 The Liaison Officer and dependents may be allowed the use of military commissaries, exchanges, theaters, and similar morale and welfare activities, in accordance with the laws, regulations, and policies of the Host Party.

6.8 To the extent permitted by the laws and regulations of the Host Government, and subject to reimbursement by the Parent Party, the Host Party may provide, if available, housing and messing facilities for the Liaison Officer and the Liaison Officer's dependents on the same basis and priority as for its own personnel of comparable rank and assignment. At locations where the Host Party does not provide housing and messing facilities, the Host Party shall use reasonable efforts to assist the Parent Party to locate such facilities for the Liaison Officer and dependents.

6.9 The Parent Party shall ensure that the Liaison Officer and dependents have all documentation required by the Host Government for entry into, and exit from, the country of the Host Government at the time of such entry or exit. Unless exempted under an applicable international agreement between the Parties, the Liaison Officers and authorized dependents entering the United States shall be required to comply with United States Customs Regulations.

6.10 The Parent Party shall ensure that the Liaison Officer and dependents accompanying the Liaison Officer in the country of the Host Party shall obtain motor vehicle liability insurance coverage for their private motor vehicles, in accordance with applicable laws, regulations and policies of the Host Government, or of any political subdivisions of the country of the Host Party in which the Liaison Officer and dependents are located.

Article VII
Discipline and Removal

7.1 Except as provided in Section 7.2, neither the Host Party nor the armed forces of the Host Government may take disciplinary action against a Liaison Officer who commits an offense under the military laws or regulations of the Host Party, nor shall the Host Party exercise disciplinary authority over the Liaison Officer's dependents. The Parent Party, however, shall take such administrative or disciplinary action against the Liaison Officer as may be appropriate under the circumstances, to ensure compliance with this Agreement, and the Parties shall cooperate in the investigation of any offenses under the laws or regulations of either Party.

7.2 The certification or approval of a Liaison Officer may be withdrawn, modified or curtailed at any time by the Host Party for any reason, including, but not limited to, the violation of the regulations or laws of the Host Party or the Host Government. In addition, at the request of the Host Party, the Parent Government shall remove the Liaison officer or dependents from the territory of the Host Government. The Host Party shall explain its request for removal but a disagreement between the Parties concerning the sufficiency of the Host Party's reasons shall not be grounds to delay the removal of the Liaison Officer.

7.3 A Liaison Officer shall not exercise any supervisory or disciplinary authority over the Host Party military or civilian personnel.

Article VIII
Claims

8.1. Claims arising under this Agreement shall be governed by any bilateral agreement between the Parties concerning the status of their armed forces in the country of the Host Party. Claims to which the provisions of any such bilateral agreements do not apply shall be dealt with as follows:

8.1.1. The Parties shall waive all their claims, other than derived from a related contractual, against each other, and against the military members and civilian employees of each other's

Department or Ministry of Defense, for damage, loss or destruction of property owned or used by its respective Department or Ministry of Defense, if damage, loss or destruction:

8.1.1.1. Was caused by a military member or a civilian employee in the performance of official duties, or

8.1.1.2. Arose from the use of any vehicle, vessel or aircraft owned by the other Party and used by its Department or Ministry of Defense, as long as the vehicle, vessel or aircraft causing the damage, loss or destruction was being used for official purposes, or that the damage, loss or destruction was caused to the property being so used.

8.2. The Parties shall waive all their claims against each other and against the military members and civilian employees of each other's Department or Ministry of Defense for injury or death suffered by any military member or civilian employee of their Department or Ministry of Defense while such member or employee was engaged in the performance of official duties.

8.3. Claims, other than contractual claims, for damage, loss, injury, or death, not covered by the waivers contained in paragraphs 1 and 2 of this Article, arising out of an act or omission by the military members or civilian employees of its Department or Ministry of Defense, or out of an act or omission for which the Parent Party is legally responsible, shall be presented to the Parent Party for consideration under its applicable laws and regulations.

Article IX
Settlement of Disputes

9.1 Disputes arising under or relating to this Agreement shall be resolved only through consultations between the Parties, and shall not be referred to an individual, national or international tribunal, or to any other forum for settlement.

Article X
Entry into Force, Amendment, Duration and Resolution

10.1 All obligations of the Parties under this current Agreement shall be subject to national laws and the availability of appropriated funds for such purposes.

10.2 The Parent Party shall ensure that the Liaison Officer complies with all related obligations and restrictions applicable to the Liaison Officer under this Agreement and Annex.

10.3 This Agreement may be amended by the mutual written consent between the Parties.

10.4 This Agreement may be terminated at any time by written mutual agreement from both Parties. Either Party may terminate this Agreement upon written notification to the other Party one hundred and eighty (180) days prior to the termination of this Agreement. Both Parties shall consult with each other prior to the date of termination.

10.5 In the event of conflict between the terms of this Agreement and the terms of an applicable Letter of Offer and Acceptance (LOA), the terms of the LOA shall control. Any LOAs associated with or related to this Agreement shall be terminated in accordance with its terms.

10.6 The respective rights and responsibilities of the Parties under Article V (Security) shall continue, notwithstanding the termination or expiration of this Agreement.

10.7 No later than the effective date of expiration or termination of this current Agreement, each Party shall remove their Liaison Officers and dependents from the territory of the other Party and pay any money owed to the other Party under this Agreement. Any costs or expenses for which a Party is responsible pursuant to this current Agreement, but which were not billed in sufficient time to permit payment prior to termination or expiration of this current Agreement, shall be paid promptly, after such bill is received.

10.8 This Agreement shall supersede any and all prior agreements regarding Liaison officers entered into by the Parties or their organizations, units, or agencies.

10.9 This Agreement shall enter into force upon the signature and date by both Parties. This Agreement shall remain in force for ten (10) years, and may be extended by written mutual agreement of the Parties.

10.10 This current Agreement consists of ten (10) Articles and an Annex.

IN WITNESS WHEREOF, the undersigned, being duly authorized, have signed this current Agreement.

DONE this ____ day of __________ 2007, in Spanish and English, in text equally authenticated.

ON BEHALF OF The United States Navy:	ON BEHALF OF The Peruvian Navy:
____________________	____________________
[Signature]	[Signature]
P. H. DALY Rear Admiral, United States Navy Assistant Deputy Chief of Naval Operations for Information, Plans and Strategy (N3/N5)	CARLOS WESTON ZANELLI Contralmirante, Jefe del Estado Mayor de la Comandancia General de Operaciones del Pacífico de la Marina de Guerra del Perú
Washington, D.C.	Lima, Perú
OCT 31 2007	**23 NOV. 2007**
Dated:	Dated:

ANNEX A
CERTIFICATION

[Date (day month year)]

Section I
Liaison Officer
Legal Status of Certification

As a representative of the Peruvian Navy under the auspices of an Extended Visit Authorization to the United States Navy, I am subject to the jurisdiction of United States federal, state, and local laws, except as provided by treaty, other specific legal authority, or the terms of any diplomatic immunity which I may have been granted. I understand that my acceptance of the Liaison Officer position does not bestow diplomatic or other special privileges.

Section II
Liaison Officer
Conditions of Certification

(1) **Responsibilities:** I understand that my activities shall be limited to the representational responsibilities of my government and that I am expected to present the views of my government with regard to the issues which my government and the U.S. Government have a mutual interest. I shall not perform duties that are reserved by law or regulation to an officer or employee of the United States Government.

(2) **Costs:** I understand that all costs associated with my duties as a Liaison Officer shall be the responsibility of my government, including, but not limited to, travel, clerical services, housing, rations, and medical and dental services.

(3) **Extensions and Revalidation:** I understand that if my government desires to request an extension or revalidation of my position beyond the original dates for which I am certified, a new visit request shall be submitted not later than 30 days prior to the expiration date of the current Extended Visit Authorization.

(4) **Contact Officer:** I understand that when the certification process is completed, a Contact Officer(s) shall be assigned to sponsor me during my visit to the Commander U.S. Naval Forces Southern Command. I further understand that I shall coordinate, through my Contact Officer, all requests for information, visits, and other business that fall under the terms of my certification. I also understand that requests for information that are beyond the terms of my certification shall be made to my Naval Attaché, Peruvian Embassy, Washington, D.C.

(5) **Other Visits:** I understand that visits to facilities for which the purpose does not directly relate to the terms of my certification shall be made through my Naval Attaché, Peruvian Embassy, Washington, D.C.

(6) **Uniform:** I understand that I shall wear my national uniform when conducting business at Commander, U. S. Naval Forces Southern Command or other United States Department of Defense facilities, unless otherwise directed. I shall comply with my Parent Government's service uniform regulations.

(7) **Duty Hours:** I understand that my duty hours shall be comparable to those established by Commander, U.S. Naval Forces Southern Command. Should I require access to my work area during non-duty hours, I am required to request authorization from my Contact officer. I further understand that it is necessary to assign a United States Navy of America escort officer to me during my

non-duty access. Any cost incurred as a result of such non-duty access may be reimbursable to the United States Government.

(8) **Security:**

a. I understand that access to the United States Government information shall be limited to that information determined by my Contact Officer to be necessary to fulfill the functions of a Liaison Officer. I also understand that I may not have unsupervised access to U.S. Government computer systems, unless the information accessible by the computer is releasable to my government in accordance with applicable U.S. law, regulations and policy.

b. All information to which I may have access during my certification shall be treated as information provided to my government in confidence and shall not be further released or disclosed by me to any other person, firm, organization, or government without the prior written authorization of the United States Government.

c. Should I obtain or become knowledgeable of United States Government information for which I am not authorized to have access, I shall immediately report it to my Contact Officer. I further agree that I shall report to my Contact Officer any incidents of my being offered or provided information that I am not authorized to have.

d. If required, I shall display a security badge on my outer clothing so that it is clearly visible. Commander U. S. Naval Forces Southern Command shall supply this badge.

(9) **Compliance:** I have been briefed on, fully understand, and shall comply with the terms and conditions of my certification. Failure to comply with this certification may result in suspension of my certification. I further understand that the termination of my certification does not preclude further disciplinary action in accordance with any applicable Status of Forces Agreement or other international agreement.

(10) **Definitions of Terms:** Terms not defined herein shall have the definitions ascribed to them in the applicable Agreement governing my assignment as a Foreign Liaison Officer.

Section III
Liaison Officer
Terms of Certification

(1) **Contact Officer:** I understand a command Contact Officer shall be assigned.

(2) **Certification:** I am certified to the Commander, U. S. Naval Forces Southern Command in support of the following program: The Commander, U. S. Naval Forces Southern Command Foreign Liaison Officer Program.

(3) **Travel:** I am authorized to visit the following locations in accordance with the conditions of my certification, with the approval of my Contact Officer: the commands, installations and localities that are subordinate to Commander, U. S. Naval Forces Southern Command.

Section IV
Liaison Officer
Certification of In-Briefing

I, ***(NAME OF FOREIGN LIAISON OFFICER)***, understand and acknowledge that I have been certified as a Foreign Liaison Officer to Commander, United States Naval Forces Southern Command, as agreed upon between the Peruvian Navy and the United States Navy. I further acknowledge that I fully understand and have been briefed on: (1) the legal status of my certification; (2) the conditions of my certification; and (3) the terms of my certification. I further acknowledge that I shall comply with the conditions and responsibilities of my certification.

____

(SIGNATURE OF LIAISON OFFICER)

____

(TYPED Name of LIAISON OFFICER)

____

(RANK OF LIAISON OFFICER)

____

(DATE)

____

(SIGNATURE OF BRIEFER)

____

(TYPED NAME)

____

(LOCATION)

STATE DEPARTMENT DOCUMENT NUMBER: 08-22

AGREEMENT BETWEEN THE UNITED STATES OF AMERICA AND THE REPUBLIC OF THE PHILIPPINES REGARDING GRANTS UNDER THE GLOBAL PEACE OPERATIONS INITIATIVE (GPOI)

EFFECTED BY EXCHANGE OF NOTES AT MANILA AND PASAY CITY, DECEMBER 18, 2007 AND JANUARY 3, 2008
ENTERED INTO FORCE JANUARY 3, 2008

CTIA DOCUMENT NUMBER: 13392.000

No. 1723

The Embassy of the United States of America presents its compliments to the Department of Foreign Affairs of the Republic of the Philippines and has the honor to refer to earlier discussions between representatives of the two Governments regarding grants under the Global Peace Operations Initiative (GPOI) of the United States of America and the furnishing of articles and services from the United States of America to the Government of the Republic of the Philippines pursuant to the GPOI.

In accordance with these discussions, it is proposed that the Government of the Republic of the Philippines agree with respect to articles and services provided pursuant to the GPOI:

A. That unless the consent of the Government of the United States of America has been first obtained, the Government of the Republic of the Philippines shall not:

(I) Permit any use of such articles or services by anyone not an officer, employee, or agent of the Government of the Republic of the Philippines;

(II) Transfer, or permit any officer, employee, or agent of the Government of the Republic of the Philippines to transfer, such articles or services by gift, sale, or otherwise; or

(III) Use, or permit the use of, such articles or services for purposes other than those for which provided;

B. That such articles and services shall be returned to the Government of the United States of America when they are no longer needed for the purposes for which they were furnished, unless the Government of the United States of America consents to another disposition;

C. That the net proceeds of sale received by the Government of the Republic of the Philippines in disposing of, with prior written consent of the Government of the United States of America, any article furnished by the United States of America under the GPOI, including scrap from any such article, shall be paid to the Government of the United States of America; and

D. That the Government of the Republic of the Philippines shall maintain the security of such articles and services; that it shall provide substantially the same degree of security protection afforded to such articles or services by the Government of the United States of America; that it shall, as the Government of the United States of America may require, permit continuous observation and review by, and furnish necessary information to, representatives of the Government of the United States of America with regard to the use thereof by the Government of the Republic of the Philippines.

The United States Government understands that the Government of the Republic of the Philippines retains its sovereign right to determine whether to deploy its forces in support of international peacekeeping operations.

The Department of Foreign Affairs' note stating that the foregoing is acceptable to the Government of the Republic of the Philippines shall, together with this note, constitute an agreement between the two Governments, which shall enter into force on the date of the Department note.

The Embassy of the United States of America avails itself of this opportunity to renew to the Department of Foreign Affairs of the Republic of the Philippines the assurances of its highest consideration.

Enclosure: Suggested text of a reply note.

Embassy of the United States of America,
Manila, December 18, 2007.

SUGGESTED TEXT OF A REPLY NOTE

The Department of Foreign Affairs of the Republic of the Philippines presents its compliments to the Embassy of the United States of America and acknowledges receipt of the Embassy's Note No. 1723, dated 18 December 2007, which reads as follows:

"The Embassy of the United States of America presents its compliments to the Department of Foreign Affairs of the Republic of the Philippines and has the honor to refer to earlier discussions between representatives of the two Governments regarding grants under the Global Peace Operations Initiative (GPOI) of the United States of America and the furnishing of articles and services from the United States of America to the Government of the Republic of the Philippines pursuant to the GPOI.

In accordance with these discussions, it is proposed that the Government of the Republic of the Philippines agree with respect to articles and services provided pursuant to the GPOI:

A. That unless the consent of the Government of the United States of America has been first obtained, the Government of the Republic of the Philippines shall not:

(I) Permit any use of such articles or services by anyone not an officer, employee, or agent of the Government of the Republic of the Philippines;

(II) Transfer, or permit any officer, employee, or agent of the Government of the Republic of the Philippines to transfer, such articles or services by gift, sale, or otherwise; or

(III) Use, or permit the use of, such articles or services for purposes other than those for which provided;

B. That such articles and services shall be returned to the Government of the United States of America when they are no longer needed for the purposes for which they were furnished, unless the Government of the United States of America consents to another disposition;

C. That the net proceeds of sale received by the Government of the Republic of the Philippines in disposing of, with prior written consent of the Government of the United States of America, any article furnished by the United States of America on a grant basis under the GPOI, including scrap from any such article, shall be paid to the Government of the United States of America; and

D. That the Government of the Republic of the Philippines shall maintain the security of such articles and services; that it shall provide substantially the same degree of security protection afforded to such articles or services by the Government of the United States of America; that it shall, as the Government of the United States of America may require, permit continuous observation and review by, and furnish necessary information to, representatives of the Government of the United States of America with regard to the use thereof by the Government of the Republic of the Philippines.

It is understood by the two Governments that the Republic of the Philippines retains its sovereign judgment with respect to participation and deployment in international peacekeeping operations.

The Department of Foreign Affairs' note stating that the foregoing is acceptable to the Government of the Republic of the Philippines shall, together with this note, constitute an agreement between the two Governments, which shall enter into force on the date of the Department's note."

The Department of Foreign Affairs of the Government of the Republic of the Philippines has the honor to confirm that the proposals set forth in the Embassy's note are acceptable to the Government of the Republic of the Philippines and that the Embassy's note and this note in reply shall constitute an agreement between the two governments which shall enter into force on this date.

The Department of Foreign Affairs of the Republic of the Philippines avails itself of this opportunity to renew to the Embassy of the United States of America the assurances of its highest consideration.

Republic of the Philippines)
City of Manila)
Embassy of the United States of America) ss:

I certify that the attached document is a true and faithful copy of the original, and that it has been carefully examined by me, compared with the said original, and found to agree with it word for word and figure for figure.

[Signature]

Sharon A. Howe
Consular Associate of the United States of America
Indefinite Commission

Date

ACTION: POL

INFO: CHRON

The Department of Foreign Affairs of the Republic of the Philippines presents its compliments to the Embassy of the United States of America and has the honor to acknowledge receipt of the Embassy's Note No. 1723, dated 18 December 2007, which reads as follows:

"The Embassy of the United States of America presents its compliments to the Department of Foreign Affairs of the Republic of the Philippines and has the honor to refer to earlier discussions between representatives of the two Governments regarding grants under the Global Peace Operations Initiative (GPOI) of the United States of America and the furnishing of articles and services from the United States of America to the Government of the Republic of the Philippines pursuant to the GPOI.

In accordance with these discussions, it is proposed that the Government of the Republic of the Philippines agree with respect to articles and services provided pursuant to the GPOI:

A. That unless the consent of the Government of the United States of America has been first obtained, the Government of the Republic of the Philippines shall not:

(I) Permit any use of such articles or services by anyone not an officer, employee, or agent of the Government of the Republic of the Philippines;

(II) Transfer, or permit any officer, employee, or agent of the Government of the Republic of the Philippines to transfer, such articles or services by gift, sale or otherwise or

(III) Use, or permit the use of, such articles or services for purposes other than those for which provided;

B. That such articles and services shall be returned to the Government of the United States of America when they are no longer needed for the purposes for which they were furnished, unless the Government of the United States of America consents to another disposition;

C. That the net proceeds of sale received by the Government of the Republic of the Philippines in disposing of, with prior written consent of the Government of the United States of America, any article furnished by the United States of America, under the GPOI, including scrap from any such article, shall be paid to the Government of the United States of America; and

D. That the Government of the Republic of the Philippines shall maintain the security of such articles and services; that it shall provide substantially the same degree of security protection afforded to such articles or services by the Government of the United States of America; that it shall, as the Government of the United States may require, permit continuous observation and review by, and furnish necessary information to, representatives of the Government of the United States of America with regard to the use thereof by the Government of the Republic of the Philippines.

The United States Government understands that the Government of the Republic of the Philippines retains its sovereign right to determine whether to deploy its forces in support of international peace-keeping operations.

The Department of Foreign Affairs' note stating that the foregoing is acceptable to the Government of the Republic of the Philippines shall, together with this note, constitute an agreement between the two Governments, which shall enter into force on the date of the Department of Foreign Affairs of the Republic of the Philippines' note.

The Embassy of the United States of America avails itself of this opportunity to renew to the Department of Foreign Affairs of the Republic of the Philippines the assurances of its highest consideration."

The Department wishes to inform the Embassy that the abovementioned note is acceptable to the Philippine Government and that said note and this reply constitute an agreement between the two Governments, which shall enter into force on the date of the Department of Foreign Affairs of the Republic of the Philippines' note.

The Department of Foreign Affairs of the Republic of the Philippines avails itself of this opportunity to renew to the Embassy of the United States of America the assurances of its highest consideration.

Pasay City, JAN 3, 2008

STATE DEPARTMENT DOCUMENT NUMBER: 08-23

PROTOCOL BETWEEN THE NUCLEAR REGULATORY COMMISSION OF THE UNITED STATES OF AMERICA (USNRC) AND THE NATIONAL NUCLEAR SAFETY ADMINISTRATION OF THE PEOPLE'S REPUBLIC OF CHINA (NNSA) ON COOPERATION IN NUCLEAR SAFETY MATTERS, WITH ADDENDUM

SIGNED AT BEIJING, JANUARY 7, 2008
ENTERED INTO FORCE JANUARY 7, 2008

CTIA DOCUMENT NUMBER: 2548.028

The Nuclear Regulatory Commission of the United States of America (USNRC) and the National Nuclear Safety Administration of the People's Republic of China (NNSA), hereinafter the Parties;

In accordance with and subject to the "Agreement Between the Government of the United States of America and the Government of the People's Republic of China on Cooperation in Science and Technology," signed in Washington on January 31, 1979, as amended and extended (hereinafter the Agreement);

Considering also the "Protocol Between the Nuclear Regulatory Commission of the United States of America and the National Nuclear Safety Administration of the People's Republic of China on Cooperation in Nuclear Safety Matters," signed in Washington on October 17, 1981; as amended and extended in Vienna on September 26, 1986; as amended and extended in Shanghai on January 11, 1993; as amended and extended in Vienna, Austria, on September 24, 1998; and as renewed in Beijing on April 23, 2004.

In view of the joint cooperative efforts and results achieved by the Parties, the Parties' reaffirmation of the importance of continued close cooperation in nuclear safety matters, and the Parties intent to expand significantly the scope of the existing cooperation between them;

Have agreed as follows.

ARTICLE 1
Technical Information Exchange

To the extent that the USNRC and the NNSA are permitted to do so under the laws, regulations, [and policy directives of their respective governments], the Parties will exchange technical and regulatory information relating to the safety, safeguards, and environmental impacts of civil nuclear installations, materials, and activities on the basis of equality, reciprocity, and mutual benefit.

A. The cooperation on nuclear safety regulation of civil nuclear installations may include the following areas:

1. Topical reports concerning safety, safeguards, decommissioning, and waste management written by or for one of the Parties as a basis for, or in support of, regulatory decisions and policies.

2. Documents relating to significant licensing actions and safety and environmental decisions affecting civil nuclear installations.

3. Detailed documents describing the USNRC process for licensing and regulating certain U.S. facilities mutually determined to be similar to certain facilities being built or planned in China and equivalent documents on such Chinese facilities.

4. Information in the field of confirmatory safety research which the Parties have the right to disclose, either in the possession of one of the Parties or available to it. Cooperation in the safety research areas will require a separate letter of agreement.

5. Reports on operating experience, such as reports on nuclear incidents, accidents and shutdowns, and compilations of historical reliability data on components and systems.

6. Regulatory procedures for the safety, safeguards (materials accountancy and control and physical protection), waste management, and environmental impact evaluation of civilian nuclear facilities.

7. Early notification of nuclear accidents in accordance with the related provisions under the "Convention on Early Notification of a Nuclear Accident".

8. Copies of regulatory standards required to be used, or proposed for use, by the regulatory organizations of the Parties.

9. Other areas as mutually agreed.

B. Emergency Exercises

The Parties may collaborate on emergency exercises to be conducted, as the Parties jointly decide is useful and appropriate. This could include observation of the exercises and participation in their critique.

C. Training and Assignments

1. Within the limits of available resources and legal authority, the USNRC will assist the NNSA in providing certain training and experience for its nuclear safety personnel. The following are typical of the kinds of on-the-job training and experience that may be provided under this Protocol:

a. NNSA nuclear safety personnel accompaniment of USNRC inspectors on operating reactor and reactor construction (if available) inspections in the U.S.

b. Participation by NNSA nuclear safety personnel in USNRC staff training courses conducted at the USNRC's Technical Training Center in Chattanooga, Tennessee; and

c. Assignment of NNSA nuclear safety personnel to work within the USNRC staff to gain experience in the practices and procedures followed by the USNRC in its regulation of U. S. nuclear facilities.

2. Within the limits of available resources and legal authority, the NNSA will receive nuclear safety personnel of the USNRC under the following typical forms:

a. The Chinese side will welcome U.S. nuclear safety personnel in specific fields to visit China and hold joint discussions on nuclear safety regulatory matters; and

b. The Chinese side will invite U.S. nuclear safety experts to China to give lectures and hold joint discussions on nuclear safety regulatory matters.

3. Temporary assignments of qualified nuclear safety experts by one Party in the other Party's agency will be considered on a case-by-case basis and will, in general, be the subject of separate letters of agreement.

D. Cooperation in Confirmatory Nuclear Safety Research

The execution of joint programs and projects of safety research and development, or those programs and projects under which activities are divided between the Parties, including the use of test facilities and/or computer programs owned by either Party, will be agreed upon on a case-by-case basis and will be the subject of separate, specific letters of agreement which, while they are in effect, are to be appended to the Protocol. Each Party, based on its own research, will transmit immediately to the other Party information of which it becomes aware concerning research results known to have urgent safety implications for nuclear facilities operating in the country of the other Party.

E. Other Technical Advice and Assistance

To the extent that the documents and other technical assistance provided by the USNRC are not adequate to meet the needs of the NNSA for technical advice, the Parties will consult on the best means for meeting such needs.

To the extent possible, the NNSA will make every effort to assist the USNRC in meeting its requests for information on nuclear regulatory activities, or the Parties will consult on the best means for meeting such needs. This may include inviting USNRC nuclear safety experts to accompany/observe NNSA inspectors on operating reactor or reactor construction inspections in China.

ARTICLE 2
Administration

A. The exchange of information under this Protocol will be accomplished through letters, reports, and other documents, and by visits and meetings arranged in advance on a case-by-case basis. Meetings will be held at such times as mutually agreed to review the exchange of information and cooperation under this Protocol, to recommend revisions to the provisions of the Protocol, and to discuss topics coming within the scope of the cooperation. The time, place, and agenda for such meetings will be agreed upon in advance. The terms of the visits which take place under the Protocol, including their schedules, will have the prior approval of the administrators referred to in paragraph 2.B.

B. An administrator will be designated by each Party to coordinate its participation in the overall exchange under this Protocol. The administrators will be the recipients of all documents transmitted under the exchange, including copies of all letters, unless otherwise agreed. Within the terms of the exchange, the administrators will be responsible for developing the scope of the exchange, including agreement on the designation of the nuclear energy facilities subject to the exchange, and on specific documents and standards to be exchanged. One or more technical coordinators may be appointed as direct contacts for specific disciplinary areas. These technical coordinators will assure that both administrators receive copies of all transmittals. These detailed arrangements are intended to assure, among other things, that a reasonably balanced exchange giving access to equivalent available information is achieved and maintained.

C. The administrators will determine the number of copies to be provided of the documents exchanged. Each document will be accompanied by an abstract in English, 250 words or less, describing its scope and content.

D. Recognizing that some information of the type covered in this Protocol is not available within the agencies which are Parties to this Protocol, but is available from other agencies of the governments of the Parties, each Party will assist the other to the maximum extent possible by organizing visits and directing inquiries concerning such information to appropriate agencies of the government concerned. The foregoing will not constitute a commitment of other agencies to furnish such information or to receive such visitors.

ARTICLE 3
Information Exchange and Use

Exchanges of information and technology undertaken in connection with these cooperative efforts will be limited to those which are useful in the development of a nuclear safety regulatory program. Neither Party is required to take any action under this Protocol which would be inconsistent with that Parry's applicable domestic laws and regulations. No nuclear information related to proliferation-sensitive technologies will be exchanged. The exchange and use of information under this Protocol are further governed by the terms specified in Addendum A, "Exchange and Use of Information", attached hereto and made an integral part of this Protocol.

ARTICLE 4
Intellectual Property Rights

This Protocol will be subject to the Agreement and Annex on the protection of intellectual property described in the IPR Annex, attached hereto and made an integral part of this document.

ARTICLE 5

Implementation of this Protocol will be subject to the availability of appropriated funds and the budgetary approval of each Party. The payment of costs will be decided by mutual written agreement on a case-by-case basis. In principle, the sharing of costs between the Parties will be decided according to the extent of the benefit received by each Party.

ARTICLE 6

Any dispute or questions between the Parties concerning the interpretation or application of this Protocol arising during its term will be settled by mutual agreement of the Parties.

ARTICLE 7

The application or use of any information exchanged or transferred between the Parties under this Protocol will be the responsibility of the receiving Party, and the transmitting Party does not warrant the suitability of such information for any particular use or application.

ARTICLE 8

A. This Protocol will enter into force upon signature, and, subject to paragraph B of this section, will remain in force for a five-year period or for the duration of the Agreement, whichever is shorter. It may be amended or extended by mutual written agreement. The April 23, 2004 Protocol will be superseded upon entry into force of this Protocol.

B. This Protocol may be terminated at any time at the discretion of either Party upon at least six months' advance notification in writing by the Party seeking to terminate the Protocol.

C. All information protected by provisions of this Protocol as proprietary or other confidential or privileged information will remain so protected for the duration of this Protocol and after this Protocol has expired or been terminated, unless otherwise specifically agreed by the Parties in writing.

D. The termination of this Protocol will not affect the validity or duration of specific activities being undertaken hereunder.

DONE at Beijing this 7th day of January 2008, in duplicate, in the English and Chinese languages, both texts being equally authentic.

FOR THE NUCLEAR REGULATORY COMMISSION OF THE UNITED STATES OF AMERICA:

[Signature]

Dale E. Klein, Chairman

FOR THE NATIONAL NUCLEAR SAFETY ADMINISTRATION OF THE PEOPLE'S REPUBLIC OF CHINA:

[Signature]

LI Ganjie, Administrator

ADDENDUM A
EXCHANGE AND USE OF INFORMATION

Pursuant to Article 3 of this Protocol:

A. General

The Parties support the widest possible dissemination of information provided, created or exchanged under this Protocol, subject to the requirements of each Party's national laws, regulations and policies and the need to protect proprietary and other sensitive/confidential or privileged information, and subject to the provisions of the Intellectual Property Addendum, hereby incorporated into this Protocol.

B. Definitions

For the purposes of this Protocol:

1. The term "information" means nuclear energy-related regulatory, safety, safeguards, waste management, scientific, or technical data, including information on results or methods of assessment, research, and any other knowledge provided, created or exchanged under this Protocol.

2. The term "proprietary information" means information provided, created or exchanged under this Protocol which contains trade secrets or other privileged or sensitive commercial information (such that the person having the information may derive a commercial benefit from it or may have a commercial advantage over those who do not have it), and such information may only include information which:

   a. has been held in confidence by its owner;

   b. is of a type which is customarily held in confidence by its owner;

   c. has not been transmitted by the owner to other entities (including the receiving Party), except on the basis that it be held in confidence;

   d. is not otherwise available to the receiving Party from another source without restrictions on its further dissemination; and

   e. is not already in the possession of the receiving Party.

3. The term "other confidential or privileged information" means non-classified information, other than "proprietary information," which has been transmitted and received in confidence under this Protocol and is protected from public disclosure under the laws, regulations, or policies of the Party providing the information, or is otherwise restricted by the provider.

C. Marking Procedures for Documentary Proprietary Information

A Party receiving documentary proprietary information pursuant to this Protocol will respect the privileged nature thereof, provided such proprietary information is clearly marked with the following (or substantially similar) restrictive legend:

> This document contains proprietary information furnished in confidence under a Protocol dated *January 07, 2008* between the Nuclear Regulatory Commission of the United States of America and the National Nuclear Safety Administration of the People's Republic of China and will not be disseminated outside these organizations, their consultants, contractors and licensees, and concerned departments and agencies of the Government of the United States and the Government of China without the prior approval of (name of the transmitting Party). This notice will be marked on each page of any reproduction hereof, in whole or in part. These limitations will automatically terminate when this information is disclosed by the owner without restrictions.

This restrictive legend will be respected by the Parties to this Protocol. Proprietary information bearing this restrictive legend shall not be made public or otherwise disseminated in any manner unspecified or contrary to the terms of this Protocol without prior written consent of the transmitting Party. Proprietary information bearing this restrictive legend shall not be used by the receiving Party or its contractors and consultants for any commercial purposes without the prior written consent of the transmitting Party.

D. Dissemination of Documentary Proprietary Information

1. In general, proprietary information received under this Protocol may be disseminated by the receiving Party without prior consent to persons within or employed by the receiving Party, and to concerned government departments and government agencies in the country of the receiving Party, provided:

a. such dissemination is made on a case-by-case basis to persons or departments and agencies having a legitimate need for the proprietary information; and

b. such proprietary information shall bear the restrictive legend appearing in Section C of this Addendum.

2. Proprietary information received under this Protocol may be disseminated by the receiving Party without prior consent [of the transmitting party] to contractors and consultants of the receiving Party located within the geographical limits of that Party's territory, provided

a. that the proprietary information is used by such contractors and consultants only for work within the scope of their contracts with the receiving Party relating to the subject matter of the proprietary information, and shall not be used by such contractors and consultants for any other private commercial purposes; and

b. that such dissemination is made on a case-by-case basis to contractors and consultants having a legitimate need for the proprietary information and who have executed a non-disclosure agreement; and

c. that such proprietary information shall bear the restrictive legend appearing in paragraph C of this Addendum.

3. With the prior written consent of the Party furnishing proprietary information under this Protocol, the receiving Party may disseminate such proprietary information more widely than otherwise permitted under the terms set forth in this Protocol. The Parties will endeavor to grant such approval to the extent permitted by their respective national laws, regulations and policies, provided

a. that the entities receiving proprietary information under paragraph D.3 of Addendum A of this Protocol, including domestic organizations permitted or licensed by the receiving Party to construct or operate nuclear production or utilization facilities, or to use nuclear materials and radiation sources, have a legitimate need for the proprietary information and have executed a non-disclosure agreement; and

b. that the entities receiving proprietary information under paragraph D. 3 of Addendum A of this Protocol, including domestic organizations permitted or licensed by the receiving Party to construct or operate nuclear production or utilization facilities, shall not use such proprietary information for any private commercial purposes; and

c. that those entities receiving proprietary information under paragraph D. 3 of Addendum A of this Protocol, that are domestic organizations permitted or licensed by the receiving Party, agree to use the proprietary information only for activities carried out under or within the terms of their specific permit or license.

E. Marking Procedures for Other Confidential or Privileged Information of a Documentary Nature

A Party receiving under this Protocol other confidential or privileged information will respect its confidential nature, provided such information is clearly marked so as to indicate its confidential or privileged nature and is accompanied by a statement indicating

1. that the information is protected from public disclosure by the government of the transmitting Party, and
2. that the information is transmitted under the condition that it be maintained in confidence.

F. Dissemination of Other Confidential or Privileged Information of a Documentary Nature

Other confidential or privileged information may be disseminated in the same manner as that set forth in paragraph D., "Dissemination of Documentary Proprietary Information."

G. Non-Documentary Proprietary or Other Confidential or Privileged Information

Non-documentary proprietary or other confidential or privileged information provided in seminars and other meetings arranged under this Protocol, or information arising from attachments of staff, use of facilities, or joint projects, will be treated by the Parties according to the principles specified for documentary information in this Protocol; provided, however, that the Party communicating such proprietary or other confidential or privileged information has placed the recipient on notice as to the character of the information communicated.

H. Consultation

If, for any reason, one of the Parties becomes aware that it will be, or may reasonably be expected to become, unable to meet the non-dissemination provisions of Addendum A to this Protocol, it will immediately inform the other Party. The Parties will thereafter consult to define an appropriate course of action.

I. Other

Nothing contained in this Protocol will preclude a Party from using or disseminating information received without restriction by a Party from sources outside of this Protocol.

INTELLECTUAL PROPERTY ADDENDUM

Pursuant to Article 4 of this Arrangement:

> The Parties shall ensure adequate and effective protection of intellectual property created or furnished under this Arrangement and relevant implementing arrangements. The Parties agree to notify one another in a timely fashion of any inventions or copyrighted works arising under this Arrangement and to seek protection for such intellectual property in a timely fashion. Rights to such intellectual property shall be allocated as provided in this Addendum.

I. SCOPE

1. This Addendum is applicable to all cooperative activities undertaken pursuant to this Arrangement, except as otherwise specifically agreed by the Parties or their designees.

2. For purposes of this Arrangement, "intellectual property" shall mean the subject matter listed in Article 2 of the Convention Establishing the World Intellectual Property Organization, done at Stockholm, July 14, 1967, and may include other subject matter as agreed by the Parties.

3. This Addendum addresses the allocation of rights, interests, and royalties between the Parties. Each Party shall ensure that the other Party can obtain rights to intellectual property allocated in accordance with this Addendum by obtaining those rights from its own participants through contracts or other legal means, if necessary. This Addendum does not otherwise alter or prejudice the allocation between a Party and its nationals, which shall be determined by that Party's laws and practices.

4. Disputes concerning intellectual property arising under this Arrangement should be resolved through discussions between the concerned participating institutions or, if necessary, the Parties or their designees. Upon mutual agreement of the Parties, a dispute shall be submitted to an arbitral tribunal for binding arbitration in accordance with the applicable rules of international law. Unless the Parties or their designees agree otherwise in writing, the arbitration rules of the United Nations Commission on International Trade Law (UNCITRAL) shall govern.

5. Termination or expiration of this Arrangement shall not affect rights or obligations under this Addendum.

II. ALLOCATION OF RIGHTS

1. Each Party shall be entitled to a non-exclusive, irrevocable, royalty-free license in all countries to translate, reproduce, and publicly distribute scientific and technical journal articles, reports, and books directly arising from cooperation under this Arrangement. All publicly distributed copies of copyrighted work prepared under this provision shall indicate the names of the authors of the work unless an author explicitly declines to be named.

2. Rights to all forms of intellectual property, other than those rights described in Section II.1., above, shall be allocated as follows:

   a. Visiting researchers, for example, scientists visiting primarily in furtherance of their education, shall receive intellectual property rights under the policies of the host institution. In addition, each visiting researcher named as an inventor shall be entitled to share in a portion of any royalties earned by the host institution from the licensing of such intellectual property.

   b. (1). For intellectual property created during joint research, for example, when the Parties, participating institutions, or participating personnel have agreed in advance on the scope of work, each Party shall be entitled to obtain all rights and interests in its own country. Rights and interests in third countries will be determined in implementing arrangements. If research is not designated as "joint research," rights to intellectual property arising from the research will be allocated in accordance with paragraph II.2.a, above. In addition, each person named as an inventor shall be entitled to share in a portion of any royalties earned by either institution from the licensing of the property.

(2). Notwithstanding paragraph II.2.b. (1), above, if a type of intellectual property is available under the laws of one Party but not of the other Party, the Party whose laws provide for this type of protection shall be entitled to all rights and interests worldwide. Persons named as inventors of the property shall nonetheless be entitled to royalties as provided in paragraph II.2.b. (1), above.

III. BUSINESS CONFIDENTIAL

In the event that information identified in a timely fashion as business-confidential is furnished or created under this Arrangement, each Party and its participants shall protect such information in accordance with applicable laws, regulations, and administrative practices. Information may be identified as "business-confidential" if a person having the information may derive an economic benefit from it or may obtain a competitive advantage over those who do not have it, the information is not generally known or publicly available from other sources, and the owner has not previously made the information available without imposing in a timely manner an obligation to keep it confidential.

STATE DEPARTMENT DOCUMENT NUMBER: 08-24

AGREEMENT BETWEEN THE UNITED STATES OF AMERICA AND THE REPUBLIC OF MALTA CONCERNING COOPERATION TO SUPPRESS ILLICIT TRAFFIC IN NARCOTIC DRUGS AND PSYCHOTROPIC SUBSTANCES BY SEA

SIGNED AT VALLETTA, JUNE 16, 2004
ENTERED INTO FORCE JANUARY 24, 2008

CTIA DOCUMENT NUMBER: 13393.000

The Government of the United States of America and the Government of the Republic of Malta (hereinafter, "the Parties");

Bearing in mind the special nature of the problem of illicit maritime drug traffic;

Having regard to the urgent need for international cooperation in suppressing illicit maritime drug traffic, which is recognized in the 1961 Single Convention on Narcotic Drugs and its 1972 Protocol, in the 1971 Convention on Psychotropic Substances, in the 1988 United Nations Convention Against Illicit Traffic in Narcotic Drugs and Psychotropic Substances (hereafter, "the 1988 Convention"), and in the 1982 United Nations Convention on the Law of the Sea; and

Recalling that Article 17 of the 1988 Convention provides, *inter alia*, that the Parties shall consider entering into bilateral and regional agreements to carry out, or to enhance the effectiveness of, the provisions of Article 17;

Desiring to promote greater cooperation between the Parties, and thereby enhance their effectiveness, in combating illicit traffic in narcotic drugs and psychotropic substances by sea;

Based on the principles of international law, respect for the sovereign equality of States and in full respect of the freedom of navigation;

Have agreed as follows:

Article 1
Purpose and Scope

The Parties shall cooperate in combating illicit traffic by sea in narcotic drugs and psychotropic substances to the fullest extent possible, consistent with available law enforcement resources and priorities related thereto.

Article 2
Definitions

For the purposes of this Agreement, unless the context otherwise requires:

(a) "illicit traffic" has the same meaning as in Article 1(m) of the 1988 Convention.

(b) "international waters" means waters seaward of any State's territorial sea, including the contiguous zone.

(c) "contiguous zone" has the same meaning as in Article 33 of the Law of the Sea Convention.

(d) "law enforcement authorities" means, for the Government of Malta, the Armed Forces of Malta, and for the Government of the United States of America, the United States Coast Guard.

(e) "law enforcement officials" means, for the Government of Malta, the Armed Forces of Malta, the Malta Police Force and the Department of Customs, and for the Government of the United States of America, uniformed members of the United States Coast Guard who may be accompanied by other authorized personnel.

(f) "law enforcement vessels" means warships or other ships of the Parties, or of third States as may be agreed by the Parties, aboard which law enforcement officials are embarked, clearly marked and identifiable as being on government non-commercial service and authorized to that effect, including any boat or aircraft embarked on such ships.

(g) "suspect vessel" means a vessel, claiming the nationality of one of the Parties, used for commercial or private purposes in respect of which there are reasonable grounds to suspect it is engaged in illicit traffic in narcotic drugs and psychotropic substances.

Article 3
Suspect Vessels

Operations to suppress illicit traffic in narcotic drugs and psychotropic substances pursuant to this Agreement shall be carried out only against suspect vessels and vessels without nationality.

Article 4
Operations in and over National Waters

This Agreement does not authorize the conduct of operations to suppress illicit traffic in narcotic drugs or psychotropic substances by one Party in and over the waters of the other Party.

Article 5
Operations in International Waters

1. Authority to Board Suspect Vessels. Whenever the law enforcement officials of one Party ("the requesting Party") encounter a suspect vessel claiming the nationality of the other Party ("the requested Party") located in international waters, the requesting Party may request that the law enforcement authority of the requested Party:

(a) confirm the claim of nationality of the requested Party; and

(b) if such claim is confirmed:

(i) authorize the boarding and search of the suspect vessel, cargo and the persons found on board by law enforcement officials of the requesting Party; and

(ii) if evidence of illicit traffic in narcotic drugs and psychotropic substances is found, authorize the law enforcement officials of the requesting Party to detain the vessel, cargo and persons on board pending instructions from the law enforcement authorities of the requested Party as to the exercise of jurisdiction in accordance with Article 6 of this Agreement.

2. Content of Requests. Each request should contain the name of the suspect vessel, the basis for the suspicion (including all facts and other information on which the suspicion is based), the geographic position of the vessel, the registration number if available, home port, the port of origin and destination, and any other identifying information. If a request is conveyed orally, the requesting Party shall confirm the request in writing as soon as possible.

3. Responding to Requests

(a) If the nationality is verified, the requested Party may:

(i) decide to conduct the boarding and search with its own law enforcement officials;

(ii) authorize the boarding and search by the law enforcement officials of the requesting Party;

(iii) decide to conduct the boarding and search together with the requesting Party; or

(iv) deny permission to board and search.

(b) The requested Party shall answer requests made for the verification of nationality within four (4) hours of the receipt of such requests.

(c) If the nationality is not verified within the four (4) hours, the requested Party may:

(i) nevertheless authorize the boarding and search by the law enforcement officials of the requesting Party; or

(ii) refute the claim of the suspect vessel to its nationality.

(d) If there is no acknowledgement or response to a written request pursuant to paragraph 2 from the requested Party within four (4) hours of its receipt of the request, the requesting Party will be deemed to have been authorized to board the suspect vessel for the purpose of inspecting the vessel's documents, questioning the persons on board, and searching the vessel to determine if it is engaged in illicit traffic.

4. Right of Visit. Notwithstanding the foregoing paragraphs of this Article, this Agreement authorizes the law enforcement officials of one Party ("the first Party") to board suspect vessels located in international waters claiming nationality in the other Party but that are not flying the flag of the other Party, are not displaying any marks of its registration or nationality, and claiming to have no documentation on board the vessel, for the purpose of locating and examining the vessel's documentation. If documentation or other physical evidence of nationality is located, then the foregoing paragraphs of this Article apply.

5. Use of Force. The authorization to board, search and detain includes the authority to use such force as may be necessary in accordance with Article 10 of this Agreement.

6. Shipboarding Otherwise in accordance with International Law. Except as expressly provided herein, this Agreement does not apply to or limit boardings of vessels, conducted by either Party in accordance with international law in international waters, whether based, *inter alia*, on the right of visit, the rendering of assistance to persons, vessels, and property in distress or peril, the consent of the vessel master, or an authorization from the flag State to take law enforcement action.

Article 6
Jurisdiction over Detained Vessels

1. Limitations. Neither Party shall undertake the exercise of jurisdiction and performance of functions in the territory of the other Party.

2. Waiver of Right. In all cases arising pursuant to this Agreement concerning vessels having the nationality of a Party in international waters, that Party ("the first Party") shall have the right to exercise jurisdiction over a detained vessel, cargo and/or persons on board (including seizure, forfeiture, arrest, and prosecution), provided, however, the first Party may, subject to its Constitution and laws, waive its right to exercise jurisdiction and authorize the enforcement of the other Party's law against the vessel, cargo and/or persons on board.

3. Contiguous Zone. In cases arising in the contiguous zone of a Party, not involving suspect vessels fleeing from the waters of that Party or suspect vessels having the nationality of that Party, in which both Parties have the authority to exercise jurisdiction to prosecute, the Party which conducts the boarding and search shall have the right to exercise jurisdiction.

4. Requests to Waive Jurisdiction. If the evidence so warrants, the other Party may request that the first Party waive jurisdiction.

5. Instructions as to the exercise of jurisdiction pursuant to this Agreement shall be given without delay.

6. Form of Waiver. A waiver of jurisdiction may be granted verbally, but as soon as possible, it shall be recorded in a written note from the competent authority and be processed through the diplomatic authorities, without prejudice to the immediate exercise of jurisdiction over the suspect vessel by the other Party.

Article 7
Points of Contact

Each Party shall identify to the other Party, and keep current, the points of contact for communicating with its national authorities competent to receive and act at any time on requests under Article 5 for verification of nationality and authority to board, search and detain suspect vessels, and for instructions as to the exercise of jurisdiction under Article 6, and to receive and act on notifications under Article 8, and to respond to requests for technical assistance under Article 13, in addition to any other communication necessary for the implementation of this Agreement.

Article 8
Notification of Results of Shipboardings and Actions Taken

1. Notification of Results. Each Party shall promptly, and in any case not later than 48 hours, notify the other Party of the results of any boarding and search of the vessels of the other Party conducted pursuant to this Agreement.

2. Status Reports. Each Party, consistent with its procedures, shall report in a timely manner at least every month to the other Party on the status of all investigations, prosecutions and judicial proceedings resulting from enforcement action taken pursuant to this Agreement where evidence of illicit traffic was found.

Article 9
Conduct of Law Enforcement Officials

1. Compliance with Law and Practices. Each Party shall ensure that its law enforcement officials, when conducting boarding and search activities pursuant to this Agreement, act in accordance with its applicable national laws and policies and with international law and accepted international practices.

2. Boarding and Search Teams

a. Boardings and searches pursuant to this Agreement shall be carried out by law enforcement officials from law enforcement vessels or aircraft of the Parties and from such vessels and aircraft of other States, according to arrangements between the Party conducting the operation and the State providing the vessel or aircraft.

b. When conducting boardings and searches law enforcement officials may carry standard law enforcement small arms.

c. While carrying out boarding and search activities pursuant to this Agreement, the Parties shall take due account of the need not to endanger the safety of life at sea, the security of the suspect vessel and its cargo, or to prejudice the commercial and legal interests of the flag State or any other interested State; and shall observe the norms of courtesy, respect and consideration for the persons on board the suspect vessel.

d. Law enforcement vessels of a Party operating with the authorization of the other Party pursuant to this Agreement shall, during such operations, also fly, in the case of the United States of America, the Merchant Flag of Malta, and in the case of Malta, the United States Coast Guard ensign.

Article 10
Use of Force

1. Rules. All uses of force by a Party pursuant to this Agreement shall be in strict accordance with applicable laws and policies of that Party and shall in all cases be that force reasonably necessary under the circumstances.

2. Self-Defense. Nothing in this Agreement shall impair the exercise of the inherent right of self-defense by law enforcement or other officials of the Parties.

Article 11
Exchange and Knowledge of Laws and Policies of the Parties

1. Exchange of Information. To facilitate implementation of this Agreement, each Party shall ensure that the other Party is fully informed of its respective applicable laws and policies, particularly those pertaining to the use of force.

2. Ensuring Knowledge. Each Party shall ensure that all of its law enforcement officials acting pursuant to this Agreement are knowledgeable of the applicable laws and policies of both Parties.

Article 12
Disposal of Seized Property

1. Disposal of Property. Assets seized in consequence of any operation undertaken pursuant to this Agreement shall be disposed of in accordance with the laws of the Party exercising jurisdiction in accordance with Article 6 of this Agreement.

2. The seizing Party may transfer in accordance with its laws forfeited assets or proceeds of their sale to the flag State Party after deducting therefrom all expenses directly and reasonably connected with the seizure and disposal and any share thereof which any Party may in accordance with its legislation be entitled to.

Article 13
Technical Assistance

The law enforcement authority of one Party (the "first Party") may request, and the law enforcement authority of the other Party may authorize, law enforcement officials of the other Party to provide technical assistance, such as specialized assistance in the conduct of search of suspect vessels, to law enforcement officials of the first Party for the boarding and search of suspect vessels located in the territory or waters of the first Party.

Article 14
Consultations and Dispute Settlement

1. Consultations. In case a question arises in connection with implementation of this Agreement, either Party may request consultations with the other Party to resolve the matter.

2. Dispute Settlement. The Parties undertake to settle by consultation any disputes that arise from the implementation of this Agreement.

Article 15
Claims

1. Examination of Claims. Any claim for damages, injury or loss resulting from an operation carried out under this Agreement shall be examined by the Party whose authorities conducted the operation.

2. Resolution of Claims. If responsibility is established, the claim shall be resolved in favor of the claimant by that Party, in accordance with the domestic law of that Party, and in a manner consistent with international law, including paragraph 3 of Article 110 of the Law of the Sea Convention.

3. No Waiver of Other Rights. Neither Party thereby waives any rights it may have under international law to raise a claim with the other Party through diplomatic channels.

Article 16
Miscellaneous Provisions

Nothing in this Agreement:

(a) precludes the Parties from otherwise agreeing on operations or other forms of cooperation to suppress illicit traffic;

(b) is intended to alter the rights and privileges due any individual in any legal proceeding;

(c) shall be construed as creating any private right of action for any individual or entity;

(d) prejudices in any manner the positions of either Party regarding the international law of the sea.

Article 17
Entry into Force

This Agreement shall enter into force upon exchange of notes indicating that the necessary internal procedures of each Party have been completed.

Article 18
Termination

1. Notification. This Agreement may be terminated at any time by either Party upon written notification to the other Party through the diplomatic channel.

2. Effective Date. Such termination shall take effect 90 days from the date of notification.

Article 19
Continuation of Actions Taken

This Agreement shall continue to apply after termination with respect to any administrative or judicial proceedings arising out of actions taken pursuant to this Arrangement.

IN WITNESS WHEREOF, the undersigned, being duly authorized by their respective Governments, have signed this Agreement.

DONE AT VALLETTA, this 16 day of June, TWO THOUSAND AND FOUR.

[Signature]

FOR THE GOVERNMENT OF THE UNITED STATES OF AMERICA:

[Signature]

FOR THE GOVERNMENT OF THE REPUBLIC OF MALTA:

STATE DEPARTMENT DOCUMENT NUMBER: 08-25

MEMORANDUM OF UNDERSTANDING BETWEEN THE UNITED STATES OF AMERICA DEPARTMENT OF DEFENSE AND THE MINISTRY OF DEFENCE OF THE UNITED KINGDOM OF GREAT BRITAIN AND NORTHERN IRELAND REGARDING THE ASSIGNMENT OF AN OPERATIONAL LOGISTICS LIAISON OFFICER TO THE UNITED STATES TRANSPORTATION COMMAND, WITH ANNEXES

SIGNED AT SCOTT AFB (BELLEVILLE), DECEMBER 17, 2007
AND JANUARY 28, 2008
ENTERED INTO FORCE JANUARY 28, 2008

CTIA DOCUMENT NUMBER: 13394.000

INTRODUCTION

The United States Transportation Command (USTRANSCOM), on behalf of the United States Department of Defense (DOD), and the Ministry of Defence of the United Kingdom of Great Britain and Northern Ireland (MODUK) (each referred to individually as a "Defense Organization" and together as the "Defense Organizations"), recognising that the Agreement between the Parties to the North Atlantic Treaty Regarding the Status of Their Forces (NATO SOFA), signed at London on June 19, 1951; the Exchange of Notes constituting an Agreement between the Government of the United States of America and the Government of the United Kingdom of Great Britain and Northern Ireland concerning Defense Cooperation Arrangement done on 27 May 1993, as amended on 1 June 2007 (the Chapeau Defense Agreement); and, the General Security Agreement between the Government of the United States of America and the Government of the United Kingdom dated April 14, 1961, as amended, and including the Security Implementing Arrangement dated January 27, 2003 thereto, will apply to this Memorandum of Understanding, desiring to establish formal liaison between the Defense Organizations in connection with combined logistics efforts, mutually determine the following provisions regarding the assignment of individuals to serve as United Kingdom Operational Logistics Foreign Liaison Officers to USTRANSCOM.

SECTION I
DEFINITIONS

In addition to any terms defined in other provisions of this Memorandum of Understanding (MOU) the following terms will have the following meanings when used herein:

1.1 "*Classified Information*" will mean official information that has been determined to require, in the interests of national security of the owning or releasing government of a Defense

Organization, protection against unauthorized disclosure and that has been so designated by the appropriate classification authority. This will include Classified Information in any form, be it oral, visual, electronic or in the form of materiel.

1.2 "*Contact Officer*" will mean a U.S. Department of Defense (DoD) official designated in writing to oversee and control all contacts, requests for information, consultations, access, and other activities of Foreign Liaison Officers who are assigned to, or are visiting, a DoD component or subordinate organization.

1.3 "*Controlled Unclassified Information*" will mean unclassified information to which access or distribution limitations have been applied in accordance with applicable national laws or regulations, including information that has been declassified but remains controlled. Whether the information is provided or generated under this Memorandum of Understanding or any arrangement thereto, the information will be marked to identify its sensitive nature.

1.4 "*Foreign Liaison Officer*" will mean a military member of the armed forces of the United Kingdom who, upon approval of or certification by the Host Defense Organization or Government, is authorized by the Parent Defense Organization to act as its official representative in connection with programs, projects, or arrangements of interest to the Defense Organizations' Governments.

1.5 "*Host Defense Organization*" will mean the national defense organization to which personnel of the Parent Defense Organization are assigned pursuant to Section III. In this MOU, the Host Defense Organization is USTRANSCOM.

1.6 "*Host Government*" will mean the national government of the Host Defense Organization, as well as all political subdivisions thereof. In this MOU, the Host Government is that of the United States.

1.7 "*International Visits Program (IVPV)*" will mean the program established to process visits by, and assignments of, foreign representatives to DoD and DoD contractor facilities. It is designed to ensure that Classified and Controlled Unclassified Information to be disclosed to foreign nationals has been properly authorized for disclosure to their governments; that the requesting foreign government provides a security assurance on such foreign nationals and their sponsoring organization or firm, when Classified Information is involved in the visit or assignment, and that administrative arrangements (e.g., date, time, and place) for the visit or assignment are provided.

1.8 "*Parent Defense Organization*" will mean the defense organization of the Parent Government that assigns personnel to the Host Defense Organization under Section III. In this MOU, the Parent Defense Organization is MODUK.

1.9 "*Parent Government*" will mean the national government of the Parent Defense Organization, as well as all political subdivisions thereof. In this MOU, the Parent Government is that of the United Kingdom of Great Britain and Northern Ireland.

SECTION II
SCOPE

2.1 During the term of this MOU, subject to the mutual concurrence of the Defense Organizations, the MODUK may assign a military member of the armed forces of the United Kingdom to serve as a Foreign Liaison Officer to USTRANSCOM in accordance with the provisions of this MOU. The military member assigned will act as the official representative to USTRANSCOM in connection with programs, projects, or arrangements of interest to the Parent Government.

2.2 The establishment of each Foreign Liaison Officer position under this MOU will be based on the demonstrated need for, and the mutual benefit of, this position to the Defense Organizations. Once established, each Foreign Liaison Officer position will be subject to periodic review by either

Defense Organization to ensure that the position continues to be required by, and is of mutual benefit to, the Defense Organizations. A Foreign Liaison Officer position no longer required by, or of mutual benefit to, either Defense Organization will be subject to elimination.

2.3 Commencement of such a tour of duty will be subject to any requirements that may be imposed by USTRANSCOM or the United States Government regarding formal certification by or approval of Foreign Liaison Officers. Foreign Liaison Officers to be assigned by MODUK to locations in the United States will be requested pursuant to the IVP, as defined in Paragraph 1.7 of this MOU.

2.4 Unless otherwise mutually determined, the normal tour of duty for a Foreign Liaison Officer will be two (2) years.

2.5 At the discretion of the MODUK, the individual occupying the Foreign Liaison Officer position established pursuant to this MOU may concurrently occupy a position on the Defence Staff of the Embassy of the United Kingdom of Great Britain and Northern Ireland, located in Washington D.C. In the event a conflict should arise between the demands of the Foreign Liaison Officer position and that of the Defence Staff position, the MODUK will decide which position has priority.

SECTION III
DUTIES AND ACTIVITIES

3.1 The Foreign Liaison Officer will not perform duties reserved by the laws or regulations of the Host Government to officers or employees of the Host Government, nor will the Foreign Liaison Officer provide any labor or services to the Host Government or any of its agencies, including USTRANSCOM.

3.2 The Foreign Liaison Officer will comply with all applicable Host Government policies, procedures, laws and regulations. The USTRANSCOM will assign a Contact Officer to provide guidance to the Foreign Liaison Officer concerning policies, procedures, laws and regulations of the Host Government, and to arrange for activities consistent with such requirements and the purposes of this MOU.

3.3 The Foreign Liaison Officer may request access to USTRANSCOM facilities by submitting a request to the Contact Officer. Access to USTRANSCOM facilities may be granted if such access promotes the purposes of this MOU, is consistent with the provisions of any applicable certification or approval issued by the Host Government, and is permitted under the applicable policies, procedures, laws and regulations of the Host Government. Approval of such requests will be at the discretion of USTRANSCOM. Any request for access that exceeds the provisions of an applicable certification or approval will be submitted through the IVP.

3.4 The Foreign Liaison Officer will not be granted access to technical data or other information of USTRANSCOM, whether or not classified, except as authorized by USTRANSCOM, and only to the extent necessary to fulfil the Foreign Liaison Officer's functions hereunder.

3.5 All information to which the Foreign Liaison Officer is granted access while serving as a liaison to USTRANSCOM will be treated as information provided in confidence to the Parent Government, and will not be further released or disclosed by the Foreign Liaison Officer to any other person, firm, organization, or government without the prior written authorization of the Host Government. Disclosure of information to the Foreign Liaison Officer will not be deemed to be a license or authorization to use such information for any purpose other than the purposes described in Section II.

3.6 The Foreign Liaison Officer will not be permitted to participate in exercises, deployments, or civil-military actions, unless expressly authorized in writing to do so by the Defense Organizations.

3.7 USTRANSCOM will not place or keep a Foreign Liaison Officer in duty assignments in which direct hostilities with forces of third states are likely to occur or have commenced, unless approved by the Defense Organizations, in writing.

3.8 The Foreign Liaison Officer will be required to comply with the dress regulations of MODUK but, if requested by USTRANSCOM, will also wear such identification necessary to identify the Foreign Liaison Officer's nationality, rank and status as a Foreign Liaison Officer. The order of dress for any occasion will be that which most closely conforms to the order of dress for the particular organization of USTRANSCOM where the Foreign Liaison Officer is located. The Foreign Liaison Officer will be required to comply with the customs of USTRANSCOM with respect to the wearing of civilian clothing.

3.9 Prior to the commencement of a Foreign Liaison Officer's tour, the MODUK will notify USTRANSCOM of the specific MODUK organization that will exercise operational control over the Foreign Liaison Officer and, if different, the MODUK organization that will provide administrative support to the Foreign Liaison Officer and the Foreign Liaison Officer's dependents.

3.10 At the end of the Foreign Liaison Officer's tour, or as otherwise mutually determined by the Defense Organizations, the MODUK may, subject to the provisions of Section II, replace the Foreign Liaison Officer with another individual who meets the requirements of this MOU.

SECTION IV
FINANCIAL ARRANGEMENTS

4.1 The MODUK will bear all costs and expenses of the Foreign Liaison Officer, including, but not limited to:

4.1.1 All pay and allowances of the Foreign Liaison Officer;

4.1.2 All travel by the Foreign Liaison Officer and the Foreign Liaison Officer's dependents, including, but not limited to, travel to and from the duty location;

4.1.3 All costs and expenses associated with the assignment or placement of the Foreign Liaison Officer and the Foreign Liaison Officer's dependents at the duty location, including travel, office space, clerical support, housing, messing, and medical and dental services, unless specifically stated otherwise in an applicable international agreement;

4.1.4 Compensation for loss of, or damage to, the personal property of the Foreign Liaison Officer or the Foreign Liaison Officer's dependents);

4.1.5 The movement of the household effects of the Foreign Liaison Officer and the Foreign Liaison Officer's dependents;

4.1.6 Preparation and shipment of remains and funeral expenses associated with the death of the Foreign Liaison Officer or the Foreign Liaison Officer's dependent(s);

4.1.7 Formal and informal training of the Foreign Liaison Officer, other than briefings on USTRANSCOM requirements provided by the Contact Officer; and

4.1.8 All expenses in connection with the return of a Foreign Liaison Officer whose assignment has ended or been terminated, along with the Foreign Liaison Officer's dependent(s).

4.2 The USTRANSCOM will provide, upon request and subject to availability, such office facilities, communication services, access to and use of facilities, base operations support, equipment, supplies and services as may be necessary for the Foreign Liaison Officer to fulfil the purposes of this MOU. All costs associated with the provision of such support will be subject to reimbursement by the MODUK to USTRANSCOM, as required by the laws, regulations, or policies of the Host Government.

4.3 The financial arrangements set forth in this MOU will be subject to the authorization and availability of appropriated funds for such purposes.

SECTION V
SECURITY

5.1 The USTRANSCOM will establish the maximum substantive scope and classification levels within which the disclosure of any Classified Information or Controlled Unclassified Information (CUI) to the Foreign Liaison Officer will be permitted. The USTRANSCOM will inform the MODUK of the level of security clearance required to permit the Foreign Liaison Officer access to such information. The Foreign Liaison Officer's access to such information and facilities will be consistent with, and limited by the provisions of his/her assignment, the provisions of this Section and any other agreement between the Defense Organizations or their Governments concerning access to such information and facilities. Further, access will at all times be limited to the minimum required to accomplish the purposes of this MOU, and, at its discretion, USTRANSCOM may prohibit the Foreign Liaison Officer's right of access to any USTRANSCOM facility or require that such access be supervised by USTRANSCOM personnel. Nothing in this MOU shall be construed by the Defense Organizations to authorize unfettered access to Classified Information or CUI residing in USTRANSCOM facilities or computers.

5.2 The MODUK will cause security assurances to be filed, through the United Kingdom Embassy in Washington, D.C stating the security clearances for the Foreign Liaison Officer being assigned. The security assurances will be prepared and forwarded through prescribed channels in compliance with established Host Government procedures. For the United States, the prescribed channels will be the IVP, as defined in paragraph 1.7 of this MOU.

5.3 The MODUK will ensure that each assigned Foreign Liaison Officer is fully cognizant of, and complies with, applicable laws and regulations concerning the protection of proprietary information (such as patents, copyrights, know-how, and trade secrets), Classified Information and CUI disclosed to the Foreign Liaison Officer. This obligation will apply both during and after termination of an assignment as a Foreign Liaison Officer. Prior to taking up duties as a Foreign Liaison Officer, the United Kingdom Foreign Liaison Officer will be required to sign the certification at Annex A. Only individuals who execute the certification will be permitted to serve as Foreign Liaison Officers with USTRANSCOM.

5.4 The MODUK will ensure that the Foreign Liaison Officer, at all times, complies with the security laws, regulations and procedures of the Host Government. Any violation of security procedures by a Foreign Liaison Officer during his or her assignment will be reported to the MODUK for appropriate action. Upon request by USTRANSCOM, the MODUK will remove any Foreign Liaison Officer who violates security laws, regulations, or procedures during his/her assignment.

5.5 All Classified Information made available to the Foreign Liaison Officer by USTRANSCOM will be considered to be Classified Information furnished to the Government of the United Kingdom, and shall be subject to all the provisions and safeguards provided for under the General Security Agreement, as amended and implemented.

5.6 The Foreign Liaison Officer will not take custody of Classified Information or CUI in tangible form (for example, documents or electronic files), except as expressly permitted by the terms of the Host Government certification of the Foreign Liaison Officer (and requested in writing by the Parent Government) for the following situations:

5.6.1 Couriers. The Foreign Liaison Officer may take custody of Classified Information to perform courier functions, when authorized by USTRANSCOM certification for the Foreign Liaison Officer. The Classified Information will be packaged and an acknowledgement for receipt provided for in compliance with Host Government requirements.

5.6.2 On-Site Storage. The Foreign Liaison Officer may be furnished a secure container for the temporary storage of Classified Information, consistent with the terms of the certification, provided the security responsibility for the container and control of the container and its contents remains with USTRANSCOM.

SECTION VI
TECHNICAL AND ADMINISTRATIVE MATTERS

6.1 The Host Government's certification or approval of an individual as a Foreign Liaison Officer will not bestow diplomatic or other special privileges on that individual.

6.2 To the extent authorized by the laws and regulations of the Host Government, and in accordance with Section IV of this MOU, USTRANSCOM may provide such administrative support as is necessary for the Foreign Liaison Officer to fulfil the purposes of this MOU, subject to reimbursement by the MODUK.

6.3 The duties, privileges, and exemptions of the Foreign Liaison Officer and the Foreign Liaison Officer's dependent(s) will be governed by applicable laws and regulations or any applicable international agreements between the Host and Parent Governments.

6.4 If office space is provided to the Foreign Liaison Officer by USTRANSCOM, USTRANSCOM will determine the normal working hours for the Foreign Liaison Officer.

6.5 The MODUK will ensure that USTRANSCOM is informed as far in advance as possible of any absences of the Foreign Liaison Officer.

6.6 The Foreign Liaison Officer and the Foreign Liaison Officer's dependent(s) will be provided care in military medical and dental facilities to the extent permitted by applicable Host Government law, policy, and/or applicable international agreement. Where a reciprocal agreement for health care exists between the Defense Organizations, the access entitlement of the Foreign Liaison Officer and the Foreign Liaison Officer's dependent(s) is specified. For those personnel covered by such an agreement, care in military medical and dental facilities is generally provided free of charge. All Foreign Liaison Officers and their dependent(s) not covered by a reciprocal agreement may be offered health care, on a reimbursable basis, in military facilities. Where military facilities are not available, the Foreign Liaison Officer will be responsible for all medical and dental costs incurred by himself/herself and his/her dependent(s). The MODUK will ensure that the Foreign Liaison Officer and his/her dependent(s) are physically fit prior to the Foreign Liaison Officer's tour of duty. The MODUK will be responsible for familiarizing itself with the medical and dental services available to the Foreign Liaison Officer and his/her dependent(s), and the costs of, and the procedures for, use of such services.

6.7 The Foreign Liaison Officer and the Foreign Liaison Officer's dependent(s) may be accorded the use of military commissaries, exchanges, theaters and similar morale and welfare activities, in accordance with the laws, regulations, and policies of the Host Government and any applicable international agreements or arrangements between the Defense Organizations.

6.8 To the extent permitted by the laws and regulations of the Host Government, and subject to reimbursement by the MODUK, USTRANSCOM may provide, if available, housing and messing facilities for the Foreign Liaison Officer and the Foreign Liaison Officer's dependent(s) on the same basis and priority as for its own personnel of comparable rank and assignment. At locations where housing and messing facilities are not provided by USTRANSCOM, USTRANSCOM will use reasonable efforts to assist the MODUK to locate such facilities for the Foreign Liaison Officer and the Foreign Liaison Officer's dependent(s).

6.9 The MODUK will ensure that the Foreign Liaison Officer and the Foreign Liaison Officer's dependent(s) have all documentation required by the Host Government for entry into, and exit from, the country of the Host Government, under Article III of the NATO SOFA or any other applicable international agreement to which the Host and Parent Government are party.

6.10 The MODUK will ensure that the Foreign Liaison Officer and dependent(s) accompanying the Foreign Liaison Officer in the United States will obtain motor vehicle liability insurance coverage for their private motor vehicles, in accordance with applicable laws, regulations and policies of the Host Government.

SECTION VII
DISCIPLINE AND REMOVAL

7.1 Except as provided in Section 7.2, neither USTRANSCOM nor the armed forces of the Host Government may take disciplinary action against a Foreign Liaison Officer who commits an offense under the military laws or regulations of, or applicable to USTRANSCOM, nor will USTRANSCOM exercise disciplinary powers over the Foreign Liaison Officer's dependent(s). The MODUK, however, will take such administrative or disciplinary action against the Foreign Liaison Officer as may be appropriate under the circumstances, to ensure compliance with this MOU, and the Defense Organizations will cooperate in the investigation of any offenses under the laws or regulations applicable to either Defense Organization.

7.2 The certification or approval of a Foreign Liaison Officer may be withdrawn, modified or curtailed at any time by USTRANSCOM for any reason, including, but not limited to, the violation of the regulations or laws of, or applicable to, USTRANSCOM or the Host Government. In addition, at the request of USTRANSCOM, the Parent Government will remove the Foreign Liaison Officer or a dependent of the Foreign Liaison Officer from the territory of the Host Government. The USTRANSCOM will provide an explanation for its removal request, but a disagreement between the Defense Organizations concerning the sufficiency of USTRANSCOM's reasons will not be grounds to delay the removal of the Foreign Liaison Officer or the dependent(s).

7.3 A Foreign Liaison Officer will not exercise any supervisory or disciplinary authority over military or civilian personnel of USTRANSCOM.

SECTION VIII
CLAIMS

8.1 Claims arising under this MOU will be dealt with in accordance with paragraph 1 of the Chapeau Defense Agreement. The Defense Organizations will share any costs required to be shared under subparagraph 1(b) (ii) of the Chapeau Defense Agreement on the following basis:

> 8.1.1 Where the Defense Organizations mutually determine in respect of any claim that the damage, injury or death can be specifically attributed to one Defense Organization, the cost of handling and settling the claim will be the sole responsibility of that Defense Organization.
>
> 8.1.2 Where it is mutually determined that both Defense Organizations are responsible for the damage, injury or death, the Defense Organizations will enter into consultation to resolve the handling and settling of the claim, with each Defense Organization paying an apportioned share according to their degree of responsibility for the damage, injury or death; and
>
> 8.1.3 Where it is mutually determined that it is not possible to attribute responsibility for the damage, injury or death, the costs of handling and settling the claim will be distributed equally between the Defense Organizations.

SECTION IX
SETTLEMENT OF DISPUTES

9.1 Disputes arising under or relating to this MOU will be resolved only though consultations between the Defense Organizations and will not be referred to third party, national or international tribunal, or to any other forum for settlement.

SECTION X
ENTRY INTO EFFECT, AMENDMENT, DURATION AND TERMINATION

10.1 All responsibilities of the Defense Organizations under this MOU will be subject to national laws and the availability of appropriated funds for such purposes.

10.2 The MODUK will ensure that the Foreign Liaison Officer complies with all responsibilities and restrictions applicable to the Foreign Liaison Officer under this MOU.

10.3 This MOU may be amended by the mutual written concurrence of the Defense Organizations.

10.4 This MOU may be terminated at any time by written concurrence of both Defense Organizations.

10.5 Either Defense Organization may terminate this MOU upon thirty (30) days' written notification to the other Defense Organization.

10.6 The respective benefits and responsibilities of the Defense Organizations under Section V (Security) and Section VIII (Claims) will continue, notwithstanding the termination or expiration of this MOU.

10.7 No later than the effective date of expiration or termination of this MOU, MODUK will remove its Foreign Liaison Officer(s) and such Foreign Liaison Officer's dependents from the territory of the United States and pay any money owed to USTRANSCOM or the Host Government under this MOU. Any costs or expenses for which the MODUK is responsible pursuant to Section IV (Financial Arrangements) of this MOU, but which were not billed in sufficient time to permit payment prior to termination or expiration of this MOU, will be paid promptly after such billing.

10.8 This MOU will enter into effect upon signature by both Defense Organizations. This MOU will remain in force five (5) years and may be extended by written concurrence of the Defense Organizations.

10.9 This MOU consists often (10) Sections and an Annex.

IN WITNESS WHEREOF, the undersigned, being duly authorized, have signed this MOU.

ON BEHALF OF UNITED STATES
TRANSPORTATION COMMAND

____

[Signature]

NORTON A. SCHWARTZ
General, U.S. Air Force Commander

Dated: 28 Jan 08

ON BEHALF OF MINISTRY OF DEFENCE
OF THE UNITED KINGDOM

____

[Signature]

DAVID J. SHOUESMITH
Major General, UK Army Assistant Chief of Defence Staff (Logistic Operations)

Dated: 17 Dec 07

ANNEX A - CERTIFICATION

SECTION I
FOREIGN LIAISON OFFICER
CERTIFICATION

As a representative of the Ministry of Defence of the United Kingdom of Great Britain and Northern Ireland (MODUK) under the auspices of a Foreign Liaison Officer assignment to the United States Transportation Command (USTRANSCOM), I am subject to the jurisdiction of United States Federal, state, and local laws, except as provided by any applicable international agreement(s) to which the United States and the United Kingdom of Great Britain and Northern Ireland are party. I understand that my acceptance of the Foreign Liaison Officer position does not bestow upon me diplomatic or other special privileges.

SECTION II
LIAISON OFFICER
PROVISIONS OF CERTIFICATION

(1) **Responsibilities:** I understand that my activities as the Operational Logistics Foreign Liaison Officer will be limited to the representational responsibilities of my Government and that I am expected to present the views of my Government with regard to the issues in which my government and the United States Government have a mutual interest. I will not perform duties that are reserved by law or regulation to an officer or employee of the United States Government. I will work on issues pertaining to the logistics systems of the Defense Organizations, particularly as they relate to combined operations between the United States and the United Kingdom, and, when requested by USTRANSCOM, provide national operational planning and coordination in support of contingency operations.

(2) **Costs:** I understand that all costs associated with my duties as a Foreign Liaison Officer will be the responsibility of my Government, including, but not limited to, travel, office space, clerical services, housing, messing, and medical and dental services.

(3) **Extensions and Revalidation:** I understand that if my Government desires to request an extension or revalidation of my position beyond the original dates for which I am certified, a new visit request will be submitted not later than 30 days prior to the expiration date of the current Foreign Liaison Officer assignment authorization.

(4) **Contact Officer:** I understand that when the certification process is completed, a Contact Officer will be assigned to sponsor me during my visit to USTRANSCOM. I further understand that I will coordinate, through my Contact Officer, all requests for information, visits, and other business that fall under the provisions of my certification. I also understand that requests for information which are beyond the provisions of my certification will be made through the Office of the Defence Attaché in Washington D.C.

(5) **Other Visits:** I understand that visits to facilities for which the purpose does not directly relate to the provisions of my certification will be made through the Office of the Defence Attaché in Washington D.C.

(6) **Uniform:** I understand that I will wear my national uniform when conducting business at USTRANSCOM or other Department of Defense facilities, unless otherwise directed. I will comply with my United Kingdom service uniform regulations.

(7) **Security:**

a. I understand that access to United States Government information will be limited to that information determined by my Contact Officer to be necessary to fulfil the functions of a Foreign Liaison Officer. I also understand that I may not have access to United States Government computer systems, unless the information accessible by the computer is releasable to my Government in accordance with applicable United States law, regulations and policy.

b. All information to which I may have access during my certification will be treated as information provided in confidence to my Government and will not be further released or disclosed by me to any other person, firm, organization, or government without the prior written authorization of the United States Government.

c. I may be allowed to take possession of classified material in the performance of my duties provided I safeguard this material in accordance with the General Security Arrangement between the Government of the United States and the Government of the United Kingdom, as amended and implemented.

d. I will immediately report to my Contact Officer should I obtain or become knowledgeable of United States Government information for which I am not authorized to have access. I will report to my Contact Officer any incidents of my being offered or provided information that I am not authorized to have.

e. If required, I will display a security badge on my outer clothing so that it is clearly visible. The United States Government will supply this badge.

(8) **Compliance:** I have been briefed on, fully understand, and will comply with the provisions of my certification. Failure to comply may result in termination of my certification. I further understand that the termination of my certification does not preclude further disciplinary action against me.

(9) **Definitions of Terms:** Terms not defined herein will have the definitions ascribed to them in the applicable MOU governing my assignment as a Foreign Liaison Officer.

SECTION III
LIAISON OFFICER - TERMS OF CERTIFICATION

(1) Contact Officer: ________________________ has been assigned as my Contact Officer.

(2) Certification: I am certified to USTRANSCOM and will act as the official representative to USTRANSCOM in connection with programs, projects, or arrangements of interest to the Parent and Host Governments. As such, I am allowed to visit sites, offices, and briefings that support the issues stemming from the logistic systems of the MODUK and USTRANSCOM, and other venues in support of Operational Logistics Foreign Liaison Officer duties with USTRANSCOM.

(3) Travel: I may visit the following locations under the terms of my certification, with the permission of my Contact Officer:

- USTRANSCOM facilities;
- USTRANSCOM subordinate activities;
- Other such locations as my Contact Officer may permit in the future.

SECTION IV
FOREIGN LIAISON OFFICER - CERTIFICATION OF IN-BRIEFING

I, (*NAME OF FOREIGN LIAISON OFFICER*), understand and acknowledge that I have been certified as an Operational Logistics Foreign Liaison Officer to USTRANSCOM, as mutually determined upon between the MODUK and USTRANSCOM. I further acknowledge that I fully understand and have been briefed on: (1) my certification; (2) the conditions of my certification; and (3) the terms of my certification. I further acknowledge that I will comply with the provisions and responsibilities of my certification.

____________________________	____________________
Signature of Foreign Liaison Officer	Signature of Briefer
____________________________	____________________
Name of Foreign Liaison Officer	Name of Briefer
____________________________	____________________
Rank and/or title	Location
____________________________	
Date	

STATE DEPARTMENT DOCUMENT NUMBER: 08-26

PROTOCOL TO AMEND THE AGREEMENT OF SEPTEMBER 17, 1980, BETWEEN THE UNITED STATES OF AMERICA AND THE PEOPLE'S REPUBLIC OF CHINA RELATING TO CIVIL AIR TRANSPORT

SIGNED AT SEATTLE, JULY 9, 2007
ENTERED INTO FORCE FEBRUARY 14, 2008

CTIA DOCUMENT NUMBER: 2525.005

The Government of the United States of America and the Government of the People's Republic of China (hereinafter, the "Parties") desiring to:

Increase travel and tourism between their countries and promote cultural, business and governmental exchanges between them;

Promote their shared, ultimate objective of full liberalization of their bilateral air transport market; and

Facilitate cooperative agreements between their air carriers so as to enable the mutually beneficial development of their aviation industries;

Have agreed to further amend the Agreement between the Government of the United States of America and the Government of the People's Republic of China Relating to Civil Air Transport, signed September 17, 1980, as amended (hereinafter "the Agreement") as follows:

Article 1
Designations

Subparagraphs (d) and (e) of Paragraph (1) of Article 3 of the Agreement shall be deleted in their entirety and replaced by the following:

(d) The People's Republic of China may designate an unlimited number of airlines to operate the agreed services on China Routes A and B. Airlines designated pursuant to this subparagraph may begin services as of August 1, 2007.

(e) The United States may designate one additional airline to operate the agreed services on U.S. Route A or one additional airline to operate the agreed services on U.S. Route B. Airlines designated pursuant to this subparagraph may begin services as of August 1, 2007.

(f) The United States may designate one additional airline to operate the agreed services on U.S. Route A and one additional airline to operate the agreed services on U.S. Route B. Airlines designated pursuant to this subparagraph may begin services as of March 25, 2009.

(g) The United States may designate one additional airline to operate the agreed services on U.S. Route A or one additional airline to operate the agreed services on U.S. Route B. Airlines designated pursuant to this subparagraph may begin services as of March 25, 2010.

(h) The United States may designate an unlimited number of airlines to operate the agreed services on U.S. Route B. Airlines designated pursuant to this subparagraph may begin services as of March 25, 2011.

Article 2
Frequencies

Paragraphs (2) and (3) of Annex V of the Agreement shall be deleted in their entirety and replaced by the following:

(2) In addition to the frequencies available under paragraph (1) above, the designated airlines of each Party shall be entitled to operate weekly frequencies for combination services on Routes I.A or II. A of Annex I on flights to and from Beijing, Shanghai and Guangzhou (hereinafter "China Zone 1") or to and from Fujian, Guangdong (except Guangzhou), Hebei, Jiangsu, Shandong, Tianjin, and Zhejiang (hereinafter "China Zone 2") according to the following schedule:

(a) Effective August 1, 2004:	an additional 14 weekly frequencies
(b) Effective March 25, 2005:	an additional 7 weekly frequencies
(c) Effective March 25, 2006:	an additional 7 weekly frequencies
(d) Effective March 25, 2007:	an additional 7 weekly frequencies
(e) Effective August 1, 2007:	an additional 7 weekly frequencies
(f) Effective March 25, 2008:	an additional 7 weekly frequencies (restricted to nonstop Guangzhou service)
(g) Effective March 25, 2009:	an additional 28 weekly frequencies
(h) Effective March 25, 2010:	an additional 21 weekly frequencies
(f) Effective March 25, 2011:	an additional 14 weekly frequencies
(g) Effective March 25, 2012:	an additional 14 weekly frequencies

Airlines designated by the People's Republic of China may freely convert these frequencies between combination and all-cargo services, and between Route II.A and Route II.B of Annex I. U.S. airlines designated on Route I. A may use these frequencies for combination services only.

(3) In addition to the frequencies available under paragraphs (1) and (2) above, the designated airlines of each Party shall be entitled to operate additional weekly frequencies for all-cargo services on any of the routes provided in Annex I on flights to and from points in China Zone 1 or China Zone 2 according to the following schedule:

(a) Effective August 1, 2004:	an additional 21 weekly frequencies
(b) Effective March 25, 2005:	an additional 18 weekly frequencies
(c) Effective March 25, 2006:	an additional 12 weekly frequencies
(d) Effective March 25, 2007:	an additional 15 weekly frequencies
(e) Effective March 25, 2008:	an additional 15 weekly frequencies

(f) Effective March 25, 2009: an additional 15 weekly frequencies

(g) Effective March 25, 2010: an additional 15 weekly frequencies

(h) Effective March 25, 2011: unlimited frequencies for the airlines designated by each Party

Airlines designated by the People's Republic of China may freely convert the frequencies listed in (a) through (g) between combination and all-cargo services, and between Route II. A and Route II.B of Annex I. U.S. airlines designated for Route I.A may not use these frequencies for combination or passenger services.

Article 3
Special Aviation Area

Annex V of the Agreement shall also be amended by deleting paragraph (6) in its entirety and replacing it with the following:

(6) All U.S. and Chinese airlines may be designated to operate services between the United States and points in China Zone 3 notwithstanding the limitation on the number of designations provided in Article 3 of this Agreement. Such services may be operated without frequency limitations. China Zone 3 consists of the points in the following areas: Anhui, Chongqing, Gansu. Guangxi, Guizhou. Hainan Island, Heilongjiang, Henan, Hubei, Hunan, Inner Mongolia, Jiangxi, Jilin, Liaoning, Ningxia, Qinghai, Shaanxi, Shanxi, Sichuan, Tibet, Xinjiang, and Yunnan. Notwithstanding any other provisions of the Agreement, each Party may choose 5 points in China Zone 3 that its airlines may serve without limitations on the number of designations and without frequency limitations on: 1) services carrying fifth-freedom traffic between such points and intermediate or beyond points in third countries on the specified routes, and 2) combination services carrying fifth-freedom traffic between such points and Japan. Each Party shall notify the other Party of the five points it has selected, with not less than 30 days' written notice. The points selected may, at the discretion of each Party, be changed with not less than 30 days' written notice to the other Party. However, service to a point in China Zone 3 via a point in China Zone 1 or Zone 2 shall be subject to the designation, frequency and Japan fifth-freedom traffic rights limitations set forth in Annex V of this Agreement.

Article 4
Code Sharing

Subparagraphs (1)(b) and (c) of paragraph 5 of Article 11 of the Agreement shall be deleted in their entirety and replaced by the following:

(b) Airlines of each Party may code share with airlines of the same Party, on the specified routes, without an airline of the other Party, according to the following:

(i) Each Party shall be permitted one such code share arrangement as of January 1, 2006; and

(ii) Each Party shall be permitted one additional such code share arrangement as of January 1, 2008; and

(iii) Each Party shall be permitted one additional such code share arrangement as of March 25, 2009; and

(iv) One of the three arrangements under this subparagraph (b) may include two airlines and the other two may include up to three airlines.

(c) If a code share arrangement permitted under subparagraph (b) above is expanded to include an airline of the other Party, such code share arrangement shall be governed by subparagraph (a) above and therefore shall no longer count against the limit of three such arrangements permitted in subparagraph (b).

Article 5
Future Negotiations

The Parties acknowledge that their mutual, ultimate objective is the full liberalization of their bilateral air transport market. The Parties agree to begin no later than March 25, 2010, to negotiate an agreement and timetable for the full liberalization of their bilateral air transport market and to work together to complete the new agreement as soon as possible.

Article 6
Guam and the Northern Mariana Islands

A new Annex VI shall be added to the Agreement and read as follows:

ANNEX VI
Service to Guam and the Northern Mariana Islands

1. Notwithstanding any other provision of this Agreement, the airlines of the People's Republic of China may provide unlimited scheduled air services between the People's Republic of China and Guam and the Northern Mariana Islands.

2. Notwithstanding any other provision of this Agreement, the airlines of the United States may provide unlimited scheduled air services between three points in the People's Republic of China and Guam and the Northern Mariana Islands. The points selected by the United States in the People's Republic of China shall not include either Beijing or Shanghai. The United States shall notify the People's Republic of China in writing of the points it has selected with at least 30 days' advance notice. The points selected may be changed at the discretion of the United States with not less than 30 days' written notice.

3. Air services provided pursuant to paragraphs (1) and (2) of this Annex shall not be subject to limitations as to the number of designations or frequencies.

Article 7
Entry into Force

This Protocol shall enter into force upon completion of an exchange of notes through diplomatic channels confirming that each Party has completed its necessary internal procedures.

IN WITNESS WHEREOF, the undersigned being duly authorized by their respective governments, have signed the present Protocol.

DONE at Seattle, in two originals, this 9th day of July, 2007, in the English and Chinese languages, both texts being equally authentic.

[Signature]

FOR THE GOVERNMENT OF THE UNITED STATES OF AMERICA:

[Signature]

FOR THE GOVERNMENT OF THE PEOPLE'S REPUBLIC OF CHINA:

STATE DEPARTMENT DOCUMENT NUMBER: 08-27

MEMORANDUM OF AGREEMENT (NAT-I-4404) BETWEEN THE FEDERAL AVIATION ADMINISTRATION, DEPARTMENT OF TRANSPORTATION, UNITED STATES OF AMERICA, AND THE UGANDA CIVIL AVIATION AUTHORITY, REPUBLIC OF UGANDA, FOR THE PROVISION OF ASSISTANCE IN DEVELOPING AND MODERNIZING THE CIVIL AVIATION INFRASTRUCTURE OF UGANDA

SIGNED AT WASHINGTON D.C. AND KAMPALA,
NOVEMBER 10 AND 11, 2003
ENTERED INTO FORCE NOVEMBER 11, 2003

CTIA DOCUMENT NUMBER: 12843.000

WHEREAS, the Federal Aviation Administration (FAA) of the Department of Transportation of the United States of America is directed to encourage the development of civil aeronautics and the safety of air commerce, and is authorized to furnish on a reimbursable basis to foreign governments certain technical assistance to that end; and

WHEREAS, the Uganda Civil Aviation Authority (UCAA) of the Republic of Uganda has requested that such technical assistance be provided;

NOW THEREFORE, the FAA and the UCAA, collectively referred to herein as the parties, mutually agree as follows:

ARTICLE I—OBJECTIVE

A. This Memorandum of Agreement (the Agreement) establishes the terms and conditions under which the FAA may provide assistance to the UCAA in developing and modernizing the civil aviation infrastructure in the managerial, operational and technical areas. For this purpose, the FAA shall, subject to the availability of appropriated funds and necessary resources, provide personnel, resources, and related services to assist the UCAA to the extent called for in the annexes and appendices to this Agreement.

B. The FAA's ability to furnish the full scope of technical assistance provided for under this Agreement depends on the use of the systems and equipment in Uganda that are similar to those used by the FAA in the U.S. National Airspace System. To the extent that other systems and equipment are used in Uganda, the FAA may not be able to support those other systems and equipment under this Agreement.

ARTICLE II—IMPLEMENTATION

A. Specific technical assistance in areas of personnel, training, equipment, or services to be provided by the FAA for the UCAA shall be delineated in annexes and appendices to this Agreement. When signed by the parties, such annexes and appendices shall become part of this Agreement. Such annexes and appendices shall contain a description of the technical assistance to be performed by the FAA, the personnel and other resources required to accomplish the tasks, the estimated costs, implementation plans, and duration.

B. The designated office at the FAA for the coordination and management of this Agreement, and where all requests for services under this Agreement should be made, is:

Federal Aviation Administration
Office of International Aviation, AIA-500
800 Independence Ave., S.W.
Washington, D.C. 20591

Telephone: 202-267-8168
Fax: 202-267-5032

ARTICLE III—DESCRIPTION OF SERVICES

A. The technical assistance provided by the FAA at the request of the UCAA may include, but is not necessarily limited to, the following:

1. Providing technical and managerial expertise to assist the UCAA in developing, improving, and operating its civil aviation infrastructure, standards, procedures, policies, training, and equipment;

2. Providing training for UCAA personnel in the United States or in Uganda;

3. Inspecting and calibrating Uganda-owned or -operated equipment and air navigation facilities; and

4. Providing resources, logistical support, and equipment for air navigation facilities.

B. Technical assistance in these and other areas, as mutually agreed to, may be accomplished by appropriate short- and long-term in-country assignments or by other assistance offered by the FAA.

ARTICLE IV—STATUS OF FAA PERSONNEL

The FAA shall assign personnel to perform the services agreed upon in the annex or appendix. The personal assigned may be the employees of the FAA, another U.S. Government agency, or a contractor to the FAA. FAA or other U.S. Government personnel assigned to any activity shall retain their status as U.S. Government employees.

The supervision and administration of the personnel shall be in accordance with the policies and procedures of the FAA as an agency of the U.S. Government. The assigned personnel shall perform at the high level of conduct and technical execution required by the FAA.

ARTICLE V—HOST PARTY SUPPORT

A. The support by the UCAA necessary for accomplishing the FAA technical assistance shall be in accordance with pertinent FAA or other U.S. regulations, rules, or procedures. The UCAA also shall provide such additional support as may be set forth in each annex or appendix.

B. If for any reason the UCAA is unable to provide fully the support specified in each annex or appendix, or if the support provided is not equivalent to that prescribed in pertinent FAA or other U.S. regulations, rules, or procedures, the FAA shall arrange for the support and charge the costs for such support to the UCAA.

ARTICLE VI—FINANCIAL PROVISIONS

A. The UCAA shall reimburse the FAA, in accordance with the provisions set forth in this Agreement and its annexes and appendices, for all costs (including administrative overhead charges) associated with the technical assistance provided by the FAA. In the event of a termination by either party under Article X.B of this Agreement, the UCAA shall pay:

1. All costs incurred by the FAA prior to the date of such termination; and

2. All termination costs incurred by the FAA during the 120-day close-out period.

B. Each annex or appendix shall describe the specific financial arrangements for the technical assistance to be provided. However, all financial arrangements shall be subject to the following:

1. Payment of bills shall be due within sixty (60) days from date of billing. Payments shall be made in U.S. dollars and may be made either by check or electronic funds transfer. Checks shall be drawn on a U.S. bank and forwarded to the FAA at the address specified. Electronic funds transfers shall be credited to the FAA's account as follows: Federal Reserve Bank of New York, 021030004 Account Treas NYC (69001104) FAA. All payments shall include a reference to the assigned agreement number and billing number.

2. In the event that payment is not made within sixty (60) days from the date of billing, U.S. Treasury Department regulations prescribe and require the FAA to assess late payment charges—i.e., interest, penalties, and administrative handling charges—in subsequent billings. These late charges shall be assessed for each additional thirty (30) day period, or portion thereof, that payment is not received. The UCAA shall pay any such late charges.

C. Agreement number NAT-I-4404 has been assigned by the FAA to identify this technical assistance project and shall be referenced in all correspondence and bills related to this Agreement.

ARTICLE VII—LIABILITY

A. The FAA assumes no liability for any claim or loss arising out of advice or other assistance provided or work performed by it under this Agreement or its annexes and appendices, or arising out of any action or decision by the UCAA, or its current or former officers, employees or contractors, in relation to such advice, assistance or work.

B. The UCAA, on behalf of the Government of Uganda, agrees to defend any suit brought in any jurisdiction other than the United States or pay for the defense of any suit brought in the United States against the Government of the United States, the FAA, or any instrumentality or current or former officer or employee of the United States arising out of any advice or other assistance provided or work performed under this Agreement or its annexes and appendices. The UCAA, on behalf of the Government of Uganda, further agrees to hold the United States, the FAA, or any instrumentality or current or former officer or employee of the United States harmless against any claim by the Government of Uganda, or by any agency thereof, or by third persons for personal injury, death, or property damage arising out of any advice or other assistance provided or work performed under this Agreement or its annexes and appendices.

C. Exception: The conduct of an officer or employee of the U.S. that results in personal injury, death, or property damage shall not be considered advice or other assistance provided or work performed under this Agreement for purposes of the obligation to hold the United States, the FAA, or any instrumentality or current or former officer or employee of the United States harmless against any claim by the Government of the Uganda, or by any agency thereof, or by third persons for personal injury, death, or property damage undertaken by the UCAA under Article VII.A above if that conduct is determined to be outside the scope of the officer or employee's employment. Scope of employment shall be determined by the law of the forum, including choice of law rules, if the litigation is brought in a court of the United States; or, if brought in a court outside the United States, according to tie law of the District of Columbia.

ARTICLE VIII—AMENDMENTS

This Agreement or its annexes or appendices may be amended by mutual consent of the parties. The details of any such amendment shall be memorialized by written agreement signed by both parties.

ARTICLE IX—RESOLUTION OF DISAGREEMENTS

Any disagreement regarding the interpretation or application of this Agreement or its annexes and appendices shall be resolved by consultations between the parties and shall not be referred to any international tribunal or third party for settlement.

ARTICLE X—ENTRY INTO FORCE AND TERMINATION

A. This Agreement shall enter into force on the date of the last signature and shall remain in force until terminated. This Agreement supercedes Agreements NAT-I-2405, NAT-I-2405-1, NAT-I-2405-1-1 and NAT-I-2405-1-2.

B. This Agreement or its annexes or appendices may be terminated at any time by either party by providing sixty (60) days notice in writing to the other party. Termination of this Agreement shall not affect existing obligations of the UCAA under Articles IV, VI, VII, and IX. The FAA shall have one hundred and twenty (120) days to close out its activities following termination of this Agreement or its annexes or appendices. Termination of this Agreement also shall terminate all annexes and appendices subsequently concluded by the parties pursuant to this Agreement.

ARTICLE XI—SIGNATURE IN COUNTERPARTS

To facilitate execution, this Agreement or its annexes or appendices maybe executed in as many counterparts as may be required. It shall not be necessary that the signature of or on behalf of each party appear on each counterpart, but it shall be sufficient that the signature of or on behalf of each party appear on one or more of the counterparts. All counterparts shall collectively constitute a single agreement.

ARTICLE XII—AUTHORITY

The FAA and the UCAA agree to the provisions of this Agreement as indicated by the signature of their duly authorized representatives.

FEDERAL AVIATION ADMINISTRATION DEPARTMENT OF TRANSPORTATION UNITED STATES OF AMERICA	UGANDA CIVIL AVIATION AUTHORITY REPUBLIC OF UGANDA
______________________ BY: [Signature] Ava L. Wilkerson	______________________ BY: [Signature] Ambrose Akandonda
TITLE: Director, Office of International Aviation	TITLE: Managing Director/CEO
DATE: November 10, 2003	DATE: 11 Nov. 2003

STATE DEPARTMENT DOCUMENT NUMBER: 08-28

AGREEMENT EXTENDING PROVISIONAL APPLICATION OF THE MARITIME BOUNDARY AGREEMENT OF DECEMBER 16, 1977, AS EXTENDED, BETWEEN THE UNITED STATES OF AMERICA AND THE REPUBLIC OF CUBA

EFFECTED BY EXCHANGE OF NOTES AT WASHINGTON D.C. AND HAVANA, DECEMBER 12, 2005 AND MARCH 30, 2006
ENTERED INTO FORCE MARCH 30, 2006,
WITH EFFECT FROM JANUARY 1, 2006

CTIA DOCUMENT NUMBER: 2677.007

DEPARTMENT OF STATE
WASHINGTON

His Excellency
Christian Blickenstorfer,
Ambassador of the Swiss Confederation.

Excellency:

The Department of State refers the Embassy of Switzerland to its note dated December 16, 2005, forwarding the note of the Ministry of Foreign Relations of Cuba, Office of North American Affairs No. RS/3310 dated December 12, 2005, to the Embassy of Switzerland in Havana, which letter reads as follows:

> "The Ministry of Foreign Relations presents its compliments to the Embassy of Switzerland and, with respect to the Interests Section of the United States of America, has the honor to refer to the Maritime Boundary Agreement Between the Republic of Cuba and the United States of America, signed at Washington, D.C., on December 16, 1977, and the agreement by both governments to apply the terms of said Agreement on a provisional basis from January 1, 1978, for a period of two years, prior to the definitive entry into force of the Agreement, on the date of exchange of the instruments of ratification.
>
> "The Ministry wishes to refer to the subsequent agreements between the Government of the Republic of Cuba and the Government of the United States of America to extend the application this Maritime Boundary Agreement for successive periods of two-year periods, most recently through the agreement of December 16 and December 30, 2003, until December 31, 2005.
>
> "On behalf of the Government of the Republic of Cuba, the Ministry has the honor to propose that the terms of the Maritime Boundary Agreement of December 16, 1977, continue to apply, on a provisional basis, from January 1, 2006, for a two-year period, until such time as its definitive entry into force on the date of exchange of the instruments of ratification.

> "If the proposal of the Ministry of Foreign Affairs is acceptable to the Government of the United States of America, the Ministry proposes that this note and the affirmative reply thereto, through the Interests Section of the United States of America shall constitute an Agreement between the Government of the Republic of Cuba and the Government of the United States of America, which shall enter into force on the date of the reply, and take effect on January 1, 2006.
>
> "The Ministry of Foreign Relations takes this opportunity to extend to the Embassy of Switzerland the renewed assurances of its highest consideration."

The Department of State wishes to inform the Embassy and through it the Cuban Interests Section that the proposal of the Ministry of Foreign Relations of Cuba to continue to apply, on a provisional basis, from January 1, 2006, for a two-year period, the terms of the Maritime Boundary Agreement, until such time as its definitive entry into force on the date of exchange of instruments of ratification, is acceptable to the Government of the United States of America, and that the Ministry's Note and the Department's Note in reply shall constitute an agreement between the Government of the United States of America and the Government of the Republic of Cuba, which enters into force on the date of this note.

For the Secretary of State:

____

[Signature]

EMBASSY OF SWITZERLAND

U.S. Department of State
Attn.: Office of Cuban Affairs
2201 C Street, N.W.
Washington, D.C. 20520

The Embassy of Switzerland presents its compliments to the U.S. Department of State and has the honor to inform that the Cuban Ministry of Foreign Affairs wishes to continue to apply provisionally the Maritime Boundary Agreement between the United States of America and the Republic of Cuba of 1977 for a period of two years starting January 1, 2006.

The Embassy of Switzerland avails itself of this opportunity to renew to the U.S. Department of State the assurances of its highest consideration

Washington, D.C., December 16, 2005.

U.S. Department of State Office
of Language Services Translating
Division

LS No. 01-2006-0074
Spanish/English
TGR/JF

Translation

Republic of Cuba
Ministry of Foreign Relations
Office on North American Affairs

Embassy of Switzerland,
Havana.

No. [Illegible]

The Ministry of Foreign Relations presents its compliments to the Embassy of Switzerland and, with respect to the Interests Section of the United States of America, has the honor to refer to the Maritime Boundary Agreement Between the Republic of Cuba and the United States of America, signed at Washington, D.C., on December 16, 1977, and the agreement by both governments to apply the terms of said Agreement on a provisional basis from January 1, 1978, for a period of two years, prior to the definitive entry into force of the Agreement, on the date of exchange of the instruments of ratification.

The Ministry wishes to refer to the subsequent agreements between the Government of the Republic of Cuba and the Government of die United States of America to extend the application of this Maritime Boundary Agreement for successive two-year periods, most recently through the agreement of December 16 and 30, 2003, until December 31, 2005.

On behalf of the Government of the Republic of Cuba, the Ministry has the honor to propose that the terms of the Maritime Boundary Agreement of December 16, 1977, continue to apply, on a provisional basis, beginning January 1, 2006, for a two-year period, until such time as its definitive entry into force on the date of exchange of the instruments of ratification.

If the proposal of the Ministry of Foreign Affairs is acceptable to the Government of the United States of America, the Ministry proposes that this note and the affirmative reply thereto, through the Interests Section of the United States of America, shall constitute an agreement between the Government of the Republic of Cuba and the Government of the United States of America, which shall enter into force on the date of reply, and take effect on January 1, 2006.

[Complimentary close]

Havana, December 12, 2005
[Initialed]
[Ministry stamp]

STATE DEPARTMENT DOCUMENT NUMBER: 08-29

MEMORANDUM OF UNDERSTANDING AMONG THE UNITED STATES OF AMERICA, THE SWISS CONFEDERATION, AND THE REPUBLIC OF KAZAKHSTAN REGARDING FUNDS TO BE PUT TO USE FOR THE BENEFIT OF POOR CITIZENS OF KAZAKHSTAN, WITH ANNEXES

SIGNED AT WASHINGTON D.C., MAY 2, 2007
ENTERED INTO FORCE MAY 2, 2007

CTIA DOCUMENT NUMBER: 13398.000

WHEREAS, the Government of the United States of America, the Government of the Republic of Kazakhstan, and the Government of the Swiss Confederation (each a "Party" and together the "Parties") are seeking to put certain funds to use for the benefit of poor citizens of Kazakhstan (as described below);

WHEREAS, in and before July 1999, approximately $84 million was held on deposit in the account of Orel Capital Ltd. ("Orel") at Credit Agricole Indosuez ("CAI") in Geneva, Switzerland. Orel was a British Virgin Islands corporation beneficially owned by a Liechtenstein foundation, the sole beneficiaries of which were individuals;

WHEREAS, on or about July 29, 1999, the contents of the Orel account were transferred to an account held in the name of the Treasury of the Ministry of Finance of the Republic of Kazakhstan at Pictet & Cie, Geneva, Switzerland;

WHEREAS, on or about August 16, 1999, the $84 million transferred from the Orel account to the Pictet account was frozen by order of a Swiss examining magistrate;

WHEREAS, on or about April 2, 2003, Indictment 03 Cr. 404 was returned by a federal grand jury in the Southern District of New York charging defendant James H. Giffen with, *inter alia*, violation of the Foreign Corrupt Practices Act ("FCPA"), in violation of 15 U.S.C. § 78dd-2; wire fraud, in violation of 18 U.S.C. § 1343; and money laundering, in violation of 18 U.S.C. §§ 1956 and 1957;

WHEREAS, the Indictment included a criminal forfeiture allegation charging that Giffen should forfeit to the United States pursuant to 18 U.S.C. § 982 all property, real and personal, involved in the money laundering offenses and all property traceable to such property;

WHEREAS, as used herein, the "Funds" include all assets transferred from the Orel account to Account No. 4025 in the Name of the Treasury of the Ministry of Finance of the Republic of Kazakhstan at Pictet & Cie, Geneva, Switzerland, and all interest, income, benefits or other proceeds traceable thereto;

WHEREAS, the Funds have been restrained pursuant to a Mutual Legal Assistance Treaty request by the United States to Switzerland;

WHEREAS, the Government of the Republic of Kazakhstan claims that it is the sole beneficiary of the Funds and that the Funds are its property;

WHEREAS, the Government of the United States asserts that if it were to forfeit the Funds, in keeping with its practice of using forfeited funds, where practicable and not inconsistent with law, to restore forfeited property to victims of the underlying criminal violation or to protect the rights of innocent persons in the interest of justice, it would endeavor to have the Funds used for the benefit of the people of Kazakhstan;

WHEREAS, the Government of the Republic of Kazakhstan asserts that if it were to obtain release of the Funds, it would endeavor to utilize the Funds for the benefit of the people of Kazakhstan;

WHEREAS, the International Bank of Reconstruction and Development (the "World Bank"), at the request of the Governments of the United States of America, the Swiss Confederation, and the Republic of Kazakhstan, has agreed to provide technical assistance and supervision for the administration of the Funds for the benefit of the Kazakh people;

WHEREAS, in furtherance of the relationship between the Governments of the United States of America, the Swiss Confederation, and the Republic of Kazakhstan, the Parties have agreed that the Funds shall be used to benefit the most needy citizens of Kazakhstan, as set forth herein;

NOW, THEREFORE, the Parties hereto agree as follows:

1. Summary of Memorandum of Understanding

This Memorandum of Understanding (MOU) sets forth the terms and conditions by and under which the Parties will consent to release of the Funds.

1.1. Contemporaneous with the signing of this MOU, the Governments of the United States of America and the Republic of Kazakhstan shall execute a Stipulation and Order of Settlement ("Stipulation and Order") (Annex 1 hereto) proposing a resolution of forfeiture allegations of the United States and claims of the Republic of Kazakhstan with respect to the Funds. Within ten business days of the signing of this MOU and the Stipulation and Order, the Government of the United States shall file a civil action in the United States District Court for the Southern District of New York (the "Court") seeking forfeiture of the Funds to the United States (the "Civil Forfeiture Action.") As soon as practicable thereafter and no later than one business day after the filing of the Civil Forfeiture Action, the Government of the United States of America shall file the Stipulation and Order in the same Court. After the provision of notice and the expiration of the period for the filing of claims to the Funds, and provided there is no other timely, valid claim to the Funds, or any portion thereof, that complies with 18 U.S.C. § 983 and all other applicable provisions of law, the United States will request that the Court endorse the Stipulation and Order of Settlement and issue a Final Order (the "Final Order") in the action implementing its terms.

1.2. The Parties acknowledge and agree that prior to the release of the Funds, or any portion thereof, any and all other claims as to the Funds must have been resolved or extinguished and that the Stipulation and Order must be accepted and approved by the Court.

1.3. The release of the Funds, or any portion thereof, is expressly contingent upon the establishment and implementation of three programs to the satisfaction of each Party and" in accordance with this MOU and the Stipulation and Order, including:

(a) a **"BOTA Program,"** for the establishment and administration of projects to benefit poor children in Kazakhstan, as set forth in more detail in Section 3 below. The BOTA program shall be implemented by creation of a non-profit, non-governmental foundation known as the BOTA Foundation. The BOTA Foundation shall be established under the laws of Kazakhstan, and shall be independent of the Government of the Republic of Kazakhstan, its officials, and their personal or business associates. The BOTA Program shall be subject to the monitoring of the Governments of the United States of America and the Swiss Confederation. The administration, management, and expenditures of the BOTA Foundation shall be conducted by a reputable international non-governmental organization serving as the BOTA Program Manager. The World Bank shall supervise and monitor the BOTA Program and the administration and expenditures of the Funds, as set forth in the Service Agreement that appears as Annex 2 hereto.

(b) a **"Public Finance Management Review (PFMR) Program,"** through which the Government of the Republic of Kazakhstan, with the support of the World Bank, shall undertake a programmatic Public Finance Management Review over a period of five years to examine and analyze the budget management process in order to formulate a comprehensive, realistic and strategic plan for improving public financial management in Kazakhstan, as set forth in the Memorandum of Understanding between the World Bank and the Government of the Republic of Kazakhstan annexed hereto as Annex 3, the reports of which shall be provided by the Government of the Republic of Kazakhstan to the other Parties; and

(c) an **"Extractive Industries Transparency Initiative (EITI) Program,"** through which the Government of the Republic of Kazakhstan, with the support of the World Bank, will prepare and implement a comprehensive strategy and action plan to increase transparency over payments and revenues of the extractive industries operating in Kazakhstan (including oil, gas, and mining), as set forth in the Memorandum of Understanding between the World Bank and the Government of the Republic of Kazakhstan annexed hereto as Annex 4, the reports of which shall be provided by the Government of the Republic of Kazakhstan to the other Parties.

1.4. The Parties agree that within nine (9) months of the Effective Date, the Program Manager shall certify to each of the Parties that all necessary steps have been taken to establish the BOTA Foundation and engage a BOTA Program Manager. In addition, by August 31, 2007, the Government of the Republic of Kazakhstan shall provide a report to the other Parties on the progress made in implementation of the PFMR and EITI Programs. If any Party, in its sole discretion, determines that actions taken to constitute the BOTA Program, as described in §§3.2, 3.3, 3.4, 3.5, and 3.6 of this MOU, have not been satisfactorily completed or that the Government of the Republic of Kazakhstan has not made substantial and demonstrable progress in implementation of either the PFMR or EITI Programs, this MOU shall terminate upon written notice from that Party to the other Parties, provided that the time to comply with the conditions set forth may be extended by written agreement of all Parties.

1.5. The Parties acknowledge that at any time during the term of this MOU the respective United States and Swiss Executive Directors of the World Bank may request an oral briefing from the World Bank with respect to the status or progress of the BOTA Program, PFMR Program, or EITI Program.

2. The Funds

2.1. The Parties acknowledge and agree that the Funds shall remain under restraint in Account No. 4025 at Pictet & Cie, Geneva, Switzerland, unless released by unanimous agreement of the Parties in accordance with this MOU and the Final Order entered by the Court, or until adjudicated in further proceedings as provided in the Stipulation and Order.

2.2. The Parties acknowledge and agree that the Funds shall be released to the BOTA Program Manager on behalf of the BOTA Foundation in installments as set forth in the Stipulation and Order. All Funds released shall be utilized for implementation of the BOTA Program in accordance with this MOU and the BOTA Program Operational Manual. At the individual discretion of either the Government of the United States of America or the Swiss Confederation, the release of any installment may be made contingent upon its satisfaction of adequate implementation of any of the programs described in Section 1.3.

2.3. The Government of the Republic of Kazakhstan hereby guarantees continuing and timely financial support for the BOTA Program up to the full amount of the Funds in the event that the Government of the Republic of Kazakhstan withdraws from participation in either the PFMR or EITI Programs or a Party objects to further release of the Funds based upon failure to implement the PFMR or EITI Programs.

2.4. In accordance with terms as set forth in Section 3, the BOTA Program Manager, on behalf of the BOTA Foundation, will make requests to the Parties for release of installments of the Funds for implementation of the BOTA Program. Any such request shall include notice to the World Bank and shall specify how the amounts sought shall be used. No such request shall be granted unless the World Bank provides notice to the Parties that it has no objection to the request. Any redistribution of the Funds among projects or to newly-identified projects must be approved in writing by the World Bank and each of the Parties.

2.5. **Costs**. The Parties agree that each Party shall be responsible for its own costs in undertaking its respective activities under this MOU. The Parties further agree that the World Bank shall receive a service fee for its participation in the BOTA Program based on cost recovery for its services rendered under and as specified in the Service Agreement. Should any monies be necessary for start-up costs of the BOTA Program prior to the release of the first installment of the Funds, such monies will be advanced by the Government of the Republic of Kazakhstan. Any such reasonable costs may be reimbursed by the Program Manager, acting on behalf of the BOTA Foundation, from the first installment of the Funds.

2.6. **Prohibited Uses**. The Parties agree that the Funds shall not be used for payments (a) prohibited by a decision of the United Nations Security Council taken under Chapter VII of the Charter of the United Nations; (b) for which corrupt, fraudulent, collusive or coercive practices were engaged in to receive any of the Funds; (c) that would support any corrupt or fraudulent activities; or (d) to the Government of the Republic of Kazakhstan, its officials, or their personal or business associates. The Parties further agree that in the event of a determination by any of the Parties that this clause has been violated, whether by the BOTA Program Manager, recipients of grants from the Funds or any other natural or legal person, the termination provisions of Section 9 and the return provisions of Section 8.3 shall become applicable in the individual discretion of me Governments of the United States of America or the Swiss Confederation.

3. BOTA Program

3.1. **Scope of the BOTA Program**. Subject to the terms and conditions set forth herein and in the Final Order upon its entry by the Court, the Funds shall be utilized for the preparation, administration, and implementation of the "BOTA Program," which shall constitute a program for the benefit of poor children and youth in Kazakhstan. The BOTA Program shall utilize the Funds for conditional cash payments to Kazakh families, scholarships to Kazakh residents, and grants to local and international NGOs in accordance with the BOTA Program Operational Manual. The Funds will be utilized to support activities aimed at improving child and youth welfare, including: reducing child labor, provision of community-based services to disabled children, shelters for runaway and homeless children, improving child nutrition, promoting and developing family-based care for children deprived of parental care, raising awareness of and decreasing child abuse and violence, reducing juvenile delinquency, expanding youth activities and resource centers, and skills development for school drop-outs, and such other projects as may be determined by the BOTA Board of Supervisors, BOTA Program Manager and the World Bank to be of benefit to poor children and youth of Kazakhstan and their families and enumerated in the BOTA Program Operational Manual.

3.2. **Foundation.** The BOTA Program shall be implemented through the creation of an independent, nongovernmental, nonprofit foundation (the "BOTA Foundation") established to receive and disburse the Funds in accordance with this MOU and constituted under Kazakhstan's Law on Non-Commercial Organizations with the assistance of the World Bank as provided in the Service Agreement. The Parties agree that in order to receive any of the Funds, such a foundation must be a purpose-built organization, founded for purposes of implementing development projects for poor children and youth in Kazakhstan; must have the capacity to undertake the contemplated activities; must be party to the Supervisory Agreement (as set forth below); and must be entirely independent of the Government of the Republic of Kazakhstan, its officials, and their personal or business associates. The Parties further agree that the managerial capacity for the BOTA Foundation must be provided through the BOTA Program Manager as set forth below. The BOTA Foundation shall be established with the intention that it continue to operate as a functioning foundation after the BOTA Program has been completed.

3.3. **Founders.** With the assistance of the World Bank (as set forth in the Service Agreement), the BOTA Foundation shall be established by five founders ("Founders") selected by the unanimous agreement of all Parties. The Founders shall be responsible for coordinating the selection of members of the Board of Supervisors as set forth in Section 3.4, and shall not have governance or managerial responsibilities with regard to the BOTA Foundation. All Parties may nominate candidates to serve as Founders. All candidates must be completely independent of the Government of the Republic of Kazakhstan, its officials, and their personal or business associates. The Founders must be respected community figures and preferably shall be known for their championing of children's causes. The Government of the Republic of Kazakhstan shall have responsibility for notifying individual Founders of their selection.

3.4. **Board of Supervisors.** With the assistance of the World Bank (as set forth in the Service Agreement), the BOTA Foundation shall be governed by a seven-member Board of Supervisors ("Board of Supervisors"). The members of the Board of Supervisors shall be a combination of respected international individuals and Kazakh citizens, preferably known for their championing of children's causes, and must be completely independent of the Government of the Republic of Kazakhstan, its officials, and their personal or business associates. The Governments of the United States of America and the Swiss Confederation, at their option, may each select a member of the Board of Supervisors (and alternates, as appropriate), who may be a representative of their respective governments or other respected individuals (the "Government Supervisors"). The Founders shall propose selection of all other candidates (and alternates, as appropriate) for consideration by the Parties, who may object to or approve any of the Founder-proposed candidates (the "non-Government Supervisors"). The final slate of Board of Supervisors members shall be individually notified of their selection by the Founders. In the event of a vacancy on the Board of Supervisors for a Government Supervisor, the respective Government may select a replacement. In the event of a vacancy on the Board of Supervisors for a non-Government Supervisor, the Founders shall propose a replacement member for consideration by and subject to the approval or objection of each Party. A Government Supervisor may be removed at any time by the Government that selected the Supervisor. Any non-Government Supervisor may be removed at any time upon a joint decision by the Governments of the United States of America and the Swiss Confederation.

3.5. **Constitutive Documents**. With the assistance of the World Bank (as set forth in the Service Agreement), the Board of Supervisors shall prepare the Charter and any other constitutive documents of the BOTA Foundation required for its formation under Kazakh law (the "Constitutive Documents"). The Parties shall be provided opportunity to review the proposed Constitutive Documents, which must be approved by all Parties prior to their adoption. After approval of the Constitutive Documents by all Parties, the Board of Supervisors as a first order of business shall convene to adopt the agreed Constitutive Documents. If the Board of Supervisors desires any changes to the Constitutive Documents, either initially or subsequently during the term of this MOU, they must be approved by all Parties before becoming effective.

3.6. **BOTA Program Manager**. The implementation, administration, management, and expenditures of the BOTA Program shall be conducted by a reputable international non-governmental organization serving as BOTA Program Manager ("Program Manager"), with the assistance of the World Bank.

(a) The specific responsibilities of the Program Manager shall be set forth in a Management Agreement between the BOTA Foundation and the Program Manager. The Management Agreement shall be drafted by the World Bank (as set forth in the Services Agreement), and must be approved by the Board of Supervisors and all Parties before becoming effective. The Management Agreement shall make the Program Manager subject to any obligations addressed to it in this MOU.

(b) **Selection of Program Manager**. The Board of Supervisors with the assistance of the World Bank (as set forth in the Services Agreement) will conduct an open, competitive bidding process to select the Program Manager. The Board of Supervisors, and the Parties then shall select a Program Manager by unanimous agreement. All candidates for Program Manager must be completely independent of the Government of the Republic of Kazakhstan, its officials, and their personal or business associates.

3.7. **Supervisory Agreement**. The relationship between the BOTA Foundation and the World Bank shall be governed by a supervisory agreement to be entered into by the Foundation and the World Bank (the "Supervisory Agreement"). The Supervisory Agreement must be approved by the Parties before signature and effectiveness. Supervisory services to be provided by the World Bank pursuant to the Supervisory Agreement are set forth in the Service Agreement. The Supervisory Agreement shall make the BOTA Foundation, its Founders, and the Board of Supervisors subject to any obligations addressed to them in this MOU.

3.8. **Operational Manual**. The World Bank (as set forth in the Service Agreement) shall prepare the BOTA Program's operational manual (the "Operational Manual"). The Operational Manual must be approved by the Board of Supervisors and each of the Parties before it becomes effective. The Operational Manual will govern the daily operations of each element of the BOTA Program (as specified in Section 3.1 above and the Services Agreement), and will, among other things, set forth the procedures for the award of grants and disbursement of funds. The World Bank, the Board of Supervisors, the Program Manager, and any of the Parties may recommend or request changes to the Operational Manual, either initially or subsequently during the term of this MOU. All requested or recommended changes must be approved in writing by all the Parties and the Board of Supervisors before becoming effective.

3.9. **BOTA Program Operational Account ("Operational Account")**. Funds released to the BOTA Foundation in accordance with Section 3 and the Stipulation and Order shall be deposited into a BOTA Program Operational Account to be established and maintained by the BOTA

Program Manager on behalf of the Foundation and from which the BOTA Program Manager may make payments or disbursements in accordance with the terms of the Operational Manual and this MOU. The Board of Supervisors, the World Bank and the Parties shall at all times have the right to review records of the BOTA Program Operational Account upon request.

3.10. **Accounts and Audits**. The Board of Supervisors and the Program Manager, with the assistance of the World Bank (as set forth in the Service Agreement), shall:

(a) ensure that a financial management system is maintained and financial statements are prepared, in accordance with consistently applied accounting standards acceptable to the World Bank, both in a manner adequate to reflect the operations, resources and expenditures related to the activities funded;

(b) ensure that interim unaudited financial reports for the activities funded by the BOTA Foundation are prepared and furnished to the World Bank and the Parties not later than three months after the end of each six-month period, covering the six-month period, in form and substance satisfactory to the World Bank;

(c) select independent auditors (the "Auditors"), whose appointment must be approved by all Parties, with the World Bank providing terms of reference for the Auditors' engagement and reviewing the short list of candidates on a no objection basis;

(d) have Financial Statements for the activities funded by the BOTA Foundation audited by the Auditors in accordance with consistently applied auditing standards acceptable to the World Bank, to be provided to the World Bank and the Parties not later than six months after the end of the BOTA Program's fiscal year; and

(e) ensure that: (i) all records evidencing expenditures related to activities funded by the Funds are retained until at least five years after the World Bank and Parties have received all the audited Financial Statements covering the Term of this MOU; and (ii) the representatives of the World Bank and the Parties are able to examine such records, and are provided all such information concerning such records as they may from time to time request.

3.11. **Work Plan**. With the assistance of the World Bank (as set forth in the Service Agreement), the BOTA Foundation and Program Manager shall prepare annual work plans for use of the Funds in a manner consistent with this MOU and the Operational Manual. The Foundation shall present such work plans when completed to the Parties for their approval or objection.

3.12. **Progress Reports**. The Parties will receive regular reports on the status of the BOTA Program prepared by the World Bank in accordance with terms set forth in the Service Agreement.

3.13. **Timing**. The Funds are expected to be fully disbursed by the Foundation within five years of the Final Order. The Parties anticipate that establishment of the BOTA Program and start-up of operations shall take approximately one year.

4. PFMR Program

4.1. **Scope of PFMR Program**. On December 1, 2006, the Government of the Republic of Kazakhstan and the World Bank executed a written Memorandum of Understanding regarding Public Finance Management ("PFM MOU"), attached at Annex 3, through which the Government of the Republic of Kazakhstan has requested and the World Bank has agreed to provide technical assistance and advice for a minimum of five years in preparing a programmatic Public Finance Management Review and in implementing its recommendations. As set forth in the PFM MOU, under this program, the Government of the Republic of Kazakhstan, with the support of the World Bank, will examine and analyze the budget management process in specified sectors to formulate a comprehensive, realistic and strategic plan for improving public financial management in Kazakhstan. The PFM MOU contemplates that the review will begin with priority sectors such as education and health and progressively expand coverage to reach 90 percent of the budget over the PFM Review period of five years. Emphasis will also be given to analysis of recurrent expenditures and assessment of extra-budgetary funds. Pursuant to the PFM MOU, the Government of the Republic of Kazakhstan has committed to using the PFM Review as an analytical, information and consensus-building tool for policy design and implementation, and has also committed to consider other measures for implementation through active collaboration with NGOs.

4.2. **Disclosure of PFMR analyses**. Each report resulting from a programmatic PFM Review shall be considered a report emanating from economic and sector work (ESW) of the World Bank, and, therefore, consistent with the World Bank Policy on Disclosure of Information, shall be distributed to the Board of Executive Directors of the World Bank and made publicly available. Each such report may also be provided directly to the Parties.

4.3. **Reports to the Parties**. The Parties anticipate that the World Bank shall provide to the Government of the Republic of Kazakhstan periodic supervision reports regarding the PFMR Program. The Government of the Republic of Kazakhstan shall provide all supervision reports received from the World Bank pursuant to the PFMR MOU to the other Parties. The Government of the Republic of Kazakhstan hereby agrees and authorizes the World Bank to make available all such supervision reports to the United States and Swiss Executive Directors of the World Bank. In addition, the Governments of the United States of America and the Swiss Confederation each may request, on an ad hoc basis, that the Government of the Republic of Kazakhstan provide an interim report on the status of the PFMR Program. The Government of the Republic of Kazakhstan agrees to provide such ad hoc reports upon request.

5. EITI Program

5.1. **Scope of the EITI Program**. On December 1, 2006, the Government of the Republic of Kazakhstan and the World Bank executed a written Memorandum of Understanding (the "EITI MOU"), attached as Annex 4, through which the Government of the Republic of Kazakhstan has requested and the World Bank has agreed to provide technical assistance and advice for a minimum of three years to support measures intended to increase transparency over payments and revenues of extractive industries operating in Kazakhstan. As set forth in the EITI MOU, the Government of the Republic of Kazakhstan has indicated that it has established a dedicated Secretariat to coordinate and support EITI efforts in Kazakhstan and has directed that the Secretariat develop a work plan by February 1, 2007, to improve management and transparency of extractive industries companies and to analyze actions needed for implementation of the Extractive Industries' Transparency Initiative (EITI) in Kazakhstan. Under the EITI MOU, the Government of the Republic of Kazakhstan has committed to take specified steps to implement the Extractive Industries Transparency Initiatives and its principles, including, but not limited to, ensuring full participation of all extractive industry (oil, gas, and raining) companies; ensuring integrity of reported data; establishing a comprehensive work plan; ensuring adequate and sustainable financing for EITI implementation; appointing and managing an appropriate consulting and auditing firm; conducting national and regional workshops on EITI data reporting and implementation; and such other measures as may be deemed appropriate through active collaboration with nongovernmental organizations. Under the EITI MOU, the World Bank has agreed to support the EITI process in Kazakhstan, provide technical assistance, assist in devising monitoring indicators, and provide additional implementation support, such as for civil society engagement in EITI.

5.2. **Annual Reports**. The Government of the Republic of Kazakhstan agrees to engage a qualified and independent expert to prepare reports on an annual basis regarding the actions taken and the results achieved to implement the EITI Program, which reports alternatively may be reports of independent validations performed in accordance with the guidelines and procedures issued by the Secretariat of the Extractive Industries Transparency Initiative. Such reports shall be provided to the other Parties and made publicly available.

5.3. **Reports to the Parties**. The Parties anticipate that the World Bank shall provide to the Government of the Republic of Kazakhstan periodic supervision reports regarding the EITI Program. The Government of the Republic of Kazakhstan shall provide all supervision reports received from the World Bank pursuant to the EITI MOU to the other Parties. The Government of the Republic of Kazakhstan hereby agrees and authorizes the World Bank to make available all such supervision reports to the United States and Swiss Executive Directors of the World Bank. In addition, the Governments of the United States of America and the Swiss Confederation each may request, on an ad hoc basis, that the Government of the Republic of Kazakhstan provide an interim report on the status of the EITI Program. The Government of the Republic of Kazakhstan agrees to provide such ad hoc reports upon request.

6. Disclosure

6.1. The Parties agree that this MOU and associated annexes shall be publicly disclosed upon the filing of the Stipulation and Order described in Section 1.1 above by the United States of America. The Parties shall also provide copies of the MOU and associated annexes to each Founder, member of the Board of Supervisors, and the BOTA Program Manager.

7. Communications

7.1. Communications and notices under this MOU may be made by email, fax or letter as follows (all contacts specified in (a) through (c) below hereinafter called the "Contacts"):

(a) Communications made to the Government of the United States of America shall be directed to the Deputy Assistant Attorney General for the Criminal Division, United States Department of Justice (the US Contact);

(b) Communications made to the Government of the Swiss Confederation shall be directed to the Head of the Economic Cooperation and Development Division, State Secretariat for Economic Affairs (SECO) (the Swiss Contact);

(c) Communications made to the Government of the Republic of Kazakhstan shall be directed to the Prime Minister of the Republic of Kazakhstan (the Kazakh Contact).

7.2. Upon execution of this MOU, each Party shall promptly provide notice to each other Party of the name, title, address, electronic mail address, and telephone contact information for its Contact.

7.3. The Parties agree that to the extent this MOU refers to notices or communications to the Parties, or any consents, approvals or objections from the Parties, or any decision making on the part of the Parties, any communication to or from, as the case may be, the respective Contact(s) shall constitute a communication to the Party represented by that Contact Notices, consents, approvals, or objections of any Party must be in writing and may be made by (a) a written statement or agreement signed directly or by countersignature; (b) a series of faxes signed directly or by countersignature; or (c) an exchange of emails confirming agreement, consent, approval or objection on the part of the Contact.

7.4. Each Party may amend the identity of the Contact(s) specified above by providing written notice to the other Parties of the change of identity of the person(s) designated, together with address information sufficient to communicate with the amended Contact(s). Each Party's designated Contact may delegate his/her authority to receive or provide a notice, communication, consent, approval or objection that relates to a particular issue or matter by providing notice to the other Parties of the identity of the person(s) who shall have such delegated authority, together with address information sufficient to communicate with the amended Contact(s).

8. Irregularities

8.1. In the event the World Bank detects any irregularities while performing the Services, such as noncompliance with the Operational Manual, the World Bank shall, as set forth in the Service Agreement, notify the Parties, the BOTA Board of Supervisors and the BOTA Program Manager. Thereafter no further actions shall be expected or required from the World Bank, and any remedial actions shall be decided among the Parties in consultation with the BOTA Board of Supervisors, Program Manager and the World Bank.

8.2. In the event any of the Parties detects any irregularities in the operation of the BOTA Program, it shall notify all other Parties, the World Bank, the BOTA Board of Supervisors and the BOTA Program Manager. Any remedial actions shall be decided among the Parties in consultation with the World Bank, the BOTA Board of Supervisors and the Program Manager.

8.3. The Governments of the United States of America and the Swiss Confederation each shall independently retain the right at all times, including after the Term of this MOU, to seek the return of any or all of the Funds after their release if either in its sole discretion determines that any of the Funds have been used in a manner inconsistent with the terms of this MOU, the Stipulation and Order, the Supervisory Agreement or the Operational Manual. Such request shall be made in writing to the Program Manager, with copies to the BOTA Board of Supervisors, the World Bank and the other Parties, and shall include a justification for such return. If no Party disputes the stated justification and the BOTA Program Manager fails to return any Funds so requested for deposit in the Pictet & Cie account within 60 days of the request, the Government of the Republic of Kazakhstan shall deposit into the Pictet & Cie account an amount equal to the requested sum, which amount shall be made part of the Funds remaining in the account. If the Government of the Republic of Kazakhstan disputes the stated justification, paragraph 18 of the Stipulation and Order shall apply.

9. Term and Termination

9.1.This MOU shall enter into force upon signature by all the Parties (the "Effective Date") and shall continue in force for five years or such earlier period in which all of the Funds have been fully expended, except (i) as may be extended by unanimous agreement of the Parties, or (ii) as may be earlier terminated in accordance with this MOU (the "Term"). If this MOU is extended, the World Bank may correspondingly extend the terms of the Service Agreement, Supervisory Agreement and Management Agreement, if so requested by the Parties.

9.2. If the Court does not accept and approve the Stipulation and Order and enter a Final Order, this MOU shall terminate. If the Stipulation and Order becomes void for any other reason, this MOU shall also terminate. If the Stipulation and Order is terminated, this MOU may be terminated by any Party, upon written notice to the other Parties.

9.3. This MOU may be terminated at any time upon mutual agreement of all the Parties.

9.4. This MOU may also be terminated by either the Government of the United States of America or the Government of the Swiss Confederation upon written notice to the other Parties for insufficient progress in implementation in accordance with Section 1.4, in the event of irregularities as provided in Section 8, or upon a determination of prohibited use as provided in Section 2.6. If this MOU is terminated, the return provisions of Section 8.3 shall become applicable.

9.5. If this MOU is terminated it shall have no further force or effect, except as provided in Section 9.7, and each Party shall reserve the right to assert all claims it possessed as of the Effective Date of this MOU, with respect to any portion of the Funds remaining in or which may be re-deposited into the Pictet & Cie account.

9.6. Unless otherwise agreed by the Parties, if (i) the World Bank elects to terminate the Service Agreement (as provided in that Agreement), or (ii) this MOU is terminated or expires by its Term, then the Parties and the Foundation shall take all appropriate steps to terminate the BOTA Program activities in an orderly manner, to settle promptly all outstanding BOTA Program matters; and to cause the Foundation to return and re-deposit any uncommitted portion of the Funds to the Pictet & Cie account to be made part of the Funds remaining in the account.

9.7. Notwithstanding the expiration or termination of this MOU, the provisions of this MOU and the Stipulation and Order relating to (i) liability and indemnity, and (ii) return shall continue in force for five years after expiration or termination of this MOU as to any events occurring during the Term of the MOU.

10. Limitations of Liability

10.1. Except as provided in the Stipulation and Order, nothing in this MOU is intended to be, or should be construed as, a waiver of the privileges and immunities of any Party or its officers and employees, which privileges and immunities are hereby specifically reserved.

11. General

11.1. The Stipulation and Order between the Governments of the United States of America and the Republic of Kazakhstan is expressly incorporated into this MOU.

11.2. This MOU, including any annexes, along with any other agreements referenced herein, comprises the entire agreement and understanding among the Parties relating to the subject matter hereof. It, along with the other referenced agreements, supersedes any prior or side arrangements, agreements or understandings relating to the subject matter. This MOU may not be amended except through the written agreement of all of the Parties. The Governments of the United States and the Republic of Kazakhstan shall promptly notify the Court of any such amendment.

11.3. The Parties shall implement this MOU and all activities thereunder in accordance with their respective domestic law.

11.4. This MOU does not give rise to any rights on the part of any private person or non-party.

IN WITNESS WHEREOF, the undersigned being duly authorized by their respective Governments, have signed this Agreement.

DONE at Washington, D.C., in four originals, this 2nd day of May, 2007, in the English language.

FOR THE GOVERNMENT OF THE SWISS CONFEDARATION	FOR THE GOVERNMENT OF THE UNITED STATES OF AMERICA	FOR THE GOVERNMENT OF THE REPUBLIC OF KAZAKHSTAN
[Signature]	[Signature]	[Signature]
Urs Ziswiler Ambassador of Switzerland to the United States of America	Bruce C. Swartz Deputy Assistant Attorney General, Criminal Division U.S. Department of Justice	Kanat B. Saudabayev Ambassador of Kazakhstan to the United States of America

Annex 1	Stipulation and Order of Settlement
Annex 2	Service Agreement
Annex 3	PFMR MOU
Annex 4	EITI MOU

Attachment

BOTA MOU ANNEX 1

(Omitted. Annex 1 is the Stipulation and Order of Settlement to which the MOU is an attachment.)

BOTA MOU ANNEX 2

SERVICE AGREEMENT FOR THE BOTA FOUNDATION among the International Bank for Reconstruction and Development and the Governments of the United States of America, the Swiss Confederation, and the Republic of Kazakhstan

WHEREAS the Governments of the United States of America, the Swiss Confederation, and the Republic of Kazakhstan (each a Government, and together the Governments) have agreed to establish a program for supporting the development of poor children and youth in Kazakhstan (the "BOTA Program"), which Program will be financed by approximately $84 million in funds (together with all interest, income, benefits or other proceeds traceable thereto) held in account no. 4025 in the name of the Treasury of the Ministry of Finance of the Republic of Kazakhstan at Pictet & Cie in Switzerland that have been restrained pursuant to a Mutual Legal Assistance Treaty request by the United States of America to Switzerland and which upon judicial approval will be released under a stipulation and order executed by the United States of America and the Republic of Kazakhstan as set forth in the May 2, 2007, Memorandum of Understanding between the Governments; and

WHEREAS at the request of the Governments, the International Bank for Reconstruction and Development (the "World Bank", and collectively with the Governments the Parties, and each a Party) has agreed to provide the services set forth below in support of establishment of the BOTA Program;

NOW THEREFORE the Parties hereto agree as follows as of May 2, 2007 (the Effective Date):

1. *Scope of Work*

1.1. As requested by the Governments, the World Bank will provide the Services (as defined in this Agreement) to the Governments and the foundation established under Kazakh law (the "BOTA Foundation") for purposes of supporting the development of poor children and youth in Kazakhstan through the BOTA Program, in accordance with this Agreement. The World Bank will provide the Services as an independent service provider, using its own staff and consultants. The Parties agree that the World Bank's role in the BOTA Program is limited to rendering the Services as specified in this Agreement and the Supervisory Agreement (as defined below), and it shall have no responsibility for any activities outside the scope of those Agreements.

1.2. The Governments acknowledge and agree that the BOTA Foundation and the BOTA Program Manager will be responsible for implementation of the BOTA Program in accordance with the Operational Manual (as defined in Section 2.6 below), the Supervisory Agreement (as defined in Section 2.5 below), and the Management Agreement (as defined in Section 2.4 below).

2. *Services To Be Provided by the World Bank*

2.1. *BOTA Foundation.* The World Bank will assist in the establishment of the BOTA Foundation, which shall be an independent, nongovernmental, nonprofit foundation constituted under Kazakhstan's Law on Non-Commercial Organizations. The Parties agree that in order to receive any funds for the BOTA Program, the BOTA Foundation must be a purpose-built organization, founded for purposes of implementing development projects for poor children and youth in Kazakhstan; must, with the Program Manager, have the capacity to undertake the contemplated activities; must be party to the Supervisory Agreement, and must be entirely independent of the Government of the Republic of Kazakhstan, its officials, and their personal or business associates. The Parties further agree that the managerial capacity for the BOTA Foundation shall be provided through the Program Manager (as defined below). The Parties further agree that the Governments shall be responsible for the nomination and selection of candidates to serve as founders (the "Founders') of the BOTA Foundation. The BOTA Foundation shall be established with the intention that it continue to operate as a functioning foundation after the BOTA Program under this Agreement has been completed.

2.2. *Board of Supervisors*. The World Bank will assist the Founders and the Governments in the establishment of and selection of members of a seven-member Board of Supervisors of the BOTA Foundation ("Board of Supervisors"), which shall govern the BOTA Foundation. The members of the Board of Supervisors shall be a combination of respected international individuals and Kazakh citizens, preferably known for their championing of children's causes, and must be completely independent of the Government of the Republic of Kazakhstan, its officials, and their personal or business associates. The Governments of the United States of America and the Swiss Confederation, at their option, may each select a member of the Board of Supervisors (and alternates, as appropriate), who may be representatives of their respective governments or other respected individuals (the "Government Supervisors"). The Founders shall propose selection of all other candidates (and alternates, as appropriate) for consideration by the Governments, who may object to or approve any of the Founder-proposed candidates (the "non-Government Supervisors"). The final slate of Board of Supervisors members shall be individually notified of their selection by the Founders. In the event of a vacancy on the Board of Supervisors for a Government Supervisor, the respective Government may select a replacement. In the event of a vacancy on the Board of Supervisors for a non-Government Supervisor, the Founders shall propose a replacement member for consideration by and subject to the approval or objection of each Government. A Government Supervisor may be removed at any time by the Government that selected the Supervisor. Any non-Government Supervisor may be removed at any time upon a joint decision by the Governments of the United States of America and the Swiss Confederation.

2.3. *Constitutive Documents*. The World Bank will assist the Board of Supervisors in preparing the charter and any other constitutive documents of the BOTA Foundation required for its formation under Kazakh law (the "Constitutive Documents"). The Governments shall be provided opportunity to review the proposed Constitutive Documents, which must be approved by the Governments prior to their adoption by the Board of Supervisors. If the Board of Supervisors desires any changes to the Constitutive Documents, either initially or subsequently during the term of this Agreement, they must be approved by the Governments before becoming effective.

2.4. *BOTA Program Manager*. The World Bank will assist the Board of Supervisors in conducting an open, competitive bidding process to select a reputable, international, non-governmental organization to be engaged by the BOTA Foundation for the implementation, administration, management, and expenditures of the BOTA Program (the "Program Manager"). The specific responsibilities of the Program Manager shall be set forth in a Management Agreement between the BOTA Foundation and the Program Manager (the "Management Agreement"). The Management Agreement shall make the Program Manager subject to any and all obligations established for that position in this Agreement. The World Bank shall prepare a draft Management Agreement for consideration by the Board of Supervisors and each Government before publication during the bidding process. The Management Agreement must be approved by the Board of Supervisors and each Government before signature and effectiveness. The World Bank shall further assist the Board of Supervisors in posting the terms of reference for the position of Program Manager, which shall serve as a basis for soliciting applications, screening all applicants and providing a short list of recommended candidates to the Governments for consideration. The Board of Supervisors and the Governments then shall select a Program Manager by unanimous agreement. All candidates for Program Manager must be completely independent of the Government of the Republic of Kazakhstan, its officials, and their personal or business associates.

2.5. *Supervisory Agreement*. The relationship between the BOTA Foundation and the World Bank shall be governed by a supervisory agreement to be entered into by the BOTA Foundation and the World Bank (the "Supervisory Agreement"). The Supervisory Agreement must be approved by the Governments before signature and effectiveness. Among the supervisory services to be provided by the World Bank pursuant to the Supervisory Agreement are the following: (i) reviewing progress reports and audited financial statements to monitor technical and fiduciary compliance by the BOTA Foundation with the Operational Manual; (ii) review of BOTA Foundation requests for funds; and (iii) training and capacity building for the BOTA Foundation in the areas of procurement, financial management, calls for grants, preparation of work plans, evaluation systems, and such other technical assistance as the World Bank in its discretion deems necessary or appropriate. The Supervisory Agreement shall make the BOTA Foundation and its Board of Supervisors subject to any and all obligations established for such entities in this Agreement.

2.6. *Operational Manual*. The World Bank shall prepare the BOTA Program's operational manual (the "Operational Manual"). The Operational Manual must be approved by the Board of Supervisors and each of the Governments before it becomes effective. The Operational Manual will govern the daily operations of each element of the BOTA Program and will, among other things, set forth the procedures for the award of grants and disbursement of funds. Funds released to the BOTA Foundation for the BOTA Program shall be deposited into an operational account (the "Operational Account") to be established and maintained by the Program Manager on behalf of the Foundation and from which the Program Manager may make payments or disbursements in accordance with the terms of the Operational Manual. The Board of Supervisors and the Parties shall at all times have the right to review records of the Operational Account upon request. The World Bank, the Board of Supervisors, the Program Manager, and any of the Governments may recommend or request changes to the Operational Manual, either initially or subsequently during the Term (as defined below). All requested or recommended changes must be approved in writing by all the Parties and the Board of Supervisors before becoming effective.

2.7. *Accounts and Audits*. The World Bank will provide capacity building and guidelines to assist the BOTA Foundation:

(a) to ensure that a financial management system is maintained and financial statements are prepared, in accordance with consistently applied accounting standards acceptable to the World Bank, both in a manner adequate to reflect the operations, resources and expenditures related to the activities funded;

(b) to ensure that interim unaudited financial reports for the activities funded by the BOTA Foundation are prepared and furnished to the Parties not later than three months after the end of each six-month period, covering the six-month period, in form and substance satisfactory to the World Bank;

(c) to select independent auditors (the "Auditors"), whose appointment must be approved by the Governments, with the World Bank providing terms of reference for the Auditors' engagement and reviewing the short list of candidates on a no objection basis;

(d) to have financial statements for the activities funded by the BOTA Foundation audited by the Auditors in accordance with consistently applied auditing standards acceptable to the World Bank, to be provided to the Parties not later than six months after the end of the BOTA Foundation's fiscal year; and

(e) to ensure that: (1) all records evidencing expenditures related to activities funded by the BOTA Foundation are retained until at least five years after the Parties have received all the audited Financial Statements covering the Term of this Agreement; and (ii) the representatives of the Parties are able to examine such records, and are provided all such information concerning such records as they, may from time to time request.

2.8. *Training and Capacity Building*. The World Bank will provide training and capacity building for the BOTA Foundation in the areas of procurement, financial management, calls for grants, preparation of work plans, evaluation systems, and such other technical assistance as the World Bank in its discretion deems necessary or appropriate. The Parties agree that the Program Manager shall be responsible for financial management, budgets, work plans and other aspects of BOTA Foundation management.

2.9. *Progress Reports*. The World Bank will provide supervision reports to the Governments on the status of the BOTA Program implementation m accordance with Bank policies, practices and procedures and as specified in the Operational Manual. Such reports shall be provided to the Governments on a semi-annual basis and may include information regarding the BOTA Foundation's procurement practices, financial management, audits, development impact monitoring, and evaluation systems in implementation of the BOTA Program, and such other information as the World Bank may deem necessary or appropriate. Such reports will be based in part on spot checks of implemented activity, as the World Bank considers appropriate, and will identify material discrepancies that are found.

2.10. *Funding*. The World Bank will assist the BOTA Foundation and the Governments in reviewing requests for the release or reallocation of funds as follows:

(a) The Program Manager, on behalf of the BOTA Foundation, may make requests to the Governments for release of installments of funds for implementation of the BOTA Program. Any such request shall include notice to the World Bank and shall specify how the amounts sought will be used. The World Bank shall inform the Governments whether it has any objection to each such request. No such request shall be granted unless the World Bank provides notice to the Governments that it has no objection to the request.

(b) All funds provided to the BOTA Foundation under this Agreement shall be utilized for the establishment of the BOTA Foundation in accordance with this Agreement and the preparation, administration and implementation of the BOTA Program in accordance with the Operational Manual. The BOTA Program shall constitute a program for the benefit of poor children and youth in Kazakhstan. The BOTA Foundation shall utilize funds provided under the BOTA Program for conditional cash payments to Kazakh families, scholarships to Kazakh residents, and grants to local and international NGOs in accordance with the Operational Manual. BOTA Program funds will be utilized to support activities aimed at improving child and youth welfare, including: reducing child labor, provision of community-based services to disabled children, shelters for runaway and homeless children, improving child nutrition, promoting and developing family-based care for children deprived of parental care, raising awareness of and decreasing child abuse and violence, reducing juvenile delinquency, expanding youth activities and resource centers, and skills development for school drop-outs, and such other projects as may be determined by the Board of Supervisors, the Program Manager and the World Bank to be of benefit to poor children and youth of Kazakhstan and their families and enumerated in the Operational Manual.

(c) The World Bank shall consult with the Board of Supervisors and Program Manager regarding any reallocation of funds that the World Bank, Board of Supervisors or Program Manager may propose to provide the maximum benefit to poor children and youth in Kazakhstan Any redistribution of funds among projects or to newly-identified projects must be approved in writing by each of the Parties.

(d) The Parties agree that the BOTA Program funds shall not be used for payments (i) prohibited by a decision of the United Nations Security Council taken under Chapter VII of the Charter of the United Nations; (ii) for which corrupt, fraudulent, collusive or coercive practices were engaged in to receive any of the funds; (iii) that would support any corrupt or fraudulent activities; or (iv) to the Government of the Republic of Kazakhstan, its officials, or their personal or business associates. The Parties agree that in the event of a determination by any of the Parties that this clause has been violated, whether by the Program Manager, recipients of grants from the funds or any other natural or legal person, the termination provisions of Section 4 and the return provisions of Section 9.3 shall become applicable in the individual discretion of the Governments of the United States of America or the Swiss Confederation.

3. *Administration of Services*

3.1. It is expected that the World Bank's ordinary interaction with the BOTA Foundation in connection with this Agreement will occur directly without direct coordination with or inclusion of any Government. The Parties agree that the World Bank's ability to provide Services will require that the BOTA Foundation cooperate with the World Bank, including providing access to sites and records that may be required in fulfillment of the World Bank's obligations under this Agreement. The World Bank will make reasonable efforts to obtain such access to sites and records. The World Bank will promptly notify the Governments of any problems regarding BOTA Foundation cooperation adversely affecting its ability to fulfill its obligations under this Agreement.

3.2. The Government of the Republic of Kazakhstan agrees to cooperate with the World Bank in all respects to ensure the World Bank's ability to perform the Services as set forth herein and intended by the Parties.

3.3. The World Bank will exercise the same level of care in performing the Services under this Agreement as it exercises in its monitoring activities for its own lending and grant making operations.

4. *Duration and Termination*

4.1. The funds under restraint in the Pictet & Cie account from which the BOTA Program is to be financed (the "Pictet & Cie Funds") are expected to be disbursed by the BOTA Foundation over a period of five years, of which the first year is expected to be for the establishment of the BOTA Foundation end preparation of the BOTA Program. This Agreement shall be in force from the Effective Date for five years or such earlier period in which all Pictet & Cie Funds have been fully expended, except (i) as may be extended by unanimous agreement of the Parties, or (ii) as may be terminated in accordance with this Agreement (the "Term"). If this Agreement is extended, the Supervisory Agreement and Management Agreement may correspondingly be extended, if requested by the Governments.

4.2. Sections 2 and 5 of this Agreement shall be subject to annual review and may be modified by mutual agreement of all Parties.

4.3. This Agreement may be terminated at any time upon mutual agreement of all the Parties. The effects and implications of such termination shall be mutually agreed by all the Parties in advance of such termination.

4.4. This Agreement may also be terminated by either the Government of the United States of America or the Government of the Swiss Confederation upon written notice to the other Parties in the event of irregularities as provided in Section 9 or upon a determination of prohibited use as provided in Section 2.10(d). In addition, if the May 2, 2007, Memorandum of Understanding between the Governments is terminated, this Agreement may be terminated by any Party. If this Agreement is terminated, the return provisions of Section 9.3 shall become applicable. If this Agreement is terminated, each Government shall reserve the right to assert all claims as to the Pictet & Cie Funds that it possessed as of the Effective Date; provided that the World Bank shall not be held liable for any expenditures made in good faith reliance on this Agreement.

4.5. Notwithstanding any other statement herein, the World Bank may terminate its participation in this Agreement upon ninety days' notice to the other Parties by notifying their respective Representatives. Upon such notice, the Parties shall take all appropriate steps to terminate the BOTA Program activities in an orderly manner; to settle promptly all outstanding BOTA Program matters; and to cause the BOTA Foundation to return and re-deposit any uncommitted portion of the Pictet & Cie Funds to the originating account. Subject to the unanimous agreement of the Governments, the Governments may arrange to replace the World Bank with another entity or take other steps that would enable the BOTA Program to continue operating.

4.6. Notwithstanding the expiration or termination of this Agreement, the provisions of this Agreement relating to (i) liability and indemnity, and (ii) payment shall continue in full force and effect for five years after such termination or expiration as to any events occurring within the duration of this Agreement.

5. *Payment*

5.1. *General.* The Governments have agreed that the Government of the Republic of Kazakhstan will pay a fixed annual fee to the World Bank for the Services in accordance with Section 5.2 below. Such fixed annual fee shall be calculated on a full cost recovery basis. Payment of the fixed annual fee will be made in advance at the beginning of each quarter in quarterly installments payable on each 15 March, 15 June, 15 September and 15 December; provided that if any such date is not a business day in Kazakhstan, then the payment shall be made on the next business day; and provided further that the first payment will be made on or after the Effective Date, on a date to be agreed by the Governments and the World Bank, and will be pro-rated for the period from the Effective Date until the next quarterly payment date. In the event of termination under Section 4, the World Bank shall refund to the Government of the Republic of Kazakhstan that portion of the quarterly payment made in advance to the World Bank that represents the remaining portion of the quarter after the date of termination.

5.2. *Total Fee and Cost Breakdown.* The fixed annual fee to be paid the World Bank in accordance with the conditions described in the preceding Section 5.1 shall be:

Activity	*Fee*
Preparatory Services (Year 1)	US$500,000 total
Ongoing Services (Years 2 to 5)	US$150,000 per year

5.3. *Adjustments.* The Parties agree that the descriptions and amounts shown in the preceding Section 5.2 will be reviewed annually and adjusted as appropriate to enable full cost recovery for the Services provided hereunder on the part of the World Bank.

5.4. Should any monies be necessary for start-up costs of the BOTA Program prior to the release of the first installment of the funds, such monies will be advanced by the Government of the Republic of Kazakhstan. Any such reasonable costs, not including World Bank service fees, may be reimbursed by the Program Manager, acting on behalf of the BOTA Foundation, from the first installment of the funds.

6. *Claims and Liability*

6.1. The World Bank shall not be liable to the Governments for any loss, cost, damage, suits, claims, demands or liability (Damages) that they may incur as a result of the Services. The Government of the Republic of Kazakhstan agrees that the Republic of Kazakhstan shall indemnify and hold the World Bank and its officers, directors, agents, subcontractors and employees (personnel) harmless from any Damages to which the World Bank or its personnel may be subject as a result of claims by third parties arising in the implementation of this Agreement or any activities undertaken in connection therewith, except those resulting from the gross negligence or willful misconduct of the World Bank or its personnel. The obligations under this Section shall not lapse upon expiration or termination of this Agreement but shall extend after expiration or termination of this Agreement.

6.2. Throughout the implementation of this Agreement and any activity or project pursuant thereto, each Party will maintain its usual and customary insurance for its own officers, employees and operations.

7. *Disputes*

7.1. Any dispute, controversy or claim between the World Bank and the Government of the Republic of Kazakhstan in connection with the World Bank's provision of Services under this Agreement which is not settled by agreement in writing shall be finally settled by arbitration in accordance with the United Nations Commission on International Law (UNCITRAL) Arbitration Rules then currently in force, and the Appointing Authority shall be the Secretary-General of the Permanent Court of Arbitration. The language of arbitration shall be English and the venue shall be Washington, DC. In the event of conflict between the UNCITRAL Arbitration Rules and the terms of this Agreement, the terms of this Agreement shall govern.

7.2. The rights and obligations of the Parties under this Agreement shall be valid and enforceable in accordance with their terms notwithstanding the law of any state or political subdivision thereof to the contrary.

8. *Disclosure*

8.1. The Parties agree that this Agreement and the activities contemplated herein may be disclosed upon the filing of the Stipulation and Order.

8.2. The World Bank may disclose to the public this Agreement and information with respect to activities contemplated herein in accordance with the World Bank's Policy on the Disclosure of Information.

9. *Irregularities*

9.1. In the event the World Bank detects any irregularities in connection with the BOTA Program while performing the Services, such as noncompliance with the Operational Manual or the Supervisory Agreement or any fraud or corruption, the World Bank shall notify the Governments, the BOTA Foundation and the Program Manager of the irregularities. Thereafter no further actions shall be expected or required from the World Bank, and any remedial actions shall be decided among the Governments in consultation with the World Bank and the BOTA Foundation.

9.2. In the event a Government detects any BOTA Program irregularities, it shall notify the other Governments, the World Bank, the BOTA Foundation and the Program Manager of the irregularities. Any remedial actions shall be decided among the Governments in consultation with the World Bank and the BOTA Foundation.

9.3. The Governments of the United States of America and the Swiss Confederation each shall independently retain the right at all times, including after the Term of this Agreement, to seek the return of any or all Pictet & Cie Funds after their release if either in its sole discretion determines that any of the Pictet & Cie Funds have been used in a manner inconsistent with the terms of this Agreement, the Supervisory Agreement or the Operational Manual. Such request shall be made in writing to the Program Manager, with copies to the Board of Supervisors and the other Parties, and shall include a justification for such return. If no Party disputes the stated justification and the Program Manager fails to return any Pictet & Cie Funds so requested for deposit in the Pictet & Cie account within 60 days of the request, the Government of the Republic of Kazakhstan shall deposit into the Pictet & Cie account an amount equal to the requested sum, which amount shall be made part of the remaining Pictet & Cie Funds.

10. *Communications*

10.1. The authorized representative of the World Bank with respect to this Agreement is the World Bank's Country Director for Kazakhstan, or such other person designated by her/him in writing to serve in that capacity (the World Bank Representative).

10.2. The authorized representative of the Government of the United States of America with respect to this Agreement is the Deputy Assistant Attorney General for the Criminal Division, United States Department of Justice, or such other person designated by her/him in writing to serve in that capacity (the US Representative).

10.3. The authorized representative of the Government of the Swiss Confederation with respect to this Agreement is the Head of the Economic Cooperation and Development Division, State Secretariat for Economic Affairs (SECO), or such other person designated by her/him in writing to serve in that capacity (the Swiss Representative).

10.4. The authorized representative of the Government of the Republic of Kazakhstan with respect to this Agreement is the Prime Minister of Kazakhstan, or such other person designated by her/him in writing to serve in that capacity (the Kazakh Representative).

10.5. Upon execution of this Agreement, each Party shall promptly provide notice to each other Party of the name, title, address, electronic mail address, and telephone contact information for its Representative.

10.6. The BOTA Foundation, once established, is expected to designate in writing without delay its authorized representative with respect to this Agreement.

10.7. The Parties agree that to the extent this Agreement refers to notices or communications to the Parties, or any consents, approvals or objections from the Parties, or any decision making on the part of the Parties, any communication to or from, as the case may be, the respective Representative(s) shall constitute a communication to the Party represented by that Representative. Notices, consents, approvals, or objections of any Party must be in writing and may be made by (a) a written statement provided by a Representative or written agreement signed directly or by countersignature; (b) a fax provided by a Representative or a series of faxes signed directly or by countersignature; or (c) an email provided by a Representative or an exchange of emails confirming agreement, consent, approval or objection on the part of the Representative.

10.8. Each Party may amend the identity of the Representative(s) specified above by providing written notice to the other Parties of the change of identity of the person(s) designated, together with address information sufficient to communicate with the amended Representative(s). Each Party's designated Representative may delegate his/her authority to receive or provide a notice, communication, consent, approval or objection that relates to a particular issue or matter by so informing in writing the other Parties of the identity of the person(s) who shall have such delegated authority, together with address information sufficient to communicate with the amended Representative(s).

11. *General*

11.1. This Agreement, along with any other agreements to the extent they are referenced herein, comprises the entire agreement and understanding between the World Bank and the Governments relating to the subject matter hereof, and supersedes any prior arrangements, agreements or understandings between the World Bank and the Governments relating thereto. However, this Agreement does not supersede or modify any agreements, arrangements, or understandings, among or between the Governments.

11.2. Nothing in this Agreement shall be construed as creating a joint venture, an agency relationship or a legal partnership between the World Bank and the Governments, or the World Bank and the BOTA Foundation, or any other party referenced herein.

11.3. Nothing in this Agreement is intended to be, or should be construed as, a waiver of the privileges and immunities of any Party or its officers or employees, which privileges and immunities are hereby specifically reserved.

11.4. Each Party warrants that it has the authority to enter into this Agreement. No Party may assign its rights, duties or obligations under this Agreement to any person or entity, in whole or in part, without the prior written consent of all other Parties. Any changes, variations, or amendments to the terms of this Agreement shall not be valid unless made in writing and signed by all Parties.

11.5. This Agreement does not give rise to any rights on the part of any private person or non-party.

IN WITNESS WHEREOF, the undersigned, being duly authorized by their respective Governments or organization, have signed this Agreement.

DONE at Washington, D.C., in five originals, this 2nd day of May, 2007, in the English language.

FOR THE GOVERNMENT OF THE SWISS CONFEDERATION

[Signature]

Urs Ziswiler
Ambassador of Switzerland to the United States of America

FOR THE GOVERNMENT OF THE REPUBLIC OF KAZAKHSTAN

[Signature]

Kanat B. Saudabayev
Ambassador of Kazakhstan to the United States of America

FOR THE GOVERNMENT OF THE UNITED STATES OF AMERICA

[Signature]

Bruce C. Swartz
Deputy Assistant Attorney General Criminal Division, U.S. Department of Justice

FOR THE INTERNATIONAL BANK FOR RECONSTRUCTION AND DEVELOPMENT

[Signature]

Shigeo Katsu
Vice President Europe and Central Asia Region

BOTA MOU ANNEX 3

Memorandum of Understanding Regarding Public Finance Management Between the Republic of Kazakhstan and International Bank for Reconstruction and Development December 1, 2006

WHEREAS the Republic of Kazakhstan (Kazakhstan) is committed to strengthening and increasing the efficiency of public finance management at all levels of government; and

WHEREAS Kazakhstan has requested and the International Bank for Reconstruction and Development (the World Bank) has agreed to provide technical assistance and advice to strengthen the public finance management in Kazakhstan:

NOW THEREFORE, the Parties agree that:

A. Kazakhstan is undertaking the following activities in the area of public sector modernization and public finance management:

(a) improvement of planning, implementation, monitoring, evaluation and audit for budget investments with clear positive externalities for recurrent expenditures;

(b) development of capacity to implement public–private partnerships in the provision of public goods, services and infrastructure;

(c) introduction of e-government and digital inclusion;

(d) a new stage of tax policy reform;

(e) improvement of the system of medical services, with a strong focus on improved public finance management of health expenditures (with clear positive externalities to the education sector as well);

(f) an agricultural expenditures study, aimed at improving the use of public funds to support rural development;

(g) a territorial development initiative, aimed at raising the involvement of local governments with the central government in economic and social development across the regions of Kazakhstan. This includes performance-based measures for public expenditure allocations, which should help to improve public allocations, incentives to budget managers at all levels of government, and set the stage to provide all budget managers more leeway to use their funding effectively to deliver envisaged outcomes, as opposed to strict input-based budget allocation and management, as has been the case to the present;

(h) tax administration modernization;

(i) customs administration modernization; and

(j) improved macroeconomic analysis to support policy making toward mitigation of the Dutch Disease, and its short term manifestations in the form of economic overheating.

B. Kazakhstan commits to:

(a) undertake a Programmatic PFM Review over the period of five years to examine and analyze the budget management process in specified sectors to formulate outline a comprehensive, realistic and strategic plan for improving public financial management in Kazakhstan, underscored by a sound macro-, fiscal, and contingent liability framework.

(b) begin a programmatic PFM Review with priority sectors such as education and health, and progressively expanding coverage to other sectors, eventually covering 90 percent of the budget over the PFM Review period of five years.

(c) as part of this work, give increased attention to analysis of the quality of recurrent expenditures and assessing any extra-budgetary funds.

(d) this Programmatic PFM Review would be used as an analytical, informational and consensus building tool upon which appropriate policy can be designed and implemented over the coming years.

(e) consider other measures for implementation through active collaboration with nongovernmental organizations.

C. The World Bank agrees that it will provide technical assistance in preparing the Programmatic PFM Review and in implementing its recommendations in the framework of the annual Joint Economic Research Program.

D. Nothing in this MOU is intended to be, or should be construed as a waiver of the privileges and immunities of either Party or its officers and employees, which privileges and immunities are hereby specifically reserved.

E. Any sharing of information between the Parties will be subject to their respective policies and procedures relating to the disclosure of information. Confidential information of the one Party shall be handled by the other Party with no lesser standard of care than it would use in handling its own confidential information.

F. In case of a dispute, controversy, or claim between the Parties arising out of or relating to this MOU or an agreement for any activity or project undertaken pursuant thereto, the Parties shall attempt to reach an amicable resolution in good faith. In the event an attempt to reach an amicable resolution proves unsuccessful within thirty days after the first Party has formally notified the dispute, controversy, or claim to the other Party in writing, any such dispute, controversy, or claim shall proceed to arbitration to be finally settled in accordance with the then-current UNCITRAL Arbitration Rules. The number of arbitrators shall be three. The appointing authority shall be the Secretary-General of the Permanent Court of Arbitration in The Hague. The language of arbitration shall be English.

G. This MOU shall come into force and effect upon signature by both Parties on the date set forth below with an initial term of three years, to be extended on a mutually agreed basis. At the end of the initial term of this MOU, a joint assessment by both Parties will be carried out to review the results sod lessons learned from their collaborative activities. The views of stakeholders on the nature and progress of activities or projects may be obtained by the Parties in connection therewith. The Parties will discuss and share any conclusions reached which may have a bearing on the Parties' collaboration under this MOU. On the basis of such assessment, the Parties may keep in force, modify or terminate this MOU as provided for below. This MOU may be modified or terminated at any time by mutual written agreement of the Parties. Further, the MOU may be terminated by either Party at its sole discretion with 60 days prior notice in writing to the other Party.

H. This MOU will supersede any previous intentions or agreements communicated and agreed upon between the Parties in respect of the collaborative activities and projects contemplated herein. The persons signing this MOU on behalf of each Party hereby represents and warrants to the other Party that he or she has the requisite legal power and authority to execute this MOU on behalf of the Party and bind the Party to the obligations herein.

In witness whereof, the Parties have caused this MOU to become effective as of December 1, 2006.

INTERNATIONAL BANK FOR
RECONSTRUCTION AND DEVELOPMENT

[Signature]

Shigeo Katsu
Vice President, Europe and Central Asia

REPUBLIC OF KAZAKHSTAN

[Signature]

Karim Massimov
Deputy Prime Minister

BOTA MOU ANNEX 4

Memorandum of Understanding Regarding the Extractive Industries Transparency Initiative Between the Republic of Kazakhstan and International Bank for Reconstruction and Development December 1, 2006

WHEREAS the Republic of Kazakhstan (Kazakhstan) joined the group of countries implementing the Extractive Industries Transparency Initiative (EITI) in October 2005; and

WHEREAS Kazakhstan has requested and the International Bank for Reconstruction and Development (the World Bank) has agreed to provide technical assistance and advice to support measures intended to increase transparency over payments and revenues of extractive industries operating in Kazakhstan:

NOW THEREFORE, the Parties agree that:

A. Kazakhstan has established a dedicated EITI Secretariat based in the Ministry of Energy and Mineral Resources and headed by a senior Government official for the coordination of all EITI work in Kazakhstan and support of the National Stakeholder Council for EITI. The Secretariat will develop by February 1, 2007, an EITI work plan as referred to in the Prime Minister's Directive dated November 28, 2006, and manage working groups tasked with (a) improving management and transparency of Extractive Industries (EI) Companies, and (b) analyzing legislation and submitting proposals on introducing legislative amendments and additions needed for EITI implementation.

B. Kazakhstan is committed to:

(a) ensure the full participation of all extractive industry (oil, gas, and milling) companies operating in Kazakhstan (EI companies) in the EITI consistent with EITI's Criteria # 1 (publication of all payments) and EITI's Criteria # 4 (involvement of all companies). This extends to all international, local, and state-owned EI Companies and then-production subsidiaries. This will be achieved through Government Decree by December 15, 2006;

(b) ensure integrity of reported data appearing in Kazakhstan's and EI Companies' EITI statements consistent with EITI Criteria # 2 (data is based on audited accounts). This entails having each entity's auditors provide statements verifying that such entity's EITI statements and reports are based on existing audited accounts. This will be achieved through the same Government Decree as above and will be applicable starting January 1, 2008;

(c) develop by February 1, 2007, a work plan for its participation in EITI and implementation of EITI steps over the next two years consistent with EITI Criteria # 6 (development of a work plan). Development of the work plan will be undertaken by the dedicated EITI Secretariat and occur through consultation with various stakeholders. Kazakhstan will report to the EITI Board on the implementation status of the work plan starting June 2007;

(d) ensure adequate and sustainable financing for EITI implementation, including the cost of the Secretariat and any working groups, contracting international experts, preparing annual reports and annual reconciliation of data. Until such time that the assigned working group establishes the exact budgetary requirement, the Government has assigned a budget line in the 2007 budget to cover the expenses related to the EITI Secretariat An inter-departmental working group has been established to analyze and report required expenditures to ensure such financing;

(e) appoint and manage an appropriate consulting or auditing firm to carry out audits in connection with the EITI program. The said firm will be selected competitively by end of May 2007;

(f) conduct a series of national and regional workshops, starting with the first workshop by end of March 2007 to promote and discuss EITI throughout Kazakhstan in conjunction with the EITI data reporting and aggregation process consistent with EITI Criteria # 1 (making EITI reports widely available in an understandable manner) and EITI Criteria # 5 (involving civil society in EITI discussions); and

(g) consider other measures for implementation through active collaboration with nongovernmental organizations.

C. The World Bank agrees that it will:

(a) support the EITI process in Kazakhstan;

(b) provide ongoing technical assistance from its EITI team to Kazakhstan, including with respect to the above measures;

(c) assist in devising monitoring indicators to help Kazakhstan monitor progress;

(d) assist in sharing implementation experience and best practice lessons of other EITI-implementing countries; and

(e) consider additional implementation support on an as-needed basis, such as on-the-ground consultancy support for implementation and financial support for workshops on enabling civil society engagement in EITI.

D. Nothing in this MOU is intended to be, or should be construed as, a waiver of the privileges and immunities of either Party or its officers and employees, which privileges and immunities are hereby specifically reserved.

E. Any sharing of information between the Parties will be subject to their respective policies and procedures relating to the disclosure of information. Confidential information of the one Party shall be handled by the other Party with no lesser standard of care than it would use in handling its own confidential information.

F. In case of a dispute, controversy, or claim between the Parties arising out of or relating to this MOU, or an agreement for any activity or project undertaken pursuant thereto, the Parties shall attempt to reach an amicable resolution in good faith. In the event an attempt to reach an amicable resolution proves unsuccessful within thirty days after the first Party has formally notified the dispute, controversy, or claim to the other Party in writing, any such dispute, controversy, or claim shall proceed to arbitration to be finally settled in accordance with the then-current UNCITRAL Arbitration Rules. The number of arbitrators shall be three. The appointing authority shall be the Secretary-General of the Permanent Court of Arbitration in The Hague. The language of arbitration shall be English.

G. This MOU shall come into force and effect upon signature by both Parties on the date set forth below with an initial term of three years, to be extended on a mutually agreed basis. At the end of the initial term of this MOU, a joint assessment by both Parties will be carried out to review the results and lessons learned from their collaborative activities. The views of stakeholders on the nature and progress of activities or projects may be obtained by the Parties in connection therewith. The Parties will discuss and share any conclusions reached which may have a bearing on the Parties' collaboration under this MOU. On the basis of such assessment, the Parties may keep in force, modify or terminate this MOU as provided for below. This MOU may be modified or terminated at any time by mutual written agreement of the Parties. Further, the MOU may be terminated by either Party at its sole discretion with 60 days prior notice in writing to the other Party.

H. This MOU will supersede any previous intentions or agreements communicated and agreed upon between the Parties in respect of the collaborative activities and projects contemplated herein. The persons signing this MOU on behalf of each Party hereby represents and warrants to the other Party that be or she has the requisite legal power and authority to execute this MOU on behalf of the Party and bind the Party to the obligations herein.

In witness whereof, the Parties have caused this MOU to become effective as of December 1, 2006.

INTERNATIONAL BANK FOR RECONSTRUCTION AND DEVELOPMENT

[Signature]

Shigeo Katsu
Vice President, Europe and Central Asia

REPUBLIC OF KAZAKHSTAN

[Signature]

Karim Massimov
Deputy Prime Minister

STATE DEPARTMENT DOCUMENT NUMBER: 08-30

PROTOCOL TO THE JULY 16, 1996 MEMORANDUM OF UNDERSTANDING BETWEEN THE UNITED STATES OF AMERICA AND THE RUSSIAN FEDERATION ON COOPERATION IN NATURAL AND MAN-MADE TECHNOLOGICAL EMERGENCY PREVENTION AND RESPONSE

SIGNED AT MOSCOW, JUNE 26, 2007
ENTERED INTO FORCE JUNE 26, 2007

CTIA DOCUMENT NUMBER: 8877.002

The Government of the United States of America and the Government of the Russian Federation (hereinafter referred to as "the Parties"),

Recognizing the importance of continuing international cooperation in the field of emergency management;

Acknowledging the danger of terrorist threats;

Noting the Memorandum of Understanding between the Government of the United States of America and the Government of the Russian Federation on Cooperation in Natural and Man-Made Technological Emergency Prevention and Response of July 16, 1996, as extended, will expire on July 17, 2007;

Have agreed as follows:

ARTICLE I

The Memorandum is extended for an additional period of ten years to July 18, 2017, inclusively.

ARTICLE II

Article VI of the Memorandum is amended by inserting at the end the following sentence:

> "To the extent that assistance is contemplated to implement cooperative activities under this Memorandum, such assistance will be deemed to be covered by the respective laws and regulations of the United States and the Russian Federation and by existing agreements between them."

ARTICLE III

In addition to the areas of cooperation specified in the Memorandum, under the same principles and terms, the Parties will cooperate in the field of emergency management for terrorist events.

ARTICLE IV

To reflect updated terminology and changes in the field of emergency management, the text of the Memorandum is amended to include the following technical changes:

1. The new title of the Memorandum is as follows: "MEMORANDUM OF UNDERSTANDING BETWEEN THE GOVERNMENT OF THE UNITED STATES OF AMERICA AND THE GOVERNMENT OF THE RUSSIAN FEDERATION ON COOPERATION IN EMERGENCY MANAGEMENT."

2. References to "technological" are deleted in the English text. In the Russian text, references to "техногенные чреэвычайные ситуации и стихийные бедствия" [technological and natural disasters] are replaced by "чреэвычайные ситуации" [emergencies].

3. The following phrases are replaced in the English text by "mitigation, preparedness, response and recovery": "prevention, mitigation, response and recovery"; "preparedness, prevention, response, recovery and mitigation"; "prevention and response". The following phrases are replaced in the Russian text by "предупреждение и ликвидация чреэвычайных ситуаций": "предупреждение техногенных чреэвычайных ситуаций, стихийных бедствий, реагирование в случае их возникновения и ликвидаций их последствий", "готовность к стихийным бедствиям, техногенным чреэвычайным ситуациям, их предупреждение, реагирование в случае возникновения, уменьшение и ликвидация их последствий".

4. Reference to the U.S.-Russian Joint Commission on Economic and Technological Cooperation is deleted, and reference to the Department of Humanitarian Affairs of the United Nations is replaced by the United Nations Office of Coordination of Humanitarian Affairs.

ARTICLE V

This Protocol enters into force upon the signature of the Parties.

Done at Moscow, in duplicate, this 26th day of June, 2007, in the English and Russian languages, each text being equally authentic.

FOR THE GOVERNMENT OF THE UNITED STATES OF AMERICA

[Signature]

FOR THE GOVERNMENT OF THE RUSSIAN FEDERATION

[Signature]

STATE DEPARTMENT DOCUMENT NUMBER: 08-31

AGREEMENT FOR ECONOMIC AND TECHNICAL COOPERATION BETWEEN THE UNITED STATES OF AMERICA AND BURUNDI

SIGNED AT BUJUMBURA, DECEMBER 12, 2007
ENTERED INTO FORCE DECEMBER 12, 2007

CTIA DOCUMENT NUMBER: 13399.000

THIS AGREEMENT FOR ECONOMIC AND TECHNICAL COOPERATION ("Agreement") is between the Government of United States of America ("Government of the United States") and the Government of Burundi ("Government of Burundi") (collectively, the "Parties" or individually, a "Party").

NOW, THEREFORE, in consideration of the rights and responsibilities set forth in this Agreement, the Parties agree as follows:

Article I
SCOPE OF AGREEMENT

This Agreement covers economic, technical, humanitarian and related assistance that may be furnished by the Government of the United States in Burundi. The furnishing of such assistance shall be subject to applicable United States laws and regulations. Such assistance will be made available in accordance with arrangements agreed upon by representatives of the appropriate agency or agencies of the Government of Burundi and representatives of the agency designated by the Government of the United States. Assistance may also be made available through other arrangements involving United States Government agencies, non-governmental organizations, individuals, private firms, public international organizations or other entities.

Article II
RESPONSIBILITIES OF THE GOVERNMENT OF BURUNDI

The Government of Burundi shall:

1. Make the full contribution permitted by its personnel, resources, facilities, and general economic conditions in furtherance of the purposes for which assistance is made under this Agreement;

2. Take appropriate steps to ensure the effective use of such assistance;

3. Cooperate with the Government of the United States to ensure that procurement will be at reasonable prices and on reasonable terms;

4. Permit, without restriction, continuous observation and review by the United States' representatives of programs and operations covered by this Agreement and records pertaining thereto, including the right during the period of any program or transaction and for three years thereafter to:

(a) examine property procured through financing by the Government of the United States for purposes of this Agreement, and;

(b) inspect and audit any records and accounts with respect to funds provided, and to any properties or contract services procured through financing by the Government of the United States for purposes of this Agreement; and

5. Bear a fair share of the costs of cooperative technical assistance programs under this Agreement and, to the maximum extent possible, seek full coordination and integration of technical cooperation programs being carried on in Burundi and also cooperate with other nations participating in such programs in the mutual exchange of technical knowledge and skills.

Article III
SPECIAL ACCOUNT

1. In any case where commodities or services are furnished on a grant basis under arrangements which result in the accrual of local currency proceeds to the Government of Burundi from the import or sale of such commodities or services, the Government of Burundi, except as may otherwise be mutually agreed upon by the representatives referred to in Article I hereof, will establish in its own name a special interest bearing account in a commercial bank in Burundi, and deposit promptly in such special account the amount of local currency equivalent to such proceeds.

2. Upon notification from time to time by the Government of the United States of its local currency requirement, the Government of Burundi will make available to the Government of the United States, in the manner requested by that Government, out of any balance in the special account, such sums as are stated in such notifications to be necessary for such requirements.

3. The Government of Burundi may draw upon any remaining balances in the special account for such purposes beneficial to Burundi as may be agreed upon from time to time by the representatives referred to in Article I of this Agreement.

4. Upon termination of assistance to the Government of Burundi under this Agreement, any unencumbered balances of funds which remain in the special account shall be disposed of for such purposes as maybe agreed upon by the aforesaid representatives of the Parties.

Article IV
THE SPECIAL MISSION

1. The Government of Burundi shall receive a special mission ("Special Mission") of the Government of the United States. The Special Mission will implement and discharge the responsibilities of the Government of the United States under this Agreement.

2. The Special Mission will enjoy the same privileges and immunities as are extended to the premises, property, records and archives of the diplomatic mission of the United States under the Vienna Convention on Diplomatic Relations of 1961.

Article V
PRIVILEGES AND IMMUNITIES

1. Employees of the United States Government (and family members forming part of their households) present in Burundi to perform work in connection with this Agreement shall enjoy privileges

and immunities equivalent to those granted a diplomatic agent under the Vienna Convention on Diplomatic Relations of 1961.

2. The privileges and immunities provided under paragraph 1 are not applicable to citizens or permanent residents of Burundi.

3. The Government of the United States will endeavor to ensure maximum possible compliance with the laws of the Burundi and will be prepared to discuss such disputes as may arise, and remove as promptly as feasible, either on its own initiative or on the request of the Government of Burundi, any United States Government employee covered by this Agreement who may abuse the privileges or immunities granted herein.

Article VI
EXEMPTIONS

In order to ensure the maximum benefits to the people of Burundi from the assistance to be furnished hereunder, whether initiated before or after the effective date of this Agreement:

(1) Any goods, supplies, materials, equipment, property, services or funds introduced into, acquired, or used in Burundi by the Government of the United States, or by any person or entity (including but not limited to contractors and grantees) financed by the Government of the United States, as part of, or in conjunction with, the assistance provided hereunder, are exempt from any and all taxes, including value-added taxes or other similar charges, while such goods, supplies, materials, equipment, property, services or funds are used in Burundi in connection with the assistance provided hereunder. Such goods, supplies, materials, equipment, property, services or funds are also exempt from any and all tariffs, customs duties, investment or deposit requirements, and currency controls. Such goods, supplies, materials, equipment, property, services or funds may be exported or re-exported from Burundi or sold or transferred to another person or entity in Burundi that is exempt from taxation and shall be exempt from any and all taxes, including value-added taxes or other similar charges, tariffs and customs duties on such export, re-export, sale or transfer. No tax (whether in the nature of an income, profits, business, rent, value-added, gross receipts, sales or other tax, duty, or fee of any nature, except fees which are commensurate with specific services rendered) shall be imposed in connection with work performed under this Agreement upon any person or entity (including but not limited to contractors and grantees) financed by the Government of the United States under the assistance furnished hereunder.

(2) In addition to personnel covered by Article V(1) above, all other personnel (and family members forming part of their households), except citizens and permanent residents of Burundi, who the Government of the United States, or any agency thereof, employs (whether by direct hire, contract or other arrangement) or finances (whether by contract, grant or otherwise with any person or entity) and who are present in Burundi to perform work in connection with this Agreement, are exempt from:

(a) Income and social security taxes levied under the laws of Burundi with respect to income derived from assistance programs;

(b) taxes (including but not limited to, sales or value-added taxes) on any of the following: (i) services or funds intended for their own use, (ii) residential leases, and (iii) the acquisition, ownership, or use of personal movable property (including vehicles) and the sale or transfer of such property to another person or entity exempt from taxation either under this Agreement or the laws of Burundi; and

(c) customs, import, and export duties on all personal effects (including vehicles), goods, equipment, supplies, services, or funds imported into Burundi for their own use, within six months of arriving in Burundi (provided that the six month period will be leniently applied where circumstances and fairness may so require) and from all other duties and fees of whatever nature, except fees which are commensurate with specific services rendered.

(3) The Government of Burundi will issue expeditiously and on a cost free basis any import licenses required for goods, supplies, materials, equipment, property, services or funds imported under this Agreement, and will assist, where appropriate, in expediting their movement through port and transportation facilities and their clearance through customs.

(4) The Government of Burundi will issue expeditiously and on a cost free basis any other documentation necessary to facilitate the implementation of programs, projects or activities funded under any assistance being provided in connection with this Agreement, including, but not limited to, visas required for individual employees and their families, work permits, and the registration, under Burundi law, of non-governmental organizations.

(5) The provisions of this Article VI will apply also to assistance, funded by the Government of the United States, occurring in or transiting through Burundi, intended to assist regional organizations or activities which include the Government of Burundi.

Article VII
INFORMATION AND PUBLICITY

1. The Government of Burundi will provide the Government of the United States of America with full and complete information concerning such programs and operations and other relevant information it may need to determine the nature and scope of operations and to evaluate the effectiveness of the assistance furnished or contemplated.

2. The Government of Burundi will give to the people of Burundi publicity concerning assistance programs under this Agreement.

Article VIII
FUNDS

1. Funds introduced into Burundi for purposes of furnishing assistance hereunder shall be convertible into the currency of Burundi at the highest rate of exchange not unlawful for any purpose at the time of conversion.

2. The Government of Burundi will establish a procedure whereby funds allocated to or derived from any assistance hereunder shall not be subject to any form of legal process, including, but not limited to, attachment or seizure by any person or juridical entity in Burundi, in the event that the Government of Burundi is advised by the Government of the United States that such legal process would interfere with the attainment of the objectives of such assistance.

Article IX
SUSPENSION AND TERMINATION

1. In addition to the provisions of any arrangements agreed upon pursuant to Article I, all or any part of any assistance provided hereunder may be suspended or terminated by either Party, upon written notice to the other Party. Termination of such assistance under this provision may include the termination of deliveries of any commodities not yet delivered.

2. This Agreement may be terminated 30 days after the receipt by either Party of a written termination notice from the other Party. Notwithstanding such termination, the provisions hereof shall remain in full force and effect with respect to assistance provided before the termination.

Article X
ENTRY INTO FORCE

This Agreement shall enter into force upon signature by authorized representatives of both Parties and shall remain in force until terminated by either Party in accordance with Article IX, paragraph 2.

IN WITNESS WHEREOF, the respective representatives, duly authorized for the purpose, have signed this Agreement at Bujumbura in duplicate in the English and French languages, the two texts being equally valid, on the 12th day of December, 2007.

For: The Government of the United States of America

[Signature]

By Patricia N. MOLLER

Ambassador

For: The Government of Burundi

[Signature]

By Antoinette BATUMUBWIRA

Minister of External Relations

STATE DEPARTMENT DOCUMENT NUMBER: 08-32

AGREEMENT BETWEEN THE UNITED STATES OF AMERICA AND THE FEDERATIVE REPUBLIC OF BRAZIL CONCERNING THE ACQUISITION AND RETENTION OF DIPLOMATIC AND CONSULAR PROPERTIES IN THE UNITED STATES AND BRAZIL

EFFECTED BY EXCHANGE OF NOTES AT BRASILIA, JUNE 1, 2007
ENTERED INTO FORCE JANUARY 18, 2008

CTIA DOCUMENT NUMBER: 13400.000

No. 211

The Embassy of the United States of America presents its compliments to the Ministry of External Relations of the Federative Republic of Brazil and has the honor to refer to your note No. 01 of June 1st, 2007, which reads as follows in English:

Having in mind the principles of reciprocity of treatment found in the Vienna Convention on Diplomatic Relations and the Vienna Convention on Consular Relations;

1. Considering that in relation to the performance of civil and commercial actions including the transfer of title of real estate, the Government of the United States of America does not impose on diplomatic missions and career consular posts established in the U.S. territory the obligation to participate in the host State social security system, I have the honor to propose to Your Excellency, on behalf of the Federative Republic of Brazil, the adoption, by our two governments, of the following:

— on the basis of reciprocity, the Government of Brazil shall issue, whenever requested, on behalf of the Embassy and Career Consular Posts of the United States of America, pertinent documentation to be provided by the Brazilian Federal Revenue Service that will allow for the transfer of title of diplomatic and consular properties, including residences, of the United States of America in the Brazilian territory.

— the Government of Brazil and the Government of the United States of America shall grant, according to their applicable internal legislation, the necessary approval for the acquisition, sale or other disposition of diplomatic and consular properties, including residences, in their respective territories.

2. This agreement shall bear no impact on the positions of both Parties regarding the interpretation of the Vienna Convention on Diplomatic Relations and the Vienna Convention on Consular Relations on the subject of social security matters.

3. Considering that the Government of United States of America agrees with the above proposals, this Note and the reply Note of Your Excellency, in which such concurrence is expressed, shall constitute an Agreement between the Government of the Federative Republic of Brazil and the

Government of the United States of America, that shall come into force on the date of the second Diplomatic Note in which one of the two Governments informs the other about the fulfillment of the respective internal legal requirements for its coming into effect.

4. The present Agreement shall remain effective for an indefinite period of time and may be denounced at any time by initiative of either Party, upon written notification that will come into effect one year after its receipt by the other Party.

I have the honor to inform you that the Government of the United States of America agrees with the proposals contained in your note. Therefore, your note and this note in reply constitute an agreement between the Government of the United States of America and the Government of the Federative Republic of Brazil, which shall enter into force on the date of the second diplomatic note in which one of the two governments informs the other about the fulfillment of its respective internal legal requirements for entry into force.

The Embassy of the United States of America avails itself of this opportunity to renew to the Ministry of External Relations of the Federative Republic of Brazil the assurances of its highest consideration.

Enclosure:

DipNote from Brazilian Government as stated (in Portuguese)

Embassy of the United States of America,

Brasilia, June 1, 2007.

JAN 03 2008

STATE DEPARTMENT DOCUMENT NUMBER: 08-33

AGREEMENT BETWEEN THE UNITES STATES OF AMERICA AND THE REPUBLIC OF TUNISIA REGARDING GRANTS UNDER THE FOREIGN ASSISTANCE ACT OF 1961, AS AMENDED, OR SUCCESSOR LEGISLATION, AND THE FURNISHING OF DEFENSE ARTICLES, RELATED TRAINING, AND OTHER DEFENSE SERVICES, INCLUDING PURSUANT TO THE UNITED STATES INTERNATIONAL MILITARY AND EDUCATION TRAINING (IMET) PROGRAM

EFFECTED BY EXCHANGE OF NOTES AT TUNIS,
NOVEMBER 23, 2007 AND FEBRUARY 13, 2008
ENTERED INTO FORCE FEBRUARY 13, 2008

CTIA DOCUMENT NUMBER: 13401.000

Republic of Tunisia
Ministry of Foreign Affairs

Embassy of the United States of America
- Tunis-

The Ministry of Foreign Affairs of the Republic of Tunisia presents its compliments to the Embassy of the United States of America and acknowledges receipt of the Embassy's Note N° 1657 dated November 23, 2007 which reads as follows:

> «The Embassy of the United States of America presents its compliments to the Ministry of Foreign Affairs of the Republic of Tunisia and has the honor to refer to earlier discussions between representatives of the two governments regarding grants under the Foreign Assistance Act of 1961, as amended, or successor legislation, and the furnishing of defense articles, related training and other defense services, including pursuant to the United States International Military Education and Training Program, from the United States of America to the Government of the Republic of Tunisia pursuant to the Foreign Assistance Act of 1961, or successor legislation.
>
> In this regard the Embassy refers to the Agreement concerning payment to the United States of net proceeds from the sale or disposal of defense articles furnished on a grant basis, effected by exchange of notes at Tunis on May 21 and June 29, 1974, as amended, and to the Agreement relating to a program of grants of military equipment and material to Tunisia, effected by exchange of notes at Tunis on September 12 and October 25, 1974.

In accordance with these discussions, it is proposed that the Government of the Republic of Tunisia agree:

A. That unless the consent of the Government of the United States of America has been first obtained the Government of the Republic of Tunisia shall not:

I. Permit any use of such defense articles, related training, including training materials, or other defense services by anyone not an officer, employee or agent of the Government of the Republic of Tunisia;

II. Transfer; or permit any officer, employee or agent of the Government of the Republic of Tunisia to transfer, such defense articles, related training, including training materials, or other defense services by gift, sale, or otherwise; or

III. Use, or permit the use of, such defense articles, related training, including training materials, or other defense services for purposes other than those for which provided;

B. That such defense articles, related training, including training materials, or other defense services shall be returned to the Government of the United States of America when they are no longer needed for the purposes for which they were furnished, unless the Government of the United States of America consents to another disposition;

C. That the net proceeds of sale received by the Government of the Republic of Tunisia in disposing of, with prior written consent of the Government of the United States of America, any defense article furnished by the Government of the United States of America on a grant basis, including scrap from any such defense article, shall be paid to the Government of the United States of America;

D. That the Government of the Republic of Tunisia shall maintain the security of such defense articles, related training, including training materials, and other defense services; that it shall provide substantially the same degree of security protection afforded to such defense articles, related training, including training materials, or other defense services by the Government of the United States of America; that it shall, as the Government of the United States of America may require, permit continuous information to representatives of the Government of the United States of America with regard to the use thereof by the Government of the Republic of Tunisia; and

E. That the Government of the United States of America may also, from time to time, make the provision of articles and services furnished under other authority (except the United States Arms Export control Act) subject to the terms and conditions of the agreement proposed herein. (Transfers under the United States Arms Export Control Act shall continue to be governed by the requirements of that Act and United States regulations applicable to such transfers).

It is further proposed that this Agreement shall supersede the above-referenced 1974 agreement. This Agreement shall apply to defense articles and defense services to which the superseded 1974 agreement had applied prior to entry into force on the date of the Ministry's note.

The Embassy of the United States of America in Tunis avails itself of this opportunity to renew to the Ministry of Foreign Affairs the assurances of its highest consideration.

Embassy of the United States of America Tunis, November 23, 2007»

The Ministry of Foreign Affairs of the Republic of Tunisia has the honor to confirm that the proposals set forth in the Embassy's note and this note in reply shall constitute an Agreement between the two Governments which shall enter into force on this date.

Tunis, February 13th, 2008.

No. 1657

The Embassy of the United States of America presents its compliments to the Ministry of Foreign Affairs of the Republic of Tunisia and has the honor to refer to earlier discussions between representatives of the two governments regarding grants under the Foreign Assistance Act of 1961, as amended, or successor legislation, and the furnishing of defense articles, related training, and other defense services, including pursuant to the United States International Military Education and Training Program, from the United States of America to the Government of the Republic of Tunisia pursuant to the Foreign Assistance Act of 1961, or successor legislation.

In this regard the Embassy refers to the Agreement concerning payment to the United States of net proceeds from the sale or disposal of defense articles furnished on a grant basis, effected by exchange of notes at Tunis on May 21 and June 29, 1974, as amended, and to the Agreement relating to a program of grants of military equipment and material to Tunisia, effected by exchange of notes at Tunis on September 12 and October 25, 1974.

In accordance with these discussions, it is proposed that the Government of the Republic of Tunisia agree:

A. That unless the consent of the Government of the United States of America has been first obtained the Government of the Republic of Tunisia shall not:

(I) Permit any use of such defense articles, related training, including training materials, or other defense services by anyone not an officer, employee or agent of the Government of the Republic of Tunisia;

(II) Transfer, or permit any officer, employee or agent of the Government of the Republic of Tunisia to transfer, such defense articles, related training, including training materials, or other defense services by gift, sale or otherwise; or

(III) Use, or permit the use of, such defense articles, related training, including training materials, or other defense services for purposes other than those for which provided;

B. That such defense articles, related training, including training materials, or other defense services shall be returned to the Government of the United States of America when they are no longer needed for the purposes for which they were furnished, unless the Government of the United States of America consents to another disposition;

C. That the net proceeds of sale received by the Government of the Republic of Tunisia in disposing of, with prior written consent of the Government of the United States of America, any defense article furnished by the Government of the United States of America on a grant basis, including scrap from any such defense article, shall be paid to the Government of the United States of America;

D. That the Government of the Republic of Tunisia shall maintain the security of such defense articles, related training, including training materials, and other defense services; that it shall provide substantially the same degree of security protection afforded to such defense articles, related training, including training materials, or other defense services by the Government of the United States of America; that it shall, as the Government of the United States of America may require, permit continuous information to representatives of the Government of the United States of America with regard to the use thereof by the Government of the Republic of Tunisia; and

E. That the Government of the United States of America may also, from time to time, make the provision of articles and services furnished under other authority (except the United States Arms Export Control Act) subject to the terms and conditions of the agreement proposed herein. (Transfers under the United States Arms Export Control Act shall continue to be governed by the requirements of that Act and United States regulations applicable to such transfers.)

It is further proposed that this Agreement shall supersede the above-referenced 1974 agreement. This Agreement shall apply to defense articles and defense services to which the superseded 1974 agreement had applied prior to entry into force on the date of the Ministry's note.

The Embassy of the United States of America in Tunis avails itself of this opportunity to renew to the Ministry of Foreign Affairs the assurances of its highest consideration.

Attachments: Non-Paper on 505 Agreement

Suggested Text for Ministry's Response

Embassy of the United States of America

Tunis, **23 NOV. 2007**

STATE DEPARTMENT DOCUMENT NUMBER: 08-34

AGREEMENT EXTENDING PROVISIONAL APPLICATION OF THE MARITIME BOUNDARY AGREEMENT OF DECEMBER 16, 1977, AS EXTENDED, BETWEEN THE UNITED STATES OF AMERICA AND THE REPUBLIC OF CUBA

EFFECTED BY EXCHANGE OF NOTES AT WASHINGTON D.C.
AND HAVANA, FEBRUARY 6 AND 25, 2008
ENTERED INTO FORCE FEBRUARY 25, 2008,
WITH EFFECT FROM JANUARY 1, 2008

CTIA DOCUMENT NUMBER: 2677.008

DEPARTMENT OF STATE
WASHINGTON

The Department of State refers the Embassy of Switzerland to the Embassy's note, dated February 8, 2008, which forwarded note No. RS/266, dated February 6, 2008, from the Ministry of Foreign Relations of the Republic of Cuba to the Embassy of Switzerland in Havana, which note reads as follows:

> The Ministry of Foreign Relations of the Republic of Cuba presents its compliments to the Embassy of Switzerland and, with respect to the United States Interests Section, has the honor to refer to the Maritime Boundary Agreement between the Republic of Cuba and the United States of America, signed at Washington, D.C. on December 16, 1977, and to the acceptance of both governments to apply the terms of said Agreement provisionally as of January 1, 1978, for a period of two years, pending the permanent entry into force of the Agreement on the date of the exchange of instruments of ratification.
>
> The Ministry wishes to refer to subsequent agreements between the Government of the Republic of Cuba and the Government of the United States of America to continue applying the Maritime Boundary Agreement provisionally for successive two-year periods, most recently from December 31, 2007, via the notes exchanged on December 12, 2005 and March 30, 2006.
>
> The Ministry, representing the Government of the Republic of Cuba, has the honor to propose that the terms of the Maritime Boundary Agreement of December 16, 1977 continue to be applied on a provisional basis beginning January 1, 2008, for a period of two years, pending its permanent entry into force on the date of the exchange of instruments of ratification.
>
> If the proposal of the Ministry of Foreign Relations is acceptable to the Government of the United States of America, the Ministry proposes that this note and the affirmative response on behalf of the Department of State of the United States of America shall constitute an agreement between the Governments of the Republic of Cuba and of the United States of America, which shall enter into force on the date of response, effective as of January 1, 2008.

The Ministry of Foreign Relations avails itself of this opportunity to renew to the Embassy of Switzerland the assurances of its highest consideration.

The Department of State informs the Embassy and through it the Cuban Interests Section that the proposal of the Ministry of Foreign Relations of Cuba to continue to apply, on a provisional basis, from January 1, 2008, for a two-year period, the terms of the Maritime Boundary Agreement, until such time as its definitive entry into force on the date of exchange of instruments of ratification, is acceptable to the Government of the United States of America, and that the Ministry's note and the Department's note in reply shall constitute an agreement between the Government of the United States of America and the Government of the Republic of Cuba, which enters into force on the date of this note.

Department of State,
Washington, February 25, 2008.

Schweizerische Eidgenossenschaft
Confédération suisse
Confederazione Svizzera
Confederaziun svizra

Embassy of Switzerland in the United States of America

U.S. Department of State
Office of Cuban Affairs
2201 C Street, N.W.
Washington, D.C. 20520

The Embassy of Switzerland presents its compliments to the U.S. Department of State and has the honor to inform that the Cuban Ministry of Foreign Affairs wishes to continue to apply provisionally the Maritime Boundary Agreement between the United States of America and the Republic of Cuba of 1977 for a period of two years starting January 1, 2008.

The Embassy of Switzerland avails itself of this opportunity to renew to the U.S. Department of State the assurances of its highest consideration

Washington, D.C. February 8, 2008

U.S. Department of State Office of Language Services Translating Division

LS No. 02-2008-0137
Spanish/English
JF/TGR

Translation

Republic of Cuba
Ministry of Foreign Relations

Embassy of Switzerland,
Havana.

No. RS/266

The Ministry of Foreign Relations of the Republic of Cuba presents its compliments to the Embassy of Switzerland and, with respect to the United States Interests Section, has the honor to refer to the Maritime Boundary Agreement between the Republic of Cuba and the United States of America, signed at Washington, D.C. on December 16, 1977, and to the acceptance of both governments to apply the terms of said Agreement provisionally as of January 1, 1978, for a period of two years, pending the permanent entry into force of the Agreement on the date of the exchange of instruments of ratification.

The Ministry wishes to refer to subsequent agreements between the Government of the Republic of Cuba and the Government of the United States of America to continue applying the Maritime Boundary Agreement provisionally for successive two-year periods, most recently from December 31, 2007, via the notes exchanged on December 12, 2005, and March 30, 2006.

The Ministry, representing the Government of the Republic of Cuba, has the honor to propose that the terms of the Maritime Boundary Agreement of December 16, 1977, continue to be applied on a provisional basis beginning January 1, 2008, for a period of two years, pending its permanent entry into force on the date of the exchange of instruments of ratification.

If the proposal of the Ministry of Foreign Relations is acceptable to the Government of the United States of America, the Ministry proposes that this note and the affirmative response on behalf of the Department of State of the United States of America shall constitute an agreement between the Governments of the Republic of Cuba and of the United States of America, which shall enter into force on the date of response, effective as of January 1, 2008.

The Ministry of Foreign Relations avails itself of this opportunity to renew to the Embassy of Switzerland the assurances of its highest consideration.

Havana, February 6, 2008

"Year 50 of the Revolution"

[Initialed]

[Stamp]

STATE DEPARTMENT DOCUMENT NUMBER: 08-35

AGREEMENT BETWEEN THE DEPARTMENT OF ENERGY OF THE UNITED STATES OF AMERICA AND THE MINISTRY OF THE INTERIOR OF THE REPUBLIC OF LATVIA FOR COOPERATION IN THE PREVENTION OF ILLICIT TRAFFICKING IN NUCLEAR AND OTHER RADIOACTIVE MATERIAL

SIGNED AT RIGA, DECEMBER 3, 2007
ENTERED INTO FORCE DECEMBER 3, 2007

CTIA DOCUMENT NUMBER: 13402.000

The Department of Energy of the United States of America (DOE) and the Ministry of the Interior of the Republic of Latvia (MOI), hereinafter referred to jointly as the "Parties";

Desiring to implement the Agreement between the Government of the United States of America and the Government of the Republic of Latvia Concerning Cooperation in the Area of the Prevention of Proliferation of Weapons of Mass Destruction of December 11, 2001, as amended (hereinafter referred to as the Counterproliferation Agreement), as it pertains to countering the proliferation of weapons of mass destruction, and technology, materials, and expertise related to such weapons;

Desiring to cooperate to prevent the illicit trafficking in nuclear and other radioactive material through technical and methodological cooperation, including the improvement of systems for the detection and identification of these materials at those state border crossing places of the Republic of Latvia (hereinafter Latvia) as the Parties jointly determine; and

Having regard to the obligations of Latvia deriving from its membership in the European Community and the European Atomic Energy Community;

Have agreed as follows:

ARTICLE I

For purposes of this Agreement:

1. "Special nuclear material" means plutonium, and uranium enriched to levels of 20% or higher in the isotope U-235.

2. "Other radioactive materials" include, but are not limited to, radioactive sources suitable for use in radiological dispersal devices.

ARTICLE II

1. In accordance with the terms of this Agreement, the DOE, through its National Nuclear Security Administration, may provide the MOI, assistance at no cost in the form of equipment, materials, training and services for MOI's use at those state border crossing places of Latvia as the Parties jointly determine, for the purpose of detecting and interdicting illicit trafficking in special nuclear material and other radioactive materials which are entering or exiting the territory of Latvia.

2. The MOI or its designated implementing agents shall use all materials (including supplies, equipment and instruments), training and services provided in accordance with this Agreement exclusively for the purpose of detecting and interdicting illicit trafficking in special nuclear material and other radioactive materials which are entering or exiting the territory of Latvia.

3. This Agreement and all activities undertaken in accordance with this Agreement shall be subject to the provisions of the Counterproliferation Agreement. In the event of any discrepancies between this Agreement and the Counterproliferation Agreement, the provisions of the Counterproliferation Agreement shall prevail.

ARTICLE III

1. Each Party to this Agreement shall have the right, following written notification to the other Party, to delegate responsibilities for the implementation of this Agreement to other agencies, departments or units of its respective Government.

2. Each Party to this Agreement shall have the right, following written notification to the other Party, to designate technical liaison representatives for equipment, materials, training and services provided pursuant to this Agreement.

ARTICLE IV

1. Within the framework of this Agreement, DOE's technical assistance may include:

a. Delivery and installation at those state border crossing places of Latvia as the Parties jointly determine of equipment adapted as appropriate for customs control conditions (including testing, setup and demonstration of the equipment);

b. Delivery of spare parts kits, test equipment and other maintenance equipment to maintain the DOE-supplied equipment;

c. Training of MOI personnel and other appropriate personnel in detection of special nuclear material and other radioactive materials, and in the proper use and maintenance of the equipment provided by DOE;

d. Support for maintenance of the equipment provided by DOE, as set forth in a maintenance and sustainability plan jointly agreed by the Parties; and

e. Additional areas of cooperation as may be agreed by the Parties in writing.

2. By mutual agreement of the Parties, technical workshops, consultations, site surveys and acceptance testing of materials and installed equipment may be conducted. By mutual agreement of the Parties, joint working groups of technical experts may be formed to exchange technical information and to make proposals on technical and training matters related to the effective implementation of this Agreement.

3. Conditions of assistance provided under this Agreement shall be defined by separate contracts or arrangements between DOE and MOI or their designated implementing agents. In case of any inconsistency between these contracts or arrangements and this Agreement, the provisions of this Agreement shall prevail.

4. Pursuant to the terms of this Agreement, DOE may, at its discretion, provide the MOI and its designated implementing agents with other types of assistance subject to the written agreement of both Parties.

ARTICLE V

1. The MOI and its designated implementing agents shall assist the DOE and its designated implementing agents during implementation of the Agreement.

2. The MOI and its designated implementing agents shall coordinate with other appropriate Latvian ministries, agencies and organizations to ensure that materials, including supplies, equipment and instruments, provided to the MOI under this Agreement are afforded priority processing to allow prompt engineering approvals and equipment and materials deliveries to their ultimate destination within Latvia.

3. The MOI and its designated implementing agents shall coordinate with the appropriate Latvian ministries, agencies, and organizations to ensure that appropriate security measures are provided for United States government personnel, contractors and materials, including supplies, equipment and instruments, at those facilities associated with work under this Agreement.

4. The MOI and its designated implementing agents shall facilitate the examination by the appropriate Latvian ministries, agencies and organizations of all materials, including supplies, equipment and instruments, received under this Agreement, and provide confirmation to the DOE of their acceptability within ten days of receipt of the results of such examinations. The terms and conditions for repair or replacement of non-complying materials, including supplies, equipment and instruments, will be set forth in the contract(s) under which the materials, including supplies, equipment and instruments, are provided under this Agreement.

ARTICLE VI

In addition to the audit and examination rights set forth in Article XII of the Counterproliferation Agreement, DOE representatives shall have the right to monitor the implementation of terms of contracts and the progress of work under this Agreement, at facilities on the territory of Latvia.

ARTICLE VII

The MOI shall furnish the U.S. Customs and Border Protection with data on any detections or seizures of unauthorized special nuclear material and other radioactive materials that are in breach of customs legislation, in accordance with the provisions of the Agreement between the European Community and the United States of America on Customs Cooperation and Mutual Assistance in Customs Matters of May 28, 1977, as amended.

ARTICLE VIII

As appropriate, the Parties may enter into implementing arrangements to carry out the provisions of this Agreement. In case of any inconsistency between this Agreement and any such arrangements, the provisions of this Agreement shall prevail.

ARTICLE IX

This Agreement shall enter into force upon signature and remain in force for the duration of the Counterproliferation Agreement. The Agreement may be amended by written agreement of the

Parties and may be terminated by either Party upon at least 90 days' prior written notification to the other Party.

IN WITNESS WHEREOF, the undersigned, being duly authorized by their respective Governments, have signed this Agreement.

DONE at Riga this 3rd day of December 2007, in duplicate in the English and Latvian languages, both texts being equally authentic.

FOR THE DEPARTMENT OF ENERGY OF THE UNITED STATES OF AMERICA:	FOR THE MINISTRY OF THE INTERIOR OF THE REPUBLIC OF LATVIA:
[Signature]	[Signature]

STATE DEPARTMENT DOCUMENT NUMBER: 08-36

AGREEMENT BETWEEN THE UNITED STATES OF AMERICA AND JAPAN CONCERNING NEW SPECIAL MEASURES RELATING TO ARTICLE XXIV OF THE AGREEMENT UNDER ARTICLE VI OF THE TREATY OF MUTUAL COOPERATION AND SECURITY BETWEEN THE UNITED STATES OF AMERICA AND JAPAN REGARDING FACILITIES AND AREAS AND THE STATUS OF UNITED STATES ARMED FORCES IN JAPAN, WITH AGREED MINUTES AND EXCHANGE OF NOTES

SIGNED AT TOKYO, JANUARY 25, 2008
ENTERED INTO FORCE FEBRUARY 5, 2008

CTIA DOCUMENT NUMBER: 13403.000

The United States of America and Japan,

Confirming that the United States armed forces maintained in Japan under the Treaty of Mutual Cooperation and Security between the United States of America and Japan (hereinafter referred to as "the Treaty") and the Agreement under Article VI of the Treaty of Mutual Cooperation and Security between the United States of America and Japan, Regarding Facilities and Areas and the Status of United States Armed Forces in Japan (hereinafter referred to as "the Status of Forces Agreement"), both signed at Washington on January 19, 1960 (hereinafter referred to as "the United States armed forces"), contribute to the security of Japan and the maintenance of international peace and security in the Far East,

Recalling that, for the purposes of maintaining stable employment of the workers who are employed by Japan and render labor services to the United States armed forces or to the organizations provided for in paragraph 1(a) of Article XV of the Status of Forces Agreement (hereinafter referred to as "the workers") and ensuring the effective operations of the United States armed forces, various measures were provided for, inter alia, special measures relating to Article XXIV of the Status of Forces Agreement which sets forth the principles on the sharing of expenditures incident to the maintenance of the United States armed forces in the Agreement between the United States of America and Japan concerning New Special Measures relating to Article XXIV of the Agreement under Article VI of the Treaty of Mutual Cooperation and Security between the United States of America and Japan, Regarding Facilities and Areas and the Status of United States Armed Forces in Japan, signed at Tokyo on January 23, 2006,

Noting situations involving both countries,

Recognizing that, for the purpose of ensuring the effective operations of the United States armed forces, it is necessary to take new special measures relating to Article XXIV of the Status of Forces Agreement,

Have agreed as follows:

Article I

Japan will bear, during the Japanese fiscal years 2008, 2009 and 2010, all or a part of the expenditures in paying the following wages to the workers:

(a) base pay, daily wage of daily employees, special term employees salary, hourly pay temporary employees hourly pay and theater personnel wage;

(b) regional allowance, discharge allowance, family allowance, remote area allowance, special work allowance, summer allowance, year end allowance, cold area allowance, retirement allowance including retirement allowances for workers separated by the United States armed forces or by the organizations provided for in paragraph 1(a) of Article XV of the Status of Forces Agreement through reduction in force and for workers whose employment is terminated for duty-connected disability or death due to duty-connected injury or illness, involuntary severance bonus for employees affected by reduction in force, pro rata bonus for employees affected by reduction in force, commutation allowance, conversion allowance, position conversion allowance, night duty allowance, housing allowance, unaccompanied duty allowance, wide-area transfer allowance, overtime pay, hourly pay temporary employees premium pay, holiday pay, night differential, non-work allowance and daily pay authorized for duty-connected illness or injury for hourly pay temporary employees; and

(c) allowance for lump sum payment to mariners for unexecuted annual leave, dangerous cargo allowance, engagement allowance, engine room allowance, engine work allowance, fire-fighting allowance, foreign ship bonus, foreign voyage allowance, labor allowance, reporting allowance, small vessel allowance, tanker allowance, towage allowance and master and chief engineer allowance.

Article II

Japan will bear, during the Japanese fiscal years 2008, 2009 and 2010, all or a part of the expenditures in paying costs of the following procured for official purposes in Japan by the United States armed forces, or by authorized procurement agencies of the United States armed forces upon appropriate certification:

(a) electricity, gas, water supply and sewerage from public utilities; and

(b) fuels for heating, cooking and hot water supply not included in (a) above.

Article III

With regard to training that the United States armed forces conduct using any specific facilities and areas among those facilities and areas the use of which is granted to the United States of America under Article VI of the Treaty (hereinafter referred to as "facilities and areas"), in cases where the United States of America, upon a request of the Government of Japan made at the Joint Committee provided for in paragraph 1 of Article XXV of the Status of Forces Agreement (hereinafter referred to as "the Joint Committee"), changes to the use of other facilities and areas instead of using the said specific facilities and areas all or a part of the said training, Japan will bear all or a part of the additional expenditures incident to such changes, provided that the Government of Japan, on making the above mentioned request, notifies the Government of the United States of America that Japan will bear expenditures in accordance with the provisions of this Article.

Article IV

The United States of America will make further efforts to economize the expenditures referred to in Article I, Article II and Article III.

Article V

Japan will determine, for each Japanese fiscal year, the actual amount of the expenditures that Japan will bear under Article I, Article II and Article III respectively and will promptly notify the United States of America of such determination.

Article VI

The United States of America and Japan may consult on all matters regarding the operation of this Agreement through the Joint Committee.

Article VII

This Agreement shall be approved by the United States of America and Japan in accordance with their respective internal legal procedures. This Agreement shall enter into force on the date when diplomatic notes indicating such approval are exchanged, and shall remain in force until March 31, 2011.

IN WITNESS WHEREOF the undersigned, duly authorized for the purpose, have signed the present Agreement.

DONE in duplicate at Tokyo in the English and Japanese languages, both equally authentic, this twenty-fifth day of January, 2008.

FOR THE UNITED STATES OF AMERICA:	FOR JAPAN:
[Signature]	[Signature]

AGREED MINUTES TO THE AGREEMENT BETWEEN THE UNITED STATES OF AMERICA AND JAPAN CONCERNING NEW SPECIAL MEASURES RELATING TO ARTICLE XXIV OF THE AGREEMENT UNDER ARTICLE VI OF THE TREATY OF MUTUAL COOPERATION AND SECURITY BETWEEN THE UNITED STATES OF AMERICA AND JAPAN, REGARDING FACILITIES AND AREAS AND THE STATUS OF UNITED STATES ARMED FORCES IN JAPAN, SIGNED AT TOKYO ON JANUARY 25, 2008

In connection with the discussions on Article I of the Agreement between the United States of America and Japan concerning New Special Measures relating to Article XXIV of the Agreement under Article VI of the Treaty of Mutual Cooperation and Security between the United States of America and Japan, Regarding Facilities and Areas and the Status of United States Armed Forces in Japan, signed at Tokyo on January 25, 2008 (hereinafter referred to as "the Agreement"), the representatives of the United States of America and Japan have agreed to record the following:

It is confirmed that the wages mentioned in Article I of the Agreement do not include those portions which had been already included in the part borne by Japan before the entry into force of the Agreement between the United States of America and Japan concerning Special Measures relating to Article XXIV of the Agreement under Article VI of the Treaty of Mutual Cooperation and Security between the United States of America and Japan, Regarding Facilities and Areas and the Status of United States Armed Forces in Japan, signed at Tokyo on January 30, 1987.

Tokyo, January 25, 2008

FOR THE UNITED STATES OF AMERICA:

____

[Signature]

FOR JAPAN:

____

[Signature]

Translation

Tokyo, February 5, 2008

His Excellency
Mr. John Thomas Schieffer
Ambassador Extraordinary
and Plenipotentiary
of the United States of America

Excellency,

I have the honor to refer to Japan's Law Regarding Special Measures Concerning Supply Assistance Activities in Support of Counter-Terrorism Maritime Interdiction Activities (Law No.1 of 2008, hereinafter referred to as "the Law").

The purpose of the Law is to continue active and voluntary contributions to efforts by the international community for the prevention and eradication of international terrorism, and thereby contribute to ensuring peace and security of the international community including Japan, through activities related to the provision of supplies and services of the Self-Defense Forces of Japan (limited to activities that provide fuel for vessels or rotary wing aircraft carried on vessels and water) to vessels of the armed forces or other similar entities of foreign countries which are engaged in duties related to activities that contribute to the achievement of the purposes of the Charter of the United Nations by making efforts to eradicate the threat caused by the terrorist attacks in the United States of America on September 11, 2001, and to take such necessary measures as the inspection and verification of vessels sailing the Indian Ocean with a view to interdicting and deterring the movements of terrorists, weapons or other material under international cooperation (hereinafter referred to as "counter-terrorism maritime interdiction activities"), in order to assist in the smooth and effective implementation of counter-terrorism maritime interdiction activities.

I have further the honor to refer to the discussions that have taken place between our two Governments concerning supplies and services in the field of logistic support (hereinafter referred to as "the logistic support, supplies, and services") contributed to the armed forces or other similar entities of the United States of America in accordance with the Law and to propose on behalf of the Government of Japan the following arrangements as a result of those discussions:

1. The use of logistic support, supplies and services contributed to and accepted by the armed forces or other similar entities of the United States of America in accordance with the Law shall be consistent with the Charter of the United Nations.

2. The logistic support, supplies and services contributed to and accepted by the armed forces or other similar entities of the United States of America in accordance with the Law shall not be transferred, either temporarily or permanently, by any means to persons outside of the armed forces or other similar entities of the United States of America, without prior consent of the Government of Japan.

3. The official, or officials of the Department of Defense or other similar entities of the United States of America with authority to accept logistic support, supplies and services to be contributed in accordance with the Law shall be informed, in writing, by the official, or officials of the Government of Japan of the conditions contained in Paragraphs 1 and 2 above.

4. The Government of Japan and the Government of the United States of America will consult with each other for the purpose of effective implementation of the present arrangements.

I have further the honor to propose that, if the proposals set out above are acceptable to the Government of the United States of America, this Note and Your Excellency's reply to that effect on behalf of the Government of the United States of America shall be regarded as constituting an agreement between the two Governments in this matter, which shall enter into force on the date of Your Excellency's reply.

I avail myself of this opportunity to renew to Your Excellency the assurance of my highest consideration.

Masahiko Koumura
Minister for Foreign Affairs
of Japan

Tokyo, February 5, 2008

His Excellency
Mr. Masahiko Koumura
Minister of Foreign Affairs
Of Japan

Excellency,

I have the honor to acknowledge the receipt of Your Excellency's Note of today's date concerning the discussions that have taken place between our two Governments concerning the logistic support, supplies and services contributed to the armed forces or other similar entities of the United States of America, which reads as follows:

"Excellency,

I have the honor to refer to Japan's Law Regarding Special Measures Concerning Supply Assistance Activities in Support of Counter-Terrorism Maritime Interdiction Activities (Law No.1 of 2008, hereinafter referred to as "the Law").

The purpose of the Law is to continue active and voluntary contributions to efforts by the international community for the prevention and eradication of international terrorism, and thereby contribute to ensuring peace and security of the international community including Japan, through activities related to the provision of supplies and services of the Self-Defense Forces of Japan (limited to activities that provide fuel for vessels or rotary wing aircraft carried on vessels and water) to vessels of the armed forces or other similar entities of foreign countries which are engaged in duties related to activities that contribute to the achievement of the purposes of the Charter of the United Nations by making efforts to eradicate the threat caused by the terrorist attacks in the United States of America on September 11, 2001, and to take such necessary measures as the inspection and verification of vessels sailing the Indian Ocean with a view to interdicting and deterring the movements of terrorists, weapons or other material under international cooperation (hereinafter referred to as "counter-terrorism maritime interdiction activities"), in order to assist in the smooth and effective implementation of counter-terrorism maritime interdiction activities."

I have further the honor to refer to the discussions that have taken place between our two Governments concerning supplies and services in the field of logistic support (hereinafter referred to as "the logistic support, supplies, and services") contributed to the armed forces or other similar entities of the United States of America in accordance with the Law and to propose on behalf of the Government of Japan the following arrangements as a result of those discussions:

1. The use of logistic support, supplies and services contributed to and accepted by the armed forces or other similar entities of the United States of America in accordance with the Law shall be consistent with the Charter of the United Nations.

2. The logistic support, supplies and services contributed to and accepted by the armed forces or other similar entities of the United States of America in accordance with the Law shall not be transferred, either temporarily or permanently, by any means to persons outside of the armed forces or other similar entities of the United States of America, without prior consent of the Government of Japan.

3. The official, or officials of the Department of Defense or other similar entities of the United States of America with authority to accept logistic support, supplies and services to be contributed in accordance with the Law shall be informed, in writing, by the official, or officials of the Government of Japan of the conditions contained in Paragraphs 1 and 2 above.

4. The Government of Japan and the Government of the United States of America will consult with each other for the purpose of effective implementation of the present arrangements.

I have further the honor to propose that, if the proposals set out above are acceptable to the Government of the United States of America, this Note and Your Excellency's reply to that effect on behalf of the

> Government of the United States of America shall be regarded as constituting an agreement between the two Governments in this matter, which shall enter into force on the date of Your Excellency's reply.
>
> I avail myself of this opportunity to renew to Your Excellency the assurance of my highest consideration."

I have further the honor to confirm on behalf of the Government of the United States of America that the proposals set out in Your Excellency's Note are acceptable to the Government of the United States of America and that Your Excellency's Note and this reply shall be regarded as constituting an agreement between the two Governments, which shall enter into force on the-date of this reply.

I avail myself of this opportunity to renew to Your Excellency the assurance of my highest consideration.

[Signatures]

Ambassador Extraordinary And
Plenipotentiary Of the United States of
America

Senate Treaty Document Number: 110-15

Protocol Amending the Convention Between the United States of America and Canada with Respect to Taxes on Income and on Capital Done at Washington D.C. on 26 September 1980, as Amended by the Protocols Done on 14 June 1983, 28 March 1984, 17 March 1995 and 29 July 1997

Signed at Chelsea, September 21, 2007
Approved by the U.S. Senate on September 23, 2008

CTIA Document Number: 2430.004

LETTER OF TRANSMITTAL

The White House, *March 13, 2008*

To the Senate of the United States:

I transmit herewith, for Senate advice and consent to ratification, the Protocol Amending the Convention Between the United States of America and Canada with Respect to Taxes on Income and on Capital done at Washington on September 26, 1980, as Amended by the Protocols done on June 14, 1983, March 28, 1984, March 17, 1995, and July 29, 1997, signed on September 21, 2007, at Chelsea (the "proposed Protocol"). The proposed Protocol would amend the existing income tax Convention between the United States and Canada that was concluded in 1980, as amended by prior protocols (the "existing Treaty"). Also transmitted for the information of the Senate is the report of the Department of State with respect to the proposed Protocol.

The proposed Protocol would eliminate withholding taxes on cross-border interest payments. In addition, the proposed Protocol would coordinate the tax treatment of contributions to, and other benefits of, pension funds for cross-border workers. The proposed Protocol also includes provisions related to the taxation of permanent establishments, so-called dual-resident corporations, income derived through certain entities that are considered fiscally transparent, and former U.S. citizens and long-term residents. The proposed Protocol further strengthens the existing Treaty's provisions that prevent the Treaty's inappropriate use by third-country residents. The proposed Protocol also provides for mandatory resolution of certain cases before the competent authorities.

I recommend that the Senate give early and favorable consideration to the proposed Protocol and give its advice and consent to ratification.

George W. Bush

LETTER OF SUBMITTAL

Department of State,
Washington, DC February 29, 2008.

The President:
The White House.

The President: I have the honor to submit to you, with a view to its transmission to the Senate for advice and consent to ratification, the Protocol Amending the Convention Between the United States of America and Canada with Respect to Taxes on Income and on Capital Done at Washington on 26 September 1980, as Amended by the Protocols Done on 14 June 1983, 28 March 1984, 17 March 1995, and 29 July 1997, signed on September 21, 2007, at Chelsea (the "proposed Protocol") and related exchanges of notes. The proposed Protocol would amend the existing income tax Convention between the United States and Canada which was concluded in 1980, as amended by prior protocols (the "existing Treaty").

The proposed Protocol would eliminate withholding taxes on cross-border interest payments. In addition, the proposed Protocol would coordinate the tax treatment of contributions to, and other benefits of, pension funds for cross-border workers. The proposed Protocol also includes provisions related to the taxation of permanent establishments, so-called dual-resident corporations, income derived through certain entities that are considered fiscally transparent, and former U.S. citizens and long-term residents. The proposed Protocol further strengthens the existing Treaty's provisions that prevent the treaty's inappropriate use by third-country residents. The proposed Protocol also provides for mandatory resolution of certain cases before the competent authorities.

The exchanges of notes confirm certain understandings with respect to application of the Protocol.

The proposed Protocol was concluded in recognition of the importance of the United States' economic relations with Canada. The Department of the Treasury and the Department of State cooperated in the negotiation of the proposed Protocol. The Protocol and the related exchanges of notes have the full approval of both Departments.

Respectfully submitted.

Condoleezza Rice.

Enclosure: Key Provisions of the U.S.-Canada Protocol.

KEY PROVISIONS OF THE U.S.-CANADA PROTOCOL

The attached Protocol with Canada (the "proposed Protocol") is the fifth protocol to the income tax Convention signed in 1980 and amended by prior protocols in 1983, 1984, 1995, and 1997 ("existing Treaty"). It was negotiated to address specific issues that have arisen in our tax treaty relations and changes in each country's domestic law and tax treaty policy, and to further reduce barriers to cross-border investment between our two countries. The exchanges of notes confirm certain understandings with respect to application of the Protocol. The proposed Protocol would incorporate provisions that are generally consistent with the U.S. Model tax treaty. However, there are several provisions of the proposed Protocol that deviate from the U.S. Model tax treaty to reflect the close economic and political relationship the United States shares with Canada.

One of the most important aspects of the proposed Protocol relates to the taxation of cross-border interest payments. The proposed Protocol provides for the elimination of withholding taxes on cross-border interest payments. This provision would be effective for interest paid to unrelated parties on the first day of January of the year in which the proposed Protocol enters into force, and it would be phased in for interest paid to related persons over a three-year period. Eliminating withholding taxes on cross-border interest payments is consistent with an overall view that investment income should be taxed by the country of residence, not the country of source.

The proposed Protocol also addresses the issue of so-called "dual-resident corporations." In addition to revising a provision of the existing Treaty relating to the residence of such companies, the proposed Protocol generally provides that the competent authorities of the United States and Canada shall endeavor to reach agreement on the treatment of such companies for purposes of the treaty.

The proposed Protocol also contains a provision that assures that a U.S. person generally may obtain the benefits of the treaty when that person derives income through an entity that is considered by the United States to be fiscally transparent (i.e., able to pass through the tax consequences of its activities to its owners) unless the entity is a Canadian entity and is not treated by Canada as fiscally transparent.

The existing Treaty generally follows the standard rules for taxation by the source country of the business profits of a resident of the other country. The source country's right to tax such profits is generally limited to cases in which the profits are attributable to a permanent establishment located in that country. The proposed Protocol would add two provisions related to the taxation of permanent establishments. First, the proposed Protocol, consistent with the U.S. Model tax treaty, contains provisions that recognize the "authorized OECD approach" to attributing profits to a permanent establishment. Second, the proposed Protocol includes a special rule for certain permanent services not otherwise considered to be provided through a permanent establishment.

Further, the proposed Protocol would update the existing Treaty to reflect current U.S. treaty policy with respect to several items, including (i) reduced withholding taxes on dividends paid from a real estate investment trust, (ii) the U.S. taxation of former citizens and long-term residents, and (iii) the coordination of the tax treatment of contributions to and accretions of income to pension funds for cross-border workers. The proposed Protocol also would update the existing Treaty's provisions preventing so-called treaty shopping, which is the inappropriate use of a tax treaty by third-country residents.

The proposed Protocol would update the provisions of the existing Treaty with respect to the mutual agreement procedure by incorporating mandatory resolution of certain cases that the competent authorities of the United States and Canada are unable to resolve within a specified period of time.

The Parties shall notify each other in writing, through diplomatic channels, when their respective applicable procedures for ratification have been satisfied. The proposed Protocol will enter into force upon the date of the later of the notifications or January 1, 2008, whichever is later. It will generally have effect, with respect to taxes withheld at source, for amounts paid or credited on or after the first day of the second month that begins after the date the proposed Protocol enters into force. With respect to other taxes, it will generally have effect for taxable years that begin after the calendar year in which the proposed Protocol enters into force. Certain provisions will be phased in or have a delayed effective date, and certain provisions will apply retroactively, consistent with prior Treasury Department public statements regarding specific issues.

PROTOCOL AMENDING THE CONVENTION BETWEEN THE UNITED STATES OF AMERICA AND CANADA WITH RESPECT TO TAXES ON INCOME AND ON CAPITAL DONE AT WASHINGTON ON 26 SEPTEMBER 1980 AS AMENDED BY THE PROTOCOLS DONE ON 14 JUNE 1983, 28 MARCH 1984, 17 MARCH 1995 AND 29 JULY 1997

The United States of America and Canada, hereinafter referred to as the "Contracting States".

DESIRING to conclude a Protocol amending the Convention between the United States of America and Canada with Respect to Taxes on Income and on Capital done at Washington on 26 September 1980, as amended by the Protocols done on 14 June 1983, 28 March 1984, 17 March 1995 and 29 July 1997 (hereinafter related to as the "Convention"),

HAVE AGREED as follows:

Article 1

Paragraph I of Article III (General Definitions) of the Convention shall be amended by deleting the word "and" at the end of subparagraph (i), by replacing the period at the end of subparagraph (j) with "; and", and by adding the following subparagraph:

(k) The term "national" of a Contracting State means:

(i) Any individual possessing the citizenship or nationality of that State; and

(ii) Any legal person, partnership or association deriving its status as such from the laws in force in that State.

Article 2

1. Paragraph 3 of Article IV (Residence) of the Convention shall be deleted and replaced by the following:

3. Where by reason of the provisions of paragraph 1, a company is a resident of both Contracting States, then

(a) If it is created under the laws in force in a Contracting State, but not under the laws in force in the other Contracting State, it shall be deemed to be a resident only of the first-mentioned State; and

(b) In any other case, the competent authorities of the Contracting States shall endeavor to settle the question of residency by mutual agreement and determine the mode of application of this Convention to the company. In the absence of such agreement, the company shall not be considered a resident of either Contracting State for purposes of claiming any benefits under this Convention.

2. Article IV (Residence) of the Convention shall be amended by adding the following after paragraph 5:

6. An amount of income, profit or gain shall be considered to be derived by a person who is a resident of a Contracting State where:

(a) The person is considered under the taxation law of that State to have derived the amount through an entity (other than an entity that is a resident of the other Contracting State); and

(b) By reason of the entity being treated as fiscally transparent under the laws of the first-mentioned State, the treatment of the amount under the taxation law of that State is the same as its treatment would be if that amount had been derived directly by that person.

7. An amount of income, profit or gain shall be considered not to be paid to or derived by a person who is a resident of a Contracting State where:

(a) The person is considered under the taxation law of the other Contracting State to have derived the amount through an entity that is not a resident of the first-mentioned State, but by reason of the entity not being treated as fiscally transparent under the laws of that State, the treatment of the amount under the taxation law of that State is not the same as its treatment would be if that amount had been derived directly by that person; or

(b) The person is considered under the taxation law of the other Contracting State to have received the amount from an entity that is a resident of that other State, but by reason of the entity being treated as fiscally transparent under the laws of the first-mentioned State, the treatment of the amount under the taxation law of that State is not the same as its treatment would be if that entity were not treated as fiscally transparent under the laws of that State.

Article 3

1. The first sentence of paragraph 6 of Article V (Permanent Establishment) of the Convention shall be amended by deleting the word "and" preceding the first reference to paragraph 5, inserting a comma, and adding the words "and 9," following that reference to paragraph 5.

2. Paragraph 9 of Article V (Permanent Establishment) of the Convention shall be deleted and replaced by the following two paragraphs:

9. Subject to paragraph 3, where an enterprise of a Contracting State provides services in the other Contracting State, if that enterprise is found not to have a permanent establishment in that other State by virtue of the preceding paragraphs of this Article, that enterprise shall be deemed to provide those services through a permanent establishment in that other State if and only if:

(a) Those services are performed in that other State by an individual who is present in that other State for a period or periods aggregating 183 days or more in any twelve-month period, and, during that period or periods, more than 50 percent of the gross active business revenues of the enterprise consists of income derived from the services performed in that other State by that individual; or

(b) The services are provided in that other State for an aggregate of 183 days or more in any twelve-month period with respect to the same or connected project for customers who are either residents of that other State or who maintain a permanent establishment in that other State and the services are provided in respect of that permanent establishment.

10. For the purposes of this Convention, the provisions of this Article shall be applied in determining whether any person has a permanent establishment in any State.

Article 4

Paragraph 2 of Article VII (Business Profits) of the Convention shall be deleted and replaced by the following:

2. Subject to the provisions of paragraph 3, where a resident of a Contracting State carries on, or has carried on, business in the other Contracting State through a permanent establishment situated therein, there shall in each Contracting State be attributed to that permanent establishment the business profits which it might be expected to make if it were a distinct and separate person engaged in the same or similar activities under the same or similar conditions and dealing wholly independently with the resident and with any other person related to the resident (within the meaning of paragraph 2 of Article IX (Related Persons)).

Article 5

1. Subparagraph 2(a) of Article X (Dividends) of the Convention shall be deleted and replaced by the following:

> (a) 5 percent of the gross amount of the dividends if the beneficial owner is a company which owns at least 10 percent of the voting stock of the company paying the dividends (for this purpose, a company that is a resident of a Contracting State shall be considered to own the voting stock owned by an entity that is considered fiscally transparent under the laws of that State and that is not a resident of the Contracting State of which the company paying the dividends is a resident, in proportion to the company's ownership interest in that entity);

2. Paragraph 3 of Article X (Dividends) of the Convention shall be deleted and replaced by the following:

> 3. For the purposes of this Article, the term "dividends" means income from shares or other rights, not being debt-claims, participating in profits, as well as income that is subjected to the same taxation treatment as income from shares under the laws of the State of which the payer is a resident.

3. Paragraph 4 of Article X (Dividends) of the Convention shall be deleted and replaced by the following:

> 4. The provisions of paragraph 2 shall not apply if the beneficial owner of the dividends, being a resident of a Contracting State, carries on, or has carried on, business in the other Contracting State of which the company paying the dividends is a resident, through a permanent establishment situated therein, and the holding in respect of which the dividends are paid is effectively connected to such permanent establishment. In such case, the provisions of Article VII (Business Profits) shall apply.

4. Paragraph 5 of Article X (Dividends) of the Convention shall be amended by deleting the words "or a fixed base" following the words "effectively connected with a permanent establishment".

5. Subparagraph 7(c) of Article X (Dividends) of the Convention shall be deleted and replaced by the following:

> (c) Subparagraph 2(a) shall not apply to dividends paid by a resident of the United States that is a Real Estate Investment Trust (REIT), and subparagraph 2(b) shall apply only if:
>
> > (i) The beneficial owner of the dividends is an individual holding an interest of not more than 10 percent in the REIT;
> >
> > (ii) The dividends are paid with respect to a class of stock that is publicly traded and the beneficial owner of the dividends is a person holding an interest of not more than 5 percent in any class of the REIT's stock; or
> >
> > (iii) The beneficial owner of the dividends is a person holding an interest of not more than 10 percent in the REIT and the REIT is diversified.
>
> Otherwise, the rate of tax applicable under the domestic law of the United States shall apply. Where an estate or testamentary trust acquired its interest in a REIT as a consequence of an individual's death, for purposes of this subparagraph the estate or trust shall for the five-year period following the death be deemed with respect to that interest to be an individual.

Article 6

Article XI (Interest) of the Convention shall be deleted and replaced by the following:

Article XI
Interest

1. Interest arising in a Contracting State and beneficially owned by a resident of the other Contracting State may be taxed only in that other State.

2. The term "interest" as used in this Article means income from debt-claims of every kind, whether or not secured by mortgage, and whether or not carrying a right to participate in the debtor's profits, and in particular, income from government securities and income from bonds or debentures, including premiums or prizes attaching to such securities, bonds or debentures, as well as income assimilated to income from money lent by the taxation laws of the Contracting State in which the income arises. However, the term "interest" does not include income dealt with in Article X (Dividends).

3. The provisions of paragraph 1 shall not apply if the beneficial owner of the interest, being a resident of a Contracting State, carries on, or has carried on, business in the other Contracting State in which the interest arises, through a permanent establishment situated therein, and the debt-claim in respect of which the interest is paid is effectively connected with such permanent establishment. In such case the provisions of Article VII (Business Profits) shall apply.

4. For the purposes of this Article, interest shall be deemed to arise in a Contracting State when the payer is that State itself, or a political subdivision, local authority or a resident of that State. Where, however, the person paying the interest, whether he is a resident of a Contracting State or not, has in a State other than that of which he is a resident a permanent establishment in connection with which the indebtedness on which the interest is paid was incurred, and such interest is borne by such permanent establishment, then such interest shall be deemed to arise in the State in which the permanent establishment is situated and not in the State of which the payer is a resident.

5. Where, by reason of a special relationship between the payer and the beneficial owner or between both of them and some other person, the amount of the interest, having regard to the debt-claim for which it is paid, exceeds the amount which would have been agreed upon by the payer and the beneficial owner in the absence of such relationship, the provisions of this Article shall apply only to the last-mentioned amount. In such case the excess part of the payments shall remain taxable according to the laws of each Contracting State, due regard being had to the other provisions of this Convention.

6. Notwithstanding the provisions of paragraph 1:

(a) Interest arising in the United States that is contingent interest of a type that does not qualify as portfolio interest under United States law may be taxed by the United States but, if the beneficial owner of the interest is a resident of Canada, the gross amount of the interest may be taxed at a rate not exceeding the rate prescribed in subparagraph (b) of paragraph 2 of Article X (Dividends);

(b) Interest arising in Canada that is determined with reference to receipts, sales, income, profits or other cash flow of the debtor or a related person, to any change in the value of any property of the debtor or a related person or to any dividend, partnership distribution or similar payment made by the debtor to a related person may be taxed by Canada, and according to the laws of Canada, but if the beneficial owner is a resident of the United States, the gross amount of the interest may be taxed at a rate not exceeding the rate prescribed in subparagraph (b) of paragraph 2 of Article X (Dividends); and

(c) Interest that is an excess inclusion with respect to a residual interest in a real estate mortgage investment conduit may be taxed by each State in accordance with its domestic law.

7. Where a resident of a Contracting State pays interest to a person other than a resident of the other Contracting State, that other State may not impose any tax on such interest except insofar as it arises in that other State or insofar as the debt-claim in respect of which the interest is paid is effectively connected with a permanent establishment situated in that other State.

Article 7

1. Paragraph 5 of Article XII (Royalties) of the Convention shall be deleted and replaced by the following:

> 5. The provisions of paragraphs 2 and 3 shall not apply if the beneficial owner of the royalties, being a resident of a Contracting State, carries on, or has carried on, business in the other Contracting State in which the royalties arise, through a permanent establishment situated therein, and the right or property in respect of which the royalties are paid is effectively connected to such permanent establishment. In such case the provisions of Article VII (Business Profits) shall apply.

2. Subparagraph 6(a) of Article XII (Royalties) of the Convention shall be deleted and replaced by the following:

> (a) Royalties shall be deemed to arise in a Contracting State when the payer is a resident of that State. Where, however, the person paying the royalties, whether he is a resident of a Contracting State or not, has in a State a permanent establishment in connection with which the obligation to pay the royalties was incurred, and such royalties are borne by such permanent establishment, then such royalties shall be deemed to arise in the State in which the permanent establishment is situated and not in any other State of which the payer is a resident, and

3. Paragraph 8 of Article XII (Royalties) of the Convention shall be amended by deleting the words "or a fixed base" following the words "effectively connected with a permanent establishment".

Article 8

1. Paragraph 2 of Article XIII (Gains) of the Convention shall be deleted and replaced by the following:

> 2. Gains from the alienation of personal properly forming part of the business property of a permanent establishment which a resident of a Contracting State has or had (within the twelve-month period preceding the date of alienation) in the other Contracting State, including such gains from the alienation of such a permanent establishment, may be taxed in that other State.

2. Paragraph 5 of Article XIII (Gains) of the Convention shall be deleted and replaced by the following:

> 5. The provisions of paragraph 4 shall not affect the right of a Contracting State to levy, according to its domestic law, a tax on gains from the alienation of any property derived by an individual who is a resident of the other Contracting State if:
>
> (a) The individual was a resident of the first-mentioned State:
>
> (i) For at least 120 months during any period of 20 consecutive years preceding the alienation of the property; and
>
> (ii) At any time during the 10 years immediately preceding the alienation of the property; and
>
> (b) The property (or property for which such property was substituted in an alienation the gain on which was not recognized for the purposes of taxation in the first-mentioned State):
>
> (i) Was owned by the individual at the time the individual ceased to be a resident of the first-mentioned State; and
>
> (ii) Was not a property that the individual was treated as having alienated by reason of ceasing to be a resident of the first-mentioned State and becoming a resident of the other Contracting State.

3. Paragraph 7 of Article XIII (Gains) of the Convention shall be deleted and replaced by the following:

> 7. Where at any time an individual is treated for the purposes of taxation by a Contracting State as having alienated a property and is taxed in that State by reason thereof, the individual may elect to be treated for the purposes of taxation in the other Contracting State, in the year that includes that time and all subsequent years, as if the individual had, immediately before that time, sold and repurchased the property for an amount equal to its fair market value at that time.

4. Subparagraph 9(c) of Article XIII (Gains) of the Convention shall be amended by deleting the words "or pertained to a fixed base" following the words "permanent establishment".

Article 9

Article XIV (Independent Personal Services) of the Convention shall be deleted and the succeeding Articles shall not be renumbered.

Article 10

1. The title of Article XV (Dependent Personal Services) of the Convention shall be deleted and replaced by "Income from Employment".

2. Paragraphs 1 and 2 of renamed Article XV (Income from Employment) of the Convention shall be deleted and replaced by the following:

> 1. Subject to the provisions of Articles XVIII (Pensions and Annuities) and XIX (Government Service), salaries, wages and other remuneration derived by a resident of a Contracting State in respect of an employment shall be taxable only in that State unless the employment is exercised in the other Contracting State. If the employment is so exercised, such remuneration as is derived therefrom may be taxed in that other State.
>
> 2. Notwithstanding the provisions of paragraph 1, remuneration derived by a resident of a Contracting State in respect of an employment exercised in the other Contracting State shall be taxable only in the first-mentioned State if:
>
> > (a) Such remuneration does not exceed ten thousand dollars ($10,000) in the currency of that other State; or
> >
> > (b) The recipient is present in that other State for a period or periods not exceeding in the aggregate 183 days in any twelve-month period commencing or ending in the fiscal year concerned, and the remuneration is not paid by, or on behalf of, a person who is a resident of that other State and is not borne by a permanent establishment in that other State.

Article 11

1. Paragraph 1 of Article XVI (Artistes and Athletes) shall be amended by deleting the words "XIV (Independent Personal Services)" following the words "Notwithstanding the provisions of Articles" and replacing them with the words "VII (Business Profits)" and by deleting the words "XV (Dependent Personal Services)" and replacing them with the words "XV (Income from Employment)".

2. Paragraph 2 of Article XVI (Artistes and Athletes) shall be amended by deleting the words "XIV (Independent Personal Services)" following the words "notwithstanding the provisions of Articles VII (Business Profits)," and by deleting the words "XV (Dependent Personal Services)" and replacing them with the words "XV (Income from Employment)".

3. Paragraph 4 of Article XVI (Artistes and Athletes) shall be amended by deleting the words "XIV (Independent Personal Services)" following the words "Notwithstanding the provisions of Articles" and replacing them with the words "VII (Business Profits)" and by deleting the words "(Dependent Personal Services)" in both places they appear in the paragraph and replacing them with the words "(Income from Employment)".

Article 12

Article XVII (Withholding of Taxes in Respect of Personal Services) of the Convention shall be deleted and the succeeding Articles shall not be renumbered.

Article 13

1. Paragraphs 3 and 4 of Article XVIII (Pensions and Annuities) of the Convention shall be deleted and replaced by the following:

3. For the purposes of this Convention:

(a) The term "pensions" includes any payment under a superannuation, pension or other retirement arrangement, Armed Forces retirement pay, war veterans pensions and allowances and amounts paid under a sickness, accident or disability plan, but does not include payments under an income-averaging annuity contract or, except for the purposes of Article XIX (Government Service), any benefit referred to in paragraph 5; and

(b) The term "pensions" also includes a Roth IRA, within the meaning of section 408A of the Internal Revenue Code, or a plan or arrangement created pursuant to legislation enacted by a Contracting State after September 21, 2007 that the competent authorities have agreed is similar thereto. Notwithstanding the provisions of the preceding sentence, from such time that contributions have been made to the Roth IRA or similar plan or arrangement, by or for the benefit of a resident of the other Contracting State (other than rollover contributions from a Roth IRA or similar plan or arrangement described in the previous sentence that is a pension within the meaning of this subparagraph), to the extent of accretions from such time, such Roth IRA or similar plan or arrangement shall cease to be considered a pension for purposes of the provisions of this Article.

4. For the purposes of this Convention:

(a) The term "annuity" means a stated sum paid periodically at stated times during life or during a specified number of years, under an obligation to make the payments in return for adequate and full consideration (other than services rendered), but does not include a payment that is not a periodic payment or any annuity the cost of which was deductible for the purposes of taxation in the Contracting State in which it was acquired; and

(b) An annuity or other amount paid in respect of a life insurance or annuity contract (including a withdrawal in respect of the cash value thereof) shall be deemed to arise in a Contracting State if the person paying the annuity or other amount (in this subparagraph referred to as the "payer") is a resident of that State. However, if the payer, whether a resident of a Contracting State or not, has in a State other than that of which the payer is a resident a permanent establishment in connection with which the obligation giving rise to the annuity or other amount was incurred, and the annuity or other amount is borne by the permanent establishment, then the annuity or other amount shall be deemed to arise in the State in which the permanent establishment is situated and not in the State of which the payer is a resident.

2. Paragraph 7 of Article XVIII (Pensions and Annuities) of the Convention shall be deleted and replaced by the following:

7. A natural person who is a citizen or resident of a Contracting State and a beneficiary of a trust, company, organization or other arrangement that is a resident of the other Contracting State, generally exempt from income taxation in that other State and operated exclusively to provide pension or employee benefits may elect to defer taxation in the first-mentioned State, subject to rules established by the competent authority of that State, with respect to any income accrued in the plan but not distributed by the plan, until such time as and to the extent that a distribution is made from the plan or any plan substituted therefor.

3. Article XVIII (Pensions and Annuities) of the Convention shall be amended by adding the following paragraphs:

8. Contributions made to, or benefits accrued under, a qualifying retirement plan in a Contracting State by or on behalf of an individual shall be deductible or excludible in computing the individual's taxable income in the other Contracting State, and contributions made to the plan by the individual's employer shall be allowed as a deduction in computing the employer's profits in that other State, where:

(a) The individual performs services as an employee in that other State the remuneration from which is taxable in that other State;

(b) The individual was participating in the plan (or another similar plan for which this plan was substituted) immediately before the individual began performing the services in that other State;

(c) The individual was not a resident of that other State immediately before the individual began performing the services in that other State;

(d) The individual has performed services in that other State for the same employer (or a related employer) for no more than 60 of the 120 months preceding the individual's current taxation year;

(e) The contributions and benefits are attributable to the services performed by the individual in that other State, and are made or accrued during the period in which the individual performs those services; and

(f) With respect to contributions and benefits that are attributable to services performed during a period in the individual's current taxation year, no contributions in respect of the period are made by or on behalf of the individual to, and no services performed in that other State during the period are otherwise taken into account for purposes of determining the individual's entitlement to benefits under, any plan that would be a qualifying retirement plan in that other State if paragraph 15 of this Article were read without reference to subparagraphs (b) and (c) of that paragraph.

This paragraph shall apply only to the extent that the contributions or benefits would quality for tax relief in the first-mentioned State if the individual was a resident of and performed the services in that State.

9. For the purposes of United States taxation, the benefits granted under paragraph 8 to a citizen of the United States shall not exceed the benefits that would be allowed by the United States to its residents for contributions to, or benefits otherwise accrued under, a generally corresponding pension or retirement plan established in and recognized for tax purposes by the United States.

10. Contributions made to, or benefits accrued under, a qualifying retirement plan in a Contracting State by or on behalf of an individual who is a resident of the other Contracting State shall be deductible or excludible in computing the individual's taxable income in that other State, where:

(a) The individual performs services as an employee in the first-mentioned state the remuneration from which is taxable in that State and is borne by an employer who is a resident of that State or by a permanent establishment which the employer has in that State; and

(b) The contributions and benefits are attributable to those services and are made or accrued during the period in which the individual performs those services.

This paragraph shall apply only to the extent that the contributions or benefits qualify for tax relief in the first-mentioned State.

11. For the purposes of Canadian taxation, the amount of contributions otherwise allowed as a deduction under paragraph 10 to an individual for a taxation year shall not exceed the individual's deduction limit under the law of Canada for the year for contributions to registered retirement savings plans remaining after taking into account the amount of contributions to registered retirement savings plans deducted by the individual under the law of Canada for the year. The amount deducted by an individual under paragraph 10 for a taxation year shall be taken into account in computing the individual's deduction limit under the law of Canada far subsequent taxation years for contributions to registered retirement savings plans.

12. For the purposes of United States taxation, the benefits granted under paragraph 10 shall not exceed the benefits that would be allowed by the United States to its residents for contributions to, or benefits otherwise accrued under, a generally corresponding pension or retirement plan established in and recognized for tax purposes by the United States. For purposes of determining an individual's eligibility to participate in and receive tax benefits with respect to a pension or retirement plan or other retirement arrangement established in and recognized for tax purposes by the United States, contributions made to, or benefits accrued under, a qualifying retirement plan in Canada by or on behalf of the individual shall be treated as contributions or benefits under a generally corresponding pension or retirement plan established in and recognized for tax purposes by the United States.

13. Contributions made to, or benefits accrued under, a qualifying retirement plan in Canada by or on behalf of a citizen of the United States who is a resident of Canada shall be deductible or excludable in computing the citizen's taxable income in the United States, where:

(a) The citizen performs services as an employee in Canada the remuneration from which is taxable in Canada and is borne by an employer who is a resident of Canada or by a permanent establishment which the employer has in Canada; and

(b) The contributions and benefits are attributable to those services and are made or accrued during the period in which the citizen performs those services.

This paragraph shall apply only to the extent that the contributions or benefits qualify for tax relief in Canada.

14. The benefits granted under paragraph 13 shall not exceed the benefits that would be allowed by the United States to its residents for contributions to, or benefits otherwise accrued under, a generally corresponding pension or retirement plan established in and recognized for tax purposes by the United States. For purposes of determining an individual's eligibility to participate in and receive tax benefits with respect to a pension or retirement plan or other retirement arrangement established in and recognized for tax purposes by the United States, contributions made to, or benefits accrued under, a qualifying retirement plan in Canada by or on behalf of the individual shall be treated as contributions or benefits under a generally corresponding pension or retirement plan established in and recognized for tax purposes by the United States.

15. For purposes of paragraphs 8 to 14, a qualifying retirement plan in a Contracting State means a trust, company, organization or other arrangement:

(a) That is a resident of that State, generally exempt from income taxation in that State and operated primarily to provide pension or retirement benefits;

(b) That is not an individual arrangement in respect of which the individual's employer has no involvement; and

(c) Which the competent authority of the other Contracting State agrees generally corresponds to a pension or retirement plan established in and recognized for tax purposes by that other State.

16. For purposes of this Article, a distribution from a pension or retirement plan that is reasonably attributable to a contribution or benefit for which a benefit was allowed pursuant to paragraph 8, 10 or 13 shall be deemed to arise in the Contracting State in which the plan is established.

17. Paragraphs 8 to 16 apply, with such modifications as the circumstances require, as though the relationship between a partnership that carries on a business, and an individual who is a member of the partnership, were that of employer and employee.

Article 14

Article XIX (Government Service) of the Convention shall be amended by deleting the words XIV (Independent Personal Services)" and replacing them with the words "VII (Business Profits)" and by deleting the words "XV (Dependent Personal Services)" and replacing them with the words "XV (Income from Employment)".

Article 15

Article XX (Students) of the Convention shall be deleted and replaced by the following:

Payments received by an individual who is a student, apprentice, or business trainee, and is, or was immediately before visiting a Contracting State, a resident of the other Contracting State, and who is present in the first-mentioned State for the purpose of the individual's full-time education or full-time training, shall not be taxed in that State, provided that such payments arise outside that State, and are for the purpose of the maintenance, education or training of the individual. The provisions of this Article shall apply to an apprentice or business trainee only for a period of time not exceeding one year from the date the individual first arrives in the first-mentioned State for the purpose of the individual's training.

Article 16

1. Paragraphs 4, 5 and 6 of Article XXI (Exempt Organizations) of the Convention shall be renumbered as paragraphs 5, 6 and 7 respectively.

2. Paragraphs 1 through 3 of Article XXI (Exempt Organizations) of the Convention shall be deleted and replaced by the following four paragraphs:

1. Subject to the provisions of paragraph 4, income derived by a religious, scientific, literary, educational or charitable organization shall be exempt from tax in a Contracting State if it is resident in the other Contracting State, but only to the extent that such income is exempt from tax in that other State.

2. Subject to the provisions of paragraph 4, income referred to in Articles X (Dividends) and XI (Interest) derived by a trust, company, organization or other arrangement that is a resident of a Contracting State, generally exempt from income taxation in a taxable year in that State and operated exclusively to administer or provide pension, retirement or employee benefits shall be exempt from income taxation in that taxable year in the other Contracting State.

3. Subject to the provisions of paragraph 4, income referred to in Articles X (Dividends) and XI (Interest) derived by a trust, company, organization or other arrangement that is a resident of a Contracting State, generally exempt from income taxation in a taxable year in that State and operated exclusively to earn income for the benefit of one or more of the following:

(a) An organization referred to in paragraph I; or

(b) A trust, company, organization or other arrangement referred to in paragraph 2;

shall be exempt from income taxation in that taxable year in the other Contracting State.

4. The provisions of paragraphs 1, 2 and 3 shall not apply with respect to the income of a trust, company, organization or other arrangement from carrying on a trade or business or from a related person other than a person referred to in paragraphs 1, 2 or 3.

Article 17

Article XXII (Other Income) of the Convention shall be amended by adding the following paragraph:

4. Notwithstanding the provisions of paragraph 1, compensation derived by a resident of a Contracting State in respect of the provision of a guarantee of indebtedness shall be taxable only in that State, unless such compensation is business profits attributable to a permanent establishment situated in the other Contracting State, in which case the provisions of Article VII (Business Profits) shall apply.

Article 18

Paragraph 2 of Article XXIII (Capital) of the Convention shall be amended by deleting the phrase, "or by personal property pertaining to a fixed base available to a resident of a Contracting State in the other Contracting State for the purpose of performing independent personal services".

Article 19

Subparagraph 2(b) of Article XXIV (Elimination of Double Taxation) of the Convention shall be deleted and replaced with the following:

(b) In the case of a company which is a resident of Canada owning at least 10 percent of the voting stock of a company which is a resident of the United States from which it receives dividends in any taxable year, Canada shall allow as a credit against the Canadian tax on income the appropriate amount of income tax paid or accrued to the United States by the second company with respect to the profits out of which the dividends are paid.

Article 20

1. Paragraph 1 of Article XXV (Non-Discrimination) of the Convention shall be deleted and replaced by the following:

1. Nationals of a Contracting State shall not be subjected in the other Contracting State to any taxation or any requirement connected therewith that is more burdensome than the taxation and connected requirements to which nationals of that other State in the same circumstances, particularly with respect to

taxation on worldwide income, are or may be subjected. This provision shall also apply to individuals who are not residents of one or both of the Contracting States.

2. Paragraph 2 of Article XXV (Non-Discrimination) of the Convention shall be deleted, and paragraphs 3 to 10 of Article XXV shall be renumbered accordingly.

3. Renumbered paragraph 3 of Article XXV (Non-Discrimination) of the Convention shall be amended by deleting the words "Article XV (Dependent Personal Services)" and replacing them with the words "Article XV (Income from Employment)".

Article 21

1. Paragraph 6 of Article XXVI (Mutual Agreement Procedure) of the Convention shall be deleted and replaced by the following:

6. Where, pursuant to a mutual agreement procedure under this Article, the competent authorities have endeavored but are unable to reach a complete agreement in a case, the case shall be resolved through arbitration conducted in the manner prescribed by, and subject to, the requirements of paragraph 7 and any rules or procedures agreed upon by the Contracting States by notes to be exchanged through diplomatic channels, if:

(a) Tax returns have been filed with at least one of the Contracting States with respect to the taxable years at issue in the case;

(b) The case:

(i) Is a ease that:

(A) Involves the application of one or more Articles that the competent authorities have agreed in an exchange of notes shall be the subject of arbitration; and

(B) Is not a particular case that the competent authorities agree, before the date on which arbitration proceedings would otherwise have begun, is not suitable for determination by arbitration; or

(ii) Is a particular case that the competent authorities agree is suitable for determination by arbitration; and

(c) All concerned persons agree according to the provisions of subparagraph 7(d).

7. For the purposes of paragraph 6 and this paragraph, the following rules and definitions shall apply:

(a) The term "concerned person" means the presenter of a case to a competent authority for consideration under this Article and all other persons, if any, whose tax liability to either Contracting State may be directly affected by a mutual agreement arising from that consideration;

(b) The "commencement date" for a case is the earliest date on which the information necessary to undertake substantive consideration for a mutual agreement has been received by both competent authorities;

(c) Arbitration proceedings in a case shall begin on the later of:

(i) Two years after the commencement date of that case, unless both competent authorities have previously agreed to a different date, and

(ii) The earliest date upon which the agreement required by subparagraph (d) has been received by both competent authorities;

(d) The concerned person(s), and their authorized representatives or agents, must agree prior to the beginning of arbitration proceedings not to disclose to any other person any information received during the course of the arbitration proceeding from either Contracting State or the arbitration board, other than the determination of such board;

(e) Unless a concerned person does not accept the determination of an arbitration board, the determination shall constitute a resolution by mutual agreement under this Article and shall be binding on both Contracting States with respect to that case; and

(f) For purposes of an arbitration proceeding under paragraph 6 and this paragraph, the members of the arbitration board and their staffs shall be considered "persons or authorities" to whom information may be disclosed under Article XXVII (Exchange of Information) of this Convention.

Article 22

1. Subparagraph 8(a) of Article XXVI A (Assistance in Collection) of the Convention shall be deleted and replaced by the following:

(a) Where the taxpayer is an individual, the revenue claim relates either to a taxable period in which the taxpayer was a citizen of the requested State or, if the taxpayer became a citizen of the requested State at any time before November 9, 1995 and is such a citizen at the time the applicant State applies for collection of the claim, to a taxable period that ended before November 9, 1995; and

2. Paragraph 9 of Article XXVI A (Assistance in Collection) of the Convention shall be deleted and replaced by the following:

9. Notwithstanding the provisions of Article II (Taxes Covered), the provisions of this Article shall apply to all categories of taxes collected, and to contributions to social security and employment insurance premiums levied, by or on behalf of the Government of a Contracting State.

Article 23

Article XXVII (Exchange of Information) of the Convention shall be deleted and replaced by the following:

Article XXVII
Exchange of Information

1. The competent authorities of the Contracting States shall exchange such information as may be relevant for carrying out the provisions of this Convention or of the domestic laws of the Contracting States concerning taxes to which this Convention applies insofar as the taxation thereunder is not contrary to this Convention. The exchange of information is not restricted by Article 1 (Personal Scope). Any information received by a Contracting State shall be treated as secret in the same manner as information obtained under the taxation laws of that State and shall be disclosed only to persons or authorities (including courts and administrative bodies) involved in the assessment or collection of, the administration and enforcement in respect of, or the determination of appeals in relation to the taxes to which this Convention applies or, notwithstanding paragraph 4, in relation to taxes imposed by a political subdivision or local authority of a Contracting State that are substantially similar to the taxes covered by this Convention under Article II (Taxes Covered). Such persons or authorities shall use the information only for such purposes. They may disclose the information in public court proceedings or in judicial decisions. The competent authorities may release to an arbitration board established pursuant to paragraph 6 of Article XXVI (Mutual Agreement Procedure) such information as is necessary for carrying out the arbitration procedure; the members of the arbitration board shall be subject to the limitations on disclosure described in this Article.

2. If information is requested by a Contracting State in accordance with this Article, the other Contracting State shall use its information gathering measures to obtain the requested information, even though that other State may not need such information for its own tax purposes. The obligation contained in the preceding sentence is subject to the limitations of paragraph 3 but in no case shall such limitations be construed to permit a Contracting State to decline to supply information because it has no domestic interest in such information.

3. In no case shall the provisions of paragraph 1 and 2 be construed so as to impose on a Contracting State the obligation:

(a) To carry out administrative measures at variance with the laws and administrative practice of that State or of the other Contracting State;

(b) To supply information which is not obtainable under the laws or in the normal course of the administration of that State or of the other Contracting State; or

(c) To supply information which would disclose any trade, business, industrial, commercial or professional secret or trade process, or information the disclosure of which would be contrary to public policy (ordre public).

4. For the purposes of this Article, this Convention shall apply, notwithstanding the provisions of Article II (Taxes Covered):

(a) To all taxes imposed by a Contracting State; and

(b) To other taxes to which any other provision of this Convention applies, but only to the extent that the information may be relevant for the purposes of the application of that provision.

5. In no case shall the provisions of paragraph 3 be construed to permit a Contracting State to decline to supply information because the information is held by a bank, other financial institution, nominee or person acting in an agency or a fiduciary capacity or because it relates to ownership interests in a person.

6. If specifically requested by the competent authority of a Contracting State, the competent authority of the other Contracting State shall provide information under this Article in the form of depositions of witnesses and authenticated copies of unedited original documents (including books, papers, statements, records, accounts, and writings).

7. The requested State shall allow representatives of the requesting State to enter the requested State to interview individuals and examine books and records with the consent of the persons subject to examination.

Article 24

1. Paragraph 2 of Article XXIX (Miscellaneous Rules) of the Convention shall be deleted and replaced by the following:

2. (a) Except to the extent provided in paragraph 3, this Convention shall not affect the taxation by a Contracting State of its residents (as determined under Article IV (Residence)) and, in the case of the United States, its citizens and companies electing to be treated as domestic corporations.

(b) Notwithstanding the other provisions of this Convention, a former citizen or former long-term resident of the United States, may, for the period of ten years following the loss or such status, be taxed in accordance with the laws of the United States with respect to income from sources within the United States (including income deemed under the domestic law of the United States to arise from such sources).

2. Subparagraph 3(a) of Article XXIX (Miscellaneous Rules) shall be deleted and replaced by the following:

(a) Under paragraphs 3 and 4 of Article IX (Related Persons), paragraphs 6 and 7 of Article XIII (Gains), paragraphs 1, 3, 4, 5, 6(b), 7, 8, 10 and 13 of Article XVIII (Pensions and Annuities), paragraph 5 of Article XXIX (Miscellaneous Rules), paragraphs 1, 5, and 6 of Article XXIX B (Taxes Imposed by Reason of Death), paragraphs 2, 3, 4, and 7 of Article XXIX B (Taxes Imposed by Reason of Death) as applied to estates of persons other than former citizens referred to in paragraph 2 of this Article, paragraphs 3 and 5 of Article XXX (Entry into Force), and Articles XIX (Government Service), XXI (Exempt Organizations), XXIV (Elimination of Double Taxation), XXV (Non-Discrimination) and XXVI (Mutual Agreement Procedure);

Article 25

Article XXIX A (Limitation on Benefits) of the Convention shall be deleted and replaced by the following:

Article XXIX A
Limitation on Benefits

1. For the purposes of the application of this Convention by a Contracting State,

(a) a qualifying person shall be entitled to all of the benefits of this Convention; and

(b) except as provided in paragraphs 3, 4 and 6, a person that is not a qualifying person shall not be entitled to any benefits of this Convention.

2. For the purposes of ibis Article, a qualifying person is a resident of a Contracting State that is:

(a) a natural person;

(b) a Contracting State or a political subdivision or local authority thereof, or any agency or instrumentality of any such State, subdivision or authority;

(c) a company or trust whose principal class of shares or units (and any disproportionate class of shares or units) is primarily and regularly traded on one or more recognized stock exchanges;

(d) a company, if five or fewer persons each of which is a company or trust referred to in subparagraph (c) own directly or indirectly more than 50 percent of the aggregate vote and value of the shares and more than 50 percent of the vote and value of each disproportionate class of shares (in neither case including debt substitute shares), provided that each company or trust in the chain of ownership is a qualifying person;

(e) (i) a company, 50 percent or more of the aggregate vote and value of the shares of which and 50 percent or more of the vote and value of each disproportionate class of shares (in neither case including debt substitute shares) of which is not owned, directly or indirectly, by persons other than qualifying persons; or

(ii) a trust, 50 percent or more of the beneficial interest in which and 50 percent or more of each disproportionate interest in which, is not owned, directly or indirectly, by persons other than qualifying persons;

where the amount of the expenses deductible from gross income (as determined in the State of residence of the company or trust) that are paid or payable by the company or trust, as the case may be, for its preceding fiscal period (or, in the case of its first fiscal period, that period) directly or indirectly, to persons that are not qualifying persons is less than 50 percent of its gross income for that period;

(f) an estate;

(g) a not-for-profit organization, provided that more than half of the beneficiaries, members or participants of the organization are qualifying persons;

(h) a trust, company, organization or other arrangement described in paragraph 2 of Article XXI (Exempt Organizations) and established for the purpose of providing benefits primarily to individuals who are qualifying persons, or persons who were qualifying persons within the five preceding years; or

(i) a trust, company, organization or other arrangement described in paragraph 3 of Article XXI (Exempt Organizations) provided that the beneficiaries of the trust, company, organization or other arrangement are described in subparagraph (g) or (h).

3. Where a person is a resident of a Contracting State and is not a qualifying person, and that person, or a person related thereto, is engaged in the active conduct of a trade or business in that State (other than the business of making or managing investments, unless those activities are carried on with customers in the ordinary course of business by a bank, an insurance company, a registered securities dealer or a deposit-taking financial institution), the benefits of this Convention shall apply to that resident person with respect to income derived from the other Contracting State in connection with or incidental to that trade or business (including any such income derived directly or indirectly by that resident person through one or more other persons that are residents of that other State), but only if that trade or business is substantial in relation to the activity carried on in that other State giving rise to the income in respect of which benefits provided under this Convention by that other State are claimed.

4. A company that is a resident of a Contracting State shall also be entitled to the benefits of Articles X (Dividends), XI (Interest) and XII (Royalties) if:

(a) Its shares that represent more than 90 percent of the aggregate vote and value of all of its shares and at least 50 percent of the vote and value of any disproportionate class of shares (in neither case including debt substitute shares) are owned, directly or indirectly, by persons each of whom is a qualifying person or a person who:

(i) Is a resident of a country with which the other Contracting State has a comprehensive income tax convention and is entitled to all of the benefits provided by that other State under that convention;

(ii) Would qualify for benefits under paragraphs 2 or 3 if that person were a resident of the first-mentioned State (and, for the purposes of paragraph 3, if the business it carried on in the country of which it is a resident were carried on by it in the first-mentioned State); and

(iii) Would be entitled to a rate of tax in the other Contracting State under the convention between that person's country of residence and that other State, in respect of the particular class of income for which benefits are being claimed under this Convention, that is at least as low as the rate applicable under this Convention; and

(b) The amount of the expenses deductible from gross income (as determined in the company's State of residence) that are paid or payable by the company for its preceding fiscal period (or, in the case of its first fiscal period, that period) directly or indirectly to persons that are not qualifying persons is less than 50 percent of the company's gross income for that period.

5. For the purposes of this Article,

(a) The term "debt substitute share" means:

(i) A share described in paragraph (e) of the definition "term preferred share" in the Income Tax Act, as it may be amended from time to time without changing the general principle thereof; and

(ii) Such other type of share as may be agreed upon by the competent authorities of the Contracting States.

(b) The term "disproportionate class of shares" means any class of shares of a company resident in one of the Contracting States that entitles the shareholder to disproportionately higher participation, through dividends, redemption payments or otherwise, in the earnings generated in the other State by particular assets or activities of the company;

(c) The term "disproportionate interest in a trust" means any interest in a trust resident in one of the Contracting States that entitles the interest holder to disproportionately higher participation in, or claim to, the earnings generated in the other State by particular assets or activities of the trust;

(d) The term "not-for-profit organization" of a Contracting State means an entity created or established in that State and that is, by reason of its not-for-profit status, generally exempt from income taxation in that State, and includes a private foundation, charity, trade union, trade association or similar organization;

(e) The term "principal class of shares" of a company means the ordinary or common shares of the company, provided that such class of shares represents the majority of the voting power and value of the company. If no single class of ordinary or common shares represents the majority of the aggregate voting power and value of the company, the "principal class of shares" are those classes that in the aggregate represent a majority of the aggregate voting power and value of the company; and

(f) The term "recognized stock exchange" means:

(i) The NASDAQ System owned by the National Association of Securities Dealers, Inc. and any stock exchange registered with the Securities and Exchange Commission as a national securities exchange for purposes of the Securities Exchange Act of 1934;

(ii) Canadian stock exchanges that are "prescribed stock exchanges" or "designated stock exchanges" under the Income Tax Act; and

(iii) Any other stock exchange agreed upon by the Contracting States in an exchange of notes or by the competent authorities of the Contracting States.

6. Where a person that is a resident of a Contracting State is not entitled under the preceding provisions of this Article to the benefits provided under this Convention by the other Contracting State, the competent authority of that other State shall, upon that person's request, determine on the basis of all factors including the history, structure, ownership and operations of that person whether:

(a) Its creation and existence did not have as a principal purpose the obtaining of benefits under this Convention that would not otherwise be available; or

(b) It would not be appropriate, having regard to the purpose of this Article, to deny the benefits of this Convention to that person.

The person shall be granted the benefits of this Convention by that other State where the competent authority determines that subparagraph (a) or (b) applies.

7. It is understood that this Article shall not be construed as restricting in any manner the right of a Contracting State to deny benefits under this Convention where it can reasonably be concluded that to do otherwise would result in an abuse of the provisions of this Convention.

Article 26

1. Paragraph 1 of Ankle XXIX B (Taxes Imposed by Reason of Death) of the Convention shall be deleted and replaced by the following:

1. Where the property of an individual who is a resident of a Contracting State passes by reason of the individual's death to an organization that is referred to in paragraph 1 of Article XXI (Exempt Organizations) and that is a resident of the other Contracting State,

(a) If the individual is a resident of the United States and the organization is a resident of Canada, the tax consequences in the United States arising out of the passing of the property shall apply as if the organization were a resident of the United States; and

(b) If the individual is a resident of Canada and the organization is a resident of the United States, the tax consequences in Canada arising out of the passing of the property shall apply as if the individual had disposed of the property for proceeds equal to an amount elected on behalf of the individual for this purpose (in a manner specified by the competent authority of Canada), which amount shall be no less than the individual's cost of the property as determined for purposes of Canadian tax and no greater than the fair market value of the property.

2. Paragraph 5 of Article XXIX B (Taxes Imposed by Reason of Death) of the Convention shall be deleted and replaced by the following:

5. Where an individual was a resident of the United States immediately before the individual's death, for the purposes of subcsections 70(5.2) and (6) of the Income Tax Act, both the individual and the individual's spouse shall be deemed to have been resident in Canada immediately before the individual's death. Where a trust that would be a trust described in subsection 70(6) of that Act, if its trustees that were residents or citizens of the United States or domestic corporations under the law of the United States were residents of Canada, requests the competent authority of Canada to do so, the competent authority may agree, subject to terms and conditions satisfactory to such competent authority, to treat the trust for the purposes of that Act as being resident in Canada for such time and with respect to such property as may be stipulated in the agreement.

Article 27

1. This Protocol shall be subject to ratification in accordance with the applicable; procedures in the United States and Canada. The Contracting States shall notify each other in writing, through diplomatic channels, when their respective applicable procedures have been satisfied.

2. This Protocol shall enter into force on the date of the later of the notifications referred to in paragraph 1, or January 1, 2008, whichever is later. The provisions of this Protocol shall have effect:

(a) In respect of taxes withheld at source, for amounts paid or credited on or after the first day of the second month that begins after the date on which this Protocol enters into force;

(b) In respect of other taxes, for taxable years that begin after (or, if the later of the notifications referred to in paragraph 1 is dated in 2007, taxable years that begin in and after) the calendar year in which this Protocol enters into force.

3. Notwithstanding paragraph 2,

(a) Paragraph 1 of Article 2 of this Protocol shall have effect with respect to corporate continuations effected after September 17, 2000;

(b) New paragraph 7 of Article IV (Residence) of the Convention as added by Article 2 of this Protocol shall have effect as of the first day of the third calendar year that ends after this Protocol enters into force;

(c) Article 3 of this Protocol shall have effect as of the third taxable year that ends after this Protocol enters into force, but in no event shall it apply to include, in the determination of whether an enterprise is deemed to provide services through a permanent establishment under paragraph 9 of Article V (Permanent Establishment) of the Convention, any days of presence, services rendered, or gross active business revenues that occur or arise prior to January 1, 2010;

(d) In applying Article 6 of this Protocol to interest paid or credited during the first two calendar years that end after entry into force of this Protocol, paragraph 1 of Article XI (Interest) of the Convention shall be read as follows:

1. Interest arising in a Contracting State and beneficially owned by a resident of the other Contracting State may be taxed only in that other State. However, if the interest is not exempt under paragraph 3 of Article XI (Interest) as it read on January 1, 2007, and the payer of the

interest and the beneficial owner of the interest are related, or would be deemed to be related if the provisions of paragraph 2 of Article IX (Related Persons) applied for this purpose, such interest may also be taxed in the Contracting State in which it arises, and according to the laws of that State, but the tax so charged shall not exceed the following percentage of the gross amount of the interest:

(a) If the interest is paid or credited during the first calendar year that ends after entry into force of this paragraph, 7 percent; and

(b) If the interest is paid or credited during the second calendar year that ends after entry into force of this paragraph, 4 percent;

(e) Paragraphs 2 and 3 of Article 8 of this Protocol shall have effect with respect to alienations of property that occur (including, for greater certainty, those that are deemed under the law of a Contracting State to occur) after September 17, 2000;

(f) Article 21 of this Protocol shall have effect with respect to

(i) Cases that are under consideration by the competent authorities as of the date on which this Protocol enters into force; and

(ii) Cases that come under such consideration after that time.

and the commencement date for a case described in subparagraph (f)(i) shall be the date on which the Protocol enters into force; and

(g) Article 22 of this Protocol shall have effect for revenue claims finally determined by an applicant State after November 9, 1985.

IN WITNESS WHEREOF the undersigned, being duly authorized thereto by their respective Governments, have signed this Protocol.

DONE in duplicate at Chelsea this twenty-first day of September 2007 in the English and French languages, each text being equally authentic.

FOR THE GOVERNMENT OF THE UNITED STATES OF AMERICA:	FOR THE GOVERNMENT OF CANADA:
[Signature]	[Signature]
Minister of Foreign Affairs	Ministre des Affaires etrangeres

Ottawa, Canada K1A 0G2

Note No. JLAB-0111

SEP 21, 2007

Excellency,

I have the honor to refer to the Protocol (the "Protocol") done today between Canada and the United States of America amending the Convention with Respect to Taxes on Income and on Capital done at Washington on 26 September 1980, as amended by the Protocols done on 14 June 1983, 28 March 1984, 17 March 1995, and 29 July 1997 (the "Convention"), and to propose on behalf of the Government of Canada the following:

In respect of any case where the competent authorities have endeavored but are unable to reach a complete agreement under Article XXVI (Mutual Agreement Procedure) of the Convention regarding the application of one or more of the following Articles of the Convention: IV (Residence) (but only insofar as it relates to the residence of a natural person), V (Permanent Establishment), VII (Business Profits), IX (Related Persons), and XII (Royalties) (but only (i) insofar as Article XII might apply in transactions involving related persons to whom Article IX might apply, or (ii) to an allocation of amounts between royalties that are taxable under paragraph 2 thereof and royalties that are exempt under paragraph 3 thereof), binding arbitration shall be used to determine such application, unless the competent authorities agree that the particular case is not suitable for determination by arbitration. In addition, the competent authorities may, on an ad hoc basis, agree that binding arbitration shall be used in respect of any other matter to which Article XXVI applies. If an arbitration proceeding (the "Proceeding") under paragraph 6 of Article XXVI commences, the following rules and procedures shall apply:

1. The Proceeding shall be conducted in the manner prescribed by, and subject to the requirements of, paragraphs 6 and 7 of Article XXVI and these rules and procedures, as modified or supplemented by any other rules and procedures agreed upon by the competent authorities pursuant to paragraph 17 below.

2. The determination reached by an arbitration board in the Proceeding shall be limited to a determination regarding the amount of income, expense or tax reportable to the Contracting States.

3. Notwithstanding the initiation of the Proceeding, the competent authorities may reach a mutual agreement to resolve a case and terminate the Proceeding. Correspondingly, a concerned person may withdraw a request for the competent authorities to engage in the Mutual Agreement Procedure (and thereby terminate the Proceeding) at any time.

4. The requirements of subparagraph 7(d) of Article XXVI shall be met when the competent authorities have each received from each concerned person a notarized statement agreeing that the concerned person and each person acting on the concerned person's behalf, shall not disclose to any other person any information received during the course of the Proceeding from either Contracting State or the arbitration board, other than the determination of the Proceeding. A concerned person that has the legal authority to bind any other concerned person(s) on this matter may do so in a comprehensive notarized statement.

5. Each Contracting State shall have 60 days from the date on which the Proceeding begins to send a written communication to the other Contracting State appointing one member of the arbitration board. Within 60 days of the date on which the second such communication is sent, the two members appointed by the Contracting States shall appoint a third member, who shall serve as chair of the board. If either Contracting State fails to appoint a member, or if the members appointed by the Contracting States fail to agree upon the third member in the manner prescribed by this paragraph, a Contracting State shall ask the highest ranking member of the Secretariat at the Centre for Tax Policy and Administration of the Organisation for Economic Co-operation and Development (OECD) who is not a citizen of either Contracting State, to appoint the remaining member(s) by written notice to

both Contracting States within 60 days of the date of such failure. The competent authorities shall develop a non-exclusive list of individuals with familiarity in international tax matters who may potentially serve as the chair of the board.

6. The arbitration board may adopt any procedures necessary for the conduct of its business, provided that the procedures are not inconsistent with any provision of Article XXVI or this note.

7. Each of the Contracting States shall be permitted to submit, within 60 days of the appointment of the chair of the arbitration board, a proposed resolution describing the proposed disposition of the specific monetary amounts of income, expense or taxation at issue in the case, and a supporting position paper, for consideration by the arbitration board. Copies of the proposed resolution and supporting position paper shall be provided by the board to the other Contracting State on the date on which the later of the submissions is submitted to the board. In the event that only one Contracting State submits a proposed resolution within the allotted time, then that proposed resolution shall be deemed to be the determination of the board in that case and the Proceeding shall be terminated. Each of the Contracting States may, if it so desires, submit a reply submission to the board within 120 days of the appointment of its chair, to address any points raised by the proposed resolution or position paper submitted by the other Contracting State. Additional information may be submitted to the arbitration board only at its request, and copies of the board's request and the Contracting State's response shall be provided to the other Contracting State on the date on which the request or the response is submitted. Except for logistical matters such as those identified in paragraphs 12, 14 and 15 below, all communications from the Contracting States to the arbitration board, and vice versa, shall take place only through written communications between the designated competent authorities and the chair of the board.

8. The arbitration board shall deliver a determination in writing to the Contracting States within six months of the appointment of its chair. The board shall adopt as its determination one of the proposed resolutions submitted by the Contracting States.

9. In making its determination, the arbitration board shall apply, as necessary: (1) the provisions of the Convention as amended; (2) any agreed commentaries or explanations of the Contracting States concerning the Convention as amended; (3) the laws of the Contracting States to the extent they are not inconsistent with each other; and (4) any OECD Commentary, Guidelines or Reports regarding relevant analogous portions of the OECD Model Tax Convention.

10. The determination of the arbitration board in a particular case shall be binding on the Contracting States. The determination of the board shall not state a rationale. It shall have no precedential value.

11. As provided in subparagraph 7(e) of Article XXVI, the determination of an arbitration board shall constitute a resolution by mutual agreement under this Article. Each concerned person must, within 30 days of receiving the determination of the board from the competent authority to which the case was first presented, advise that competent authority whether that concerned person accepts the determination of the board. If any concerned person fails to so advise the relevant competent authority within this time frame, the determination of the board shall be considered not to have been accepted in that case. Where the determination of the board is not accepted, the case may not subsequently be the subject of a Proceeding.

12. Any meeting(s) of the arbitration board shall be in facilities provided by the Contracting State whose competent authority initiated the mutual agreement proceedings in the case.

13. The treatment of any associated interest or penalties shall be determined by applicable domestic law of the Contracting State(s) concerned.

14. No information relating to the Proceeding (including the board's determination) may be disclosed by the members of the arbitration board or their staffs or by either competent authority, except as permitted by the Convention and the domestic laws of the Contracting States. In addition, all material prepared in the course of, or relating to, the Proceeding shall be considered to be information exchanged between the Contracting States. The Contracting States shall ensure that all members of

the arbitration board and their staffs sign and send to each Contracting State notarized statements, prior to their acting in the arbitration proceeding, in which they agree to abide by and be subject to the confidentiality and nondisclosure provisions of Articles XXVI and XXVII of the Convention and the applicable domestic laws of the Contracting States. In the event those provisions conflict, the most restrictive condition shall apply.

15. The fees and expenses of members of the arbitration board shall be set in accordance with the International Centre for Settlement of Investment Disputes (ICSID) Schedule of Fees for arbitrators, as in effect on the date on which the arbitration proceedings begin, and shall be borne equally by the Contracting States. Any fees for language translation shall also be borne equally by the Contracting States. Meeting facilities, related resources, financial management, other logistical support, and general administrative coordination of the Proceeding shall be provided, at its own cost, by the Contracting State whose competent authority initiated the mutual agreement proceedings in the case. Any other costs shall be borne by the Contracting State that incurs them.

16. For purposes of paragraphs 6 and 7 of Article XXVI and this note, each competent authority shall confirm in writing to the other competent authority and to the concerned person(s) the date of its receipt of the information necessary to undertake substantive consideration for a mutual agreement. Such information shall be:

a) in the United States, the information required to be submitted to the U.S. competent authority under Revenue Procedure 2006-54, section 4.05 (or any applicable analogous provisions) and, for cases initially submitted as a request for an Advance Pricing Agreement, the information required to be submitted to the Internal Revenue Service under Revenue Procedure 2006-9, section 4 (or any applicable analogous provisions), and

b) in Canada, the information required to be submitted to Canadian competent authority under Information Circular 71-17 (or any applicable successor publication).

However, this information shall not be considered received until both competent authorities have received copies of all materials submitted to either Contracting State by the concerned person(s) in connection with the mutual agreement procedure.

17. The competent authorities of the Contracting States may modify or supplement the above rules and procedures as necessary to more effectively implement the intent of paragraph 6 of Article XXVI to eliminate double taxation.

If the above proposal is acceptable to your Government, I further propose that this Note, which is authentic in English and in French, and your reply Note reflecting such acceptance shall constitute an agreement between our two Governments which shall enter into force on the date of entry into force of the Protocol and shall be annexed to the Convention as Annex A thereto and shall therefore be an integral part of the Convention.

Please accept, Excellency, the assurance of my highest consideration.

[Signature]
Maxime Bernier
Minister of Foreign Affairs

No. 1015

Excellency,

I have the honor to acknowledge receipt of your Note No. JLAB-0111 dated September 21, 2007, which states in its entirety as follows:

> Excellency,
>
> I have the honor to refer to the Protocol (the "Protocol") done today between Canada and the United States of America amending the Convention with Respect to Taxes on Income and on Capital done at Washington on 26 September 1980, as amended by the Protocols done on 14 June 1983, 28 March 1984, 17 March 1995, and 29 July 1997 (the "Convention"), and to propose on behalf of the Government of Canada the following:
>
> > In respect of any case where the competent authorities have endeavored but are unable to reach a complete agreement under Article XXVI (Mutual Agreement Procedure) of the Convention regarding the application of one or more of the following Articles of the Convention: IV (Residence) (but only insofar as it relates to the residence of a natural person), V (Permanent Establishment), VII (Business Profits), IX (Related Persons), and XII (Royalties) (but only (i) insofar as Article XII might apply in transactions involving related persons to whom Article IX might apply, or (ii) to an allocation of amounts between royalties that are taxable under paragraph 2 thereof and royalties that are exempt under paragraph 3 thereof), binding arbitration shall be used to determine such application, unless the competent authorities agree that the particular case is not suitable for determination by arbitration. In addition, the competent authorities may, on an ad hoc basis, agree that binding arbitration shall be used in respect of any other matter to which Article XXVI applies. If an arbitration proceeding (the "Proceeding") under paragraph 6 of Article XXVI commences, the following rules and procedures shall apply:
> >
> > 1. The Proceeding shall be conducted in the manner prescribed by, and subject to the requirements of, paragraphs 6 and 7 of Article XXVI and these rules and procedures, as modified or supplemented by any other rules and procedures agreed upon by the competent authorities pursuant to paragraph 17 below.
> >
> > 2. The determination reached by an arbitration board in the Proceeding shall be limited to a determination regarding the amount of income, expense or tax reportable to the Contracting States.
> >
> > 3. Notwithstanding the initiation of the Proceeding, the competent authorities may reach a mutual agreement to resolve a case and terminate the Proceeding. Correspondingly, a concerned person may withdraw a request for the competent authorities to engage in the Mutual Agreement Procedure (and thereby terminate the Proceeding) at any time.
> >
> > 4. The requirements of subparagraph 7(d) of Article XXVI shall be met when the competent authorities have each received from each concerned person a notarized statement agreeing that the concerned person and each person acting on the concerned person's behalf, shall not disclose to any other person any information received during the course of the Proceeding from either Contracting State or the arbitration board, other than the determination of the Proceeding. A concerned person that has the legal authority to bind any other concerned person(s) on this matter may do so in a comprehensive notarized statement.
> >
> > 5. Each Contracting State shall have 60 days from the date on which the Proceeding begins to send a written communication to the other Contracting State appointing one member of the arbitration board. Within 60 days of the date on which the second such communication is sent, the two members appointed by the Contracting States shall appoint a third member, who shall serve as chair of the board. If either Contracting State fails to appoint a member, or if the members appointed by the Contracting States fail to agree upon the third member in the manner prescribed by this paragraph, a Contracting State shall ask the highest ranking member of the Secretariat at the Centre for Tax Policy and Administration of the Organisation for Economic Co-operation and Development (OECD) who is not a citizen of either Contracting State, to appoint the remaining members) by written notice to both Contracting States within 60 days of the date of such failure.

The competent authorities shall develop a non-exclusive list of individuals with familiarity in international tax matters who may potentially serve as the chair of the board.

6. The arbitration board may adopt any procedures necessary for the conduct of its business, provided that the procedures are not inconsistent with any provision of Article XXVI or this note.

7. Each of the Contracting States shall be permitted to submit, within 60 days of the appointment of the chair of the arbitration board, a proposed resolution describing the proposed disposition of the specific monetary amounts of income, expense or taxation at issue in the case, and a supporting position paper, for consideration by the arbitration board. Copies of the proposed resolution and supporting position paper shall be provided by the board to the other Contracting State on the date on which the later of the submissions is submitted to the board. In the event that only one Contracting State submits a proposed resolution within the allotted time, then that proposed resolution shall be deemed to be the determination of the board in that case and the Proceeding shall be terminated. Each of the Contracting States may, if it so desires, submit a reply submission to the board within 120 days of the appointment of its chair, to address any points raised by the proposed resolution or position paper submitted by the other Contracting State. Additional information may be submitted to the arbitration board only at its request, and copies of the board's request and the Contracting State's response shall be provided to the other Contracting State on the date on which the request or the response is submitted. Except for logistical matters such as those identified in paragraphs 12, 14 and 15 below, all communications from the Contracting States to the arbitration board, and vice versa, shall take place only through written communications between the designated competent authorities and the chair of the board.

8. The arbitration board shall deliver a determination in writing to the Contracting States within six months of the appointment of its chair. The board shall adopt as its determination one of the proposed resolutions submitted by the Contracting States.

9. In making its determination, the arbitration board shall apply, as necessary: (1) the provisions of the Convention as amended; (2) any agreed commentaries or explanations of the Contracting States concerning the Convention as amended; (3) the laws of the Contracting States to the extent they are not inconsistent with each other, and (4) any OECD Commentary, Guidelines or Reports regarding relevant analogous portions of the OECD Model Tax Convention.

10. The determination of the arbitration board in a particular case shall be binding on the Contracting States. The determination of the board shall not state a rationale. It shall have no precedential value.

11. As provided in subparagraph 7(e) of Article XXVI, the determination of an arbitration board shall constitute a resolution by mutual agreement under this Article. Each concerned person must, within 30 days of receiving the determination of the board from the competent authority to which the case was first presented, advise that competent authority whether that concerned person accepts the determination of the board. If any concerned person fails to so advise the relevant competent authority within this time frame, the determination of the board shall be considered not to have been accepted in that case. Where the determination of the board is not accepted, the case may not subsequently be the subject of a Proceeding.

12. Any meeting(s) of the arbitration board shall be in facilities provided by the Contracting State whose competent authority initiated the mutual agreement proceedings in the case.

13. The treatment of any associated interest or penalties shall be determined by applicable domestic law of the Contracting State(s) concerned.

14. No information relating to the Proceeding (including the board's determination) may be disclosed by the members of the arbitration board or their staffs or by either competent authority, except as permitted by the Convention and the domestic laws of the Contracting States. In addition, all material prepared in the course of, or relating to, the Proceeding shall be considered to be information exchanged between the Contracting States. The Contracting States shall ensure that all members of the arbitration board and their staffs sign and send to each Contracting State notarized statements, prior to their acting in the arbitration proceeding, in which they agree to

abide by and be subject to the confidentiality and nondisclosure provisions of Articles XXVI and XXVII of the Convention and the applicable domestic laws of the Contracting States. In the event those provisions conflict, the most restrictive condition shall apply.

15. The fees and expenses of members of the arbitration board shall be set in accordance with the International Centre for Settlement of Investment Disputes (ICSID) Schedule of Fees for arbitrators, as in effect on the date on which the arbitration proceedings begin, and shall be borne equally by the Contracting States. Any fees for language translation shall also be borne equally by the Contracting States. Meeting facilities, related resources, financial management, other logistical support, and general administrative coordination of the Proceeding shall be provided, at its own cost, by the Contracting State whose competent authority initiated the mutual agreement proceedings in the case. Any other costs shall be borne by the Contracting State that incurs them.

16. For purposes of paragraphs 6 and 7 of Article XXVI and this note, each competent authority shall confirm in writing to the other competent authority and to the concerned person(s) the date of its receipt of the information necessary to undertake substantive consideration for a mutual agreement. Such information shall be:

a) in the United States, the information required to be submitted to the U.S. competent authority under Revenue Procedure 2006-54, section 4.05 (or any applicable analogous provisions) and, for cases initially submitted as a request for an Advance Pricing Agreement, the information required to be submitted to the Internal Revenue Service under Revenue Procedure 2006-9, section 4 (or any applicable analogous provisions), and

b) in Canada, the information required to be submitted to Canadian competent authority under Information Circular 71-17 (or any applicable successor publication).

However, this information shall not be considered received until both competent authorities have received copies of all materials submitted to either Contracting State by the concerned person(s) in connection with the mutual agreement procedure.

17. The competent authorities of the Contracting States may modify or supplement the above rules and procedures as necessary to more effectively implement the intent of paragraph 6 of Article XXVI to eliminate double taxation.

If the above proposal is acceptable to your Government, I further propose that this Note, which is authentic in English and in French, and your reply Note reflecting such acceptance shall constitute an agreement between our two Governments which shall enter into force on the date of entry into force of the Protocol and shall be annexed to the Convention as Annex A thereto and shall therefore be an integral part of the Convention.

Please accept, Excellency, the assurance of my highest consideration.

I am pleased to inform you that the Government of the United States of America accepts the proposal set forth in your Note. The Government of the United States of America further agrees that your Note, which is authentic in English and in French, together with this reply, shall constitute an Agreement between the United States of America and Canada, which shall enter into force on the date of entry into force of the Protocol amending the Convention between the United States of America and Canada with Respect to Taxes on Income and on Capital done at Washington on 26 September 1980, as amended by the Protocols done on 14 June 1983, 28 March 1984, 17 March 1995, and 29 My 1997 (the "Convention"), and shall be annexed to the Convention as Annex A thereto, and shall therefore be an integral part of the Convention.

Accept, Excellency, the renewed assurances of my highest consideration.

Embassy of the United States of America
Ottawa, September 21, 2007

Minister of Foreign Affairs Ministre des Affaires etrangeres

Ottawa, Canada K1A 0G2

Note No. JLAB-0112

SEP 27 2007

Excellency,

I have the honor to refer to the Protocol (the "Protocol") done today between Canada and the United States of America amending the Convention with Respect to Taxes on Income and on Capital done at Washington on 26 September 1980, as amended by the Protocols done on 14 June 1983, 28 March 1984, 17 March 1995, and 29 July 1997 (the "Convention").

In the course of the negotiations leading to the conclusion of the Protocol done today, the negotiators developed and agreed upon a common understanding and interpretation of certain provisions of the Convention. These understandings and interpretations are intended to give guidance both to the taxpayers and to the tax authorities of our two countries in interpreting various provisions contained in the Convention.

I, therefore, have the further honor to propose on behalf of the Government of Canada the following understandings and interpretations:

1. Meaning of undefined terms

For purposes of paragraph 2 of Article III (General Definitions) of the Convention, it is understood that, as regards the application at any time of the Convention, and any protocols thereto by a Contracting State, any term not defined therein shall, unless the context otherwise requires or the competent authorities otherwise agree to a common meaning pursuant to Article XXVI (Mutual Agreement Procedure), have the meaning which it has at that time under the law of that State for the purposes of the taxes to which the Convention, and any protocols thereto apply, any meaning under the applicable tax laws of that State prevailing over a meaning given to the term under other laws of that State.

2. Meaning of connected projects

For the purposes of applying subparagraph (*b*) of paragraph 9 of Article V (Permanent Establishment) of the Convention, it is understood that projects shall be considered to be connected if they constitute a coherent whole, commercially and geographically.

3. Definition of the term "dividends"

It is understood that distributions from Canadian income trusts and royalty trusts that are treated as dividends under the taxation laws of Canada shall be considered dividends for the purposes of Article X (Dividends) of the Convention.

4. Deletion of Article XIV (Independent Personal Services)

It is understood that the deletion of Article XIV (Independent Personal Services) of the Convention confirms the negotiators' shared understanding that no practical distinction can be made between a "fixed base" and a "permanent establishment", and that independent personal services of a resident of a Contracting State, to the extent that such resident is found to have a permanent establishment in the other Contracting State with respect to those services, shall be subject to the provisions of Article VII (Business Profits).

5. Former permanent establishments and fixed bases

It is understood that the modifications of paragraph 2 of Article VII (Business Profits), paragraph 4 of Article X (Dividends), paragraph 3 of Article XI (Interest) and paragraph 5 of Article XII (Royalties) of the Convention to refer to business having formerly been carried on through a permanent establishment confirm the negotiators' shared understanding of the meaning of the existing provisions, and thus are clarifying only.

6. Stock options

For purposes of applying Article XV (Income from Employment) and Article XXIV (Elimination of Double Taxation) of the Convention to income of an individual in connection with the exercise or other disposal (including a deemed exercise or disposal) of an option that was granted to the individual as an employee of a corporation or mutual fund trust to acquire shares or units ("securities") of the employer (which is considered, for the purposes of this Note, to include any related entity) in respect of services rendered or to be rendered by such individual, or in connection with the disposal (including a deemed disposal) of a security acquired under such an option, the following principles shall apply:

(*a*) Subject to subparagraph 6(b) of this Note, the individual shall be deemed to have derived, in respect of employment exercised in a Contracting State, the same proportion of such income that the number of days in the period that begins on the day the option was granted, and that ends on the day the option was exercised or disposed of, on which the individual's principal place of employment for the employer was situated in that Contracting State is of the total number of days in the period on which the individual was employed by the employer; and

(*b*) Notwithstanding subparagraph 6(a) of this Note, if the competent authorities of both Contracting States agree that the terms of the option were such that the grant of the option will be appropriately treated as transfer of ownership of the securities (e.g., because the options were in-the-money or not subject to a substantial vesting period), then they may agree to attribute income accordingly.

7. Taxes imposed by reason of death

It is understood that,

(*a*) Where a share or option in respect of a share is property situated in the United States for the purposes of Article XXIX B (Taxes Imposed by Reason of Death) of the Convention, any employment income in respect of the share or option shall be, for the purpose of clause 6(a)(ii) of that Article, income from property situated in the United States;

(*b*) Where property situated in the United States for the purposes of Article XXIX B (Taxes Imposed by Reason of Death) of the Convention is held by an entity that is a resident of Canada and that is described in subparagraph 1(b) of Article IV (Residence) of the Convention, any income out of or under the entity in respect of the property shall be, for the purpose of subparagraph 6(a)(ii) of Article XXIX B (Taxes Imposed by Reason of Death), income from property situated in the United States; and

(*c*) Where a tax is imposed in Canada by reason of death in respect of an entity that is a resident of Canada and that is described in subparagraph 1(b) of Article IV (Residence) of the Convention, that tax shall be, for the purpose of paragraph 7 of Article XXIX B (Taxes Imposed by Reason of Death) of the Convention, imposed in respect of property situated in Canada.

8. Royalties – information in connection with franchise agreement

It is understood that the reference in subparagraph 3(c) of Article XII (Royalties) of the Convention to information provided in connection with a franchise agreement shall generally refer only to information that governs or otherwise deals with the operation (whether by the payer or by another person) of the franchise, and not to other information concerning industrial, commercial or scientific experience that is held for resale or license.

9. With reference to Article VII (Business Profits)

It is understood that the business profits to be attributed to a permanent establishment shall include only the profits derived from the assets used, risks assumed and activities performed by the permanent establishment. The principles of the OECD Transfer Pricing Guidelines shall apply for purposes of determining the profits attributable to a permanent establishment, taking into account the different economic and legal circumstances of a single entity. Accordingly, any of the methods described therein as acceptable methods for determining an arm's length result may be used to determine the income of a permanent establishment so long as those methods are applied in accordance with the Guidelines. In particular, in determining the amount of attributable profits, the permanent establishment shall be treated as having the same amount of capital that it would need to support its activities if it were a distinct and separate enterprise engaged in the same or similar activities. With respect to financial institutions other than insurance companies, a Contracting State may determine the amount of capital to be attributed to a permanent establishment by allocating the institution's total equity between its various offices on the basis of the proportion of the financial institution's risk-weighted assets attributable to each of them. In the case of an insurance company, there shall be attributed to a permanent establishment not only premiums earned through the permanent establishment, but that portion of the insurance company's overall investment income from reserves and surplus that supports the risks assumed by the permanent establishment.

10. Qualifying retirement plans

For purposes of paragraph 15 of Article XVIII (Pensions and Annuities) of the Convention, it is understood that

(*a*) In the case of Canada, the term "qualifying retirement plan" shall include the following and any identical or substantially similar plan that is established pursuant to legislation introduced after the date of signature of the Protocol: registered pension plans under section 147.1 of the Income Tax Act, registered retirement savings plans under section 146 that are part of a group arrangement described in subsection 204.2(1.32), deferred profit sharing plans under section 147, and any registered retirement savings plan under section 146 or registered retirement income fund under section 146.3 that is funded exclusively by rollover contributions from one or more of the preceding plans; and

(*b*) In the case of the United States, the term "qualifying retirement plan" shall include the following and any identical or substantially similar plan that is established pursuant to legislation introduced after the date of signature of the Protocol: qualified plans under section 401(a) of the Internal Revenue Code (including section 401(k) arrangements), individual retirement plans that are part of a simplified employee pension plan that satisfies section 408(k), section 408(p) simple retirement accounts, section 403(a) qualified annuity plans, section 403(b) plans, section 457(g) trusts providing benefits under section 457(b) plans, the Thrift Savings Fund (section 7701 (j)), and any individual retirement account under section 408(a) that is funded exclusively by rollover contributions from one or more of the preceding plans.

11. Former long-term residents

The term "long-term resident" shall mean any individual who is a lawful permanent resident of the United States in eight or more taxable years during the preceding 15 taxable years. In determining whether the threshold in the preceding sentence is met, there shall not count any year in which the individual is treated as a resident of Canada under the Convention, or as a resident of any country other than the United States under the provisions of any other U.S. tax treaty, and, in either case, the individual does not waive the benefits of such treaty applicable to residents of the other country.

12. Special source rules relating to former citizens and long-term residents

For purposes of subparagraph 2 (b) of Article XXIX (Miscellaneous Rules) of the Convention, "income deemed under the domestic law of the United States to arise from such sources" shall consist of gains from the sale or exchange of stock of a U.S. company or debt obligations of a U.S. person, the United States, a State, or a political subdivision thereof, or the District of Columbia, gains from property (other than stock or debt obligations) located in the United States, and, in certain cases, income or gain derived from the sale of stock of a non-U.S. company or a disposition of property contributed to such non-U.S. company where such company would be a controlled foreign corporation with respect to the person if such person had continued to be a U.S. person. In addition, an individual who exchanges property that gives rise or would give rise to U.S.-source income for property that gives rise to foreign-source income shall be treated as if he or she had sold the property that would give rise to U.S. source income for its fair market value, and any consequent gain shall be deemed to be income from sources within the United States.

13. Exchange of Information

It is understood that the standards and practices described in Article XXVII (Exchange of Information) of the Convention are to be in no respect less effective than those described in the Model Agreement on Exchange of Information on Tax Matters developed by the OECD Global Forum Working Group on Effective Exchange of Information.

14. Limitation on Benefits

The United States and Canada are part of the same regional free trade area and, as a result, the Convention reflects the fact that publicly traded companies resident in one country may be traded on a stock exchange of the other country. Nevertheless, the Contracting States agree that in making future amendments to the Convention, they shall consult on possible modifications to subparagraph 2(c) of Article XXIX A (Limitation on Benefits) of the Convention (including, modifications necessary to discourage corporate inversion transactions).

If the above proposal is acceptable to your Government, 1 further propose that this Note, which is authentic in English and in French, and your reply Note reflecting such acceptance shall constitute an agreement between our two Governments which shall enter into force on the date of entry into force of the Protocol and shall be annexed to the Convention as Annex B thereto and shall therefore be an integral part of the Convention.

Please accept, Excellency, the assurance of my highest consideration.

[Signature]
Maxime Bernier
Minister of Foreign Affairs

No. 1014

Excellency,

I have the honor to acknowledge receipt of your Note No. JLAB-0112 dated September 21, 2007, which states in its entirety as follows:

Excellency,

I have the honor to refer to the Protocol (the "Protocol") done today between Canada and the United States of America amending the Convention with Respect to Taxes on Income and on Capital done at Washington on 26 September 1980, as amended by the Protocols done on 14 June 1983, 28 March 1984, 17 March 1995, and 29 July 1997 (the "Convention")

In the course of the negotiations leading to the conclusion of the Protocol done today, the negotiators developed and agreed upon a common understanding and interpretation of certain provisions of the Convention. These understandings and interpretations are intended to give guidance both to the taxpayers and to the tax authorities of our two countries in interpreting various provisions contained in the Convention.

I, therefore, have the further honor to propose on behalf of the Government of Canada the following understandings and interpretations:

1. Meaning of undefined terms

For purposes of paragraph 2 of Article III (General Definitions) of the Convention, it is understood that, as regards the application at any time of the Convention, and any protocols thereto by a Contracting State, any term not defined therein shall, unless the context otherwise requires or the competent authorities otherwise agree to a common meaning pursuant to Article XXVI (Mutual Agreement Procedure), have the meaning which it has at that time under the law of that State for the purposes of the taxes to which the Convention, and any protocols thereto apply, any meaning under the applicable tax laws of that State prevailing over a meaning given to the term under other laws of that State.

2. Meaning of connected projects

For the purposes of applying subparagraph (*b*) of paragraph 9 of Article V (Permanent Establishment) of the Convention, it is understood that projects shall be considered to be connected if they constitute a coherent whole, commercially and geographically.

3. Definition of the term "dividends"

It is understood that distributions from Canadian income trusts and royalty trusts that are treated as dividends under the taxation laws of Canada shall be considered dividends for the purposes of Article X (Dividends) of the Convention.

4. Deletion of Article XIV (Independent Personal Services)

It is understood that the deletion of Article XIV (Independent Personal Services) of the Convention confirms the negotiators' shared understanding that no practical distinction can be made between a "fixed base" and a "permanent establishment", and that independent personal services of a resident of a Contracting State, to the extent that such resident is found to have a permanent establishment in the other Contracting State with respect to those services, shall be subject to the provisions of Article VII (Business Profits).

5. Former permanent establishments and fixed bases

It is understood that the modifications of paragraph 2 of Article VII (Business Profits), paragraph 4 of Article X (Dividends), paragraph 3 of Article XI (Interest) and paragraph 5 of Article XII (Royalties) of the Convention to refer to business having formerly been carried on through a permanent establishment confirm the negotiators' shared understanding of the meaning of the existing provisions, and thus are clarifying only.

6. Stock options

For purposes of applying Article XV (Income from Employment) and Article XXIV (Elimination of Double Taxation) of the Convention to income of an individual in connection with the exercise or other disposal (including a deemed exercise or disposal) of an option that was granted to the individual as an employee of a corporation or mutual fund trust to acquire shares or units ("securities") of the employer (which is considered, for the purposes of this Note, to include any related entity) in respect of services rendered or to be rendered by such individual, or in connection with the disposal (including a deemed disposal) of a security acquired under such an option, the following principles shall apply:

(*a*) Subject to subparagraph 6(b) of this Note, the individual shall be deemed to have derived, in respect of employment exercised in a Contracting State, the same proportion of such income that the number of days in the period that begins on the day the option was granted, and that ends on the day the option was exercised or disposed of, on which the individual's principal place of employment for the employer was situated in that Contracting State is of the total number of days in the period on which the individual was employed by the employer; and

(*b*) Notwithstanding subparagraph 6(a) of this Note, if the competent authorities of both Contracting States agree that the terms of the option were such that the grant of the option will be appropriately treated as transfer of ownership of the securities (e.g., because the options were in-the-money or not subject to a substantial vesting period), then they may agree to attribute income accordingly.

7. Taxes imposed by reason of death

It is understood that,

(*a*) Where a share or option in respect of a share is property situated in the United States for the purposes of Article XXIX B (Taxes Imposed by Reason of Death) of the Convention, any employment income in respect of the share or option shall be, for the purpose of clause 6(a)(ii) of that Article, income from property situated in the United States;

(*b*) Where property situated in the United States for the purposes of Article XXIX B (Taxes Imposed by Reason of Death) of the Convention is held by an entity that is a resident of Canada and that is described in subparagraph 1(b) of Article IV (Residence) of the Convention, any income out of or under the entity in respect of the property shall be, for the purpose of subparagraph 6(a)(ii) of Article XXIX B (Taxes Imposed by Reason of Death), income from property situated in the United States; and

(*c*) Where a tax is imposed in Canada by reason of death in respect of an entity that is a resident of Canada and that is described in subparagraph 1(b) of Article IV (Residence) of the Convention, that tax shall be, for the purpose of paragraph 7 of Article XXIX B (Taxes Imposed by Reason of Death) of the Convention, imposed in respect of property situated in Canada.

8. Royalties – information in connection with franchise agreement

It is understood that the reference in subparagraph 3(c) of Article XII (Royalties) of the Convention to information provided in connection with a franchise agreement shall generally refer only to information that governs or otherwise deals with the operation (whether by the payer or by another person) of the franchise, and not to other information concerning industrial, commercial or scientific experience that is held for resale or license.

9. With reference to Article VII (Business Profits)

It is understood that the business profits to be attributed to a permanent establishment shall include only the profits derived from the assets used, risks assumed and activities performed by (he permanent establishment. The principles of the OECD Transfer Pricing Guidelines shall apply for purposes of determining the profits attributable to a permanent establishment, taking into account the different economic and legal circumstances of a single entity. Accordingly, any of the methods described therein as acceptable methods for determining an arm's length result may be used to determine the income of a permanent establishment so long as those methods are applied in accordance with the Guidelines. In particular, in determining the amount of attributable profits, the permanent establishment shall be treated as having the same amount of capital that it would need to support its activities if it were a distinct and separate enterprise engaged in the same or similar activities. With respect to financial institutions other than insurance companies, a Contracting State may determine the amount of capital to be attributed to a permanent establishment by allocating the institution's total equity between its various offices on the basis of the proportion of the financial institution's risk-weighted assets attributable to each of them. In the case of an insurance company, there shall be attributed to a permanent establishment not only premiums earned through the permanent establishment, but that portion of the insurance company's overall investment income from reserves and surplus that supports the risks assumed by the permanent establishment.

10. Qualifying retirement plans

For purposes of paragraph 15 of Article XVIII (Pensions and Annuities) of the Convention, it is understood that

(*a*) In the case of Canada, the term "qualifying retirement plan" shall include the following and any identical or substantially similar plan that is established pursuant to legislation introduced after the date of signature of the Protocol: registered pension plans under section 147.1 of the Income Tax Act, registered retirement savings plans under section 146 that are part of a group arrangement described in subsection 204.2(1.32), deferred profit sharing plans under section 147, and any registered retirement savings plan under section 146 or registered retirement income fund under section 146.3 that is funded exclusively by rollover contributions from one or more of the preceding plans; and

(*b*) In the case of the United States, the term "qualifying retirement plan" shall include the following and any identical or substantially similar plan that is established pursuant to legislation introduced after the date of signature of the Protocol: qualified plans under section 401(a) of the Internal Revenue Code (including section 401(k) arrangements), individual retirement plans that are part of a simplified employee pension plan that satisfies section 408(k), section 408(p) simple retirement accounts, section 403(a) qualified annuity plans, section 403(b) plans, section 457(g) trusts providing benefits under section 457(b) plans, the Thrift Savings Fund (section 7701 (j)), and any individual retirement account under section 408(a) that is funded exclusively by rollover contributions from one or more of the preceding plans.

11. Former long-term residents

The term "long-term resident" shall mean any individual who is a lawful permanent resident of the United States in eight or more taxable years during the preceding 15 taxable years. In determining whether the threshold in the preceding sentence is met, there shall not count any year in which the individual is treated as a resident of Canada under the Convention, or as a resident of any country other than the United States under the provisions of any other U.S. tax treaty, and, in either case, the individual does not waive the benefits of such treaty applicable to residents of the other country.

12. Special source rules relating to former citizens and long-term residents

For purposes of subparagraph 2 (b) of Article XXIX (Miscellaneous Rules) of the Convention, "income deemed under the domestic law of the United States to arise from such sources" shall consist of gains from the sale or exchange of stock of a U.S. company or debt obligations of a U.S. person, the United States, a State, or a political subdivision thereof, or the District of Columbia, gains from property (other than stock or debt obligations) located in the United States, and, in certain cases, income or gain derived from the sale of stock of a non-U.S. company or a disposition of property contributed to such non-U.S. company where such company would be a controlled foreign corporation with respect to the person if such person had continued to be a U.S. person. In addition, an individual who exchanges property that gives rise or would give rise to U.S.-source income for property that gives rise to foreign-source income shall be treated as if he or she had sold the property that would give rise to U.S. source income for its fair market value, and any consequent gain shall be deemed to be income from sources within the United States.

13. Exchange of Information

It is understood that the standards and practices described in Article XXVII (Exchange of Information) of the Convention are to be in no respect less effective than those described in the Model Agreement on Exchange of Information on Tax Matters developed by the OECD Global Forum Working Group on Effective Exchange of Information.

14. Limitation on Benefits

The United States and Canada are part of the same regional free trade area and, as a result, the Convention reflects the fact that publicly traded companies resident in one country may be traded on a stock exchange of the other country. Nevertheless, the Contracting States agree that in making future amendments to the Convention, they shall consult on possible modifications to subparagraph 2(c) of Article XXIX A (Limitation on Benefits) of the Convention (including, modifications necessary to discourage corporate inversion transactions).

If the above proposal is acceptable to your Government, I further propose that this Note, which is authentic in English and in French, and your reply Note reflecting such acceptance shall constitute an agreement between our two Governments which shall enter into force on the date of entry into force of the Protocol and shall be annexed to the Convention as Annex B thereto, and shall therefore be an integral part of the Convention.

Please accept, Excellency, the assurance of my highest consideration.

I am pleased to inform you that the Government of the United States of America accepts the proposal set forth in your Note. The Government of the United States of America further agrees that your Note, which is authentic in English and in French, together with this reply, shall constitute an Agreement between the United States of America and Canada, which shall enter into force on the date of entry into force of the Protocol amending the Convention between the United States of America and Canada with Respect to Taxes on Income and on Capital done at Washington on 26 September 1980, as amended by the Protocols done on 14 June 1983, 28 March 1984, 17 March 1995, and 29 July 1997 (the "Convention"), and shall be annexed to the Convention as Annex B thereto, and shall therefore be an integral part of the Convention.

Accept, Excellency, the renewed assurances of my highest consideration.

Embassy of the United States of America

Ottawa, September 21, 2007

SENATE TREATY DOCUMENT NUMBER: 110-16

AMENDMENTS TO THE CONSTITUTION AND CONVENTION OF THE INTERNATIONAL TELECOMMUNICATION UNION, AS AMENDED, TOGETHER WITH THE DECLARATIONS AND RESERVATIONS BY THE UNITED STATES OF AMERICA, ALL AS CONTAINED IN THE FINAL ACTS OF THE PLENIPOTENTIARY CONFERENCE

SIGNED AT ANTALYA, TURKEY, NOVEMBER 24, 2006
APPROVED BY THE U.S. SENATE ON SEPTEMBER 25, 2008

CTIA DOCUMENT NUMBER: 9296.003

LETTER OF TRANSMITTAL

THE WHITE HOUSE, *April 8, 2008.*

To the Senate of the United States:

With a view to receiving the advice and consent of the Senate to ratification, I transmit herewith the amendments to the Constitution and Convention of the International Telecommunication Union (Geneva, 1992), as amended by the Plenipotentiary Conference (Kyoto, 1994) and the Plenipotentiary Conference (Marrakesh, 2002), together with the declarations and reservations by the United States, all as contained in the Final Acts of the Plenipotentiary Conference (Antalya, 2006). I transmit also, for the information of the Senate, the report of the Department of State concerning the amendments.

The Plenipotentiary Conference (Antalya, 2006) adopted amendments that, among other things: clarify the functions of certain International Telecommunication Union (ITU) officials and bodies; reduce the frequency of certain ITU conferences; clarify eligibility for re-election to certain ITU positions; enhance oversight of the ITU budget and provide for results-based (as well as cost-based) budget proposals; expand the scale of available contribution levels for Member States and Sector Members; and, clarify the definition of and role of observers participating in ITU proceedings.

Consistent with longstanding practice in the ITU, the United States, in signing the 2006 amendments, made certain declarations and reservations. Subject to those declarations and reservations, I believe the United States should ratify the 2006 amendments to the International Telecommunication Union Constitution and Convention. These amendments will contribute to the ITU's ability to adapt to changes in the global telecommunications sector and, in so doing, serve the needs of the United States Government and United States industry.

It is my hope that the Senate will take early action on this matter and give its advice and consent to ratification.

George W. Bush

LETTER OF SUBMITTAL

Department of State,
Washington, May 29, 2007

The President,
The White House

THE PRESIDENT: I have the honor to submit to you, with a view to their transmission to the Senate for advice and consent to ratification, amendments to the Constitution and Convention of the International Telecommunication Union (Geneva, 1992), as amended by the Plenipotentiary Conference (Kyoto, 1994), the Plenipotentiary Conference (Minneapolis, 1998), and the Plenipotentiary Conference (Marrakesh, 2002). The United States signed these amendments to the Constitution and Convention on November 24, 2006, at the Plenipotentiary Conference in Antalya, Turkey. I also have the honor to submit to you certain U.S. declarations and reservations made upon signature of these amendments that also require Senate advice and consent.

The Department of State and the other agencies involved recommend that these declarations and reservations be confirmed in the U.S. instrument of ratificatiun of the amendments. The Department of State and the other interested agencies are of the view that no additional reservations are required. These amendments will not require implementing U.S. legislation. The National Telecommunications and Information Administration of the Department of Commerce, the Department of Defense, the Federal Communications Commission, and the National Aeronautics and Space Administration concur in my recommendation that the amendments, with the U.S. declarations and reservations discussed above, be submitted to the Senate for its consideration and advice and consent to ratification.

Respectfully submitted,

Condoleezza Rice

Enclosure: Overview of the amendments

2006 Amendments to the ITU Constitution and Convention

Overview

These amendments to the ITU Constitution and Convention were signed by the United States on November 24, 2006, at the Plenipotentiary Conference that convened in Antalya, Turkey during the period November 6-24, 2006. The amendments, as well as the declarations and reservations made by the U.S. delegation, are contained in the Final Acts of the Plenipotentiary Conference, which also includes texts of the following documents that do not require ratification by the United States: (1) declarations and reservations of other governments; (2) General Rules of Conferences, Assemblies, and Meetings of the Union, as amended; (3) Decisions, as amended; (4) Resolutions, as amended; and (5) a list of Resolutions abrogated by the Plenipotentiary Conference. The certified English language text of the Final Acts is submitted herewith.

The amendments to the Constitution and Convention will each, respectively, enter into force as a whole and in the form of one single instrument, on January 1, 2008, between Member States that have by that date deposited their instruments of ratification, acceptance, or approval of, or accession to, the amendments. The amendments will thereafter be open to accession.

Description and Effect of Amendments

Amendments concerning certain functions of ITU officials and bodies.

The Convention was amended to clarify that the Secretary-General, the Deputy Secretary-General, or a representative of the Secretary-General may participate in ITU conferences or other ITU meetings in an advisory, vice consultative, capacity (See Convention, Art. 5, paragraph 2 (MOD 105)). The Convention currently provides that world telecommunication development conferences may, as part of the work program of the Telecommunication Development Sector, set up study groups. The Convention was amended to amplify this function, specifying that such conferences shall decide on the need to maintain, terminate, or establish study groups and allocate to them the matters to be studied (See Convention, Art. 16, paragraph 1(a) (MOD 209)). In addition, the provision in the Convention relating to the functions of the Telecommunication Development Advisory Group was amended to state that this Group shall act through the Director of the Telecommunication Development Bureau. This provides more direct control by the Director over the activities of the Telecommunication Development Advisory Group (See Convention, Art. 17A, paragraph 1 (MOD 215C)).

Amendments concerning scheduling of meetings.

Under the current Constitution, world radiocommunication conferences and radiocommunication assemblies are normally to be convened every two to three years. In an effort to reduce ITU expenditures, the Conference amended the Constitution to provide that world radiocommunication conferences and radiocommunication assemblies shall normally be convened every three to four years (See Constitution, Art. 13, paragraphs 2 and 3 (MOD 90, MOD 91)).

Amendments concerning elections.

The Convention provides that elected officials of the ITU (the Secretary-General, the Deputy Secretary-General, and the Directors of the Bureaus) shall be eligible for re-election only once. An amendment clarifies that this applies only to re-election for the same position. Also, it clarifies that the restriction on re-election for a second term applies regardless of whether the terms are consecutive (See Convention, Art. 2, "Elected Officials" paragraph 1 (MOD 13)). A similar amendment clarifies that the existing restriction on re-election for a second term for members of the Radio Regulations Board applies regardless of whether the terms are consecutive. See Convention, Art. 2, "Members of the Radio Regulations Board" paragraph 1 (MOD 20).

Amendments concerning financial matters.

In an effort to enhance oversight of the budget of the ITU, the Convention was amended to require that the Council carry out an annual review of income and expenditures in order to make adjustments, as appropriate, in accordance with resolutions and decisions of the plenipotentiary conference (See Convention, Art. 4, paragraph 11(7) (MOD 73)). In addition, the Convention was amended to provide that, in preparing and submitting to the Council a biennial draft budget covering ITU expenditures, the Secretary-General shall include results-based as well as cost-based budget information (See Convention, Art. 5, paragraph 1(q) (MOD 100)). Under the Convention, each Member State and Sector Member must choose its class of contribution to the ITU from a scale of contribution units. The Conference amended that scale by adding two new levels (11 unit class and 6 unit class), bringing the total of available contribution levels to 24 (See Convention, Art, 33, paragraph 1 (MOD 468)). Also, a provision was added to the Convention permitting the Council, in exceptional circumstances, to authorize a reduction in the number of contributory units when so requested by a Sector Member that can no longer maintain its original level of contribution (See Convention, Art. 33, paragraph 4(5ter) (ADD 480B)). The Constitution provides that, prior to each plenipotentiary conference, the Council shall fix the provisional amount of the contributory unit on the basis of the draft financial plan and the total number of contributory units. The Secretary-General is then to inform the Member States and the Sector Members of the provisional amount of the contributory unit and invite Member States to notify the class of contribution they have provisionally chosen. The Conference changed the deadline for such notification from no later than one week prior to the opening of the plenipotentiary conference to no later than four weeks prior to the opening of the plenipotentiary conference, thereby providing the Secretariat with more time to process the notifications and incorporate any financial implications into fiscal planning (See Constitution, Art. 28, paragraph 2(3bis)(2) (MOD 161C)). The Constitution further provides that the plenipotentiary conference shall determine the definitive upper limit of the amount of the contributory unit and fix a deadline by which Member States must announce their definitive choice of class of contribution. That deadline was changed from a date within the penultimate week of the plenipotentiary conference to the Monday of the final week of the plenipotentiary conference (See Constitution, Art. 28, paragraph 2(3bis)(4) (MOD 161E)). The article in the Convention on Finances was amended to identify with more precision the organizations and Sector Members that are obligated to share in defraying the expenses of the conferences, assemblies, and meetings in which they participate (See Convention, Art. 33, paragraph 4(1) (MOD 476)).

Amendment concerning participation by Sector Members.

The Convention authorizes certain entities to participate in the activities of the ITU as Sector Members. The Convention currently provides that, when a Sector Member elects to withdraw from such participation, this becomes effective one year from the date of notification to the Secretary-General. The Conference changed this period of time to six months in order to increase the likelihood of payment after notification of withdrawal (See Convention, Art. 19, paragraph 10 (MOD 240)).

Amendments concerning the role of observers.

The definition of "observer" in the Annex to the Convention was simplified to state that an observer is "[a] person sent by a Member State, organization agency, or entity to attend a conference, assembly, or meeting of the Union or the Council, without the right to vote and in accordance with the relevant provisions of the basic texts of the Union" (See Convention, Annex (MOD 1002)). The Conference deleted a provision in the Convention giving the representative of each Member State of the Council the right to attend, as an observer, all meetings of the ITU Sectors (See Convention, Art. 4, paragraph 7 (SUP 58)). The Convention was amended to clarify that Sector Members may attend – and not merely be represented at – meetings of the Council, its committees, and its working groups, subject to certain conditions (See Convention, Art. 4, paragraph 9ter (MOD 60B)). The Convention was amended to clarify that observers of specified organizations, agencies, and entities may participate in plenipotentiary conferences in an advisory capacity (See Convention, Art. 23, paragraph 1(d) (MOD 269)). Such observers include certain Sector Members, but no longer organizations of an international character representing such Sector Members (See Convention, Art. 23, paragraph 1(e) (MOD 269E)). Another amendment clarifies that observers of certain organizations and agencies, including international organizations, may participate in radiocommunication conferences in an advisory capacity (See Convention, Art. 24, paragraph 1(b) (MOD 278); Art. 24, paragraph 1(c) (MOD 279)). There is no longer a requirement that observers from Sector Members of the Radiocommunication Sector participating in radiocommunication conferences be "duly authorized by the Member State concerned" (See Convention, Art. 24, paragraph 1(d) (MOD 280)). With respect to admission to radiocommunication assemblies, world telecommunication standardization assemblies, and telecommunications development conferences, an amendment clarifies that observers from certain organizations and agencies may participate in an advisory capacity; other amendments restructure the relevant article without changing its substance (See Convention, Art. 25, paragraph 1 (ADD 296bis; MOD 297; ADD 297bis; SUP 298A; SUP 298B; MOD 298C; SUP 298D; SUP 298E; SUP 298F)).

Amendments of a technical nature.

The languages of the ITU (Arabic, Chinese, English, French, Russian, and Spanish) are now described in the Constitution as "official" only rather than as "official and working" (See Constitution, Art. 29, paragraph 1 (MOD 171)). Conforming changes were made in several references in the Convention to languages of the ITU (See Convention, Art. 12, paragraph 2(4)(b) (MOD 178); Convention, Art. 15, paragraph 2(d) (MOD 203); and Convention, Art. 18, paragraph 2(c) (MOD 220)). In order to improve transparency, reports of the proceedings of the Coordination Committee are now to be made available to all Member States without the need for a specific request (See Convention, Art. 6, paragraph 4 (MOD 111)). Several amendments were made to change references in the text to conform to earlier revisions in the numbering of various provisions (See Convention, Art. 4, paragraph 11(14) (MOD 80); Convention Art. 5, paragraph 1(m) (MOD 96); Convention, Art. 19, paragraph 5 (MOD 235); Convention, Art. 19, paragraph 6 (MOD 236); Convention, Art. 19, paragraph 7 (MOD 237); Convention, Art. 21, paragraph 2 (MOD 251); and Convention, Art. 33, paragraph 4(5bis) (MOD 480A)). One amendment merely moved a provision to a different place in the same article (See Constitution, Art. 11, paragraph 1 (ADD 73bis, SUP 76).

Declarations and Reservations

ITU practice provides for declarations and reservations to be submitted by governments prior to signature of the Final Acts of the Plenipotentiary Conference. In 2006, the United States submitted six declarations and reservations that are included in the 2006 Final Acts. The six declarations and reservations made by the United States require Senate advice and consent.

Consistent with long-standing U.S. practice at ITU treaty-making conferences, the first of these declarations and reservations (No. 70(1)) makes three key points: (1) The United States reserved the right to make additional reservations or declarations at the time of deposit of its instruments of ratification of the amendments to the Constitution and Convention; (2) The United States reiterated and incorporated by reference all reservations and declarations made at earlier ITU conferences; and (3) The United States reiterated the position that the United States cannot be considered bound by the Administrative Regulations adopted previously, or revisions thereto adopted subsequently, without specific notification to the ITU of its consent to be bound. The U.S. statement also makes reference to concerns expressed at the Plenipotentiary Conference regarding procedures followed in certain committee proceedings. The relevant text reads as follows:

> The United States of America refers to the provisions on reservations of Article 32B of the Convention of the International Telecommunication Union (Geneva, 1992), and notes that in considering the Final Acts of the Plenipotentiary Conference (Antalya, 2006), the United States of American may find it necessary to make additional reservations or declarations. The United States of America also wishes to reiterate its concerns, as reflected in the summary minutes of the Plenary, with respect to certain procedures that were followed during committee proceedings. Accordingly, the United States of America reserves the right to make additional reservations or declarations at the time of deposit of its instrument of ratification of the amendments to the Constitution and the Convention (Geneva, 1992) which are adopted by the Plenipotentiary Conference (Antalya, 2006).
>
> The United States of America reiterates and incorporates by reference all reservations and declarations made at world administrative conferences and world radiocommunication conferences prior to signature of these Final Acts.
>
> The United States of America does not, by signature to or by any subsequent ratification of the amendments to the Constitution and the Convention adopted by the Plenipotentiary Conference (Antalya, 2006), consent to be bound by the Administrative Regulations adopted prior to the date of signature of these Final Acts. Nor shall the United States of America be deemed to have consented to be bound by revisions of the Administrative Regulations, whether partial or complete, adopted subsequent to the date of signature of these Final Acts, without specific notification to the International Telecommunication Union of its consent to be bound.

The second of these declarations and reservations (No. 70(2)) states the view of the United States that the ITU, in carrying out the mandates of the Plenipotentiary Conference, should adhere to the principles of accountability, responsibility, and transparency. It reads as follows:

> The United States of America, recalling the principles of accountability, responsibility, and transparency that are fundamental to United Nations reform, notes that it is essential that the International Telecommunication Union, in carrying out the mandates of the Plenipotentiary Conference (Antalya, 2006) adhere to those principles in order to achieve lasting reform.

The third of these declarations and reservations (No. 70(3)), referring to a related statement made by the United States at an earlier Plenipotentiary Conference, provides that the United States will interpret the Resolution on the "Status of Palestine in the ITU," as revised at the Plenipotentiary Conference in Antalya, in accordance with relevant international agreements. It reads as follows:

> The United States of America refers to its Statement 92 made at the Plenipotentiary Conference (Minneapolis, 1998) and states that it will interpret Resolution 99 (Rev. Antalya, 2006) in accordance with relevant international agreements, including agreements between Israel and the Palestinians.

In keeping with prior U.S. practice in the ITU, the fourth of these declarations and reservations (No. 104(1)) preserves the right of the United States to take such actions as it deems necessary in response to actions taken by other Member States that are detrimental to U.S. telecommunication interests. It reads as follows:

> The United States of America refers to declarations made by various Member States reserving their right to take such action as they may consider necessary to safeguard their interests with respect to application of provisions of the Constitution and Convention of the International Telecommunication Union (Geneva, 1992), and any amendments thereto. The United States of America reserves the right to take whatever measures it deems necessary to safeguard U.S. interests in response to such actions.

Also in keeping with prior U.S. practice in the ITU, the fifth of these declarations and reservations (No. 104(2)) responds to a statement by Cuba reserving its right to take any steps that it may deem necessary against U.S. radio and television broadcasting to Cuba and denouncing U.S. use of radio frequencies at Guantanamo, Cuba. The U.S. response, which is similar to those made by the United States at previous ITU conferences, reads as follows:

> The United States of America, noting Statement 80 entered by the delegation of Cuba, recalls its right to broadcast to Cuba on appropriate frequencies free of jamming or other wrongful interference and reserves its rights with respect to existing interference and any future interference by Cuba with U.S. broadcasting. Furthermore, the United States of America notes that its presence in Guantanamo is by virtue of an international agreement presently in force and that the United States of America reserves the right to meet its radiocommunication requirements there as it has in the past.

The sixth of these declarations and reservations (No. 106), in which the United States joined with eight other Member States, responds to statements by other countries concerning the use of the geostationary-satellite orbit or related claims. It reads as follows:

> The delegations of the above-mentioned States, referring to the declarations made by the Republic of Colombia (No. 58), Mexico (No. 34), and Ecuador (No. 55), inasmuch as these and any similar statements refer to the Bogota Declaration of 3 December 1976 by equatorial countries and to the claims of those countries to exercise sovereign rights over segments of the geostationary-satellite orbit, or to any related claims, consider that the claims in question cannot be recognized by this Conference.
>
> The above-mentioned delegations also wish to state that the reference in Article 44 of the Constitution to the "geographical situation of particular countries" does not imply recognition of a claim to any preferential rights to the geostationary-satellite orbit.

International Telecommunication Union

Final Acts of the Plenipotentiary Conference (Antalya, 2006)

**Instrument amending
the Constitution
of the International Telecommunication Union (Geneva, 1992)
as amended by the
Plenipotentiary Conference (Kyoto, 1994),
by the
Plenipotentiary Conference (Minneapolis, 1998)
and by the
Plenipotentiary Conference (Marrakesh, 2002)**

**Instrument amending
the Convention
of the International Telecommunication Union (Geneva, 1992)
as amended by the
Plenipotentiary Conference (Kyoto, 1994),
by the
Plenipotentiary Conference (Minneapolis, 1998)
and by the
Plenipotentiary Conference (Marrakesh, 2002)**

General Rules of Conferences, Assemblies and Meetings of the Union

Decisions and Resolutions

EXPLANATORY NOTES

Symbols used in the Final Acts

The symbols given in the margin indicate changes adopted by the Plenipotentiary Conference (Antalya, 2006) in relation to the texts of the Constitution and Convention (Geneva, 1992) as amended by the Plenipotentiary Conference (Kyoto, 1994), by the Plenipotentiary Conference (Minneapolis, 1998) ad by the Plenipotentiary Conference (Marrakesh, 2002), and have the following meaning:

ADD	=	addition of a new provision
MOD	=	modification of an existing provision
(MOD)	=	editorial modification of an existing provision
SUP	=	deletion of an existing provision
SUP*	=	provision moved to another place in the Final Acts
ADD*	=	an existing provision moved from another place in the Final Acts to the place indicated

These symbols are followed by the number of the existing provision. For new provisions (symbol ADD), the point at which they are to be inserted is shown by the number of the preceding provision, followed by a letter.

INSTRUMENT AMENDING THE CONSTITUTION OF THE INTERNATIONAL TELECOMMUNICATION UNION (GENEVA, 1992)

as amended by the Plenipotentiary Conference (Kyoto, 1994), by the Plenipotentiary Conference (Minneapolis, 1998) and by the Plenipotentiary Conference (Marrakesh, 2002)

(Amendments adopted by the Plenipotentiary Conference (Antalya, 2006))

CONSTITUTION OF THE INTERNATIONAL TELECOMMUNICATION UNION* (GENEVA, 1992)

PART I. Foreword

By virtue of and in implementation of the relevant provisions of the Constitution of the International Telecommunication Union (Geneva, 1992), as amended by the Plenipotentiary Conference (Kyoto, 1994), by the Plenipotentiary Conference (Minneapolis, 1998) and by the Plenipotentiary Conference (Marrakesh, 2002), in particular those in Article 55 thereof, the Plenipotentiary Conference of the International Telecommunication Union (Antalya, 2006) has adopted the following amendments to the said Constitution:

ARTICLE 11
General Secretariat

ADD*	**73*bis***	The Secretary-General shall act as the legal representative of the Union.
SUP*	**76**	

ARTICLE 13
Radiocommunication Conferences and Radiocommunication Assemblies

MOD PP-98	90	2. World radiocommunication conferences shall normally be convened every three to four years; however, following the application of the relevant provisions of the Convention, such a conference need not be convened or an additional one may be convened.
MOD PP-98	91	3. Radiocommunication assemblies shall also normally be convened every three to four years, and may be associated in place and time with world radiocommunication conferences so as to improve the efficiency and effectiveness of the Radiocommunication Sector. Radiocommunication assemblies shall provide the necessary technical bases for the work of the world radiocommunication conferences and respond to all requests from world radiocommunication conferences. The duties of the radiocommunication assemblies are specified in the Convention.

* The language used in the basic instruments of the Union (Constitution and Convention) is to be considered as gender neutral.

ARTICLE 28
Finances of the Union

MOD PP-98	161C	2) The Secretary-General shall inform the Member States and Sector Members of the provisional amount of the contributory unit as determined under No. 161B above and invite the Member States to notify, no later than four weeks prior to the date set for the opening of the plenipotentiary conference, the class of contribution they have provisionally chosen.
MOD PP-98 PP-02	161E	4) Bearing in mind the draft financial plan as revised, the plenipotentiary conference shall, as soon as possible, determine the definitive upper limit of the amount of the contributory unit and set the date, which shall be at the latest on Monday of the final week of the plenipotentiary conference, by which Member States, upon invitation by the Secretary-General, shall announce their definitive choice of class of contribution.

ARTICLE 29
Languages

MOD	171	1 1) The official languages of the Union shall be Arabic, Chinese, English, French, Russian and Spanish.

PART II. Date of Entry into Force

The amendments contained in the present instrument shall, as a whole and in the form of one single instrument, enter into force on 1 January 2008 between Member States being at that time parties to the Constitution and the Convention of the International Telecommunication Union (Geneva, 1992), and having deposited before that date their instrument of ratification, acceptance or approval of, or accession to, the present amending instrument.

IN WITNESS WHEREOF, the respective plenipotentiaries have signed the original of the present instrument amending the Constitution of the International Telecommunication Union (Geneva, 1992), as amended by the Plenipotentiary Conference (Kyoto, 1994), by the Plenipotentiary Conference (Minneapolis, 1998) and by the Plenipotentiary Conference (Marrakesh, 2002).

Done at Antalya, 24 November 2006

INSTRUMENT AMENDING THE CONVENTION OF THE INTERNATIONAL TELECOMMUNICATION UNION (GENEVA, 1992)

as amended by the Plenipotentiary Conference (Kyoto, 1994), by the Plenipotentiary Conference (Minneapolis, 1998) and by the Plenipotentiary Conference (Marrakesh, 2002)

(Amendments adopted by the Plenipotentiary Conference (Antalya, 2006))

CONVENTION OF THE INTERNATIONAL TELECOMMUNICATION UNION* (GENEVA, 1992)

PART I. Foreword

By virtue of and in implementation of the relevant provisions of the Convention of the International Telecommunication Union (Geneva, 1992), as amended by the Plenipotentiary Conference (Kyoto, 1994), by the Plenipotentiary Conference (Minneapolis, 1998) and by the Plenipotentiary Conference (Marrakesh, 2002), in particular those in Article 42 thereof, the Plenipotentiary Conference of the International Telecommunication Union (Antalya, 2006) has adopted the following amendments to the said Convention:

ARTICLE 2
Elections and Related Matters

Elected officials

MOD	13	1. The Secretary-General, the Deputy Secretary-General and the Directors of the Bureaux shall take up their duties on the dates determined by the Plenipotentiary Conference at the time of their election. They shall normally remain in office until dates determined by the following Plenipotentiary Conference, and they shall be eligible for re-election once only for the same post. Re-election shall mean that it is possible for only a second term, regardless of whether it is consecutive or not.

Members of the Radio Regulations Board

MOD	20	1. The members of the Radio Regulations Board shall take up their duties on the dates determined by the Plenipotentiary Conference at the time of their election. They shall remain in office until dates determined by the following Plenipotentiary Conference, and shall be eligible for re-election once only. Re-election shall mean that it is possible for only a second term, regardless of whether it is consecutive or not.

* The language used in the basic instruments of the Union (Constitution and Convention) is to be considered as gender neutral.

ARTICLE 4
The Council

SUP	58	
MOD PP-02	60B	9 *ter)* Sector Members may attend, as observers, meetings of the Council, its committees and its working groups, subject to the conditions established by the Council, including conditions relating to the number of such observers and the procedures for appointing them.
MOD PP-98 PP-02	73	7) review and approve the biennial budget of the Union, and consider the budget forecast (included in the financial operating report prepared by the Secretary-General under No. 101 of this Convention) for the two-year period following a given budget period, taking account of the decisions of the Plenipotentiary Conference in relation to No. 50 of the Constitution and of the financial limits set by the Plenipotentiary Conference in accordance with No. 51 of the Constitution; it shall ensure the strictest possible economy but be mindful of the obligation upon the Union to achieve satisfactory results as expeditiously as possible. In so doing, the Council shall take into account the priorities established by the Plenipotentiary Conference as expressed in the strategic plan for the Union, the views of the Coordination Committee as contained in the report by the Secretary-General mentioned in No. 86 of this Convention and the financial operating report mentioned in No. 101 of this Convention. The Council shall carry out an annual review of income and expenditure with a view to effecting adjustments, where appropriate, in accordance with resolutions and decisions of the Plenipotentiary Conference;
MOD PP-94	80	14) be responsible for effecting the coordination with all international organizations referred to in Articles 49 and 50 of the Constitution and to this end, conclude, on behalf of the Union, provisional agreements with the international organizations referred to in Article 50 of the Constitution and in Nos. 269B and 269C of the Convention, and with the United Nations in application of the Agreement between the United Nations and the International Telecommunication Union; these provisional agreements shall be submitted to the Plenipotentiary Conference in accordance with the relevant provision of Article 8 of the Constitution;

ARTICLE 5
General Secretariat

MOD	96	*m)* prepare recommendations for the first meeting of the heads of delegation referred to in No. 49 of the General Rules of conferences, assemblies and meetings of the Union, taking into account the results of any regional consultation;

MOD PP-98	100	*q)* after consultation with the Coordination Committee and making all possible economies, prepare and submit to the Council a biennial draft budget covering the expenditures of the Union, taking account of the financial limits laid down by the Plenipotentiary Conference. This draft shall consist of a consolidated budget, including cost-based and results-based budget information for the Union, prepared in accordance with the budget guidelines issued by the Secretary-General, and comprising two versions. One version shall be for zero growth of the contributory unit, the other for a growth less than or equal to any limit fixed by the Plenipotentiary Conference, after any drawing on the Reserve Account. The budget resolution, after approval by the Council, shall be sent for information to all Member States;
MOD	105	2. The Secretary-General or the Deputy Secretary-General may participate, in an advisory capacity, in conferences of the Union; the Secretary-General or his representative may participate in an advisory capacity in all other meetings of the Union.

ARTICLE 6
Coordination Committee

MOD PP-02	111	4. A report shall be made of the proceedings of the Coordination Committee and shall be made available to the Member States.

ARTICLE 12
Radiocommunication Bureau

MOD PP-98	178	*b)* exchange with Member States and Sector Members data in machine-readable and other forms, prepare and keep up to date any documents and databases of the Radiocommunication Sector, and arrange, with the Secretary-General, as appropriate, for their publication in the languages of the Union in accordance with No. 172 of the Constitution;

ARTICLE 15
Telecommunication Standardization Bureau

MOD PP-98	203	*d)* exchange with Member States and Sector Members data in machine-readable and other forms, prepare and, as necessary, keep up to date any documents and databases of the Telecommunication Standardization Sector, and arrange with the Secretary-General, where appropriate, for their publication in the languages of the Union in accordance with No. 172 of the Constitution;

ARTICLE 16
Telecommunication Development Conferences

MOD	209	a) world telecommunication development conferences shall establish work programmes and guidelines for defining telecommunication development questions and priorities and shall provide direction and guidance for the work programme of the Telecommunication Development Sector. They shall decide, in the light of the above-mentioned programmes of work, on the need to maintain, terminate or establish study groups and allocate to each of them the questions to be studied;

ARTICLE 17A
Telecommunication Development Advisory Group

MOD	215C	1. The telecommunication development advisory group shall be open to representatives of administrations of Member States and representatives of Sector Members and to chairmen and vice-chairmen of study groups and other groups, and will act through the Director.

ARTICLE 18
Telecommunication Development Bureau

MOD	220	*c)* exchange with members data in machine-readable and other forms, prepare and, as necessary, keep up to date any documents and databases of the Telecommunication Development Sector, and arrange with the Secretary-General, as appropriate, for their publication in the languages of the Union in accordance with No. 172 of the Constitution;

ARTICLE 19
Participation of Entities and Organizations Other than Administrations in the Union's Activities

(MOD)	235	5. Any request from any entity or organization listed in No. 231 above (other than those referred to in Nos. 269B and 269C of this Convention) to participate in the work of a Sector shall be sent to the Secretary-General and acted upon in accordance with procedures established by the Council.
(MOD)	236	6. Any request from an organization referred to in Nos. 269B to 269D of this Convention to participate in the work of a Sector shall be sent to the Secretary-General, and the organization concerned shall be included in the lists referred to in No. 237 below.
(MOD) PP-98	237	7. The Secretary-General shall compile and maintain lists of all entities and organizations referred to in Nos. 229 to 231 and Nos. 269B to 269D of this Convention that are authorized to participate in the work of each Sector and shall, at appropriate intervals, publish and distribute these lists to all Member States and Sector Members concerned and to the Director of the Bureau concerned. That Director shall advise such entities and organizations of the action taken on their requests, and shall inform the relevant Member States.

MOD PP-98	240	10. Any Sector Member has the right to denounce such participation by notifying the Secretary-General. Such participation may also be denounced, where appropriate, by the Member State concerned or, in case of the Sector Member approved pursuant to No. 234C above, in accordance with criteria and procedures determined by the Council. Such denunciation shall take effect at the end of six months from the date when notification is received by the Secretary-General.

ARTICLE 21
Recommendations from One Conference to Another

(MOD)	251	2. Such recommendations shall be sent to the Secretary-General in good time for assembly, coordination and communication, as laid down in No. 44 of the General Rules of conferences, assemblies and meetings of the Union.

ARTICLE 23
Admission to Plenipotentiary Conferences

PP-02		
MOD PP-94 PP-02	269	*d)* observers of the following organizations, agencies and entities, to participate in an advisory capacity:
MOD PP-02	269E	*e)* observers from the Sector Members referred to in Nos. 229 and 231 of this Convention.

ARTICLE 24
Admission to Radiocommunication Conferences

PP-02		
MOD PP-02	278	*b)* observers of organizations and agencies referred to in Nos. 269A to 269D of this Convention, to participate in an advisory capacity;
MOD PP-02	279	*c)* observers of other international organizations invited in accordance with the relevant provisions of Chapter I of the General Rules of conferences, assemblies and meetings of the Union, to participate in an advisory capacity;
MOD PP-98	280	*d)* observers from Sector Members of the Radiocommunication Sector;

ARTICLE 25
Admission to Radiocommunication Assemblies, World Telecommunication Standardization Assemblies and Telecommunication Development Conferences

PP-98 PP 02		
ADD	296*bis*	*b)* representatives of Sector Members concerned;
MOD PP-02	297	*c)* observers, to participate in an advisory capacity, from:

ADD	297*bis*	*i)* the organizations and agencies referred to in Nos. 269A to 269D of this Convention;
SUP	298A	
SUP	298B	
(MOD) PP-02	298C	*ii)* any other regional organization or other international organization dealing with matters of interest to the assembly or conference.
SUP	298D	
SUP	298E	
SUP*	298F	

ARTICLE 33
Finances

MOD PP-98	468	1 1) The scale from which each Member State, subject to the provisions of No. 468A below, and Sector Member, subject to the provisions of No. 468B below, shall choose its class of contribution, in conformity with the relevant provisions of Article 28 of the Constitution, shall be as follows:	
		40 unit class	8 unit class
		35 unit class	6 unit class
		30 unit class	5 unit class
		28 unit class	4 unit class
		25 unit class	3 unit class
		23 unit class	2 unit class
		20 unit class	1 1/2 unit class
		18 unit class	1 unit class
		15 unit class	1/2 unit class
		13 unit class	1/4 unit class
		11 unit class	1/8 unit class
		10 unit class	1/16 unit class

MOD PP-94 PP-98 PP-02	476	4 1) The organizations referred to in Nos. 269A to 269E of this Convention and other organizations also specified in Chapter II thereof (unless they have been exempted by the Council, subject to reciprocity) and Sector Members referred to in No. 230 of this Convention which participate, in accordance with the provisions of this Convention, in a plenipotentiary conference, in a conference, assembly or meeting of a Sector of the Union, or in a world conference on international telecommunications, shall share in defraying the expenses of the conferences, assemblies and meetings in which they participate on the basis of the cost of these conferences and meetings and in accordance with the Financial Regulations. Nevertheless, Sector Members will not be charged separately for their attendance at a conference, assembly or meeting of their respective Sectors, except in the case of regional radiocommunication conferences.
(MOD) PP-98	480A	5 *bis)* When a Sector Member contributes to defraying the expenses of the Union under No. 159A of the Constitution, the Sector for which the contribution is made should be identified.
ADD	480B	5 *ter*) Under exceptional circumstances, the Council may authorize a reduction in the number of contributory units when so requested by a Sector Member which has established that it can no longer maintain its contribution at the class originally chosen.

ANNEX
Definition of Certain Terms Used in this Convention and the Administrative Regulations of the International Telecommunication Union

MOD PP-94 PP-98	1002	*Observer:* A person sent by a Member State, organization, agency or entity to attend a conference, assembly or meeting of the Union or the Council, without the right to vote and in accordance with the relevant provisions of the basic texts of the Union.

PART II. Date of Entry into Force

The amendments contained in the present instrument shall, as a whole and in the form of one single instrument, enter into force on 1 January 2008 between Member States being at that time parties to the Constitution and the Convention of the International Telecommunication Union (Geneva, 1992), and having deposited before that date their instrument of ratification, acceptance or approval of, or accession to, the present amending instrument.

IN WITNESS WHEREOF, the respective plenipotentiaries have signed the original of the present instrument amending the Convention of the International Telecommunication Union (Geneva, 1992), as amended by the Plenipotentiary Conference (Kyoto, 1994), by the Plenipotentiary Conference (Minneapolis, 1998) and by the Plenipotentiary Conference (Marrakesh, 2002).

Done at Antalya, 24 November 2006

GENERAL RULES OF CONFERENCES, ASSEMBLIES AND OTHER MEETINGS OF THE UNION

CHAPTER I
General Provisions Regarding Conferences and Assemblies

		2. Invitation to radiocommunication conferences when there is an inviting government
MOD	12	2.1) Subject to the relevant provisions of Article 24 of the Convention, the provisions of Nos. 5 to 10 above shall apply to radiocommunication conferences.
MOD	14	3.1) The inviting government, in agreement with or on a proposal by the Council, may notify the international organizations other than those referred to in Nos. 269A to 269D of the Convention which may be interested in sending observers to participate in the conference.
		8. Time-limits and conditions for submission of proposals and reports to conferences
MOD	44	6. The Secretary-General shall assemble and coordinate the proposals received from Member States and shall communicate them to Member States as they are received, but in any case at least two months before the opening of the conference, making them available by electronic means. Elected officials and staff members of the Union, as well as those observers that may attend conferences in accordance with the relevant provisions of the Convention, shall not be entitled to submit proposals.

CHAPTER II
Rules of Procedure of Conferences, Assemblies and Meetings

		13. Composition of committees
		13.1. Plenipotentiary conferences
MOD	75	Subject to No. 66 of these General Rules, committees shall be composed of the delegates of Member States. Unless otherwise decided by the plenary meeting, the observers referred to in Nos. 269A to 269E of the Convention shall be authorized to attend such committees, with the exception of the steering, credentials, budget control and editorial committees.
		13.2. Radiocommunication conferences and world conferences on international telecommunications
MOD	76	1. Subject to No. 66 of these General Rules, committees of radiocommunication conferences shall be composed of the delegates of Member States. Unless otherwise decided by the plenary meeting, the observers referred to in Nos. 278, 279, 280 and, as appropriate, 282 of the Convention, shall be authorized to attend such committees, with the exception of the steering, credentials, budget control and editorial committees.

ADD	76*bis*	2. Subject to No. 66 of these General Rules, committees of world conferences on international telecommunications shall be composed of the delegates of Member States. Unless otherwise decided by the plenary meeting, the observers referred to in Nos. 278 and 279 of the Convention, and observers of Sector Members shall be authorized to attend such committees, with the exception of the steering, credentials, budget control and editorial committees.
SUP	77	
		13.3. Radiocommunication assemblies, world telecommunication standardization assemblies and telecommunication development conferences
MOD	**78**	In addition to delegates of Member States and representatives of any entity or organization included in the relevant list referred to in No. 237 of the Convention, the committees of radiocommunication assemblies, of world telecommunication standardization assemblies and of telecommunication development conferences, with the exception of the steering, budget control and editorial committees, may be attended by the observers referred to in Article 25 of the Convention.

CHAPTER III
Election Procedures

		31. General rules on election procedures
MOD	**172**	5) Elections shall begin on the fourth calendar day of the conference.
		33. Specific rules of procedure for the election of the members of the Radio Regulations Board
(MOD)	**195**	1) The total number of members of the Radio Regulations Board and the number of seats per region of the world shall be decided in accordance with Nos. 63 and 93A of the Constitution.

DECISIONS

RESOLUTIONS

List of PP-06 Decisions/Resolutions – Final numbering

DECISIONS AND RESOLUTIONS OF THE PLENIPOTENTIARY CONFERENCE (ANTALYA, 2006)		
Provisional numbering	**Final numbering***	**Title**
	Decisions	
	5 (Rev. Antalya, 2006)	Income and expenditure for the Union for the period 2008 to 2011
GT-PLEN/A	9 {Antalya, 2006)	Fourth World Telecommunication Policy Forum
COM6/1	10 (Antalya, 2006)	Implementation of additional corrective measures relating to cost recovery on satellite network filings.
	Resolutions	
	11 (Rev. Antalya, 2006)	World and regional telecommunication/information and communication technology exhibitions and forums.
	14 (Rev. Antalya, 2006)	Recognition of the rights and obligations of all Sector Members of the Union
	21 (Rev. Antalya, 2006)	Special measures concerning alternative calling procedures on international telecommunication networks
	22 (Rev. Antalya, 2006)	Apportionment of revenues in providing international telecommunication services
	25 (Rev. Antalya, 2006)	Strengthening the regional presence
	30 (Rev. Antalya, 2006)	Special measures for the least developed countries and small island developing states
	34 (Rev. Antalya, 2006)	Assistance and support to countries in special need for rebuilding their telecommunication sector
	36 (Rev. Antalya, 2006)	Telecommunications/information and communication technologies in. the service of humanitarian assistance
	41 (Rev. Antalya 2006)	Arrears and special arrears accounts
	48 (Rev. Antalya. 2006)	Human resources management and development

* Final publication to be made available in due course. (05/02/07)

	64 (Rev, Antalya, 2006)	Non-discriminatory access to modern telecommunication/information and communication technology facilities and services
	68 (Rev. Antalya, 2006)	World Telecommunication and Information Society Day
	70 (Rev. Antalya, 2006)	Gender mainstreaming in ITU and promotion of gender equality towards all-inclusive information societies
	71 (Rev. Antalya, 2006)	Strategic plan for the Union for 2008-2011
	72 (Rev. Antalya, 2006)	Linking strategic, financial and operational planning in ITU
	77 (Rev. Antalya, 2006)	Future conferences, assemblies and forums of the Union (2008-2011)
	91 (Rev. Antalya, 2006)	Cost recovery for some ITU products and services
	94 (Rev. Antalya, 2006)	Auditing of the accounts of the Union
	99 (Rev. Antalya, 2006)	Status of Palestine in ITU
	101 (Rev. Antalya, 2006)	Internet Protocol-based networks
	102 (Rev. Antalya, 2006)	ITU's role with regard to international public policy issues pertaining to the Internet and the management of Internet resources, including domain names and addresses
	111 (Rev. Antalya, 2006)	Scheduling of ITU conferences and assemblies
	115 (Rev. Antalya, 2006)	Methods to improve the efficiency and effectiveness of the Radio Regulations Board
	122 (Rev. Antalya, 2006)	The evolving role of the World Telecommunication Standardization Assembly
	123 (Rev. Antalya, 2006)	Bridging the standardization gap between developing and developed countries
	124 (Rev, Antalya, 2006)	Support for the New Partnership for Africa's Development
	126 (Rev. Antalya, 2006)	Assistance and support to the Republic of Serbia for rebuilding its destroyed public broadcasting system
	128 (Rev. Antalya, 2006)	Support for the Agenda for Connectivity in the Americas and Quito Action Plan
	130 (Rev. Antalya, 2006)	Strengthening the role of ITU in building confidence and security in the use of information and communication technologies
	131 (Rev. Antalya, 2006)	Information and communication technology index and community connectivity indicators
	133 (Rev. Antalya, 2006)	Role of administrations of Member States in the management of internationalized (multilingual) domain names

PLEN/1	134 (Antalya, 2006)	Number of Council Member States
GT-PLEN/1	135 (Antalya, 2006)	The role of the International Telecommunication Union in the development of telecommunications/ information and communication technologies, in providing technical assistance and advice to developing countries, and in implementing relevant national, regional and inter-regional projects
GT-PLEN/2	136 (Antalya, 2006)	The use of telecommunications/information and communication technologies for monitoring and management in emergency and disaster situations for early warning, prevention, mitigation and relief
GT-PLEN/3	137 (Antalya, 2006)	Next-generation network deployment in developing countries
GT-PLEN/4	138 (Antalya, 2006)	The Global Symposium for Regulators
GT-PLEN/5	139 (Antalya, 2006)	Telecommunications/information and communication technologies to bridge the digital divide
GT-PLEN/6	140 (Antalya, 2006)	ITU's role in implementing the outcomes of the World Summit on the Information Society
GT-PLEN/7	141 (Antalya, 2006)	Study on the participation of all relevant stakeholders in the activities of the Union related to the World Summit on the Information Society
GT-PLEN/8	142 (Antalya, 2006)	Review of terminology used in the Constitution and Convention of the International Telecommunication Union
COM5/1	143 (Antalya, 2006)	Extending the provisions in ITU documents relating to developing countries to apply to countries with economies in transition
COM5/2	144 (Antalya, 2006)	Availability of model host-country agreements in advance for conferences and assemblies of the Union held away from Geneva
COM5/3	145 (Antalya, 2006)	Participation of observers in conferences, assemblies and meetings of the Union
COM5/4	146 (Antalya, 2006)	Review of the International Telecommunication Regulations
COM5/5	147 (Antalya, 2006)	Study on the management and functioning of the Union
COM5/6	148 (Antalya, 2006)	Tasks and functions of the Deputy Secretary-General
COMS/7	149 (Antalya, 2006)	Study of definitions and terminology relating to building confidence and security in the use of information and communication technologies

COM6/1	150 (Antalya, 2006)	Approval of the accounts of the Union for the years 2002 to 2005
COM6/2	151 (Antalya, 2006)	Implementation of results-based management in ITU
COM6/3	152 (Antalya, 2006)	Improvement of management and follow-up of the defrayal of ITU expenses by Sector Members and Associates
COM6/4	153 (Antalya, 2006)	Scheduling of Council sessions and plenipotentiary conferences
COM6/5	154 (Antalya, 2006)	Use of the six official languages of the Union on an equal footing
COM6/6	155 (Antalya, 2006)	Establishment of a management and budget group of the Council
COM6/7	156 (Antalya, 2006)	Scheduling of conferences
COM6/8	157 (Antalya, 2006)	Resolution of the project execution function in ITU
COM6/9	158 (Antalya, 2006)	Financial issues for consideration by the Council
COM6/10	159 (Antalya, 2006)	Assistance and support to Lebanon for rebuilding its telecommunication networks (fixed and mobile)
COM6/11	160 (Antalya, 2006)	Assistance to Somalia
COM6/12	161 (Antalya, 2006)	Assistance and support for the Democratic Republic of the Congo for rebuilding its telecommunication network

DECISION 5 (Rev. Antalya, 2006)
Income and expenditure for the Union for the period 2008 to 2011

The Plenipotentiary Conference of the International Telecommunication Union (Antalya, 2006),

considering

the strategic plans and goals established for the Union and its Sectors for the period 2008 to 2011, and the priorities identified therein,

considering farther

a) Resolution 91 (Rev. Antalya, 2006) of this conference on general principles for cost recovery;

b) that, in the consideration of the draft financial plan of the Union for 2008-2011, the gap between income and expenditure was substantial;

noting

that this conference has adopted Resolution COM6/2 (Antalya, 2006) concerning the implementation of results-based management in ITU, an important component of which relates to planning, programming, budgeting, monitoring and evaluation, and which should lead, *inter alia*, to further strengthening of the financial management system of the Union,

noting further

that Resolution 48 (Rev. Antalya, 2006) of this conference, stresses the importance of the human resources of the Union for the fulfilment of its goals and objectives,

decides

1. that the Council is authorized to draw up the two biennial budgets of the Union in such a way that the total expenditure of the General Secretariat and the three Sectors of the Union is balanced by the anticipated income, on the basis of Annex 1 to this decision, taking into account the following:

1.1. that the upper limit of the amount of the contributory unit of Member States for the years 2008-2011 shall be CHF 330 000;

1.2. that, for the years 2008-2009, the contributory unit of Member States shall not exceed CHF 318 000;

1.3. that expenditure on interpretation, translation and text processing in respect of the official languages of the Union shall not exceed CHF 85 million for the years 2008 to 2011;

1.4. that, when adopting the biennial budgets of the Union, the Council may decide to give the Secretary-General the possibility, in order to meet unanticipated demand, to increase the budget for products or services which are subject to cost recovery, within the limit of the income from cost recovery for that activity;

1.5. that the Council shall each year control the expenditure and income in the budget as well as the different activities and the related expenditure contained therein;

2. that, if no plenipotentiary conference is held in 2010, the Council shall establish the biennial budgets of the Union for 2012 and thereafter, having first obtained approval for the budgeted annual values of the contributory unit from a majority of the Member States of the Union;

3. that the Council may authorize expenditure in excess of the limits for conferences, meetings and seminars if such excess can be compensated by sums within the expenditure limits accrued from previous years or charged to the following year;

4. that the Council shall, during each budgetary period, assess the changes that have taken place and the changes likely to take place in the current and coming budgetary periods under the following items:

4.1. salary scales, pension contributions and allowances, including post adjustments, established by the United Nations common system and applicable to the staff employed by the Union;

4.2. the exchange rate between the Swiss franc and the United States dollar in so far as this affects the staff costs for those staff members on United Nations scales;

4.3. the purchasing power of the Swiss franc in respect of non-staff items of expenditure;

5. that the Council shall have the task of effecting every possible economy, in particular taking into account the options for reducing expenditure contained in Annex 2 to this decision, and considering the application of the concept of unfunded mandatory activities (UMACs)[1], and, to this end, that it shall establish the lowest possible authorized level of expenditure commensurate with the needs of the Union, within the limits established by *decides* 1, if necessary taking into account the provisions of *decides* 7 below; a set of options for reducing expenditure is given in Annex 2 to this decision;

6. that the Council may exceed the limit set in *decides* 1.2 above for the years 2008-2009 by up to 1 per cent, in order to meet expenditure on unforeseen and urgent activities which are in the interests of the Union; within the upper limit established in *decides* 1.1 above, the Council may exceed the limit of CHF 318 000 by more than 1 per cent only with the approval of a majority of the Member States of the Union, after they have been duly consulted, within the upper limit of CHF 330 000; they shall be presented with a full statement of the facts justifying this step;

7. that, in determining the value of the contributory unit in any budgetary period, the Council shall take into account the future programme of conferences and meetings and the estimated related costs, as well as other sources of income, in order to avoid wide fluctuations from period to period;

8. that, in determining the value of the contributory unit, the Council should also take into account the budgetary impact of the introduction of new cost-recovery charges for activities that were previously funded from assessed contributions and should, to the greatest extent possible, reduce the value of the contributory unit by an appropriate amount;

9. that the following guidelines should be applied in relation to any expenditure reductions:

a) the internal audit function of the Union should be maintained at a strong and effective level;

b) there should be no expenditure reductions which would affect cost-recovery income;

c) fixed costs such as those related to the reimbursement of loans or after-service health insurance should not be subject to expenditure reductions;

d) there should be no expenditure reductions in regular maintenance costs for ITU buildings which would affect the security or the health of staff;

e) the information services function in the Union should be maintained at an effective level,

10. that the Council, in determining the amount of withdrawals from or allocations to the Reserve Account, should aim under normal circumstances at keeping the Reserve Account (after integration of unused appropriations) at a level above 3 per cent of the total budget,

---

[1] The concept of UMACs may be applied, where necessary, as a means of highlighting a number of activities within the overall programme of work mandated by the governing bodies of the Union, as well as those support activities which are deemed essential to implement the mandated activities, which could not be accommodated within the financial limits set by the Plenipotentiary Conference. The Secretary-General would be authorized to incur expenditure on these activities provided that savings are achieved or additional income is generated.

instructs the Secretary-General, with the assistance of the Coordination Committee

1. to prepare the draft biennial budgets for the years 2008-2009, as well as 2010-2011, on the basis of the associated guidelines in the *decides* above, the Annexes to this decision and all relevant documents submitted to the Plenipotentiary Conference;

2. to ensure that, in each biennial budget, income and expenditure are balanced;

3. to draw up and implement a programme of appropriate cost efficiencies and reductions across all ITU operations so as to ensure a balanced budget;

4. to implement the aforementioned programme as soon as possible,

instructs the Secretary-General

to provide to the Council, no less than seven weeks before its 2007 and 2009 ordinary sessions, complete and accurate data as needed for the development, consideration and establishment of the biennial budget,

instructs the Council

1. to review and approve the biennial budgets for 2008-2009 and 2010-2011, giving due consideration to the associated guidelines in *decides* above, the Annexes to this decision and all documents submitted to the Plenipotentiary Conference;

2. to ensure that, in each biennial budget, income and expenditure are balanced;

3. to consider further appropriations in the event that additional sources of revenue are identified or savings achieved;

4. to examine the cost-efficiency and cost-reduction programme drawn up by the Secretary-General;

5. to take account of the impact of any cost reduction programme on the staff of the Union, including the implementation of a voluntary retirement scheme.

ANNEX 1 TO DECISION 5 (Rev. Antalya, 2006)
Financial plan 2008-2011: Income and expenditure estimates

	Amount of the contributory unit (in CHF)	318 000 000 CHF
1	Income estimates	
2	Assessed contributions (403.08 full units)*	511 445
3	Cost-recovery income	105 369
4	Other income	10 800
5	Reduction due to free access to ITU-T recommendations**	−7 000
6	Increase in the price of publications (10% on average)	4 000
7	**Income estimates**	**624 614**
8	Expenditure estimates***	673 662
9	Estimated financial impact of PP-06 resolutions and decisions (COM5/1, COM5/4, GT-PLEN/A)	1 490
10	RRC-06 post-conference work	5 200
11	WTDC-06 Doha Action Plan	4 500
12	IPSAS implementation	2 500
13	Security projects	0
14	WSIS outcomes	0
15	WTSA-04 outcomes	0
16	WTDC-06 outcomes	0
17	Staff costs	− 2 000
18	Travel on duty	− 2 000
19	Fellowships	− 1 000
20	External consultants	− 1 000
21	Public services	− 1 000
22	Documentation	− 11 500
23	Advisory groups	− 560
24	Council working groups	− 490
25	WRC/RA/CPM	− 600
26	Study group meetings	− 2 000
27	Interpretation	− 1 500
28	**Expenditure estimates**	**663 702**
29	**Income estimates less expenditure estimates****	− 39 088

** Based on the number of contributory as at 22 November 2006*

*** Subject to Council 2007 decision*

**** Reference Document PP-06/5 7 (Annex 1)*

***** Reduction of expenditure and/or increase of income to be identified*

ANNEX 2 TO DECISION 5 (Rev, Antalya, 2006)
Options for reducing expenditure

1) Identification of possible duplications (functions, activities, workshops, seminars) and centralization of finance and administrative tasks.

2) Coordination and harmonization of seminars and workshops in order to avoid duplication of the subjects covered and to optimize secretariat attendance.

3) Coordination with regional organizations with a view to sharing the available resources of the regional organizations and minimizing the costs of participation (workshops, seminars, preparatory meetings for world conferences).

4) Possible savings from natural attrition (opportunity for keeping vacant positions unfilled and for the redeployment of staff).

5) New activities are to be implemented through staff redeployment.

6) Reduction in the cost of documentation of conferences and meetings by:

a) requesting at the time of registration whether paper copies are required;

b) setting of a maximum number of copies by the Plenipotentiary Conference or by the Council;

c) setting of a maximum of three sets per delegation;

d) reducing the number of paper copies sent to administrations from the current five to a maximum of two or three.

7) Consideration of savings in languages (translation, interpretation) for study group meetings and publications.

8) Implementation of WSIS activities through staff redeployment within the existing resources.

9) Review of the costs of study groups, working parties, task groups.

10) Limitation of the number of study group meetings and in their duration.

11) Limitation of the number of days of meetings for the advisory groups to three days per year maximum. Additional meetings may be held on cost recovery basis, i.e. costs are financed by the requesting Sectors.

12) Elimination as much as possible of physical meetings of working groups of the Council.

13) Reduction of 2 working days for WRC, 1 for RA and 1 for CPM. The scope and complexity of the agenda will have to be taken into consideration and adapted to the new durations of these events.

14) Identification of the level of achievement of the different programmes with a view to utilizing resources for other new activities.

15) For new programmes or those having additional financial resource implications, a "value-added impact statement" should justify how the proposed programmes differ from current and/or similar programmes in order to avoid overlap and duplication.

16) Sound consideration of the resources allocated to regional initiatives, programmes and assistance to members, to the regional presence both in the regions and at headquarters, as well as those resulting from the outcome of WTDC and the Doha Action Plan.

17) Reduce the cost of travel on duty, by limiting the time on mission as well as the participation to meetings, and benefiting from reductions in air fares.

18) Radio Regulations Board - reduce the number of meetings in one calendar year from 4 to 3.

DECISION GT-PLEN/A (Antalya, 2006)
Fourth World Telecommunication Policy Forum

The Plenipotentiary Conference of the International Telecommunication Union (Antalya, 2006),

considering

a) Resolution 2 (Rev. Marrakesh, 2002) of the Plenipotentiary Conference on the maintaining of the World Telecommunication Policy Forum (WTPF) in order to discuss and exchange views and information on telecommunication policy and regulatory matters, especially on global and cross-sectoral issues;

b) Resolution COM5/4 (Antalya, 2006) of this conference on the review of the International Telecommunication Regulations,

noting

a) the relevant outcomes of the World Summit on the Information Society;

b) that the purposes of the Union are, *inter alia*, to promote, at international level, the adoption of a broader approach to the issues of telecommunications in the global information economy and society, to promote the extension of the benefits of the new telecommunication technologies to all the world's inhabitants and to harmonize the actions of Member States and Sector Members in the attainment of those ends;

c) that ITU is uniquely positioned and has the necessary experience to provide a forum for the coordination of, exchange of information on, discussion of and harmonization of national, regional and international telecommunication strategies and policies;

d) that WTPF has provided a venue for discussion of global and cross-sectoral issues by high-level participants, thus contributing to the advance of world telecommunications,

considering further

a) that convergence, including Internet-related public policy matters, is one of the topics of high current interest to ITU Member States and Sector Members;

b) that the continued development of convergence, next-generation networks, and Internet also has significant implications for several domains, particularly for capacity building, especially in developing countries;

c) that a study of emerging telecommunications policy and regulatory issues is also amongst the topics of high current interest to ITU Member States and Sector Members;

d) that a study of new and emerging issues as referred to in Resolution COM5/4 (Antalya, 2006) is also among the topics of high current interest to ITU Member States and Sector Members,

decides

1. to convene the fourth WTPF in Geneva in the first quarter of 2009, in order to discuss and exchange views on the themes listed above, with the draft agenda shown in the Annex to this Decision;

2. that the fourth WTPF shall draw up a report and, if possible, opinions for consideration by ITU Member States and Sector Members and relevant ITU meetings;

3. that arrangements for the fourth WTPF shall be in accordance with applicable Council decisions for such fora.

ANNEX TO DECISION GT-PLEN/A (Antalya, 2006)

Draft agenda

Fourth World Telecommunication Policy Forum

1. Inauguration of the fourth World Telecommunication Policy Forum
2. Election of the chairman
3. Opening remarks and presentations
4. Organization of the work of the Forum
5. Presentation of the Secretary-General's report
6. Presentation of comments by the membership on the report
7. Discussion
8. Consideration of draft opinions
9. Adoption of the chairman's report and opinions
10. Other business

DECISION COM6/1 (Antalya, 2006)
Implementation of additional corrective measures relating to cost recovery on satellite network filings

The Plenipotentiary Conference of the International Telecommunication Union (Antalya, 2006),

considering

a) the revision of the methodology and scale of charges for cost recovery for the processing of satellite network filings established in Decision 482 modified by the Council at its 2002 session;

b) that, in Decision 513, Council-03 agreed on the need to address this issue on a temporary basis, pending a review of the charging methodology by Council-04;

c) that the application of Decision 513 still resulted in some invoices having values significantly higher than CHF 100 000;

d) that Council-04 did not adopt a new charging methodology;

e) that Council-05 identified and corrected several anomalies regarding the cost-recovery fees for satellite network filings with invoices issued in the 2004-2005 biennium;

f) that corrective measures set forth in some Couneil-05 decisions for invoices issued for the 2002-2003 period were not implementable due to the closure of the accounts for 2002-2003,

noting

a) that Council-06 instructed the Secretary-General to transmit to the Plenipotentiary Conference (Antalya, 2006) the relevant matters relating to the implementation of cost recovery for satellite network filings (C-05 Decision 531, C-05 Decision 532, C-05 Decision 534) for which invoices were issued during the 2002-2003 period, and which were subject to actions by Council-05;

b) the Radio Regulations Board (RRB), at its 41st meeting (Geneva, 4-8 September 2006), concluded that the publication of special sections pertaining to the coordination of some satellite networks was not correct, and therefore requested the cancellation of the relevant invoices issued during the 2002-2003 period,

decides

1. to implement the corrective measures set forth in the Council-05 Decisions 531, 532 and 534 and in the RRB decision (41st meeting, Geneva, 4-8 September 2006) in respect of invoices issued for the 2002-2003 period, taking into account *considering f)* above;

2. that, in respect of those satellite network filings affected by *decides* 1 above, and not nominated for the free entitlement, the Radiocommunication Bureau shall issue revised invoices and shall credit the responsible administration, as appropriate;

3. to withdraw the amount of CHF 6 204 956.40 from the Reserve Account, noting, however, that Decision 5 (Rev, Antalya, 2006) of this conference requires that in no circumstances should the Reserve Account be reduced below 3 per cent as a result of the present decision.

SUP DECISION 4 (Minneapolis, 1998)

Procedure concerning choice of class of contribution

SUP DECISION 8 (Marrakesh, 2002)

ITU input to the Declaration of Principles and Plan of Action of the World Summit on the Information Society and the information document on ITU activities related to the Summit

RESOLUTION 11 (Rev. Antalya, 2006)
World and regional telecommunication/information and communication technology exhibitions and forums

The Plenipotentiary Conference of the International Telecommunication Union (Antalya, 2006),

considering

a) that telecommunication/ICT exhibitions and associated forums (ITU TELECOM) are of considerable assistance in keeping the membership of the Union and the wider telecommunication/ICT community informed of the latest advances in all fields of telecommunications/ICT and the possibilities of applying them for the benefit of all Member States and Sector Members, particularly the developing countries;

b) that world and regional ITU TELECOM events fulfil the mandate to keep Member States and Sector Members informed of, and offer a universal opportunity for the display of, state-of-the-art technology concerning all aspects of telecommunications/ICT and related fields of activity;

c) that some developing countries that have not had the opportunity to host world and regional ITU TELECOM events now have the capability, willingness and commitment to host such events;

d) that regional ITU TELECOMs bring the potential benefits of telecommunications/ICT closer to the people of all continents by emphasizing the specific problems of each region and indicating possible solutions to them;

e) that such regional exhibitions and forums organized on a regular basis by ITU, staged at the invitation of Member States, are an excellent means of catering for the needs of both developed and developing countries and facilitate the transfer of technology and of essential information to developing countries;

f) the commitments made by Switzerland towards ITU;

g) the commitments made by the countries which have signed the Convention on the Privileges and Immunities of the Specialized Agencies,

noting

a) that an ITU TELECOM Board has been established to assist the Secretary-General in the management of ITU TELECOM activities;

b) that many developing countries have moved significantly forward in the development of their telecommunication/ICT sector;

c) that some of these countries have already hosted regional ITU TELECOM events which have proved successful;

d) that ITU has been successfully organizing world and regional ITU TELECOM events for many years;

e) that the principles governing ITU's activities in this field have proved to be extraordinarily useful for the membership of the Union and the wider telecommunication/ICT community;

f) that the operational flexibility which the ITU TELECOM management needs in order to meet all the challenges in its field of activity and compete in its semi-commercial environment has proved to be useful, *resolves*

1. that the Union should, in collaboration with its Member States and its Sector Members, continue to organize world and regional telecommunication/ICT exhibitions and forums on a regular basis, taking due account of the need to ensure the financial success of such exhibitions;

2. that the Union, in its venue selection process for ITU TELECOM exhibitions and forums, should, taking into account *resolves* 5 below, give due consideration to:

2.1. ensuring that such decisions are based on an open and transparent process, with objective criteria – including financial viability – as well as on the results of preliminary market and feasibility studies, including consultations with exhibitors from all regions, guaranteeing preferential or discounted hotel prices to participants and exhibitors;

2.2. balancing the need for generating surplus income with the capability and willingness of countries, and developing countries in particular, to host and stage world and regional ITU TELECOM events;

3. that the Secretary-General is fully accountable for ITU TELECOM activities (including planning, organization and finance), which are an integral part of the permanent activities of the Union;

4. that ITU TELECOM activities are subject to the ITU Staff Regulations and Staff Rules, publication practices and Financial Regulations, including internal control and internal audit;

5. that the venue selection for world ITU TELECOM events be based on a fair and transparent process open to all interested parties and that, in the case when several countries have submitted competitive offers, taking into account *resolves* 2.1 above, the principle of rotation applies;

6. that the audit of ITU TELECOM accounts shall be carried out by the External Auditor of the Union;

7. that, once all the expenditures have been recovered, a significant part of any surplus income over expenditure derived from ITU TELECOM activities should be used as extrabudgetary income for the Telecommunication Development Bureau, for specific telecommunication development projects, primarily in the least developed countries,

instructs the Secretary-General

1. to ensure the appropriate management of all ITU TELECOM activities, in line with the regulations of the Union and in particular with this resolution;

2. to consider measures that will enable and assist Member States which are capable and willing, particularly developing countries, to host and stage regional ITU TELECOM events;

3. in respect of these measures, to take into account the following:

— flexibility in implementing ITU requirements for regional telecommunication/ICT exhibitions and forums, i.e. space requirements, pricing regimes for exhibition, forum and office space;

— establishing a rotation system in deciding the venue of regional ITU TELECOM events which will give due consideration, on a neutral basis, to countries which have not had the opportunity to host such an event but are willing and capable of doing so;

4. to take advice from the ITU TELECOM Board, the mandate and the principles governing the composition of which are approved by the Council on the proposal of the Secretary-General, with due consideration to ensuring transparency and to appointing some individuals with experience in the organization of exhibitions and forums;

5. to ensure the transparency of ITU TELECOM activities and report on them in a separate annual report to the Council, including on:

— all ITU TELECOM business activities;

— all activities of the ITU TELECOM Board;

— the reasons for the selection of venues for future world and regional ITU TELECOM exhibitions and forums;

— future events and their financial implications, the future strategy and risks to be considered;

— action taken with respect to the use of surplus income,

6. to establish a mechanism to implement *resolves* 2.1 and *resolves* 5 above;

7. not to stage regional ITU TELECOM events in a year in which a world ITU TELECOM event will be organized;

8. that a world ITU TELECOM event is held every four years, provided that it does not coincide with one of the most important ITU conferences or assemblies, thus reverting to the previous cycle;

9. to ensure the internal control and internal and external audits of the accounts for the different ITU TELECOM activities,

instructs the Council

1. to review the annual report on ITU TELECOM activities as described under *instructs the Secretary-General* 5 above and give guidance on future trends for those activities;

2. to review and approve the ITU TELECOM accounts, after having examined the reports of the External Auditor and of the internal auditor of the Union;

3. to review and approve the use of ITU TELECOM surplus fonds and to decide annually on the amount to be transferred to the ICT Development Fund;

4. to review and approve proposals of the Secretary-General on the principles for a transparent decision-making process on the venues of world and regional ITU TELECOM events, including the criteria which serve as a basis for that process; such criteria shall include cost elements as well as the rotation system as referred to in *resolves* 5 above and the additional costs which may result from holding the event outside the city of the seat of the Union;

5. to review and approve proposals of the Secretary-General on the mandate and on the composition of the ITU TELECOM Board, with due consideration to ensuring transparency and to appointing some individuals with experience in the organization of exhibitions and forums.

RESOLUTION 14 (Rev. Antalya, 2006)
Recognition of the rights and obligations of all Sector Members of the Union

The Plenipotentiary Conference of the International Telecommunication Union (Antalya, 2006),

considering

a) that the rights and obligations of Member States and Sector Members of the Union are set out in Article 3 of the ITU Constitution;

b) that Article 19 of the ITU Convention lists the types of entities and organizations which may be authorized to participate in the activities of the Sectors as Sector Members;

c) that, except for the provisions of Nos 239 and 340C of the Convention, only Member States have the right to vote, particularly for the approval of recommendations and questions, in accordance with Article 3 of the Constitution,

recognizing

that Sector Members referred to in the lists established by the Secretary-General in accordance with No. 237 of the Convention may participate in all activities of the Sector concerned, with the exception of formal votes and some treaty-making conferences, and in this regard each Sector Member is entitled to:

a) receive from the Bureau of that Sector all the documents which they have requested relating to the Sector's study groups, assemblies or conferences in which they may participate under the relevant provisions of the Convention and under the working methods and procedures of the Sector concerned;

b) send contributions to study groups, notably those in which they have requested to participate in due time, in accordance with the Sector's working methods and procedures;

c) send representatives to such meetings, after having announced their names to the Bureau in due time, in accordance with the Sector's working methods and procedures;

d) propose items for inclusion in the agendas of such meetings, except in relation to the structure and functioning of the Union;

e) take part in all discussions, and may assume responsibilities such as chairmanship or vice-chairmanship of a study group, working party, expert group, rapporteur's group or any other ad hoc group, according to the competence and availability of their experts;

f) take part in the drafting work and editorial work necessary prior to the adoption of recommendations,

recognizing further

that coordination between Member States and Sector Members at the national level has proved to increase the efficiency of the work,

resolves

to invite Sector Members to take part in any decision-finding procedure aimed at facilitating the achievement of a consensus in study groups, in particular in the field of standardization,

invites the world telecommunication development conference, radiocommunication assembly and world telecommunication standardization assembly

to adopt respective provisions in the working methods and procedures of their Sectors,

invites administrations of Member States

to conduct, at the national level, broad coordination among all Sector Members from their countries.

RESOLUTION 21 (Rev. Antalya, 2006)
Special measures concerning alternative calling procedures on international telecommunication networks

The Plenipotentiary Conference of the International Telecommunication Union (Antalya, 2006),

recognizing

a) that each Member State has the sovereign right to allow or prohibit certain or all alternative calling procedures in order to avoid negative effects on or harm to its national telecommunication networks;

b) the interests of developing countries;

c) the interests of consumers and users of telecommunication services,

considering

a) that the use of some alternative calling procedures may adversely affect the economies of developing countries and may seriously hamper the efforts made by those countries to ensure the sound development of their telecommunication/information and communication technology networks and services;

b) that some forms of alternative calling procedures may have an impact on traffic management and network planning and degrade the quality and performance of the public switched telephone network (PSTN);

c) that the use of certain alternative calling procedures that are not harmful to networks may contribute to competition in the interests of consumers;

d) that a number of relevant Telecommunication Standardization Sector (ITU-T) recommendations specifically address, from several points of view, including technical and financial, the effects of alternative calling procedures (including call-back and refile) on the performance and development of telecommunication networks,

recalling

a) Resolution 21 (Rev. Marrakesh, 2002) of the Plenipotentiary Conference, on alternative calling procedures on telecommunication networks, which:

— urged Member States to cooperate among themselves to resolve difficulties in order to ensure that national laws and regulations of ITU Member States are respected;

— instructed ITU-T to accelerate its studies with a view to developing appropriate solutions and recommendations;

b) Resolution 29 (Rev. Florianópolis, 2004) of the World Telecommunication Standardization Assembly (WTSA), which resolved that:

— administrations and recognized operating agencies (ROA) should take all reasonable measures, within the constraints of their national law, to suspend alternative calling procedures which seriously degrade the quality and performance of the PSTN;

— administrations and ROAs should take a cooperative and reasonable approach to respecting the national sovereignty of others;

— further studies are required to evaluate the economic effects of call-back on the effort of countries with economies in transition, developing countries, and especially least developed countries, for sound development of their local telecommunication networks and services, and to evaluate the effectiveness of the suggested guidelines for consultation on call-back;

c) Resolution 22 (Rev. Doha, 2006) of the World Telecommunication Development Conference, the final version of which is based on amendments to Resolutions 20 and 29 (Rev. Florianópolis, 2004) of WTSA,

aware

a) that, as at October 2006, 114 Member States had notified the Telecommunication Standardization Bureau that call-back is prohibited on their territory;

b) that ITU-T has concluded that certain alternative calling procedures such as constant calling (or bombardment or polling) and answer suppression seriously degrade the quality and the performance of the PSTN;

c) that appropriate ITU-T study groups are cooperating on issues related to alternative calling procedures, including refile, call-back, and telecommunication origin identification,

resolves

1. to encourage administrations and international telecommunication operators to implement the ITU-T recommendations referred to in *considering d)* in order to limit the negative effects that, in some cases, alternative calling procedures have on developing countries;

2. to request administrations and international operators which permit the use of alternative calling procedures on their territory in accordance with their national regulations to pay due regard to the decisions of other administrations and international operators whose regulations do not permit such services;

3 to request the appropriate ITU-T study groups, through contributions of Member States and Sector Members, to continue to study alternative calling procedures, such as refile and call-back, and issues related to identification of origin, in order to take into account the importance of these studies as they relate to next-generation networks (NGN) and network degradation,

instructs the Director of the Telecommunication Development Bureau and the Director of the Telecommunication Standardization Bureau

1. to collaborate in the effective implementation of this resolution;

2. to collaborate so as to avoid overlap and duplication of effort in studying issues related to refile, call-back and identification of origin.

RESOLUTION 22 (Rev. Antalya, 2006)
Apportionment of revenues in providing international telecommunication services

The Plenipotentiary Conference of the International Telecommunication Union (Antalya, 2006),

considering

a) the importance of telecommunications/information and communication technology (ICT) for the social and economic development of all countries;

b) the continued leading role of the International Telecommunication Union in stimulating the universal development of telecommunication/ICT;

c) the increasing imbalance, under the current circumstances, between developed and developing countries, in terms of economic growth and technological progress;

d) that the Independent Commission for World-Wide Telecommunications Development, in its report "The Missing Link", recommended, inter alia, that Member States should consider setting aside a small portion of revenues from calls between developing and industrialized countries to be devoted to telecommunications in developing countries;

e) that Recommendation D. 150 of the Telecommunication Standardization Sector (ITU-T), which provides for the apportionment of accounting revenues from international traffic between terminal countries, in principle on a 50/50 basis, has been amended to provide for sharing in a different proportion where there are differences in the costs of providing and operating telecommunication services, although ITU-T has not obtained any information on its implementation;

f) Resolution 3 (Melbourne, 1988) adopted by the World Administrative Telegraph and Telephone Conference;

g) that ITU, in pursuance of Resolution 23 of the Plenipotentiary Conference (Nice, 1989) and as a follow-up to the recommendation in "The Missing Link", carried out a study of the costs of providing and operating international telecommunication services between developing and industrialized countries and established that the cost of providing telecommunication services is much higher in developing countries than in developed ones and this remains the case;

h) that ITU-T has conducted the necessary studies for completion of Recommendation D.140 which establish the principles of cost-orientated accounting rates and accounting rate shares in each relation,

recognizing

a) that the continuing social and economic underdevelopment of a large part of the world is one of the most serious problems affecting not only the countries concerned but also the international community as a whole;

b) that the development of telecommunication/ICT infrastructure and services is a precondition for social and economic development;

c) that inequalities in access to telecommunication facilities globally result in a widening of the gap between the developed and the developing world in terms of economic growth and technological progress;

d) that the trend is towards falling costs of international telecommunication transmission and switching, contributing towards a lowering of accounting rate levels, especially between developed nations, but that the conditions for lowering rates are not uniformly present throughout the world;

e) that raising telecommunication network quality and telephone access levels to developed-country levels throughout the world would assist significantly in achieving economic equilibrium and in diminishing existing call and cost imbalances, *recalling*

a) the relevant resolutions of various development conferences, especially their declarations on the recognition of the need to pay special attention to the requirements of the least developed countries (LDCs) when devising development cooperation programmes;

b) the recommendation in "The Missing Link" that Member States should consider a rearrangement of their international traffic accounting procedures in relations between developing and industrialized countries such that a small proportion of call revenue be used for development purposes;

c) Recommendation 3 (Kyoto, 1994) of the Plenipotentiary Conference, which recommends that developed countries take into account requests for favourable treatment made by developing countries in service, commercial or other relations in telecommunications, thus helping to achieve the desired economic equilibrium conducive to a relaxation of present world tensions,

noting

a) that the concept of network externalities may apply to international traffic between developing and developed countries;

b) that information regarding the concept of network externalities and its possible application to international traffic may be found in an ITU-T Report;

c) that if the concept of network externalities were found to apply, it might be appropriate, subject to certain conditions being fulfilled, for the apportionment of accounting revenues to be on a basis other than 50/50, with the higher proportion being payable by the developed country to take account of the value of the network externalities;

d) that ITU-T is studying the applicability of network externalities to international traffic,

resolves to urge the Telecommunication Standardization Sector

1. to expedite its work on completing its study on the concept of network externalities for international traffic in relation to both fixed and mobile services;

2. to follow up its work on developing the appropriate costing methodologies for both fixed and mobile services;

3. to agree on transitional arrangements which may allow for some flexibility, taking into account the situation of the developing countries and the rapidly changing international telecommunication environment;

4. to take into consideration the interests of all users of telecommunications as a high priority,

invites administrations of the Member States

1. to make available to the General Secretariat all the information necessary for the implementation of this resolution;

2. to contribute to the work of ITU-T on network externalities, with a view to completing the required studies, taking due account of the legitimate interests of all involved parties,

instructs the Secretary-General and the Director of the Telecommunication Standardization Bureau

to monitor, and report to the Council on progress achieved,

instructs the Director of the Telecommunication Standardization Bureau

to submit a report to the Council on the implementation of this resolution, *instructs the Council*

1. to review achieved results, and to take all necessary measures so as to contribute to the achievement of the objectives of this resolution;

2. to report to the next plenipotentiary conference on the progress made with respect to this resolution.

RESOLUTION 25 (Rev. Antalya, 2006)
Strengthening the regional presence

The Plenipotentiary Conference of the International Telecommunication Union (Antalya, 2006),

recalling

a) Resolution 25 (Rev. Minneapolis, 1998) of the Plenipotentiary Conference, which instructed the Director of the Telecommunication Development Bureau (BDT), in close consultation with the Secretary-General and the Directors of the Radiocommunication Bureau (BR) and the Telecommunication Standardization Bureau (TSB), to strengthen gradually the regional presence;

b) Resolution 25 (Rev. Marrakesh, 2002) of the Plenipotentiary Conference, which resolved that the regional presence should be further strengthened and kept under review in the interests of meeting the continually evolving requirements and priorities of each region;

c) Resolution COM5/1 (Antalya, 2006) of this conference, which resolves that the provisions of all ITU documents relating to developing countries shall be extended adequately to apply to countries with economies in transition;

d) Resolutions 1143 and 1183 adopted by the Council at its 1999 and 2001 sessions, respectively, specifying a series of measures to be taken by the Director of BDT, aimed at strengthening the regional presence;

e) that, at its 2002 session, the Council approved a plan of action for the implementation of Resolution 1183;

f) resolutions adopted by the Council at its 2006 session, and resolutions of the World Telecommunication Development Conference (Doha, 2006);

g) that the ITU Strategic Plan for 2008-2011 recommends strengthening communication channels among BDT, the Member States and the Sector Members and Associates of the Telecommunication Development Sector (ITU-D), and ensuring effective and cooperative communication and coordination between BDT – both headquarters and the regional offices – and the General Secretariat, the Radiocommunication Sector (ITU-R) and the Telecommunication Standardization Sector (ITU-T);

h) the instruction given in the relevant Council resolutions to the Director of BDT, in collaboration with the Secretary-General and the Directors of TSB and BR, to seek new sources of financing for regional presence and investigate the possible arrangements for, and impact of, expanding the role of the regional presence to serve the needs of countries wishing to benefit from the full range of the Union's activities,

reaffirming

a) the importance of the regional presence in enabling ITU to work as closely as possible with its Member States and Sector Members, improve the dissemination of information on its activities and develop closer ties with regional and subregional organizations;

b) the importance of continuing to strengthen coordination between BDT, the other Bureaux and the General Secretariat,

considering

a) the outcomes of the Geneva (2003) and Tunis (2005) phases of the World Summit on the Information Society;

b) that many countries are coping with a complex array of issues, some of which are currently being addressed in ail three Sectors of the Union;

c) that ITU should remain a leading intergovernmental organization in which the Member States, Sector Members and Associates work together to foster the growth and sustained development of telecommunication and information networks and facilitate universal access, so that everyone, everywhere may participate in and benefit from the world information economy and society;

d) that means must continue to be established to enable the regional presence to respond effectively and tangibly to the crucial needs of the developing countries, which in the end will benefit the developed world as well,

recognizing

a) the difficulty faced by many countries, particularly developing countries, least developed countries, countries with economies in transition and small island developing states, with stringent budgetary constraints, in participating in the activities of ITU, including the conferences and meetings of the three Sectors;

b) the urgent need to adapt the expertise and working methods of the regional presence towards partnerships in project implementation and activities, which would necessarily involve strengthening the relationship between ITU and regional telecommunication organizations, as foreseen in Resolution 58 (Kyoto, 1994) of the Plenipotentiary Conference;

c) the decision by the World Radiocommunication Conference, in its Resolution 72 (WRC-97), to instruct the Director of BR to consult regional telecommunication organizations on the means by which assistance can be given to their preparations for future world radiocommunication conferences, including the facilitation of regional and interregional preparatory meetings, and to report on those consultations;

d) that the regional offices facilitate participation in preparations under Resolution 112 (Marrakesh, 2002) of the Plenipotentiary Conference;

e) the decision by the World Telecommunication Development Conference (WTDC), through its Resolutions 21 (Rev. Doha, 2006) and 32 (Rev. Doha, 2006), to highlight the need for ITU-D to institute active coordination and collaboration and organize joint activities in areas of common interest with regional and subregional organizations and training institutions, and to consider the establishment of regional rapporteur groups, as a complement to the two ITU-D study groups, so as to permit wider participation by some countries, at lower cost, in addressing certain questions;

f) that WTDC, in Resolution 17 (Rev. Doha, 2006) called for equitable budget allotments for each region to implement regional initiatives;

g) that the regional offices enable ITU to be more responsive to and more aware of the specific needs of the regions;

h) that the regional offices provide important technical assistance to countries with development needs;

i) that resources are limited, and that efficiency and effectiveness are therefore key considerations for activities to be undertaken by ITU;

j) that, to be effective, the regional presence must have the necessary level of authority to meet the diverse requirements of the Member States;

k) that adequate online access between headquarters and the field offices would enhance technical cooperation activities significantly;

l) that all relevant electronic information available at headquarters should also be available to regional offices;

m) that strengthened regional presence will create efficiencies and greater convenience for Member States, *noting*

a) that joint projects involving the collaborative efforts of the ITU regional offices and certain regional telecommunication organizations have already been very successfully implemented in some regions;

b) that both the Plenipotentiary Conference and the Council have endorsed the principle that regional offices should be entrusted with clear and specific functions;

c) that there should be greater cooperation among BDT, the other Bureaux and the General Secretariat in order to encourage participation by the regional offices in their respective spheres;

d) that the regional and area offices are inadequately staffed,

noting also

that it is essential to evaluate the outcomes of the work accomplished by the regional offices, draw conclusions, and, if appropriate, make, with a view to the future, such adjustments as may be required to ensure that they operate in accordance with the imperatives of efficiency and effectiveness, to optimize the use of resources and to avoid duplication of effort, so as to continue to take decisions that will strengthen the regional presence,

resolves

1. to undertake an evaluation of the ITU regional presence;

2. that, within the scarce existing resources of the Union, the regional presence shall be further strengthened and kept under review in the interests of meeting the continually evolving requirements and priorities of each region, the first objective being to maximize the benefits of the regional presence for the whole of the Union's membership;

3. that a broadening of the information dissemination functions of the regional presence is required to ensure that all of the activities and programmes of the Union are represented, while avoiding the duplication of such functions between headquarters and the regional offices;

4. that the regional offices shall be empowered to make decisions within their mandate, while the coordination functions and the balance between ITU headquarters and the regional offices should be facilitated and improved, in accordance with the Strategic Plan 2008-2011, in order to achieve a better balance of work between headquarters and the regional offices;

5. that priority shall be given to implementing all elements of the ITU Strategic Plan 2008-2011 with a view to strengthening the regional presence, in particular:

a) to expand and strengthen the regional offices by identifying functions which could be decentralized and implementing them as soon as possible;

b) to review the internal administrative procedures pertaining to the work of the regional offices, with a view to their simplification and transparency and enhancement of work efficiency;

c) to assist countries in implementing the projects defined in Resolution 17 (Rev. Doha, 2006);

d) to establish clear procedures for consulting Member States, giving Member States the opportunity to review the consolidated regional initiatives and provide feedback to help prioritize them and keeping them informed on project selection and funding;

e) to provide the regional offices with greater autonomy in terms both of decision-making and of addressing the crucial needs of the Member States in the region, including but not limited to:

— functions relating to the dissemination of information, provision of expert advice and hosting of meetings, courses and seminars;

— any functions and tasks that may be delegated to them relating to the preparation and implementation of their own budgets;

— ensuring their effective participation in discussions on the future of Union and on strategic issues concerning the telecommunication/information and communication technology (ICT) sector;

6. that cooperation between the ITU regional offices, relevant regional organizations and other international organizations dealing with development and financial matters should continue to be improved, in the interests of optimizing the use of resources and avoiding duplication, and that Member States should be kept updated through BDT, where necessary, to ensure that their needs are being met in a coordinated and consultative fashion;

7. that regional meetings should be organized in the various regions by the relevant Sectors, particularly ITU-D, in collaboration with regional organizations, in order to improve the effectiveness of the corresponding global meetings and facilitate better participation;

8. that substantial resources have to be made available in order for BDT to be able to operate effectively in the interests of narrowing the telecommunication gap between the developing and developed countries, thereby supporting endeavours towards bridging the digital divide; accordingly the regional offices should, in coordination with ITU headquarters, take measures with a view to:

— supporting pilot projects for the implementation of e-services/applications, analysing and disseminating their results and managing their further adaptation and development within the region;

— creating a mechanism for the purpose:

i) developing a suitable and sustainable business model that will result in private-sector participation (companies and academic communities);

ii) assisting in the determination of an appropriate and affordable technology to meet the needs and requirements of rural populations;

iii) formulating a rural deployment strategy that takes account of the ICT literacy of rural populations and is relevant to their conditions and needs;

— actively assisting Member States in the area of funds-in-trust projects or projects financed from the ICT Development Fund,

instructs the Council

1. to continue to include the regional presence as an item on the agenda of each session of the Council in order to examine its evolution and adopt decisions for its continuing structural adaptation and operation, with the aim of fully meeting the requirements of the Union's membership and giving effect to the decisions adopted at meetings of the Union, and of consolidating the coordination and complementary aspects of activities between ITU and regional and subregional telecommunication organizations;

2. to allocate the appropriate financial resources within the financial limits established by the Plenipotentiary Conference;

3. to report to the next plenipotentiary conference on the progress made in implementing this resolution,

instructs the Secretary-General

1. facilitate the task of the Council by providing all necessary support for strengthening the regional presence as described in this resolution;

2. to adapt where necessary the agreements between ITU and the host countries of the regional and area offices to the changing environment in the host countries;

3. to submit each year to the Council for consideration a detailed report on the regional presence, covering its staffing, a financial overview and the evolution and development of its activities, including the extension of its activities to the three Sectors, and, if appropriate, proposing any changes that would be conducive to the better accomplishment of its mission, and to disseminate this report to all Member States and Sector Members,

further instructs the Secretary-General

to suggest including evaluation of the effectiveness of ITU's regional presence in the United Nations Joint Inspection Unit (JIU) work programme, or to refer it to any other independent entity, if appropriate, taking into account the elements set out in the annex to this resolution,

instructs the Director of Telecommunication Development Bureau, in close consultation with the Secretary-General and the Directors of the Radiocommunication Bureau and the Telecommunication Standardization Bureau

1. to take the necessary measures for further strengthening of the regional presence, as described in this resolution;

2. to support the evaluation of the effectiveness of the ITU's regional presence, taking into account the elements set out in the annex to this resolution;

3. to develop specific operational and financial plans for the regional presence, in collaboration with the regional offices, to be included as part of ITU's annual operational and financial plans;

4. to review and determine the appropriate posts, including permanent posts, in regional and area offices, and provide specialized staff on an as-needed basis to meet particular needs;

5. to fill the vacant posts in the regional offices, where appropriate, giving due consideration to the regional distribution of staff positions;

6. to ensure that the regional offices are given sufficient priority among the activities and programmes of the Union as a whole, and that, to supervise the implementation of funds-in-trust projects and projects financed from the ICT Development Fund, they have the required autonomy, the decision-making authority and the appropriate means;

7. to take the necessary measures to improve the exchange of information between headquarters and field offices;

8. to strengthen the human resource capabilities and provide the regional and area offices with a measure of flexibility in terms of the recruitment of professional staff as well as support staff;

9. to take the necessary measures to ensure the effective incorporation of BR and TSB activities in the regional offices,

instructs the Directors of the Radiocommunication Bureau and the Telecommunication Standardization Bureau

to continue cooperating with the Director of BDT in enhancing the ability of the regional and area offices to provide information on their Sectors' activities, as well as the necessary expertise, to strengthen cooperation and coordination with the relevant regional organizations and to facilitate the participation of all Member States and Sector Members in the activities of the three Sectors of the Union.

ANNEX TO RESOLUTION 25 (Rev. Antalya, 2006)
Elements for evaluation of the ITU regional presence

The evaluation of the ITU's regional presence should be based on the functions assigned to its regional offices under Council-99 Resolution 1143, Annex A: "Generic activities expected of the regional presence," in *resolves* 2 to 8 of Resolution 25 (Rev. Antalya, 2006) and other pertinent decisions.

The evaluation of the regional presence should take into account, but not be limited to, the following elements:

a) the extent of fulfilment of the provisions of Resolution 25 (Rev. Antalya, 2006) by BDT, the General Secretariat and the other two Sectors, as appropriate;

b) how further decentralization could ensure greater efficiency at lower cost, taking into consideration accountability and transparency;

c) a survey of the level of satisfaction of Member States, Sector Members and regional telecommunication organizations with the ITU's regional presence, including the effectiveness of its regional programmes and offices;

d) the extent of possible duplication between the functions of ITU headquarters and the regional offices;

e) the degree of autonomy in decision-making currently accorded to regional offices, and whether greater autonomy could enhance their efficiency and effectiveness;

f) the effectiveness of collaboration between the ITU regional offices, regional telecommunication organizations and other regional and international development and financial organizations;

g) how regional presence and the organization of activities in the regions can enhance the effective participation of all countries in ITU work;

h) the resources currently made available to the regional offices for reducing the digital divide;

i) the identification of functions and powers that might be assigned to the regional presence in implementing the WSIS Plan of Action;

j) the optimal structure of the ITU regional presence, including the location and number of regional and area offices.

In preparing this evaluation, input should be sought from Member States and Sector Members which benefit from the ITU's regional presence, as well as from the regional offices, from regional and international organizations and from any other relevant entities.

A report on this evaluation exercise should be submitted by the Secretary-General to Council at its 2008 session. The Council should then consider the appropriate course of action to be taken, with a view to reporting to the 2010 plenipotentiary conference on the matter.

RESOLUTION 30 (Rev. Antalya, 2006)
Special measures for the least developed countries and small island developing states

The Plenipotentiary Conference of the International Telecommunication Union (Antalya, 2006),

considering

United Nations resolutions on programmes of action for the least developed countries (LDCs) and small island developing states (SIDS),

recognizing

the importance of telecommunications/information and communication technologies (ICTs) for the development of the countries concerned,

having noted

Resolution 49 (Doha, 2006) of the World Telecommunication Development Conference and the Doha Action Plan which provides for extending these measures to include SIDS,

concerned

that the number of LDCs has continued to rise and that it is necessary to address the situation of SIDS,

instructs the Secretary-General and the Director of the Telecommunication Development Bureau

1. to continue to review the state of telecommunication/ICT services in LDCs and SIDS so identified by the United Nations and needing special measures for the development and provision of telecommunications/ICTs, and to identify areas of critical weakness requiring priority action;

2. to propose to the Council concrete measures intended to bring about genuine improvements and provide effective assistance to these countries from the Special Voluntary Programme for Technical Cooperation, the Union's own resources and other sources of finance;

3. within existing resources, to provide the necessary administrative and operational structure for proper administration of the resources appropriated for the LDCs and the SIDS;

4. to report annually on the matter to the Council,

instructs the Council

1. to consider the above-mentioned reports and take appropriate action so that the Union may continue to display its keen interest and cooperate actively in the development of telecommunication/ICT services in these countries;

2. to make appropriations for this purpose from the Special Voluntary Programme for Technical Cooperation, the Union's own resources and any other sources of finance;

3. to keep the situation under constant review and to report on the matter to the next plenipotentiary conference.

RESOLUTION 34 (Rev. Antalya, 2006)
Assistance and support to countries in special need for rebuilding their telecommunication sector

The Plenipotentiary Conference of the International Telecommunication Union (Antalya, 2006),

recalling

a) the noble principles, purpose and objectives enshrined in the Charter of the United Nations and in the Universal Declaration of Human Rights, as well as in the Declaration of Principles adopted by the World Summit on the Information Society;

b) the efforts of the United Nations to promote sustainable development;

c) the purposes of the Union as enshrined in Article 1 of the ITU Constitution,

recalling further

a) Resolution 127 (Marrakesh, 2002) of the Plenipotentiary Conference;

b) Resolution 25 (Rev. Doha, 2006), Resolution 26 (Rev. Doha, 2006), Resolution 51 (Doha, 2006) and Resolution 57 (Doha, 2006) of the World Telecommunication Development Conference,

recognizing

a) that reliable telecommunication systems are indispensable for promoting the socio-economic development of countries, in particular of countries in special need, which are those having suffered from natural disasters, domestic conflicts or war;

b) that, under the present conditions and in the foreseeable future, these countries will not be able to ensure effective operation of their telecommunication sector without help from the international community, provided bilaterally or through international organizations,

noting

that the conditions of order and security sought by United Nations resolutions have been only partially achieved and hence Resolution 34 (*Rev.* Minneapolis, 1998) has only been partially implemented,

resolves

that the special action undertaken by the Secretary-General and the Director of the Telecommunication Development Bureau, with specialized assistance from the ITU Radiocommunication Sector and the ITU Telecommunication Standardization Sector, should be continued or initiated in order to provide appropriate assistance and support to countries in special need referred to in the annex to this resolution in rebuilding their telecommunication sector,

calls upon Member States

to offer all possible assistance and support to the countries in special need, either bilaterally or through the special action of the Union referred to above, and, in any case, in coordination with that action,

instructs the Council

to allocate the necessary funds to the aforesaid action, within the financial limits set by the Plenipotentiary Conference, and proceed with its implementation, *instructs the Director of the Telecommunication Development Bureau*

1. to carry out an assessment of the particular needs of each of these countries;

2. to ensure adequate resource mobilization, including under the internal budget and the Information and Communication Technology (ICT) Development Fund, for the implementation of the proposed actions,

instructs the Secretary-General

1. to coordinate the activities carried out by the three Sectors of the Union in accordance with *resolves* above, to ensure that the Union's action in favour of the countries in special need is as effective as possible, and to report annually on the matter to the Council;

2. with the approval of the Council, upon request from the countries concerned, to update the annex to this resolution as needed.

ANNEX TO RESOLUTION 34 (Rev. Antalya, 2006)

Afghanistan

As the result of the past 24 years of war in Afghanistan, the telecommunication system has been destroyed and needs urgent attention for its basic reconstruction.

Within the framework of Resolution 34 (Rev. Antalya, 2006), appropriate assistance and support shall be provided to the Government of Afghanistan in rebuilding its telecommunication system.

Burundi, Timor Leste, Eritrea, Ethiopia, Guinea, Guinea-Bissau, Liberia, Rwanda, Sierra Leone

Within the framework of Resolution 34 (Rev. Antalya, 2006), appropriate assistance and support shall be provided to these countries in rebuilding their telecommunication networks.

Democratic Republic of the Congo

The basic telecommunication infrastructure of the Democratic Republic of the Congo has been severely damaged by the conflicts and wars from which the country has suffered for more than a decade.

As part of the reform of the telecommunication sector undertaken by the Democratic Republic of the Congo, involving the separation of the operating and regulatory functions, two regulatory bodies have been instituted along with a basic telecommunication network, which requires adequate financial resources in order to be built.

Within the framework of Resolution 34 (Rev. Antalya, 2006), appropriate assistance and support for rebuilding its basic telecommunication network shall be provided to the Democratic Republic of the Congo.

Iraq

The telecommunication infrastructure in the Republic of Iraq has been destroyed by two and a half decades of war and the systems currently in use have become antiquated through long years of use.

Iraq has received no assistance from ITU for a long time due to the conditions of war it has experienced.

Within the framework of Resolution 34 (Rev. Antalya, 2006), the Republic of Iraq shall be supported in rebuilding and overhauling its telecommunication infrastructure, establishing institutions, developing human resources and establishing tariffs, through the provision of all forms of assistance, including technical assistance.

Lebanon

Lebanon's telecommunication facilities have been severely damaged due to wars in that country.

Within the framework of Resolution 34 (Rev. Antalya, 2006), Lebanon shall be provided with appropriate assistance and support in rebuilding its telecommunication network.

Somalia

The telecommunication infrastructure in Somalia has been completely destroyed by a decade and half of war and, in addition, the regulatory framework in the country needs to be re-established.

Somalia has not benefited adequately from the Union's assistance over a long period due to war in the country and lack of government.

Within the framework of Resolution 34 (Rev. Antalya, 2006), and using funds allocated to the programme of assistance for the least developed countries, a special initiative shall be launched, aimed at providing assistance and support to Somalia, in rebuilding and modernizing its telecommunication infrastructure, re-establishing a well-equipped ministry of telecommunications and establishing institutions, and developing telecommunication/ICT policy, legislation and regulation, including a numbering plan, spectrum management, tariff and human resource capacity building, and all other necessary forms of assistance.

RESOLUTION 36 (Rev. Antalya, 2006)
Telecommunications/information and communication technologies in the service of humanitarian assistance

The Plenipotentiary Conference of the International Telecommunication Union (Antalya, 2006),

endorsing

a) Resolution 644 (Rev.WRC-2000) of the World Radiocommunication Conference on telecommunication resources for disaster mitigation and relief operations;

b) Resolution 646 (WRC-03) of the World Radiocommunication Conference on public protection and disaster relief,

c) Resolution 34 (Rev. Doha, 2006) of the World Telecommunication Development Conference on the role of telecommunications/information and communication technology (ICT) in early warning and mitigation of disasters and humanitarian assistance;

d) § 91 of the Tunis Agenda for the Information Society adopted by the second phase of the World Summit on the Information Society,

considering

a) that the Intergovernmental Conference on Emergency Telecommunications (Tampere, 1998) adopted the Tampere Convention on the provision of telecommunication resources for disaster mitigation and relief operations, which entered into force on 8 January 2005;

b) that the second Tampere Conference on Disaster Communications (Tampere, 2001) invited ITU to study the use of public mobile networks for early warning and the dissemination of emergency information, and the operational aspects of emergency telecommunications such as call prioritization;

c) that the third Tampere Conference on Disaster Communications (Tampere, 2006) encouraged wider understanding and cooperation between governments on implementation of the Tampere Convention;

d) that the United Nations World Conference on Disaster Reduction (Kobe, Hyogo, 2005) encouraged all States, taking into account their domestic legal requirements, to consider, as appropriate, acceding to, approving or ratifying relevant international legal instruments relating to disaster reduction, such as the Tampere Convention,

recognizing

a) the seriousness and magnitude of potential disasters that may cause dramatic human suffering;

b) that the recent tragic events in the world clearly demonstrate the need for high-quality communications services to assist public safety and disaster relief agencies in minimizing risk to human life and to cover the necessary general public information and communication needs in such situations,

convinced

that the unhindered use of telecommunication/ICT equipment and services is indispensable for the provision of effective and appropriate humanitarian assistance,

further convinced

that the Tampere Convention provides the necessary framework for such use of telecommunication/ICT resources, *resolves to instruct the Secretary-General and the Director of the Telecommunication Development Bureau*

1 to work closely with the United Nations Emergency Relief Coordinator to support Member States which so request in their work towards their national accession to the Tampere Convention;

2 to assist Member States which so request with the development of their practical arrangements for implementation of the Tampere Convention, in close collaboration with the United Nations Emergency Relief Coordinator,

invites Member States

to work towards their accession to the Tampere Convention as a matter of priority,

urges Member States Parties to the Tampere Convention

to take all practical steps for the application of the Tampere Convention and to work closely with the operational coordinator as provided for therein.

RESOLUTION 41 (Rev. Antalya 2006)
Arrears and special arrears accounts

The Plenipotentiary Conference of the International Telecommunication Union (Antalya, 2006),

in view of

the report of the Council to the Plenipotentiary Conference on the situation with regard to amounts owed to the Union by Member States, Sector Members and Associates,

regretting

the increasing level of arrears and slow settlement of special arrears accounts,

considering

that it is in the interest of all Member States, Sector Members and Associates to maintain the finances of the Union on a sound footing,

having noted

that a number of Member States and Sector Members for which special arrears accounts have been established, notwithstanding the provisions of No. 168 of the ITU Constitution, have up to now not complied with their obligation to submit a repayment schedule to the Secretary-General, and to agree on such a schedule with the Secretary-General, and that their special account has accordingly been cancelled,

urges

all Member States in arrears, especially those for which special arrears accounts have been cancelled, as well as Sector Members and Associates in arrears, to submit a repayment schedule to the Secretary-General, and to agree on such a schedule with the Secretary-General,

confirms the decision

to open any new special arrears account only after the conclusion of an agreement with the Secretary-General establishing a specific repayment schedule at the latest within one year of the receipt of the request for such a special arrears account,

resolves

that the amounts due shall not be taken into account when applying No. 169 of the Constitution provided that the Member States concerned have submitted their repayment schedules to the Secretary-General, and agreed on those schedules with the Secretary-General, and for as long as they strictly comply with them and with the associated conditions, and that failure to comply with the repayment schedule and associated conditions shall result in the cancellation of the special arrears account,

resolves further

that No. 480B of the ITU Convention adopted by this conference shall provisionally apply as from the date of signature of its Final Acts,

instructs the Council

1. to review the guidelines for repayment schedules, including a maximum duration, which would be up to five years for developed countries, up to ten years for developing countries and up to fifteen years for least developed countries, as well as up to five years for Sector Members and Associates,

2. to consider appropriate additional measures such as, for example, in exceptional circumstances, temporary reduction in class of contribution in conformity with No. 165A of the Constitution and

No. 480B of the Convention, and the write-off of interest on overdue payments, subject to each Member State, Sector Member and Associate concerned complying strictly with the agreed repayment schedule for the settlement of the unpaid contributions;

3. to take additional measures in respect of non-compliance with the agreed terms of settlement and/or arrears in payment of annual contributory shares not included in repayment schedules, including, in particular, suspending the participation of Sector Members and Associates in the work of the Union,

further instructs the Council

to review the appropriate level of the Reserve for Debtors' Accounts, to provide appropriate coverage, and to report to the next plenipotentiary conference on the results obtained in pursuance of this resolution,

authorizes the Secretary-General

to negotiate and agree upon, with all Member States in arrears, especially those for which special arrears accounts have been cancelled, as well as with Sector Members and Associates in arrears, schedules for the repayment of their debts in accordance with the guidelines established by the Council, and, where appropriate, to submit for decision by the Council proposals for additional measures as indicated under *instructs the Council* above, including those related to non-compliance,

instructs the Secretary-General

to inform all Member States, Sector Members and Associates in arrears or having special arrears accounts or cancelled special arrears accounts of this resolution and to report to the Council on the measures taken and progress made towards the settlement of debts in respect of special arrears accounts or cancelled special arrears accounts, as well as on any non-compliance with the agreed terms of settlement,

urges Member States, Sector Members and Associates

to assist the Secretary-General and the Council in the application of this resolution.

RESOLUTION 48 (Rev. Antalya, 2006)
Human resources management and development

The Plenipotentiary Conference of the International Telecommunication Union (Antalya, 2006),

recalling

a) Resolution 48 (Rev. Marrakesh, 2002) of the Plenipotentiary Conference on human resources management and development;

b) No. 154 of the ITU Constitution,

noting

a) the strategic plan for the Union as described in Resolution 71 (Rev. Antalya, 2006) of this conference;

b) the report submitted to the 2002 session of the Council (Document C02/27) on effective human resources management in the Union;

c) the Standards of Conduct for the International Civil Service established by the International Civil Service Commission (ICSC) and implemented by ITU in July 2002;

d) Decision 517, adopted by the Council at its 2004 session, on strengthening the dialogue between the Secretary-General and the ITU Staff Council;

e) the report introduced to the 2006 session of the Council (Document C06/EP/3) on ITU human resources management;

f) Resolution 1253, adopted by the Council at its 2006 session, establishing the Tripartite Group on Human Resources Management,

recognizing

a) the value of the human resources of the Union to the fulfilment of its goals;

b) that the human resources strategy should emphasize the continued importance of maintaining a well-trained workforce and providing more training to serving staff members, while recognizing budget constraints,

further recognizing

a) the value, both to the Union and to the staff, of developing those resources to the fullest extent possible through various human resources development activities, including in-service training and training activities in accordance with staffing levels;

b) the impact on the Union and its staff of the continuing evolution of activities in the field of telecommunications and the need for the Union and its human resources to adapt to this evolution through training and staff development;

c) the importance of human resources management and development in support of ITU's strategic orientations and goals,

considering

a) the need to follow a recruitment policy appropriate to the requirements of the Union, including the redeployment of posts and recruitment of specialists at the start of their career;

b) the need to continue to improve the geographical distribution of appointed staff of the Union;

c) the need to encourage the recruitment of more women in the Professional and higher categories, especially at the senior levels;

d) the constant advances made in telecommunications and information and communication technology and operation and the corresponding need to recruit specialists of the highest standard of competence;

e) that it is likely that the definitive upper limit of the contributory unit approved by this conference for the years 2008-2011 will affect the amount spent on human resources in the Union;

f) that there are a number of factors that will affect the finances of the Union which cannot be accurately predicted up to the end of 2011, such as the fluctuations in the rate of exchange between the US dollar and the Swiss franc, and actual income that will be generated from cost recovery,

resolves

1. that the management and development of ITU's human resources should be compatible with the goals and activities of the Union and with the United Nations common system;

2. that ICSC recommendations approved by the United Nations General Assembly should continue to be implemented;

3. that, with immediate effect, within available financial resources, and to the extent practicable, vacancies should be filled through greater mobility of existing staff;

4. that internal mobility should, to the extent practicable, be coupled with training so that staff can be used where they are most needed;

5. that internal mobility should be applied, to the extent feasible, to cover needs when staff retire or leave ITU in order to reduce staffing levels without terminating contracts,

resolves further

1. that appointed staff in the Professional and higher categories shall continue to be recruited on an international basis and that posts identified for external recruitment shall be advertised as widely as possible and communicated to the administrations of all Member States of the Union; however, reasonable promotion possibilities must continue to be offered to existing staff;

[Editor's Note: The remainder of this document was omitted in the version provided by the U.S. Government Printing Office. It appears that the omitted text may have included the remainder of Resolution 48 as well as Resolutions 64 through 161 and a list of resolutions abrogated by the Plenipotentiary Conference. A version containing the omitted materials is available through the website of the International Telecommunication Union, http://www.itu.int.]

STATE DEPARTMENT DOCUMENT NUMBER: 110-17

CONVENTION BETWEEN THE UNITED STATES OF AMERICA AND ICELAND FOR THE AVOIDANCE OF DOUBLE TAXATION AND THE PREVENTION OF FISCAL EVASION WITH RESPECT TO TAXES ON INCOME, AND ACCOMPANYING PROTOCOL

SIGNED AT WASHINGTON D.C., OCTOBER 23, 2007
APPROVED BY THE U.S. SENATE ON SEPTEMBER 23, 2008

CTIA DOCUMENT NUMBER: 16900.000

LETTER OF TRANSMITTAL

The White House, *May 6, 2008.*

To the Senate of the United States:

I transmit herewith, for Senate advice and consent to ratification, the Convention Between the Government of the United States of America and the Government of Iceland for the Avoidance of Double Taxation and the Prevention of Fiscal Evasion with Respect to Taxes on Income, and accompanying Protocol, signed on October 23, 2007, at Washington, D.C. (the "proposed Treaty"). The proposed Treaty would replace the existing income tax Convention with Iceland that was concluded in 1975 (the "existing Treaty"). Also transmitted for the information of the Senate is the report of the Department of State with respect to the proposed Treaty.

The proposed Treaty contains a comprehensive provision designed to prevent so-called treaty shopping. The existing Treaty contains no such protections, resulting in substantial abuse of the existing Treaty's provisions by third-country investors. The proposed Treaty also reflects changes to U.S. and Icelandic law and tax treaty policy since 1975.

I recommend that the Senate give early and favorable consideration to the proposed Treaty and give its advice and consent to ratification.

George W. Bush

LETTER OF SUBMITTAL

The Secretary of State,
Washington, February 29, 2008.

The President,
The White House.

THE PRESIDENT: I have the honor to submit to you, with a view to its transmission to the Senate for advice and consent to ratification, the Convention Between the Government of the United States of America and the Government of Iceland for the Avoidance of Double Taxation and the Prevention of Fiscal Evasion with Respect to Taxes on Income, and accompanying Protocol, signed on October 23, 2007, at Washington (the "proposed Treaty"). The proposed Treaty will replace the existing income tax Convention which was concluded in 1975 (the "existing Treaty").

The proposed Treaty contains a comprehensive provision designed to prevent so-called treaty shopping. The existing Treaty contains no such protections, resulting in substantial abuse of the existing Treaty's provisions by third-country investors. As with the existing Treaty, the proposed Treaty eliminates or significantly reduces withholding taxes on certain cross-border payments of dividends, interest, and royalties.

Ratification of the proposed Treaty would recognize the importance of the United States' economic relations with Iceland. The Department of the Treasury and the Department of State cooperated in the negotiation of the proposed Treaty. It has the full approval of both Departments.

Respectfully submitted.

Condoleezza Rice.

Enclosure: Key Provisions of the U.S.-Iceland Income Tax Convention and Protocol.

Key Provisions of the U.S.-Iceland Income Tax Convention and Protocol

The attached Convention and accompanying Protocol with Iceland (the "proposed Treaty") would replace the existing Convention, concluded in 1975 (the "existing Treaty"). Although the proposed Treaty would bring our tax treaty relations with Iceland into closer conformity with current U.S. tax treaty policy, there are, as with all bilateral tax conventions, some variations from these norms. In the proposed Treaty, these differences reflect particular aspects of Icelandic law and treaty policy, the interaction of U.S. and Icelandic law, and U.S.-Icelandic economic relations.

The most important change from the existing Treaty is the addition of a comprehensive provision to address "treaty shopping," which is the inappropriate use of a tax treaty by third-country residents. The existing Treaty does not contain treaty shopping protections and, as a result, has been abused by third-country investors in recent years.

The proposed Treaty generally provides for withholding rates on investment income that are the same as or lower than those in the existing Treaty. Like the existing Treaty, the proposed Treaty provides for reduced source-country taxation of cross-border dividends. In addition, the proposed Treaty would eliminate source-country withholding tax on cross-border dividend payments to pension funds. As with the existing Treaty, the proposed Treaty generally would eliminate source-country withholding tax on cross-border interest payments. While the existing Treaty eliminates source-country withholding taxes on all cross-border payments of royalties, the proposed Treaty would allow the country in which certain cross-border trademark royalties arise to impose a withholding tax of up to five percent.

The proposed Treaty provides, in addition, for the exchange between the tax authorities of each country of information relevant to carrying out the provisions of the Treaty or the domestic tax laws of either country. The proposed Treaty allows the United States to obtain information (including information from financial institutions) from Iceland whether or not Iceland needs the information for its own tax purposes.

The proposed Treaty also reflects changes to U.S. and Icelandic law since 1975. For example, the proposed Treaty updates the "saving clause" to provide that former citizens or long-term residents of the United States may, for the period of ten years following the loss of such status, be taxed in accordance with the laws of the United States. The proposed Treaty also makes various other changes to modernize our treaty relationship with Iceland and brings it into closer conformity with current U.S. tax treaty policy.

The Parties shall notify each other in writing, through diplomatic channels, when their respective applicable procedures for ratification have been satisfied.

The proposed Treaty will enter into force on the date of the later of the notifications. It will have effect, with respect to taxes withheld at source, on income derived on or after the first day of January of the calendar year next following entry into force, and with respect to other taxes, for taxable years beginning on or after the first day of January next following the date upon which the proposed Treaty enters into force. The existing Treaty will, with respect to any tax, cease to have effect as of the date on which this proposed Treaty has effect with respect to such tax. However, where any person would be entitled to greater benefits under the existing Treaty, the existing Treaty, at the election of the person, shall continue to have effect in its entirety with respect to such person for a period of twelve months from the date the provisions of the proposed Treaty are effective.

CONVENTION BETWEEN THE GOVERNMENT OF THE UNITED STATES OF AMERICA AND THE GOVERNMENT OF ICELAND FOR THE AVOIDANCE OF DOUBLE TAXATION AND THE PREVENTION OF FISCAL EVASION WITH RESPECT TO TAXES ON INCOME

The Government of the United States of America and the Government of Iceland, desiring to conclude a Convention for the avoidance of double taxation and the prevention of fiscal evasion with respect to taxes on income,

HAVE AGREED as follows:

ARTICLE 1
General Scope

1. This Convention shall apply only to persons who are residents of one or both of the Contracting States, except as otherwise provided in the Convention.

2. This Convention shall not restrict in any manner any benefit now or hereafter accorded:

a) by the laws of either Contracting State; or

b) by any other agreement between the Contracting States.

3. a) Notwithstanding the provisions of subparagraph b) of paragraph 2:

(i) the provisions of Article 24 (Mutual Agreement Procedure) of this Convention exclusively shall apply to any dispute concerning whether a measure is within the scope of this Convention, and the procedures under this Convention exclusively shall apply to that dispute; and

(ii) unless the competent authorities determine that a taxation measure is not within the scope of this Convention, the non-discrimination obligations of this Convention exclusively shall apply with respect to that measure, except for such national treatment or most-favored-nation obligations as may apply to trade in goods under the General Agreement on Tariffs and Trade. No national treatment or most-favored-nation obligation under any other agreement shall apply with respect to that measure.

(b) For the purposes of this paragraph, a "measure" is a law, regulation, rule, procedure, decision, administrative action, or any similar provision or action.

4. Notwithstanding any provision of the Convention except paragraph 5 of this Article, a Contracting State may tax its residents (as determined under Article 4 (Resident)), and by reason of citizenship may tax its citizens, as if the Convention had not come into effect. Notwithstanding the other provisions of this Convention, a former citizen or long-term resident of the United States may, for the period often years following the loss of such status, be taxed in accordance with the laws of the United States.

5. The provisions of paragraph 4 shall not affect:

a) the benefits conferred by a Contracting State under paragraph 2 of Article 9 (Associated Enterprises), paragraphs 2 and 4 of Article 17 (Pensions, Social Security, and Annuities), and Articles 22 (Relief from Double Taxation), 23 (Non-Discrimination), and 24 (Mutual Agreement Procedure); and

b) the benefits conferred by a Contracting State under Articles 18 (Government Service), 19 (Students and Trainees), and 26 (Members of Diplomatic Missions and Consular Posts), upon individuals who are neither citizens of, nor have been admitted for permanent residence in, that State.

6. An item of income derived through an entity that is a partnership, trust or estate under the laws of either Contracting State shall be considered to be derived by a resident of a State to the extent that the item is treated for purposes of the taxation law of such Contracting State as the income of a resident, either in its hands or in the hands of its partners or beneficiaries,

ARTICLE 2
Taxes Covered

1. This Convention shall apply to taxes on income imposed on behalf of a Contracting State, irrespective of the manner in which they are levied.

2. There shall be regarded as taxes on income all taxes imposed on total income, on total capital, or on elements of income, including taxes on gains from the alienation of movable or immovable property (real property), taxes on the total amounts of wages or salaries paid by enterprises, but excluding social security taxes, as well as taxes on capital appreciation.

3. The existing taxes to which the Convention shall apply are:

a) in Iceland:

(i) the income taxes to the state (tekjuskattar rikissjóðs); and

(ii) the income tax to the municipalities *(útsvar)*,

(hereinafter referred to as "Icelandic tax");

b) in the United States:

(i) the Federal income taxes imposed by the Internal Revenue Code; and

(ii) the Federal excise taxes imposed with respect to private foundations

(hereinafter referred to as "United States tax").

4. The Convention shall apply also to any identical or substantially similar taxes that are imposed after the date of signature of the Convention in addition to, or in place of, the existing taxes. The competent authorities of the Contracting States shall notify each other of any significant changes that have been made in their respective taxation or other laws that significantly affect their obligations under this Convention.

ARTICLE 3
General Definitions

1. For the purposes of this Convention, unless the context otherwise requires:

a) the term "Iceland" means Iceland and, when used in a geographical sense, means the territory of Iceland, including its territorial sea, and any area beyond the territorial sea within which Iceland, in accordance with international law, exercises jurisdiction or sovereign rights with respect to the sea bed, its subsoil and its superjacent waters, and their natural resources;

b) the term "United States" means the United States of America, and includes the states thereof and the District of Columbia; such term also includes the territorial sea thereof and the sea bed and subsoil of the submarine areas adjacent to that territorial sea, over which the United States exercises sovereign rights in accordance with international law; the term, however, does not include Puerto Rico, the Virgin Islands, Guam or any other United States possession or territory;

c) the term "person" includes an individual, an estate, a trust, a partnership, a company and any other body of persons;

d) the term "company" means any body corporate or any entity that is treated as a body corporate for tax purposes according to the laws of the state in which it is organized;

e) the term "enterprise" applies to the carrying on of any business;

f) the terms "enterprise of a Contracting State" and "enterprise of the other Contracting State" mean respectively an enterprise carried on by a resident of a Contracting State and an enterprise carried on by a resident of the other Contracting State;

g) the terms "a Contracting State" and "the other Contracting State" mean Iceland or the United States as the context requires;

h) the term "international traffic" means any transport by a ship or aircraft, except when such transport is solely between places in a Contracting State;

i) the term "competent authority" means:

(i) in the case of Iceland: the Minister of Finance or his authorized representative; and

(ii) in the case of the United States: the Secretary of the Treasury or his delegate;

j) the term "national" means:

(i) any individual possessing the nationality or citizenship of a Contracting State;

(ii) any legal person, partnership or association deriving its status as such from the laws in force in a Contracting State;

k) the term "business" includes the performance of professional services and of other activities of an independent character;

l) the term "pension scheme" means any plan, scheme, fund, trust or other arrangement established in a Contracting State that:

(i) is generally exempt from income taxation in that State; and

(ii) operates principally to administer or provide pension or retirement benefits or to earn income for the benefit of one or more such arrangements.

2. As regards the application of the Convention at any time by a Contracting State any term not defined therein shall, unless the context otherwise requires, or the competent authorities agree to a common meaning pursuant to the provisions of Article 24 (Mutual Agreement Procedure), have the meaning that it has at that time under the law of that State for the purposes of the taxes to which the Convention applies, any meaning under the applicable tax laws of that State prevailing over a meaning given to the term under other laws of that State.

ARTICLE 4
Resident

1. For the purposes of this Convention, the term "resident of a Contracting State" means any person who, under the laws of that State, is liable to tax therein by reason of his domicile, residence, citizenship, place of management, place of incorporation or any other criterion of a similar nature, and also includes that State and any political subdivision or local authority thereof. This term, however, does not include any person who is liable to tax in that State in respect only of income from sources in that State or capital situated therein or of profits attributable to a permanent establishment in that State.

2. The term "resident of a Contracting State" includes:

a) a pension scheme;

b) a plan, scheme, fund, trust, company or other arrangement established in a Contracting State that is operated exclusively to administer or provide employee benefits and that, by reason of its nature as such, is generally exempt from income taxation in that State; and

c) an organization that is established exclusively for religious, charitable, scientific, artistic, cultural, or educational purposes and that is a resident of a Contracting State according to its laws,

notwithstanding that all or part of its income or gains may be exempt from tax under the domestic law of that State.

3. Where by reason of the provisions of paragraph 1 an individual is a resident of both Contracting States, then his status shall be determined as follows:

a) he shall be deemed to be a resident only of the State in which he has a permanent home available to him; if he has a permanent home available to him in both States, he shall be deemed to be a resident only of the State with which his personal and economic relations are closer (center of vital interests);

b) if the State in which he has his center of vital interests cannot be determined, or if he has not a permanent home available to him in either State, he shall be deemed to be a resident only of the State in which he has an habitual abode;

c) if he has an habitual abode in both States or in neither of them, he shall be deemed to be a resident only of the State of which he is a national;

d) if he is a national of both States or of neither of them, the competent authorities of the Contracting States shall settle the question by mutual agreement.

4. Where by reason of the provisions of paragraphs 1 and 2 of this Article a person other than an individual is a resident of both Contracting States, the competent authorities of the Contracting States shall endeavor to determine by mutual agreement the mode of application of this Convention to that person. If the competent authorities do not reach such an agreement, that person shall not be entitled to claim any benefit provided by this Convention, except those provided by Article 23 (Non-Discrimination) and Article 24 (Mutual Agreement Procedure).

ARTICLE 5
Permanent Establishment

1. For the purposes of this Convention, the term "permanent establishment" means a fixed place of business through which the business of an enterprise is wholly or partly carried on.

2. The term "permanent establishment" includes especially:

a) a place of management;

b) a branch;

c) an office;

d) a factory;

e) a workshop; and

f) a mine, an oil or gas well, a quarry or any other place of extraction of natural resources.

3. A building site or construction or installation project, or an installation or drilling rig or ship used for the exploration of natural resources constitutes a permanent establishment only if it lasts or the activity continues for more than twelve months.

4. Notwithstanding the preceding provisions of this Article, the term "permanent establishment" shall be deemed not to include;

a) the use of facilities solely for the purpose of storage, display or delivery of goods or merchandise belonging to the enterprise;

b) the maintenance of a stock of goods or merchandise belonging to the enterprise solely for the purpose of storage, display or delivery;

c) the maintenance of a stock of goods or merchandise belonging to the enterprise solely for the purpose of processing by another enterprise;

d) the maintenance of a fixed place of business solely for the purpose of purchasing goods or merchandise, or of collecting information for the enterprise;

e) the maintenance of a fixed place of business solely for the purpose of carrying on, for the enterprise, any other activity of a preparatory or auxiliary character;

f) the maintenance of a fixed place of business solely for any combination of activities mentioned in subparagraphs a) to e), provided that the overall activity of the fixed place of business resulting from this combination is of a preparatory or auxiliary character.

5. Notwithstanding the provisions of paragraphs 1 and 2, where a person -- other than an agent of an independent status to whom paragraph 6 applies -- is acting on behalf of an enterprise and has, and habitually exercises, in a Contracting State an authority to conclude contracts in the name of the enterprise, that enterprise shall be deemed to have a permanent establishment in that State in respect of any activities which that person undertakes for the enterprise, unless the activities of such person are limited to those mentioned in paragraph 4 which, if exercised through a fixed place of business, would not make this fixed place of business a permanent establishment under the provisions of that paragraph.

6. An enterprise shall not be deemed to have a permanent establishment in a Contracting State merely because it carries on business in that State through a broker, general commission agent or any other agent of an independent status, provided that such persons are acting in the ordinary course of their business as independent agents.

7. The fact that a company which is a resident of a Contracting State controls or is controlled by a company which is a resident of the other Contracting State, or which carries on business in that other State (whether through a permanent establishment or otherwise), shall not constitute either company a permanent establishment of the other.

ARTICLE 6
Income from Immovable Property (Real Property)

1. Income derived by a resident of a Contracting State from immovable property (real property), including income from agriculture or forestry, situated in the other Contracting State may be taxed in that other State.

2. The term "immovable property (real property)" shall have the meaning which it has under the law of the Contracting State in which the property in question is situated. The term shall in any case include property accessory to immovable property (real property), livestock and equipment used in agriculture and forestry, rights to which the provisions of general law respecting landed property apply, usufruct of immovable property (real property) and rights to variable or fixed payments as consideration for the working of, or the right to work, mineral deposits, sources and other natural resources; ships, boats and aircraft shall not be regarded as immovable property (real property).

3. The provisions of paragraph 1 shall apply to income derived from the direct use, letting or use in any other form of immovable property (real property).

4. The provisions of paragraphs 1 and 3 shall also apply to the income from immovable property (real property) of an enterprise.

ARTICLE 7
Business Profits

1. The profits of an enterprise of a Contracting State shall be taxable only in that State unless the enterprise carries on business in the other Contracting State through a permanent establishment situated therein. If the enterprise carries on business as aforesaid, the profits of the enterprise may be taxed in the other State but only so much of them as is attributable to that permanent establishment.

2. Subject to the provisions of paragraph 3 of this Article, where an enterprise of a Contracting State carries on business in the other Contracting State through a permanent establishment situated therein, there shall in each Contracting State be attributed to that permanent establishment the business profits that it might be expected to make if it were a distinct and separate enterprise engaged in the same or similar activities under the same or similar conditions and dealing wholly independently with the enterprise of which it is a permanent establishment. For this purpose, the business profits to be attributed to the permanent establishment shall include only the profits derived from the assets used, risks assumed and activities performed by the permanent establishment.

3. In determining the profits of a permanent establishment, there shall be allowed as deductions expenses which are incurred for the purposes of the permanent establishment, including executive and general administrative expenses so incurred, whether in the State in which the permanent establishment is situated or elsewhere.

4. No profits shall be attributed to a permanent establishment by reason of the mere purchase by that permanent establishment of goods or merchandise for the enterprise.

5. For the purposes of the preceding paragraphs, the profits to be attributed to the permanent establishment shall be determined by the same method year by year unless there is good and sufficient reason to the contrary.

6. Where profits include items of income which are dealt with separately in other Articles of this Convention, then the provisions of those Articles shall not be affected by the provisions of this Article.

7. In applying this Article, paragraph 6 of Article 10 (Dividends), paragraph 3 of Article 11 (Interest), paragraph 4 of Article 12 (Royalties), paragraph 3 of Article 13 (Capital Gains) and paragraph 2 of Article 20 (Other Income), any income or gain attributable to a permanent establishment during its existence is taxable in the Contracting State where such permanent establishment is situated even if the payments are deferred until such permanent establishment has ceased to exist.

ARTICLE 8
Shipping and Air Transport

1. Profits of an enterprise of a Contracting State from the operation of ships or aircraft in international traffic shall be taxable only in that State.

2. For the purposes of this Article, profits from the operation of ships or aircraft include profits derived from the rental of ships or aircraft on a full (time or voyage) basis. They also include profits from the rental of ships or aircraft on a bareboat basis if such ships or aircraft are operated in

international traffic by the lessee, or if the rental income is incidental to profits from the operation of ships or aircraft in international traffic. Profits derived by an enterprise from the inland transport of property or passengers within either Contracting State shall be treated as profits from the operation of ships or aircraft in international traffic if such transport is undertaken as part of international traffic.

3. Profits of an enterprise of a Contracting State from the use, maintenance, or rental of containers (including trailers, barges, and related equipment for the transport of containers) used in international traffic shall be taxable only in that State.

4. The provisions of paragraphs 1 and 3 shall also apply to profits from the participation in a pool, a joint business or an international operating agency.

ARTICLE 9
Associated Enterprises

1. Where

a) an enterprise of a Contracting State participates directly or indirectly in the management, control or capital of an enterprise of the other Contracting State, or

b) the same persons participate directly or indirectly in the management, control or capital of an enterprise of a Contracting State and an enterprise of the other Contracting State,

and in either case conditions are made or imposed between the two enterprises in their commercial or financial relations which differ from those which would be made between independent enterprises, then any profits which would, but for those conditions, have accrued to one of the enterprises, but, by reason of those conditions, have not so accrued, may be included in the profits of that enterprise and taxed accordingly.

2. Where a Contracting State includes in the profits of an enterprise of that State — and taxes accordingly — profits on which an enterprise of the other Contracting State has been charged to tax in that other State and the other Contracting State agrees that the profits so included are profits which would have accrued to the enterprise of the first-mentioned State if the conditions made between the two enterprises had been those which would have been made between independent enterprises, then that other State shall make an appropriate adjustment to the amount of the tax charged therein on those profits. In determining such adjustment, due regard shall be had to the other provisions of this Convention and the competent authorities of the Contracting States shall if necessary consult each other.

ARTICLE 10
Dividends

1. Dividends paid by a company which is a resident of a Contracting State to a resident of the other Contracting State may be taxed in that other State.

2. However, such dividends may also be taxed in the Contracting State of which the company paying the dividends is a resident and according to the laws of that State, but if the beneficial owner of the dividends is a resident of the other Contracting State, the tax so charged shall not exceed:

a) 5 per cent of the gross amount of the dividends if the beneficial owner is a company which holds directly at least 10 per cent of the share capital of the company paying the dividends;

b) 15 per cent of the gross amount of the dividends in all other cases. This paragraph shall not affect the taxation of the company in respect of the profits out of which the dividends are paid.

3. Subparagraph a) of paragraph 2 shall not apply in the case of dividends paid by a Regulated Investment Company (RIC) or a Real Estate Investment Trust (REIT). In the case of dividends paid by a RIC, subparagraph b) of paragraph 2 shall apply. In the case of dividends paid by a REIT, subparagraph b) of paragraph 2 also shall not apply unless:

a) the beneficial owner of the dividends is an individual holding an interest of not more than 10 percent in the REIT;

b) the dividends are paid with respect to a class of stock that is publicly traded and the beneficial owner of the dividends is a person holding an interest of not more than 5 percent of any class of the REIT's stock; or

c) the beneficial owner of the dividends is a person holding an interest of not more than 10 percent in the REIT and the REIT is diversified.

The rules of this paragraph shall also apply to dividends paid by companies resident in Iceland that are similar to the United States companies referred to in this paragraph. Whether companies that are residents of Iceland are similar to the United States companies referred to in this paragraph will be determined by mutual agreement of the competent authorities.

4. Notwithstanding paragraphs 2 or 3, dividends shall not be taxed in the Contracting State of which the company paying the dividends is a resident if the beneficial owner of the dividends is resident in the other Contracting State and is described in subparagraph a) or b) of paragraph 2 of Article 4 (Resident), provided that such dividends are not derived from the carrying on of a business, directly or indirectly, by such pension scheme or employee benefit organization.

5. For purposes of this Article, the term "dividends" means income from shares or other rights, not being debt-claims, participating in profits, as well as income that is subjected to the same taxation treatment as income from shares under the laws of the State of which the payer is a resident.

6. The provisions of paragraphs 1 through 4 shall not apply if the beneficial owner of the dividends, being a resident of a Contracting State, carries on business in the other Contracting State of which the company paying the dividends is a resident, through a permanent establishment situated therein and the holding in respect of which the dividends are paid is effectively connected with such permanent establishment. In such case the provisions of Article 7 (Business Profits) shall apply.

7. A Contracting State may not impose any tax on dividends paid by a resident of the other State, except insofar as the dividends are paid to a resident of the first-mentioned State or the dividends are attributable to a permanent establishment, nor may it impose tax on a corporation's undistributed profits, except as provided in paragraph 8, even if the dividends paid or the undistributed profits consist wholly or partly of profits or income arising in that State.

8. A company that is a resident of one of the States and that has a permanent establishment in the other State or that is subject to tax in the other State on a net basis on its income that may be taxed in the other State under Article 6 (Income from Immovable Property (Real Property)) or under paragraph 1 of Article 13 (Capital Gains) may be subject in that other State to a tax in addition to the tax allowable under the other provisions of this Convention. Such tax, however, may be imposed on only the portion of the business profits of the company attributable to the permanent establishment and the portion of the income referred to in the preceding sentence that is subject to tax under Article 6 or under paragraph 1 of Article 13 that, in the case of the United States, represents the dividend equivalent amount of such profits or income and, in the case of Iceland, is an amount that is analogous to the dividend equivalent amount.

9. The tax referred to in paragraph 8 may not be imposed at a rate in excess of the rate specified in subparagraph 2 a).

ARTICLE 11
Interest

1. Interest arising in a Contracting State and beneficially owned by a resident of the other Contracting State shall be taxable only in that other State.

2. The term "interest" as used in this Article means income from debt-claims of every kind, whether or not secured by mortgage and whether or not carrying a right to participate in the debtor's profits, and in particular, income from government securities and income from bonds or debentures, including premiums and prizes attaching to such securities, bonds or debentures, and all other income that is subjected to the same taxation treatment as income from money lent by the taxation law of the Contracting State in which the income arises. Income dealt with in Article 10 (Dividends) and penalty charges for late payment shall not be regarded as interest for the purpose of this Article.

3. The provisions of paragraph 1 shall not apply if the beneficial owner of the interest, being a resident of a Contracting State, carries on business in the other Contracting State in which the interest arises, through a permanent establishment situated therein and the debt-claim in respect of which the interest is paid is effectively connected with such permanent establishment. In such case the provisions of Article 7 (Business Profits) shall apply.

4. Where, by reason of a special relationship between the payer and the beneficial owner or between both of them and some other person, the amount of the interest, having regard to the debt-claim for which it is paid, exceeds the amount which would have been agreed upon by the payer and the beneficial owner in the absence of such relationship, the provisions of this Article shall apply only to the last-mentioned amount. In such case, the excess part of the payments shall remain taxable according to the laws of each Contracting State, due regard being had to the other provisions of this Convention.

5. Notwithstanding the provisions of paragraph 1:

a) interest paid by a resident of a Contracting State and that is determined with reference to receipts, sales, income, profits or other cash flow of the debtor or related person, to any change in the value of any property of the debtor or a related person or to any dividend, partnership distribution or similar payment made by the debtor to a related person also may be taxed in the Contracting State in which it arises, and according to the laws of that State, but if the beneficial owner is a resident of the other Contracting State, the gross amount of the interest may be taxed at a rate not exceeding the rate prescribed in subparagraph b) of paragraph 2 of Article 10 (Dividends); and

b) interest that is an excess inclusion with respect to a residual interest in a real estate mortgage investment conduit may be taxed by each State in accordance with its domestic law.

ARTICLE 12
Royalties

1. Royalties arising in a Contracting State and beneficially owned by a resident of the other Contracting State may be taxed only in that other State.

2. Notwithstanding the provisions of paragraph 1, such royalties may also be taxed in the Contracting State in which they arise if they constitute consideration for the use of, or the right to use

a) a trademark and any information concerning industrial, commercial or scientific experience provided in connection with a rental or franchise agreement that includes rights to use a trademark, or

b) a motion picture film or work on film or videotape or other means of reproduction for use in connection with television,

however the tax so charged shall not exceed 5 percent of the gross amount of the royalties.

3. The term “royalties” as used in this Article means payments of any kind received as a consideration for the use of, or the right to use, any copyright of literary, artistic, scientific or other work (including computer software, and cinematographic films), any patent, trade mark, design or model, plan, secret formula or process, or for information concerning industrial, commercial or scientific experience,

4. The provisions of paragraphs 1, 2 and 3 shall not apply if the beneficial owner of the royalties, being a resident of a Contracting State, carries on business in the other Contracting State in which the royalties arise, through a permanent establishment situated therein and the right or property in respect of which the royalties are paid is effectively connected with such permanent establishment. In such case the provisions of Article 7 (Business Profits) shall apply.

5. For the purposes of this Article,

a) Royalties shall be deemed to arise in a Contracting State when the payer is a resident of that State. Where, however, the person paying the royalties, whether he is a resident of a Contracting State or not, has in a State a permanent establishment in connection with which the obligation to pay the royalties was incurred, and such royalties are borne by such permanent establishment, then such royalties shall be deemed to arise in the State in which the permanent establishment is situated and not in any other State of which the payer is a resident;

b) Where subparagraph a) does not operate to treat royalties as arising in either Contracting State, and the royalties are for the use of, or the right to use, in one of the Contracting States, any property or right described in paragraph 3, the royalties shall be deemed to arise in that State.

6. Where, by reason of a special relationship between the payer and the beneficial owner or between both of them and some other person, the amount of the royalties, having regard to the use, right or information for which they are paid, exceeds the amount which would have been agreed upon by the payer, and the beneficial owner in the absence of such relationship, the provisions of this Article shall apply only to the last-mentioned amount. In such case, the excess part of the payments shall remain taxable according to the laws of each Contracting State, due regard being had to the other provisions of this Convention.

ARTICLE 13
Capital Gains

1. Gains derived by a resident of a Contracting State from the alienation of immovable property (real property) situated in the other Contracting State may be taxed in that other State.

2. For the purposes of this Article the term “immovable property (real property) situated in the other Contracting State” shall include:

a) immovable property (real property) referred to in Article 6 (Income from Immovable Property (Real Property));

b) rights to assets to be produced by the exploration or exploitation of the sea bed and sub-soil of that other State and their natural resources, including rights to interests in or the benefit of such assets;

c) where that other State is the United States, a United States real property interest; and

d) where that other State is Iceland,

(i) shares, including rights to acquire shares, other than shares in which there is regular trading on a stock exchange, deriving their value or the greater part of their value directly or indirectly from immovable property (real property) situated in Iceland; and

(ii) an interest in a partnership or trust to the extent that the assets of the partnership or trust consist of immovable property (real property) situated in Iceland, or of shares referred to in clause i) of this subparagraph.

3. Gains from the alienation of movable property forming part of the business property of a permanent establishment which an enterprise of a Contracting State has in the other Contracting State and gains from the alienation of such a permanent establishment (alone or with the whole enterprise) may be taxed in that other State.

4. Gains derived by an enterprise of a Contracting State from the alienation of ships, aircraft, or containers operated or used in international traffic or personal property pertaining to the operation or use of such ships, aircraft, or containers shall be taxable only in that State.

5. Gains from the alienation of any property other than that referred to in the preceding paragraphs shall be taxable only in the Contracting State of which the alienator is a resident.

6. The provisions of paragraph 5 shall not affect the right of each of the Contracting States to levy according to its own law a tax on gains from the alienation of shares or rights in a company, the capital of which is wholly or partly divided into shares and which under the laws of that State is a resident of that State, derived by an individual who is a resident of the other Contracting State and has been a resident of the first-mentioned State in the course of the last five years preceding the alienation of the shares or rights.

ARTICLE 14
Income from Employment

1. Subject to the provisions of Articles 15 (Directors' Fees), 17 (Pensions, Social Security, and Annuities), and 18 (Government Service), salaries, wages and other similar remuneration derived by a resident of a Contracting State in respect of an employment shall be taxable only in that State unless the employment is exercised in the other Contracting State. If the employment is so exercised, such remuneration as is derived therefrom may be taxed in that other State.

2. Notwithstanding the provisions of paragraph 1, remuneration derived by a resident of a Contracting State in respect of an employment exercised in the other Contracting State shall be taxable only in the first-mentioned State if:

a) the recipient is present in the other State for a period or periods not exceeding in the aggregate 183 days in any twelve-month period commencing or ending in the fiscal year or the taxable year concerned, and

b) the remuneration is paid by, or on behalf of, an employer who is not a resident of the other State, and

c) the remuneration is not borne by a permanent establishment which the employer has in the other State.

3. Notwithstanding the preceding provisions of this Article, remuneration described in paragraph 1 that is derived by a resident of a Contracting State in respect of an employment as a member of the regular complement of a ship or aircraft operated in international traffic shall be taxable only in that State.

ARTICLE 15
Directors' Fees

Directors' fees and other similar payments derived by a resident of a Contracting State in his capacity as a member of the board of directors of a company which is a resident of the other Contracting State may be taxed in that other State.

ARTICLE 16
Artistes and Sportsmen

1. Income derived by a resident of a Contracting State as an entertainer, such as a theater, motion picture, radio, or television artiste, or a musician, or as a sportsman, from his personal activities as such exercised in the other Contracting State, which income would be exempt from tax in that other Contracting State under the provisions of Articles 7 (Business Profits) and 14 (Income from Employment) may be taxed in that other State, except where the amount of the gross receipts derived by such entertainer or sportsman, including expenses reimbursed to him, or borne on his behalf, from such activities does not exceed twenty thousand United States dollars ($20,000) or its equivalent in Icelandic kronur for the taxable year concerned.

2. Where income in respect of activities exercised by an entertainer or a sportsman in his capacity as such accrues not to the entertainer or sportsman himself but to another person, that income, notwithstanding the provisions of Article 7 (Business Profits), may be taxed in the Contracting State in which the activities of the entertainer or sportsman are exercised, unless such other person establishes that neither the entertainer or sportsman nor persons related thereto participate directly or indirectly in the profits of that other person in any manner, including the receipt of deferred remuneration, bonuses, fees, dividends, partnership distributions, or other distributions.

ARTICLE 17
Pensions, Social Security, and Annuities

1. Subject to the provisions of paragraph 2 of Article 18 (Government Service), pensions and other similar remuneration paid to a resident of a Contracting State in consideration of past employment shall be taxable only in that State.

2. Notwithstanding the provisions of paragraph 1, payments made by a Contracting State under provisions of the social security or similar legislation of that State to a resident of the other Contracting State or to a citizen of the United States shall be taxable only in the first-mentioned State.

3. Annuities derived and beneficially owned by an individual resident of a Contracting State shall be taxable only in that State. The term "annuities" as used in this paragraph means a stated sum paid periodically at stated times during a specified number of years, under an obligation to make the payments in return for adequate and full consideration (other than services rendered).

4. Where a resident of a Contracting State is a beneficiary of a pension scheme resident in the other Contracting State, income earned but not distributed by the pension scheme may be taxed in the first-mentioned State only at such time as and, subject to paragraph 1, to the extent that a distribution is made from the pension scheme.

ARTICLE 18
Government Service

1. a) Salaries, wages and other similar remuneration, other than a pension, paid from the public funds of a Contracting State or a political subdivision or a local authority thereof to an individual in respect of services rendered to that State or subdivision or authority in the discharge of functions of a governmental nature shall be taxable only in that State.

b) However, such salaries, wages and other similar remuneration shall be taxable only in the other Contracting State if the services are rendered in that State and the individual is a resident of that State who:

(i) is a national of that State; or

(ii) did not become a resident of that State solely for the purpose of rendering the services.

2. a) Any pension paid by, or out of funds created by, a Contracting State or a political subdivision or a local authority thereof to an individual in respect of services rendered to that State or subdivision or authority in the discharge of functions of a governmental nature (other than a payment to which paragraph 2 of Article 17 (Pensions, Social Security, and Annuities) applies) shall be taxable only in that State.

b) However, such pension shall be taxable only in the other Contracting State if the individual is a resident of, and a national of, that State.

3. The provisions of Articles 14 (Income from Employment), 15 (Directors' Fees), 16 (Artistes and Sportsmen), and 17 (Pensions, Social Security, and Annuities) shall apply to salaries, wages and other similar remuneration and to pensions in respect of services rendered in connection with a business carried on by a Contracting State or a political subdivision or a local authority thereof.

ARTICLE 19
Students and Trainees

1. a) An individual who is a resident of one of the Contracting States at the time he becomes temporarily present in the other Contracting State and who is temporarily present in that other Contracting State for the primary purpose of:

(i) studying at a university or other recognized educational institution in that other Contracting State, or

(ii) securing training required to qualify him to practice a profession or professional specialty, or

(iii) studying or doing research as a recipient of a grant, allowance, or award from a governmental, religious, charitable, scientific, literary, or educational organization,

shall be exempt from tax by that other Contracting State with respect to amounts described in subparagraph b) for a period not exceeding 5 taxable years from the date of his arrival in that other Contracting State.

b) The amounts referred to in subparagraph a) are:

(i) gifts from abroad for the purpose of his maintenance, education, study, research, or training;

(ii) the grant, allowance, or award; and

(iii) income from personal services performed in that other Contracting State in an amount not in excess of nine thousand United States dollars ($9,000) or its equivalent in Icelandic kronur for any taxable year.

2. An individual who is a resident of one of the Contracting States at the time he becomes temporarily present in the other Contracting State and who is temporarily present in that other Contracting State as an employee of, or under Contract with, a resident of the first-mentioned Contracting State, for the primary purpose of:

a) acquiring technical, professional, or business experience from a person other than that resident of the first-mentioned Contracting State or other than a person related to such resident, or

b) studying at a university or other recognized educational institution in that other Contracting State, shall be exempt from tax by that other Contracting State for a period of 12 consecutive months with respect to his income from personal services in an aggregate amount not in excess of nine thousand United States dollars ($9,000) or its equivalent in Icelandic kronur.

3. An individual who is a resident of one of the Contracting States at the time he becomes temporarily present in the other Contracting State and who is temporarily present in that other Contracting State for a period not exceeding 1 year, as a participant in a program sponsored by the Government of that other Contracting State, for the primary purpose of training, research, or study, shall be exempt from tax by that other Contracting State with respect to his income from personal services in respect of such training, research, or study performed in that other Contracting State in an aggregate amount not in excess of nine thousand United States dollars ($9,000) or its equivalent in Icelandic kronur.

ARTICLE 20
Other Income

1. Items of income beneficially owned by a resident of a Contracting State, wherever arising, not dealt with in the foregoing Articles of this Convention shall be taxable only in that State.

2. The provisions of paragraph 1 shall not apply to income, other than income from immovable property (real property) as defined in paragraph 2 of Article 6 (Income from Immovable Property (Real Property)), if the beneficial owner of such income, being a resident of a Contracting State, carries on business in the other Contracting State through a permanent establishment situated therein and the right or property in respect of which the income is paid is effectively connected with such permanent establishment. In such case the provisions of Article 7 (Business Profits) shall apply.

ARTICLE 21
Limitation on Benefits

1. A resident of a Contracting State shall be entitled to benefits otherwise accorded to residents of a Contracting State by this Convention only to the extent provided in this Article.

2. A resident of a Contracting State shall be entitled to all the benefits of this Convention if the resident is:

a) an individual;

b) a Contracting State or any political subdivision or local authority thereof;

c) a company if,

(i) its principal class of shares is regularly traded on one or more recognized stock exchanges, and either

A) its principal class of shares is primarily traded on a recognized stock exchange located in the Contracting State of which the company is a resident; or

B) the company's primary place of management and control is in the Contracting State of which it is a resident; or

(ii) at least 50 percent of the aggregate vote and at least 50 percent of the aggregate value of the shares in the company are owned directly or indirectly by five or fewer companies entitled to benefits under clause (i) of this subparagraph, provided that, in the case of indirect ownership, each intermediate owner is a resident of either Contracting State;

d) a person described in paragraph 2 of Article 4 (Resident) of this Convention, provided that, in the case of a person described in subparagraph a) or subparagraph b) of that paragraph, more than

50 percent of the person's beneficiaries, members or participants are individuals resident in either Contracting State; or

e) a person other than an individual, if;

(i) on at least half the days of the taxable year at least 50 percent of each class of shares or other beneficial interests in the person is owned, directly or indirectly, by residents of that State that are entitled to the benefits of this Convention under subparagraph a), subparagraph b), clause (i) of subparagraph c), or subparagraph d) of this paragraph, provided that, in the case of indirect ownership, each intermediate owner is a resident of that Contracting State; and

(ii) less than 50 percent of the person's gross income for the taxable year, as determined in the person's State of residence, is paid or accrued, directly or indirectly, to persons who are not residents of either Contracting State entitled to the benefits of this Convention under subparagraph a), subparagraph b), clause (i) of subparagraph c), or subparagraph d) of this paragraph in the form of payments that are deductible for purposes of the taxes covered by this Convention in the person's State of residence (but not including arm's length payments in the ordinary course of business for services or tangible property and payments in respect of financial obligations to a bank, provided that where such a bank is not a resident of a Contracting State such payment is attributable to a permanent establishment of that bank located in one of the Contracting States).

3. a) A company that is a resident of a Contracting State shall also be entitled to the benefits of the Convention if:

(i) at least 95 percent of the aggregate vote and at least 95 percent of the value of all its shares is owned, directly or indirectly, by seven or fewer persons that are residents of Member States of the European Union, or of the European Economic Area, or parties to the North American Free Trade Agreement or the European Free Trade Agreement that, in any case, meet the requirements of subparagraph b), or any combination thereof; and

(ii) less than 50 percent of the company's gross income for the taxable year is paid or accrued, in the form of deductible payments, directly or indirectly, to persons who are not residents of Member States of the European Union, or of the European Economic Area, or parties to the North American Free Trade Agreement or the European Free Trade Agreement that, in any case, meet the requirements of subparagraph b), or any combination thereof.

b) For purposes of subparagraph a), a person will be treated as a resident of a Member State of the European Union or of the European Economic Area or party to the North American Free Trade Agreement or the European Free Trade Agreement only if such person:

(i) is a resident of a Contracting State entitled to the benefits of this Convention by reason of subparagraph a), subparagraph b), clause (i) of subparagraph c), or subparagraph d) of paragraph 2; or

(ii)(A) would be entitled to the benefits of a comprehensive income tax convention in force between any Member State of the European Union or of the European Economic Area or party to the North American Free Trade Agreement or the European Free Trade Agreement and the Contracting State from which the benefits of this Convention are claimed, analogous to subparagraph a), subparagraph b), clause (i) of subparagraph c) or subparagraph d) of paragraph 2, provided that if such other convention does not contain a comprehensive limitation on benefits article, the person would be entitled to the benefits of this Convention under subparagraph a), subparagraph b), clause (i) of subparagraph c), or subparagraph d) of paragraph 2 if such person were a resident of one of the Contracting States under Article 4 (Resident) of this Convention; and

(B) with respect to income referred to in Articles 10 (Dividends), 11 (Interest) or 12 (Royalties), would be entitled under the convention referred to in clause (ii) of this subparagraph to a rate of tax with respect to the particular class of income for which benefits are being claimed under this Convention that is at least as low as the rate applicable under this Convention.

4. a) A resident of a Contracting State will be entitled to benefits of the Convention with respect to an item of income derived from the other State, regardless of whether the resident is entitled to benefits under paragraph 2 or 3 of this Article, if the resident is engaged in the active conduct of a trade or business in the first-mentioned State (other than the business of making or managing investments for the resident's own account, unless these activities are banking, insurance or securities activities carried on by a bank, insurance company or registered securities dealer), and the income derived from the other Contracting State is derived in connection with, or is incidental to, that trade or business and that resident satisfies any other conditions for obtaining such benefits.

b) If the resident or any of its associated enterprises carries on a trade or business activity in the other Contracting State which gives rise to an item of income, subparagraph a) of this paragraph shall apply to such item only if the trade or business activity in the first-mentioned State is substantial in relation to the trade or business activity in the other State. Whether a trade or business activity is substantial for purposes of this paragraph will be determined based on all the facts and circumstances.

c) In determining whether a person is "engaged in the active conduct of a trade or business" in a Contracting State under subparagraph a) of this paragraph, activities conducted by a partnership in which that person is a partner and activities conducted by persons connected to such person shall be deemed to be conducted by such person. A person shall be connected to another if one possesses at least 50 percent of the beneficial interest in the other (or, in the case of a company, at least 50 percent of the aggregate vote and at lease 50 percent of the aggregate value of the shares in the company or of the beneficial equity interest in the company) or another person possesses, directly or indirectly, at least 50 percent of the beneficial interest (or, in the case of a company, at least 50 percent of the aggregate vote and at least 50 percent of the aggregate value of the shares in the company or of the beneficial equity interest in the company) in each person. In any case, a person shall be considered to be connected to another if, based on all the relevant facts and circumstances, one has control of the other or both are under the control of the same person or persons.

5. Notwithstanding the preceding provisions of this Article, where an enterprise of a Contracting State derives income from the other Contracting State, and that income is attributable to a permanent establishment which that enterprise has in a third jurisdiction, the tax benefits that would otherwise apply under the other provisions of the Convention will not apply to any item of income if the combined tax that is actually paid with respect to such income in the first-mentioned State and in the third jurisdiction is less than 60 percent of the tax that would have been payable in the first-mentioned State if the income were earned in that State by the enterprise and were not attributable to the permanent establishment in the third jurisdiction. Any dividends, interest or royalties to which the provisions of this paragraph apply shall be subject to tax at a rate that shall not exceed 15 percent of the gross amount thereof. Any other income to which the provisions of this paragraph apply will be subject to tax under the provisions of the domestic law of the other Contracting State, notwithstanding any other provision of the Convention. The provisions of this paragraph shall not apply if:

a) in the case of royalties, the royalties are received as compensation for the use of, or the right to use, intangible property produced or developed by the permanent establishment itself; or

b) in the case of any other income, the income derived from the other Contracting State is derived in connection with, or is incidental to, the active conduct of a trade or business carried on by the permanent establishment in the third jurisdiction (other than the business of making, managing or simply holding investments for the person's own account, unless these activities are banking or securities activities carried on by a bank or registered securities dealer).

6. Notwithstanding the preceding provisions of this Article, if a company that is a resident of a Contracting State, or a company that controls directly or indirectly such a company, has outstanding a class of shares:

a) which is subject to terms or other arrangements which entitle its holders to a portion of the income of the company derived from the other Contracting State that is larger than the portion such holders would receive absent such terms or arrangements ("the disproportionate part of the income"); and

b) 50 percent or more of which is owned by persons who are not entitled to benefits under paragraph 2 of this Article;

the benefits of this Convention shall not apply to the disproportionate part of the income.

7. A resident of a Contracting State that is not entitled to benefits pursuant to the preceding paragraphs of this Article shall, nevertheless, be granted benefits of the Convention if the competent authority of the other Contracting State determines that the establishment, acquisition or maintenance of such person and the conduct of its operations did not have as one of its principal purposes the obtaining of benefits under the Convention. The competent authority of the other Contracting State shall consult with the competent authority of the first-mentioned State before denying the benefits of the Convention under this paragraph.

8. a) For purposes of this Article the term "principal class of shares" means the ordinary or common shares of the company, provided that such class of shares represents the majority of the voting power and value of the company. If no single class of ordinary or common shares represents the majority of the aggregate voting power and value of the company, the "principal class of shares" is that class or those classes that in the aggregate represent a majority of the aggregate voting power and value of the company.

b) For purposes of this Article the term "recognized stock exchange" means:

(i) the NASDAQ System owned by the National Association of Securities Dealers, Inc. and any stock exchange registered with the U.S. Securities and Exchange Commission as a national securities exchange under the U.S. Securities Exchange Act of 1934;

(ii) the Icelandic Stock Exchange;

(iii) the stock exchanges of Amsterdam, Brussels, Copenhagen, Frankfurt, Hamburg, Helsinki, London, Oslo, Paris, Stockholm, Sydney, Tokyo, and Toronto; and

(iv) any other stock exchange agreed upon by the competent authorities of both Contracting States.

(c) For purposes of this Article a company's primary place of management and control will be in the State of which it is a resident only if executive officers and senior management employees exercise day-to-day responsibility for more of the strategic, financial and operational policy decision making for the company (including its direct and indirect subsidiaries) in that State than in any other state, and the staffs conduct more of the day-to-day activities necessary for preparing and making those decisions in that State than in any other state.

ARTICLE 22
Relief from Double Taxation

1. in accordance with the provisions and subject to the limitations of the law of the United States (as it may be amended from time to time without changing the general principle hereof), the United States shall allow to a resident or citizen of the United States as a credit against the United States tax on income:

a) the income tax paid or accrued to Iceland on behalf of such citizen or resident; and

b) in the case of a United States company owning at least 10 percent of the voting stock of a company that is a resident of Iceland and from which the United States company receives dividends, the income tax paid or accrued to Iceland by or on behalf of the payer with respect to the profits out of which the dividends are paid.

For the purposes of this paragraph, the taxes referred to in subparagraph a) of paragraph 3 and paragraph 4 of Article 2 (Taxes Covered) shall be considered income taxes.

2. For the purposes of applying paragraph 1 of this Article,

a) subject to subparagraph b) of this paragraph, an item of gross income, as determined under the laws of the United States, derived by a resident of the United States that, under this Convention, may be taxed in Iceland shall be deemed to be income from sources in Iceland;

b) however, gains derived by an individual while that individual was a resident of the United States, that are taxed by the United States in accordance with the Convention, and that may also be taxed in Iceland by reason only of paragraph 5 of Article 13 (Capital Gains), shall be deemed to be gains from sources in the United States.

3. In the case of Iceland, double taxation shall be avoided as follows:

a) When a resident of Iceland derives income which, in accordance with the provisions of this Convention, may be taxed in the United States, Iceland shall allow as a deduction from the tax on the income of that resident an amount equal to the income tax paid in the United States;

b) Such deduction shall not, however, exceed that part of the income tax, as computed before the deduction is given, which is attributable to the income that may be taxed in the United States;

c) When a resident of Iceland derives income which, in accordance with the provisions of this Convention, shall be taxable only in the United States, Iceland may include this income in the tax base but shall allow as a deduction from income tax that part of the income tax which is attributable to the income derived from the United States.

For the purposes of this paragraph, the United States taxes referred to in subparagraph b) of paragraph 3 and paragraph 4 of Article 2 (Taxes Covered) shall be considered income taxes, and shall be allowed as a deduction against the Icelandic tax on income.

4. Where a United States citizen is a resident of Iceland:

a) with respect to items of income that under the provisions of this Convention are exempt from United States tax or that are subject to a reduced rate of United States tax when derived by a resident of Iceland who is not a United States citizen, Iceland shall allow as a credit against Icelandic tax, only the tax paid, if any, that the United States may impose under the provisions of this Convention, other than taxes that may be imposed solely by reason of citizenship under the saving clause of paragraph 4 of Article 1 (General Scope);

b) for purposes of computing United States tax on those items of income referred to in subparagraph a), the United States shall allow as a credit against United States tax the income tax paid to Iceland after the credit referred to in subparagraph a); the credit so allowed shall not reduce the portion of the United States tax that is creditable against the Icelandic tax in accordance with subparagraph a); and

c) for the exclusive purpose of relieving double taxation in the United States under subparagraph b), items of income referred to in subparagraph a) shall be deemed to arise in Iceland to the extent necessary to avoid double taxation of such income under subparagraph b).

ARTICLE 23
Non-Discrimination

1. Nationals of a Contracting State shall not be subjected in the other Contracting State to any taxation or any requirement connected therewith, which is other or more burdensome than the taxation and connected requirements to which nationals of that other State in the same circumstances, in particular with respect to residence, are or may be subjected. This provision shall, notwithstanding the provisions of Article 1 (General Scope), also apply to persons who are not residents of one or both of the Contracting States. However, for the purposes of United States taxation, United States nationals who are subject to tax on a worldwide basis are not in the same circumstances as nationals of Iceland who are not residents of the United States.

2. The taxation on a permanent establishment which an enterprise of a Contracting State has in the other Contracting State shall not be less favourably levied in that other State than the taxation levied on enterprises of that other State carrying on the same activities. This provision shall not be construed as obliging a Contracting State to grant to residents of the other Contracting State any personal allowances, reliefs and reductions for taxation purposes on account of civil status or family responsibilities which it grants to its own residents.

3. Except where the provisions of paragraph 1 of Article 9 (Associated Enterprises), paragraph 4 of Article 11 (Interest), or paragraph 6 of Article 12 (Royalties), apply, interest, royalties and other disbursements paid by an enterprise of a Contracting State to a resident of the other Contracting State shall, for the purpose of determining the taxable profits of such enterprise, be deductible under the same conditions as if they had been paid to a resident of the first-mentioned State. Similarly, any debts of an enterprise of a Contracting State to a resident of the other Contracting State shall, for the purpose of determining the taxable capital of such enterprise, be deductible under the same conditions as if they had been contracted to a resident of the first-mentioned State.

4. Enterprises of a Contracting State, the capital of which is wholly or partly owned or controlled, directly or indirectly, by one or more residents of the other Contracting State, shall not be subjected in the first-mentioned State to any taxation or any requirement connected therewith which is other or more burdensome than the taxation and connected requirements to which other similar enterprises of the first-mentioned State are or may be subjected.

5. Nothing in this Article shall be construed as preventing either Contracting State from imposing a tax as described in paragraph 8 of Article 10 (Dividends).

6. The provisions of this Article shall, notwithstanding the provisions of Article 2 (Taxes Covered), apply to taxes of every kind and description imposed by a Contracting State or a political subdivision or local authority thereof.

ARTICLE 24
Mutual Agreement Procedure

1. Where a person considers that the actions of one or both of the Contracting States result or will result for him in taxation not in accordance with the provisions of this Convention, he may, irrespective of the remedies provided by the domestic law of those States, and the time limits prescribed in such laws for presenting claims for refunds, present his case to the competent authority of either State.

2. The competent authority shall endeavor, if the objection appears to it to be justified and if it is not itself able to arrive at a satisfactory solution, to resolve the case by mutual agreement with the competent authority of the other Contracting State, with a view to the avoidance of taxation which is not in accordance with the Convention. Any agreement reached shall be implemented notwithstanding any time limits or other procedural limitations in the domestic law of the Contracting States.

3. The competent authorities of the Contracting States shall endeavor to resolve by mutual agreement any difficulties or doubts arising as to the interpretation or application of the Convention. In particular the competent authorities of the Contracting States may agree:

a) to the same attribution of income, deductions, credits, or allowances of an enterprise of a Contracting State to its permanent establishment situated in the other Contracting State;

b) to the same allocation of income, deductions, credits, or allowances between persons;

c) to the same characterization of particular items of income, including the same characterization of income that is assimilated to income from shares by the taxation law of one of the Contracting States and that is treated as a different class of income in the other State;

d) to the same characterization of persons;

e) to the same application of source rules with respect to particular items of income;

f) to a common meaning of a term; and

g) to the application of the provisions of domestic law regarding penalties, fines, and interest in a manner consistent with the purposes of the Convention.

They may also consult together for the elimination of double taxation in cases not provided for in the Convention.

4. The competent authorities of the Contracting States may communicate with each other directly, for the purpose of reaching an agreement in the sense of the preceding paragraphs.

ARTICLE 25
Exchange of Information and Administrative Assistance

1. The competent authorities of the Contracting States shall exchange such information as is relevant for carrying out the provisions of this Convention or of the domestic laws concerning taxes of every kind imposed by a Contracting States, insofar as the taxation thereunder is not contrary to the Convention including information relating to the assessment or collection of, the enforcement or prosecution in respect of, or the determination of appeals in relation to, the taxes covered by the Convention, The exchange of information is not restricted by paragraph 1 of Article 1 (General Scope) and Article 2 (Taxes Covered). Any information received by a Contracting State shall be treated as secret in the same manner as information obtained under the domestic laws of that State and shall be disclosed only to persons or authorities (including courts and administrative bodies) involved in the assessment, collection or administration of, the enforcement or prosecution in respect

of, or the determination of appeals in relation to the taxes referred to above, or the oversight of the above. Such persons or authorities shall use the information only for such purposes. They may disclose the information in public court proceedings or in judicial decisions.

2. If information is requested by a Contracting State in accordance with this Article, the other Contracting State shall obtain that information in the same manner and to the same extent as if the tax of the first-mentioned State were the tax of that other State and were being imposed by that other State, notwithstanding that the other State may not, at that time, need such information for purposes of its own tax.

3. In no case shall the provisions of paragraphs 1 and 2 be construed so as to impose on a Contracting State the obligation:

a) to carry out administrative measures at variance with the laws and administrative practice of that or of the other Contracting State;

b) to supply information which is not obtainable under the laws or in the normal course of the administration of that or of the other Contracting State;

c) to supply information which would disclose any trade, business, industrial, commercial or professional secret or trade process, or information, the disclosure of which would be contrary to public policy (ordre public).

4. If specifically requested by the competent authority of a Contracting State, the competent authority of the other Contracting State shall provide information under this Article in the form of depositions of witnesses and authenticated copies of unedited original documents (including books, papers, statements, records, accounts, and writings), to the same extent such depositions and documents can be obtained under the laws and administrative practices of that other State with respect to its own taxes.

5. Each of the Contracting States shall endeavor to collect on behalf of the other Contracting State such amounts as may be necessary to ensure that relief granted by the Convention from taxation imposed by that other State does not inure to the benefit of persons not entitled thereto. This paragraph shall not impose upon either of the Contracting States the obligation to carry out administrative measures that would be contrary to its sovereignty, security, or public policy.

6. The competent authority of a Contracting State intending to send officials of that State to the other Contracting State to interview individuals and examine books and records with the consent of the persons subject to examination shall notify the competent authority of the other Contracting State of that intention.

ARTICLE 26
Members of Diplomatic Missions and Consular Posts

Nothing in this Convention shall affect the fiscal privileges of members of diplomatic missions or consular posts under the general rules of international law or under the provisions of special agreements.

ARTICLE 27
Entry Into Force

1. This Convention shall be subject to ratification in accordance with the applicable procedures of each Contracting State. The Contracting States shall notify each other in writing, through diplomatic channels, when their respective applicable procedures have been satisfied.

2. The Convention shall enter into force on the date of the later of the notifications referred to in paragraph 1, and its provisions shall have effect in both Contracting States:

a) in respect of taxes withheld at source, on income derived on or after 1 January in the calendar year next following the year in which the Convention enters into force;

b) in respect of other taxes, for taxes chargeable for any tax year beginning on or after 1 January in the calendar year next following the year in which the Convention enters into force.

3. The Convention between the United States of America and the Republic of Iceland for the Avoidance of Double Taxation and the Prevention of Fiscal Evasion with Respect to Taxes on Income and Capital, signed May 7, 1975, ("the prior Convention") shall cease to have effect in relation to any tax from the date on which this Convention has effect in relation to that tax in accordance with paragraph 2 of this Article. Notwithstanding the preceding sentence, where any person entitled to benefits under the prior Convention would have been entitled to greater benefits thereunder than under this Convention, the prior Convention shall, at the election of such person, continue to have effect in its entirety with respect to such person for a twelve-month period from the date on which the provisions of this Convention otherwise would have effect under paragraph 2 of this Article. The prior Convention shall terminate on the last date on which it has effect in relation to any tax in accordance with the foregoing provisions of this paragraph.

4. Notwithstanding the entry into force of this Convention, an individual who was entitled to benefits of Article 21 (Teachers) of the prior Convention at the time of the entry into force of this Convention shall continue to be entitled to such benefits until such time as the individual would cease to be entitled to benefits if the prior Convention remained in force.

ARTICLE 28
Termination

This Convention shall remain in force until terminated by a Contracting State. Either Contracting State may terminate the Convention, through diplomatic channels, by giving notice of termination in writing at least six months before the end of any calendar year. In such event, the Convention shall cease to have effect in both Contracting States:

a) in respect of taxes withheld at source, on income derived on or after 1 January in the calendar year next following the year in which the notice is given;

b) in respect of other taxes, for taxes chargeable for any tax year beginning on or after 1 January in the calendar year next following the year in which the notice is given.

IN WITNESS WHEREOF the undersigned, being duly authorized thereto by their respective Governments, have signed this Convention.

Done in duplicate at Washington on this twenty-third day of October 2007, in the English and Icelandic languages, both texts being equally authentic.

FOR THE GOVERNMENT OF THE UNITED STATES OF AMERICA:	FOR THE GOVERNMENT OF ICELAND:
[Signature]	[Signature]

Protocol

At the signing of the Convention concluded today between the Government of the United States of America and the Government of Iceland for the Avoidance of Double Taxation and the Prevention of Fiscal Evasion with Respect to Taxes on Income, the undersigned have agreed upon the following additional provisions which shall form an integral part of the said Convention.

1. With reference to Article 3 (General Definitions)

The following shall be considered to meet the requirements of subparagraph 1) of paragraph 1:

a) in Iceland: any pension fund or pension plan qualified under the Pension Act or any identical or substantially similar schemes which are created under any law enacted after the signature of the Convention.

b) in the United States, qualified plans under section 401(a) of the Internal Revenue Code, individual retirement plans (including individual retirement plans that are part of a simplified employee pension plan that satisfies section 408(k), individual retirement accounts, individual retirement annuities, section 408(p) accounts, and Roth IRAs under section 408A), section 457(g) governmental plans, section 403(a) qualified annuity plans, and section 403(b) plans, or any identical or substantially similar schemes which are created under any law enacted after the signature of the Convention.

2. With reference to Article 7 (Business Profits)

The principles of the OECD Transfer Pricing Guidelines shall apply, by analogy, for the purposes of determining the profits attributable to a permanent establishment. Accordingly, any of the methods described therein, including profits methods, may be used to determine the income of a permanent establishment so long as those methods are applied in accordance with the Guidelines.

3. Articles 7 (Business Profits) and 23 (Non-Discrimination) shall not prevent Iceland from continuing to tax permanent establishments of United States insurance companies in accordance with Article 70, paragraph 2, section 3 of the Icelandic Tax Code, nor shall it prevent the United States from continuing to tax permanent establishments of Icelandic insurance companies in accordance with section 842 (b) of the Internal Revenue Code.

4. With reference to paragraphs 8 and 9 of Article 10 (Dividends)

The general principle of the "dividend equivalent amount", as used in United States law, is to approximate that portion of the income mentioned in paragraph 7 of Article 10 that is comparable to the amount that would be distributed as a dividend if such income were earned by a subsidiary incorporated in the United States. For any year, a foreign corporation's dividend equivalent amount is equal to the after-tax earnings attributable to the foreign corporation's (i) income attributable to a permanent establishment in the United States, (ii) income from real property in the United States that is taxed on a net basis under Article 6 (Income from Immovable Property (Real Property)), and (iii) gain from a real property interest taxable by the United States under paragraph 1 of Article 13 (Capital Gains), reduced by any increase in the foreign corporation's net investment in U.S. assets or increased by any reduction in the foreign corporation's net investment in U.S. assets.

5. With reference to Article 16 (Artistes and Sportsmen)

Nothing shall preclude a Contracting State from withholding tax from such payments according to its domestic laws. However, if according to the provisions of this Article, such remuneration or income may only be taxed in the other Contracting State, the first-mentioned Contracting State shall make a refund of the tax so withheld upon a duly filed claim. Such claim must be filed with the tax authorities that have collected the withholding tax within five years after the close of the calendar year in which the tax was withheld.

6. With reference to Article 21 (Limitation on Benefits)

The competent authorities of the Contracting States shall consult together with a view to developing a commonly agreed application of the provisions of this Article. The competent authorities shall, in accordance with the provisions of Article 25 (Exchange of Information and Administrative Assistance), exchange such information as is necessary for carrying out the provisions of this Article.

7. With reference to Article 25 (Exchange of Information and Administrative Assistance) The powers of each Contracting State's competent authority to obtain information include powers to obtain information held by financial institutions, nominees, or persons acting in an agency or fiduciary capacity (not including information that would reveal confidential communications between a client and an attorney, solicitor or other legal representative, where the client seeks legal advice), and information relating to the ownership of legal persons, and that each Contracting State's competent authority are able to exchange such information in accordance with the Article.

IN WITNESS WHEREOF the undersigned, being duly authorized thereto by their respective Governments, have signed this Protocol.

Done in duplicate at Washington on this twenty-third day of October 2007 in the English and Icelandic languages, both texts being equally authentic.

FOR THE GOVERNMENT OF THE UNITED STATES OF AMERICA:	FOR THE GOVERNMENT OF ICELAND:
[Signature]	[Signature]

SENATE TREATY DOCUMENT NUMBER: 110-18 (FIRST PART)

CONVENTION BETWEEN THE UNITED STATES OF AMERICA AND THE REPUBLIC OF BULGARIA FOR THE AVOIDANCE OF DOUBLE TAXATION AND THE PREVENTION OF FISCAL EVASION WITH RESPECT TO TAXES ON INCOME, WITH ACCOMPANYING PROTOCOL

SIGNED AT WASHINGTON D.C., FEBRUARY 23, 2007
APPROVED BY THE U.S. SENATE ON SEPTEMBER 23, 2008

CTIA DOCUMENT NUMBER: 16901.000

LETTER OF TRANSMITTAL

THE WHITE HOUSE, *June 4, 2008.*

To the Senate of the United States:

I transmit herewith, for Senate advice and consent to ratification, the Convention Between the Government of the United States of America and the Government of the Republic of Bulgaria for the Avoidance of Double Taxation and the Prevention of Fiscal Evasion With Respect to Taxes on Income, with accompanying Protocol, signed at Washington on February 23, 2007 (the "Proposed Treaty"), as well as the Protocol Amending the Convention Between the Government of the United States of America and the Government of the Republic of Bulgaria for the Avoidance of Double Taxation and the Prevention of Fiscal Evasion With Respect to Taxes on Income, signed at Sofia on February 26, 2008 (the "Proposed Protocol of Amendment"). The Proposed Treaty and Proposed Protocol of Amendment are consistent with U.S. tax treaty policy. Also transmitted for the information of the Senate is the report of the Department of State with respect to the Proposed Treaty and Proposed Protocol of Amendment.

The Proposed Treaty generally reduces the withholding tax on cross-border dividend, interest, and royalty payments. Importantly, the Proposed Treaty generally eliminates withholding tax on cross-border dividend payments to pension funds and cross-border interest payments made to financial institutions. The Proposed Treaty also contains provisions, consistent with current U.S. tax treaty policy, that are designed to prevent so-called treaty shopping. The Proposed Protocol of Amendment further strengthens these treaty shopping provisions.

I recommend that the Senate give early and favorable consideration to the Proposed Treaty and give its advice and consent to ratification to both the Proposed Treaty and the Proposed Protocol of Amendment.

George W. Bush

LETTER OF SUBMITTAL

Department of State,
Washington, May 7, 2008.

The President,
The White House.

THE PRESIDENT: I have the honor to submit to you, with a view to their transmission to the Senate for advice and consent to ratification, the Convention Between the Government of the United States of America and the Government of the Republic of Bulgaria for the Avoidance of Double Taxation and the Prevention of Fiscal Evasion with Respect to Taxes on Income, with accompanying Protocol, signed at Washington on February 23, 2007 (the "Proposed Treaty"), and the Protocol Amending the Convention Between the Government of the United States of America and the Government of the Republic of Bulgaria for the Avoidance of Double Taxation and the Prevention of Fiscal Evasion with Respect to Taxes on Income, signed at Sofia on February 26, 2008 (the "Proposed Protocol of Amendment"). The Proposed Treaty is the first income tax treaty between our two countries.

The Proposed Treaty generally reduces the rate of withholding tax on cross-border dividends, interest, and royalties. Importantly, however, the Proposed Treaty generally eliminates withholding tax on cross-border dividend payments to pension funds and cross-border interest payments made to financial institutions. The Proposed Treaty also contains provisions, consistent with current U.S. tax-treaty policy, that are designed to prevent so-called treaty shopping. The Proposed Protocol of Amendment further strengthens these treaty shopping provisions.

The Proposed Treaty and Proposed Protocol of Amendment were concluded in recognition of the importance of the United States' economic relations with Bulgaria. The Department of the Treasury and the Department of State cooperated in the negotiation of the Proposed Treaty and Proposed Protocol of Amendment. They have the full approval of both Departments.

Respectfully submitted,

Condoleezza Rice.

Enclosure: Key Features of Proposed Treaty and Proposed Protocol of Amendment Between the United States and Bulgaria.

Key Features of Proposed Treaty and Proposed Protocol of Amendment Between the United States and Bulgaria

The Convention Between the Government of the United States of America and the Government of the Republic of Bulgaria for the Avoidance of Double Taxation and the Prevention of Fiscal Evasion with Respect to Taxes on Income, with accompanying Protocol, signed at Washington on February 23, 2007 (the "Proposed Treaty"), and the Protocol Amending the Convention Between the Government of the United States of America and the Government of the Republic of Bulgaria for the Avoidance of Double Taxation and the Prevention of Fiscal Evasion with Respect to Taxes on Income, signed at Sofia on February 26, 2008 (the "Proposed Protocol of Amendment"), were negotiated to further facilitate the cross-border economic activity between our countries. The Proposed Treaty and Proposed Protocol of Amendment are consistent with current U.S. tax treaty policy. There are, as with all bilateral tax treaties, some variations from these norms. In the Proposed Treaty and Proposed Protocol of Amendment, these differences reflect particular aspects of Bulgarian law and treaty policy, the interaction of U.S. and Bulgarian law, and U.S.-Bulgarian economic relations.

The Proposed Treaty provides for a withholding rate of ten percent on cross-border portfolio dividend payments, and five percent on dividends when the beneficial owner of the dividend is a company that directly owns at least ten percent of the stock of the company paying the dividend. However, no withholding is permitted on dividends paid by a company resident in one of the countries to a pension fund that is a resident in the other country provided the dividend is not derived from the carrying on of a trade or business by such pension fund.

Further, withholding taxes on cross-border interest payments may be imposed at a maximum rate of five percent. No withholding in the source state on a cross-border interest payment is generally permitted, however, when the interest is beneficially owned by the government of the other country (or a bank operated or controlled by that government), a pension fund resident in the other country, or a financial institution (including a bank or insurance company) resident in the other country.

Cross-border royalty payments are generally sourced to the country of the payer of the royalty and may be subject to a maximum withholding tax rate of five percent in that source state.

The Proposed Treaty also provides that the United States and Bulgaria will reconsider the permissible positive withholding rates with respect to interest and royalties when Bulgarian sourced interest and royalty payments made to other members of the European Union are required to be exempt from source state withholding taxes under certain EU Directives.

The Proposed Treaty follows the standard rules for taxation by the source country of the business profits of a resident of the other country. The source country's right to tax such profits is generally limited to cases in which the profits are attributable to a permanent establishment located in that country. The Proposed Treaty also includes a special rule for certain long-term services not otherwise considered to be provided through a permanent establishment.

The Proposed Treaty includes the "Limitation on Benefits" Article, which is designed to deny "treaty-shoppers" the benefits of the Convention. The Proposed Protocol of Amendment further strengthens the Limitation on Benefits article of the Proposed Treaty. The Proposed Treaty also preserves the U.S. right to tax a former citizen or long-term resident of the United States for the period of ten years following the loss of such status, in accordance with the laws of the United States.

The Proposed Treaty also provides for an exchange of information between our countries, which will facilitate the enforcement of U.S. domestic tax rules. Specifically, the Proposed Treaty allows the United States to obtain information (including bank information) from Bulgaria whether or not Bulgaria needs the information for its own tax purposes. The Proposed Treaty allows the General Accounting Office and the tax writing Committees of Congress to obtain access to certain tax information exchanged under the Convention for use in their oversight of the administration of U.S. tax laws and treaties.

The Proposed Treaty will enter into force on the date of receipt of the later of the notifications exchanged between the parties indicating that their respective requirements for entry into force have been satisfied. It will have effect, with respect to taxes withheld at source, for amounts paid or credited on or after the first day of January next following the year in which the Proposed Treaty enters into force and, with respect to other taxes, for taxable years beginning on or after the first day of January next following the year in which the Proposed Treaty enters into force. The Proposed Protocol of Amendment will enter into force on the date of entry into force of the Proposed Treaty.

CONVENTION BETWEEN THE GOVERNMENT OF THE UNITED STATES OF AMERICA AND THE GOVERNMENT OF THE REPUBLIC OF BULGARIA FOR THE AVOIDANCE OF DOUBLE TAXATION AND THE PREVENTION OF FISCAL EVASION WITH RESPECT TO TAXES ON INCOME

The Government of the United States of America and the Government of the Republic of Bulgaria, desiring to conclude a Convention for the avoidance of double taxation and the prevention of fiscal evasion with respect to taxes on income, have agreed as follows:

CHAPTER I
SCOPE OF THE CONVENTION

Article 1
GENERAL SCOPE

1. This Convention shall apply only to persons who are residents of one or both of the Contracting States, except as otherwise provided in this Convention.

2. This Convention shall not restrict in any manner any benefit now or hereafter accorded:

a) by the laws of either Contracting State; or

b) by any other agreement to which the Contracting States are party,

3. a) Notwithstanding the provisions of subparagraph b) of paragraph 2 of this Article:

i) for purposes of paragraph 3 of Article XXII (Consultation) of the General Agreement on Trade in Services, the Contracting States agree that any question arising as to the interpretation or application of this Convention and, in particular, whether a taxation measure is within the scope of this Convention, shall be determined exclusively in accordance with the provisions of Article 24 (Mutual Agreement Procedure) of this Convention; and

ii) the provisions of Article XVII (National Treatment) of the General Agreement on Trade in Services shall not apply to a taxation measure unless the competent authorities agree that the measure is not within the scope of Article 23 (Non-Discrimination) of this Convention.

b) For the purposes of this paragraph, a "taxation measure" is a law, regulation, rule, procedure, decision, administrative action, or any similar provision or action, relating to taxation.

4. a) Notwithstanding any provision of this Convention except paragraph 5 of this Article, a Contracting State may tax its residents (as determined under Article 4 (Resident)), and by reason of citizenship may tax its citizens, as if this Convention had not come into effect.

b) Notwithstanding the other provisions of this Convention, a former citizen or long-term resident of the United States may, for the period often years following the loss of such status, be taxed in accordance with the laws of the United States. This paragraph shall apply only in respect of income from sources within the United States (including income deemed under the domestic law of the United States to arise from such sources).

5. The provisions of paragraph 4 shall not affect:

a) the benefits conferred by a Contracting State under paragraph 2 of Article 9 (Associated Enterprises), paragraphs 1 and 2 of Article 17 (Pensions, Social Security Payments, Annuities, Alimony, and Child Support), and Articles 22 (Relief From Double Taxation), 23 (Non-Discrimination), and 24 (Mutual Agreement Procedure); and

b) the benefits conferred by a Contracting State under Articles 18 (Government Service), 19 (Students, Trainees, Teachers and Researchers), and 26 (Members of Diplomatic Missions and

Consular Posts), upon individuals who are neither citizens of, nor have been admitted for permanent residence in, that State.

6. An item of income derived through an entity that is fiscally transparent under the laws of either Contracting State shall be considered to be derived by a resident of a Contracting State to the extent that the item is treated for purposes of the taxation law of such Contracting State as the income of a resident.

Article 2
TAXES COVERED

1. This Convention shall apply to taxes on income imposed on behalf of a Contracting State irrespective of the manner in which they are levied.

2. There shall be regarded as taxes on income all taxes on total income, or on elements of income, including taxes on gains from the alienation of movable or immovable property, but excluding social security taxes.

3. The existing taxes to which this Convention shall apply are:

a) in the case of Bulgaria:

i) the personal income tax; and

ii) the corporate income tax.

b) in the case of the United States: the Federal income taxes imposed by the Internal Revenue Code (but excluding social security taxes), and the Federal taxes imposed on the investment income of foreign private foundations.

4. This Convention shall apply also to any substantially similar taxes that are imposed after the date of signature of this Convention in addition to, or in place of, the existing taxes. The competent authorities of the Contracting States shall notify each other of any changes that have been made in their respective taxation or other laws that significantly affect their obligations under this Convention.

CHAPTER II
DEFINITIONS

Article 3
GENERAL DEFINITIONS

1. For the purposes of this Convention, unless the context otherwise requires:

a) the term "Bulgaria" means the Republic of Bulgaria and, when used in a geographical sense, means the territory and the territorial sea over which it exercises its State sovereignty, as well as the continental shelf and the exclusive economic zone over which it exercises sovereign rights and jurisdiction in conformity with international law;

b) the term "United States" means the United States of America, and includes the states thereof and the District of Columbia; such term also includes the territorial sea thereof and the sea bed and subsoil of the submarine areas adjacent to that territorial sea, over which the United States exercises sovereign rights in accordance with international law; the term, however, does not include Puerto Rico, the Virgin Islands, Guam or any other United States possession or territory;

c) the terms "a Contracting State" and "the other Contracting State" mean Bulgaria or the United States, as the context requires;

d) the term "person" includes an individual, a company, and any other body of persons;

e) the term "company" means any body corporate or any entity that is treated as a body corporate for tax purposes according to the laws of the state in which it is organized;

f) the terms "enterprise of a Contracting State" and "enterprise of the other Contracting State" mean respectively an enterprise carried on by a resident of a Contracting State, and an enterprise carried on by a resident of the other Contracting State;

g) the term "enterprise" applies to the carrying on of any business;

h) the term "business" includes the performance of professional services and of other activities of an independent character;

i) the term "business profits" also includes income from the performance of professional services and of other activities of an independent character;

j) the term "international traffic" means any transport by a ship or aircraft, except when such transport is solely between places in a Contracting State;

k) the term "competent authority" means:

i) in Bulgaria: the Minister of Finance or an authorized representative; and

ii) in the United States: the Secretary of the Treasury or his delegate;

l) the term "national" of a Contracting State means:

i) any individual possessing the citizenship of that State; and

ii) any legal person, partnership or association deriving its status as such from the laws in force in that State;

m) the term "pension fund" means any person established in a Contracting State that is:

i) generally exempt from income taxation in that State; and

ii) operated principally to administer or provide pension or retirement benefits or to earn income for the benefit of one or more such arrangements.

2. As regards the application of this Convention at any time by a Contracting State any term not defined therein shall, unless the context otherwise requires, or the competent authorities agree to a common meaning pursuant to the provisions of Article 24 (Mutual Agreement Procedure), have the meaning which it has at that time under the law of that State for the purposes of the taxes to which this Convention applies, any meaning under the applicable tax laws of that State prevailing over a meaning given to the term under other laws of that State.

Article 4
RESIDENT

1. For the purposes of this Convention, the term "resident of a Contracting State" means any person who, under the laws of that State, is liable to tax therein by reason of his domicile, residence, citizenship, place of management, place of incorporation, or any other criterion of a similar nature, and also includes that State and any political subdivision or local authority thereof. This term, however, does not include any person who is liable to tax in that State in respect only of income from sources in that State.

2. The term "resident of a Contracting State" includes:

a) a pension fund established in that State; and

b) an organization that is established and maintained in that State exclusively for religious, charitable, scientific, artistic, cultural, or educational purposes, notwithstanding that all or part of its income or gains may be exempt from tax under the domestic law of that State.

3 . Where, by reason of the provisions of paragraph 1, an individual is a resident of both Contracting States, then his status shall be determined as follows:

a) he shall be deemed to be a resident only of the State in which he has a permanent home available to him; if he has a permanent home available to him in both States, he shall be deemed to be a resident only of the State with which his personal and economic relations arc closer (center of vital interests);

b) if the State in which he has his center of vital interests cannot be determined, or if he does not have a permanent home available to him in either State, he shall be deemed to be a resident only of the State in which he has an habitual abode;

c) if he has an habitual abode in both States or in neither of them, he shall be deemed to be a resident only of the State of which he is a national;

d) if he is a national of both States or of neither of them, the competent authorities of the Contracting States shall endeavor to settle the question by mutual agreement.

4. Where by reason of the provisions of paragraphs 1 and 2 of this Article a person other than an individual is a resident of both Contracting States, the competent authorities of the Contracting States shall by mutual agreement endeavor to determine the mode of application of this Convention to that person. In the absence of a mutual agreement by the competent authorities of the Contracting States, the person shall not be considered a resident of either Contracting State for the purposes of claiming any benefits provided by this Convention.

Article 5
PERMANENT ESTABLISHMENT

1. For the purposes of this Convention, the term "permanent establishment" means a fixed place of business through which the business of an enterprise is wholly or partly carried on.

2. The term "permanent establishment" includes especially:

a) a place of management;

b) a branch;

c) an office;

d) a factory;

e) a workshop; and

f) a mine, an oil or gas well, a quarry, or any other place of extraction of natural resources.

3. A building site or construction or installation project, or an installation used for the exploration of natural resources, constitutes a permanent establishment only if it lasts or the activity continues for more than six months.

4. Notwithstanding the preceding provisions of this Article, the term "permanent establishment" shall be deemed not to include:

a) the use of facilities solely for the purpose of storage, display or delivery of goods or merchandise belonging to the enterprise;

b) the maintenance of a stock of goods or merchandise belonging to the enterprise solely for the purpose of storage, display or delivery;

c) the maintenance of a stock of goods or merchandise belonging to the enterprise solely for the purpose of processing by another enterprise;

d) the maintenance of a fixed place of business solely for the purpose of purchasing goods or merchandise, or of collecting information, for the enterprise;

e) the maintenance of a fixed place of business solely for the purpose of carrying on, for the enterprise, any other activity of a preparatory or auxiliary character;

f) the maintenance of a fixed place of business solely for any combination of the activities mentioned in subparagraphs a) through e), provided that the overall activity of the fixed place of business resulting from this combination is of a preparatory or auxiliary character.

5. Notwithstanding the provisions of paragraphs 1 and 2, where a person--other than an agent of an independent status to whom paragraph 6 applies — is acting in a Contracting State on behalf of a enterprise of the other Contracting State, that enterprise shall be deemed to have a permanent establishment in the first-mentioned Contracting State in respect of any activities which that person undertakes for the enterprise, if such a person:

a) has and habitually exercises in that State an authority to conclude contracts in the name of the enterprise, unless the activities of such person are limited to those mentioned in paragraph 4 which, if exercised through a fixed place of business, would not make this fixed place of business a permanent establishment under the provisions of that paragraph; or

b) has no such authority, but habitually maintains in the first-mentioned State a stock of goods or merchandise belonging to the enterprise from which such person regularly fills orders or makes deliveries on behalf of the enterprise, and additional activities conducted in that State on behalf of the enterprise have contributed to the conclusion of the sale of such goods or merchandise.

6. An enterprise shall not be deemed to have a permanent establishment in a Contracting State merely because it carries on business in that State through a broker, general commission agent, or any other agent of an independent status, provided that such persons are acting in the ordinary course of their business as independent agents.

7. The fact that a company that is a resident of a Contracting State controls or is controlled by a company that is a resident of the other Contracting State, or that carries on business in that other State (whether through a permanent establishment or otherwise), shall not constitute either company a permanent establishment of the other.

8. Subject to the provisions of paragraph 4, where an enterprise of a Contracting State provides services in the other Contracting State, if that enterprise is found not to have a permanent establishment in that other Contracting State by virtue of the preceding paragraphs of this Article, that enterprise shall be deemed to provide those services through a permanent establishment in that other State if and only if:

a) those services are performed in that other State by an individual who is present in that other State for a period or periods aggregating 183 days or more in any twelve month period, and, during that period or periods, more than 50 percent of the gross active business revenues of the enterprise consists of income derived from the services performed in that State by the individual; or

b) the services are provided in that other State for an aggregate of 183 days or more in any twelve month period with respect to the same or connected project for customers who are either residents of that other State or who maintain a permanent establishment in that other State with respect to which the services are provided.

CHAPTER III
TAXATON OF INCOME

Article 6
INCOME FROM IMMOVABLE PROPERTY (REAL PROPERTY)

1. Income derived by a resident of a Contracting State from immovable property (real property), including income from agriculture or forestry, situated in the other Contracting State may be taxed in that other State.

2. The term "immovable property (real property)" shall have the meaning which it has under the law of the Contracting State in which the property in question is situated. The term shall in any case include property accessory to immovable property (real property), including livestock and equipment used in agriculture and forestry, rights to which the provisions of general law respecting landed property apply, usufruct of immovable property (real property) and rights to variable or fixed payments as consideration for the working of, or the right to work, mineral deposits, sources and other natural resources. Ships and aircraft shall not be regarded as immovable property (real property).

3. The provisions of paragraph 1 shall apply to income derived from the direct use, letting, or use in any other form of immovable property (real property).

4. The provisions of paragraphs 1 and 3 shall also apply to the income from immovable properly (real property) of an enterprise. However, the provisions of paragraphs 1 and 3 shall not apply if the beneficial owner of the income referred to in paragraph 1 or 3, being a resident of a Contracting State, carries on a business in the other Contracting State through a permanent establishment situated therein and the immovable property (real property) in respect of which the income is paid is effectively connected with such permanent establishment. In such case, the provisions of Article 7 shall apply.

5. However, as long as a resident of the United States is not entitled under Bulgarian law to make an election to compute the tax on income from immovable property (real property) situated in Bulgaria on a net basis as if such income were business profits attributable to a permanent establishment in Bulgaria, the Bulgarian tax permitted to be charged under paragraph 1 shall not exceed 10 percent of the gross amount of the income.

Article 7
BUSINESS PROFITS

1. The business profits of an enterprise of a Contracting State shall be taxable only in that State unless the enterprise carries on business in the other Contracting State through a permanent establishment situated therein. If the enterprise carries on business as aforesaid, the business profits of the enterprise may be taxed in the other State but only so much of them as are attributable to that permanent establishment.

2. Subject to the provisions of paragraph 3, where an enterprise of a Contracting State carries on business in the other Contracting State through a permanent establishment situated therein, there shall in each Contracting State be attributed to that permanent establishment the business profits that it might be expected to make if it were a distinct and independent enterprise engaged in the same or similar activities under the same or similar conditions.

3. In the determination of the profits of a permanent establishment, there shall be allowed as deductions expenses which are incurred for the purposes of the business of the permanent establishment, including executive and general administrative expenses so incurred, whether in the State in which the permanent establishment is situated or elsewhere.

4. No business profits shall be attributed to a permanent establishment by reason of the mere purchase by that permanent establishment of goods or merchandise for the enterprise.

5. For the purposes of the preceding paragraphs, the business profits to be attributed to the permanent establishment shall be determined by the same method year by year unless there is good and sufficient reason to the contrary.

6. Where business profits include items of income that are dealt with separately in other Articles of this Convention, then the provisions of those Articles shall not be affected by the provisions of this Article.

Article 8
INTERNATIONAL TRAFFIC

1. Profits of an enterprise of a Contracting State from the operation of ships or aircraft in international traffic shall be taxable only in that State.

2. For purposes of this Article, profits from the operation of ships or aircraft include, but are not limited to:

a) profits from the rental of ships or aircraft on a full (time or voyage) basis; and

b) profits from the rental on a bareboat basis of ships or aircraft if the rental income is incidental to profits from the operation of ships or aircraft in international traffic.

3. Profits of an enterprise of a Contracting State from the use, maintenance, or rental of containers (including trailers, barges, and related equipment for the transport of containers) used for the transport of goods or merchandise shall be taxable only in that Contracting State, except insofar as those containers or trailers and related equipment are used for transport solely between places within the other Contracting State.

4. The provisions of paragraphs 1 and 3 shall also apply to profits from participation in a pool, a joint business, or an international operating agency.

Article 9
ASSOCIATED ENTERPRISES

1. Where:

a) an enterprise of a Contracting State participates directly or indirectly in the management, control or capital of an enterprise of the other Contracting State; or

b) the same persons participate directly or indirectly in the management, control, or capital of an enterprise of a Contracting State and an enterprise of the other Contracting State,

and in either case conditions are made or imposed between the two enterprises in their commercial or financial relations that differ from those that would be made between independent enterprises, then any profits that, but for those conditions, would have accrued to one of the enterprises, but by reason of those conditions have not so accrued, may be included in the profits of that enterprise and taxed accordingly.

2. Where a Contracting State includes in the profits of an enterprise of that State, and taxes accordingly, profits on which an enterprise of the other Contracting State has been charged to tax in that other State, and the other Contracting State agrees that the profits so included are profits that would have accrued to the enterprise of the first-mentioned State if the conditions made between the two enterprises had been those that would have been made between independent enterprises, then that

other State shall make an appropriate adjustment to the amount of the tax charged therein on those profits. In determining such adjustment, due regard shall be had to the other provisions of this Convention and the competent authorities of the Contracting States shall if necessary consult each other.

Article 10
DIVIDENDS

1. Dividends paid by a company that is a resident of a Contracting State to a resident of the other Contracting State may be taxed in that other State.

2. However, such dividends may also be taxed in the Contracting State of which the company paying the dividends is a resident and according to the laws of that State, but if the dividends are beneficially owned by a resident of the other Contracting State, except as otherwise provided, the tax so charged shall not exceed:

a) 5 percent of the gross amount of the dividends if the beneficial owner is a company that owns directly at least 10 percent of the voting stock of the company paying the dividends;

b) 10 percent of the gross amount of the dividends in all other cases.

This paragraph shall not affect the taxation of the company in respect of the profits out of which the dividends are paid.

3. a) Subparagraph a) of paragraph 2 shall not apply in the case of dividends paid by a U.S. Regulated Investment Company (RIC) or a U.S. Real Estate Investment Trust (REIT). In the case of dividends paid by a RIC, subparagraph b) of paragraph 2 and paragraph 4 shall apply. In the case of dividends paid by a REIT, subparagraph b) of paragraph 2 and paragraph 4 shall apply only if:

i) the beneficial owner of the dividends is an individual or a pension fund, in either case, holding an interest of not more than 10 percent in the REIT;

ii) the dividends are paid with respect to a class of stock that is publicly traded and the beneficial owner of the dividends is a person holding an interest of not more than 5 percent of any class of the REIT's stock; or

iii) the beneficial owner of the dividends is a person holding an interest of not more than 10 percent in the REIT and the REIT is diversified.

b) The rules of subparagraph a) shall also apply to dividends paid by companies resident in Bulgaria that are similar to the U.S. companies referred to in this paragraph. Whether companies that are residents of Bulgaria are similar to the U.S. companies referred to in this paragraph will be determined by mutual agreement of the competent authorities.

c) For purposes of this paragraph, a REIT or similar company referred to in paragraph 3 b) shall be "diversified" if the value of no single interest in real property exceeds 10 percent of its total interests in real property. For the purposes of this rule, foreclosure property shall not be considered an interest in real property. Where a REIT or such similar company holds an interest in a partnership, it shall be treated as owning directly a proportion of the partnership's interests in real property corresponding to its interest in the partnership.

4. Notwithstanding paragraph 2, dividends shall not be taxed in the Contracting State of which the company paying the dividends is a resident if:

a) the beneficial owner of the dividends is a pension fund that is a resident of the other Contracting State; and

b) such dividends are not derived from the carrying on of a trade or business by such pension fund nor from an associated enterprise other than a person referred to in subparagraph a).

5. For purposes of this Article, the term "dividends" means income from shares or other rights, not being debt-claims, participating in profits, as well as income that is subjected to the same taxation treatment as income from shares under the laws of the State of which the payer is a resident.

6. The provisions of paragraphs 1 through 4 shall not apply if the beneficial owner of the dividends, being a resident of a Contracting State, carries on business in the other Contracting State, of which the payer is a resident, through a permanent establishment situated therein, and the holding in respect of which the dividends are paid is effectively connected with such permanent establishment. In such case the provisions of Article 7 (Business Profits) shall apply.

7. A Contracting State may not impose any tax on dividends paid by a resident of the other State, except insofar as the dividends are paid to a resident of the first-mentioned State or the dividends are attributable to a permanent establishment in the first-mentioned State, nor may it impose lax on a corporation's undistributed profits, except as provided in paragraph 8, even if the dividends paid or the undistributed profits consist wholly or partly of profits or income arising in that other State.

8. a) A company that is a resident of one of the States and that has a permanent establishment in the other State or that is subject to tax in the other State on a net basis on its income that may be taxed in the other State under Article 6 (Income from Immovable Property (Real Property)) or under paragraph 1 of Article 13 (Capital Gains) may be subject in that other State to a tax in addition to the tax allowable under the other provisions of this Convention.

b) Such tax, however, may be imposed:

i) on only the portion of the business profits of the company attributable to the permanent establishment and the portion of the income referred to in the preceding sentence that is subject to tax under Article 6 (Immovable Property (Real Property)) or under paragraph 1 of Article 13 (Capital Gains) that, in the case of the United States, represents the dividend equivalent amount of such profits or income and, in the case of Bulgaria, is an amount that is analogous to the dividend equivalent amount; and

ii) at a rate not in excess of 5 percent.

Article 11
INTEREST

1. Interest arising in a Contracting State and paid to a resident of the other Contracting State may be taxed in that other State.

2. However, such interest may also be taxed in the Contracting State in which it arises and according to the laws of that State, but if the beneficial owner of the interest is a resident of the other Contracting State, the tax so charged shall not exceed 5 per cent of the gross amount of the interest.

3. Notwithstanding the provisions of paragraph 2, interest arising in a Contracting State shall be taxable only in the other Contracting State if:

a) the interest is beneficially owned by that other Contracting State, a political subdivision or local authority thereof, or the central bank of that other Contracting State or any institution wholly owned by that Contracting State;

b) the interest is beneficially owned by a resident of that other Contracting State with respect to debt-claims guaranteed, insured or indirectly financed by the Government of that other Contracting

State, a political subdivision or local authority thereof, or the central bank of that other Contracting State or any institution wholly owned by that Contracting State;

c) the interest is beneficially owned by a resident of the other Contracting State that is a financial institution (including, for example, a bank or an insurance company), unless the interest is paid as a part of a back-to-back loan or an arrangement that is economically similar to and has the effect of a back-to-back loan; or

d) the interest is beneficially owned by a pension fund that is a resident of that other Contracting State, provided that such interest is not derived from the carrying on of a business, directly or indirectly, by such pension fund.

4. The term "interest" as used in this Article means income from debt-claims of every kind, whether or not secured by mortgage, and whether or not carrying a right to participate in the debtor's profits, and in particular, income from government securities and income from bonds or debentures, including premiums or prizes attaching to such securities, bonds or debentures, and all other income that is subjected to the same taxation treatment as income from money lent by the taxation law of the Contracting State in which the income arises. Income dealt with in Article 10 (Dividends) and penalty charges for late payment shall not be regarded as interest for the purposes of this Convention.

5. The provisions of paragraphs 1, 2 and 3 shall not apply if the beneficial owner of the interest, being a resident of a Contracting State, carries on business in the other Contracting State, in which the interest arises, through a permanent establishment situated therein, and the debt-claim in respect of which the interest is paid is effectively connected with such permanent establishment. In such case the provisions of Article 7 (Business Profits) shall apply.

6. Interest shall be deemed to arise in a Contracting State when the payer is a resident of that State. Where, however, the person paying the interest, whether a resident of a Contracting State or not, has in a Contracting State a permanent establishment in connection with which the indebtedness on which the interest is paid was incurred, and such interest is borne by such permanent establishment, then such interest shall be deemed to arise in the State in which the permanent establishment is situated.

7. Where, by reason of a special relationship between the payer and the beneficial owner or between both of them and some other person, the amount of the interest, having regard to the debt-claim for which it is paid, exceeds the amount which would have been agreed upon by the payer and the beneficial owner in the absence of such relationship, the provisions of this Article shall apply only to the last-mentioned amount. In such case the excess part of the payments shall remain taxable according to the laws of each State, due regard being had to the other provisions of this Convention.

8. Notwithstanding the provisions of paragraph 1:

a) interest arising in the United States that is contingent interest of a type that does not qualify as portfolio interest under United States law may be taxed by the United States but, if the beneficial owner of the interest is a resident of Bulgaria, the interest may be taxed at a rate not exceeding 10% of the gross amount of the interest;

b) interest arising in Bulgaria that is determined with reference to receipts, sales, income, profits or other cash flow of the debtor or a related person, to any change in the value of any property of the debtor or a related person or to any dividend, partnership distribution or similar payment made by the debtor or a related person may be taxed in Bulgaria, and according to the laws of Bulgaria, but if the beneficial owner is a resident of the United States, the interest may be taxed at a rate not exceeding 10% of the gross amount of the interest; and

c) Interest that is an excess inclusion with respect to a residual interest in a real estate mortgage investment conduit may be taxed by each State in accordance with its domestic law.

9 Where interest expense is deductible in determining the income of a company that is a resident of a Contracting State, being income which:

a) is attributable to a permanent establishment of that company situated in the other Contracting State; or

b) may be taxed in the other Contracting State under Article 6 (Immovable Property (Real Property)) or paragraph 1 of Article 13 (Capital Gains);

and that interest expense exceeds the interest paid by that permanent establishment or paid with respect to the debt secured by immovable property (real property) situated in that other Contracting State, the amount of that excess shall be deemed to be interest arising in that other Contracting State and beneficially owned by a resident of the first-mentioned Contracting State. That deemed interest may be taxed in that other Contracting State at a rate not to exceed the rate provided for in paragraph 2, unless the company is described in paragraph 3 in which case it shall be exempt from such taxation in that other Contracting State.

Article 12
ROYALTIES

1. Royalties arising in a Contracting State and paid to a resident of the other Contracting State may be taxed in that other State.

2. However, such royalties may also be taxed in the Contracting State in which they arise and according to the laws of that State, but if the beneficial owner of the royalties is a resident of the other Contracting State, the tax so charged shall not exceed 5 per cent of the gross amount of the royalties.

3. The term "royalties" as used in this Article means:

a) payments of any kind received as a consideration for the use of, or the right to use, any copyright of literary, artistic, scientific or other work (including cinematographic films and films, tapes or other means of image or sound reproduction for radio or television broadcasting), any patent, trademark, design or model, plan, secret formula or process, or for information concerning industrial, commercial or scientific experience; and

b) gain derived from the alienation of any property described in subparagraph a), to the extent that such gain is contingent on the productivity, use, or disposition of the properly.

4. The provisions of paragraphs 1 and 2 shall not apply if the beneficial owner of the royalties, being a resident of a Contracting State, carries on business in the other Contracting State through a permanent establishment situated therein and the right or property in respect of which the royalties are paid is effectively connected with such permanent establishment. In such case the provisions of Article 7 (Business Profits) shall apply.

5. Royalties shall be deemed to arise in a Contracting State when the payer is a resident of that State. Where, however, the person paying the royalties, whether he is a resident of a Contracting State or not, has in a Contracting State a permanent establishment with which the right or property in respect of which the royalties are paid is effectively connected, and such royalties are borne by such permanent establishment, then such royalties shall be deemed to arise in the State in which the permanent establishment is situated. Where the person paying the royalties is not a resident of either Contracting State, and the royalties are not borne by a permanent establishment in either Contracting State, but the royalties relate to the use of, or the right to use, in one of the Contracting States, any property or right described in paragraph 3, the royalties shall be deemed to arise in that State.

6. Where, by reason of a special relationship between the payer and the beneficial owner or between both of them and some other person, the amount of the royalties, having regard to the use, right, or information for which they are paid, exceeds the amount which would have been agreed upon by the payer and the beneficial owner in the absence of such relationship, the provisions of this Article shall apply only to the last-mentioned amount. In such case the excess part of the payments shall remain taxable according to the laws of each Contracting State, due regard being had to the other provisions of this Convention.

Article 13
CAPITAL GAINS

1. Gains derived by a resident of a Contracting State that are attributable to the alienation of immovable property (real property) situated in the other Contracting State may be taxed in that other State.

2. For the purposes of this Article the term "immovable property (real property) situated in the other Contracting State" shall include:

a) immovable property (real property) referred to in Article 6 (Income from Immovable Property (Real Property));

b) where that other State is the United States, a United States real property interest as defined under U.S. law; and

c) where that other State is Bulgaria,

i) shares, including rights to acquire shares, other than shares regularly traded on an established securities market, deriving more than 50 percent of their value directly or indirectly from immovable property (real property) referred to in subparagraph a) of this paragraph situated in Bulgaria; and

ii) an interest in a partnership or trust to the extent that the assets of the partnership or trust consist of immovable property (real property) situated in Bulgaria, or of shares referred to in clause i) of this subparagraph.

3. Gains from the alienation of movable property forming part of the business property of a permanent establishment which an enterprise of a Contracting State has in the other Contracting State, including such gains from the alienation of such a permanent establishment (alone or with the whole enterprise), may be taxed in that other State.

4. Gains derived by an enterprise of a Contracting State from the alienation of ships or aircraft operated or used in international traffic or movable property (personal property) pertaining to the operation or use of such ships or aircraft shall be taxable only in that State.

5. Gains derived by an enterprise of a Contracting State from the alienation of containers (including trailers and related equipment for the transport of containers) used for the transport of goods or merchandise shall be taxable only in that State, unless those containers or trailers and related equipment are used for transport solely between places within the other Contracting state.

6. Gains derived by a resident of a Contracting State from the alienation of shares of a company that is a resident of the other Contacting State may be taxed in that other State if the alienation of such shares occurs within 12 months of the date that such shares are acquired and if the recipient of the gain, at any time during the 12-month period preceding such alienation, had a participation, directly or indirectly, of at least 25 percent in the capital of that company. This paragraph, however, shall not apply with respect to the alienation of shares of stock of public companies, traded on an established securities market.

7. Gains described in paragraph 3 of Article 12 (Royalties) shall be taxable only in accordance with the provisions of Article 12 (Royalties).

8. Gains from the alienation of any property other than property referred to in paragraphs 1 through 7 shall be taxable only in the Contracting State of which the alienator is a resident.

Article 14
INCOME FROM EMPLOYMENT

1. Subject to the provisions of Articles 15 (Directors' Fees), 17 (Pensions, Social Security Payments, Annuities, Alimony, and Child Support) and 18 (Government Service), salaries, wages, and other remuneration derived by a resident of a Contracting State in respect of an employment shall be taxable only in that State unless the employment is exercised in the other Contracting State. If the employment is so exercised, such remuneration as is derived therefrom may be taxed in that other State.

2. Notwithstanding the provisions of paragraph 1, remuneration derived by a resident of a Contracting State in respect of an employment exercised in the other Contracting State shall be taxable only in the first-mentioned State if:

a) the recipient is present in the other State for a period or periods not exceeding in the aggregate 183 days in any twelve month period commencing or ending in the taxable year concerned;

b) the remuneration is paid by, or on behalf of, an employer who is not a resident of the other State; and

c) the remuneration is not borne by a permanent establishment which the employer has in the other State.

3. Notwithstanding the preceding provisions of this Article, remuneration described in paragraph 1 that is derived by a resident of a Contracting State in respect of an employment as a member of the crew of a ship or aircraft, or as other personnel regularly employed to serve aboard a ship or aircraft operated in international traffic shall be taxable only in that State.

Article 15
DIRECTORS' FEES

Directors' fees and other compensation derived by a resident of a Contracting State for services rendered in his capacity as a member of the board of directors (including the managing board or supervisory board or a functionally similar body) of a company that is a resident of the other Contracting State may be taxed in that other Contracting State.

Article 16
ENTERTAINERS AND SPORTSMEN

1. Income derived by a resident of a Contracting State as an entertainer, such as a theater, motion picture, radio, or television artiste, or a musician, or as a sportsman, from his personal activities as such exercised in the other Contracting State, which income would be exempt from tax in that other Contracting State under the provisions of Articles 7 (Business Profits) or Article 14 (Income from Employment) may be taxed in that other State, except where the amount of the gross receipts derived by such entertainer or sportsman, including expenses reimbursed to him or borne on his behalf, from such activities does not exceed fifteen thousand United States dollars ($15,000) or its equivalent in Bulgarian currency for the taxable year concerned.

2. Where income in respect of personal activities exercised by an entertainer or a sportsman in his capacity as such accrues not to the entertainer or sportsman himself but to another person, that income may, notwithstanding the provisions of Articles 7 (Business Profits) and Article 14 (Income from Employment), be taxed in the Contracting State in which the activities of the entertainer or sportsman are exercised, but only in cases in which the contract pursuant to which the personal activities are performed

a) designates (by name or description) the entertainer or sportsman; or

b) allows the other party to the contract (or a person other than the entertainer, sportsman or the person to whom the income accrues) to designate the individual who is to perform the personal activities.

Article 17
PENSIONS, SOCIAL SECURITY PAYMENTS, ANNUITIES, ALIMONY, AND CHILD SUPPORT

1. Pensions and other similar remuneration beneficially owned by a resident of a Contracting State shall be taxable only in that State.

2. Notwithstanding paragraph 1, payments made by a Contracting State under provisions of the social security or similar legislation of that State to a resident of the other Contracting State or to a citizen of the United States shall be taxable only in the first-mentioned State.

3. Annuities derived and beneficially owned by an individual resident of a Contracting State shall be taxable only in that State. The term "annuities" as used in this paragraph means a stated sum paid periodically at stated times during a specified number of years, or for life, under an obligation to make the payments in return for adequate and full consideration (other than services rendered).

4. Alimony and payments for the support of a child, paid by a resident of a Contracting State to a resident of the other Contracting State shall be taxable only in the first-mentioned Contracting State. However, such payments shall not be taxable in either Contracting State if the individual making such payments is not entitled to a deduction for such payments in computing taxable income in the Contracting State of which he is a resident. The term "alimony" as used in this Article means periodic payments, made pursuant to a written separation agreement or a decree of divorce, separate maintenance, or compulsory support.

5. Where an individual who is a resident of one of the States is a member or beneficiary of, or participant in, a pension fund that is a resident of the other State, income earned by the pension fund may be taxed as income of that individual only when, and, subject to the provisions of paragraphs 1 and 2 of this Article, to the extent that, it is paid to, or for the benefit of, that individual from the pension fund (and not transferred to another pension fund in that other State).

Article 18
GOVERNMENT SERVICE

1. Notwithstanding the provisions of Articles 14 (Income from Employment), 15 (Directors' Fees) and 16 (Entertainers and Sportsmen):

a) Salaries, wages and other remuneration, other than a pension, paid to an individual in respect of services rendered to a Contracting State or a political subdivision or local authority thereof shall, subject to the provisions of subparagraph b), be taxable only in that State;

b) such remuneration, however, shall be taxable only in the other Contracting State if the services are rendered in that State and the individual is a resident of that State who:

i) is a national of that State; or

ii) did not become a resident of that State solely for the purpose of rendering the services.

2. Notwithstanding the provisions of paragraph 1 of Article 17 (Pensions, Social Security Payments, Annuities, Alimony, and Child Support):

a) any pension paid by, or out of funds created by, a Contracting State or a political subdivision or a local authority thereof to an individual in respect of services rendered to that State or subdivision or authority (other than a payment to which paragraph 2 of Article 17 applies) shall, subject to the provisions of subparagraph b), be taxable only in that State;

b) such pension, however, shall be taxable only in the other Contracting State if the individual is a resident of, and a national of, that State.

3. The provisions of Articles 14 (Income from Employment), 15 (Directors' Fees), 16 (Entertainers and Sportsmen) and 17 (Pensions, Social Security Payments, Annuities, Alimony, and Child Support) shall apply to salaries, wages and other remuneration, and to pensions, in respect of services rendered in connection with a business carried on by a Contracting State or a political subdivision or a local authority thereof.

Article 19
STUDENTS, TRAINEES, TEACHERS AND RESEARCHERS

1. a) Payments, other than compensation for personal services, received by a student or business trainee who is, or was immediately before visiting a Contracting State, a resident of the other Contracting State, and who is present in the first-mentioned State for the purpose of his full-time education at a college, university or other recognized educational institution of a similar nature, or for his full-time training, shall not be taxed in that State, provided that such payments arise outside that-State, and are for the purpose of his maintenance, education or training. The exemption from tax provided by this paragraph shall apply to a business trainee only for a period of time not exceeding two years from the date the business trainee first arrives in the first-mentioned Contracting State for the purpose of training.

b) A student or business trainee within the meaning of subparagraph a) shall be exempt from tax by the Contracting State in which the student or trainee is temporarily present with respect to income from personal services in an aggregate amount equal to $9,000 or its equivalent in Bulgarian currency annually. The competent authorities shall, every five years, adjust the amount provided in this subparagraph.

c) For purposes of this paragraph, a business trainee is an individual:

i) who is temporarily in a Contracting State for the purpose of securing training required to qualify the individual to practice a profession or professional specialty; or

ii) who is temporarily in a Contracting State as an employee of, or under contract with, a resident of the other Contracting State, for the primary purpose of acquiring technical, professional, or business experience from a person other than

A) that resident of the other Contracting State, and

B) a person related to such resident of the other Contracting State.

2. An individual who is a resident of a Contracting State at the beginning of his visit to the other Contracting State and who is temporarily present in the other Contracting State for the purpose of

teaching or carrying on research at a school, college, university or other recognized educational or research institution shall be exempt from tax in the other Contracting State, for a period not exceeding two years from the date of the individual's arrival in that other State. This paragraph shall not apply to income from research if such research is undertaken not in the public interest but primarily for the private benefit of a specific person or persons.

Article 20
OTHER INCOME

1. Items of income beneficially owned by a resident of a Contracting State, wherever arising, not dealt with in the foregoing Articles of this Convention shall be taxable only in that State.

2. The provisions of paragraph 1 shall not apply to income, other than income from immovable property (real property) as defined in paragraph 2 of Article 6 (Income from Immovable Property (Real Property)), if the beneficial owner of the income, being a resident of a Contracting State, carries on business in the other Contracting State through a permanent establishment situated therein and the income is attributable to such permanent establishment. In such case the provisions of Article 7 (Business Profits) shall apply.

CHAPTER IV
LIMITATION ON BENEFITS

Article 21
LIMITATION ON BENEFITS

1. Except as otherwise provided in this Article, a resident of a Contracting State that derives income from the other Contracting State shall not be entitled to the benefits of this Convention otherwise accorded to residents of a Contracting State unless such resident is a "qualified person" as defined in paragraph 2.

2. A resident of a Contracting State shall be a qualified person for a taxable year if the resident is:

a) an individual;

b) a Contracting State, or a political subdivision or local authority thereof;

c) a company, if:

i) the principal class of its shares (and any disproportionate class of shares) is regularly traded on one or more recognized stock exchanges, and either

A) its principal class of shares is primarily traded on one or more recognized stock exchanges located in the Contracting State of which the company is a resident; or

B) the company's primary place of management and control is in the Contracting State of which it is a resident; or

ii) at least 50 percent of the aggregate vote and value of the shares (and at least 50 percent of any disproportionate class of shares) in the company is owned directly or indirectly by five or fewer companies entitled to benefits under clause i) of this subparagraph, provided that, in the case of indirect ownership, each intermediate owner is a resident of either Contracting State;

d) a person described in paragraph 2 of Article 4 of this Convention, provided that, in the case of a person described in subparagraph a) of that paragraph, more than 50 percent of the person's beneficiaries, members or participants are individuals resident in either Contracting State, or

e) a person other than an individual, if:

i) on at least half the days of the taxable year, persons who are residents of that Contracting State and that are entitled to the benefits of this Convention under subparagraphs a), b), c) i) or d) own, directly or indirectly, shares or other beneficial interests representing al least 50 percent of the aggregate voting power and value (and at least 50 percent of any disproportionate class of shares) of the person, provided that, in the case of indirect ownership, each intermediate owner is a resident of that Contracting State, and

ii) less than 50 percent of the person's gross income for the taxable year, as determined in that person's State of residence, is paid or accrued, directly or indirectly, to persons who are not residents of either Contracting State entitled to the benefits of this Convention under subparagraph a), subparagraph b), clause i), of subparagraph c), or subparagraph d) of this paragraph in the form of payments that are deductible for purposes of the taxes covered by this Convention in the persons State of residence (but not including arm's length payments in the ordinary course of business for services or tangible property).

3. A company that is a resident of a Contracting State shall also be entitled to the benefits of the Convention if:

a) at least 95 percent of the aggregate voting power and value of its shares (and at least 50 percent of any disproportionate class of shares) is owned, directly or indirectly, by seven or fewer persons that are equivalent beneficiaries; and

b) less than 50 percent of the company's gross income, as determined in the company's State of residence, for the taxable year is paid or accrued, directly or indirectly, to persons who are not equivalent beneficiaries, in the form of payments (but not including arm's length payments in the ordinary course of business for services or tangible property), that are deductible for the purposes of the taxes covered by this Convention in the company's State of residence.

4. a) A resident of a Contracting State will be entitled to benefits of the Convention with respect to an item of income derived from the other State, regardless of whether the resident is a qualified person, if the resident is engaged in the active conduct of a trade or business in the first-mentioned State (other than the business of making or managing investments for the resident's own account, unless these activities are banking, insurance or securities activities carried on by a bank, insurance company or registered securities dealer), and the income derived from the other Contracting State is derived in connection with, or is incidental to, that trade or business.

b) If a resident of a Contracting State derives an item of income from a trade or business activity in the other Contracting State, or derives an item of income arising in the other Contracting State from a related person, the conditions described in subparagraph a) shall be considered to be satisfied with respect to such item only if the trade or business activity carried on by the resident in the first-mentioned Contracting State is substantial in relation to the trade or business activity carried on by the resident or such person in the other Contracting State. Whether a trade or business activity is substantial for the purposes of this paragraph will be determined based on all the facts and circumstances.

c) In determining whether a person is "engaged in the active conduct of a trade or business" in a Contracting State under subparagraph a) of this paragraph, activities conducted by persons connected to such person shall be deemed to be conducted by such person. For the purposes of this subparagraph, a person shall be connected to another if one possesses at least 50 percent of the beneficial interest in the other (or, in the case of a company, at least 50 percent of the aggregate vote and value of the company's shares or of the beneficial equity interest in the company) or another person possesses, directly or indirectly, at least 50 percent of the beneficial interest (or, in the case of a company, at least 50 percent of the aggregate vote and value of the company's shares or of the beneficial equity interest in the company) in each person. In any case, for the purposes of this subparagraph, a person shall be considered to be connected to another if, based on all the relevant facts and circumstances, one has control of the other or both are under the control of the same person or persons.

5. A resident of a Contracting State that is neither a qualified person pursuant to the provisions of paragraph 2 nor entitled to benefits under paragraph 3 or, with respect to an item of income, under paragraph 4 of this Article shall, nevertheless, be granted benefits of the Convention if the competent authority of the other Contracting State determines that the establishment, acquisition or maintenance of such person and the conduct of its operations did not have as one of its principal purposes the obtaining of benefits under the Convention.

6. For purposes of this Article:

a) the term "recognized stock exchange" means:

i) the NASDAQ System owned by the National Association of Securities Dealers, Inc. and any stock exchange registered with the U.S. Securities and Exchange Commission as a national securities exchange under the U.S. Securities Exchange Act of 1934:

ii) the Bulgarian Stock Exchange – Sofia, and any other stock exchange licensed to trade securities and financial instruments under the Bulgarian law;

iii) any other stock exchange agreed upon by the competent authorities;

b) the term "principal class of shares" means the ordinary or common shares of the company, provided that such class of shares represents the majority of the voting power and value of the company. If no single class of ordinary or common shares represents the majority of the aggregate voting power and value of the company, the "principal class of shares" are those classes that in the aggregate represent a majority of the aggregate voting power and value of the company;

c) the term "disproportionate class of shares" means any class of shares of a company resident in one of the Contracting States that entitles the shareholder to disproportionately higher participation, through dividends, redemption payments or otherwise, in the earnings generated in the other State by particular assets or activities of the company;

d) a company's "primary place of management and control" will be in the Contracting State of which it is a resident only if executive officers and senior management employees exercise day-to-day responsibility for more of the strategic, financial and operational policy decision making for the company (including its direct and indirect subsidiaries) in that State than in any other state and the staff of such persons conducts more of the day-to-day activities necessary for preparing and making those decisions in that State than in any other state;

e) an "equivalent beneficiary" is a resident of a member state of the European Union or of a European Economic Area State or of a party to the North American Free Trade Agreement but only if that resident:

i) A) would be entitled to all the benefits of a comprehensive convention for the avoidance of double taxation between any member state of the European Union or European Economic Area State or any party to the North American Free Trade Agreement and the State from which benefits of this Convention are claimed under provisions analogous to subparagraph a), b), clause i) of subparagraph c) or subparagraph d) of paragraph 2 of this Article, provided that if such convention does not contain a comprehensive limitation on benefits article, the person would be a qualified person under subparagraph a), b), clause i) of subparagraph c) or subparagraph d) of paragraph 2 of this Article if such person were a resident of one of the states under Article 4 (Resident) of this Convention;

B) with respect to income referred to in Article 10 (Dividends), 11 (Interest), or 12 (Royalties) of this Convention, would be entitled under such convention to a rate of tax with respect to the particular class of income for which benefits are being claimed under this Convention that is at least as low as the rate applicable under this Convention; or

ii) is a resident of one of the Contracting States and is a qualified person by reason of subparagraph a), b), clause i) of subparagraph c) or subparagraph d) of paragraph 2 of this Article;

f) with respect to dividends, interest or royalties arising in Bulgaria and beneficially owned by a company that is a resident of the United States, a company that is a resident of a member state of the European Union will be treated as satisfying the requirements of subparagraph c) i) B) of this paragraph for purposes of determining whether such United States resident is entitled to benefits under this paragraph if a payment of dividends, interest or royalties arising in Bulgaria and paid directly to such resident of a member state of the European Union would have been exempt from tax pursuant to any directive of the European Union, notwithstanding that the income tax convention between Bulgaria and that other member state of the European Union would provide for a higher rate of tax with respect to such payment then the rate of tax applicable to such United States company under Article 10 (Dividends), 11 (Interest), or 12 (Royalties) of this Convention;

g) with respect to paragraph 2, the shares in a class of shares are considered to be regularly traded on one or more recognized stock exchanges in a taxable year if the aggregate number of shares of that class traded on such stock exchange or exchanges during the twelve months ending on the day before the beginning of that taxable year is at least six percent of the average number of shares outstanding in that class during the twelve-month period.

CHAPTER V
RELIEF FROM DOUBLE TAXATION

Article 22
RELIEF FROM DOUBLE TAXATION

1. In the case of Bulgaria, double taxation will be relieved as follows;

a) where a resident of Bulgaria derives income which in accordance with the provisions of this Convention may be taxed in the United States, Bulgaria shall, subject to the provisions of subparagraphs (b) and (c) of this paragraph, exempt such income from tax;

b) where a resident of Bulgaria derives dividends, interest or royalties which in accordance with the provisions of Articles 10 (Dividends), 11 (Interest)or 12(Royalties)of this Convention may be taxed in the United States, Bulgaria shall allow as a deduction from the tax on the dividends, interest or royalties of that resident an amount equal to the tax paid in the United States. Such deduction shall not, however, exceed that part of the tax, as computed before the deduction is given, which is attributable to such dividends, interest or royalties derived from the United States;

c) where in accordance with any provision of this Convention income derived by a resident of Bulgaria is exempt from tax in Bulgaria, Bulgaria may nevertheless, in calculating the amount of the tax on the remaining income of such resident, take into account the exempted income.

2. In accordance with the provisions and subject to the limitations of the law of the United States (as it may be amended from time to time without changing the general principle hereof), the United States shall allow to a resident or citizen of the United States as a credit against the United States tax on income;

a) the income tax paid or accrued to Bulgaria by or on behalf of such resident or citizen; and

b) in the case of a United States company owning at least 10 percent of the voting stock of a company that is a resident of Bulgaria and from which the United States company receives dividends, the income tax paid or accrued to Bulgaria by or on behalf of the payer with respect to the profits out of which the dividends are paid.

For the purposes of this paragraph, the taxes referred to in paragraphs 3 a) i) and ii) and 4 of Article 2 (Taxes Covered) shall be considered income taxes.

3. For the purposes of applying paragraph 2 of this Article, an item of gross income, as determined under the laws of the United States, derived by a resident of the United States that, under this Convention, may be taxed in Bulgaria shall be deemed to be income from sources in Bulgaria.

4. For the purposes of applying the preceding paragraphs of this Article, where the United States taxes, in accordance with paragraph 4 of Article 1 (General Scope), a citizen, or a former citizen or long-term resident, of the United States who is a resident of Bulgaria:

a) Bulgaria shall take into account for the purposes of computing the credit to be allowed under paragraph 1 only the amount of tax, if any, that the United States may impose on income under the provisions of this Convention that is derived by a resident of Bulgaria who is neither a citizen, nor a former citizen nor long-term resident, of the United States;

b) for purposes of computing the United States tax on income referred to in subparagraph a), the United States shall allow as a credit against the United States tax the Bulgarian tax after the credit referred to in that subparagraph; the credit so allowed shall not reduce the portion of the United States tax that is creditable against the Bulgarian tax in accordance with that subparagraph; and

c) for the exclusive purpose of allowing the credit by the United States provided for under subparagraph b), income referred to in subparagraph a) shall be deemed to arise in Bulgaria to the extent necessary to allow the United States to grant the credit provided for in subparagraph b).

CHAPTER VI
SPECIAL PROVISIONS

Article 23
NON-DISCRIMINATION

1. Nationals of a Contracting State shall not be subjected in the other Contracting State to any taxation or any requirement connected therewith that is more burdensome than the taxation and connected requirements to which nationals of that other State in the same circumstances, in particular with respect to residence, are or may be subjected. This provision shall also apply to persons who are not residents of one or both of the Contracting States. However, for the purposes of United States taxation, United States nationals who are subject to tax on a worldwide basis are not in the same circumstances as nationals of Bulgaria who are not residents of the United States.

2. The taxation on a permanent establishment that an enterprise of a Contracting State has in the other Contracting State shall not he less favorably levied in that other State than the taxation levied on enterprises of that other State carrying on the same activities.

3. The provisions of paragraphs 1 and 2 shall not be construed as obliging a Contracting State to grant to residents of the other Contracting State any personal allowances, reliefs, and reductions for taxation purposes on account of civil status or family responsibilities that it grants to its own residents.

4. Except where the provisions of paragraph 1 of Article 9 (Associated Enterprises), paragraph 7 of Article 11 (Interest), or paragraph 6 of Article 12 (Royalties) apply, interest, royalties, and other disbursements paid by a resident of a Contracting State to a resident of the other Contracting State shall, for the purpose of determining the taxable profits of the first-mentioned resident, be deductible under the same conditions as if they had been paid to a resident of the first-mentioned State. Similarly, any debts of a resident of a Contracting State to a resident of the other Contracting State shall, for the purpose of determining the taxable capital of the first-mentioned resident, be deductible under the same conditions as if they had been contracted to a resident of the first-mentioned State.

5. Enterprises of a Contracting State, the capital of which is wholly or partly owned or controlled, directly or indirectly, by one or more residents of the other Contracting State, shall not be subjected in the first-mentioned State to any taxation or any requirement connected therewith that is more burdensome than the taxation and connected requirements to which other similar enterprises of the first-mentioned State are or may be subjected.

6. Nothing in this Article shall be construed as preventing either Contracting State from imposing a tax as described in paragraph 8 of Article 10 (Dividends) or paragraph 9 of Article 11 (Interest).

7. The provisions of this Article shall, notwithstanding the provisions of Article 2 (Taxes Covered), apply to taxes of every kind and description imposed by a Contracting State or a political subdivision or local authority thereof.

Article 24
MUTUAL AGREEMENT PROCEDURE

1. Where a person considers that the actions of one or both of the Contracting States result or will result for such person in taxation not in accordance with the provisions of this Convention, it may, irrespective of the remedies provided by the domestic law of those States, and the time limits prescribed in such laws for presenting claims for refund, present its case to the competent authority of either Contracting State.

2. The competent authority shall endeavor, if the objection appears to it to be justified and if it is not itself able to arrive at a satisfactory solution, to resolve the case by mutual agreement with the competent authority of the other Contracting State, with a view to the avoidance of taxation which is not in accordance with the Convention. Any agreement reached shall be implemented notwithstanding any time limits or other procedural limitations in the domestic law of the Contracting States.

3. The competent authorities of the Contracting States shall endeavor to resolve by mutual agreement any difficulties or doubts arising as to the interpretation or application of the Convention. They also may consult together for the elimination of double taxation in cases not provided for in the Convention. In particular the competent authorities of the Contracting States may agree:

a) to the same attribution of income, deductions, credits, or allowances of an enterprise of a Contracting State to its permanent establishment situated in the other Contracting State;

b) to the same allocation of income, deductions, credits, or allowances between persons;

c) to the same characterization of particular items of income;

d) to the same characterization of persons;

e) to the same application of source rules with respect to particular items of income;

f) to a common meaning of a term; and

g) to advance pricing arrangements.

4. The competent authorities also may agree to increases in any specific dollar amounts; referred to in the Convention to reflect economic or monetary developments.

5. The competent authorities of the Contracting States may communicate with each other directly for the purpose of reaching an agreement in the sense of the preceding paragraphs.

Article 25
EXCHANGE OF INFORMATION AND ADMINISTRATIVE ASSISTANCE

1. The competent authorities of the Contracting States shall exchange such information as may be relevant for carrying out the provisions of this Convention or of the domestic laws of the Contracting States concerning taxes of every kind imposed by a Contracting State insofar as the taxation thereunder is not contrary to the Convention, including information relating to the assessment or collection of, the enforcement or prosecution in respect of, or the determination of appeals in relation to, the taxes covered by the Convention. The exchange of information is not restricted by paragraph 1 of Article 1 (General Scope) or Article 2 (Taxes Covered).

2. If specifically requested by the competent authority of a Contracting State, the competent authority of the other Contracting State shall provide information under this Article in the form of depositions of witnesses and authenticated copies of unedited original documents (including books, papers, statements, records, accounts, and writings).

3. Any information received under this Article by a Contracting State shall be treated as secret in the same manner as information obtained under the domestic laws of that State and shall be disclosed only to persons or authorities (including courts and administrative bodies) involved in the assessment, collection, or administration of, the enforcement or prosecution in respect of, or the determination of appeals in relation to, the taxes referred to above, or the oversight of the above. Such persons or authorities shall use the information only for such purposes. They may disclose the information in public court proceedings or in judicial decisions.

4. In no case shall the provisions of the preceding paragraphs be construed so as to impose on a Contracting State the obligation:

a) to carry out administrative measures at variance with the laws and administrative practice of that or of the other Contracting State;

b) to supply information that is not obtainable under the laws or in the normal course of the administration of that or of the other Contracting State;

c) to supply information that would disclose any trade, business, industrial, commercial, or professional secret or trade process, or information the disclosure of which would be contrary to public policy (ordre public).

5. If information is requested by a Contracting State in accordance with this Article, the other Contracting State shall use its information gathering measures to obtain the requested information, even though that other State may not need such information for its own purposes. The obligation contained in the preceding sentence is subject to the limitations of paragraph 4 but in no case shall such limitation be construed to permit a Contracting State to decline to supply information because it has no domestic interest in such information.

6. In no case shall the provisions of paragraph 4 be construed to permit a Contracting State to decline to supply information because the information is held by a bank, other financial institution, nominee or person acting in an agency or fiduciary capacity or because it relates to ownership interests in a person.

Article 26
MEMBERS OF DIPLOMATIC MISSIONS AND CONSULAR POSTS

Nothing in this Convention shall affect the fiscal privileges of members of diplomatic missions or consular posts under the general rules of international law or under the provisions of special agreements.

CHAPTER VII
FINAL PROVISIONS

Article 27
ENTRY INTO FORCE

1. The Contracting States shall notify each other, through diplomatic channels, when their respective requirements for the entry into force of this Convention have been satisfied. This Convention shall enter into force on the date of receipt of the later of these notifications.

2. The provisions of the Convention shall have effect in both Contracting States:

a) in respect of taxes withheld at source, on income paid or credited on or after the first day of January in the calendar year next following the year in which this Convention enters into force;

b) in respect of other taxes on income, for any taxable period beginning on or after the first day of January in the calendar year next following the year in which this Convention enters into force.

Article 28
TERMINATION

1. This Convention shall remain in force indefinitely but either of the Contracting States may terminate the Convention through the diplomatic channel, by giving to the other Contracting State written notice of termination not later than June 30th of any calendar year.

2. In such event the Convention shall cease to have effect in both Contracting States:

a) in respect of taxes withheld at source, on income paid or credited on or after the first day of January in the calendar year next following the year in which the notice has been given;

b) in respect of other taxes on income, for any taxable period beginning on or after the first day of January in the calendar year next following the year in which the notice has been given.

IN WITNESS WHEREOF, the undersigned, being duly authorized thereto by their respective Governments, have signed this Convention.

DONE at Washington in duplicate, in the English and Bulgarian languages, both texts being equally authentic, this twenty-third day of February, 2007.

FOR THE GOVERNMENT OF THE UNITED STATES OF AMERICA:

[Signature]

FOR THE GOVERNMENT OF THE REPUBLIC OF BULGARIA:

[Signature]

Protocol

At the signing of the Convention concluded today between the Government of the United States of America and the Government of the Republic of Bulgaria for the Avoidance of Double Taxation and the Prevention of Fiscal Evasion with Respect to Taxes on Income (hereinafter referred to as the "the Convention"), the undersigned have agreed upon the following additional provisions which shall form an integral part of the Convention.

1. With respect to paragraph 4 of Article I (General Scope)

The term "long-term resident" as used in subparagraph b) shall mean any individual who is a lawful permanent resident of the United States in eight or more taxable years during the preceding 15 taxable years. In determining whether the threshold in the preceding sentence is met, there shall not count any year in which the individual is treated as a resident of Bulgaria under this Convention, or as a resident of any country other than the United States under the provisions of any other tax treaty of the United States, and, in either case, the individual does not waive the benefits of such treaty applicable to residents of the other country.

2. With respect to paragraph 3 of Article 2 (Taxes Covered)

The personal income tax and corporate income tax referred to in subparagraph a) i) and ii) include the patent tax.

3. With respect to paragraph 1 of Article 3 (General Definitions)

The term "any other body of persons" as used in subparagraph d) includes an estate, trust, and partnership.

4. With respect to Article 4 (Resident)

A company that is or would be a resident of a Contracting State pursuant to that State's domestic law will not be treated as a resident of that State for purposes of the Convention if it is treated as a resident of a third state pursuant to an income tax convention between that State and the third state.

A person who is liable to lax in respect only of profits attributable to a permanent establishment in a Contracting State is not liable to tax therein by reason of domicile, residence, citizenship, place of management, place of incorporation or a criterion of a similar nature.

5. With respect to Article 7 (Business Profits)

For this purpose, the business profits to be attributed to the permanent establishment shall include only the business profits derived from the assets used, risks assumed and activities performed by the permanent establishment.

The principles of the OECD Transfer Pricing Guidelines will apply for purposes of determining the profits attributable to a permanent establishment, taking into account the different economic and legal circumstances of a single entity. Accordingly, any of the methods described therein as acceptable methods for determining an arm's length result may be used to determine the income of a permanent establishment so long as those methods are applied in accordance with the Guidelines. In determining the amount of business profits attributable to a permanent establishment, the permanent establishment shall be treated as having the same amount of capital that it would need to support its activities if it were a distinct and separate enterprise engaged in the same or similar activities. With respect to financial institutions other than insurance companies, a Contracting State may determine the amount of capital to be attributed to a permanent establishment by allocating the institution's total equity between its various offices on the basis of the proportion of the financial institution's risk-weighted assets attributable to each of them. In the case of an insurance company, there shall be attributed to a permanent establishment not only premiums earned through the permanent establishment, but that portion of the insurance company's overall investment income from reserves and surplus that supports the risks assumed by the permanent establishment.

In applying Article 7, paragraph 4 of Article 6 (Income from Immovable Property (Real Property)), paragraph 6 of Article 10 (Dividends), paragraph 5 of Article 11 (Interest), paragraph 4 of Article 12 (Royalties), paragraph 3 of Article 13 (Capital Gains) and paragraph 2 of Article 20 (Other Income), any income or gain attributable to a permanent establishment during its existence is taxable in the Contracting State where such permanent establishment is situated even if the payments are deferred until such permanent establishment has ceased to exist.

6. With respect to Article 8 (International Traffic)

Profits derived by an enterprise from the transport of tangible property or passengers within either Contracting State shall be treated as profits from the operation of ships or aircraft in international traffic if such transport is undertaken as part of international traffic.

7. With respect to Articles 11 (Interest) and 12 (Royalties)

The Convention permits positive rates of taxation on interest and royalties. With respect to interest and royalties deemed to arise in Bulgaria where the beneficial owner of the income is a resident of the United States under the Convention, the Contracting States agree to reconsider the provisions of Articles 11 and 12 at an appropriate time, consistent with the conclusion of the transition period applicable to interest and royalties deemed to arise in Bulgaria that are beneficially owned by a resident of the European Union pursuant to Council Directive 2003/49/EC of 3 June 2003 on a common system of taxation applicable to interest and royalty payments made between associated companies of different Member States.

8. With respect to paragraph 3 of Article 11 (Interest)

The term "back to back loan" as used in subparagraph c) means a loan structured to obtain the benefits of subparagraph c) in which the loan is made to a financial institution that in turn lends the funds directly to the intended borrower.

9. With respect to paragraph 2 c) and paragraph 6 of Article 13 (Capital Gains)

The term "established securities market" means a national securities exchange which is officially recognised, sanctioned, or supervised by a governmental authority as well as an over the counter market. An over the counter market is any market reflected by the existence of an interdealer quotation system. An interdealer quotation system is any system of general circulation to brokers and dealers which regularly disseminates quotations of stocks and securities by identified brokers or dealers, other than by quotation sheets which are prepared and distributed by a broker or dealer in the regular course of business and which contain only quotations of such broker or dealer.

10. With respect to paragraph 2 of Article 24 (Mutual Agreement Procedure)

An agreement reached would not affect any court proceedings or any final court decisions or final tax assessment acts, unless, in the case of final court decisions or final tax assessment acts, the requirements under Bulgarian law for revision or repeal of final acts are fulfilled.

If an examination is completed and closed (and is not a matter pending before a court or for which a settlement or court decision has been reached) in a Contracting State, that Contracting State's competent authority may nonetheless accept a request for assistance if an adjustment causing double taxation is made in the other Contracting State.

11. With respect to Article 27 (Entry into Force)

The provisions of Article 25 (Exchange of Information and Administrative Assistance) shall have effect from the date of entry into force of the Convention without regard to the taxable period to which the matter relates.

IN WITNESS WHEREOF, the undersigned, being duly authorized thereto by their respective Governments, have signed this Protocol.

DONE at Washington in duplicate, in the English and Bulgarian languages, both texts being equally authentic, this twenty-third day of February, 2007.

FOR THE GOVERNMENT OF THE UNITED STATES OF AMERICA:

[Signature]

FOR THE GOVERNMENT OF THE REPUBLIC OF BULGARIA:

[Signature]

STATE DEPARTMENT DOCUMENT NUMBER: 110-18 (SECOND PART)

PROTOCOL AMENDING THE CONVENTION BETWEEN THE UNITED STATES OF AMERICA AND THE REPUBLIC OF BULGARIA FOR THE AVOIDANCE OF DOUBLE TAXATION AND THE PREVENTION OF FISCAL EVASION WITH RESPECT TO TAXES ON INCOME

SIGNED AT SOFIA, FEBRUARY 26, 2008
APPROVED BY THE U.S. SENATE ON SEPTEMBER 23, 2008

CTIA DOCUMENT NUMBER: 16901.001

The Government of the United States of America and the Government of the Republic of Bulgaria, desiring to amend the Convention Between the Government of the United States of America and the Government of the Republic of Bulgaria for the Avoidance of Double Taxation and the Prevention of Fiscal Evasion with Respect to Taxes on Income, signed at Washington on February 23, 2007 (hereinafter referred to as "the Convention").

Have agreed as follows:

ARTICLE I

With respect to Article I (General Scope), subparagraph a) of paragraph 5 shall be amended to read as follows:

"5. The provisions of paragraph 4 shall not affect:

a) the benefits conferred by a Contracting State under paragraph 2 of Article 9 (Associated Enterprises), paragraphs 2 and 5 of Article 17 (Pensions, Social Security Payments, Annuities, Alimony, and Child Support), and Articles 22 (Relief From Double Taxation), 23 (Non-Discrimination), and 24 (Mutual Agreement Procedure); and"

ARTICLE II

With respect to Article II (Interest), paragraph 8, the reference to "paragraph 1" shall be changed to "paragraphs 2 and 3" as follows:

"8. Notwithstanding the provisions of paragraphs 2 and 3:"

ARTICLE III

With respect to Article 19 (Students, Trainees, Teachers and Researchers), paragraph 2 shall be amended to read as follows:

"2. An individual who is a resident of a Contracting State at the beginning of his visit to the other Contracting State and who is temporarily present in the other Contracting State for the purpose of teaching or carrying on research at a school, college, university or other recognized educational or research institution shall be exempt from tax in the other Contracting State, for a period not exceeding two years from the date of the individual's arrival in that other State on the remuneration received in consideration of teaching or carrying on research. This paragraph shall not apply to income from research if such research is undertaken not in the public interest but primarily for the private benefit of a specific person or persons."

ARTICLE IV

With respect to Article 21 (Limitation on Benefits), paragraphs 5 and 6 shall be renumbered as paragraphs 6 and 7, respectively, and a new paragraph 5 shall be added to read us follows:

"5. Notwithstanding the preceding provisions of this Article, where an enterprise of Bulgaria derives interest, or royalties from the United States, and the income consisting of such interest, or royalties is exempt from taxation in Bulgaria because it is attributable to a permanent establishment which that enterprise has in a third state, the tax benefits that would otherwise apply under the other provisions of the Convention will not apply to such income if the tax that is actually paid with respect to such income in the third state is less than 60 percent of the tax that would have been payable in Bulgaria if the income were earned in Bulgaria by the enterprise and were not attributable to the permanent establishment in the third state. Any interest or royalties to which the provisions of this paragraph apply may be taxed in the United States at a rate that shall not exceed 15 percent of the gross amount thereof. The provisions of this paragraph shall not apply if:

a) in the case of interest, as defined in Article 11 (Interest), the income from the United States is derived in connection with, or is incidental to, the active conduct of a trade or business carried on by the permanent establishment in the third state (other than the business of making, managing, or simply holding investments for the enterprise's own account, unless these activities are banking, or securities activities carried on by a bank, or registered securities dealer); or

b) in the case of royalties, as defined in Article 12 (Royalties), the royalties are received as compensation for the use of, or the right to use, intangible property produced or developed by the permanent establishment itself."

ARTICLE V

1. This Protocol shall enter into force on the date of entry into force of the Convention.

IN WITNESS WHEREOF, the undersigned, being duly authorized thereto by their respective Governments, have signed this Protocol.

DONE at Sofia, in duplicate, this 26th day of February, 2008, in the English and Bulgarian languages, both texts being equally authentic.

[Signature]

FOR THE GOVERNMENT OF THE UNITED STATES OF AMERICA:

[Signature]

FOR THE GOVERNMENT OF THE REPUBLIC OF BULGARIA:

SENATE TREATY DOCUMENT NUMBER: 110-19

INTERNATIONAL TREATY ON PLANT GENETIC RESOURCES FOR FOOD AND AGRICULTURE, WITH ANNEXES. ADOPTED BY THE FOOD AND AGRICULTURE ORGANIZATION OF THE UNITED NATIONS ON NOVEMBER 3, 2001

SIGNED BY THE UNITED STATES OF AMERICA ON NOVEMBER 1, 2002
ENTERED INTO FORCE (BUT NOT FOR THE U.S.) ON JUNE 29, 2004

CTIA DOCUMENT NUMBER: 10785.000

LETTER OF TRANSMITTAL

THE WHITE HOUSE, *July 7, 2008*

To the Senate of the United States:

I transmit herewith for advice and consent of the Senate to ratification the International Treaty on Plant Genetic Resources for Food and Agriculture, adopted by the Food and Agriculture Organization of the United Nations on November 3, 2001, and signed by the United States on November 1, 2002 (the "Treaty"). The Treaty entered into force in June 2004.

The centerpiece of the Treaty is the establishment of a multilateral system under which a party provides access to other parties, upon request, to listed plant genetic resources held in national genebanks. These resources are to be used solely for purposes of research, breeding, and training in agriculture. A recipient of such a resource must then share the benefits from its use, e.g., a recipient who commercializes a product containing an accessed plant genetic resource must generally pay a percentage of any gross sales into a trust account.

Transfers under the multilateral system are to be accompanied by a standard material transfer agreement, the current version of which was concluded in June 2006.

Provision of plant genetic resources from U.S. genebanks is fully consistent with the Department of Agriculture's long-standing general practice of providing access to such plant genetic resources upon request. Ratification of the Treaty will provide U.S. agricultural interests with similar access to other parties' genebanks, thus helping U.S. farmers and researchers sustain and improve their crops and promote food security.

The Treaty may be implemented under existing U.S. authorities.

I also transmit, for the information of the Senate, the report of the Department of State concerning the Treaty, which contains an understanding regarding Article 12.

George W. Bush

LETTER OF SUBMITTAL

Department of State,
Washington, February 11, 2008

The President,
The White House

THE PRESIDENT: I have the honor to submit to you, with a view to its transmittal to the Senate for advice and consent to ratification, the International Treaty on Plant Genetic Resources for Food and Agriculture, adopted by the Conference of the Food and Agriculture Organization of the United Nations on November 3, 2001 (the "Treaty"), and signed by the United States on November 1, 2002.

The Treaty establishes a system of access to plant genetic resources held in a Party's national gene banks with concomitant sharing of benefits by the recipient arising from their use. It also commits Parties to promote the conservation and sustainable use of plant genetic resources integral to global food security. Throughout the complex negotiations, the United States was firmly committed to creating a system that promotes U.S. and global food security and protects U.S. access to genetic resources held outside of our borders.

All interested agencies in the Executive Branch favor ratification of the Treaty, which can be implemented under existing authorities. I recommend, therefore, that the Treaty be transmitted to the Senate as soon as possible for its advice and consent to ratification.

Respectfully submitted

Condoleezza Rice

Enclosures: As stated

INTERNATIONAL TREATY ON PLANT GENETIC RESOURCES FOR FOOD AND AGRICULTURE

PREAMBLE

The Contracting Parties,

Convinced of the special nature of plant genetic resources for food and agriculture, their distinctive features and problems needing distinctive solutions;

Alarmed by the continuing erosion of these resources;

Cognizant that plant genetic resources for food and agriculture are a common concern of all countries, in that all countries depend very largely on plant genetic resources for food and agriculture that originated elsewhere;

Acknowledging that the conservation, exploration, collection, characterization, evaluation and documentation of plant genetic resources for food and agriculture are essential in meeting the goals of the Rome Declaration on World Food Security and the World Food Summit Plan of Action and for sustainable agricultural development for this and future generations, and that the capacity of developing countries and countries with economies in transition to undertake such tasks needs urgently to be reinforced;

Noting that the Global Plan of Action for the Conservation and Sustainable Use of Plant Genetic Resources for Food and Agriculture is an internationally agreed framework for such activities;

Acknowledging further that plant genetic resources for food and agriculture are the raw material indispensable for crop genetic improvement, whether by means of farmers' selection, classical plant breeding or modern biotechnologies, and are essential in adapting to unpredictable environmental changes and future human needs;

Affirming that the past, present and future contributions of farmers in all regions of the world, particularly those in centres of origin and diversity, in conserving, improving and making available these resources, is the basis of Farmers' Rights;

Affirming also that the rights recognized in this Treaty to save, use, exchange and sell farm-saved seed and other propagating material, and to participate in decision-making regarding, and in the fair and equitable sharing of the benefits arising from, the use of plant genetic resources for food and agriculture, are fundamental to the realization of Farmers' Rights, as well as the promotion of Farmers' Rights at national and international levels;

Recognizing that this Treaty and other international agreements relevant to this Treaty should be mutually supportive with a view to sustainable agriculture and food security;

Affirming that nothing in this Treaty shall be interpreted as implying in any way a change in the rights and obligations of the Contracting Parties under other international agreements;

Understanding that the above recital is not intended to create a hierarchy between this Treaty and other international agreements;

Aware that questions regarding the management of plant genetic resources for food and agriculture are at the meeting point between agriculture, the environment and commerce, and convinced that there should be synergy among these sectors;

Aware of their responsibility to past and future generations to conserve the World's diversity of plant genetic resources for food and agriculture;

Recognizing that, in the exercise of their sovereign rights over their plant genetic resources for food and agriculture, states may mutually benefit from the creation of an effective multilateral system for facilitated access to a negotiated selection of these resources and for the fair and equitable sharing of the benefits arising from their use; and

Desiring to conclude an international agreement within the framework of the Food and Agriculture Organization of the United Nations, hereinafter referred to as FAO, under Article XIV of the FAO Constitution;

Have agreed as follows:

PART I – INTRODUCTION

Article 1 – Objectives

1.1 The objectives of this Treaty are the conservation and sustainable use of plant genetic resources for food and agriculture and the fair and equitable sharing of the benefits arising out of their use, in harmony with the Convention on Biological Diversity, for sustainable agriculture and food security.

1.2 These objectives will be attained by closely linking this Treaty to the Food and Agriculture Organization of the United Nations and to the Convention on Biological Diversity.

Article 2 – Use of terms

For the purpose of this Treaty, the following terms shall have the meanings hereunder assigned to them. These definitions are not intended to cover trade in commodities:

"*In situ* conservation" means the conservation of ecosystems and natural habitats and the maintenance and recovery of viable populations of species in their natural surroundings and, in the case of domesticated or cultivated plant species, in the surroundings where they have developed their distinctive properties.

"*Ex situ* conservation" means the conservation of plant genetic resources for food and agriculture outside their natural habitat.

"Plant genetic resources for food and agriculture" means any genetic material of plant origin of actual or potential value for food and agriculture.

"Genetic material" means any material of plant origin, including reproductive and vegetative propagating material, containing functional units of heredity.

"Variety" means a plant grouping, within a single botanical taxon of the lowest known rank, defined by the reproducible expression of its distinguishing and other genetic characteristics.

"*Ex situ* collection" means a collection of plant genetic resources for food and agriculture maintained outside their natural habitat.

"Centre of origin" means a geographical area where a plant species, either domesticated or wild, first developed its distinctive properties.

"Centre of crop diversity" means a geographic area containing a high level of genetic diversity for crop species in *in situ* conditions.

Article 3 – Scope

This Treaty relates to plant genetic resources for food and agriculture.

PART II – GENERAL PROVISIONS

Article 4 – General Obligations

Each Contracting Party shall ensure the conformity of its laws, regulations and procedures with its obligations as provided in this Treaty.

Article 5 – Conservation, Exploration, Collection, Characterization, Evaluation and Documentation of Plant Genetic Resources for Food and Agriculture

5.1 Each Contracting Party shall, subject to national legislation, and in cooperation with other Contracting Parties where appropriate, promote an integrated approach to the exploration, conservation and sustainable use of plant genetic resources for food and agriculture and shall in particular, as appropriate:

(a) Survey and inventory plant genetic resources for food and agriculture, taking into account the status and degree of variation in existing populations, including those that are of potential use and, as feasible, assess any threats to them;

(b) Promote the collection of plant genetic resources for food and agriculture and relevant associated information on those plant genetic resources that are under threat or are of potential use;

(c) Promote or support, as appropriate, farmers and local communities' efforts to manage and conserve on-farm their plant genetic resources for food and agriculture;

(d) Promote *in situ* conservation of wild crop relatives and wild plants for food production, including in protected areas, by supporting, *inter alia*, the efforts of indigenous and local communities;

(e) Cooperate to promote the development of an efficient and sustainable system of *ex situ* conservation, giving due attention to the need for adequate documentation, characterization, regeneration and evaluation, and promote the development and transfer of appropriate technologies for this purpose with a view to improving the sustainable use of plant genetic resources for food and agriculture;

(f) Monitor the maintenance of the viability, degree of variation, and the genetic integrity of collections of plant genetic resources for food and agriculture.

5.2 The Contracting Parties shall, as appropriate, take steps to minimize or, if possible, eliminate threats to plant genetic resources for food and agriculture.

Article 6 – Sustainable Use of Plant Genetic Resources

6.1 The Contracting Parties shall develop and maintain appropriate policy and legal measures that promote the sustainable use of plant genetic resources for food and agriculture.

6.2 The sustainable use of plant genetic resources for food and agriculture may include such measures as:

(a) pursuing fair agricultural policies that promote, as appropriate, the development and maintenance of diverse farming systems that enhance the sustainable use of agricultural biological diversity and other natural resources;

(b) strengthening research which enhances and conserves biological diversity by maximizing intra-and inter-specific variation for the benefit of farmers, especially those who generate and use their own varieties and apply ecological principles in maintaining soil fertility and in combating diseases, weeds and pests;

(c) promoting, as appropriate, plant breeding efforts which, with the participation of farmers, particularly in developing countries, strengthen the capacity to develop varieties particularly adapted to social, economic and ecological conditions, including in marginal areas;

(d) broadening the genetic base of crops and increasing the range of genetic diversity available to farmers;

(e) promoting, as appropriate, the expanded use of local and locally adapted crops, varieties and underutilized species;

(f) supporting, as appropriate, the wider use of diversity of varieties and species in on-farm management, conservation and sustainable use of crops and creating strong links to plant breeding and agricultural development in order to reduce crop vulnerability and genetic erosion, and promote increased world food production compatible with sustainable development; and

(g) reviewing, and, as appropriate, adjusting breeding strategies and regulations concerning variety release and seed distribution.

Article 7 – National Commitments and International Cooperation

7.1 Each Contracting Party shall, as appropriate, integrate into its agriculture and rural development policies and programmes, activities referred to in Articles 5 and 6, and cooperate with other Contracting Parties, directly or through FAO and other relevant international organizations, in the conservation and sustainable use of plant genetic resources for food and agriculture.

7.2 International cooperation shall, in particular, be directed to:

(a) establishing or strengthening the capabilities of developing countries and countries with economies in transition with respect to conservation and sustainable use of plant genetic resources for food and agriculture;

(b) enhancing international activities to promote conservation, evaluation, documentation, genetic enhancement, plant breeding, seed multiplication; and sharing, providing access to, and exchanging, in conformity with Part IV, plant genetic resources for food and agriculture and appropriate information and technology;

(c) maintaining and strengthening the institutional arrangements provided for in Part V; and

(d) implement the funding strategy of Article 18.

Article 8 – Technical Assistance

The Contracting Parties agree to promote the provision of technical assistance to Contracting Parties, especially those that are developing countries or countries with economies in transition, either bilaterally or through the appropriate international organizations, with the objective of facilitating the implementation of this Treaty.

PART III – FARMERS' RIGHTS

Article 9 – Farmers' Rights

9.1 The Contracting Parties recognize the enormous contribution that the local and indigenous communities and farmers of all regions of the world, particularly those in the centres of origin and crop diversity, have made and will continue to make for the conservation and development of plant genetic resources which constitute the basis of food and agriculture production throughout the world.

9.2 The Contracting Parties agree that the responsibility for realizing Farmers' Rights, as they relate to plant genetic resources for food and agriculture, rests with national governments. In accordance with their needs and priorities, each Contracting Party should, as appropriate, and subject to its national legislation, take measures to protect and promote Farmers' Rights, including:

(a) protection of traditional knowledge relevant to plant genetic resources for food and agriculture;

(b) the right to equitably participate in sharing benefits arising from the utilization of plant genetic resources for food and agriculture; and

(c) the right to participate in making decisions, at the national level, on matters related to the conservation and sustainable use of plant genetic resources for food and agriculture.

9.3 Nothing in this Article shall be interpreted to limit any rights that farmers have to save, use, exchange and sell farm-saved seed/propagating material, subject to national law and as appropriate.

PART IV – THE MULTILATERAL SYSTEM OF ACCESS AND BENEFIT-SHARING

Article 10 – Multilateral System of Access and Benefit-sharing

10.1 In their relationships with other States, the Contracting Parties recognize the sovereign rights of States over their own plant genetic resources for food and agriculture, including that the authority to determine access to those resources rests with national governments and is subject to national legislation.

10.2 In the exercise of their sovereign rights, the Contracting Parties agree to establish a multilateral system, which is efficient, effective, and transparent, both to facilitate access to plant genetic resources for food and agriculture, and to share, in a fair and equitable way, the benefits arising from the utilization of these resources, on a complementary and mutually reinforcing basis.

Article 11 – Coverage of the Multilateral System

11.1 In furtherance of the objectives of conservation and sustainable use of plant genetic resources for food and agriculture and the fair and equitable sharing of benefits arising out of their use, as stated in Article 1, the Multilateral System shall cover the plant genetic resources for food and agriculture listed in Annex I, established according to criteria of food security and interdependence.

11.2 The Multilateral System, as identified in Article 11.1, shall include all plant genetic resources for food and agriculture listed in Annex I that are under the management and control of the Contracting Parties and in the public domain. With a view to achieving the fullest possible coverage of the Multilateral System, the Contracting Parties invite all other holders of the plant genetic resources for food and agriculture listed in Annex I to include these plant genetic resources for food and agriculture in the Multilateral System.

11.3 Contracting Parties also agree to take appropriate measures to encourage natural and legal persons within their jurisdiction who hold plant genetic resources for food and agriculture listed in Annex I to include such plant genetic resources for food and agriculture in the Multilateral System.

11.4 Within two years of the entry into force of the Treaty, the Governing Body shall assess the progress in including the plant genetic resources for food and agriculture referred to in paragraph 11.3 in the Multilateral System. Following this assessment, the Governing Body shall decide whether access shall continue to be facilitated to those natural and legal persons referred to in paragraph 11.3 that have not included these plant genetic resources for food and agriculture in the Multilateral System, or take such other measures as it deems appropriate.

11.5 The Multilateral System shall also include the plant genetic resources for food and agriculture listed in Annex I and held in the *ex situ* collections of the International Agricultural Research Centres of the Consultative Group on International Agricultural Research (CGIAR), as provided in Article 15.1a, and in other international institutions, in accordance with Article 15.5.

Article 12 – Facilitated access to plant genetic resources for food and agriculture within the Multilateral System

12.1 The Contracting Parties agree that facilitated access to plant genetic resources for food and agriculture under the Multilateral System, as defined in Article 11, shall be in accordance with the provisions of this Treaty.

12.2 The Contracting Parties agree to take the necessary legal or other appropriate measures to provide such access to other Contracting Parties through the Multilateral System. To this effect, such access shall also be provided to legal and natural persons under the jurisdiction of any Contracting Party, subject to the provisions of Article 11.4.

12.3 Such access shall be provided in accordance with the conditions below:

(a) Access shall be provided solely for the purpose of utilization and conservation for research, breeding and training for food and agriculture, provided that such purpose does not include chemical, pharmaceutical and/or other non-food/feed industrial uses. In the case of multiple-use crops (food and non-food), their importance for food security should be the determinant for their inclusion in the Multilateral System and availability for facilitated access.

(b) Access shall be accorded expeditiously, without the need to track individual accessions and free of charge, or, when a fee is charged, it shall not exceed the minimal cost involved;

(c) All available passport data and, subject to applicable law, any other associated available non-confidential descriptive information, shall be made available with the plant genetic resources for food and agriculture provided;

(d) Recipients shall not claim any intellectual property or other rights that limit the facilitated access to the plant genetic resources for food and agriculture, or their genetic parts or components, in the form received from the Multilateral System;

(e) Access to plant genetic resources for food and agriculture under development, including material being developed by farmers, shall be at the discretion of its developer, during the period of its development;

(f) Access to plant genetic resources for food and agriculture protected by intellectual and other property rights shall be consistent with relevant international agreements, and with relevant national laws;

(g) Plant genetic resources for food and agriculture accessed under the Multilateral System and conserved shall continue to be made available to the Multilateral System by the recipients of those plant genetic resources for food and agriculture, under the terms of this Treaty; and

(h) Without prejudice to the other provisions under this Article, the Contracting Parties agree that access to plant genetic resources for food and agriculture found in *in situ* conditions will be provided according to national legislation or, in the absence of such legislation, in accordance with such standards as may be set by the Governing Body.

12.4 To this effect, facilitated access, in accordance with Articles 12.2 and 12.3 above, shall be provided pursuant to a standard material transfer agreement (MTA), which shall be adopted by the

Governing Body and contain the provisions of Articles 12.3a, d and g, as well as the benefit-sharing provisions set forth in Article 13.2d(ii) and other relevant provisions of this Treaty, and the provision that the recipient of the plant genetic resources for food and agriculture shall require that the conditions of the MTA shall apply to the transfer of plant genetic resources for food and agriculture to another person or entity, as well as to any subsequent transfers of those plant genetic resources for food and agriculture.

12.5 Contracting Parties shall ensure that an opportunity to seek recourse is available, consistent with applicable jurisdictional requirements, under their legal systems, in case of contractual disputes arising under such MTAs, recognizing that obligations arising under such MTAs rest exclusively with the parties to those MTAs.

12.6 In emergency disaster situations, the Contracting Parties agree to provide facilitated access to appropriate plant genetic resources for food and agriculture in the Multilateral System for the purpose of contributing to the re-establishment of agricultural systems, in cooperation with disaster relief co-ordinators.

Article 13 – Benefit-sharing in the Multilateral System

13.1 The Contracting Parties recognize that facilitated access to plant genetic resources for food and agriculture which are included in the Multilateral System constitutes itself a major benefit of the Multilateral System and agree that benefits accruing therefrom shall be shared fairly and equitably in accordance with the provisions of this Article.

13.2 The Contracting Parties agree that benefits arising from the use, including commercial, of plant genetic resources for food and agriculture under the Multilateral System shall be shared fairly and equitably through the following mechanisms: the exchange of information, access to and transfer of technology, capacity-building, and the sharing of the benefits arising from commercialization, taking into account the priority activity areas in the rolling Global Plan of Action, under the guidance of the Governing Body:

(a) Exchange of information:

The Contracting Parties agree to make available information which shall, *inter alia*, encompass catalogues and inventories, information on technologies, results of technical, scientific and socio-economic research, including characterization, evaluation and utilization, regarding those plant genetic resources for food and agriculture under the Multilateral System. Such information shall be made available, where non-confidential, subject to applicable law and in accordance with national capabilities. Such information shall be made available to all Contracting Parties to this Treaty through the information system, provided for in Article 17.

(b) Access to and transfer of technology

(i) The Contracting Parties undertake to provide and/or facilitate access to technologies for the conservation, characterization, evaluation and use of plant genetic resources for food and agriculture which are under the Multilateral System. Recognizing that some technologies can only be transferred through genetic material, the Contracting Parties shall provide and/or facilitate access to such technologies and genetic material which is under the Multilateral System and to improved varieties and genetic material developed through the use of plant genetic resources for food and agriculture under the Multilateral System, in conformity with the provisions of Article 12. Access to these technologies, improved varieties and genetic material shall be provided and/or facilitated, while respecting applicable property rights and access laws, and in accordance with national capabilities.

(ii) Access to and transfer of technology to countries, especially to developing countries and countries with economies in transition, shall be carried out through a set of measures, such as the establishment and maintenance of, and participation in, crop-based thematic groups on utilization of plant genetic resources for food and agriculture, all types of partnership in research and development and in commercial joint ventures relating to the material received, human resource development, and effective access to research facilities.

(iii) Access to and transfer of technology as referred to in (i) and (ii) above, including that protected by intellectual property rights, to developing countries that are Contracting Parties, in particular least developed countries, and countries with economies in transition, shall be provided and/or facilitated under fair and most favourable terms, in particular in the case of technologies for use in conservation as well as technologies for the benefit of farmers in developing countries, especially in least developed countries, and countries with economies in transition, including on concessional and preferential terms where mutually agreed, *inter alia*, through partnerships in research and development under the Multilateral System. Such access and transfer shall be provided on terms which recognize and are consistent with the adequate and effective protection of intellectual property rights.

(c) Capacity-building

Taking into account the needs of developing countries and countries with economies in transition, as expressed through the priority they accord to building capacity in plant genetic resources for food and agriculture in their plans and programmes, when in place, in respect of those plant genetic resources for food and agriculture covered by the Multilateral System, the Contracting Parties agree to give priority to (i) establishing and/or strengthening programmes for scientific and technical education and training in conservation and sustainable use of plant genetic resources for food and agriculture, (ii) developing and strengthening facilities for conservation and sustainable use of plant genetic resources for food and agriculture, in particular in developing countries, and countries with economies in transition, and (iii) carrying out scientific research preferably, and where possible, in developing countries and countries with economies in transition, in cooperation with institutions of such countries, and developing capacity for such research in fields where they are needed.

(d) Sharing of monetary and other benefits of commercialization

(i) The Contracting Parties agree, under the Multilateral System, to take measures in order to achieve commercial benefit-sharing, through the involvement of the private and public sectors in activities identified under this Article, through partnerships and collaboration, including with the private sector in developing countries and countries with economies in transition, in research and technology development;

(ii) The Contracting Parties agree that the standard Material Transfer Agreement referred to in Article 12.4 shall include a requirement that a recipient who commercializes a product that is a plant genetic resource for food and agriculture and that incorporates material accessed from the Multilateral System, shall pay to the mechanism referred to in Article 19.3f, an equitable share of the benefits arising from the commercialization of that product, except whenever such a product is available without restriction to others for further research and breeding, in which case the recipient who commercializes shall be encouraged to make such payment.

The Governing Body shall, at its first meeting, determine the level, form and manner of the payment, in line with commercial practice. The Governing Body may decide to establish different levels of payment for various categories of recipients who commercialize such products; it may also decide on the need to exempt from such payments small farmers in developing countries and in countries with economies in transition. The Governing Body may, from time to time, review the levels of payment with a view to achieving fair and equitable sharing of benefits, and it may also assess, within a period of five years from the entry into force of this Treaty, whether the mandatory payment requirement in the MTA shall apply also in cases where such commercialized products are available without restriction to others for further research and breeding.

13.3 The Contracting Parties agree that benefits arising from the use of plant genetic resources for food and agriculture that are shared under the Multilateral System should flow primarily, directly and indirectly, to farmers in all countries, especially in developing countries, and countries with economies in transition, who conserve and sustainably utilize plant genetic resources for food and agriculture.

13.4 The Governing Body shall, at its first meeting, consider relevant policy and criteria for specific assistance under the agreed funding strategy established under Article 18 for the conservation of plant genetic resources for food and agriculture in developing countries, and countries with economies in transition whose contribution to the diversity of plant genetic resources for food and agriculture in the Multilateral System is significant and/or which have special needs.

13.5 The Contracting Parties recognize that the ability to fully implement the Global Plan of Action, in particular of developing countries and countries with economies in transition, will depend largely upon the effective implementation of this Article and of the funding strategy as provided in Article 18.

13.6 The Contracting Parties shall consider modalities of a strategy of voluntary benefit-sharing contributions whereby Food Processing Industries that benefit from plant genetic resources for food and agriculture shall contribute to the Multilateral System.

PART V – SUPPORTING COMPONENTS

Article 14 – Global Plan of Action

Recognizing that the rolling Global Plan of Action for the Conservation and Sustainable Use of Plant Genetic Resources for Food and Agriculture is important to this Treaty, Contracting Parties should promote its effective implementation, including through national actions and, as appropriate, international cooperation to provide a coherent framework, *inter alia,* for capacity-building, technology transfer and exchange of information, taking into account the provisions of Article 13.

Article 15 – Ex Situ Collections of Plant Genetic Resources for Food and Agriculture held by the International Agricultural Research Centres of the Consultative Group on International Agricultural Research and other International Institutions

15.1 The Contracting Parties recognize the importance to this Treaty of the *ex situ* collections of plant genetic resources for food and agriculture held in trust by the International Agricultural Research Centres (IARCs) of the Consultative Group on International Agricultural Research (CGIAR). The Contracting Parties call upon the IARCs to sign agreements with the Governing Body with regard to such *ex situ* collections, in accordance with the following terms and conditions:

(a) Plant genetic resources for food and agriculture listed in Annex I of this Treaty and held by the IARCs shall be made available in accordance with the provisions set out in Part IV of this Treaty.

(b) Plant genetic resources for food and agriculture other than those listed in Annex I of this Treaty and collected before its entry into force that are held by IARCs shall be made available in accordance with the provisions of the MTA currently in use pursuant to agreements between the IARCs and the FAO. This MTA shall be amended by the Governing Body no later than its second regular session, in consultation with the IARCs, in accordance with the relevant provisions of this Treaty, especially Articles 12 and 13, and under the following conditions:

(i) The IARCs shall periodically inform the Governing Body about the MTAs entered into, according to a schedule to be established by the Governing Body;

(ii) The Contracting Parties in whose territory the plant genetic resources for food and agriculture were collected from *in situ* conditions shall be provided with samples of such plant genetic resources for food and agriculture on demand, without any MTA;

(iii) Benefits arising under the above MTA that accrue to the mechanism mentioned in Article 19.3f shall be applied, in particular, to the conservation and sustainable use of the plant genetic resources for food and agriculture in question, particularly in national and regional programmes in developing countries and countries with economies in transition, especially in centres of diversity and the least developed countries; and

(iv) The IARCs shall take appropriate measures, in accordance with their capacity, to maintain effective compliance with the conditions of the MTAs, and shall promptly inform the Governing Body of cases of non-compliance.

(c) IARCs recognize the authority of the Governing Body to provide policy guidance relating to *ex situ* collections held by them and subject to the provisions of this Treaty.

(d) The scientific and technical facilities in which such *ex situ* collections are conserved shall remain under the authority of the IARCs, which undertake to manage and administer these *ex situ* collections in accordance with internationally accepted standards, in particular the Genebank Standards as endorsed by the FAO Commission on Genetic Resources for Food and Agriculture.

(e) Upon request by an IARC, the Secretary shall endeavour to provide appropriate technical support.

(f) The Secretary shall have, at any time, right of access to the facilities, as well as right to inspect all activities performed therein directly related to the conservation and exchange of the material covered by this Article.

(g) If the orderly maintenance of these *ex situ* collections held by IARCs is impeded or threatened by whatever event, including *force majeure,* the Secretary, with the approval of the host country, shall assist in its evacuation or transfer, to the extent possible.

15.2 The Contracting Parties agree to provide facilitated access to plant genetic resources for food and agriculture in Annex I under the Multilateral System to IARCs of the CGIAR that have signed agreements with the Governing Body in accordance with this Treaty. Such Centres shall be included in a list held by the Secretary to be made available to the Contracting Parties on request.

15.3 The material other than that listed in Annex I, which is received and conserved by IARCs after the coming into force of this Treaty, shall be available for access on terms consistent with those mutually agreed between the IARCs that receive the material and the country of origin of such resources or the country that has acquired those resources in accordance with the Convention on Biological Diversity or other applicable law.

15.4 The Contracting Parties are encouraged to provide IARCs that have signed agreements with the Governing Body with access, on mutually agreed terms, to plant genetic resources for food and agriculture not listed in Annex I that are important to the programmes and activities of the IARCs.

15.5 The Governing Body will also seek to establish agreements for the purposes stated in this Article with other relevant international institutions.

Article 16 – International Plant Genetic Resources Networks

16.1 Existing cooperation in international plant genetic resources for food and agriculture networks will be encouraged or developed on the basis of existing arrangements and consistent with the terms of this Treaty, so as to achieve as complete coverage as possible of plant genetic resources for food and agriculture.

16.2 The Contracting Parties will encourage, as appropriate, all relevant institutions, including governmental, private, non-governmental, research, breeding and other institutions, to participate in the international networks.

Article 17 – The Global Information System on Plant Genetic Resources for Food and Agriculture

17.1 The Contracting Parties shall cooperate to develop and strengthen a global information system to facilitate the exchange of information, based on existing information systems, on scientific, technical and environmental matters related to plant genetic resources for food and agriculture, with the expectation that such exchange of information will contribute to the sharing of benefits by making information on plant genetic resources for food and agriculture available to all Contracting Parties. In developing the Global Information System, cooperation will be sought with the Clearing House Mechanism of the Convention on Biological Diversity.

17.2 Based on notification by the Contracting Parties, early warning should be provided about hazards that threaten the efficient maintenance of plant genetic resources for food and agriculture, with a view to safeguarding the material.

17.3 The Contracting Parties shall cooperate with the Commission on Genetic Resources for Food and Agriculture of the FAO in its periodic reassessment of the state of the world's plant genetic resources for food and agriculture in order to facilitate the updating of the rolling Global Plan of Action referred to in Article 14.

PART VI – FINANCIAL PROVISIONS

Article 18 – Financial Resources

18.1 The Contracting Parties undertake to implement a funding strategy for the implementation of this Treaty in accordance with the provisions of this Article.

18.2 The objectives of the funding strategy shall be to enhance the availability, transparency, efficiency and effectiveness of the provision of financial resources to implement activities under this Treaty.

18.3 In order to mobilize funding for priority activities, plans and programmes, in particular in developing countries and countries with economies in transition, and taking the Global Plan of Action into account, the Governing Body shall periodically establish a target for such funding.

18.4 Pursuant to this funding strategy:

(a) The Contracting Parties shall take the necessary and appropriate measures within the Governing Bodies of relevant international mechanisms, funds and bodies to ensure due priority and attention to the effective allocation of predictable and agreed resources for the implementation of plans and programmes under this Treaty.

(b) The extent to which Contracting Parties that are developing countries and Contracting Parties with economies in transition will effectively implement their commitments under this Treaty will depend on the effective allocation, particularly by the developed country Parties, of the resources referred to in this Article. Contracting Parties that are developing countries and Contracting Parties with economies in transition will accord due priority in their own plans and programmes to building capacity in plant genetic resources for food and agriculture.

(c) The Contracting Parties that are developed countries also provide, and Contracting Parties that are developing countries and Contracting Parties with economies in transition avail themselves of, financial resources for the implementation of this Treaty through bilateral and regional and multilateral channels. Such channels shall include the mechanism referred to in Article 19.3f.

(d) Each Contracting Party agrees to undertake, and provide financial resources for national activities for the conservation and sustainable use of plant genetic resources for food and agriculture in accordance with its national capabilities and financial resources. The financial resources provided shall not be used to ends inconsistent with this Treaty, in particular in areas related to international trade in commodities. ;

(e) The Contracting Parties agree that the financial benefits arising from Article 13.2d are part of the funding strategy.

(f) Voluntary contributions may also be provided by Contracting Parties, the private sector, taking into account the provisions of Article 13, non-governmental organisations and other sources. The Contracting Parties agree that the Governing Body shall consider modalities of a strategy to promote such contributions;

18.5 The Contracting Parties agree that priority will be given to the implementation of agreed plans and programmes for farmers in developing countries, especially in least developed countries, and in countries with economies in transition, who conserve and sustainably utilize plant genetic resources for food and agriculture.

PART VII – INSTITUTIONAL PROVISIONS

Article 19 – Governing Body

19.1 A Governing Body for this Treaty is hereby established, composed of all Contracting Parties.

19.2 All decisions of the Governing Body shall be taken by consensus unless by consensus another method of arriving at a decision on certain measures is reached, except that consensus shall always be required in relation to Articles 23 and 24.

19.3 The functions of the Governing Body shall be to promote the full implementation of this Treaty, keeping in view its objectives, and, in particular, to:

(a) provide policy direction and guidance to monitor, and adopt such recommendations as necessary for the implementation of this Treaty and, in particular, for the operation of the Multilateral System;

(b) adopt plans and programmes for the implementation of this Treaty;

(c) adopt, at its first session, and periodically review the funding strategy for the implementation of this Treaty, in accordance with the provisions of Article 18;

(d) adopt the budget of this Treaty;

(e) consider and establish subject to the availability of necessary funds such subsidiary bodies as may be necessary, and their respective mandates and composition;

(f) establish, as needed, an appropriate mechanism, such as a Trust Account, for receiving and utilizing financial resources that will accrue to it for purposes of implementing this Treaty;

(g) establish and maintain cooperation with other relevant international organizations and treaty bodies, including in particular the Conference of the Parties to the Convention on Biological Diversity, on matters covered by this Treaty, including their participation in the funding strategy;

(h) consider and adopt, as required, amendments to this Treaty, in accordance with the provisions of Article 23;

(i) consider and adopt, as required, amendments to annexes to this Treaty, in accordance with the provisions of Article 24;

(j) consider modalities of a strategy to encourage voluntary contributions, in particular, with reference to Articles 13 and 18;

(k) perform such other functions as may be necessary for the fulfilment of the objectives of this Treaty;

(l) take note of relevant decisions of the Conference of the Parties to the Convention on Biological Diversity and other relevant international organizations and treaty bodies;

(m) inform, as appropriate, the Conference of the Parties to the Convention on Biological Diversity and other relevant international organizations and treaty bodies of matters regarding the implementation of this Treaty; and

(n) approve the terms of agreements with the IARCs and other international institutions under Article 15, and review and amend the MTA in Article 15.

19.4 Subject to Article 19.6, each Contracting Party shall have one vote and may be represented at sessions of the Governing Body by a single delegate who may be accompanied by an alternate, and by experts and advisers. Alternates, experts and advisers may take part in the proceedings of the Governing Body but may not vote, except in the case of their being duly authorized to substitute for the delegate.

19.5 The United Nations, its specialized agencies and the International Atomic Energy Agency, as well as any State not a Contracting Party to this Treaty, may be represented as observers at sessions of the Governing Body. Any other body or agency, whether governmental or non-governmental, qualified in fields relating to conservation and sustainable use of plant genetic resources for food and agriculture, which has informed the Secretary of its wish to be represented as an observer at a session of the Governing Body, may be admitted unless at least one third of the Contracting Parties present object. The admission and participation of observers shall be subject to the Rules of Procedure adopted by the Governing Body.

19.6 A Member Organization of FAO that is a Contracting Party and the member states of that Member Organization that are Contracting Parties shall exercise their membership rights and fulfil their membership obligations in accordance, *mutatis mutandis*, with the Constitution and General Rules of FAO.

19.7 The Governing Body shall adopt and amend, as required, its own Rules of Procedure and financial rules which shall not be inconsistent with this Treaty.

19.8 The presence of delegates representing a majority of the Contracting Parties shall be necessary to constitute a quorum at any session of the Governing Body.

19.9 The Governing Body shall hold regular sessions at least once every two years. These sessions should, as far as possible, be held back-to-back with the regular sessions of the Commission on Genetic Resources for Food and Agriculture.

19.10 Special Sessions of the Governing Body shall be held at such other times as may be deemed necessary by the Governing Body, or at the written request of any Contracting Party, provided that this request is supported by at least one third of the Contracting Parties.

19.11 The Governing Body shall elect its Chairperson and Vice-Chairpersons (collectively referred to as "the Bureau"), in conformity with its Rules of Procedure.

Article 20 – Secretary

20.1 The Secretary of the Governing Body shall be appointed by the Director-General of FAO, with the approval of the Governing Body. The Secretary shall be assisted by such staff as may be required.

20.2 The Secretary shall perform the following functions:

(a) arrange for and provide administrative support for sessions of the Governing Body and for any subsidiary bodies as may be established;

(b) assist the Governing Body in carrying out its functions, including the performance of specific tasks that the Governing Body may decide to assign to it;

(c) report on its activities to the Governing Body.

20.3 The Secretary shall communicate to all Contracting Parties and to the Director-General:

(a) decisions of the Governing Body within sixty days of adoption;

(b) information received from Contracting Parties in accordance with the provisions of this Treaty.

20.4 The Secretary shall provide documentation in the six languages of the United Nations for sessions of the Governing Body.

20.5 The Secretary shall cooperate with other organizations and treaty bodies, including in particular the Secretariat of the Convention on Biological Diversity, in achieving the objectives of this Treaty.

Article 21 – Compliance

The Governing Body shall, at its first meeting, consider and approve cooperative and effective procedures and operational mechanisms to promote compliance with the provisions of this Treaty and to address issues of non-compliance. These procedures and mechanisms shall include monitoring, and offering advice or assistance, including legal advice or legal assistance, when needed, in particular to developing countries and countries with economies in transition.

Article 22 – Settlement of Disputes

22.1 In the event of a dispute between Contracting Parties concerning the interpretation or application of this Treaty, the parties concerned shall seek solutions by negotiation.

22.2 If the parties concerned cannot reach agreement by negotiation, they may jointly seek the good offices of, or request mediation by, a third party.

22.3 When ratifying, accepting, approving or acceding to this Treaty, or at any time thereafter, a Contracting Party may declare in writing to the Depositary that for a dispute not resolved in accordance with Article 22.1 or Article 22.2 above, it accepts one or both of the following means of dispute settlement as compulsory:

(a) Arbitration in accordance with the procedure laid down in Part 1 of Annex II to this Treaty;

(b) Submission of the dispute to the International Court of Justice.

22.4 If the parties to the dispute have not, in accordance with Article 22.3 above, accepted the same or any procedure, the dispute shall be submitted to conciliation in accordance with Part 2 of Annex II to this Treaty unless the parties otherwise agree.

Article 23 – Amendments of the Treaty

23.1 Amendments to this Treaty may be proposed by any Contracting Party.

23.2 Amendments to this Treaty shall be adopted at a session of the Governing Body. The text of any proposed amendment shall be communicated to Contracting Parties by the Secretary at least six months before the session at which it is proposed for adoption.

23.3 All amendments to this Treaty shall only be made by consensus of the Contracting Parties present at the session of the Governing Body.

23.4 Any amendment adopted by the Governing Body shall come into force among Contracting Parties having ratified, accepted or approved it on the ninetieth day after the deposit of instruments of ratification, acceptance or approval by two-thirds of the Contracting Parties. Thereafter the amendment shall enter into force for any other Contracting Party on the ninetieth day after that Contracting Party deposits its instrument of ratification, acceptance or approval of the amendment.

23.5 For the purpose of this Article, an instrument deposited by a Member Organization of FAO shall not be counted as additional to those deposited by member states of such an organization.

Article 24 – Annexes

24.1 The annexes to this Treaty shall form an integral part of this Treaty and a reference to this Treaty shall constitute at the same time a reference to any annexes thereto.

24.2 The provisions of Article 23 regarding amendments to this Treaty shall apply to the amendment of annexes.

Article 25 – Signature

This Treaty shall be open for signature at the FAO from 3 November 2001 to 4 November 2002 by all Members of FAO and any States that are not Members of FAO but are Members of the United Nations, or any of its specialized agencies or of the International Atomic Energy Agency.

Article 26 – Ratification, Acceptance or Approval

This Treaty shall be subject to ratification, acceptance or approval by the Members and non-Members of FAO referred to in Article 25. Instruments of ratification, acceptance, or approval shall be deposited with the Depositary.

Article 27 – Accession

This Treaty shall be open for accession by all Members of FAO and any States that are not Members of FAO but are Members of the United Nations, or any of its specialized agencies or of the International Atomic Energy Agency from the date on which the Treaty is closed for signature. Instruments of accession shall be deposited with the Depositary.

Article 28 – Entry into force

28.1 Subject to the provisions of Article 29.2, this Treaty shall enter into force on the ninetieth day after the deposit of the fortieth instrument of ratification, acceptance, approval or accession, provided that at least twenty instruments of ratification, acceptance, approval or accession have been deposited by Members of FAO.

28.2 For each Member of FAO and any State that is not a Member of FAO but is a Member of the United Nations, or any of its specialized agencies or of the International Atomic Energy Agency that ratifies, accepts, approves or accedes to this Treaty after the deposit, in accordance with Article 28.1, of the fortieth instrument of ratification, acceptance, approval or accession, the Treaty shall enter into force on the ninetieth day following the deposit of its instrument of ratification, acceptance, approval or accession.

Article 29 – Member Organizations of FAO

29.1 When a Member Organization of FAO deposits an instrument of ratification, acceptance, approval or accession for this Treaty, the Member Organization shall, in accordance with the provisions of Article II.7 of the FAO Constitution, notify any change regarding its distribution of competence to its declaration of competence submitted under Article II.5 of the FAO Constitution as may be necessary in light of its acceptance of this Treaty. Any Contracting Party to this Treaty may, at any time, request a Member Organization of FAO that is a Contracting Party to this Treaty to provide information as to which, as between the Member Organization and its member states, is responsible for the implementation of any particular matter covered by this Treaty. The Member Organization shall provide this information within a reasonable time.

29.2 Instruments of ratification, acceptance, approval, accession or withdrawal, deposited by a Member Organization of FAO, shall not be counted as additional to those deposited by its Member States.

Article 30 – Reservations

No reservations may be made to this Treaty.

Article 31 – Non-Parties

The Contracting Parties shall encourage any Member of FAO or other State, not a Contracting Party to this Treaty, to accept this Treaty.

Article 32 – Withdrawals

32.1 Any Contracting Party may at any time after two years from the date on which this Treaty has entered into force for it, notify the Depositary in writing of its withdrawal from this Treaty. The Depositary shall at once inform all Contracting Parties.

32.2 Withdrawal shall take effect one year from the date of receipt of the notification.

Article 33 – Termination

33.1 This Treaty shall be automatically terminated if and when, as the result of withdrawals, the number of Contracting Parties drops below forty, unless the remaining Contracting Parties unanimously decide otherwise.

33.2 The Depositary shall inform all remaining Contracting Parties when the number of Contracting Parties has dropped to forty.

33.3 In the event of termination the disposition of assets shall be governed by the financial rules to be adopted by the Governing Body.

Article 34 – Depositary

The Director-General of FAO shall be the Depositary of this Treaty.

Article 35 – Authentic Texts

The Arabic, Chinese, English, French, Russian and Spanish texts of this Treaty are equally authentic.

ANNEX I
LIST OF CROPS COVERED UNDER THE MULTILATERAL SYSTEM

Food crops

Crop	Genus	Observations
Breadfruit	*Artocarpus*	Breadfruit only.
Asparagus	*Asparagus*	
Oat	*Avena*	
Beet	*Beta*	
Brassica complex	*Brassica et al.*	Genera included are: *Brassica, Armoracia, Barbarea, Camelina, Crambe, Diplotaxis, Eruca, Isatis, Lepidium, Raphanobrassica, Raphanus, Rorippa,* and *Sinapis*. This comprises oilseed and vegetable crops such as cabbage, rapeseed, mustard, cress, rocket, radish, and turnip. The species *Lepidium meyenii* (maca) is excluded.
Pigeon Pea	*Cajanus*	
Chickpea	*Cicer*	
Citrus	*Citrus*	Genera *Poncirus* and *Fortunella* are included as root stock.
Coconut	*Cocos*	
Major aroids	*Colocasia,*	Major aroids include taro, cocoyam, dasheen and tannia.
	Xanthosoma	
Carrot	*Daucus*	
Yams	*Dioscorea*	
Finger Millet	*Eleusine*	
Strawberry	*Fragaria*	
Sunflower	*Helianthus*	
Barley	*Hordeum*	
Sweet Potato	*Ipomoea*	
Grass pea	*Lathyrus*	
Lentil	*Lens*	
Apple	*Malus*	
Cassava	*Manihot*	*Manihot esculenta* only.
Banana / Plantain	*Musa*	Except *Musa textilis*.
Rice	*Oryza*	
Pearl Millet	*Pennisetum*	
Beans	*Phaseolus*	Except *Phaseolus polyanthus*.

Pea	*Pisum*	
Rye	*Secale*	
Potato	*Solanum*	Section tuberosa included, except *Solanum phureja*.
Eggplant	*Solanum*	Section melongena included.
Sorghum	*Sorghum*	
Triticale	*Triticosecale*	
Wheat	*Triticum et al.*	Including *Agropyron, Elymus*, and *Secale*.
Faba Bean / Vetch	*Vicia*	
Cowpea et al.	*Vigna*	
Maize	*Zea*	Excluding *Zea perennis, Zea diploperennis,* and *Zea luxurians*.

Forages

Genera	Species
LEGUME FORAGES	
Astragalus	*chinensis, cicer, arenarius*
Canavalia	*ensiformis*
Coronilla	*varia*
Hedysarum	*coronarium*
Lathyrus	*cicera, ciliolatus, hirsutus, ochrus, odoratus, sativus*
Lespedeza	*cuneata, striata, stipulacea*
Lotus	*corniculatus, subbiflorus, uliginosus*
Lupinus	*albus, angustifolius, luteus*
Medicago	*arborea, falcata, sativa, scutellata, rigidula, truncatula*
Melilotus	*albus, officinalis*
Onobrychis	*viciifolia*
Ornithopus	*sativus*
Prosopis	*affinis, alba, chilensis, nigra, pallida*
Pueraria	*phaseoloides*
Trifolium	*alexandrinum, alpestre, ambiguum, angustifolium, arvense, agrocicerum, hybridum, incarnatum, pratense, repens, resupinatum, rueppellianum, semipilosum, subterraneum, vesiculosum*
GRASS FORAGES	
Andropogon	*gayanus*
Agropyron	*cristatum, desertorum*
Agrostis	*stolonifera, tenuis*
Alopecurus	*pratensis*

Arrhenatherum	*elatius*
Dactylis	*glomerata*
Festuca	*arundinacea, gigantea, heterophylla, ovina, pratensis, rubra*
Lolium	*hybridum, multiflorum, perenne, rigidum, temulentum*
Phalaris	*aquatica, arundinacea*
Phleum	*pratense*
Poa	*alpina, annua, pratensis*
Tripsacum	*laxum*
OTHER FORAGES	
Atriplex	*halimus, nummularia*
Salsola	*vermiculata*

ANNEX II

Part 1
ARBITRATION

Article 1

The claimant party shall notify the Secretary that the parties to the dispute are referring it to arbitration pursuant to Article 22. The notification shall state the subject-matter of arbitration and include, in particular, the articles of this Treaty, the interpretation or application of which are at issue. If the parties to the dispute do not agree on the subject matter of the dispute before the President of the tribunal is designated, the arbitral tribunal shall determine the subject matter. The Secretary shall forward the information thus received to all Contracting Parties to this Treaty.

Article 2

1. In disputes between two parties to the dispute, the arbitral tribunal shall consist of three members. Each of the parties to the dispute shall appoint an arbitrator and the two arbitrators so appointed shall designate by common agreement the third arbitrator who shall be the President of the tribunal. The latter shall not be a national of one of the parties to the dispute, nor have his or her usual place of residence in the territory of one of these parties to the dispute, nor be employed by any of them, nor have dealt with the case in any other capacity.

2. In disputes between more than two Contracting Parties, parties to the dispute with the same interest shall appoint one arbitrator jointly by agreement.

3. Any vacancy shall be filled in the manner prescribed for the initial appointment.

Article 3

1. If the President of the arbitral tribunal has not been designated within two months of the appointment of the second arbitrator, the Director-General of FAO shall, at the request of a party to the dispute, designate the President within a further two-month period.

2. If one of the parties to the dispute does not appoint an arbitrator within two months of receipt of the request, the other party may inform the Director-General of FAO who shall make the designation within a further two-month period.

Article 4

The arbitral tribunal shall render its decisions in accordance with the provisions of this Treaty and international law.

Article 5

Unless the parties to the dispute otherwise agree, the arbitral tribunal shall determine its own rules of procedure.

Article 6

The arbitral tribunal may, at the request of one of the parties to the dispute, recommend essential interim measures of protection.

Article 7

The parties to the dispute shall facilitate the work of the arbitral tribunal and, in particular, using all means at their disposal, shall:

(a) Provide it with all relevant documents, information and facilities; and

(b) Enable it, when necessary, to call witnesses or experts and receive their evidence.

Article 8

The parties to the dispute and the arbitrators are under an obligation to protect the confidentiality of any information they receive in confidence during the proceedings of the arbitral tribunal.

Article 9

Unless the arbitral tribunal determines otherwise because of the particular circumstances of the case, the costs of the tribunal shall be borne by the parties to the dispute in equal shares. The tribunal shall keep a record of all its costs, and shall furnish a final statement thereof to the parties to the dispute.

Article 10

Any Contracting Party that has an interest of a legal nature in the subject-matter of the dispute which may be affected by the decision in the case, may intervene in the proceedings with the consent of the tribunal.

Article 11

The tribunal may hear and determine counterclaims arising directly out of the subject-matter of the dispute.

Article 12

Decisions both on procedure and substance of the arbitral tribunal shall be taken by a majority vote of its members.

Article 13

If one of the parties to the dispute does not appear before the arbitral tribunal or fails to defend its case, the other party may request the tribunal to continue the proceedings and to make its award. Absence of a party to the dispute or a failure of a party to the dispute to defend its case shall not constitute a bar to the proceedings. Before rendering its final decision, the arbitral tribunal must satisfy itself that the claim is well founded in fact and law.

Article 14

The tribunal shall render its final decision within five months of the date on which it is fully constituted unless it finds it necessary to extend the time-limit for a period which should not exceed five more months.

Article 15

The final decision of the arbitral tribunal shall be confined to the subject-matter of the dispute and shall state the reasons on which it is based. It shall contain the names of the members who have participated and the date of the final decision. Any member of the tribunal may attach a separate or dissenting opinion to the final decision.

Article 16

The award shall be binding on the parties to the dispute. It shall be without appeal unless the parties to the dispute have agreed in advance to an appellate procedure.

Article 17

Any controversy which may arise between the parties to the dispute as regards the interpretation or manner of implementation of the final decision may be submitted by either party to the dispute for decision to the arbitral tribunal which rendered it.

Part 2
CONCILIATION

Article 1

A conciliation commission shall be created upon the request of one of the parties to the dispute. The commission shall, unless the parties to the dispute otherwise agree, be composed of five members, two appointed by each party concerned and a President chosen jointly by those members.

Article 2

In disputes between more than two Contracting Parties, parties to the dispute with the same interest shall appoint their members of the commission jointly by agreement. Where two or more parties to the dispute have separate interests or there is a disagreement as to whether they are of the same interest, they shall appoint their members separately.

Article 3

If any appointments by the parties to the dispute are not made within two months of the date of the request to create a conciliation commission, the Director-General of FAO shall, if asked to do so by the party to the dispute that made the request, make those appointments within a further two-month period.

Article 4

If a President of the conciliation commission has not been chosen within two months of the last of the members of the commission being appointed, the Director-General of FAO shall, if asked to do so by a party to the dispute, designate a President within a further two-month period.

Article 5

The conciliation commission shall take its decisions by majority vote of its members. It shall, unless the parties to the dispute otherwise agree, determine its own procedure. It shall render a proposal for resolution of the dispute, which the parties shall consider in good faith.

Article 6

A disagreement as to whether the conciliation commission has competence shall be decided by the commission.

STATE DEPARTMENT DOCUMENT NUMBER: 110-20

PROTOCOLS TO THE NORTH ATLANTIC TREATY OF 1949 ON THE ACCESSION OF THE REPUBLIC OF ALBANIA AND THE REPUBLIC OF CROATIA

ADOPTED AT BRUSSELS, JULY 9, 2008
APPROVED BY THE U.S. SENATE ON SEPTEMBER 25, 2008

CTIA DOCUMENT NUMBER: 8347.004

LETTER OF TRANSMITTAL

To the Senate of the United States:

I transmit herewith, for Senate advice and consent to ratification, Protocols to the North Atlantic Treaty of 1949 on the Accession of the Republic of Albania and the Republic of Croatia. These Protocols were adopted at Brussels on July 9, 2008, and signed that day on behalf of the United States and the other Parties to the North Atlantic Treaty. Also transmitted for the information of the Senate is the report of the Department of State, which includes an overview of the Protocols.

NATO enlargement remains an historic success in advancing freedom, stability, and democracy in the Euro-Atlantic area. Albania and Croatia serve as two more examples of countries motivated by the prospect of NATO membership to advance significant and difficult political, economic, and military reforms. Their efforts and success demonstrate to other countries in the Balkans and beyond that NATO's door remains open to nations willing to shoulder the responsibilities of membership. I am pleased that, with the advice and consent of the Senate, these new democracies can soon join us as members of this great Alliance.

I ask the Senate to join me in advancing the cause of freedom and strengthening NATO by providing its prompt advice and consent to ratification of these Protocols of Accession. My Administration stands ready to assist you in any way we can in your deliberations.

George W. Bush.

THE WHITE HOUSE, *July 23, 2008.*

LETTER OF SUBMITTAL

Department of State,
Washington, July 16, 2008.

The President,
The White House.

The President: I have the honor to submit to you, with a view to their transmission to the Senate for advice and consent to ratification, Protocols to the North Atlantic Treaty of 1949 on the accession of the Republic of Albania and the Republic of Croatia. These Protocols were opened for [Signature] at Brussels on July 9, 2008, and were signed on that day on behalf of the United States of America and the other parties to the North Atlantic Treaty.

The Protocols propose adding the Republic of Albania and the Republic of Croatia to NATO as members, with all the privileges and responsibilities that apply to current Allies. The core commitment to these states will be embodied in the existing text of the North Atlantic Treaty of 1949, including the central collective defense provision in Article 5. I believe these countries merit this commitment on our part and that they share our common commitment to democratic values and are prepared to act as responsible Allies. The U.S. decision to pursue the enlargement of NATO has had bipartisan support across several administrations. I am therefore confident that the Senate will grant its advice and consent to ratification of these Protocols, after due deliberation, without hesitation.

These two countries have made the difficult decisions needed to advance reforms and become vibrant democracies with vigorous market economies. Their accession to the Alliance will be a major step toward realizing your vision of a Europe whole, free, and at peace.

Respectfully submitted.

Condoleezza Rice.

Overview

The Protocols are identical in structure and composed of three Articles. Article I provides that, once the Protocol has entered into force, the Secretary General of NATO shall extend an invitation to the named state to accede to the North Atlantic Treaty, and that, in accordance with Article 10 of the Treaty, the state shall become a Party to the Treaty on the date it deposits its instrument of accession with the Government of the United States of America. Article II provides that the Protocol shall enter into force when each of the parties to the North Atlantic Treaty has notified the Government of the United States of America of its acceptance of the Protocol. Article III provides that the English and French texts shall be equally authentic, and calls for deposit of the Protocol in the Archives of the Government of the United States of America, the depositary state for the North Atlantic Treaty.

PROTOCOL TO THE NORTH ATLANTIC TREATY ON THE ACCESSION OF THE REPUBLIC OF ALBANIA

PROTOCOLE AU TRAITÉ DE L'ATLANTIQUE NORD SUR L'ACCESSION DE LA RÉPUBLIQUE D'ALBANIE

The Parties to the North Atlantic Treaty, signed at Washington on April 4, 1949,

Being satisfied that the security of the North Atlantic area will be enhanced by the accession of the Republic of Albania to that Treaty,

Agree as follows:

Article I

Upon the entry into force of this Protocol, the Secretary General of the North Atlantic Treaty Organisation shall, on behalf of all the Parties, communicate to the Government of the Republic of Albania an invitation to accede to the North Atlantic Treaty. In accordance with article 10 of the Treaty, the Republic of Albania shall become a Party on the date when it deposits its instrument of accession with the Government of the United States of America.

Article II

The present Protocol shall enter into force when each of the Parties to the North Atlantic Treaty has notified the Government of the United States of America of its acceptance thereof. The Government of the United States of America shall inform all the Parties to the North Atlantic Treaty of the date of receipt of each such notification and of the date of the entry into force of the present Protocol.

Article III

The present Protocol, of which the English and French texts are equally authentic, shall be deposited in the Archives of the Government of the United States of America. Duly certified copies thereof shall be transmitted by that Government to the Governments of all the Parties to the North Atlantic Treaty.

In witness whereof, the undersigned plenipotentiaries have signed the present Protocol.	Signed at Brussels on this 9th day of July 2008
En foi de quoi, les plénipotentiaires désignés ci-dessous ont signé le présent Protocole.	Signé à Bruxelles le 9 juillet 2008
For the Kingdom of Belgium:	
Pour le Royaume de Belgique:	[[Signature]]
For the Republic of Bulgaria:	
Pour la République de Bulgarie:	[Signature]
For Canada:	
Pour le Canada:	[Signature]
For the Czech Republic:	
Pour la République tchèque:	[Signature]

For the Kingdom of Denmark:
Pour le Royaume de Danemark: [Signature]
For the Republic of Estonia:
Pour la République d'Estonie: [Signature]
For the French Republic:
Pour la République française: [Signature]
For the Federal Republic of Germany:
Pour la République fédérale d'Allemagne: [Signature]
For the Hellenic Republic:
Pour la République hellénique: [Signature]
For the Republic of Hungary:
Pour la République de Hongrie: [Signature]
For the Republic of Iceland:
Pour la République d'Islande: [Signature]
For the Italian Republic:
Pour la République italienne: [Signature]
For the Republic of Latvia:
Pour la République de Lettonie: [Signature]
For the Republic of Lithuania:
Pour la République de Lituanie: [Signature]
For the Grand Duchy of Luxembourg:
Pour le Grand-Duché de Luxembourg: [Signature]
For the Kingdom of the Netherlands:
Pour le Royaume des Pays-Bas: [Signature]
For the Kingdom of Norway:
Pour le Royaume de Norvège: [Signature]
For the Republic of Poland:
Pour la République de Pologne: [Signature]
For the Portuguese Republic:
Pour la République portugaise: [Signature]
For Romania:
Pour la Roumanie: [Signature]
For the Slovak Republic:
Pour la République slovaque: [Signature]
For the Republic of Slovenia:
Pour la République de Slovénie: [Signature]

For the Kingdom of Spain:	
Pour le Royaume d'Espagne:	[Signature]
For the Republic of Turkey:	
Pour la République de la Turquie:	[Signature]
For the United Kingdom of Great Britain and Northern Ireland:	
Pour le Royaume-Uni de Grande-Bretagne et d'Irlande du Nord:	[Signature]
For the United States of America:	
Pour les États-Unis d'Amérique:	[Signature]

I CERTIFY THAT the foregoing is a true copy of the Protocol to the North Atlantic Treaty on the Accession of the Republic of Albania, signed at Brussels on July 9, 2008, in the English and French languages, the signed original of which is deposited in the archives of the Government of the United States of America.

IN TESTIMONY WHEREOF. I, CONDOLEEZZA RICE, Secretary of State of the United States of America, have hereunto caused the seal of the Department of State to be affixed and my name subscribed by the Authentications Officer of the said Department, at the city of Washington, in the District of Columbia, this fourteenth day of July, 2008.

[Condoleezza Rice]
Secretary of State

By [Denitra T. Hawkins]
Authentications Officer
Department of State

PROTOCOL
TO THE NORTH ATLANTIC TREATY ON THE ACCESSION OF THE REPUBLIC OF CROATIA

PROTOCOLE AU TRAITÉ DE L'ATLANTIQUE NORD SUR L'ACCESSION DE LA RÉPUBLIQUE DE CROATIE

The Parties to the North Atlantic Treaty, signed at Washington on April 4, 1949,

Being satisfied that the security of the North Atlantic area will be enhanced by the accession of the Republic of Croatia to that Treaty,

Agree as follows:

Article I

Upon the entry into force of this Protocol, the Secretary General of the North Atlantic Treaty Organisation shall, on behalf of all the Parties, communicate to the Government of the Republic of Croatia an invitation to accede to the North Atlantic Treaty. In accordance with article 10 of the Treaty, the Republic of Croatia shall become a Party on the date when it deposits its instrument of accession with the Government of the United States of America.

Article II

The present Protocol shall enter into force when each of the Parties to the North Atlantic Treaty has notified the Government of the United States of America of its acceptance thereof. The Government of the United States of America shall inform all the Parties to the North Atlantic Treaty of the date of receipt of each such notification and of the date of the entry into force of the present Protocol.

Article III

The present Protocol, of which the English and French texts are equally authentic, shall be deposited in the Archives of the Government of the United States of America. Duly certified copies thereof shall be transmitted by that Government to the Governments of all the Parties to the North Atlantic Treaty.

In witness whereof, the undersigned plenipotentiaries have signed the present Protocol.	Signed at Brussels on this 9th day of July 2008
En foi de quoi, les plénipotentiaires désignés ci-dessous ont signé le présent Protocole.	Signé à Bruxelles le 9 juillet 2008
For the Kingdom of Belgium:	
Pour le Royaume de Belgique:	[Signature]
For the Republic of Bulgaria:	
Pour la République de Bulgarie:	[Signature]
For Canada:	
Pour le Canada:	[Signature]
For the Czech Republic:	
Pour la République tchèque:	[Signature]

For the Kingdom of Denmark:	
Pour le Royaume de Danemark:	[Signature]
For the Republic of Estonia:	
Pour la République d'Estonie:	[Signature]
For the French Republic:	
Pour la République française:	[Signature]
For the Federal Republic of Germany:	
Pour la République fédérale d'Allemagne:	[Signature]
For the Hellenic Republic:	
Pour la République hellénique:	[Signature]
For the Republic of Hungary:	
Pour la République de Hongrie:	[Signature]
For the Republic of Iceland:	
Pour la République d'Islande:	[Signature]
For the Italian Republic:	
Pour la République italienne:	[Signature]
For the Republic of Latvia:	
Pour la République de Lettonie:	[Signature]
For the Republic of Lithuania:	
Pour la République de Lituanie:	[Signature]
For the Grand Duchy of Luxembourg:	
Pour le Grand-Duché de Luxembourg:	[Signature]
For the Kingdom of the Netherlands:	
Pour le Royaume des Pays-Bas:	[Signature]
For the Kingdom of Norway:	
Pour le Royaume de Norvège:	[Signature]
For the Republic of Poland:	
Pour la République de Pologne:	[Signature]
For the Portuguese Republic:	
Pour la République portugaise:	[Signature]
For Romania:	
Pour la Roumanie:	[Signature]
For the Slovak Republic:	
Pour la République slovaque:	[Signature]
For the Republic of Slovenia:	
Pour la République de Slovénie:	[Signature]

For the Kingdom of Spain:	
Pour le Royaume d'Espagne:	[Signature]
For the Republic of Turkey:	
Pour la République de la Turquie:	[Signature]
For the United Kingdom of Great Britain and Northern Ireland:	
Pour le Royaume-Uni de Grande-Bretagne et d'Irlande du Nord:	[Signature]
For the United States of America:	
Pour les États-Unis d'Amérique:	[Signature]

I CERTIFY THAT the foregoing is a true copy of the Protocol to the North Atlantic Treaty on the Accession of the Republic of Croatia, signed at Brussels on July 9, 2008, in the English and French languages, the signed original of which is deposited in the archives of the Government of the United States of America.

IN TESTIMONY WHEREOF, I, CONDOLEEZZA RICE, Secretary of State of the United States of America, have hereunto caused the seal of the Department of State to be affixed and my name subscribed by the Authentications Officer of the said Department, at the city of Washington, in the District of Columbia, this fourteenth day of July, 2008.

[Condoleezza Rice]
Secretary of State

By [Denitra T. Hawkins]
Authentications Officer
Department of State

APPENDIX I
INDEX BY COUNTRY

Argentina

Nuclear Materials and Safety

Arrangement Between the Nuclear Regulatory Commission of the United States of America and the Autoridad Regulatoria Nuclear de Argentina for the Exchange of Technical Information and Cooperation in Regulatory and Safety Research Matters, with Addendums. Signed at Rockville and Buenos Aires, December 4 and 28, 2007. Entered into force December 28, 2007. **08-1 CTIA 139, DOS 08-18.**

Azerbaijan

Defense

Agreement Between the United States of America and the Republic of Azerbaijan Concerning the Provision of Training Relating to Defense Articles Under the United States International Military Education and Training (IMET) Program. Effected by Exchange of Notes at Baku, May 8 and June 14, 2002. Entered into force June 14, 2002. **08-1 CTIA 7, DOS 08-02.**

Belize

Military Operations

Agreement Between the United States of America and Belize Regarding the Status of Members of the Armed Forces of the United States and Civilian Personnel of the United States Department of Defense Temporarily Present in Belize in Connection with Military Training, Exercises, Humanitarian Activities and Other Agreed Purposes. Effected by Exchange of Notes at Belmopan, July 2 and October 29, 2007. Entered into force October 29, 2007, with effect from April 24, 2007. **08-1 CTIA 17, DOS 08-04.**

Brazil

Diplomatic Relations

Agreement Between the United States of America and the Federative Republic of Brazil Concerning the Acquisition and Retention of Diplomatic and Consular Properties in the United States and Brazil. Effected by Exchange of Notes at Brasilia, June 1, 2007. Entered into force January 18, 2008. **08-1 CTIA 269, DOS 08-32.**

Bulgaria

Income Taxation

Convention Between the United States of America and the Republic of Bulgaria for the Avoidance of Double Taxation and the Prevention of Fiscal Evasion with Respect to Taxes on Income, with Accompanying Protocol. Signed at Washington D.C., February 23, 2007. Approved by the U.S. Senate on September 23, 2008. **08-1 CTIA 415, Senate Treaty Document Number 110-18 (first part).**

Protocol Amending the Convention Between the United States of America and the Republic of Bulgaria for the Avoidance of Double Taxation and the Prevention of Fiscal Evasion with Respect to Taxes on Income. Signed at Sofia, February 26, 2008. Approved by the U.S. Senate on September 23, 2008. **08-1 CTIA 445, Senate Treaty Document Number 110-18 (second part).**

Burundi

Economic Cooperation

Agreement for Economic and Technical Cooperation Between the United States of America and Burundi. Signed at Bujumbura, December 12, 2007. Entered into force December 12, 2007. **08-1 CTIA 263, DOS 08-31.**

Canada

Income Taxation

Protocol Amending the Convention Between the United States of America and Canada with Respect to Taxes on Income and on Capital Done at Washington D.C. on 26 September 1980, as Amended by the Protocols Done on 14 June 1983, 28 March 1984, 17 March 1995 and 29 July 1997. Signed at Chelsea, September 21, 2007. Approved by the U.S. Senate on September 23, 2008. **08-1 CTIA 291, Senate Treaty Document Number 110-15.**

China

Aviation

Protocol to Amend the Agreement of September 17, 1980, Between the United States of America and the People's Republic of China Relating to Civil Air Transport. Signed at Seattle, July 9, 2007. Entered into force February 14, 2008. **08-1 CTIA 219, DOS 08-26.**

Health

Agreement Between the Department of Health and Human Services of the United States of America and the General Administration of Quality Supervision, Inspection and Quarantine of the People's Republic of China on the Safety of Food and Feed. Signed at Beijing, December 11, 2007. Entered into force December 11, 2007. **08-1 CTIA 73, DOS 08-12.**

Agreement Between the Department of Health and Human Services of the United States of America and the State Food and Drug Administration of the People's Republic of China on the Safety of Drugs and Medical Devices. Signed at Beijing, December 11, 2007. Entered into force December 11, 2007. **08-1 CTIA 85, DOS 08-13.**

Income Taxation

Memorandum of Understanding Between the United States of America and the People's Republic of China Regarding Certain Measures Granting Refunds, Reductions or Exemptions from Taxes or Other Payments. Signed at Geneva, November 29, 2007. Entered into force November 29, 2007. **08-1 CTIA 23, DOS 08-05.**

Nuclear Materials and Safety

Protocol Between the Nuclear Regulatory Commission of the United States of America (USNRC) and the National Nuclear Safety Administration of the People's Republic of China (NNSA) on

Iceland

Income Taxation

Convention Between the United States of America and Iceland for the Avoidance of Double Taxation and the Prevention of Fiscal Evasion with Respect to Taxes on Income, and Accompanying Protocol. Signed at Washington D.C., October 23, 2007. Approved by the U.S. Senate on September 23, 2008. **08-1 CTIA 387, Senate Treaty Document Number 110-17.**

Italy

Space

Memorandum of Understanding Between the United States National Aeronautics and Space Administration and the Italian Space Agency Concerning the Gamma-Ray Large Area Space Telescope Mission. Signed on February 22 and March 7, 2007. Entered into force December 4, 2007. **08-1 CTIA 51, DOS 08-09.**

Japan

Defense

Agreement Between the United States of America and Japan Concerning New Special Measures Relating to Article XXIV of the Agreement Under Article VI of the Treaty of Mutual Cooperation and Security Between the United States of America and Japan Regarding Facilities and Areas and the Status of United States Armed Forces in Japan, with Agreed Minutes and Exchange of Notes. Signed at Tokyo, January 25, 2008. Entered into force February 5, 2008. **08-1 CTIA 283, DOS 08-36.**

Telecommunications

Agreement on Mutual Recognition of Results of Conformity Assessment Procedures Between the United States of America and Japan, with Annex. Signed at Washington D.C., February 16, 2007. Entered into force January 1, 2008. **08-1 CTIA 149, DOS 08-19.**

Kazakhstan

Customs

Agreement Between the United States of America and the Republic of Kazakhstan Regarding Cooperation and Mutual Assistance Between Their Customs Services. Signed at Washington D.C., November 18, 1997. Entered into force August 21, 2000. **08-1 CTIA 1, DOS 08-01.**

Latvia

Nuclear Materials and Safety

Agreement Between the Department of Energy of the United States of America and the Ministry of the Interior of the Republic of Latvia for Cooperation in the Prevention of Illicit Trafficking in Nuclear and Other Radioactive Material. Signed at Riga, December 3, 2007. Entered into force December 3, 2007. **08-1 CTIA 279, DOS 08-35.**

Sierra Leone

Debts

Agreement Between the United States of America and the Republic of Sierra Leone Regarding the Reduction of Certain Debts Owed to, Guaranteed by, or Insured by the United States Government and Its Agency. Signed at Freetown, June 7, 2007. Entered into force January 29, 2008. **08-1 CTIA 165, DOS 08-20.**

Tunisia

Defense

Agreement Between the Unites States of America and the Republic of Tunisia Regarding Grants Under the Foreign Assistance Act of 1961, as Amended, or Successor Legislation, and the Furnishing of Defense Articles, Related Training, and Other Defense Services, Including Pursuant to the United States International Military and Education Training (IMET) Program. Effected by Exchange of Notes at Tunis, November 23, 2007 and February 13, 2008. Entered into force February 13, 2008. **08-1 CTIA 271, DOS 08-33.**

Uganda

Aviation

Memorandum of Agreement (NAT-I-4404) Between the Federal Aviation Administration, Department of Transportation, United States of America, and the Uganda Civil Aviation Authority, Republic of Uganda, for the Provision of Assistance in Developing and Modernizing the Civil Aviation Infrastructure of Uganda. Signed at Washington D.C. and Kampala, November 10 and 11, 2003. Entered into force November 11, 2003. **08-1 CTIA 223, DOS 08-27.**

Peace Corps

Agreement Between the United States of America and the Republic of Uganda Concerning the Program of the Peace Corps in the Republic of Uganda. Signed at Kampala, December 10, 2007. Entered into force December 10, 2007. **08-1 CTIA 69, DOS 08-11.**

United Kingdom

Defense

Memorandum of Understanding Between the United States of America Department of Defense and the Ministry of Defence of the United Kingdom of Great Britain and Northern Ireland Regarding the Assignment of an Operational Logistics Liaison Officer to the United States Transportation Command, with Annexes. Signed at Scott AFB (Belleville), December 17, 2007 and January 28, 2008. Entered into force January 28, 2008. **08-1 CTIA 207, DOS 08-25.**

APPENDIX II
INDEX TO MULTILATERAL AGREEMENTS

Agriculture and Agricultural Commodities
International Treaty on Plant Genetic Resources for Food and Agriculture, with Annexes. Adopted by the Food and Agriculture Organization of the United Nations on November 3, 2001. Signed by the United States of America on November 1, 2002. (Entered into force (but not for the U.S.) on June 29, 2004.) **08-1 CTIA 447, Senate Treaty Document Number 110-19.**

Economic Assistance
Memorandum of Understanding Among the United States of America, the Swiss Confederation, and the Republic of Kazakhstan Regarding Funds to Be Put to Use for the Benefit of Poor Citizens of Kazakhstan, with Annexes. Signed at Washington D.C., May 2, 2007. Entered into force May 2, 2007. **08-1 CTIA 233, DOS 08-29.**

North Atlantic Treaty Organization (NATO)
Protocols to the North Atlantic Treaty of 1949 on the Accession of the Republic of Albania and the Republic of Croatia. Adopted at Brussels, July 9, 2008. **08-1 CTIA 473, Senate Treaty Document Number 110-20.**

Telecommunications
Amendments to the Constitution and Convention of the International Telecommunication Union, as Amended, Together with the Declarations and Reservations by the United States of America, All as Contained in the Final Acts of the Plenipotentiary Conference. Signed at Antalya, Turkey, November 24, 2006. Approved by the U.S. Senate on September 25, 2008. **08-1 CTIA 329, Senate Treaty Document Number 110-16.**

APPENDIX III
TOPICAL INDEX

Documents are listed by topic and, within each topic, by the country which is the other party to the agreement. References are to page numbers within this volume and to Department of State numbers or Senate treaty document numbers, as applicable.

Economic Cooperation

Burundi, **08-1 CTIA 263, DOS 08-31.**

Egypt, **08-1 CTIA 11, DOS 08-03.**

Mozambique, **08-1 CTIA 39, DOS 08-07; 08-1 CTIA 45, DOS 08-08.**

Emergency Preparedness

Russian Federation, **08-1 CTIA 261, DOS 08-30.**

Health

China, **08-1 CTIA 73, DOS 08-12; 08-1 CTIA 85, DOS 08-13.**

Income Taxation

Bulgaria, **08-1 CTIA 415, Senate Treaty Document Number 110-18 (first part); 08-1 CTIA 445, Senate Treaty Document Number 110-18 (second part).**

Canada, **08-1 CTIA 291, Senate Treaty Document Number 110-15.**

China, **08-1 CTIA 23, DOS 08-05.**

Iceland, **08-1 CTIA 387, Senate Treaty Document Number 110-17.**

Limitation

Malta, **08-1 CTIA 97, DOS 08-14.**

Military Operations

Belize, **08-1 CTIA 17, DOS 08-04.**

Narcotics

Colombia, **08-1 CTIA 119, DOS 08-15.**

Malta, **08-1 CTIA 199, DOS 08-24.**

North Atlantic Treaty Organization (NATO)

Multilateral, **08-1 CTIA 473, Senate Treaty Document Number 110-20.**

Nuclear Materials and Safety

Argentina, **08-1 CTIA 139, DOS 08-18.**

China, **08-1 CTIA 189, DOS 08-23.**

Latvia, **08-1 CTIA 279, DOS 08-35.**

www.ingramcontent.com/pod-product-compliance
Ingram Content Group UK Ltd.
Pitfield, Milton Keynes, MK11 3LW, UK
UKHW051048150926
475595UK00005B/175